Population Reference Bureau, Inc.

Region or Country *	Population Estimate Mid-1976 (millions) †	Birth Rate ‡	Death Rate ‡	Rate of Population Growth (annual, percent) §	Number of Years to Double Population ¶	Population Projection to 2000 (millions) ‖	Infant Mortality Rate **	Population under 15 Years (percent) ††	Median Age (years) ††	Life Expectancy at Birth (years)	Urban Population (percent) ‡‡	Per Capita Gross National Product (USA) $$
Namibia	0.9	46	23	2.2	32	1.6	177	41	19.7	41	23	1,200
South Africa	25.6	43	16	2.7	26	50.6	117	41	19.5	52	48	
Swaziland	0.5	49	22	3.2	22	1.0	149	46	16.7	44	8	400
ASIA	**2,287**	**33**	**13**	**2.0**	**35**	**3,612**	**121**	**38**	**21.1**	**56**	**25**	**450**
SOUTHWEST ASIA	**87**	**43**	**14**	**2.9**	**24**	**166**	**144**	**44**	**18.2**	**55**	**41**	**1,050**
Bahrain	0.2	44	15	2.9	24	0.5	78	44	17.8	61	78	2,250
Cyprus	0.7	18	10	0.8	87	0.8	28	32	24.7	71	43	1,380
Gaza	0.4	50	16	3.4	20	0.9	—	49	—	52	79	—
Iraq	11.4	48	15	3.3	21	24.3	99	48	16.0	53	61	970
Israel	3.5	28	7	2.9	24	5.5	23	33	25.1	71	86	3,380
Jordan	2.8	48	15	3.3	21	5.9	97	48	16.2	53	43	400
Kuwait	1.1	45	8	5.9	12	3.0	44	43	19.1	69	22	11,640
Lebanon	2.7	40	10	3.0	23	5.7	59	48	18.6	63	61	1,080
Oman	0.8	50	19	3.1	22	1.6	138	—	—	—	—	1,250
Qatar	0.1	50	19	3.1	22	0.2	138	—	—	—	—	5,830
Saudi Arabia	6.4	49	20	2.9	24	12.9	152	45	17.6	45	18	2,080
Syria	7.6	45	15	3.0	23	16.0	93	49	15.4	54	44	490
Turkey	40.2	39	12	2.6	27	71.3	119	42	19.0	57	39	690
United Arab Emirates	0.2	50	19	3.1	22	0.5	138	34	21.3	—	65	13,500
Yemen Arab Republic	6.9	50	21	2.9	24	13.8	152	45	17.6	45	7	120
Yeman (People's Republic of)	1.7	50	21	2.9	24	3.4	152	45	17.6	45	26	120
MIDDLE SOUTH ASIA	**851**	**37**	**16**	**2.2**	**32**	**1,493**	**137**	**41**	**19.2**	**49**	**20**	**160**
Afghanistan	19.5	43	21	2.2	32	36.3	182	44	17.9	40	15	100
Bangladesh	76.1	47	20	2.7	26	144.8	132	46	16.7	43	9	100
Bhutan	1.2	44	21	2.3	30	2.2	—	42	18.9	44	3	70
India	620.7	35	15	2.0	35	1,051.4	139	40	19.6	50	20	130
Iran	34.1	45	16	3.0	23	67.0	139	47	16.4	51	43	1,060
Maldive Islands	0.1	50	23	3.3	21	0.2	—	44	—	—	11	90
Nepal	12.9	43	20	2.3	30	23.2	[illegible]	40	20.3	44	4	110
Pakistan	72.5	44	15	2.9	24	146.4	124	46	16.6	50	26	130
Sikkim	0.2	—	—	2.0	35	0.4	208	40	19.5	—	5	90
Sri Lanka	14.0	28	8	2.0	35	21.0	45	39	19.9	68	22	130
SOUTHEAST ASIA	**327**	**38**	**15**	**2.4**	**29**	**583**	**108**	**43**	**18.3**	**51**	**20**	**220**
Burma	31.2	40	16	2.4	29	53.5	126	41	19.6	50	19	90
Indonesia	134.7	38	17	2.1	33	230.3	125	44	18.1	48	18	150
Khmer Republic	8.3	47	19	2.8	25	15.8	127	45	17.2	45	19	—
Laos	3.4	45	23	2.4	29	5.7	123	42	18.9	40	15	—
Malaysia	12.4	39	10	2.9	24	22.0	75	44	17.7	59	27	660
Philippines	44.0	41	11	3.0	23	86.3	74	43	18.4	58	32	310
Portuguese Timor	0.7	44	23	2.1	33	1.1	184	42	18.9	40	10	130
Singapore	2.3	20	5	1.6	43	3.1	16	39	19.7	67	100	2,120
Thailand	43.3	36	11	2.5	28	86.0	81	45	17.3	58	13	300
Vietnam (Dem. Republic of)	24.8	32	14	1.8	38	44.1	—	41	19.1	48	12	130
Vietnam (Republic of)	21.6	42	16	2.6	27	34.9	—	41	19.3	40	19	170
EAST ASIA	**1,023**	**26**	**9**	**1.7**	**41**	**1,369**	**23**	**33**	**23.9**	**63**	**30**	**710**
China (People's Republic of)	836.8	27	10	1.7	41	1,126.0	—	33	23.5	62	23	300
Hong Kong	4.4	19	5	2.1	33	5.8	18	36	22.0	71	90	1,540
Japan	112.3	19	6	1.2	58	132.7	11	24	29.6	73	72	3,880
Korea (Dem. People's Republic of)	16.3	36	9	2.7	26	27.5	—	42	18.5	61	38	390
Korea (Republic of)	34.8	29	9	2.0	35	52.3	47	40	19.6	61	41	470
Macau	0.3	25	7	1.8	38	0.4	78	38	18.9	—	97	270
Mongolia	1.5	40	10	3.0	23	2.7	—	44	18.1	61	46	620
Taiwan (Republic of China) ¶¶	16.3	23	5	1.9	36	22.0	26	43	18.2	69	63	720
NORTH AMERICA	**239**	**15**	**9**	**0.8**	**87**	**294**	**16**	**27**	**27.9**	**71**	**74**	**6,580**
Canada	23.1	15	7	1.3	53	31.6	16	29	26.5	73	76	6,080

7.60 | mc
10/15/84
TSU
Bookstore.

JUDAH MATRAS
Hebrew University of Jerusalem

Introduction to Population

A Sociological Approach

Prentice-Hall, Inc., Englewood Cliffs, New Jersey 07632

Library of Congress Cataloging in Publication Data

MATRAS, JUDAH.
Introduction to population.

Bibliography: p.
1. Population. I. Title.
HB871.M28 301.32 76-49577
ISBN 0-13-493122-X

To PHILIP M. HAUSER

PRINTED IN THE UNITED STATES OF AMERICA

10 9 8 7 6 5 4 3 2 1

World Population Data Sheet on the endpapers prepared by the Population Reference Bureau, Inc., 1754 N Street, N.W., Washington, D.C. 20036.

Prentice-Hall International, Inc., *London*
Prentice-Hall of Australia Pty. Limited, *Sydney*
Prentice-Hall of Canada, Ltd., *Toronto*
Prentice-Hall of India Private Limited, *New Delhi*
Prentice-Hall of Japan, Inc., *Tokyo*
Prentice-Hall of Southeast Asia Pte. Ltd., *Singapore*
Whitehall Books Limited, *Wellington, New Zealand*

Contents

Preface

This is a textbook on population, and its main purpose is to take the student—and teacher—farther and deeper into the intersection of population and social structure than has previously been attempted at the introductory level. The book is intended to be exploratory rather than encyclopedic, provocative rather than summarily definitive, and sometimes speculative rather than strictly inductive, and it is concerned with raising new issues more than with settling old ones. In the book I draw extensively on ideas of my earlier book, *Populations and Societies,* about relationships between population and social structure. But I extend and expand the discussions dealing with social consequences of population changes very considerably, and—except for the most essential measures outlined in an Appendix—in this volume I bypass the technical detail taken up in the earlier one.

The first part of the book, Chapters 1 through 5, comprises a general introduction to population issues and problems, their historical background, and their bearing on social, economic, and political organization generally, and in the United States in particular. The second part, Chapters 6 through 10, takes up the elements of population structure and change: mortality, fertility, and migration. And the third part, Chapters 11 through 17, deals with the consequences of population shifts —demographic, social, economic, and political—and with issues and prospects of population policy.

Much of the work on this book was done during the summer of 1975, when I had an opportunity to be at two distinguished centers for studies in demography and ecology: at the University of Washington, in Seattle, and at the University of Wisconsin, in Madison. Samuel Preston and James Sweet, the Directors, and the staffs and students at these remarkable centers provided not only access to materials and all manner of technical assistance, but a large measure of stimulus and critical feedback as well. Larry H. Long called my attention to comparative migration studies which I had overlooked earlier.

Neil J. Smelser, Barbara Phillips, David Heer, Roy Kass, Shirley Foster Hartley, Charles B. Nam, and Paul Tschetter read early versions of the manuscript and provided helpful suggestions for its improvement. Special thanks are due to Phillips Cutright, whose critical reading and comments were especially detailed, mercilessly penetrating, and therefore the more helpful and the more appreciated. Finally and especially, Edward H. Stanford and Irene Fraga, my cronies and alter-egos at Prentice-Hall, provided the whips, carrots, and friendly persuasion, and saw to the morale and good humor, indispensable to all.

Judah Matras
Jerusalem, The Hebrew University

One

Perspectives on People, Populations, and Societies

1

The Population Explosion: Crisis, Opportunity, or Slogan?

This is a book about population, the causes of population growth and change, and the consequences of population trends for human society. At the outset of the book, we will look at the current worldwide concern with the population explosion and the efforts that have been made to achieve zero population growth. Next, we turn to analysis of the components of population growth and the factors, especially social factors, which affect them. We then proceed to consider the ways societies and cultures are responding to population change. And we conclude with a summary and overview of the questions and issues concerning the socio-demographic future of America and the rest of the world.

OUR EXPLODING POPULATION: THE FACT AND THE MESSAGE

The world population has exploded in the twentieth century. World population has grown from about 1.5 billion at the turn of the century to about four billion in 1975; and it seems likely to exceed six billion by the year 2000—in other words, a growth of 4.5 billion, or roughly a quadrupling of the population of the world in a single century. In the last century, world population also grew at a previously unprecedented rate.[1] But neither the absolute growth nor the rate of growth in the previous century is even remotely comparable to the current population growth (see Fig. 1.1).

Not only is the current rate of world population growth unprecedented in human history, but it is easy to show by simple calculations of person-space relationships that such growth cannot go on indefinitely. The population growth of the recent past has already had profound effects on mankind. And how long it continues will affect all of mankind's future welfare, his culture and social forms, and probably his very existence.

One of the most remarkable aspects of the recent population explosion is that it has been so widely noted and discussed, even if it hasn't always been well-understood. In large measure, this is so because the population explosion has coincided with the development and extension of the mass media—newspapers, motion pictures, radio, and especially television. People everywhere understand that the populations to which they belong, or the numbers of persons around them, have grown very rapidly in the recent past and are continuing to grow at unprecedented rates.

In literate societies everywhere the message of the population explosion has gone out; and there are very few literate individuals who have heard, read, or absorbed nothing at all of the message. There are more people, and less empty space, than there were in even the recent past. And for those who haven't noticed it themselves, this fact has been pointed out and driven home in an extensive public information campaign. Pamphlets, books, and slogans have poured forth to inform, alert, educate, and influence the public. Some have been utopian, looking to near-imminent solutions. Others have been apocalyptic: the explosion spells doom. While it is hard to measure the public reaction, many students of population believe they can already see both individual and collective responses; and some analysts believe that recent unprecedented declines in birth rates reflect a loud and clear reading of the population explosion message.

The widespread awareness of the population explosion is not the same as agreement or consensus about its implications. On the contrary, there is considerable disagreement about implications of rapid population growth. Thus, though the fact of the population explosion is beyond

[1] World population grew from .9 billion in 1800 to about 1.6 billion in 1900—i.e., by about 78 percent.

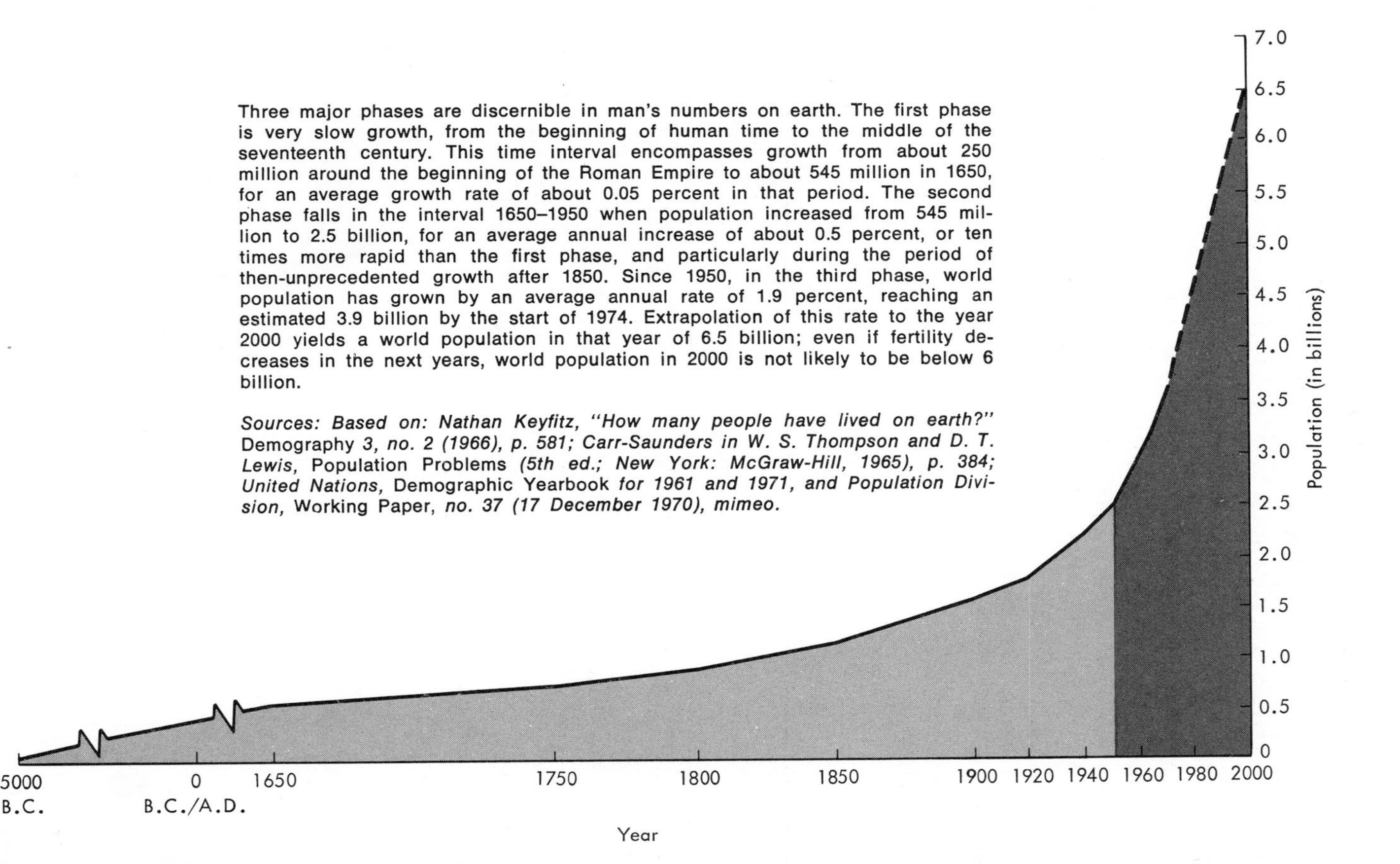

Figure 1.1 World Population through History. *Source: B. Berelson,* et al., *"World Population: Status Report 1974. A Guide for the Concerned Citizen,"* Reports on Population/Family Planning, *No. 15, January 1974. By permission of the Population Council.*

dispute, its meanings and interpretations have been topics of lively controversy.

One school of thought views the world population growth as a crisis for mankind, for human sustenance, and for living space. A second school views the current population growth as presenting an unprecedented opportunity for economic and social development, innovation, and human progress in most areas of the world. Finally, a third point of view asserts that the population explosion is the basic ingredient of most, if not all, the nation's and the world's current social, political, and welfare problems. We turn below to a brief review of these different points of view.

The Population Explosion as a Crisis

The view of the population explosion as a crisis for mankind was first heard from a few isolated voices in the early years after World War II. It later rose to a chorus of concern, and more recently it has become a crescendo of alarm. According to this view, if man does not take immediate control of his numbers, the world will run out of food, land, clean water and breatheable air, energy, and other resources. The shortage of food and other resources will ultimately control or reduce man's numbers, but not without widespread starvation, disorganization, warfare, and all manner of suffering.

World population is currently growing at a rate of about two percent each year, a rate at which the population doubles about every 35 years. From this has come a long list of colorful phrases, book titles, and slogans: "The Population Bomb," "Standing Room Only," "The Garbage Explosion," "America the Dirty," and "The Human Zoo." Whether the problems depicted are worldwide, national, or local, they usually reduce to a few types of consequences which may be anticipated from such an enormous rate of growth.

First, there is likely to be increased pressure upon food, space, and other resources, and also upon the social and community relationships that determine who gets what and how much. The result of scarcities in resources is likely to be increases in economic hardship, malnutrition, and perhaps death rates, too. In 1970, population densities of 1,500 to 2,000 persons per block were very common on New York's Manhattan Island; it is hard to imagine the pressures that would result from a doubling of that density.

In the second place, it is widely believed that the resource drain resulting from rapid population growth may frustrate efforts of new underdeveloped nations to accelerate economic and social development and close the gap between rich and poor nations (see Fig. 1.2). If India's

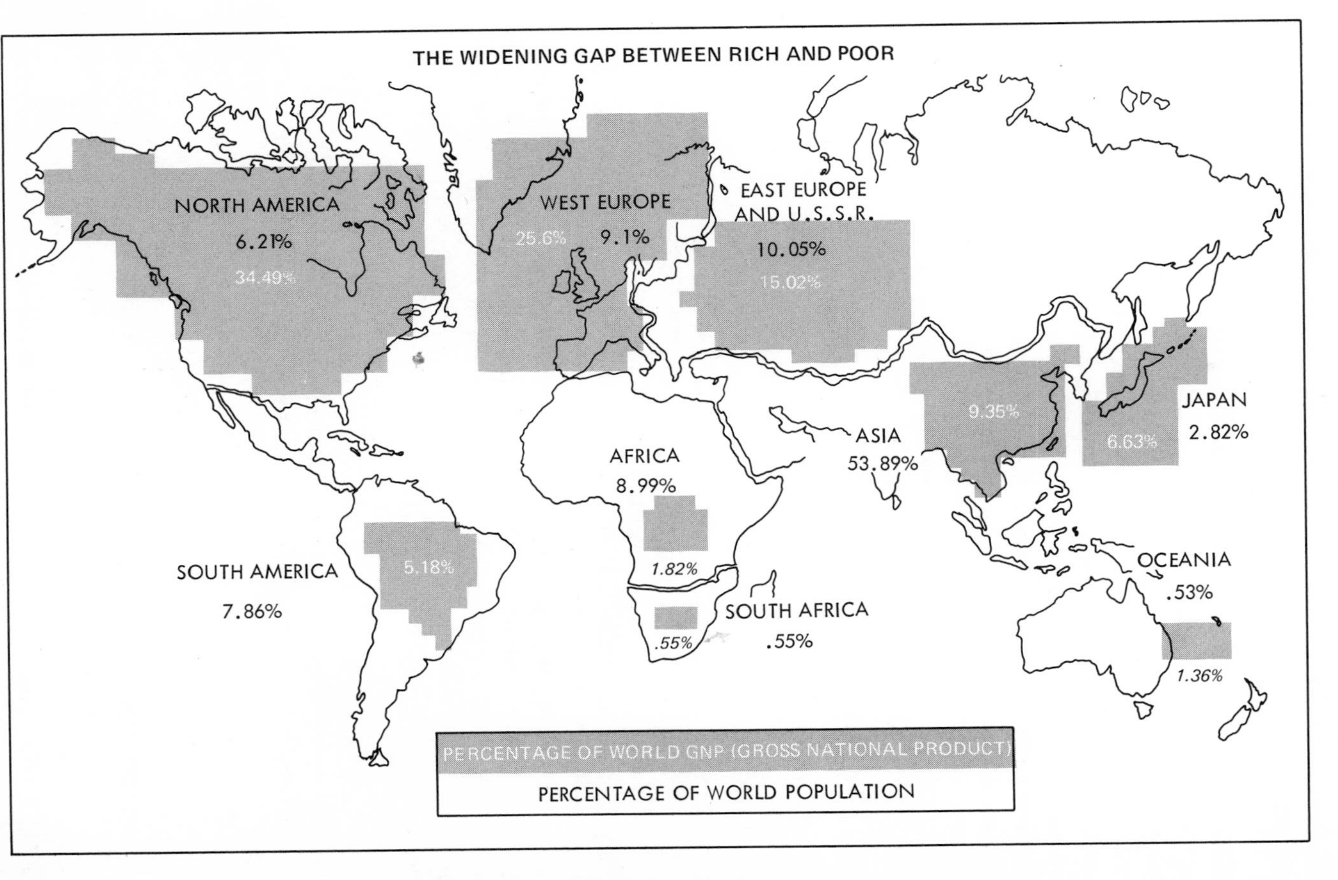

Figure 1.2 The Widening Gap between Rich and Poor.

growth rate is not reduced, her population will probably double in the next generation from 613 million to about 1,226 million, with no comparable growth of national product. Such a grim projection implies a doubling of the homelessness, the starvation, and the suffering already so common in that country.

Finally, the differences in rates of growth among the different areas of the world (see Column 4 of end papers) will produce a redistribution of the world's population which will probably have major implications for international politics. Europe's population, which accounted for an estimated 15 percent of the world population in the year 1000, increased to almost 25 percent by 1900. But 50 years later, it was reduced to 16.4 percent of the total, and by 1975 this figure was down to 11.9 percent. Many observers are alarmed by prospects of accompanying cultural, political, and economic declines in the West.

These three types of consequences of population growth recur in virtually every kind of social and cultural setting. Rapid population growth or change puts pressures on the resources—including jobs, campgrounds, housing, and education—of the state of California. In New York City, too, some of the demands and expectations of residents for resources like space, air, and water, as well as for educational, employment, residential, or recreational opportunities, are frustrated by population turnover and newcomers' needs for basic amenities. And the delicate class, racial, and ethnic political balance of the cities of Chicago, Atlanta, Los Angeles, and for that matter Centerville, U.S.A., is constantly threatened by population shifts into, out of, or within these places. Busing conflicts, teachers' strikes, and zoning controversies are well-publicized examples. Thus, the problem of amounts and distribution of the earth's resources is accompanied by many other problems: poverty and want; space and clean air and environment; equality of opportunity and segregation of residences, schools, and employment; health, and access to care and treatment; and the availability (or, conversely, hoarding) of national goods, air and environment, health and medical care, entertainment, leisure, culture, and all manner of resources in any of the societies of the world today.

A crucial twentieth-century—perhaps post-World War II—development is that the various parts of the world have discovered one another to an extent previously unknown in human history. All are increasingly aware of how the other half lives, and, in particular, the have-not peoples, nations, and societies are no longer ignorant of the worlds and the pleasures of the haves. Leaders and governments increasingly are seeking to better the lives and conditions of their have-not constituents; the have-nots make more and more demands upon their own rulers and upon the haves. But knowing about the haves is not the same as being one!

A crowded market in Naples, Italy. *(United Nations)*

And the political commitment of rulers and the elites to development and to increased levels of living is not the same as its actual achievement. Whether, and by what means, the have-nots can hope to become haves is a central issue in which population growth patterns have a crucial influence.

In the modern world homogeneous societies are the exception, not the rule. Most large-scale societies maintain a balance between two or more quite distinct population groups. Whites and blacks, Catholics and Protestants, Czechs and Slovaks, Hindus and Moslems, Spaniards and Indians, Jews and Arabs, Swedes and Finns may coexist in a more or less delicately balanced, more or less equalitarian, more or less segregated, more or less open, pluralistic society. In many societies such coexistence is a matter of tradition, pride, and harmonious cooperation and mutual respect. But increasingly, under the new visibility afforded by the revolution in communication, literacy, and information, pluralism has come to be synonymous with inequality. In all societies and all communities, an ongoing balance between majority and minority populations, between dominant and subordinate population groups, or between groups of divergent interests, outlooks, traditions, or needs is *always* threatened by the different growth patterns of different groups.

In sum, there are two key dimensions of the view of the population explosion as a crisis. First, the food and resource shortages and the destruction or pollution of the environment are either imminent or they are already taking place. And second, measures other than the control or reduction of the population can delay or prolong, but cannot possibly resolve these problems. It is the urgency for population control that, from this viewpoint, renders the trend of recent growth a clear and present danger for mankind—a crisis already upon us.

The Population Explosion as an Opportunity

The population crisis view holds that population growth has unfavorable effects upon economic development for two reasons. The first is the fixity of natural resources, especially land: agricultural productivity and average per capita food resources and income must eventually decline. The second reason is that rapid population growth brings a high ratio of dependent children to adult workers. This causes families to spend rather than save, thus depressing the rate of savings and the resulting investment in the economy. But the actual instances of decline in per capita income are few even in countries with very rapid population growth. And the fact that death rates have universally declined may indicate generally *improved* levels of living.

Historically, industrialization and rising income in Europe were accompanied by—and followed—very rapid population growth. In Europe's case, it seems clear not only that great population growth has been successfully sustained, but also that levels of living and the quality of life in general have enjoyed great improvement. Thus, it has also been argued that population growth may sometimes enhance the prospects for economic development. Two basic reasons are cited. First, economies of scale (greater output per unit of input) are made possible by larger markets and by a larger, more specialized labor force. And second, the pressure of increased family size or community size causes people to work harder and, especially, it causes both individuals and organizations to develop or adopt innovations or improved methods and processes of production. A further argument connecting population growth to economic development holds that health improvements are responsible for increased productivity.

The idea that population growth is good for business and enhances both economic and political power has deep roots in social thought. Moreover, the prescription in the Western religions to "be fruitful and multiply, and fill up the earth," along with its counterparts in non-Western religious teachings, remains a pervasive value especially in societies where religious observance, ritual, and institutions loom large in personal and community life. Thus, both objective and normative ideas about right and wrong have led more than a few scholars to seek out systematically the positive economic and social consequences of population growth. Three economic benefits of population growth traditionally are cited:

1. Larger population permits production in larger scale. This in turn permits production of standardized items for impersonal markets, rather than made-to-order items sold directly to consumers. The result is enormous increases in productivity and profit. The cost per unit of a thousand identical chairs is much lower than the cost of a single chair fashioned individually; the same holds true for dresses, doors, toys, guns, butter, station wagons, and so forth.
2. Larger population means a larger work force, which permits much more extensive division of labor, much greater occupational specialization, and much more efficient performance of more specialized tasks.
3. Growing population sustains demands. As the numbers of children, couples, and households expand, there is less danger of product saturization—of situations where the market for future production is exhausted because everyone already owns a chair, dress, door, toy, or a gun.

More recently, an additional argument for population growth has emerged. This links population growth with innovation, with social and economic change, and with the search for, discovery, and exploitation of new resources, opportunities, and social forms.

Thus, this point of view sees population growth as a key to many recent historical patterns like industrialization, urbanization, technological and social innovations, and enhanced standards of living—for all of these developments were preceded, or accompanied, or in some cases made possible by the population growth. This viewpoint also sees the current population growth in underdeveloped areas of the world as both a challenge and an opportunity for these countries to extend the exploitation of resources and to make the social and technological innovations which can catapult them into the modern era of computors and mass communications, consumption, leisure, greater longevity, and family planning.

The Population Explosion as a Slogan

One result of the discovery and popularization of the population explosion has been its widespread invocation as an explanation of all manner of social, economic, and political ills. The list includes crowding and food shortages; pollution of the air, water and the environment; inflation, unemployment, and underemployment; the economic gap between developed and developing countries; poverty and want; shortages of recreational space and facilities; shortages of travel and communication facilities; crowded streets and highways; the energy crisis; social complexity and social formality; deteriorated housing; alienation and individual powerlessness; and riots and group competition for power.

A corollary to this analysis is the idea that at least partial solutions to these problems are implied by reducing or halting population growth (by zero population growth—slogan and objective of an organization and a worldwide movement as well!). Put in other words, no solutions to these problems are possible *without* reduction or halting of population growth. For many natural and social scientists as well as laymen, social and economic inequality are to be dealt with not by improvement in income distribution, welfare provisions, or enhanced access to social opportunity, but, rather, by population control. Similarly, the solution to air, water, noise, or environmental pollution is viewed not in terms of control of large industrial and business polluters—not even in obliging them to pay for the cleaning and restoring necessitated by their pollution—but by checking population growth. And in this approach, the solution to shortages of recreational facilities lies not in the provision of more parks, nor of more effective preservation of public lands and facilities. Instead, it lies in birth control! Thus, the population explosion and population control have become rhyme and verse for transferring responsibility for social improvement away from business and government (where many thoughtful observers believe it should lie) to the people themselves who are responsible for the population explosion.

POPULATION RHETORIC AND POPULATION ANALYSIS

There can be no doubt that under some circumstances population growth really does imply social, economic, political, or cultural crises—just as it may also present social, economic, political, or cultural opportunities. Clearly, if there were no people there would be no pressure on recreational areas or food supplies; nor would there be poverty, unemployment, or social alienation. Thus population growth must surely affect the severity, if not the very origins and nature of pressing social problems. It is the task of population studies to inquire about the nature of these relationships: about the circumstances under which population growth enhances or impairs human welfare, dignity, and satisfaction; and about the general nature of relationships between population and social structure.

How and why are populations, societies, and social organizations related? Under what conditions do they vary and change together, and when do they seem to be independent of one another? How can we explain demographic and social transformations, and how can we account for the *absence* of such changes? How can we explain variations in the direction of change? For example, why does one population lean toward growth while another tends to stabilize? Or why does one population move rapidly toward agglomeration and urbanization, while others do so very slowly or not at all? A *scientific theory of populations and societies* seeks to answer these questions by developing propositions that are empirically verifiable based on observation in the real world. It is the beginning and outline of such a theory that we intend to develop in this book.

Curiosity and speculation about man's numbers on earth may be as ancient as man himself. But it is the recognition that man's numbers relate to and influence his safety, his well-being, his social relations and community organization, and perhaps his very survival that has given impetus to the modern systematic study of populations. Unfortunately, such studies have been obscured too often by a spate of statistical tables, graphs, and charts which portray populations in such extreme detail that the important relationships are lost. In this book we shall attempt to make such relationships explicit and explore them in some depth. At the same time, we shall attempt to introduce the study of populations, their variations, and their relationships with social structure in different places and at different times.

We shall try to show, on the one hand, that the central determinants of variations and changes in population size, composition, and distribution are *social structural,* and that we must turn to sociology, social anthropology, and human ecology for basic concepts and research tools. However, we shall also see that population structure is itself determinant of social structure, bounding all its other aspects. Populations naturally tend to grow and change in the absence of constraints. And population processes and transformations are themselves processes and transformations in social structure; they are also direct causes of other major social structural and cultural changes.

SUMMARY

We have introduced the study of population by pointing out the dimensions of recent world population growth (the population explosion) and by describing briefly some alternative views about its nature. World population has grown from about 1.5 billion in 1900 to about four billion in 1975, and it will probably reach six billion by the year 2000—a growth pattern unprecedented in human history. Many people see the rapid growth of world population and the pressures of human numbers on space, food, and other resources available on a finite earth as constituting a crisis for mankind. Others think population growth encourages economic growth, development, progress, and opportunity by providing larger and more specialized markets and working forces and by encouraging inventiveness and innovation. A frequent theme in scholarly and popular discussions alike has been the imputation of population explosion causes to a large variety of social problems, implying or asserting that their solution or alleviation depends first and foremost upon population control.

A task of population studies is the analysis of the actual relationships between population growth and social problems. More generally, population studies address questions of the size, composition, and structure of human populations; their implications for social organization; and the elements, causes, and consequences of their growth and change. We turn next to examination of the concept of zero population growth (ZPG) and prospects for its realization, and then to consideration of the full range of cultural, historical, social, economic, and political causes and consequences of population variations and changes.

2

On the Brink of Zero Population Growth

In this chapter we introduce the concept of zero population growth (ZPG) and review both its origins and the movement and organization to which it has given rise. We will look at several of the ongoing debates that surround the issue of ZPG: the goals and methods it advocates; the prospects for, and implications of, its realization; the nature of population policy and public intervention; and the role of population science in formulating and implementing public policy.

ZPG: THE PHRASE, THE GOAL, AND THE MOVEMENT

Population growth in any given period of time consists of the difference between the number of people entering the population (by birth or in-migration) and the number departing (by death or out-migration). In the United States we are accustomed, from long history, to positive population growth—an excess of births over deaths. But negative population growth, or an excess of deaths over births, is not only conceivable but has actually occurred fairly often in many countries throughout history. Many American communities, too, have experienced negative population growth during periods when out-migrants have outnumbered in-migrants. A third condition besides positive and negative population growth is possible. ZPG occurs when the number of births and other entrances to a community are exactly equal to the number of deaths and other departures. On a world-wide basis, and for all practical purposes for most national populations as well, ZPG describes the demographic situation in which the number of births is equal to the number of deaths.

In a paper published in the widely read journal, *Science* (1967), Kingsley Davis notes that public and private groups and agencies are increasingly trying to influence family formation practices and encourage family planning and birth control. These groups and agencies had initially focused their activities on the promotion of individual happiness. Their main objective was success in planning families, enabling couples to avoid unwanted births or to achieve the number of children desired at the times deemed most convenient or appropriate. However, Davis notes that more recently these organizations are citing the dangers of world population explosion and the economic, social, and ecological disadvantages of population growth for individual countries as a primary justification for family planning.

While these groups agree on the public's need for population control, there is, as Davis points out, a certain confusion about their specific goals and their prospects of achieving them by the means they advocate. If the goal is to halt the growth of population, that is, to arrive at zero population growth, these groups have not declared so explicitly. And even if their aim *is* ZPG, there is no chance of achieving it by the means they advocate. For even in a situation where all couples successfully plan and control their fertility so that they have exactly the number of children they want, the population will continue to grow. This is because the number of children that all couples want, when viewed in the aggregate, assures not only replacement of the existing population, but further growth of the population—and all the economic, social, and ecological consequences that further growth entails. Thus, the voluntary birth control practices advocated by private and public groups and agencies cannot alone stop population growth. If ZPG is to be the goal, then other kinds of programs involving sanctions and possibly government coercion must be considered in addition to voluntary family planning and birth control.

Scientists and laymen alike have not been slow to meet the challenge. Individuals and groups have used both learned forums and popular media to declare that ZPG is indeed the appropriate goal for those concerned with population growth and its consequences. They recognize that this goal demands individual and collective commitment not only to voluntary family planning, but also to additional measures designed to bring population growth to a standstill. For instance, couples might be penalized for bearing too many (more than two) children.

ZPG has caught on as both a slogan and a goal, especially among groups concerned with pollution and the quality of the environment—and a movement has been born. In 1969, a national organization called Zero Population Growth, Inc. was formed under the sponsorship of a distinguished group of scientists and public figures. This group has started a campaign to publicize its goals, to seek additional public support, and to lobby for legislative action (Piotrow, 1973, pp. 187-90). The organization claims large numbers of members and even larger numbers of supporters.

The organized Zero Population Growth movement tries to publicize the population problem and their solution. *(Zero Population Growth)*

THE SCHOLARLY DEBATE

Space and atmosphere are finite, so population must also ultimately be finite. Serious and responsible demographers and other scholars recognize that world population growth must ultimately come to a halt, that zero population growth is inevitable in the long run—whether because of man's decision and activities, or despite them.

There are many different opinions about just how urgent the population explosion problem is in the world as a whole and in specific parts of the world. Paul Ehrlich, the biologist whose best-selling book *The Population Bomb* (1968) has been the clarion call of the American antipopulation-growth movements, asserts that the world is rapidly running out of food and that widespread famine is inevitable. Moreover, the continuing deterioration of the environment due to excess numbers of people and overexploitation of natural resources poses threats to mankind no less frightening than starvation. While acknowledging that the problems of less developed countries (LDCs) are more severe than those of more developed countries (MDCs), Ehrlich says that even the MDCs are overpopulated and face urgent social and environmental crises. And in any case, the MDCs cannot escape the worldwide political and economic cataclysm attending starvation and overcrowding in the LDCs. So urgent is the situation, according to Ehrlich, that governments (and first and foremost the United States Government) must immediately reverse domestic policies of encouraging reproduction and replace them with a series of financial rewards and penalties designed to discourage people from having babies. Moreover, LDCs should be ready to use coercive measures to control numbers of births. These actions are not only acceptable and justifiable, but should be considered as conditions for receipt of food aid from the United States.

Not all population scholars agree with Ehrlich's assessment. Frank Notestein is a demographer and an early supporter of the planned parenthood movement who attacks the call for drastic and coercive measures to control population and achieve ZPG. He argues that coercion is either unnecessary or unfeasible (Notestein, 1970). In the MDCs, population growth does not in fact pose anything like the threat envisaged by the ZPG movement: it does not endanger food supply, energy, environment, or resources. Instead, it encourages intelligence and effective organization to assure both that new resources will be developed and that the environment will be preserved and enhanced. Notestein favors the eventual stabilization of population or even moderate population decline in the MDCs in the near future, but he stresses that we must not be indifferent to the consequences of alternative means and schedules for attaining these goals. It is very likely that voluntary family planning, when universally accepted and practiced, will alone be sufficient to bring reproduction close to the level of population replacement. In all events, the situation in the MDCs does not yet justify departure from voluntary methods of family planning.

If the situation is not critical in the MDCs, Notestein acknowledges that the need to reduce population growth (and indeed to reach negative growth) in the less developed areas *is* very urgent. But Notestein points out that while population growth there is much more rapid, by and large neither the leadership nor the public in these countries favors a complete halt to population growth. Family planning has been widely encouraged and approved as a service to citizens who want it, but there is little support or administrative capability to implement more effective or coercive measures.

> It is at best idle to talk of governments in this position drastically coercing their people's reproductive behavior. There are governments that can do something to educate and lead, but, save in the most primitive matters of public order they cannot coerce.
>
> The inability to coerce is perhaps fortunate in this field. I think that we have reason to believe that voluntarism through education and service is the most direct route, as it is certainly the most civilized. (Notestein, 1970, p. 451)

Notestein's faith in the promise of voluntary family planning has been echoed by other demographers and social scientists, especially by those who are closely associated with birth control and planned parenthood activities. But two critiques of this viewpoint have emerged from among fellow demographers. Both assert that we cannot depend on voluntary family planning alone to move us to ZPG in any reasonable span of time. The first line of critique is represented especially by the writings of Philip M. Hauser. According to this argument, birth control has never been the primary factor in observed declines in fertility, either historically or currently. And it cannot reasonably be expected to lead to significant fertility declines—much less to ZPG—by itself, regardless of how smoothly it is sold to leadership and public in the LDCs. Instead, social and economic development and reform have been largely responsible for past and current fertility declines, *and* for adoption of more and more effective methods of birth control. Some minimal affluence, literacy, and even higher aspirations are required as well as sheer availability of means. And visions of future fertility and population control are meaningless without programs of social, economic, educational, and cultural improvements (Hauser, 1967).

A second line of critique is represented by the writings of Kingsley Davis and Judith Blake. They reiterate the idea that voluntary family planning—even if it is universally adopted and is successful in achieving couples' desired family sizes—cannot bring an end to population growth. Indeed, it is inconsistent with the concept of zero population growth. In Davis and Blake's view, the very notions of voluntarism, voluntary family planning, and individual reproductive freedom—as well as the revulsion against coercion or compulsory means of birth control—are themselves deeply pronatalist (favoring high birth rates) values and sentiments. Such ideas are traditional in the sense that they are aligned with the established pronatalist institutions of a society whose mores and institutions were formed under an entirely different demographic regime: under historical conditions of mortality, societies could survive only if the number of births was sufficiently high. Davis and Blake advocate a reconsideration of the *meaning* of birth control measures in terms of what is acceptable and what is not acceptable and what should be coercive and what should be voluntary, under modern demographic conditions. By implication, they suggest that as leaders and public recognize both the desirability and the urgency of population control, and the incompatibility of population control and reproductive freedom, they must opt increasingly and decisively for population control (Davis, 1973; Blake, 1965).

Having one-child or two-children families will help achieve zero population growth. *(United Nations)*

THE FALL OF THE BIRTH RATE

Although world population as a whole continues to grow at an alarming rate, it seems increasingly clear that the early 1970s have witnessed measurable and often very substantial declines in the birth rates of many countries, both developed and less developed. The crude birth rate (the number of births per 1,000 population) in the United States reached a post-World War II baby boom peak of about 25 to 27 per 1,000 between 1955 and 1957. But then it declined to about 18 per 1,000 in 1966, a level which had previously (in 1935, the bottom of the Great Depression) been an all-time low for the birth rate. And it has continued to decline, reaching a new all-time low of 15 births per 1,000 in 1973 (see Figure 2.1). European countries, whose post-World War II baby booms

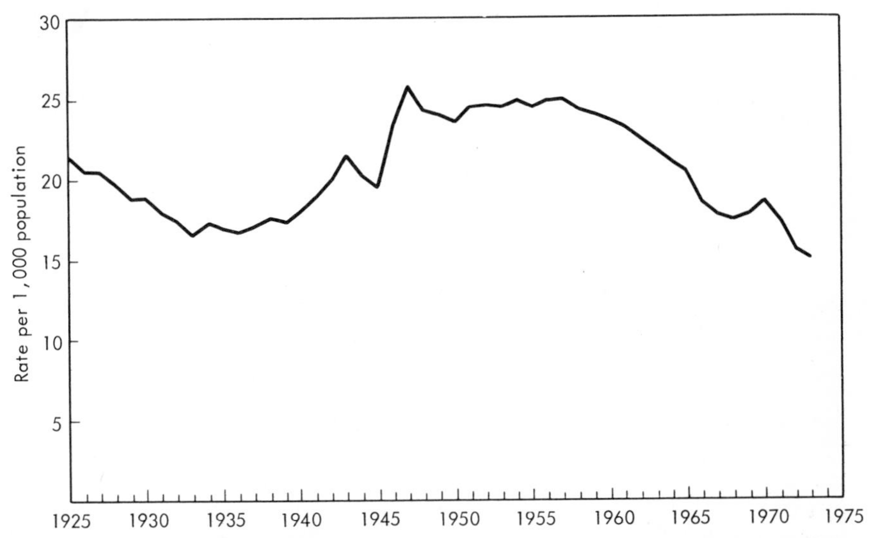

Figure 2.1 U.S. Crude Birth Rate, 1925–1972. *Source: "Vital Statistics Rates: 1925–1973," Statistical Abstract of the United States, 1974, U.S. Bureau of the Census.*

never reached the prolonged high level reached in the United States have recently experienced declines to even lower levels in their birth rates: the United Kingdom's crude birth rate dropped to 14 per 1,000 in 1973, Sweden's to 13.5, and Finland's to 12.2. Both East Germany and West Germany, with birth rates of 10.6 and 10.2 respectively, have experienced net population declines. They have passed ZPG and experienced negative population growth (NPG) in 1973 (see Fig. 2.2).

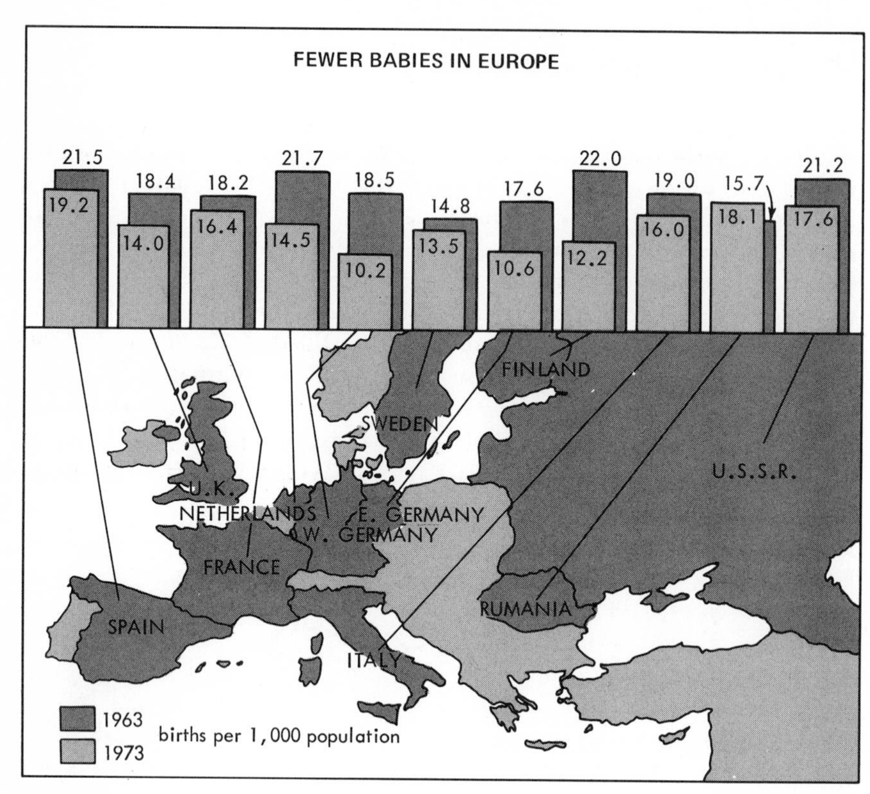

Figure 2.2 Fewer Babies in Europe. *Source:* TIME, *September 16, 1974. Reprinted by permission from* TIME, *The Weekly Newsmagazine; Copyright Time, Inc.*

Outside of Europe and North America, birth rates tend to be much higher. They are almost always higher than 20 per 1,000 (except in Japan); and they exceed 40 per 1,000 in countries of Latin America and South Asia, and 50 per 1,000 in the Middle East and parts of Africa south of the Sahara. But some of these countries have also experienced declines in birth rates, sometimes spectacular ones. Probably best known are the cases of Hong Kong (whose birth rate fell from 36 in 1963 to 19.4 in 1974); Singapore (from 38.7 in 1960 to 21.2 in 1974); and Taiwan (from 39.5 in 1960 to 24 in 1974). Egypt, Sri Lanka (formerly Ceylon), El Salvador, Chile, Malaysia, Jamaica, Costa Rica, and other high-fertility countries have experienced major declines in the birth rate in the same period.

There is no single simple explanation for this recent decline in the birth rates of so many different countries. Instead, several social, economic, and cultural factors seem to be responsible. In Europe, North America, and other countries settled by Europeans the most important factors tend to be widespread education, more effective and more widely available contraception and abortion, environmental concerns, delay of marriage, unemployment and inflation, and women's liberation—the changing status, occupational opportunities, and aspirations of women. In the LDCs, the factors include expanded education, especially for the female population; continuing urbanization and nonagricultural employment; expanding mass communication; and, especially, the deliberate introduction of family planning programs. The exact effect of each separate factor is difficult to measure, and indeed there is considerable difference of opinion especially about the impact of family planning programs first introduced by outside agencies and later supported by LDC governments. Some observers credit most or all of the fall of the birth rate to these activities, while others hold that these trends were based on social and economic development instead, and that the birth rate was declining in these countries even before family planning programs were ever introduced.

In all events, the declining birth rate is a fact, and many demographers now see zero population growth as a realistic possibility for many areas of the world within the next half century. The United States Commission on Population Growth and the American Future was appointed by President Nixon in 1969 to study United States population trends and make policy recommendations. It concluded that if the average family size in the United States should drop to two children per couple, the rate of population growth would decline to zero in about 2015 to 2025 (U.S. Commission on Population Growth and the American Future, 1972). According to *Time* magazine's report of September, 1974, "most European demographers believe most of Europe will hit zero population growth by the turn of the century, about 25 years before the United States." While either or both of these projections may turn out to have been in error, the point is that the MDCs are already close enough to view ZPG as an attainable goal which requires preparation and planning for beyond the sloganeering which has to date characterized discussions. For the LDCs, ZPG seems a much more distant possibility. But here, too, the facts of rapid development, urbanization, and expanded literacy coupled with the recent fall in birth rates say together that ZPG is far more than a utopian concept for the rest of the world as well.

THE ROLE OF POPULATION SCIENCE AND POPULATION POLICY

To say that ZPG is inevitable in the long run is not to say that there are not alternative paths to ZPG, that it is a matter of indifference how the world or any one country reaches ZPG, or that man cannot influence the path taken to ZPG. There *are* alternative paths; it *does* make a difference which path is taken; and man *does,* in general, influence demographic trends and *can* in particular influence the path and speed to zero population growth.

Population Science and Paths to Zero Population Growth

It is clear that even if birth rates decline to no more than replacement levels (about an average of 2.1–2.2 births per woman), populations still retain great potential for growth. High birth rates in the recent past have resulted in a large proportion of young people in the population, many of whom are still unmarried. Their reproductive years are still in the future, which means that there will be large numbers of births even if the rates are low, before zero population growth can be achieved. Thus, even in the United States, if fertility persists at a replacement level, ZPG must still be 50 or 60 years in the future. And by that time, the population will be about 40 percent larger (Freedman & Berelson, 1974).

Population science attempts to ascertain what are the alternative paths to ZPG, to determine the conditions under which each different path is likely to be followed, and to analyze the likely demographic, social organizational, and economic consequences of several types of population developments which would lead in the long run to ZPG in the United States (Frejka, 1968). Frejka (1973) has worked out demographic consequences of the alternative ways of attaining ZPG for the United States and for world population.

The situation Frejka investigates for the United States is one in which there is an immediate (as of 1965) halt to the growth of the United States population—a situation where the annual number of births equals the annual number of deaths. Since death rates at each age are assumed to be fixed,[1] the annual *total* number of deaths fluctuates with the num-

[1] This assumption about mortality in the near future is overall the most likely to correspond to reality, though death rates at some ages might change slightly.

bers of persons in the population at each age. With this fact, Frejka shows that the annual number and rate of births would have to fluctuate very sharply in order to keep pace with deaths—so sharply as to render this a very unlikely path to ZPG.

Frejka has studied subsequent demographic situations for the United States where fertility declines gradually, leading to zero population growth in 2030, in 2035, in 2040 . . . in 2070. Under these conditions the population would gradually achieve a stable age distribution, ultimately characterized by a large proportion of elderly people (18-20 percent of the population over 65) and a relatively small proportion of children (18-19 percent under 15). The total size of the population would depend on how soon the fertility diminished to a replacement level of ZPG, and on the average age of women at childbirth (see Fig. 2.3).

Frejka considers the paths to worldwide population equilibrium by means of the same kinds of projections and computations carried out for the United States. Again, these include the unrealistic conditions necessary for "immediate" achievement of zero population growth, and the alternative gradual paths to ZPG. Frejka also considers and works out possibilities of *uneven* rates of fertility decline in the various areas or types of countries in the world. Assuming a very rapid decline of fertility in the LDCs, Frejka projects a world population of 5.8 billion by the year 2000 (with 1.3 billion in the MDCs and 4.5 billion in the LDCs) and 7.9 billion by 2050 (1.4 billion in the MDCs and 6.5 billion in the LDCs) (see Fig. 2.4). Slower decline of fertility in the LDCs would lead to projected LDC populations of 5.3 billion by 2000 and 11.6 billion by the 2050—to a world population total of 13 billion in the year 2050 (see Fig. 2.5).

Determining the Impact of Social Intervention

We have seen that while demographers and other scientists generally agree about the need to achieve zero population growth, there is no such consensus about the means, or the time schedule, for reaching this goal. This question is a central focus, sometimes direct, sometimes indirect, of scientific population studies. Whether a study attempts to measure the effectiveness of some method of reducing fertility in a contemporary population (a direct study of the impact of social intervention on fertility) or of some factors which affected shifts in fertility in historical populations (an indirect study), virtually all fertility research today bears on this issue.

It is the task of population science to enumerate and evaluate as fully as possible *both* the factors that bear on population and especially

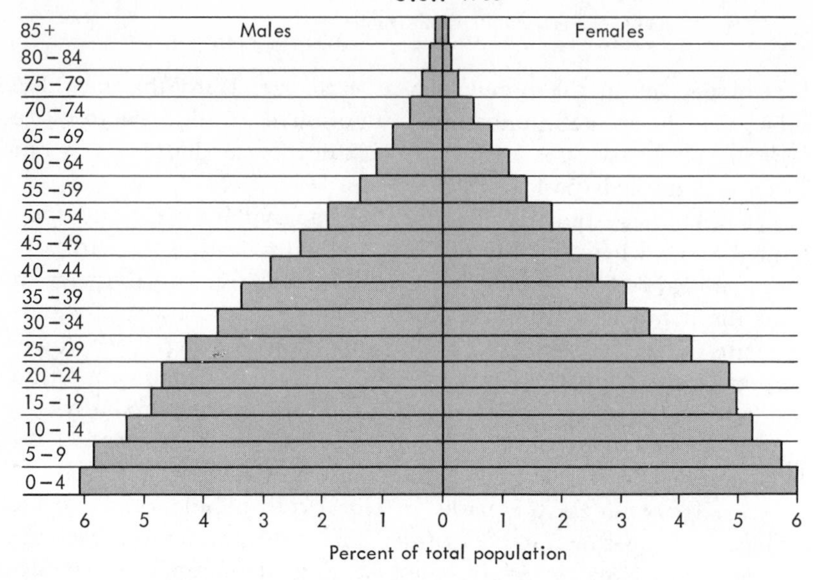

U.S. POPULATION OF 1900 had the age composition shown in this pyramid. Its shape is characteristic of a fast-growing population with high birth and death rates where the average life expectancy is under 60. A third of Americans were under 15 years of age.

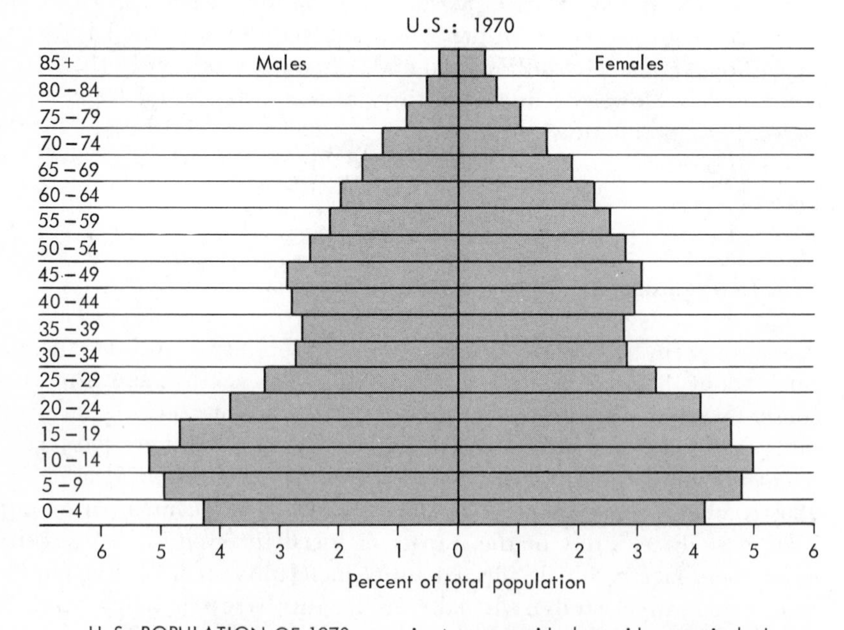

U.S. POPULATION OF 1970 gave rise to a pyramid whose sides are pinched in because of low birth rates that prevailed during the years of the Great Depression. The bulge centered on the 10 to 14 year old age group is a consequence of the postwar baby boom.

Figure 2.3 Age and Sex of the Population of the United States: 1900, 1970, Projections for 2000, and Ultimate ZPG. *Source:* Scientific American. *September 1974.*

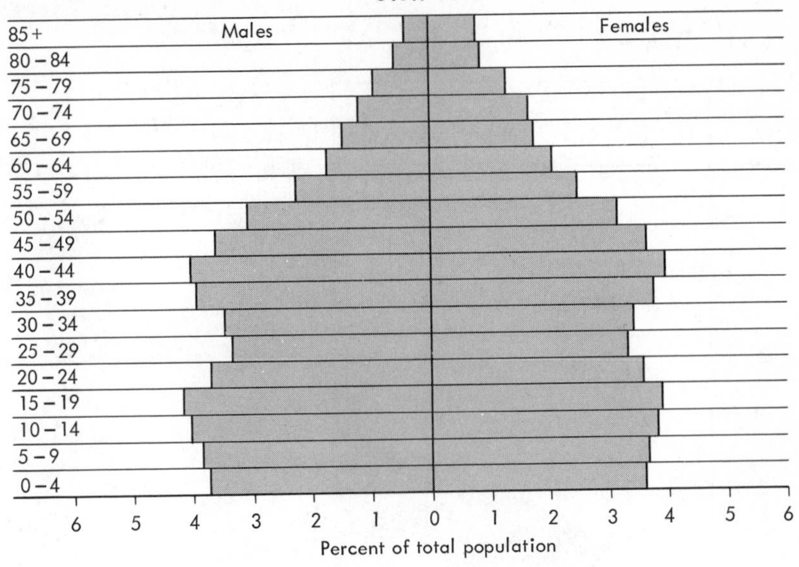

U.S. POPULATION OF YEAR 2000 will form this age pyramid if fertility stabilizes at replacement levels from now until the end of the century. Five to 19 year olds of 1970, who will then be 30 years older, will have produced a second bulge of 5 to 19 year olds.

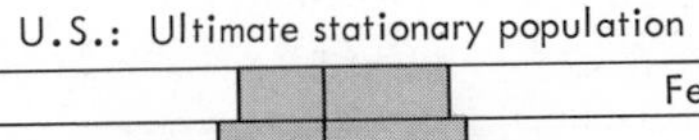

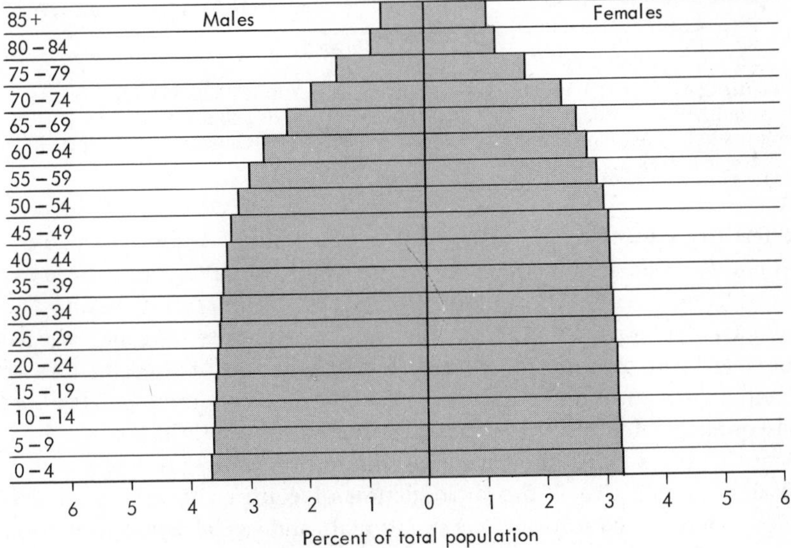

ULTIMATE STATIONARY POPULATION, if it is achieved in the U.S. during the next century, will have the age composition shown here. A third of the population will be under 25 years of age, a third will be between 25 and 50 and another third will be over 50.

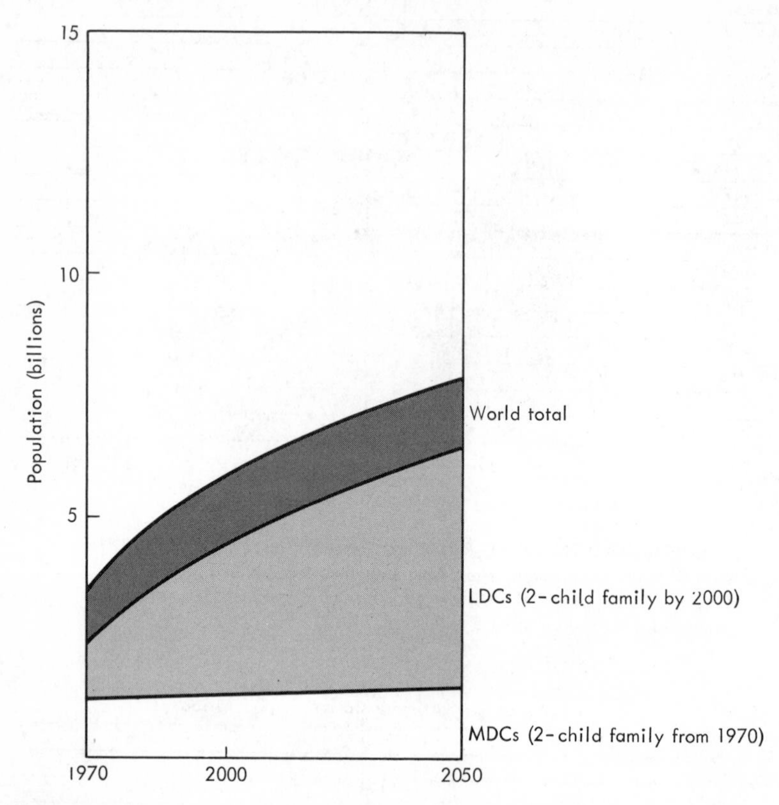

Figure 2.4 World Population Projections under Immediate Fertility Declines. Assuming "rapid demographic transition" in less developed countries (LDCs) with stable situation in more developed countries (MDCs). *Source:* People, *Vol. 1, No. 4 (1974).*

on fertility (since we are all agreed that a higher death rate is an *unacceptable*—even if sometimes inevitable—path to ZPG); and the extent, manner, and circumstances under which these factors can be manipulated by social decisions. Population science also attempts to gauge the consequences, spin-offs, or side effects of manipulation of these factors. For example: what would be the demographic, the economic, and the social consequences of prohibiting marriage below some minimum age in the twenties, rather than the teenage minimum now widely in effect in many areas? How effective is the introduction of contraception and abortion unless women's educational, occupational, and social opportunities are changed? Exactly how would the aging of the population under different paths to ZPG affect the economic and political structure of societies? These and a wide range of similar questions are the province of demographers and other social scientists. And it is population science which

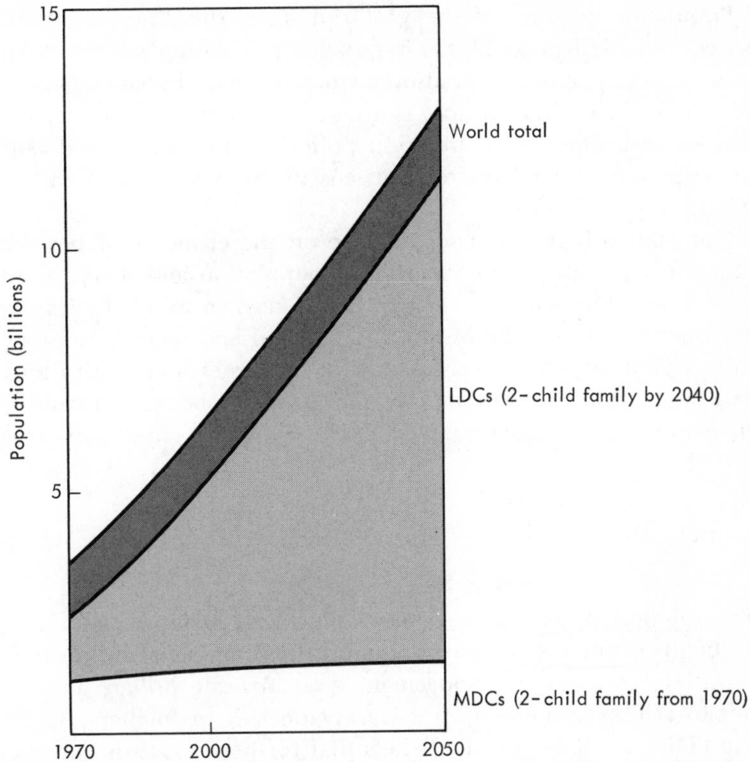

Figure 2.5 World Population Projections under Intermediate Fertility Declines. Assuming "traditional demographic transition" in LDCs. *Source:* People, *Vol. 1, No. 4 (1974).*

has the skills and knowledge to lay out the social options and analyze their implications.

Making the Social Choices: Population Science and Population Policy

The decisions to favor one course of action or inaction over another, or many other, courses always involves some evaluation of tradeoffs. In everyday life, we must balance the conveniences and pleasures of urban living against the noise and crowding of city life; the pleasures of children against the burdens and drains of resources; the joys of personal freedom against the burdens of social and community responsibility. On a worldwide scale, these choices are made by a political process. This process can be aided greatly by scientific knowledge, but ultimately other extrascientific considerations will be brought to bear as well.

Population policies of the past can be studied, and their effects measured and evaluated. This is a task for population science. Current population policy options can also be studied, their effects analyzed, projected, and compared. This, too, is a task for population science. But in making and carrying out population policy, demographers and population scientists must participate as citizens in the political process, acting along with other citizens.

Our emphasis in this book will be on the elements of population science, and especially of the bearing of population and social structure on each other. Throughout, we shall try to keep in mind the important place of population science in modern political and social processes. For regardless of the type of decision-making processes and institutions involved, population policy will have no chance of being constructive or effective unless it is informed by a fully developed population science.

SUMMARY

Zero population growth is the demographic situation in which the number of births in the population is equal to the number of deaths. Several organizations and indeed a movement now advocate private and public actions to achieve a national and worldwide halt to further population growth. They are based on the beliefs that further growth is detrimental to the point of being a menace to well-being, security, and stability; and that voluntary family planning has not by itself been able to reduce population growth enough to resolve either the issues or the crises of the population explosion. The ZPG movement has held—or at least not precluded the idea—that some coercive means are likely to be necessary to achieve ZPG. Some critics of the ZPG movement assert that voluntary family planning will suffice, while others contend that the importance of the population explosion and environmental crises are very much exaggerated relative to other social problems.

Even as the debate goes on, birth rates in countries of the West, including the United States, have been falling to new lows. And in some less developed countries as well, the birth rates have undergone very significant declines. These trends have led many demographers to anticipate actual achievement of zero population growth in the near future —in this century or in the early decades of the next century in Europe and North America, and somewhat later in the entire world. The prospects for realizing ZPG have led to more detailed attention to its implications and side effects. It is very clear that ZPG implies that population will be much *older,* including larger proportions of aged persons and substantially smaller proportions of young persons. In addition, it is believed that the nature of further economic growth—if it is to continue at all—must change under ZPG. But a detailed understanding of what ZPG means is yet to be worked out.

Analysis of the implications of zero population growth depends in large part on the level and detail of our understanding of the causes and consequences of general population variations. Population science has a special role in formulating and examining the range of population policy options and their implications. But the choice of population policies and the adoption of measures to promote and implement them are political processes, and these processes involve all of us.

3

World Population Growth: Demographic Transitions and Societal Adaptations

In this chapter we will review briefly the growth of the world's population and the background of the population explosion. We will present an overview of the patterns of population changes that have occurred from place to place throughout the history of civilization. In this chapter and throughout the book, we shall try to show that population variations over space and transformations over time are always accompanied by changes in societies and social structure. An underlying goal of the book will be to outline a theory which seeks to explain how and why these concomitant variations occur.

INTRODUCTION: WORLD POPULATION AND POPULATIONS OF THE WORLD

There are two areas of concern in the study of population history. The first is that of description and analysis: the description of world population, the development of specific populations, and various patterns of settlement; and the analysis of the factors that are involved in population change and growth. Included in this area of concern is the problem of determining the population setting of social, economic, and political situations or events throughout history. What was the population setting of colonial America? of Ancient Rome at various stages of its growth and decline? of England on the eve of the Industrial Revolution? of France at the time of Louis XIV? of Japan at the beginning of World War II? The answers are crucial if we are to understand the events of the periods indicated and their causes and consequences.

The second area of concern is the more scientific interest in deriving generalizations about population per se. The study of colonial America's population growth, expansion of settlement, and changing social institutions may suggest general conclusions about the interaction of geographical and social-structural consequences of population growth. Such conclusions might help us to understand current demographic and social changes in Australia, or the Middle East, or Asiatic Russia. In the same way, the study of marriage patterns in medieval European towns gives us general information about the overall relationships between urbanization, matchmaking, and family formation.

Prehistoric Populations

It has been possible to identify human habitation in certain areas from about the early Paleolithic through the late Neolithic periods. But at most this has told us only that human activity existed, giving us some very general insight into the kinds of technological adaptations made by people in very early times.

E. S. Deevey, Jr., has recently attempted a quantitative representation of prehistoric population growth (Deevey, 1960; Coale, 1974). According to Deevey's calculations, the total population of the world a million years ago, during the Lower Paleolithic period, was about 125,000. Seven hundred thousand years later, during the Middle Paleolithic period, the population of the world reached one million. And some 275,000 years later, during the Upper Paleolithic period, it reached 3,340,000.

The Bronze Age or Mesolithic Period began in about 8000 B.C., and by this time the total world population had reached about 5,320,000. Four thousand years later, at the onset of the Neolithic period, or Iron Age (which also witnessed the beginnings of settled agriculture), it reached some 86 million. And by the time of Christ, the total world population was about 133 million (see Table 3.1), with most ancient civilizations based on both agricultural and urban settlements.

Early Paleolithic man. *(Courtesy of The American Museum of Natural History)*

TABLE 3.1 Estimated Prehistoric World Population

Years Ago	*Cultural Stage*	*Estimated Population*
1,000,000	Lower Paleolithic	125,000
300,000	Middle Paleolithic	1,000,000
25,000	Upper Paleolithic	3,340,000
10,000	Mesolithic (Bronze Age)	5,320,000
6,000	Neolithic (Iron Age)	86,000,000
2,000	Common Era	133,000,000

Source: Based on data from Edward S. Deevey, Jr., The human population, Scientific American, *September, 1960.*

Population in Ancient Times Through the Middle Ages

We know much more about the populations of the ancient world than about prehistoric populations. In fact, we have comparatively substantial information on the ancient populations of the Mediterranean, the Indian peninsula, China, and Middle and South America. Ancient Mesopotamia had a population of four or five million. And it has been estimated that the population of Ancient Egypt reached some seven or eight million with a density of roughly 200 persons per square kilometer —somewhat higher than the density of present-day western Europe.

Historians have estimated the population of ancient Athens in the fifth century B.C. at about 200,000 (Clark, 1967; Reinhard, Armengaud, Dupaquier, 1968). The population of Rome was about 130,000 in 508 B.C.;

337,000 in 164 B.C.; and 900,000 in 70 B.C. Despite these estimates, however, the gaps in our knowledge of population and settlement patterns in ancient and premodern times are so great as to make it almost impossible to estimate the total population of the world for dates before 1650, much less to trace the development and growth of world population and its components.

There is evidence of major population declines in the transition from the beginning of the Roman Empire in Europe to the more localized polities and societies of the Middle Ages (Clark, 1967; Reinhard, Armengaud, Dupaquier, 1968). During the Middle Ages, populations grew, but only very slowly, and often the growth was wiped out or reversed by recurring famines, wars, or plagues. Great famines were experienced throughout India in 650 A.D.; over the entire world in 879; in India in 941, 1022, and 1033; in England in 1005; and throughout Europe in 1016. A seven-year famine depopulated Egypt between 1064 and 1072 A.D., and many of the German lands are said to have lost half their population from hunger in 1125. There was an eleven-year famine between 1148 and 1159 in India, and in 1162 there was another, worldwide, famine (Ross, 1927). Malaria is believed to have been the major disease threatening ancient Near Eastern populations, and the Black Death was responsible for a great number of deaths in Europe. Between 1348 and 1375, it is thought to have reduced the population of England from about 5 million to 2.3 million. Spain suffered continuous warfare from the eighth to the fifteenth centuries. Her population declined from a peak of about eight million in the second century A.D. to 3.6 million in 600 A.D.; and it took until late in the thirteenth century for the population to reach the eight-million mark again (Clark, 1967).

Such patterns characterized much of the world until very recently. But progress was also being made during Medieval times. There were improvements in agriculture, food preservation, transport, and communication. Technological progress combined with the increasing use of money to produce a more sophisticated economy, as food was grown for markets rather than for subsistence only. A considerable number of ancient cities —including Lacydon (Marseilles), Alexandria, Rome, Athens, and Byzantium—were revived and rebuilt. Many new cities were founded, too: London, Paris, Bruges, Cologne, Venice, Florence, Genoa, and Milan. By 1650, world population had reached about 500 million, and the modern period of population growth had begun.

World Population Since 1650

As Table 3.2 shows, there has been tremendous population growth in recent times. World population increased more than eightfold between 1600 and 1975, from under 500 million to just under 4 billion. It took

TABLE 3.2 Estimates of World Population by Regions, A.D. 14 to 1975 (in millions)

Date A.D.	*World Total*	*Africa*	*North America*	*Latin America*	*Asia*[a]	*Europe*[a]	*Oceania*
14	256	23	. . .	3	184	44	1
350	254	30	. . .	5	185	33	1
600	237	37	. . .	7	168	24	1
800	261	43	. . .	10	173	34	1
1000	280	50	. . .	13	172	44	1
1200	384	61	. . .	23	242	57	1
1340	378	70	. . .	29	186	90	2
1500	427	85	1	40	225	74	2
1600	498	95	1	14	305	95	2
1750	791	106	2	16	498	167	2
1800	978	107	7	24	630	208	2
1850	1262	111	26	38	801	284	2
1900	1650	133	82	74	925	430	6
1950	2486	217	166	162	1335	572	13
1965	3289	303	214	246	1833	675	18
1975	3967	401	237	324	2255	728	21

[a] Estimates for Asia exclude Asiatic Russia. *Source: Figures for A.D. 14–1600 are taken from C. Clark,* Population Growth and Land Use *(London: Macmillan, 1967), Table 3. By permission of Macmillan London and Basingstoke. For 1750–1965 from the United Nations,* Determinants and Consequences of Population Trends, *2nd ed., "Durand Medium Variants Estimates"; for 1975 from endpapers.*

all of human history before 1650 to reach a world population of one-half billion. But the second half billion was achieved in less than 200 years, the third in 50 years, the fourth in 30 years, the fifth in just over 20 years, the sixth in a little more than a decade, and the seventh in only eight or nine years. The growth rate of the world's population has increased from about 0.3 percent per annum in the period from 1600 to 1750 to 2 percent per annum by 1971.

A look at Table 3.2 also shows that population growth has not taken place uniformly in different parts of the world. Between 1750 and 1850, for example, the population of the area of European settlement—including Europe, Asiatic Russia, North and South America, and Oceania—virtually doubled. But at the same time, the population of Asia (excluding Russia) increased by only about 60 percent, and the population of Africa hardly increased at all. The growth pattern looks much different later on. Between 1900 and 1975, Europe's population increased by only 69 percent. But Africa's grew by 202 percent, Asia's by 144 percent, North America's by 189 percent, and Latin America's by 338 percent. As of 1975, the total population of the world is growing at an annual rate of about 1.9 percent, but the rate for Europe is only about 0.6 percent. Asia's growth rate is 2.1 percent (a rate at which the population doubles every 33 years), Africa's is 2.6 percent, and Latin America's is about 2.7 percent (a rate at which the population doubles every 26 years).

CHANGING PATTERNS OF BIRTHS AND DEATHS

Both the phenomenal growth of the world's population in modern times and the different patterns of growth in different parts of the world can be explained mainly by changing patterns of births and deaths. Population growth has two components: *natural increase,* which is the numerical difference between births and deaths; and *net migration,* which is the difference between the number of in-migrants and out-migrants. In the case of the total population of the world, of course, only natural increase need be considered. And in the case of the separate continents, only during certain periods in North and South America and Oceania has net migration accounted for a substantial part of population growth.

Data on population size, numbers of births and deaths, and migratory movements are nonexistent for most countries for most years. However, there are long statistical series available for a number of countries, notably those of Scandinavia. And with these, we can reconstruct Europe's fertility and mortality profile at about the time of the Industrial Revolution. In addition, the census-taking and statistical activities now conducted throughout the world give us data about most recent trends, although this hardly presents a complete body of information.

On the basis of historical data from European countries and data collected more recently throughout the world, we can tentatively say that preindustrial populations are characterized by both very high mortality and very high fertility rates. A crude birth rate [1] of between 30 and 40 per thousand of population may have characterized the European countries in preindustrial periods, and even higher rates (between 40 and 50 per thousand) characterize unindustrialized countries (or LDCs) today. The crude death rate [2] in preindustrial Europe fluctuated widely from

[1] The crude birth rate is the annual number of births per thousand of population, computed as

$$\frac{\text{total number of births in a given year}}{\text{average total population during the year}} \times 1{,}000$$

[2] The crude death rate is the annual number of deaths per thousand, computed as

$$\frac{\text{total number of deaths in a given year}}{\text{average total population alive during the year}} \times 1{,}000$$

The crude rate of natural increase is simply the crude birth rate minus the crude death rate.

year to year in accordance with climate, wars, famines, and pestilence, but it averaged about 30 to 35 deaths per thousand. Even higher crude death rates may have characterized non-European preindustrial countries until fairly recently. But conditions have improved so much that today, it can be said that nowhere do national crude death rates exceed 32 per thousand. Under past high fertility–high mortality conditions, preindustrial populations could grow only very slowly. Indeed, in many periods they actually declined in size. Recent improvements in conditions are one factor which has contributed to the modern population boom.

The preindustrial–postindustrial picture is reflected in data from England. We have records of the burials, marriages, and baptisms that took place in Coylton, England from 1550 to 1830, and these are shown in Figure 3.1. It can be seen that at several points in the preindustrial period, burials exceeded baptisms or births: from 1640 to 1650; from 1665 to 1735; and again from 1765 to 1775. We can see a similar pattern in other parts of England. Figure 3.2 shows population changes in the town of Nottingham and in industrial and agricultural villages in the Vale of Trent. Growth was very slow, and there were occasional declines. After 1750, growth accelerated, especially in Nottingham and the industrial villages.

DEMOGRAPHIC TRANSITIONS

Death rates began to decline in northern and western Europe during the second half of the eighteenth century; this pattern continued until the early twentieth century. Because birth rates remained high through most of this time, the gap between birth and death rates became wider and wider, generating unprecedented rates of population growth. But by the second half of the nineteenth century, birth rates also began to decline in northern and western Europe. This narrowed the gap between birth and deaths and diminished the rate of population growth somewhat.

This process, represented in data for Sweden in Figure 3.3, was repeated in other European countries, though not exactly at the same time. In general, mortality rates began to decline with the beginning of several social and technological movements: these included industrialization, the agricultural revolution, the consolidation of nation-states, and the improvement of transportation and communication. The entire process described above has been outlined in the *theory of demographic*

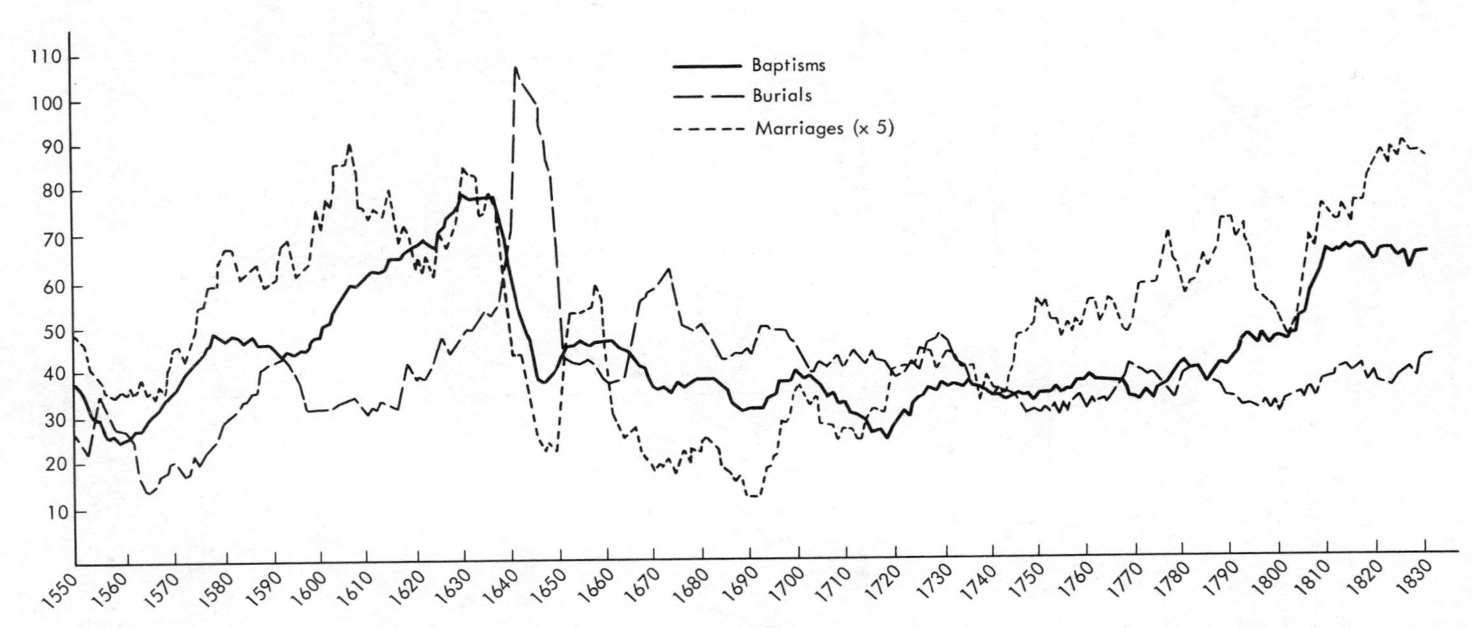

Figure 3.1 **Baptisms, burials, and marriages in Colyton, England (nine-year moving averages).** ***Source: E. A. Wrigley,*** **Population and History** ***(London: George Weidenfeld & Nicholson Ltd., 1969), Fig. 3.4, pp. 82–83.***

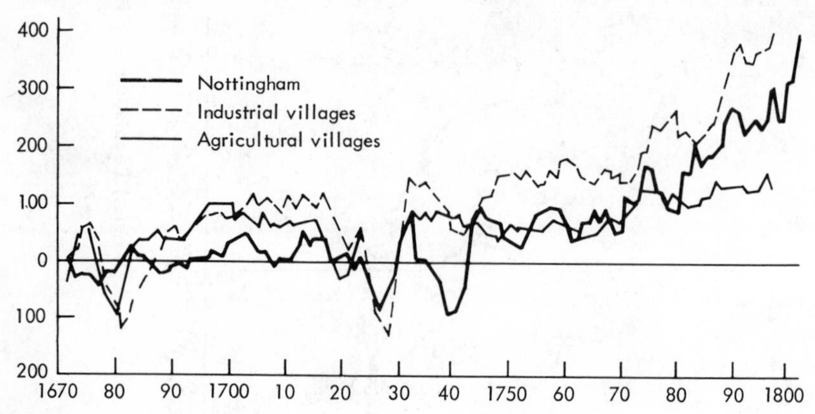

Figure 3.2 Population growth in the town of Nottingham, and in industrial and agricultural villages in the Vale of Trent, 1670–1800. *Source: P. Guillaume and J. P. Poussou,* Demographie Historique *(Paris: Armand Colin, 1976).*

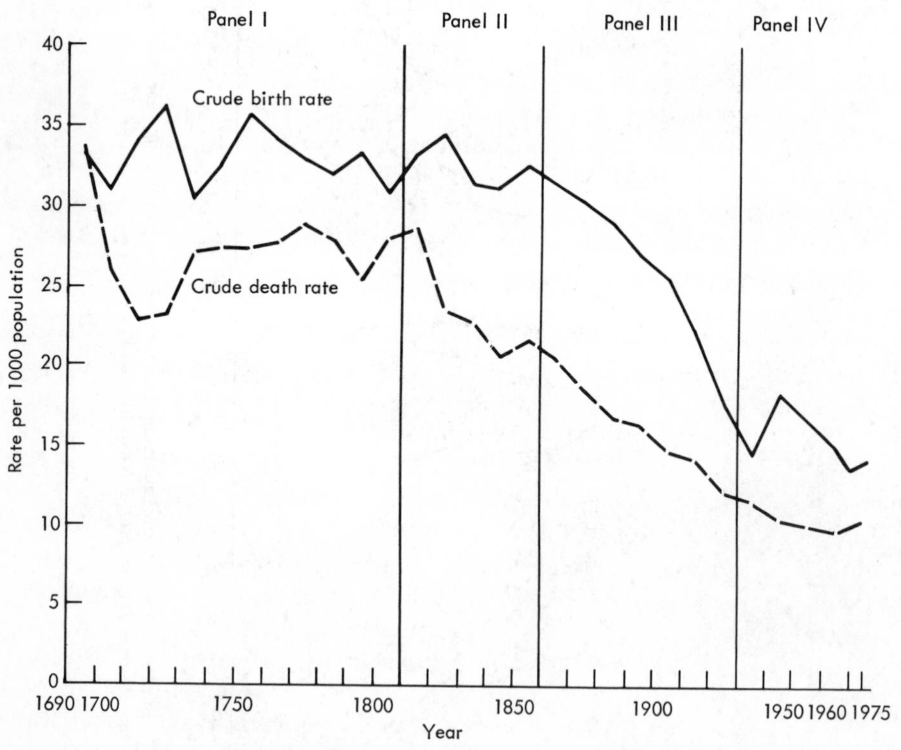

Figure 3.3 Crude birth and death rate in Sweden, 1691–1975. *Data from: G. Utterström, "Population in Eighteenth-Century Scandinavia," in D. V. Glass and D. E. C. Eversley, eds.,* Population in History *(Chicago, 1965), Table 1, p. 538; and W. S. and E. S. Woytinsky,* World Population and Production, Trends and Outlook *(New York: © 1953, Twentieth Century Fund), Tables 66 and 84.*

transition. The general model of the process is typically viewed as having three stages:

1. a period of high fertility and high mortality
2. a stage of declining mortality and high or medium fertility
3. a final stage of low fertility and low mortality

The first stage has been called the *high growth potential stage* because a decline in mortality, in the absence of other changes, would result in very high rates of population growth. Panel I in Figure 3.3 shows that Sweden's high growth potential stage took place in the period before 1810.

The second stage may be called the stage of *transitional growth*. It is characterized by continued high fertility but low or declining mortality rates. In this second stage of demographic transition, population not only grows very rapidly, but it also undergoes changes in age composition. There is typically a slight increase in the proportion of elderly persons (aged 60 and over) which may be imputed in a general way to increased longevity. There is an even more marked increase in the proportion of young persons (under 20 years of age), which derives especially from high fertility and also from a greatly reduced infant and child mortality. And there is a contraction in the proportion of "middle-aged" people—the in-between group from ages 20 to 59.[3] Figure 3.3 shows that Sweden's transitional growth stage took place from about 1810 to 1930, and during this time her population increased from 2.4 to 6.1 million. The stage of transitional growth is often partitioned into two substages—one in which high fertility is maintained while mortality declines, one in which both fertility and mortality decline. In the case of Sweden, the first substage would be from about 1810 through 1860 and the second from 1860 to 1930.

The third stage has been called the stage of *incipient decline*. It is characterized by both low mortality and low fertility. Fertility in this stage is, presumably, deliberately controlled to a considerable degree. The term incipient decline is used because during this stage, populations are capable of depressing fertility to levels so low as to produce negative natural increase (an excess of deaths over births) and hence a decline in population size. France experienced negative natural increase between 1937 and 1945, as did Belgium between 1940 and 1944. As Figure 3.3 shows, Sweden has been in this third stage since about 1930.

[3] Relationships between a population's fertility, mortality, and age composition are discussed later in this volume. For a precise and detailed analysis of these relationships, see Pressat, 1972.

The most recent expositions of the theory of demographic transition have elaborated on this third stage by adding an hypothesis of unstable fertility rates. This says that fertility rates fluctuate with economic, social, and political trends and cycles while mortality rates remain low.

In its general outlines, this model does describe the course of population trends in many European countries, even if some modifications are required in a few cases. The three stages are thought to be related to, and in part are caused by, industrialization, urbanization, and the spread of literacy and education. These are trends with which demographic transitions have certainly been associated in Europe. But a major issue confronting demographers, scientists, and administrators is whether or not the model of the demographic transition can be applied to newly developing countries. Will declining birth rates follow the already spectacularly declining mortality rates and phenomenal population growth of the underdeveloped world? [4] The data in Table 3.3 are relevant to this question.

TABLE 3.3 Recent Trends in Crude Rates of Birth, Death, and Natural Increase: Selected Countries, 1940 to 1975

	Crude Death Rates			*Crude Birth Rates*			*Crude Rates of Natural Increase*		
Country	*1940*	*1960*	*1975*	*1940*	*1960*	*1975*	*1940*	*1960*	*1975*
Mexico	23.2	11.4	8.6	44.3	45.0	42.0	21.1	33.6	33.4
Costa Rica	17.3	8.6	5.9	44.6	42.9	33.4	27.3	34.3	27.5
Chile	21.6	11.9	9.2	33.4	35.4	27.9	11.8	23.5	18.7
Venezuela	16.6	8.0	7.1	36.0	49.6	36.1	19.4	41.6	29.0
Sri Lanka	20.6	9.1	6.4	35.8	37.0	28.6	15.2	27.9	22.2
Malaysia	20.1	9.5	9.9	40.7	37.7	38.7	20.6	28.2	28.8
Singapore	20.9	6.3	5.2	45.0	38.7	21.2	24.1	32.4	16.0
Japan	16.8	7.6	6.6	29.4	17.2	19.2	12.6	9.6	12.6

Source: 1940 and 1960 figures: Dorn 1963, pp. 7–29; 1975 figures: Endpapers.

The eight countries represented in Table 3.3 all had fairly high crude death rates in the period before 1940, when the table begins. In each country, the years after 1940 have been marked by a steep decline in the death rate. All the countries (except Japan, whose crude birth rate has fallen sharply since 1940) had sustained high fertility rates through 1960, even after mortality rates declined. Hence they show increases in crude rates of natural increase. For example, Mexico's crude rate of nat-

[4] For a recent summary of the current debate, see Drake, 1969, pp. 1–13.

ural increase rose from 21.1 per thousand in 1940 (roughly a doubling time of 33 years) to 33.4 per thousand in 1975 (a doubling time of 21 years). Some of the countries, e.g., Venezuela, Sri Lanka, Singapore, have more recently experienced fertility declines.

Throughout the rest of this book, we will see that the general pattern of demographic transition discussed above is a phenomenon which

A crowded commuter-train station in Tokyo, Japan. *(United Nations)*

has recurred and is recurring with many variations at many times and places. A major objective of the study of populations is to describe and analyze the variations in different demographic transitions and to investigate their correlates, causes, and consequences. We are interested in the downward and upward turns of death rates; the inflections of birth rates; the spread, and the time intervals and lags, between birth and death rates; the fluctuations of these intervals and lags; and, in general, the whole class of sociohistorical phenomena related to demographic transitions. Our interest extends beyond the question of whether the demographic transition is a general pattern or strictly a European one. It extends to the range of variations in all such patterns and to their causes and consequences.

THE PRESSURES OF POPULATION GROWTH AND SOCIETAL ADAPTATIONS

The social, economic, and technological arrangements by which a population assures its sustenance and survival are always subject to a certain amount of tension and threat of disruption. This tension or threat may come from external sources: natural or climatic disaster, crop failure, epidemic, war, or any number of other disturbances. The smaller and more isolated the society, the greater the susceptibility to external tension. In addition to outside sources of tension and pressure, an internal source is always present, too. Every population is put under pressure by its own tendency to increase in numbers. This tendency spells opportunity for some societies and disaster for others; in either case, it is a source of change. The pressures of population growth force changes in settlement and in the social-organizational, economic, and technological arrangements of a population. They may even bring about institutionalized constraints on mating or procreation.

In studying any society, we can see that there is an ongoing interaction between a population and its social organization, technology, and environment. Any change in one element must be counterbalanced by shifts in other elements. If a fixed technology and social organization is confronted with substantial population growth, it must adapt to this growth. If it doesn't expand its environment by settlement, cultivation, or exploitation of new areas, it may suffer a decline in per capita level of subsistence. Other options are open to the society confined to a fixed geographical area. It may be able to look after its growing numbers by making adaptations in either social organization or technology. The society which cannot alter its social or technological patterns and which is unable to expand its physical environment must adapt in other ways. It must find a way to control population growth. Otherwise, it will either suffer substantial decreases in its levels of living, or it will lose all of its potential growth through high mortality.

To recapitulate: In any given period of time, a society's strategy of survival and adaptation is bounded and limited by the size of its population, the area and the nature of the territory in which it resides, and the population density of the area in question. Every society must confront the pressure of fertility and potentially expanding populations. This pressure usually generates changes in the societal strategy of survival and adaptation. Only in special cases, as in societies which have very high mortality rates or which deliberately control population growth, does fertility *not* necessarily exert pressure toward change.

Alternative Strategies of Adaptation

We can now consider in some depth a society with a given population size, a given territory, and a given strategy (pastoral, horticultural, agricultural, or industrial) of adaptation. We can assume that any society has a natural potential for population growth. And when population grows, it generates pressures which force the society to make adaptations and expand its effective environment, either extensively or intensively. What alternative strategies are open to such a society?

The First Alternative: Territorial Expansion. One alternative is for a society to expand its area of settlement. The society may divide, developing a second group which simply migrates, leaves the original society, and forms its own settlement in another place. Two cases in point are the Greek colonization in the Mediterranean and the Roman conquests. Other possibilities are the movement of some, many, or even all members of the society to less crowded, peripheral areas, and the expansion of the areas in which food is collected or produced. Both of these alternatives were used in the westward expansion of the United States.

Often, though, there are factors which prevent a society from expanding its area of settlement. Neighboring societies may have territorial rights which they can enforce to prevent such expansion. This restricted expansion for the Italian city-states of the late Middle Ages and the primitive circum-Caribbean societies. Or, a society may not have the means of transport and communication to cover a wider area of settlement. This would mean that the group would either have to break up or lose contact if it expanded its territory. This kind of situation eventually imposes severe strains on a society—witness the case of the overexpanded Roman Empire. Finally, physical expansion may be limited if the neighboring territory is not habitable. A settlement may be surrounded by sea, desert, or some other terrain which it is unable to live on or to exploit for food. This was the case in Ancient Egypt, where the population settled primarily along the banks of the Nile River, leaving the surrounding desert unpopulated.

The Second Alternative: Adoption of Technological and Social Innovations. If a society can't deal with the pressures of population increase by expanding its territory, it may try to intensify its exploitation of the territory it has. This intensification may be effected in two general

Grain harvesting in North Dakota. Extensive mechanization of agriculture has helped provide sustenance for expanding populations. *(United Nations)*

ways. First, the society may improve its technology in order to raise the sustenance yield per unit of area and per unit of labor. This permits the society to absorb and maintain a significant population increase. Technological improvements in the past have included the adoption of cultivation, the change from digging-stick cultivation to hoe cultivation, and from hoe agriculture to plow agriculture. The adoption of hybrid corn in North America and the Green Revolution in Asia are more recent examples. Similarly, the domestication of animals and the development of new forms of power and energy conversion, transportation, communication, and storage all increase either the yield per unit of land or the ability to distribute sustenance among a larger number of people. New technologies for extracting and processing resources and fabricating manufactured products also allow a society to sustain higher population sizes and densities.

Another way to intensify the exploitation of a given territory is to make changes in social organization. Changes like specialization and the division of labor increase very significantly the yield per unit of land; thus they provide an alternative strategy to cope with population pressures.

R. L. Carneiro compared the Kuikuru Indians and other horticultural tribes of the Amazon Basin with horticultural societies of the circum-Caribbean region and the Andean highlands to show how social adaptations may be forced by population pressures. In the Amazon Basin, wide stretches of habitable land allowed the population to grow and expand with no great density concentrations or technological or social-organizational changes. But in the circum-Caribbean and Andean areas, the settlements were circumscribed by uncultivable land. In the mountain valleys of Colombia, the coastal strips of Venezuela, the islands of the Greater Antilles, and the Peruvian coastal valleys, there was no room for settlements to spread out. Here, the result of population growth was competition, warfare, increased political organization, stratification, division of labor, and intensification of agricultural activity (Carneiro, 1968).

The Third Alternative: Population Control. When a society of given size and area can neither expand its territory nor intensify its exploitation of the land, population growth will exert pressure on resources so that the standard of living is reduced. This usually causes a rise in mortality rates, which in turn reduces or even neutralizes the pressure of population growth. This has been the pattern of population growth throughout most of human history.

But there is another alternative to this cycle. Another way to diminish the pressures of growing population is to control fertility deliberately. Celibacy, delayed marriage, birth control, and abortion within marriage are the most familiar means of controlling population growth in modern Western societies. However, some societies have been known to engage in considerably more drastic means of population control: the abandonment of elderly and deformed persons, infanticide, human sacrifice, cannibalism, and slave trading. The Aztecs practiced human sacrifice on a large scale; the ancient Greeks killed disabled infants; the Tikopia practiced infanticide. Hobhouse, Wheeler, and Ginsberg (1965) note ten societies which practice cannibalism,[5] 42 which practice human sacrifice, and 45 which practice infanticide.

Societal Adaptations: Some Examples Over Time. We can look at a few examples of the ways different societies have coped with population growth. The most familiar example is that of the United States, where both high rates of natural increase and a great influx of immigrants made the nineteenth century a time of tremendous population growth. The well-known westward expansion of the frontier took place throughout most of the century, and it provided an initial solution to population pressures. But late in the nineteenth century, industrialization and changing technology produced new, more concentrated patterns of settlement as urbanization began. This social-technological reorganization rendered the earlier geographical expansion relatively obsolete, or at least less advantageous as a social strategy, and it has remained the key to our coping strategy until recent years. We will return to this example in Chapter 5.

Ireland and Spain have another means of population control. Both are Catholic, both have low levels of urbanization and industrialization; both also have low mortality rates. Yet these populations have experienced very little growth for generations. The two cultures have traditions of very late marriage and high proportions of unmarried people. These factors both act as substitutes for birth control to limit population growth.

Newly developing countries in Asia have recently enjoyed spectacular declines in mortality and are now experiencing correspondingly spectacular increases in population. With available land already intensively settled, cultivated, and exploited, these populations are seeking to preserve and even improve their levels of living by introducing new technologies and at the same time promoting fertility control practices. They are making a deliberate, conscious, planned attempt to revise social strategies of adaptation. Asia's (and some other LDCs,) attempt to control population pressure illustrates the urgency of our need to understand population processes and social strategies, both current and historical.

In Europe's case, it seems clear not only that great population growth was successfully sustained in the demographic transition, but also that levels of living and the quality of life in general were improved. The case is not so clear in the newly developing countries today. Their spectacular population growth is itself evidence that these countries have succeeded in altering their strategies of survival and adaptation—

[5] Although they do not distinguish between those practicing it on enemies or strangers and those practicing it on members of their own society.

otherwise, their high fertility would be neutralized by high mortality, as indeed it was in the past. What is in question is whether or not, under conditions of rapid population growth, the already low levels of living in these countries can be prevented from falling further (or whether they can be raised as they were in Europe). Because of the widespread political commitment of national elites to raising levels of living, and because of the increasing visibility (due to education, improved information, and communication) of the extreme differences in standard of living between developed and underdeveloped countries, any failure to improve conditions in the LDCs can be seen as a threat to local and world political stability. It is here that the social-scientific questions of how population size, structure, and change are related to production, distribution, and levels of living take on their current urgency.

SUMMARY

In this chapter, we have outlined world population growth from the earliest times to the present. We have introduced some basic ideas and concepts in the analysis of demographic transitions and presented the outlines of a theory of societal adaptations to actual or potential population growth. Two major population explosions are identified in world history: the first is associated with the introduction of agriculture and agricultural settlement in ancient times, and the second with the industrial revolution. We have only sketchy information about the size and distribution of world population before the modern period. But we think the world's population reached about one-half billion before the onset of the industrial revolution. It reached about one billion in the mid-nineteenth century; almost three billion by the mid-twentieth century; and four billion by 1975. In the early modern period Europe's population grew much faster than the rest of the world. But in this century, Europe's population growth has been moderate while that of Asia, Africa, and especially Latin America has been very rapid.

The modern patterns of rapid population growth have been characterized as *demographic transitions,* the name given to shifts from demographic situations of high death rates and high birth rates (little or no net population growth) to low death and birth rates (again, with relatively little net population growth) which have recurred in many countries. In the course of this demographic transition, there is characteristically a middle stage: a lag between the early decline of death rates and the later decline of birth rates which is a period of great population growth. In western Europe, this demographic transition and the corresponding population boom took place largely in the nineteenth and early twentieth centuries (in southern and eastern Europe it happened somewhat later and also more rapidly). The countries of Asia, Africa, and Latin America are now experiencing what appears to be the beginnings of demographic transition—rapidly declining death rates, with continued high birth rates and ensuing rapid population growth. The question of whether, when, and under what circumstances they will complete their demographic transitions with lowered birth rates and diminished or zero population growth is at the heart of the world population explosion riddle.

Population changes, and especially population growth, subject societies' social, political-organizational, economic, and technological arrangements to new pressures and requirements—and also opportunities—for providing sustenance and for ordering social interactions. To assure that levels of living will remain acceptable, societies confronted with population growth may either expand their areas of settlement or adopt technological or social innovations to increase production within a constrained environment. In this way, population growth generates distributional and social-organizational responses and adaptations. If a society is unable to provide for increased population by expanding its environment, its technology, or its organizational abilities, it will lose its potential population growth through other means. High death rates are historically the most common pattern. But a society may also prevent the increase itself by adopting some means of population control. Different historical patterns of population growth, and different societal strategies of adaptation to this growth potential, have generated variations in population size, distribution, and structure. It is to these that we turn in the next chapter.

4

Contemporary Population Variations and Social Structures

About the most obvious demographic statement we can make is that populations vary from one society to the next. In this chapter, we introduce several ways of classifying populations, and we use these to look at the variations among contemporary populations. We shall argue that differences in population size, composition, and attributes correspond to variations in social-organizational features and interactional arrangements—an analysis which is a continuation of the theories of societal adaptations to population changes introduced in Chapter 3.

POPULATION VARIATION AND POPULATION STUDIES

In this era of long-distance travel, widespread literacy, and highly developed communications media, almost everybody has some elementary acquaintance with the demographic differences among communities, states, regions, or nations. The populations of India, the United States, Australia, Mexico, Belgium, and Ghana differ from one another in many ways. At least some of these kinds of differences are so widely recognized as to make it self-evident that there are in the world, at any moment in time, a large number of delineable populations which differ from one another in many ways. The observable variations in population size, structure, and other characteristics, and the determinants and consequences of these variations, are the subject matter of scientific population studies. In dealing with population variations in this book, we shall be particularly concerned with their social-structural causes, effects, and correlates.

Delineating Populations

Populations can be distinguished from one another by several different criteria. The most common of these is political integration. Persons belonging to the same political unit—be it a nation, tribe, township, municipality, or kinship network—as well as people living in territory which belongs to that political unit, are "in" the population of the unit. Everyone else is considered to be outside it.

Populations may also be delineated in terms of natural geographic criteria, as are the populations of islands or continents and the populations of some naturally bordered regions or distinct geomorphological units (for instance, Appalachia, the Low Countries of Northwest Europe, and the Gulf Coast of the United States). Populations may also be defined and bounded according to a recognized range of economic integration—examples are metropolitan New York and the Cotton Belt. Finally, cultural criteria like language, religion, or ethnic origin, and other bases for social solidarity like race, occupational attachments, previous military service, physical ability or disabilities may be used to define distinct population groups.

NATIONAL POPULATIONS

Probably the most frequently encountered classification of populations is that of the nation-state, or national population. National populations can be classified according to several characteristics: population size; the kinds of areas in which people live; population density; composition in terms of sizes of places of settlement or in terms of urban or rural settlement; age structure and growth characteristics; and social, cultural, and economic characteristics.

Variations in Population Size

In most contemporary sovereign nations the population is 30 million or less. The smallest of these, the countries with populations of one million or less, are mostly Arab sheikdoms in the Near East (Kuwait, Qatar, Oman, and Bahrein) and a few tiny principalities in Europe, like Andorra, Liechtenstein, Luxembourg, Monaco, and San Marino.

The largest group of nations have populations in the 1–5 million class. Included are all the Central American republics and about half of the independent states of Africa. Twelve populations number between 30 and 75 million. These include Nigeria and Egypt on the African continent; Mexico on the North American continent; Turkey, the Philippines, and Thailand in the two extremes of Asia; and France, West Germany, Italy, Poland, Spain and the United Kingdom in Europe. Finally, there are only eight countries with giant populations of 75 million persons or more. The United States is the only giant in North America. Similarly, Brazil is the only one in South America, and the Soviet Union is the only one in Europe. By contrast, Asia has five giant populations: Mainland China, India, Indonesia, Japan, and Pakistan.

Variations in Area Size

The populations of just over one-fourth of contemporary sovereign nations of the world are confined to land areas under 50 thousand square kilometers (where one square kilometer = .3861 square miles). Over a third of the countries have areas between 100,000 and 500,000 square kilometers, and only seven nations have land areas of over three million square kilometers.

Europe and Asia are each represented in the smallest class by twelve populations. In Europe, these include Belgium, Denmark, the Vatican, Luxembourg, the Netherlands, and Switzerland; and in Asia, Taiwan, Israel, Kuwait, Lebanon, Cyprus, Singapore, and Hong Kong. North American countries in this group include the small Central American and Caribbean republics of El Salvador, the Dominican Republic, and Haiti. African countries in the smallest area category include Zambia, Mauritius, Burundi, and Rwanda. New Zealand and the Fiji Islands in Oceania also belong to this group. No South American populations occupy such small areas.

The 100,000 to 500,000 square kilometer category includes a large number of nations in Africa, Asia, and Europe, but relatively few in North and South America. Some of the African populations in this group are Ghana, Guinea, the Ivory Coast, Morocco, Tunisia, and Dahomey; and a sample of the European countries includes Bulgaria, Czechoslovakia, East Germany, West Germany, Greece, Norway, Poland, Rumania, and the United Kingdom. The Asian countries in this category include Iraq, Japan, Malaysia, Nepal, the Philippines, Syria, both North and South Vietnam, and Yemen.

Of the seven with the greatest amount of land, two are in North America (Canada and the United States); two are in Asia (Mainland China and India); and South America, Oceania and Europe each have one. These giants are Brazil, Australia, and the Soviet Union.

Variations in Population Density

The relationship between population and area is expressed in terms of population density, the number of persons per areal unit. In this case we are concerned with the number of persons per square kilometer. Because of the innumerable possible combinations of population size and area, singularly different types of populations can have the same population density. For example, a population of 1,000 persons living in an area of 100 square kilometers will have a density of ten persons per square kilometer—and so will a population of 10,000 persons living in an area of 1,000 square kilometers. Africa, South America, and Oceania have largely low-density nations; North America and Asia have a broad range of density patterns; and the nations of Europe are predominantly of high density.

Population density is very high in both Europe and Asia. In Europe, no fewer than eight populations have densities of 200 persons per square kilometer or more. These are Belgium, West Germany, the Vatican, Malta, Monaco, the Netherlands, San Marino, and the United Kingdom. Some of the eight Asian countries in the highest density class include Taiwan, Japan, South Korea, and Lebanon, and those in the next highest include India, Pakistan, Israel, the Philippines, and Sri Lanka. Note, again, that very different types of populations can have the same density. Some countries have high densities because they have very small territories but large populations. This is the case of Burundi, Rwanda, Sri Lanka, Hong Kong, Taiwan, Singapore, South Korea, and the Netherlands. Other countries have high density because they have moderately large territories but huge populations: Japan, Pakistan, the Philippines, Turkey, West Germany, and the United Kingdom are cases in point. Conversely, countries like Sarawak, Gabon, and Iceland have very low densities because their small populations live on large land areas; while Libya, Mali, Canada, Bolivia, and Saudi Arabia have low densities because their moderately large populations live in enormous areas.

To this point, our purpose has been to indicate the range of variation among populations. We now turn to a discussion of the way such variations affect the social, economic, and political make-up of a population and, in particular, how a change in population size, density, or composition may affect the political, economic, and social structure of a population.

CLASSIFYING POPULATIONS BY PATTERNS OF SETTLEMENT

Populations may be classified according to type or size of settlement: urban, rural, metropolitan, rural farm, and rural nonfarm. This means of classification may tell us more about a population's character than do the size, area, and density classifications. This is because there are significant differences between towns and villages with respect to work, residence, family, government, religion, recreation, education, voluntary organizations, social stratification, norms and values, and interpersonal relations. In addition, the urban proportion in a population influences the social structure and relationships in both the urban and in rural sectors of the society (Sjoberg, 1964; Gibbs & Schnore, 1960; Hauser & Schnore, 1965; Tilly, 1974).

Classification by settlement patterns may be especially informative, but it poses certain technical problems. There are few universal definitions of the concepts involved. In some countries, a place of settlement is considered urban if it is of a certain size—if it has 2,000 persons, or 10,000, or more. In other countries, the kind of local political administration is taken as the relevant criterion. And in still others, characteristics like the economy or the degree of population density determine what is an "urban place."

In the United States, we consider a place to be urban if it is incorporated and includes 2,500 or more inhabitants, or if it is contiguous to an urban settlement and is densely settled. In Honduras, settlements of 1,000 or more inhabitants are considered urban. In Yugoslavia, the criterion is 15,000 population or a large proportion of the labor force engaged in nonagricultural occupations. In Denmark, places are urban if they have 200 residents or more, but in Czechoslovakia, urban places must have populations of 5,000 and a density level of 100 or more per square kilometer. In Italy, places are urban if no more than 50 percent of their inhabitants are engaged in agriculture. Great Britain's county boroughs and districts are urban regardless of population size or occupational composition (Hauser, 1965a). Thus, there is a real problem of noncomparability with regard to the "urban" sectors of various national populations.

Nevertheless, all urban populations have in common high densities, fairly large agglomerations of populations, and generally nonagricultural occupations—and this makes it possible at least to compare countries in terms of their urban proportions. Table 4.1 shows the urban proportions of selected countries in about 1950 and in 1970. We can see that urban proportions in the mid-twentieth century ranged from 9.9 percent in Thailand, to 71.3 in Israel, to 80.3 in the United Kingdom. The table also shows what proportions of the populations of these countries live in localities of several different sizes, from 2,000 persons or more on up to 100,000 persons or more. Not all of these are necessarily considered urban, for while one country may designate a place of 2,000 persons as urban, another may not. However, nearly all countries consider places of 20,000 or more to be urban. In any event, size designations like those in Table 4.1 do not depend on any one country's definition; they are descriptive and nonsubjective. By showing, for instance, that Thailand has the smallest percent of its population living in localities of 2,000 or over, and that the United Kingdom has the largest, the table gives us a good idea of the comparative urbanization of the five countries included.

Most countries have at least one city with a population of over 100,000, and the percentage of people living in cities of this size has risen in the last 30 years. In about 1950, more than half of Australia's population lived in places of 100,000 or more, as did almost half the populations of Israel and the United States. This was in contrast to only 5 percent of the Pakistani population and 7 percent of the Indian population. By 1970, the proportion of the population in urban areas had increased in all countries (except the United Kingdom, where it remained nearly stable) although as Table 4.1 shows, the range of urbanization is still great. This change is the result of rural migration to the cities which has been stimulated by continuing industrialization and urban development.

The process of urbanization varies over space and time. Australia and Israel are examples of countries in which initial modern settlement took place largely in the cities. Early immigrants to colonial America, by contrast, settled in rural places. The United States, at first a largely rural society, underwent a process of urbanization that began with its independence, was accelerated after the Civil War, and is only now nearing completion. India and Pakistan, despite their very ancient and large

TABLE 4.1 Urban Population and Population Living in Agglomerations of Different Sizes: Selected Countries, circa 1950 and 1970 (in percentages)

	1950							1970	
Country	*Percent urban*	*2,000+*	*5,000+*	*10,000+*	*20,000+*	*50,000+*	*100,000+*	*Percent urban*	*100,000+*
Australia[a]	68.9	74.2	66.4	61.6	57.3	52.4	51.4	88.5	64.7
India[b]	17.3	37.7	21.1	15.3	12.0	8.7	6.6	18.8	10.0
Israel	71.3	73.6	66.2	61.9	51.3	45.6	45.6	81.3	55.1
United States	64.0	65.1	60.5	56.2	52.0	46.8	43.9	75.2	58.4
Thailand[c]	9.9	9.9	9.8	8.9	6.7	4.5	4.5	13.0	7.8
United Kingdom[d]	80.3	79.7	77.6	74.0	66.9	50.8	36.1	79.1	71.8

[a] 1943 data.
[b] 1951 data.
[c] 1947 data. Cities and towns defined administratively.
[d] 1951 data. Cities and towns defined administratively.

Sources: figures circa 1950 adapted from J. P. Gibbs and Kingsley Davis, Conventional versus metropolitan data in the international study of urbaniaztion, American Sociological Review, *Vol. 23, No. 5, October 1958; 1970 figures from Kingsley Davis,* World Urbanization 1950–1970, Vol. 1 *(Berkeley: Institute for International Studies, 1969); reprinted by Greenwood Press, 1976.*

cities and their recent upsurge in urbanization, are still at only the beginning of a process of rural-to-urban migration and population redistribution.

CLASSIFYING POPULATIONS BY AGE STRUCTURE AND GROWTH CHARACTERISTICS

Populations are classified in terms of their age structures and growth characteristics (primarily fertility). However, it is not always recognized that age structure and growth characteristics are very intimately related. A *young population* is one with a relatively high proportion of children,

(United Nations)

adolescents, and young adults, and a relatively low proportion of middle-aged and aged persons: such a population has high potential for growth. An *old population* has a relatively high proportion of middle-aged and aged people, and it usually has lower growth potential. Figure 4.1 shows young and old populations graphically in the form of population pyramids for the United States in 1870, 1940, 1970, and 1974. Populations which have both high mortality and high fertility tend to be quite young populations; the United States in 1870 had medium mortality and high fertility. Populations characterized by both low mortality and low fertility—such as the United States in 1940—tend to be old populations. The pyramid for 1970 reflects the low fertility prior to World War II, the high fertility of the extended postwar baby boom, and the tapering off of fertility in the 1960s.

Thus, the population pyramid shown in Figure 4.1 for 1870 is broadest at the base and narrower at each higher and older age group. This reflects continued high fertility, with each aggregate of new babies larger than that of the previous year for some time before 1870. After World War I, the number of births in the United States declined, and it did not begin to recover until 1940. This trend is reflected in the population pyramid for 1940, in which the base is narrower than the middle. After World War II, the number of births increased annually, reaching a peak in 1959–1961 and then declining sharply. This is reflected in the 1970 population pyramid in the small base which becomes sharply broader in the 5–9 and 10–14 year age groups. The population pyramid for 1974 shows that this trend is still continuing.

We have already noted that countries and continents differ from each other in respect to their patterns of population growth. Table 4.2

TABLE 4.2 Age Composition and Dependency Ratio, Selected Countries, 1969 and 1974

	Age (in percentages)			*Dependency Ratio*
Country	*<15*	*15–64*	*65+*	$\left(\frac{<15 \text{ and } 65+}{15\text{–}64}\right) \times 100$
United States, 1974	25.8	64.2	10.0	56
Dominican Republic, 1969	47.3	49.7	3.0	101
Paraguay, 1969	45.9	50.2	3.9	99
Egypt, 1969	42.7	53.8	3.5	86
Denmark, 1969	23.8	64.8	11.4	54
United Kingdom, 1969	23.5	63.7	12.8	57
Austria, 1969	24.1	62.1	13.8	61

Source: United Nations, Demographic Yearbook, *1969.*

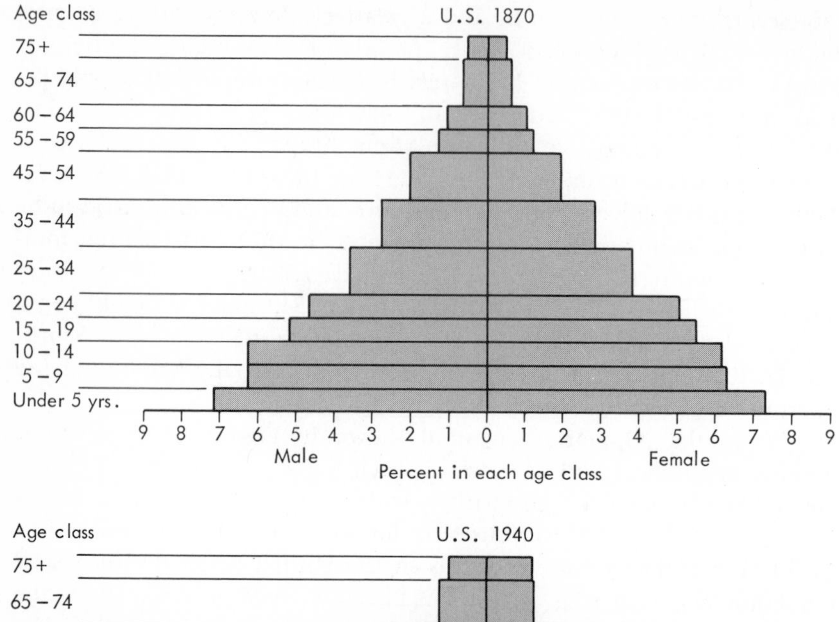

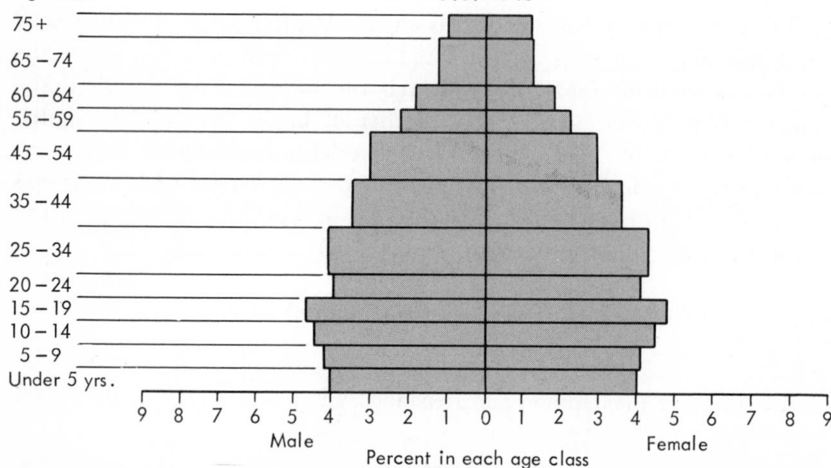

Figure 4.1 Population pyramids for the United States, 1870, 1940, 1970, and 1974. *Source: U.S. Bureau of the Census,* U.S. Census of the Population, 1870, 1940, and 1970; Characteristics of the Population and 1974 Current Population Reports, No. 529, p. 25.

indicates some of the variations among selected populations in 1969 and 1974. For instance, the proportion under 15 years of age ranged from about 24 percent in Austria to about 47 percent in the Dominican Republic. The proportion aged 15 to 64 ranged from about 50 percent in the Dominican Republic to nearly 65 percent in Denmark. For ages 65 and over, the range was from three percent in the Dominican Republic to nearly 14 percent in Austria.

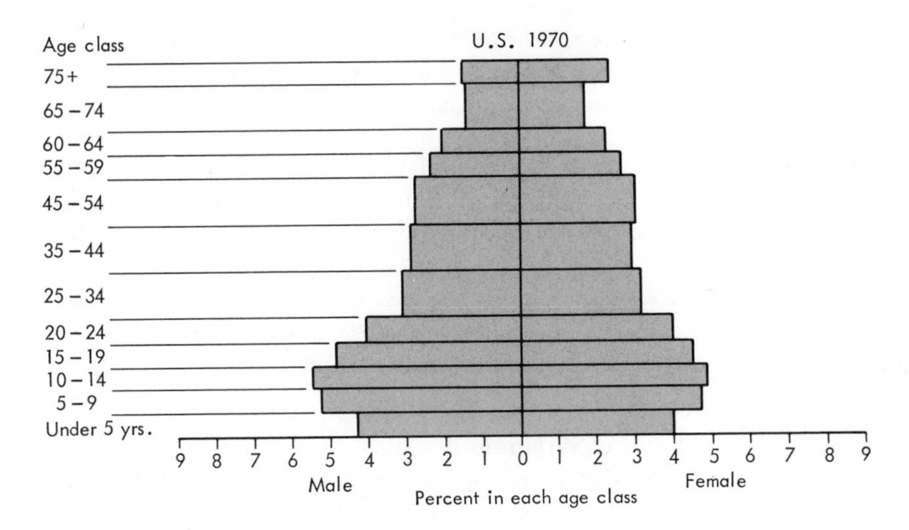

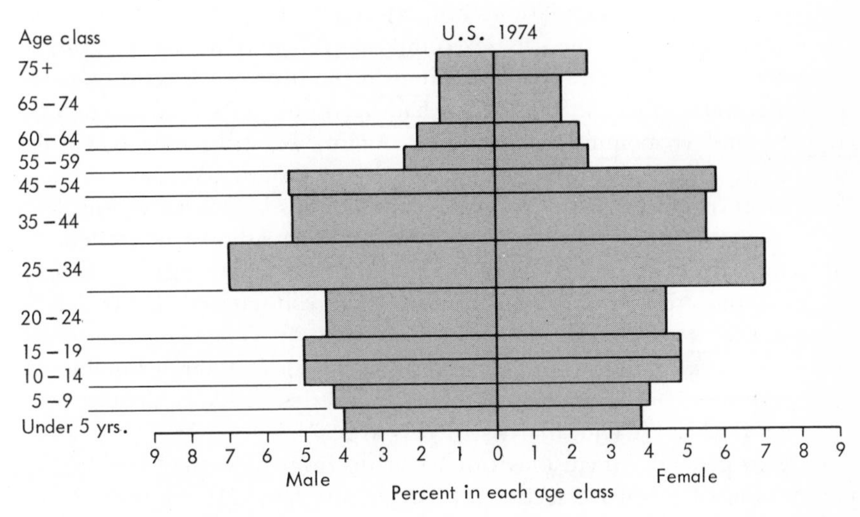

The last column of Table 4.2 shows ratios of the population total of the "under 15s" and the "65 and over's" to the middle population group between ages 15 and 64. This is called the *dependency ratio.* It is so named because it measures the ratio of the population in ages too young or too old to work (but consumers, just the same) to the population of working age. The table shows that the Dominican Republic, Paraguay, and Egypt had very high dependency ratios because of the large percentages under 15 years of age. The dependency ratios of the United States and Denmark are lowest. Denmark's is slightly lower than that of the United States despite a larger percentage of the elderly.

Variations like those shown in Table 4.2 could be sketched for the 50 American states; for the country's major racial and religious populations; for each of the community areas of any major city; for the population employed in, or dependent upon, each of the various economic sectors; or more generally for any population group. The demographic, social, economic, and political implications of variations and change in age structure will be examined in more detail in Parts II and III of this book.

PRELITERATE AND SMALL-SCALE SOCIETIES

In principle, the kinds of variations described above can be studied for populations of nonliterate tribes or communities, for nomadic groupings, and for isolated village populations of every type. In practice, however, data for such populations are extremely difficult to obtain. We know very little about the size, sex composition, age structure, or growth characteristics of American Indian tribes in the nineteenth century, even though ethnographers and historians had begun to study their languages, customs, and economies by that time. Again, we still know relatively little about the demographic characteristics of groups like the Eskimos, the African pygmies, or the Arapesh made famous by Margaret Mead.

However, demographers are becoming increasingly interested in the populations of preliterate and small-scale societies; just as anthropologists and ethnographers are becoming more interested in the demographic characteristics of the societies they study. The *Cross Cultural Summary* (Textor, 1967), an extensive work which includes a number of demographic variables among small-scale societies, is likely to stimulate even more research and analysis in this area.

Two general conclusions can be made from data we have on the populations of primitive societies. First, despite frequent suppositions to the contrary, primitive populations are often very unstable. Fluctuations in size due to changes in mortality levels and migrations are very common. Primitive populations also have fluctuating marriage and fertility rates, although less is known of these. Petersen (1969) cites several examples of changing mortality levels in small-scale societies. In some cases, like those of the Polynesians, American Indians, the Hispaniola Indians in Haiti, and the Omagua in the Caribbean, population size dropped sharply following contact with Europeans. (This is not always the case. Another Caribbean tribe called the Cocama have retained their initial population size since contact with Europeans, while some New Hebrides Islands groups and the Angmagssalik Eskimos in Greenland have increased their populations.) Petersen concludes that the factor most directly responsible for population decimations, where they occurred, was the new diseases brought by the Europeans, but that the extent of such direct depopulation has probably been exaggerated. Armed conflict and the slave trade caused depopulation, too. Probably more of this was indirect—through disease and by prevention of marriage and reproduction—than was direct, by personal casualties.

In general, changes within populations of primitive societies are much less well known, and still less understood, than the variations among these societies. And the second general conclusion that can be made about primitive populations is that there is indeed considerable variation —in size, density, structure, growth rate, and composition.[1] The *Cross Cultural Summary* records 222 fixed-settlement cultures, and 110 nomadic cultures historically with no fixed patterns of settlement. The Shoshonean Indian tribes were one nomadic population in America. They foraged for vegetable foods and small game in family bands in spring and summer, but clustered in multifamily encampments during the winter months. In British Columbia, the Carrier Indians summered in permanent villages near lake or river fishing areas, and in the winter families traveled alone in small bands to hunt and trap meat- and fur-bearing animals (Steward, 1955).

Table 4.3 shows how local communities of small-scale and preliterate

TABLE 4.3 Cross-Cultural Survey: Mean Size of Local Communities[a]

Mean Size of Local Communities	*Number of Cultures*
1. Fewer than 50 persons	46 cultures
2. 50 to 99 persons	43 cultures
3. 100 to 199 persons	46 cultures
4. 200 to 399 persons	21 cultures
5. 400 to 1,000 persons	24 cultures
6. More than 1,000 persons; no indigenous urban aggregation of more than 5,000 persons	5 cultures
7. One or more indigenous towns of more than 5,000 inhabitants but none of more than 50,000 persons	16 cultures
8. One or more indigenous cities with more than 50,000 inhabitants	23 cultures

[a] Among a sample of 224 preliterate and small-scale populations.
Source: R. B. Textor, A cross-cultural summary *(New Haven: Human Relations Area Files Press, 1967).*

[1] For a pioneer work on the demography of primitive societies, see Krzywicki, 1934.

societies can be classified by size (Textor, 1967). Approximately 46 cultures of the 224-culture sample comprise communities of fewer than 50 persons (for example, the Andamanese). Forty-five have medium-sized communities of 200 to 1,000 persons (including the Cherokee, Kikuyu, and Tikopia); and 44 cultures (including the Ashanti, Yoruba, and Zuñi) have either an average community size of 1,000 or more or a town or city of at least 5,000.

Classification by Technology

Primitive or nonliterate societies can be classified according to many other critera besides community size: by geographic location, such as continent or region (the Pacific Islands, the Great Plains North America, or East Africa); by type of environment (mountain, seacoast, forest, or plains); or by racial stock (American Indians, Asiatic Mongoloids, Polynesians, or Indo-Australians). Most frequently, however, they are classified in terms of their technologies and sustenance-producing arrangements, that is, according to whether the dominant feature of their material adaptation is hunting or gathering, pastoral nomadism, some form of horticulture or agriculture, or industry—and according to whether their residence is nomadic or settled. Every category in such a classification is typically associated with a range of forms of social differentiation, social roles, and social division of labor; and with various political, religious, educational, and family institutions. Population densities are typically associated with the different technological classifications, too.

Different technologies are also associated with the size of population groupings. Hunting and gathering cultures usually live in small groups of 25 to 30 persons, while agricultural village societies more typically number between 500 and 1,000 persons (Peterson, 1961; Hawley, 1950; Murdock, 1949; Ottenberg & Ottenberg, 1960; Forde, 1964; and Textor, 1967).

SOCIETAL TAXONOMIES AND THE SIZE-DENSITY MODEL

We saw above that societies and social structures vary according to population variations. In this section we will look more closely at the ways in which population and societal structure are mutually dependent—how changes in population size and structure are fundamental factors and indeed causes of societal change.

A Definition of Society and its Relevant Characteristics

As a working definition, we may say that a *society* is a human population organized or characterized by patterns of social relationships for the purpose of collective survival in, and adaptation to, its environment. Recalling our earlier discussion of the delineation of population, this definition demands that the members of a society occupy the same physical area. It also demands that they be associated in patterns of social interaction and that the society (but not necessarily all the social relationships in it) have at least the implicit purpose of promoting the survival and adaptation of its members in their environment. Thus, tribal, regional, or national societies may be identified and distinguished by the geophysical environments in which their populations are located and according to which their social organization evolves.

From our definition of society, it seems to follow that in many characteristics besides population density, societies vary according to their methods of collective survival and adaptation. A number of authors have taken note of the differences in social structure and social relationships associated with different adaptations and technologies, and some have based societal *taxonomies*—schemes for classifying societies based on their distinctive characteristics—upon these distinctions.

Forde's Taxonomy

The classic study by C. Daryll Forde, *Habitat, Economy and Society* (1964), classifies a number of non-European societies in terms of food-production technologies and economies. The relationships between technology and the elements of social organization are examined in some detail for three types of societies: hunting and gathering societies like the Semang and Sakai of Malaya, the Bushmen of the Kalahari desert in Africa, and the North American Paiute Indians; agricultural and animal-husbanding societies like the Yoruba of the Congo Basin of Africa, the Hopi Indians of Arizona, and the Cochin of southwest India; and nomadic pastoral societies like the Masai of East Africa and the Kazak and Kirghiz of Central Asia.

Societies with food-gathering and hunting enomomies, Forde points out, tend to live in relatively small groups. They are sparsely settled or migrate within specified territories. Populations are concentrated in small areas, and they are typically very small and of low density (not more than two or three persons per square mile)—a factor which limits the scope of political institutions and, indeed, of social differentiation and organization in general.

Societies with food-cultivation economies and technologies, whether they cultivate by digging sticks, hoes, or ploughs, are almost always composed of larger and denser population clusters than are hunters and gatherers. For some, like the Boro in the Western Amazon Basin, the food cultivation is also migratory. Others, like the Hawaiian Polynesians or the Cochin, cultivate food in permanent settlements. The introduction of more efficient methods of cultivation apparently results in food surpluses that release some members of the population to spend part or all of their working time in nonagricultural occupations. Accordingly, the more "advanced" food-cultivating societies are characterized by a differentiation of economic roles, and by the presence of more elaborate social, religious, and political roles and organization.

Pastoral societies are typically nomadic, roaming within well-defined areas, and they may combine animal husbandry and herding with some food cultivation. They generally maintain some contact with more sedentary food-cultivating societies. The size of population groupings and the nature of social and political organization vary among pastoral societies as they do in food-cultivating groups. More than the other types of economy and technology, pastoralism appears to be related to geographical characteristics. It is associated with latitudes, altitudes, and climates in which systematic crop cultivation is difficult, and it is rarely found in forested areas. Forde shows that a few pastoral societies like the Kirghiz are in fact food-cultivating societies which have been dispossessed or otherwise uprooted.

The Duncan-Goldschmidt Taxonomy and the Principle of Ecological Expansion

Another societal taxonomy has been presented by Otis Dudley Duncan (1964). It is based on a combination of two factors: the society's subsistence technology (hunting and gathering, horticulture, agriculture, herding, or industry); and the nature and scope of the local territorial unit (nomadic band, nomadic tribal band, sedentary tribal village, peasant village, or urban community).[2] The taxonomy includes the following types of societies:

1. Nomadic hunting and gathering bands

[2] Duncan notes that the taxonomy was originally proposed by Walter Goldschmidt in *Man's Way: A Preface to the Understanding of Human Society*, © 1959 by Walter Goldschmidt. Adapted material used by permission of Holt, Rinehart and Winston.

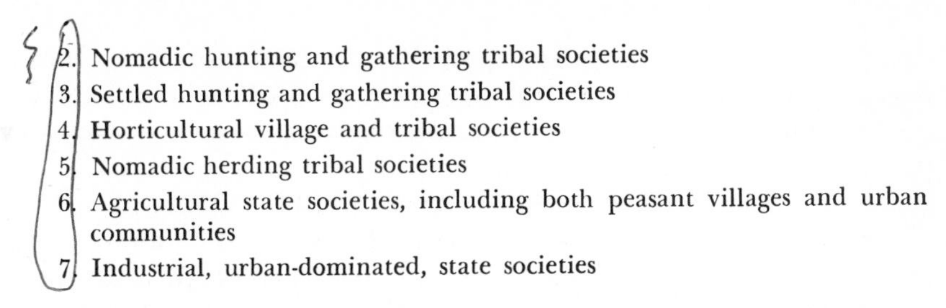

2. Nomadic hunting and gathering tribal societies
3. Settled hunting and gathering tribal societies
4. Horticultural village and tribal societies
5. Nomadic herding tribal societies
6. Agricultural state societies, including both peasant villages and urban communities
7. Industrial, urban-dominated, state societies

These categories represent a sequence of stages in the evolution of society. They are also related to a number of key structural variables, including political organization (whether it is *local* or *interlocal,* involving a single or several distinct settlements or communities); type of territorial occupation (nomadic or sedentary); method of obtaining food (collection or production); the economic pattern (self-sufficiency or exchange); and the utilization of energy (preindustrial or industrial) (Duncan, 1964). The categories also comprise a typology of basic ecological forms based upon the distinction between different exploitative technologies.

Figure 4.2 shows how Duncan's taxonomy works. It also shows the directions of the evolutionary stages which Duncan suggests. The settled hunting and gathering tribal society evolves from the hunting and gathering band society. The horticultural village society evolves from the hunting and gathering village society and from it, in turn, evolves

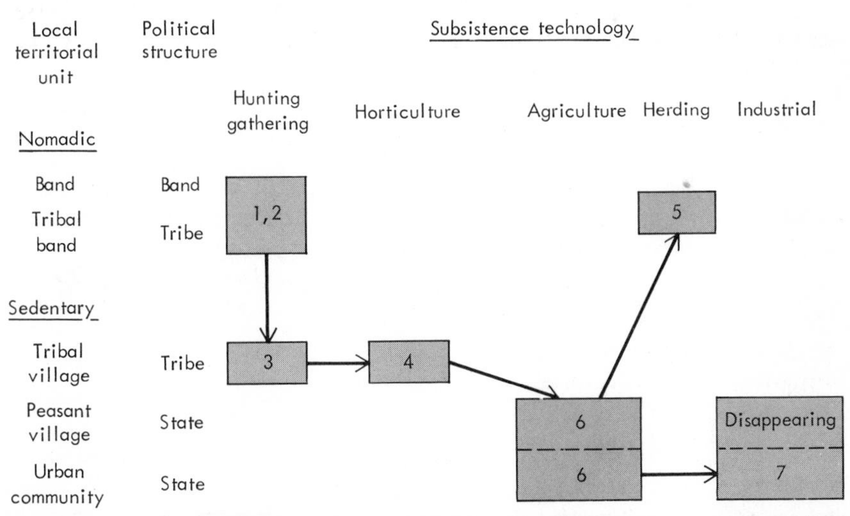

Figure 4.2 Duncan's taxonomy of societies, after Goldschmidt. *Source: Otis Dudley Duncan, "Social Organization and the Ecosystem," in Robert E. L. Faris,* Handbook of Modern Sociology, © *1964 by Rand McNally and Company, Chicago, Figure 4, p. 53. Reproduced and adapted by permission of Rand McNally College Publishing Company.*

the agricultural state society of peasant villages and urban communities. Nomadic herding societies may evolve either from or together with agricultural state societies. Finally, the industrial urban society evolves from the agricultural state society, retaining the urban communities of the agricultural state, but ultimately losing the peasant villages.

To Duncan's taxonomy of societies, we may add a final category of "metropolitan-megalopolitan societies," and later we shall discuss in some detail the characteristics of this category and the justification for its addition. In general, we can find most real—historical or contemporary —societies in one of the categories of this expanded taxonomy.

Duncan raises the problem of accounting for evolutionary transitions from one societal level to the next, and he suggests *ecological expansion* as an explanatory principle. Ecological expansion is defined as: (a) an increase in numbers sustained by (b) increasing human resourcefulness in extracting the requisite supplies of energy and material from the environment and (c) an elaboration of the patterns of organization of the human collective efforts involved in this activity (Duncan, 1964).

Clearly, Duncan and Goldschmidt's societal types are strongly related to both population size and density of settlement. Moreover, as Table 4.4 shows, evolutionary transitions almost always entail an increase in population size or population density, or both. This means that we can simplify the explanatory principle of ecological expansion somewhat by redefining it as *the population growth and economic, tech-*

TABLE 4.4 The Duncan-Goldschmidt Taxonomy of Societal Types, Modified to Associated Population Size and Density

Societal Type	*Population Size*	*Population Density*
1. Nomadic hunting and gathering bands	very small	low
2. Nomadic hunting and gathering tribal societies	small	low
3. Settled hunting and gathering tribal societies	small	medium
4. Horticultural village and tribal societies	medium	medium
5. Nomadic herding tribal societies	medium	low
6. Agricultural state societies, including both peasant villages and urban communities	large	medium
7. Industrial, urban-dominated, state societies	large	high
8. Metropolitan-megalopolitan societies	very large	very high

Source: Otis Dudley Duncan, "Social Organization and the Ecosystem," in Robert E. L. Faris, Handbook of Modern Sociology, *© 1964 by Rand McNally & Company, Chicago, Figure 3, p. 51. Reproduced and adapted by permission of Rand McNally College Publishing Company.*

nological, and social-organizational changes that are mutually required to sustain one another. Let us look more closely at the Duncan-Goldschmidt taxonomy with the added metropolitan-megalopolitan category in terms of population size and density.

The Size-Density Model

We can extend the above line of approach somewhat by considering a classification of societies according to population size and the size of the territory available for exploitation to assure survival and sustenance. Aside from the fact that it fits neatly with the sustenance-technology taxonomies, such a classification has its own justification. First, the absolute population size of a society bounds, or sets limits upon, the range of social and economic differentiation and division of labor possible in that society. Japan, Indonesia, and the United States, with 1975 populations of 111 million, 136 million, and 214 million respectively, have available more alternatives for social differentiation than do Canada, Australia, or Libya, with 1975 populations of 23 million, 14 million, and 2 million.

Secondly, the society is also bounded by its territorial scope in terms of the variety of environmental conditions and resources which it can exploit for sustenance. Brazil, with a population of 110 million and a territory of 8,500,000 square kilometers, has more environmental opportunities than does Indonesia, whose population is even greater but is confined to an area of only 1,500,000 square kilometers. Canada's population of 23 million has access to the resources of an area totaling ten million square kilometers, while North Vietnam's 24 million people have only 159,000 square kilometers of land.

Finally, the density of population settlement limits the number, frequency, and variety of human contacts and social and economic relationships possible in day-to-day affairs. Ireland, with a population of about three million and a density of about 44 persons per square kilometer, has residential patterns, an economy, and a social structure quite different from those of Israel, whose population is the same but whose density is about 164 persons per square kilometer. Again, Afghanistan and Taiwan have populations of 19 million and 16 million. Population density in Afghanistan is about 30 persons per square kilometer, while Taiwan's is 444 per square kilometer. Correspondingly, the two countries have extreme differences in social, economic, and political structure, in technology and levels of living, and in virtually all aspects of individual and community life. Table 4.5 outlines the possible extremes in such a classification in a four-fold scheme.

TABLE 4.5 Four Alternatives Within the Size-Density Classification System

	Territorial Scope	
Population size	*Small area*	*Large area*
Small society	Small society Small area	Small society Large area
Large society	Large society Small area	Large society Large area

We can best illustrate our model by looking at some of the most extreme contrasts possible. There are wide differences in both physiographic environment and cultural adaptation between the isolated nomadic food-gathering groups located at the smallest size, lowest density extreme and the large, urban-industrial societies located at the largest size, highest density extreme. The isolated nomadic group is at the mercy of its environment; life and death themselves depend on how successfully the population withstands daily environmental perils. By contrast, the mass urban-industrial society has the technology to transform its environment, virtually creating its own geography by manipulating and exploiting geophysical features of the land to its own benefit.

There is no hard-and-fast relationship between the territorial and population sizes of societies and their levels of technological, social, political, or economic development. Thus, though both India and China have large territories, large populations, and high population densities, we would not necessarily expect India and China to be the world's most advanced societies. However, their large areas, tremendous populations, and high densities do present certain basic social, political, and economic imperatives.

Among the pioneers of sociological theory, Emile Durkheim first drew attention to the way in which population size, distribution, density, and composition affect society and social structure. In his classic *The Division of Labor in Society* (1933), the French sociologist proposes that the development of social differentiation is a universal phenomenon. He contrasts relatively undifferentiated societies with highly differentiated ones in terms of the nature and basis of their social solidarity. He distinguishes between "mechanical solidarity," the social solidarity of similar individuals, of the undifferentiated societies and an "organic solidarity" of the differentiated ones. Organic solidarity is seen as resulting from the division of labor and mutual interdependence of dissimilar individuals.

In considering the causes of the division of labor, Durkheim poses this central proposition:

> The division of labor varies in direct ratio with volume and density of societies, and, if it progresses in a continuous manner in the course of social development, it is because societies become regularly denser and generally more voluminous. (Durkheim, 1933, p. 262)

Durkheim initiated, and his students continued, a subfield of sociology called *social morphology,* which is concerned with the study of social, economic, political, and other characteristics of human communities as they relate to population size, composition, and geographic distribution (Duncan & Pfautz, 1960). More recently, Hawley has worked out an analysis of population balance, where the adjustment a population makes to the opportunities for living involve the three factors of population size, resource abundance, and organization of the population (Hawley, 1950, chap. 9). Hawley determined that societies which are small, isolated, and self-sufficient characteristically have constant social organizational forms, like the family, church, or political institutions. But since resource materials are highly variable, the populations of these societies must vary in size according to fluctuations in the habitat. Conversely, the extensive interdependence that obtains among large, spatially-dispersed population aggregates allows for a stabilization of resources by means of exchange. But here the social-organizational factor may be variable. Under such circumstances, adjustment and balance are effected by mobility of population and of all agents of production, rather than by mortality (Hawley, 1950; also Schnore, 1958; Duncan, 1959; and Hauser, 1963).

Having already shown briefly some lines of change within, and variations among, populations, we can conclude by exploring very tentatively the proposition that societies and social structure vary in time and space concomitantly with populations.

Again, we can draw upon the familiar example of the United States to illustrate concomitant variations of population and social structure. The original 13 states of early America comprised a small, low density, essentially rural population whose character was reflected in its large families, its educational and religious institutions, and its economic and political organization. These institutions contrast sharply with their counterparts in contemporary United States, with its enormous high density and largely urban population. But even within contemporary American society, there are sharp contrasts between the social life and institutions of the very densely populated communities on the West Coast or the Eastern Seaboard and those of the sparsely populated areas like the Great Plains or Rocky Mountains.

Similar contrasts exist between the England of Shakespeare and the England of the Beatles, or between contemporary England and contemporary Ireland and again, both the population differences and social institutional differences are equally striking. Finally, we can see the corresponding changes in population size and social structure through broad international contrasts among existing societies—from isolated nomadic bands or small settled tribes, through small national populations, to the largest, most densely packed urban societies. The contrasts in population size and density typically correspond in at least some measure to variations in the role that family and kinship play in social structure; to variations in the extent of individual social differentiation and in extent of institutional specialization and differentiation; and to variations in the content and forms of relationships among individuals and institutions.

How and why are populations and societies related, how do such relationships vary, and how do these relationships change over time? We will begin a more detailed consideration of these questions in the next chapter.

SUMMARY

In this chapter we have looked at several ways populations may be classified: by total size; areal density; patterns of geographic distribution and residential settlement; age composition; and cultural and technological characteristics. We have looked at the variations among real populations with respect to each of these factors, and found that these variations typically correspond to variations in organizational and social-structural features of societies. The smallest and least densely settled populations tend also to exhibit the simplest and least differentiated social forms, institutions, and relationships; while the largest and most densely settled populations form highly complex, differentiated, and very elaborately organized societies. The absolute population size, the territory, and the density of population settlement bound, or create imperatives for, several societal traits: the degree of social and economic differentiation and division of labor; the variety of sustenance-producing activities; and the number, frequency, and variety of human contacts and interaction in daily affairs.

The evolutionary transitions of societies from one level of organizational complexity to the next can be accounted for by the principle of ecological expansion: by population growth together with the corresponding economic, technological, and social-organizational adaptations which the society makes in order to sustain this growth. In the next chapter we turn to a brief review of the population and social history of the United States. In addition to its intrinsic interest and importance, this will afford us an opportunity to illustrate both that social-structural variations correspond closely to variations in population; and that shifts over time in population size and composition are a major source of social-structural change.

5

Population and American Society, Past and Present

INTRODUCTION: A GROWING NATION AND A GROWING POPULATION

In this chapter, we put to use the concepts and approaches presented in the previous chapters in a review of the major changes in population and social structure in the United States. The main theme of our analysis will be the interaction of population trends with changes in technology and societal strategies of settlement and adaptation. We will look at the population history of the United States in two chronological stages. In rural America of the pre-Civil War period, we focus on population growth and territorial expansion, and the social patterns and institutional features associated with these trends. America became more urbanized after the Civil War. In this period, we examine the changing patterns of growth and settlement, and social and institutional characteristics that were associated with new technologies and the influx of immigrants.

The growth of the population of the United States and the development of American society are not results of social processes indigenous to the American continent. Instead, they are consequences of European population growth and the migration of Europeans to the relatively unsettled Western Hemisphere. But although the American colonies began as Europe's hinterland, their distance from the more developed European centers, along with their own size and density of population and great natural wealth, allowed them relatively early economic and political independence. Thus the post-independence patterns of settlement—and to some extent even colonial patterns—can be viewed as largely indigenous to America. So, too, can the accompanying forms of social and economic organization.[1]

Table 5.1 outlines the main features of the analysis presented in this chapter. The first two columns of the table show the growth of the total land area and population of the United States for census years from 1790 to 1970. By 1850, the United States' total land area had more than tripled since 1790, and virtually all its land acquisitions were completed. In this same period the population had increased almost sixfold, so that population density in 1860, on the eve of the Civil War, was slightly more than double the density at the time of the first United States census. Most important, in the pre-Civil War period from 1790 to 1860, the great bulk (some 78 percent) of the population increase was absorbed by an increase in the rural population. The pre-Civil War strategy of adaptation to sharp population increases was expansion of rural settlement and of agriculture, forestry, mining, and other primary extractive economic activities.

During the decade of the Civil War, the overall strategy of adaptation to the still increasing population changed to urbanization, with expansion of existing urban centers and rapid growth of new urban agglomerations. Between 1860 and 1970, the total population of the United States increased more than sixfold. Of the total population increase in this period, some 83 percent can be accounted for by the growth of the urban population.

Because the land area of the United States remained almost fixed while the total population virtually sextupled, the total population density also increased more than fivefold, from 10.6 persons per square mile in 1860 to 57.5 persons per square mile in 1970. Most of this increase was in urban areas: rural population density increased by only 6.7 persons per square mile.

[1] In recent years there has appeared an important series of historical studies dealing with the prerevolutionary population and society of the United States. A major concern of these studies is the direct connection of patterns of population growth and density of agricultural settlement in the colonies (mainly New England, so far) to family structure and inheritance, local political and economic organization, and ultimately, migration and frontier resettlement. See K. B. Lockridge, 1968; P. J. Greven, Jr., 1970; and J. Demos, 1968.

TABLE 5.1 Population of the United States, Urban and Rural, and Intercensal Change, 1790–1970

Year	*Total land area (in thousand sq. miles)*	*Population (in millions)*			*Intercensal Increase (in millions)*			*Population Density (total pop. per sq. mile)*	*Rural Population Density*
		Total	*Urban*	*Rural*	*Total*	*Urban*	*Urban as percentage of total*		
1790	865	3.9	0.2	3.7	. . .	. . .	. . .	4.5	4.3
1800	865	5.3	0.3	5.0	1.4	0.1	6.9	6.1	5.8
1810	1,682	7.2	0.5	6.7	1.9	0.2	10.5	4.3	4.0
1820	1,749	9.6	0.7	8.9	2.4	0.2	7.0	5.5	5.1
1830	1,749	12.9	1.1	11.8	3.2	0.4	13.4	7.4	6.7
1840	1,749	17.1	1.8	15.3	4.2	0.7	17.1	9.8	8.7
1850	2,940	23.2	3.5	19.7	6.1	1.7	27.7	7.9	6.7
1860	2,970	31.4	6.2	25.2	8.3	2.7	32.4	10.6	8.5
1870	2,970	38.6	9.9	28.7	7.1	3.7	51.8	13.0	9.6
1880	2,970	50.2	14.1	36.1	11.6	4.2	36.5	16.9	12.1
1890	2,970	62.9	22.1	40.8	12.8	8.0	62.4	21.2	13.7
1900	2,970	76.0	30.2	45.8	13.0	8.1	61.7	25.6	15.4
1910	2,970	92.0	42.0	50.0	16.0	11.8	74.1	31.0	16.8
1920	2,969	105.7	54.2	51.5	13.7	12.2	88.5	35.6	17.3
1930	2,947	122.8	69.0	53.8	17.1	14.8	86.7	41.2	18.1
1940	2,977	131.7	74.4	57.3	8.9	5.5	61.5	44.2	19.2
1950	3,552	151.3	96.8	54.5	19.1	a	a	42.6	15.3
1960	3,549	179.3	125.3	54.0	28.0	28.5	101.8	50.5	15.2
1970	3,537	203.2	149.3	53.9	23.9	24.0	100.4	57.5	15.2

Source: U.S. Bureau of the Census, Census of Population 1970: Characteristics of the Population, ***Vol. 1, Part 1, Tables 2 and 3.***

a Definitional change in 1950.

An Overview

We will be looking at American population and society basically in terms of changing strategies of settlement, absorption, and adaptation undertaken by a rapidly growing population, and in terms of the social and economic accompaniments to this change. Of course, the change did not take place uniformly or even simultaneously throughout the country. The flow of immigrants entered the country on the Eastern Seaboard, and both rural and urban settlement and population growth took place there first.

Urban concentrations have nearly always existed in the United States despite the early rural character of the country as a whole. On the other hand, many areas of the United States are still predominantly rural, despite the overall urban character of the population and the low proportion now engaged in or directly supported by agriculture and other primary economic activities.

In the same way, the American economy has always been varied. Some parts (perhaps more correctly, certain local or regional American economies) have always been market economies of a highly differentiated and interdependent nature. Others began as extremely localized subsistence economies and only gradually became integrated into progressively larger, more differentiated, and more interdependent regional or national complexes.

The differences in patterns of settlement and in scope of economy have always been associated with sectional differences, competition, and tension in national politics: the North *vs.* the South; the Eastern Seaboard *vs.* the Midwest and West; industrial and commercial sectors *vs.* the agricultural sector. Urban and rural differences have always been sources of cleavage and conflict in regional and national politics. And local politics have always been characterized by competition between economic and social classes and between ethnic, religious, racial or neighborhood groups. This competition in many instances has been affected by patterns of immigration and differential fertility.

Finally, family formation and population growth itself have been affected by the changes in societal strategies of survival and adaptation. The correlates of technological change and social differentiation, education and mobility, have, along with urbanization, affected the nuclear family (adult couple and their children) and its relationship to the other institutions of American society. These same factors—education and mobility—also have generated the shift in the American society's adaptation strategies from the expansion of settlements to the expansion of industry, the economy, and the general urban-megalopolitan character of the society.

Population Growth and Expansion of Settlement, 1790–1860

Between 1790 and 1800, the population of the United States grew from 3,929,000 to 5,308,000, in increase of 35 percent. But during this decade there was no increase in the nation's land area. The increase in population was divided almost equally between the northeastern states and the South, and some 93 percent of the growth took place in the rural population. The North Central states had a population of about 51,000 in 1800.

In the next decade, the territory of the United States practically doubled because of the Louisiana Purchase. In this period, too, the total population grew by some 36 percent, to 7,240,000 in 1810. Again, the bulk of the growth—about 90 percent—took place in the rural population. And the total increase was divided about equally between the northeastern states and the South. But the population of the North Central states increased almost sixfold, numbering about 292,000 by 1810.

The following three decades—from 1810 to 1840—were characterized by steady population growth at an average rate of some 3.3 percent per annum, so that population had reached 17,069,000 by the 1840 census. Land area increased slightly during this period, primarily because of the acquisition of Florida and other areas ceded by Spain. Beginning in 1819, a count was maintained of overseas immigrants to the United States; and in the years between 1819 and 1840 their number totaled some 750,000. In these decades, 1810 to 1840, the populations of the northeastern and southern regions both increased by nearly 200 percent. But the population of the North Central states, the frontier of the early nineteenth century, grew more than elevenfold, from 292,000 in 1810 to 3,352,000 in 1840. Again, the bulk of the growth was absorbed by the rural population: the total number of urban places increased from only 46 in 1810 to 113 in 1840, and there were just three cities with more than 100,000 inhabitants each and nine with more than 25,000.

Between 1840 and 1860, the bulk of the territorial expansion of the United States was completed with the Mexican Cession, the Gadsden Purchase, and the acquisition of Texas and Oregon. The total population grew by 83 percent, from 17,069,000 in 1840 to 31,443,000 in 1860. During this period, the settlement of the West began, and the population there reached some 619,000 by 1860. By 1860, too, the population of the North Central states nearly equaled that of the Northeast. Overseas immigration in these two decades totaled some 4,311,000 persons, and the urban population began to absorb a substantial part of the overall population increase (28 percent between 1840 and 1850, and 32 percent between 1850 and 1860). By 1860, the number of urban places had increased to 392. There were now nine cities of 100,000 residents or more and 26 cities of 25,000 or more.

FAMILIES AND ECONOMIC, SOCIAL, AND POLITICAL INSTITUTIONS OF RURAL AMERICA

Contemporary America has an extremely rich heritage of literature and lore from colonial and nineteenth-century rural America. And many of the nation's most deeply cherished traditions, institutions, and values are rooted in frontier life and in the rural social, economic, and political organization of the late nineteenth and early twentieth centuries.

A number of historical studies of rural communities in the nineteenth century or earlier employ sociological or ecological concepts. With these, along with other historical analyses and census and other data, we can sketch some of the main features of social structure in premechanized rural America.

Three Salient Aspects of Rural Settlement in America

In considering the major social institutions of nineteenth-century rural America, it is important to bear in mind three separate aspects of the history of the nation's rural settlement. In the first place, any area of settlement always included a large proportion of migrants—either from areas of the United States farther east or northeast, or from foreign countries. Population turnover in any given rural area was, in the nineteenth century, quite high. Some migrants remained only briefly in one place, then moved on to more promising places; others remained for a number of years and then resettled. In many areas, only a small minority of migrants ever settled permanently. Thus, many areas had a very heterogeneous mix of national, ethnic, and linguistic groups. More often than not, this heterogeneity was reflected also in the residents' period of arrival or length of stay. Accordingly, those social institutions that involved members of many families tended to be characterized by changing numbers and composition.

In the second place, farm families of rural United States were characterized by considerable physical isolation, and certain types of family self-sufficiency were in fact demanded by this isolation. Since frontier land was cheap and, in the eastern United States, an extremely promising investment, settlers sought to claim or purchase the largest homestead or farm which they could afford, regardless of their ability, experience, or actual expectations to cultivate it. In contrast both to European rural settlement and to the earliest agricultural settlements in New England, most of the rural settlement in the United States took place on relatively isolated farms or homesteads. Each settler family was usually physically isolated from other settler families. Villages, which abounded in rural America no less than in rural areas elsewhere, were generally not the farmers' places of residence. They were, rather, places of business and of residence for the nonagricultural rural population engaged in one or another service to the farmers. While farm families were isolated, though, most rural communities throughout the United States organized social, economic, or political units which helped to reduce this isolation by developing road networks and transportation and communication services.

Finally, rural settlement in the United States did not ordinarily, if ever, occur spontaneously. Instead, it was organized and promoted by various individuals, groups, and agencies who were interested first in the settlement of the western frontier areas and later in the more dense or intensive settlement of nonfrontier areas. National and local governments, land and real estate speculators and promoters, and merchants, traders, and transportation companies were all involved in promotional schemes for settlement. For the most part, the promoting agents understood the need to organize personal services and services essential to farm maintenance and development. In addition, they also organized marketing and retailing services that would give access to the eastern or overseas market and to urban manufacturers and services.

In other words, subsistence agriculture, although frequent enough, was hardly ever a way of life in rural America. Instead it was a transitional stage between initial settlement of the land and the development of the communication, transportation, and institutions that provided access to neighboring or distant markets and sources. American farmers generally were well acquainted with the more elaborate socioeconomic organization of the European countries of origin or the more densely settled, already partly-urban East. The isolated, large western holdings implied for many people, perhaps, the promise of eventual personal wealth and security. But in fact, rural settlement in the United States was promoted and developed in the direction of intricate social, economic, and political relationships within larger regional and national economies.

The Family

The basic family unit in rural America was the nuclear family. Broader kinship ties were also recognized, but they never determined rural residence units. As we saw earlier, a very large proportion of the rural families were either migrant families or families which had been formed by migrants at the new places of settlement. Migration took place almost exclusively among single persons, or among nuclear family groups, but almost never among extended families (Eblen, 1965). Rural American families were usually quite large, a tendency which reflected the relatively early marriage, high fertility, and low child mortality of early rural America.[2]

Families in rural areas were usually isolated both from one another and from villages and towns. Partly as a consequence of their isolation, and presumably partly because of traditional family patterns, the American rural family was what may be termed a *multifunctional* family. Like the modern family, it was the social institution in which legitimate sex, childbearing, and child-rearing were carried out. But it also had many other functions, as a production and consumption unit, a religious unit, a recreational unit, and an associational unit involved in a very large proportion of the individual member's contacts with the outside world. Age-sex differentiation was the rule in American rural families, as in all families. But there was relatively little internal differentiation among age-sex categories with respect to occupations, interests, religious activities, social associations, and the allocation of time. Family members were typically all involved (to the extent that their individual ages and sex permitted) in the production activities of the farm or the family business. Family members typically shared the same small social world of contacts with other families, school, church, business establishments, and community agencies and institutions. The same life cycle was more or less repeated by each family member in the relatively small and undifferentiated social world of the rural American community. Since there was little or no individual or personal access to private transportation or communication, there was little opportunity for different family members to embark on separate social paths.

The Economy

There were three distinct but overlapping and interrelated economic units in the rural American community: the household, the village, and the region. In any given region, the relative importance of each of these economies and the relationship of each to the others reflected, first, the quality of communication and transportation, and only

[2] In the United States and Canada, marriage has always occurred earlier among rural than among urban females. This contrasts with the pattern in Scandinavia or Ireland, where the reverse is true, or in England, where there are no substantial urban-rural differences in age at marriage.

secondarily the elaborateness of mediating economic institutions like brokerages, banks, or transport or marketing institutions. In general, economic institutions as elaborate as necessary were founded as soon as political and communication conditions permitted their operation. And the establishment of modern economic institutions like factories, storage and distribution firms, and transport companies did not often have to overcome any obstacles except those of a pragmatic nature.

The household economy. The household economy was in simplest terms a production-consumption unit. It produced a combination of cash crops and products for home consumption, and it consumed a combination of home-produced and purchased products. The nature of the overall combination varied with the family's ability to produce cash crops for a market. This was a function of the individual family, its land, and its access to the knowledge, techniques, and equipment necessary for such production. It also varied with the family's physical and economic ability to gain access to the market. If a farm was physically isolated, it could produce little or nothing for a market, regardless of its own production potential. In such a case, the household would itself have to produce all its own goods. In the same way, if a farm family was able to produce for a cash market but had little or no access to markets for home consumption products, it was obliged to produce for its own consumption. But it could probably market a considerable portion of its output, too.

In spite of the nostalgic tendency of literature, and sometimes even history books, to glorify the self-sufficiency and home production of rural families, the extent to which the household economy relied on the market or on home production varied mostly according to market accessibility or the socioeconomic situation of the household. If Granny could earn more cash or goods by manufacturing flower pots than by baking pies, and if she could buy the equivalent or near-equivalent pies in the local grocery store, she generally gave up baking pies, switched to flower pots, and pocketed the difference.

The village economy. The village in rural America consisted of a number of small businesses (usually family-owned and family-operated), some personal and professional services, and some community institutions like schools, churches, and hospitals—all serving the farm families of the more or less immediately surrounding area. Although the villagers were often only part-time tradesmen, physicians, clergymen, or merchants (since they were part-time farmers as well) the American village itself was almost never a self-sufficient unit. Instead, it was part of a village economy involving farmers, villagers, and often external markets or sources of goods and services. In many parts of the United States, villages were deliberately planned and constructed by railroad companies, land speculators, promoters, and so forth, for purposes like enhancing the attractiveness of surrounding farm lands.

The typical village business was owned and operated by a family living on the same or nearby property. The village family was similar to the farm family in a number of ways, especially in its size and in its tendency for the entire family to be economically involved in the business. Village businesses might be engaged in mediating exchange among the farmers; in providing services (like transportation, construction, contracting, milling, storage, or the marketing or brokerage of local crops into the regional or national system) to the farmers; in the local distribution of manufactured products from other areas; or in providing personal and household services through such specialists as physicians, barbers, and blacksmiths. In addition, village businesses typically included public services like newspapers, churches, schools, and occasionally, commercial entertainment.

The regional economy. The regional economy included the town or city which was the major marketing, transportation, or manufacturing center of the area and the surrounding village economies which were connected with it by waterways, rail, or road. The regional centers processed rural products or marketed them to nearby or distant consumers. They fabricated consumer products from raw materials, then distributed them throughout the region. The regional center did not have a rural social structure, but it was always a fundamental part of the rural economy.

People did not usually migrate to new rural settlements in the United States in order to establish some elementary level of subsistence: typically, they had enjoyed that modicum of sustenance—or more—in their places of origin. Instead, migrants sought to better their styles of life. And in agricultural settlement this always involved the production of cash crops for a market which was usually at least regional in scope.

Of course in many areas, conditions were such that farm families had no alternative but to engage in subsistence farming. In these cases, the absence of knowledge, capital, tools, or productive land rendered anything other than subsistence farming impossible. In the United States there have always been impoverished rural families and, indeed, impoverished rural areas. But the nation's rural agricultural settlement—to the extent that it was planned or guided at all—was always organized with reference to some potential or expected market, usually regional in scope.

Social Institutions

Schools. Schools were accessible, in principle if not always in fact, to all children regardless of social or economic status, creed, language, or origin in rural as well as urban America. And a large number of laws and ordinances made the public schools a major American institution. Typically, state or territorial constitutions required county or township authorities to organize school districts for the purpose of levying school taxes and building, staffing, and maintaining public schools. These laws were implemented to a greater or lesser degree, depending upon local conditions, available state aid, and the enthusiasm of the various persons and public agencies involved.

This is not to say that rural America always had model educational systems. Most rural primary schools in the nineteenth century had inadequate physical facilities and untrained and poorly paid teachers. In addition, their needs were usually met with either indifference or systematic attempts to cut school costs and budgets on the part of the population charged with their support. Worse than that, the typical school term in farm areas was very short, as brief as one month per year and seldom longer than four months. Many school-aged children were not enrolled in the schools, many enrolled children did not attend the schools, and teachers of any calibre were difficult to mobilize at any price.

Nevertheless, tens of thousands of schools were built and attended by millions of children. Virtually every rural community had at least a one-room schoolhouse. Only very much later—well into the twentieth century, when the organization of free bus transportation made it possible to consolidate rural schools into institutions serving much greater areas—did rural schools become substantially improved. Then, teachers' standards and salaries were raised, their working conditions were improved, and the educational opportunities available to rural children were made comparable to those available to urban youngsters.

Churches. Rural churches typically received considerably more support than rural schools, perhaps because they made fewer demands upon the working time of the farm families. Rural churches were ordinarily quite small, serving very specific congregations. Often the church would be a rural neighborhood one, located in open country, while a rural village might contain three or four churches of different denominations.

No one religion practiced in rural America ever became the indigenous or established religion of the country or of any area. Migrating families tended to bring their religious practices and beliefs with them, keeping their old denominations after settling in a new land. Small numbers of families with the same beliefs or religious background sufficed to give birth to a church, often with a part-time preacher who, like his flock, farmed on weekdays.

Many churches were born, and many died, in nineteenth-century rural America. In any given region, a number of Protestant sects or denominations might establish churches in competition with one another. Some or several of them would not survive. Typically, different ethnic or language groups formed their own churches, and many of these did not survive even minor population movements. Most important, improvements in roads and transportation rendered many neighborhood churches superfluous and brought larger numbers of worshippers to the central village churches.

Voluntary organizations. Even in the nineteenth century, rural America was characterized by innumerable voluntary organizations. Most of these were of mutual-aid, civic, or recreational nature, and they catered to a variety of interests: athletic, educational, fraternal, musical, patriotic, youth-serving, and so on. Some were entirely indigenous to the local area; others were carry-overs brought in by migrants.

The outstanding characteristic of voluntary organizations in rural America was their instability (Kolb & de Brunner, 1935). Even more than churches, many of these organizations were born and many died. However, at any point in time and in any given rural community, it was possible to find a substantial number and variety of organizations for individuals, families, couples, or children. Later on, broader-scale rural services were organized in many places on a township, county, or statewide basis. Many of the voluntary organizations received professional or semiprofessional assistance and some financial support, and some ultimately achieved a considerable measure of stability.

Political Institutions

The ordinances and legislation which provided for local self-government on the American frontier generally preceded the arrival and settlement of newcomers. Territorial ordinances and state constitutions, codes, and statutes were usually patterned after those of Eastern Seaboard states. They defined the state, county, township, and village organs of government, the key administrative and judicial roles, the institutions of the town meeting, and the organs for choosing and controlling officials and reviewing their activities. The standardization of political institutions and patterns over so much of rural America was the result of restrictions imposed by the national Constitution and the fact that so many state codes were patterned on a few New England and middle-Atlantic state constitutions.

Villages or townships were ordinarily the smallest or "most local" political units. In many states they were established by law, complete with governing machinery that usually consisted of a periodic town or village meeting and the election of committees and officials. Official roles might include those of the town clerk, the town assessor, the justice of the peace, the town treasurer, and the town supervisors, among others. The requirements and duties of these roles usually were spelled out in great detail by statute. Township or village business included the building of roads and bridges, the provision of schools, assistance to the needy, the licensing of businesses, and the registering of mortgages and deeds.

In the sparsely settled rural areas, county government was also quite localized. The economic welfare of individuals was associated to a great degree with the county's road-opening and road-maintenance services. In addition, the county had broad judicial, administrative, educational, law enforcement, and social welfare functions. In most areas, the county was the area's most important employer, consumer, and entrepreneur: as such, it was quite wealthy in comparison to individuals and even to other corporate groups.

State government was generally far more removed from the rural community than township or county governments, and of course the federal government was even more distant. Nevertheless, local people often participated with a lively interest in elections, referenda, and attempts to influence state and national governing bodies.

Political parties operated on the local level in each county and often in each township. Different population groups were attracted to the separate political parties, and there were differences, too, in the degree to which groups backed candidates and participated in politics. However, researchers have apparently found it difficult to make any generalizations about the directions of these differences. In particular, the social bases of political cleavage are difficult to determine.

Social Differentiation

The rural population of the country as a whole, and of individual states and countries as well, was generally characterized by limited social differentiation along a number of separate, but overlapping axes. For instance, "new settlers" were inevitably differentiated from "old settlers," at least in terms of local political power and influence and very often in terms of economic well-being. Again, the settlers' places of origin and related abilities like language, literacy, and special skills were also sources of differentiation. In the community as a whole, open-country settlers or farmers were ordinarily distinguished from village settlers, and within the village there was some occupational differentiation.

How meaningful these differentiating characteristics were in terms of prestige or social standing cannot be assessed in any comprehensive fashion, nor is it easy to determine how rigid the distinctions were. A part of the American creed holds that mobility and self-improvement are possible for any person. But the extent to which this was actually the case in nineteenth-century rural America is not easy to ascertain.

POPULATION GROWTH AND REDISTRIBUTION, 1870–1975

The main trends in the development of the United States population since the Civil War are fairly well known and have already been described in considerable detail (Bogue, 1959; U.S. Bureau of the Census, "Historical Statistics," 1960; Taeuber & Taeuber, 1971; I. B. Taeuber, 1972a). We review here only the highlights of these trends.

The nation's population virtually doubled between 1870 and 1900, from about 38.6 million to nearly 76 million. It doubled again after 1900, to about 150.7 million in 1950, and it reached some 214 million by mid-1975. However, with the exception of a small gain between 1920 and 1930, the rate of increase declined steadily from 1870 until 1940.

Beginning in 1840, foreign immigration became a major component of population growth (see Table 5.2). The net number of immigrants reached a peak of 6.3 million between 1900 and 1910, accounting for about 39 percent of the decade's total population increase. We can only partially assess the contribution of foreign-born immigrants to the growth of the population from the census statistics. Aside from their own contribution to the population, immigrants also added births to the "native-born" population. Although these were separately identifiable in censuses as "native of foreign-born or mixed parentage" (or, together with immigrants, as "foreign stock"), their children were "native-born of native parentage" and therefore indistinguishable in the census data.

The second half of the nineteenth century witnessed the settlement and development of the north central region and the beginning of the settlement of the West. (see Table 5.3). While the total population grew

TABLE 5.2 Increase in Population, Net Arrivals (Foreign-Born Immigrants), and Natural Increase, 1810 to 1970 (thousands)

	Total Increase			
Period	*Number*	*Percent Over Initial Population*	*Natural Increase*	*Net Arrivals*
1810–1820	2,399	33.1	2,328	71
1820–1830	3,228	33.5	3,105	123
1830–1840	4,203	32.7	3,710	493
1840–1850	6,122	35.9	4,702	1,420
1850–1860	8,251	35.6	5,614	2,593
1860–1870	8,375	26.6	6,291	2,102
1870–1880	10,337	26.0	7,675	2,622
1880–1890	12,792	25.5	7,527	4,966
1890–1900	13,047	20.7	9,345	3,711
1900–1910	15,978	21.0	9,656	6,294
1910–1920	13,738	14.9	11,489	2,484
1920–1930	17,064	16.1	14,500	3,187
1930–1940	9,894	7.2	9,962	— 85
1940–1950	19,429	14.7	17,426	1,789
1950–1960	28,289	18.6	25,310	2,975
1960–1970	24,344	13.5	20,413	3,920

Source: Irene B. Taeuber 1972a, Table 1.

TABLE 5.3 Population of Regions and the Nation, 1850 to 1974

	Population (in thousands)				*Percentage increase*		
Regions	*1850*	*1900*	*1950*	*1974*	*1850 to 1900*	*1900 to 1950*	*1950 to 1974*
United States total	23,192	75,995	150,697	211,390	228	98	40
Northeast	8,627	21,047	39,478	49,426	144	88	25
North Central	5,404	26,333	44,461	57,543	387	69	29
South	8,983	24,524	47,197	67,180	173	93	42
West	179	4,091	19,562	37,243	2,186	378	90

Sources: Figures for 1850–1950 adapted from Taeuber and Taeuber, 1958, Table 2; for 1974 from U.S. Bureau of the Census, Current Population Reports, *Series P-20.*

by some 228 percent between 1850 and 1900, the population of the North Central states increased almost fivefold, from 5.4 million in 1850 to 26.3 million in 1900. In the same period the population of the West increased sharply, from only 179,000 to four million.

In the first half of the twentieth century, the population of the North Central states grew at a rate lower than that of the rest of the country, while in the West population continued to grow at a rate several times higher. The settlement of the north central and western regions occurred largely as a consequence of westward, and some northward, migration. From 1950 to the present, the West has continued its rapid growth, and the South has grown more rapidly than either northeastern or north central regions. This has been due largely to net migration southward in the recent period.

In addition to interstate movements of population, two other kinds of geographic movements have characterized America in the century since the Civil War. These are migration away from the farm to urban areas, and the suburbanization of metropolitan areas.

Since 1870, urban population growth has accounted for more than half of the nation's total population increase. However, estimates of the volume of rural-to-urban migration are available only for the period after 1920. Between 1920 and 1930, net migration from rural to urban areas amounted to about 5.7 million persons, or 11 percent of the total rural population in 1920 (Taeuber & Taeuber, 1958). One 1958 study of residence histories found that 62 percent of all farm-born adults in the United States no longer lived on farms. Fifty-three percent of 18 to 24 year-olds had moved away from farms, as had 68 percent of people 65 and older (Taeuber, Chiazze, & Haenszel, 1968). This rural-to-urban movement meant that by 1958, 16 percent of all nonfarm residents were persons of farm origin.

In addition to the movement away from the farm, accelerated foreign migration in the post-Civil War period contributed to the rapid increase in the number, size, and density of urban places (see Table 5.4). Although cities of 100,000 persons or more contained only 5 percent of the population in 1850, they accounted for about 19 percent in 1900 and about 30 percent in 1930. Immigrants have always been heavily represented in urban areas, especially in the largest cities. In 1900, two-thirds of the foreign-born population (compared to only 40 percent of the total population) lived in urban places. In 1950, more than half the foreign-born, but less than one-fourth of native-born whites, lived in urban areas of over one million. More than a third of the foreign born lived in areas of three million or more.

TABLE 5.4 Number of Urban Places by Population Size: Selected Years, 1850 to 1970

Size of Place	*1850*	*1900*	*1930*	*1950*	*1960*	*1970*
Total (2,500 and over)	236	1,737	3,165	4,284	5,445	6,435
1,000,000 or more	—	3	5	5	5	6
500,000 to 1,000,000	1	3	8	13	16	20
250,000 to 500,000	—	9	24	23	30	30
100,000 to 250,000	5	23	56	65	81	100
50,000 to 100,000	4	40	98	126	201	240
25,000 to 50,000	16	82	185	252	432	520
10,000 to 25,000	36	280	606	778	1,134	1,385
5,000 to 10,000	85	465	851	1,176	1,394	1,839
2,500 to 5,000	89	832	1,332	1,846	2,152	2,295

Source: U.S. Bureau of the Census, U.S. Census of Population, *1950, Vol. II, and 1960, Vol. I:* Statistical Abstract of the U.S., *1974, Table 17.*

In this century, especially since 1920, there has been large-scale movement of city dwellers to the outskirts of urban areas. This suburbanization has taken place in all of the largest American cities, and has resulted in the phenomenon of the *metropolitan area* which includes a central city and a satellite area (or "metropolitan ring") of socially and economically related population. Metropolitan growth in recent decades has taken place largely as a twofold process of migration which includes first, the movement of large numbers of migrants from outside the metropolitan area to the largest cities; and second, the accompanying displacement and exodus of urban dwellers to the suburbs or metropolitan ring (Bogue, 1953; Bogue & Hawley, 1956, Taeuber & Taeuber, 1971).

Thus, movement off the farm, foreign immigration, and the additional factor of high fertility rates among both groups of migrants have combined to produce the nation's tremendous urban growth from under ten million in 1870 to 149 million in 1970. Together with great investment and development, these movements have transformed a rural, agriculturally oriented America into the urban-industrial society that it is today. By 1870, nearly half (47 percent) of the total number of gainfully employed were in nonagricultural occupations, and by 1920 the proportion had risen to nearly three-fourths (73 percent).

But since 1970, nonmetropolitan areas are not only retaining population, but are receiving net in-migration as well. In a recent study, Beale and Fuguitt (1975) conclude that America has entered a period of greatly reduced growth for its major metropolitan areas and of demographic revival for most of its rural and small town areas. We seem to be entering a new phase of adaptation to population pressures.

The Changing Strategy of Adaptation: Variations in Time and Space

It is important to see that the change from a rural to urban absorption of population growth (what we have termed the changing societal strategy of adaptation) did not occur uniformly in time or space in the United States. To be sure, only since 1870 has urban growth accounted for the bulk of the country's population increase; and the industrialization of the United States is conventionally seen as a post-Civil War phenomenon (in part, we might add, because relevant data on occupations and industries are not generally available for the years before 1870). In addition, the major developments in the mechanization of agriculture did not actually get under way in the United States until after the Civil War.

However, the urbanization of several of the northeastern and middle-Atlantic states began well before 1870. More than half the population of Massachusetts and Rhode Island was urban by 1850. And in the decade between 1850 and 1860, almost all the population growth of Massachusetts (97 percent) was accounted for by urban growth. In the same period Rhode Island actually experienced a decline in rural population, its total and urban populations growing by some 27,000 and 28,000 respectively (see Table 5.5).

In the same decade, urban areas absorbed 75 percent of the total population growth in Connecticut, 85 percent in New York, and 73 percent in New Jersey. Thus, although only some 20 percent of the total American population was urban at the onset of the Civil War, important

TABLE 5.5 Total and Urban Population Growth: Selected States, 1850–1860

	Percent Urban		*1850–1860 Increase (in thousands)*		*(in percent)*
State	*1850*	*1860*	*Total*	*Urban*	*Urban*
U.S. total	15	20	8,300	2,700	32
Massachusetts	51	60	236	229	97
Rhode Island	56	63	27	28	104
Connecticut	16	26	89	67	79
New York	28	39	764	651	85
New Jersey	18	33	183	134	73
Pennsylvania	24	31	584	350	60
Maryland	32	34	104	45	42
Ohio	12	17	360	158	44

Source: U.S. Bureau of the Census, U.S. Census of Population, *1950, Vol. II.*

areas of the country were already characterized by an urban strategy of adaptation and by substantially higher proportions of urban than rural residents.

FAMILIES AND ECONOMIC, SOCIAL, AND POLITICAL INSTITUTIONS IN TWENTIETH-CENTURY URBAN AMERICA

The post-Civil War population trends just discussed have had major implications for American social structure. Technological changes and increased population density have multiplied greatly the number and variety of social roles, and they have also multiplied and diversified the nation's social institutions.

The Family

The urban American family is still basically a nuclear family unit. But, especially since the spread of birth-control practices, it has become smaller than it was in the past. Although urban dwellers generally marry later than people in rural areas, they still marry at a relatively early age. Childbearing tends to be concentrated in the earliest years of marriage. The combination of early marriage, small planned families completed early in marriage, and increased longevity of both husbands and wives has lengthened the family cycle. The American family cycle now often includes a period of childbearing and a period in which the couple is still relatively young but already relatively free of childbearing duties. Women are increasingly active in the labor force. And both the joint retirement of couples and the individual retirement of widowers or widows are prolonged.

Urban families are, physically, not at all isolated from other families or from other elements of the social structure. However, the urban family cannot be characterized as *socially* integrated into, or isolated from, the rest of society. Instead, individual families are characterized by varying degrees of integration or isolation. Of course, different subpopulations of families may characteristically be more or less integrated or isolated than others, and these patterns of differentiation are important topics of research.

The urban family's physical proximity to the rest of the social structure is associated with its changing (most often diminishing) functions. Sex, childbearing, childrearing, and child socialization are still key family functions, and they help integrate the family into the rest of the social structure. However, the urban family is rarely a production unit, and its function as a consumption unit is somewhat less than that of the rural family. Often, too, the family is not a religious, recreational, political, or other social unit. This is because individual family members often seek their own entertainment, religious experiences, and political and social activities outside the home. Family members tend more to develop their own individual relationships to the economy through occupational choice and individual paths of education and employment. In the American family of today integration into the social structure is now more an individual than a family affair.

The Economy

Mechanization of agriculture and the spread of cheap and efficient land transport are the primary developments that led to accelerating urbanization and new social strategies of settlement. These developments also significantly altered the local and regional economies and their institutions. The mechanization of agriculture freed resources and labor from primary agricultural and extractive activities for employment in secondary, then tertiary, sectors of the economy. The development of cheap land transport promoted both rural agricultural and urban specialization as well as the social and economic institutions—financial, storage, brokerage, informational—that were devoted to the mediation of exchange. These developments led to the emergence of the regional urban economy, dominated usually by some regional metropolis with its smaller satellite cities and surrounding rural areas. They also have made the functions of the rural villages increasingly superfluous (Bogue, 1949). Both cities and rural areas have become functionally specialized in the regional economy, with the internal structure of a city or rural community strongly influenced by the nature of its economic base.

The urban-regional economy is characterized by relatively large businesses, especially in manufacturing, distribution, transport, and finance, which operate over large areas. Ownership, management, and work are often—perhaps usually—differentiated and bureaucratized. An individual's role in the economy tends to be highly specialized. But the urban scene is characterized by a very large variety of types, sizes, and proprietary arrangements of economic activity. The internal organization of business establishments ranges from one-person neighborhood businesses to giant corporations. Individual attachment to economic activity also varies widely in the urban economy, from casual or temporary jobs, to long-term careers, to proprietorship.

Social Institutions

Schools. The schools of twentieth-century urban America play a much more important role, in every respect, than did their nineteenth-century predecessors. They are larger, have far more resources invested in them, account for a much greater proportion of the time and life cycle of children, and are much more intimately connected with other facets of the social and economic structure.

Modern urban U.S.A. *(© Russell Abraham, 1976; Jeroboam, Inc.)*

Today, American children's time is not ordinarily taken up with chores or with involvement in a family economic enterprise. This means that they have more time to attend school. And, in most American communities throughout most of the twentieth century, children of certain ages have been obliged by law to do so. In addition, urban occupational roles have traditionally demanded more minimal skill in the manipulation of words, numbers, and abstractions than have occupational roles in the agricultural sector. Finally, while the rural and social-economic situation has traditionally been one in which successful farming, increased land holdings, or successful merchandising are the keys to mobility and advancement, the urban path to success much more frequently involves a hierarchy of skills or of professional or technical competence. In other words, it is a path than can be traveled only with considerable formal education.

Accordingly, urban American schools are key institutions. And access to them and the opportunities offered by such access have been the theme of major social movements and issues. Probably the best indication of the integration of schools and educational institutions into the rest of the economy and social structure is the tendency of both economists and laymen to view the schools increasingly as a community investment rather than as an item of consumption.

Churches. The distinguishing feature of churches in twentieth-century America is probably the fact that they must compete with other social and economic institutions in making claims upon, or offering diversion to, the urban population. This means that the twentieth-century American church plays many roles: it may sponsor the Thursday night bingo game; hold lectures on everything from sex to social justice; give dances and church suppers; and sponsor nursery schools, theatre groups, and summer camps for children. Not only did the early rural church meet with relatively little serious competition for the attention of the family, but it was often able to benefit from local legislation which restrained or barred potential competition by stores and places of amusement. The "blue laws," for example, prohibited work, commerce, and amusement on Sundays. Churches in many urban communities are still able to benefit from such blue laws and so they enjoy a partial monopolization of the sabbath. But individuals and families are typically much more mobile and may develop more effective strategies for finding non-church sabbath diversions than they could in the past.

Of course, the basic relationship of very large numbers of individuals to churches is still one of religious belief and practice. But urban churches have typically sought to attract the less enthusiastic and less deeply committed believers and practitioners of the religion rather than depend entirely upon the support of the very religious.

Urban churches of all denominations tend to be quite large. Like other institutions, they have a large number and variety of roles. These are divided between clerical and lay roles, with different churches having different internal organizations. Large cities may have churches of many different sizes, resources, and volumes of activity. These may range from the once-a-week storefront church with an unpaid or even itinerant preacher to the vast and complex operations of a Catholic diocese. The latter typically includes not only the conventional pursuits of religion but also its own school system, social welfare system, youth and lay adult movements and organizations, property interests, and recreational, cultural, and political activities.

Voluntary organizations. Voluntary organizations, like other social institutions in twentieth-century America, range widely in internal organization and intensity of interest and activity. The urban organization with a large membership may have an extremely active nucleus, a larger number of moderately active members, and an even larger number of members who are occasionally aroused to group involvement. Urban voluntary organizations are much more stable than their rural counterparts, at least potentially, because of their size and the differentiation among their memberships. An organization may be entirely local in nature or it may be connected to regional or national parent organizations. For individuals, organizational membership is a key avenue of communication and of integration into the larger social structure.

The very heterogeneity of urban society serves as the raison d'être for a large number of voluntary organizations. Individuals of similar characteristics or interests seek each other out and, upon finding others, institutionalize organized social contact and activities. The same types of voluntary organizations are found in urban areas as in rural communities, although there is a greater variety in the cities. A number of types are peculiar to the urban setting itself. Groups interested in particular facets of music, science, literature, art, and sports thrive in the urban setting. Foreign-language groups and ethnic associations of mutual aid (*landsmannschaften*) are ordinarily found in cities, as are foreign-language newspapers and other publications, and foreign-language theater. The labor union in the United States, too, has thus far been limited mostly to cities and to one-industry rural communities.

Political Instituitons

Many of the institutions of local, state, and national government in twentieth-century urban America duplicate, at least in form, their counterparts of the nineteenth century. However, the changes in population size and distribution and in economic structure have generated some far-reaching functional changes in these institutions and also in the general political structure.

Probably the greatest change is the increase in both size and function of federal and municipal governments. In addition to its traditional responsibility for defense, foreign trade, international relations, and immigration, the federal government has assumed the initiative in establishing and regulating many other matters: among them, economy and trade, resource development and conservation, and social welfare and health. Today, the federal government is responsible for mobilizing and channeling enormous resources comprising a considerable proportion of the total national product. City governments, for their part, have become deeply involved in matters of health, welfare, housing, local transportation, delinquency, social disorganization, education, and the promotion of the local economy.

Both the expansion of the federal and urban governments and the decline of smaller local government bases have made direct individual participation in politics relatively less influential than organizational participation. As a result, individual political participation is usually organized and mediated by voluntary associations, political parties and clubs, labor unions, and professional groups which command far more resources than any individual. Political parties and organizations are very complex and elaborate in urban settings, having to contend both with the complexities of government and with the problem of reaching, or being reached by, large numbers and many different types of constituents and supporters.

COMMUNITY, ETHNICITY, AND SOCIAL CLASS: CHANGING AXES OF SOCIAL SOLIDARITY AND POLITICAL CLEAVAGE

Those differences in social characteristics, behavior, interaction, and solidarity that are associated with size and type of residence (community); race, religion, or national origin (ethnicity); and socioeconomic status (social class) have been clearly recognized and documented in American social science. We can already see such differences in the earliest United States censuses—which distinguishes between urban and rural populations, whites and nonwhites, freemen and slaves, and native-born and foreign-born, although never between the different religious groups. Censuses, government and private surveys, community studies, historical studies, and case studies have all revealed residential, ethnic, and class-based variations in all types of social phenomena: marriage and fertility, socialization and education, employment and consumption, voting and political participation, and so on. Often these variables overlap. Residential differences in employment characteristics often reflect educational, ethnic, color, or social-class differences; and ethnic group differences in fertility sometimes reflect differences in social-class composition or women's employment roles. But geographic and residential, racial and ethnic, and social status differences are often found to persist even when the other variables are taken into account.

America: A "Melting Pot" or Still a Pluralistic Society?

To what extent do residence, ethnicity, and class retain their importance as bases of social differentiation and solidarity under the impact of population and social change? This is an important question to any student of American social patterns, and from it follow many other questions. To what extent have migration and improved transportation reduced differences in social relations and behavior between urban and rural areas, different regional sectors, and different communities? To what extent have legal equality and the process of assimilation rendered race, religion, or national origin socially (and sociologically) irrelevant? To what extent have occupation and status mobility neutralized social-class differences in behavior, associations, and political activity? [3]

The answers to such questions are not easy ones, nor are they tidily documented. Theories (or ideologies) of the "melting pot" of ethnic amalgamation, acculturation, and assimilation anticipate the eventual convergence of the different racial, religious, and national-origin groups. Among white Protestants, it probably can be said that the different national groups (Scandinavian, British, German, etc.) are much less dissimilar today than they were two generations, or even one generation, ago. Indeed, there has been a considerable amount of intermarriage among the white Protestant ethnic groups. Similarly, white Catholics of different national origins are probably less dissimilar than they were in the past, although they have probably intermarried less than have Protestant groups. But white Catholics remain "different" from white Protestants, and in many respects they are socially segregated from them; and Jews, by and large, remain "different" and socially segregated from Christians of both groups. Blacks and other nonwhites remain even more "different," and, even worse, they still remain segregated residentially, occupationally, and socially from whites of all religions and types. Table 5.6 shows the estimated composition of the population by religious denominations and the differences in age and social characteristics among the major religious and ethnic groups.

Similar conclusions can be drawn with regard to social class. The skilled-worker and craftsmen groups are overtaking the lower clerical and sales groups in income levels and consumption, and the styles of life of these and other groups are exhibiting increasing similarities. In addition,

[3] For penetrating analyses of this question, see Gordon (1964), Blau and Duncan (1967, Chaps. 6 and 12), and Duncan, Featherman, and Duncan (1972).

TABLE 5.6 American Religioethnic Groups, Based on Seven NORC[a] Surveys: 1963 to 1972: Social and Demographic Characteristics

Religioethnic Group	*Percent of Total Population*	*Average Years of Education*	*Average Age*[b]	*Average Occupation Prestige*	*Percent White Collar*	*Average Number of Children*[c]	*Average Family Income*	*Percent Married*
Protestants								
British (1303)	13.6	11.9	47.5	3.98	53	2.3	$ 8309	79.1
German (1205)	12.6	11.0	45.8	3.46	40	2.5	7858	83.8
Scandinavian (359)	3.7	11.3	45.1	3.38	42	2.7	7869	80.5
Irish (530)	5.5	10.6	46.2	3.17	38	2.7	7022	79.7
Other (1883)	19.7	10.5	45.5	3.33	41	2.6	7275	80.9
Catholics								
Irish (328)	3.4	12.2	44.5	4.27	49	2.8	9255	80.8
German (342)	3.6	11.3	44.4	3.88	45	3.1	8903	85.1
Italian (346)	3.6	10.7	44.6	3.48	39	2.8	7979	81.8
Polish (136)	1.4	10.0	45.1	2.69	34	2.9	7940	75.4
Slavic (237)	2.5	10.4	45.0	3.48	31	2.3	7693	75.5
French (156)	1.6	10.4	43.9	3.30	25	2.8	7478	75.0
Spanish-speaking (122)	1.3	9.3	38.2	3.10	24	3.1	6145	86.9
Other (609)	6.4	11.0	41.1	3.46	38	2.7	8105	78.6
Jews								
German (30)	0.3	12.9	48.0	5.36	57	2.3	9326	80.6
Eastern European (160)	1.7	13.3	45.0	4.77	79	1.7	11,114	78.8
Other (50)	0.5	13.3	43.6	4.38	73	2.0	11,218	74.5
Blacks (1285)	13.4	9.7	43.3	2.47	18	2.9	5425	66.8
Orientals (20)	0.2	11.6	42.0	2.60	35	2.6	7918	70.0
No religion[d] (304)	3.2	12.0	41.7	3.49	45	1.9	9046	67.0
Other (150)	1.6	11.2	45.2	3.72	44	2.3	7654	69.5
National average (9593)	100	10.9	44.8	3.42	39	2.6	7588	78.1

Numbers in parentheses are numbers of respondents in each population category.
[a] National Opinion Research Center, University of Chicago. [b] Adults over age 18. [c] Per women ever married.
[d] Those who described their religious affiliation as "none," no matter what their ethnic background.
Source: A. M. Greeley, Ethnicity in the United States: A Preliminary Reconnaissance *(New York: John Wiley & Sons, 1974). Tables 4 and 6.*

social-class fertility differentials have diminished greatly (Ryder & Westoff, 1972; Kiser et al., 1968). But these groups remain distinct in many elements of life-style: when and whether they marry; how many children they have and how they rear them; participation or nonparticipation in voluntary organizations; and political orientation and activity at both community and national levels.

Finally, although the rural population has declined proportionally and absolutely, what we refer to as the urban population is differentiated within itself in several respects: city size, proximity to the metropolitan centers, and the "functional classes" (manufacturing, commercial, administrative, and so forth) within the city. Thus, though there are fewer rural, urban, and size-of-place differences in fertility and numbers marrying, there are still many differences in age at marriage, in labor-force participation and employment, in political organization, in types of economic and voluntary organizations, and in types of public institutions.

Social Change as a Permanent Fixture of American Society

Careful study of United States census data would almost surely reveal that in some counties or areas of the United States there have been periods of three or four decades when there were no substantial changes in population size, distribution, and composition; in the number, size, and economic orientation of business establishments; or in the size, occupational distribution, or industrial composition of the labor force. But these instances of stability are the exception rather than the rule, and in any case they do not necessarily reflect social stability. For more likely than not, seemingly stable areas have been deeply affected by population changes and related social transformations in both neighboring and distant parts of the country. Moreover, even in areas of unchanging population size and composition, we can be sure that some changes have occurred: some youngsters have had more schooling than their parents; transportation and communication have changed; and methods of work and production, both within and outside of agriculture, have changed considerably. Thus it may be said that social change itself has been a most enduring aspect of American social structure.

Our descriptions in this chapter have been meant to present an ideal type of analytical model of the social-structural features of nineteenth-century rural America and twentieth-century urban America. At no time has the social structure of the United States corresponded perfectly, or even approximately, to our description of rural and urban social structure in the nineteenth and twentieth centuries. However, areas in the United States have at different times had social structures characterized by the features we have described for nineteenth-century rural and for twentieth-century urban America. And for at least some parts of America, the transformation we have described from a nineteenth-century rural social structure to a twentieth-century urban one does indeed correspond to the social changes that have already occurred or are even now taking place.

SUMMARY

In this chapter we have looked briefly at population growth, distribution, and patterns of settlement in the United States, and we have related these to variations and changes in a number of major institutional features of American society. The first United States census in 1790 recorded a total population of just under four million, and the total reported by the most recent census exceeded 204 million. Every census since 1810 (the beginning of immigration and emigration records) shows that the bulk of the population increase was due to natural increase, though in some decades as much as 32 to 40 percent of the increase was due to net immigration. Until 1860, the bulk of American population growth was absorbed in rural communities, but after the Civil War population growth was absorbed mostly in urban communities. In the 1970 census, almost three-quarters of the population was urban, with 27.6 percent living in places of 100,000 or more inhabitants.

Just as the various regions and states were populated and settled at different times in American history, urbanization and metropolitanization have taken place at different periods in the various sections of the country. The Eastern Seaboard was already highly urbanized early in the nineteenth century, while parts of the South, Midwest, and mountain states are largely rural even today. However, the population and social structure of a "nineteenth century rural America" can be generally contrasted with those of "twentieth century urban America" both as overall characterization and as an analytical device. The small, sparsely populated, and relatively isolated communities of nineteenth century rural America were characterized by large multifunctional families. They were childbearing, residential, economic, religious, recreational, and associational units all at the same time, and they mediated much of the individual's activities and social contacts. A large proportion of work activity was in and surrounding agriculture and closely related pursuits. Communities tended to be very homogeneous in this respect, with village and town business, and professional and public service highly oriented to agriculture and the farm population.

The large, densely populated, and economically and politically integrated communities of twentieth-century urban America, in contrast, tend to have small families with much more restricted, though still crucial, social functions. Sex, childbearing and early socialization, residential organization, and household consumption are still largely family functions. Economic, political, religious, or recreational activity may or may not take place in family units or settings. Work is very highly differentiated in the urban setting, as are the competing arrays of social, political, recreational, and religious activities and institutions.

Historically Americans have always had a propensity to change their places of residence. Patterns of settlement of the different regions are closely connected to the interstate streams of migration in every period of American history. More recently, rural-to-urban, central-city-to-suburb, and intermetropolitan migration have influenced the geographical distribution of the population and the patterns of residential settlement. The evolution of huge, complex megalopolitan networks of urban places has characterized the post-1950 period but there have been some indications of a reversal of this trend. The recession years of the 1970s have been characterized by net gains for the smaller urban and rural communities.

Even beyond the redistribution of population, the American tradition of migration may have generated a kind of often-migrant population pool, with new bases of social solidarity and differentiation. Traditional ties like religion, ethnicity, community of origin, length of residence in the community, and family and neighborhood connections have become less important, while other factors like occupational affiliation, leisure, recreational and consumption patterns, or participation in the community or in groups have been upgraded as bases of association. There still remains a large part of the American population which is strongly rooted in its communities of origin, and for whom race, religion, ethnicity, and social class are still the basic axes of social solidarity and differentiation. Increasingly, American urban communities of all types—cities, suburbs, and megalopolitan agglomerations—comprise elements of often-migrant and never-migrant populations in varying mixes.

In Part II, we will turn to a consideration of the factors which bear directly on changes in population size and structure like those described in this and previous chapters. We will review the variations and trends in mortality, marriage, fertility, and migration, studying the factors which cause or influence them. We will begin Part II with an overview of the elements of population change in the next chapter.

Two

Components and Determinants of Population Trends

6

The Elements of Population Change

We will begin our discussion of the components of population trends with an overview of the elements of population change and the way in which they are studied. First, we introduce the concept of population composition. Then we turn to the basic demographic "balancing equation" which shows population growth in its separate elements—births, deaths, in-migrants, and out-migrants—and we will look briefly at some methods of measuring these elements. We conclude with a brief discussion of sources of population data and the various approaches to population measurement and analysis.

POPULATION COMPOSITION

Any human population may be viewed as an aggregate of individuals of different types and characteristics. It is these types, and their absolute or relative numbers in the population, that are the subject of concern in the analysis of population composition.

Hawley (1959) has observed that the analysis of population composition constitutes a quantitative description of a society's human resources. Historically, as in the case of census population counts, the delineation of human resources has been the major purpose of analyses of population composition. Demographers, however, have always given first priority to the age-sex factor. This is because they have recognized that a population's age-sex characteristics are intimately related not only to its human resources, but also to its rate and pattern of growth.

Thus, in population studies, an understanding of a population's composition is seen as particularly relevant to understanding both actual or potential population growth and the society's stock of human resources. (And techniques of demographic analysis have, in turn, been involved in the study of changes in human resources.) For a population's changing size and its changing composition by sex, age, and geographic distribution are certainly the fundamental factors in changes in its human resources.

Composition by Sex

The very earliest demographers noted that the number of male births in a population always exceeds the number of female births, and that, at virtually all ages, the number of male deaths exceeds the number of female deaths. Typically, the number of males in a population exceeds the

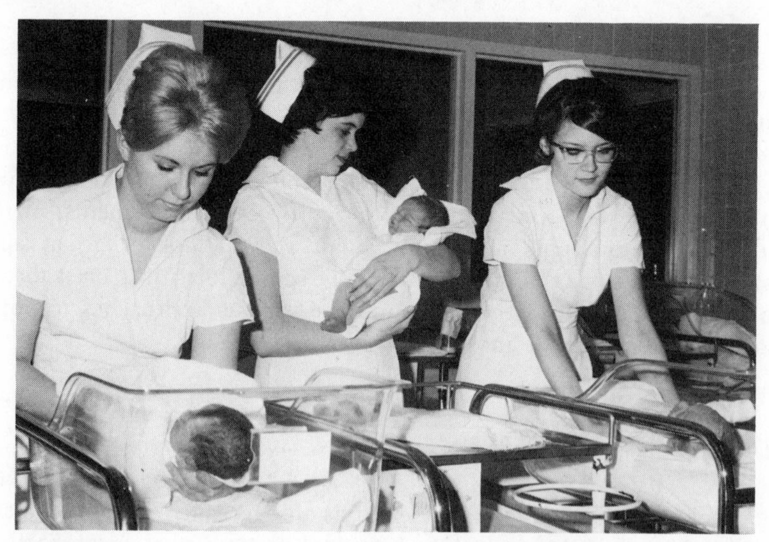

Demographers generally start their studies here to determine a population's birth rate and age-sex characteristics. *(Courtesy of Englewood Hospital, Englewood, New Jersey)*

number of females at the very earliest ages. At later ages this male excess is reduced by an excess of male mortality. And at the most advanced ages, females outnumber males.

The exact ratio of males to females in a population may vary with mortality patterns (including foetal mortality, which affects the sex ratio at birth). It may also vary with the age composition of the population and with patterns of migration. Thus, other things being equal, populations with low general mortality or large proportions of younger persons have higher proportions of males than do populations with high general mortality or large proportions of older persons, respectively. Countries attracting overseas migrants also have high proportions of males, as do industrial communities. Cities that attract large numbers of rural-to-urban migrants have high proportions of females.

Composition by Age

Populations are considered "young" or "old," depending upon whether they have high proportions of young or old persons. Populations with large proportions of adults, and relatively small proportions in both the younger and older ages of dependency are generally believed to be in a favorable position with regard to levels of living, investment, and development. Age divides a population into groups of potential producers and consumers: the independent adults in the middle range of the population are both producers and consumers, while the dependent children and the retired or infirm are consumers only. (The reader may wish to refer to Table 4.2, which shows the age composition of selected countries.)

A population's age composition has a wide-ranging influence on social and economic arrangements and institutions, from maternity wards, kindergartens, and schools to entertainment, transportation, religion, and homes for the aged. Moreover, central social and economic processes such as family formation and home-purchasing, job-seeking, retirement, savings, migration, and mobility are closely related to the age composition of a population.

A population's age composition depends first and foremost upon its level of fertility and only secondarily upon its level of mortality. However, migratory movements are important factors determining age composition, especially in relatively small or localized populations. *Aging of population* describes a gradual process where the proportions of adults and elderly persons increase and the proportions of children and adolescents decrease over time. Aging is always a consequence of low or declining fertility.

Composition by Marital Status

Next to sex and age, the most familiar compositional characteristic of the population is marital status: people are either single, married, widowed, or divorced. Without a doubt, marital status varies sharply with age and sex; it is also closely connected with fertility and population growth.

A profile of a population's composition by marital status gives the demographer important information. It is indicative of the number of family units, the potential number of marriages, the composition of the population eligible for marriage (the "marriage market"), and many other factors. Table 6.1 shows the composition of the population (aged 14 and over) by sex, age, and marital status.

Household status, or an individual's relationship to the head of the household, is often used to plot population composition according to numbers of people in or not in households, numbers of people with each possible kinship and nonkinship relationship to the head of the household, and numbers of family and nonfamily household groupings. A population's marital characteristics (like year of present or first marriage, age at marriage, number of marriages) and its fertility characteristics are often studied, too.

Composition by Origin

After sex, age, and marital status, the most important questions in analyzing population composition concern the origins of the population: place of birth, citizenship, race, religion, language, ethnic characteristics, and migrant or refugee status. In the United States, census and vital statistics operations avoid ascertaining or publishing data concerning the population's religious composition.[1] Nevertheless, there is great interest in this topic, and many students of American population and society have sought to study religious composition in the absence of census data.

Data on composition by origins allow us to classify population groups by origin; they also provide a basis for the study of population movements. When birthplaces are tabulated, a population can be classified by geographic origins and also by whether or not people still reside in their place of birth. This tabulation makes it possible to study the volume of migration.

[1] An important exception was the Current Population Survey conducted in March 1957 by the Bureau of the Census, in which religious preference was asked. Results of this survey are still the most important source available on the religious composition of the United States population.

TABLE 6.1 Marital Status and Presence of Spouse According to Sex and Age, 1972 (in thousands of persons 18 years old and over, except percent. As of March 1972.)

Sex and Age	Total	Single	Married	Widowed	Divorced	Percent Distribution				
						Total	Single	Married	Widowed	Divorced
Male	64,228	12,558	48,054	1,834	1,781	100.0	19.6	74.8	2.9	2.8
18–19 years	3,629	3,336	290	–	3	100.0	91.9	8.0	–	0.1
20–24 years	8,247	4,690	3,465	1	101	100.0	56.9	41.9	(z)	1.2
25–29 years	7,117	1,375	5,539	4	109	100.0	19.3	77.8	0.1	2.8
30–34 years	5,913	732	4,996	12	173	100.0	12.4	84.5	0.2	2.9
35–44 years	10,988	964	9,578	55	451	100.0	8.2	87.2	0.5	4.1
45–54 years	11,212	613	10,057	154	390	100.0	5.5	89.7	1.4	3.5
55–64 years	8,848	452	7,769	307	321	100.0	5.1	87.8	3.5	3.6
65–74 years	5,410	314	4,391	593	112	100.0	5.8	81.2	11.0	2.1
75 years and over	2,862	141	1,980	708	33	100.0	4.9	69.2	24.7	1.1
Female	71,557	9,856	49,047	9,601	3,052	100.0	13.8	68.5	13.4	4.3
18–19 years	3,783	2,912	816	6	20	100.0	77.0	22.4	0.2	0.5
20–24 years	8,992	3,275	5,464	21	231	100.0	36.4	60.8	0.2	2.6
25–29 years	7,361	909	6,059	35	357	100.0	12.4	82.3	0.5	4.9
30–34 years	6,126	412	5,347	58	309	100.0	6.7	87.3	1.0	5.0
35–44 years	11,614	522	10,069	335	689	100.0	4.5	86.7	2.9	6.0
45–54 years	12,142	514	9,926	991	711	100.0	4.2	81.7	8.2	5.9
55–64 years	9,981	550	6,935	2,056	413	100.0	5.5	69.5	20.6	1.4
65–74 years	7,046	470	3,395	2,962	219	100.0	6.7	48.2	42.0	3.1
75 years and over	4,509	292	1,007	3,138	73	100.0	6.5	22.3	69.6	1.6

– Represents zero. Z less than 0.05 percent. *Source:* Statistical Abstract of the United States, 1973, *Table 47, p. 38.*

Composition by Other Characteristics

Another key element of population composition is that of economic activity or participation in the labor force. Individuals in a population are often classified by the extent of their participation in the labor force; by occupation or industry group; by employment or unemployment; by employment status (employee, self-employed, or employer); and sometimes by the amount of time they have worked, their secondary occupations, and their annual, monthly, or other incomes.

Another element is the level of literacy, educational achievement, and school attendance of population groups. There has traditionally been great interest in the relative numbers of a population able to read and write. More recently, in countries where literacy is virtually universal, composition by literacy is no longer investigated. In these countries, composition by educational achievement may be studied in great detail, with attention given to both the number of school years completed and the types of education completed.

Finally, composition of the population may also be studied by geographic location or by type of place of residence. Such studies typically distinguish rural from urban residence, residence in places of different size classes, and residence in places of different types such as metropolitan and nonmetropolitan places.

Population Composition as Role Distribution

It should be obvious from the foregoing discussion that the compositional characteristics of populations most commonly studied by demographers and other students of population are social roles and categories of social roles. A female's role is different from a male's, a child's different from an adult's, a migrant's different from a nonmigrant's. The fact that all social roles are not seen as compositional characteristics is due primarily to the difficulty, or lack of interest, in enumerating them in censuses, surveys, and records of vital statistics (Hawley, 1959).

Role distribution describes a population's composition by categories. Any change in population composition means a change in role distribution. Such changes fundamentally originate in two ways:

1. as the result of differential rates of increment to the population. Thus, higher-than-average birth rates among lower socioeconomic level population groups imply a changing role distribution for the society as a whole.
2. as the net result of the aggregate of individual role changes. Net rural-to-urban migration implies a changing role distribution. Individual

marriages and divorces, completion of education, and occupational changes all contribute to population-wide changes in role distributions.

Data on population composition allow us to specify and analyze role distributions and composition changes over time. And analysis of population composition and changes is a powerful tool for analyzing social structure. Thus, the study of population composition and distribution is a natural complement to the study of social roles and social systems.

STUDYING POPULATION GROWTH

The growth of a population is always studied with reference to the size of that population at some initial point in time. The basic relationship is expressed:

$$\begin{pmatrix}\text{Size of population}\\ \text{at terminal point}\end{pmatrix} = \begin{pmatrix}\text{Size of population}\\ \text{at initial point}\end{pmatrix} + \begin{pmatrix}\text{Growth in the}\\ \text{interval of time}\end{pmatrix}.$$

Population growth is usually measured in two ways. The first measure is the percentage change in the size of the population during the interval. It is obtained by calculating the ratio of the growth in the interval of time to the initial population size and then multiplying by 100:

$$\text{Percentage change} = \frac{\text{growth in the interval}}{\text{initial population size}} \times 100.$$

Thus, drawing upon the data in Table 6.2, we can determine the percentage change in the size of the United States population between April, 1960 and April, 1970:

$$\begin{aligned}\text{Percentage change} &= \frac{(\text{1970 total pop.}) - (\text{1960 total pop.})}{(\text{1960 total pop.})} \times 100\\ &= \frac{203{,}184{,}772 - 179{,}323{,}175}{179{,}323{,}175} \times 100\\ &= 13.3 \text{ percent.}\end{aligned}$$

The corresponding change in the intercensal period from 1 April, 1950, to 1 April, 1960, was:

$$\frac{179{,}323{,}175 - 151{,}325{,}798}{151{,}325{,}798} \times 100 = 18.5 \text{ percent.}$$

TABLE 6.2 Estimates of Total Resident U.S. Population and Components of Change, United States, 1950–1971 (in thousands)

Components of Change	*April 1, 1970*[a] *to Jan. 1, 1971*	*April 1, 1960 to April 1, 1970*	*April 1, 1950 to April 1, 1960*
Population at beginning of period	203,185	179,323	151,326
Births in period	2,866	39,033	40,963
Deaths in period	1,413	18,192	15,608
Net migration in period[b]	437	3,020	2,642
Population at end of period	206,488	203,185	179,323
Net change	3,303	23,862	27,997

[a] Preliminary estimates.

[b] Includes net civilian migration less movement of armed forces overseas and error of closure.

Source: U.S. Bureau of the Census, Current Population Reports, *"Population Estimates," Series P-25, no. 460 (June 7, 1971) and no. 465 (Sept. 8, 1971).*

The second measure of population growth is the average annual rate of change in population size during the interval. It is obtained by calculating the ratio of the growth in the interval to the initial population size and dividing that ratio by the number of years in the interval:

$$\text{Average annual rate of change} = \frac{\left(\text{Growth in the interval}\right) / \left(\text{Initial population size}\right)}{\text{Number of years in the interval}}.$$

For the United States in the 1960–1970 period, the average annual rate of change was 1.33 percent. This represents a sharp decline from the average annual rate of change of 1.85 percent in the 1950–1960 interval. Besides the two measures of population growth described here, there are other, somewhat more elaborate measures which may be employed. We have not described them here because they are less frequently used and beyond the scope of our introductory discussion.

Components of Population Growth: An Overview

The growth of a population during a given interval of time may be divided into four major components:

$$\begin{pmatrix}\text{Growth}\\ \text{in the}\\ \text{interval}\end{pmatrix} = \begin{pmatrix}\text{Births}\\ \text{in the}\\ \text{interval}\end{pmatrix} - \begin{pmatrix}\text{Deaths}\\ \text{in the}\\ \text{interval}\end{pmatrix} + \begin{pmatrix}\text{No. of}\\ \text{in-migrants}\end{pmatrix} - \begin{pmatrix}\text{No. of}\\ \text{out-migrants}\end{pmatrix}.$$

Combining the birth and death components yields:

$$\begin{pmatrix}\text{Growth due to}\\ \text{natural increase}\end{pmatrix} = \begin{pmatrix}\text{Number of births}\\ \text{in the interval}\end{pmatrix} - \begin{pmatrix}\text{Number of deaths}\\ \text{in the interval}\end{pmatrix},$$

and combining the in-migration and out-migration components yields

$$\begin{pmatrix}\text{Growth}\\ \text{due to net}\\ \text{migration}\end{pmatrix} = \begin{pmatrix}\text{Number of}\\ \text{in-migrants in}\\ \text{the interval}\end{pmatrix} - \begin{pmatrix}\text{Number of}\\ \text{out-migrants}\\ \text{in the interval}\end{pmatrix}.$$

Measurements of population growth due to natural increase, and of growth due to net migration, are analogous to the measurement of total population growth. Thus

$$\begin{matrix}\text{Percentage change due}\\ \text{to natural increase}\end{matrix} = \frac{\text{Growth due to natural increase}}{\text{Initial population size}} \times 100,$$

and

$$\begin{matrix}\text{Average annual rate}\\ \text{of growth due to}\\ \text{natural increase}\end{matrix} = \frac{(\text{Growth due to natural increase})/(\text{Initial population}).}{\text{Number of years in the interval}}$$

Similarly,

$$\begin{matrix}\text{Percentage change due}\\ \text{to net migration}\end{matrix} = \frac{\text{Growth due to net migration}}{\text{Initial population size}} \times 100,$$

and

$$\begin{matrix}\text{Average annual rate}\\ \text{of growth due to}\\ \text{net migration}\end{matrix} = \frac{(\text{Growth due to net migration})/(\text{Initial population}).}{\text{Number of years in the interval.}}$$

In the United States in the 1960–1970 period,

$$\begin{matrix}\text{Percentage change due}\\ \text{to natural increase}\end{matrix} = \frac{20{,}841{,}000}{179{,}323{,}175} \times 100 = 11.6 \text{ percent.}$$

Thus, the average annual rate of growth due to natural increase was 1.16 percent. The table also shows that:

$$\text{Percent change due to net international migration} = \frac{3,020,000}{179,323,175} \times 100 = 1.7 \text{ percent.}$$

Thus, the average annual change due to net migration was 0.17 percent. When growth rates are studied on a year-to-year basis, the midyear (rather than the beginning-of-the-year) population is often taken as the denominator. Under this procedure, the measures of change due to each component correspond to the crude birth rate, crude death rate, and so on. Thus, for the United States, the components of growth in 1974 were:

	Number	*Rate per 1,000 Midyear Population*
Initial 1974 Population	211,205,000	
Births	3,166,000	14.9
Deaths	1,933,000	9.1
Net Civilian Immigration	360,000	1.7
Population at Beginning of 1975	212,796,000	

Components of change from 1930 to 1974 are shown for the United States in Figure 6.1.

Mortality

Mortality has always been a subject of reflection, speculation, and discourse by poets and philosophers, generals and chiefs of state, and priests and medicine men as well as the "common man." But not until John Graunt made a systematic study, *Natural and Political Observations . . . Made Upon the Bills of Mortality* (London, 1662), of the number of deaths in relation to the total population in London did man's interest in mortality launch modern demography and population studies. Today, the study of mortality and its relationship to population size, composition, and change retains a central position in population research. In the eighteenth and nineteenth centuries there was a flood of investigations of mortality, fertility, and population size in Europe. This deluge coincided with the increasing availability of data about populations and vital events and with the emergence of far-reaching population trends associated with the transformation of European societies and culture.

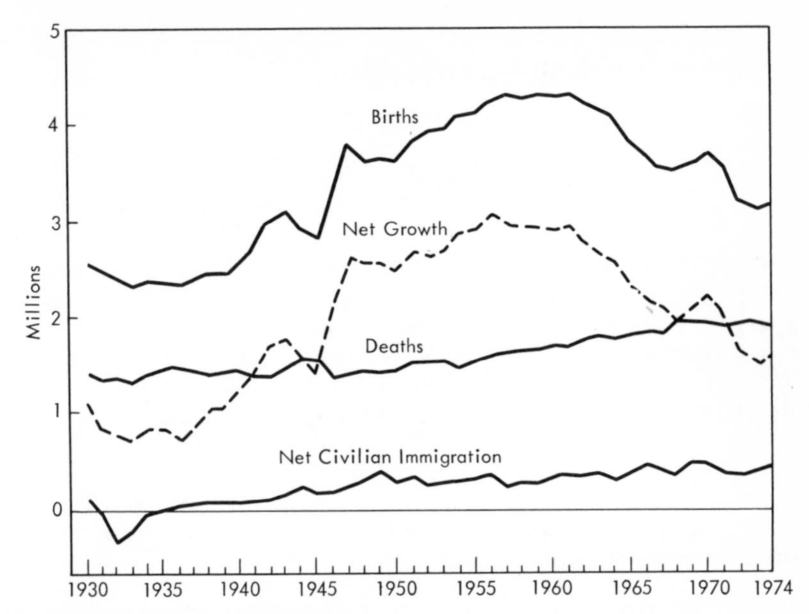

Figure 6.1 Estimates of the population of the United States and components of change: 1974, with annual data from 1930. *Source: Data from U.S. Bureau of the Census,* Current Population Reports, *Series P-25, no. 545 (April, 1975).*

(Among the most important of the European trends were declining mortality and both rural-to-urban and overseas migration.) In the same period, social reformers and their opponents, too, were increasingly concerned with conditions of life and health among the various population groups. And this interest generated more and increasingly detailed studies of disease and mortality.

Today, our concern with health conditions centers on the availability and equality of access to medical and health services. And just as mortality studies served to highlight the misfortunes of the nineteenth-century industrial and rural poor in Europe, they can be used today to document one of America's gravest social problems in the twentieth century: the persistence and inadequacy of archaic institutions and systems for the provision of medical care.

Measures of mortality. The most commonly seen measure of mortality is the crude death rate, taken as the number of deaths per thousand population (shown for the United States from 1900 to 1969 in Figure 6.2). More detailed measures are the age-specific mortality rates, and these are discussed in detail in the Appendix. There is a universal age variation in mortality rates: a fairly high rate immediately following

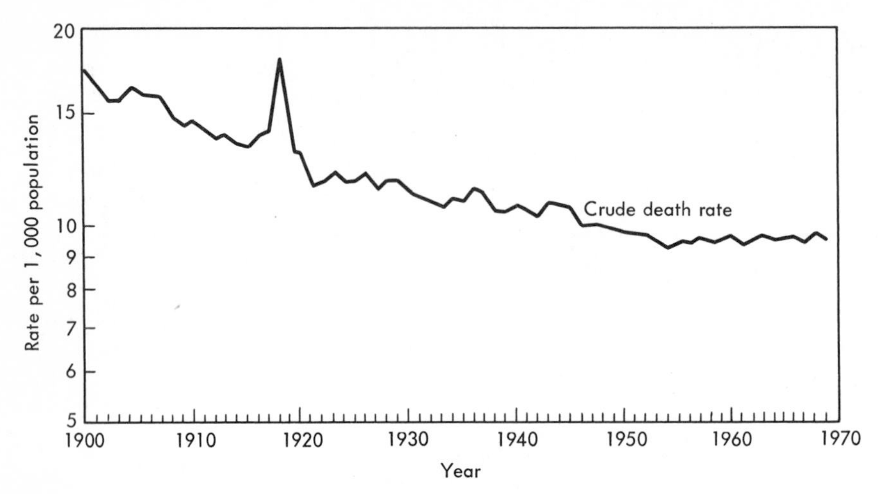

Figure 6.2 Crude death rates in the United States, 1900–1969. *Source: Data for 1900–32 from state death registrations; 1933–69 data from U.S. Bureau of the Census,* Statistical Abstract of the United States, 1970.

birth (around 20 to 30 deaths per 1,000 births in Western Europe, North America, and Oceania, but as high as 200 to 300 deaths per thousand births in underdeveloped countries); a diminishing rate throughout the ages of childhood, reaching a minimum between ages 10 and 14 (about 0.5 to 1.0 death per 1,000 in Western populations); and, finally, an increasing rate at subsequent ages (about 30 to 50 deaths per 1,000 at age 65 in Western populations, then rising very sharply). Figure 6.3 depicts this age variation in mortality rates with regard to both male and female populations in 1969.

Male mortality is usually higher than female mortality at all ages.[2] For example, infant mortality in the United States in 1969 was 24 per 1,000 for white males but only 19 per 1,000 for white females; [3] and the death rate at ages 75–84 in the same year was 98 per 1,000 for white males but only 66 per 1,000 for white females (See Figure 6.3) Thus, the overall pattern of mortality for any population is described by a set of mortality rates by age and sex. Such a set of age-sex-specific mortality rates is con-

[2] For a recent analysis of some South Asian exceptions, see El-Badry, 1969.

[3] It might be noted here that the United States infant mortality rate has been consistently higher in the past several decades than the rates of a number of other Western countries, among them the Netherlands, Sweden, Norway, Australia, and New Zealand. Moreover, the United States rate has been declining at a slower pace than the rates of other Western countries, so that countries with previously higher levels of infant mortality, like England and Wales, Denmark, and Scotland, have rates below that of the United States. See Table 6.9 and, for much more detail, H. C. Chase, 1969.

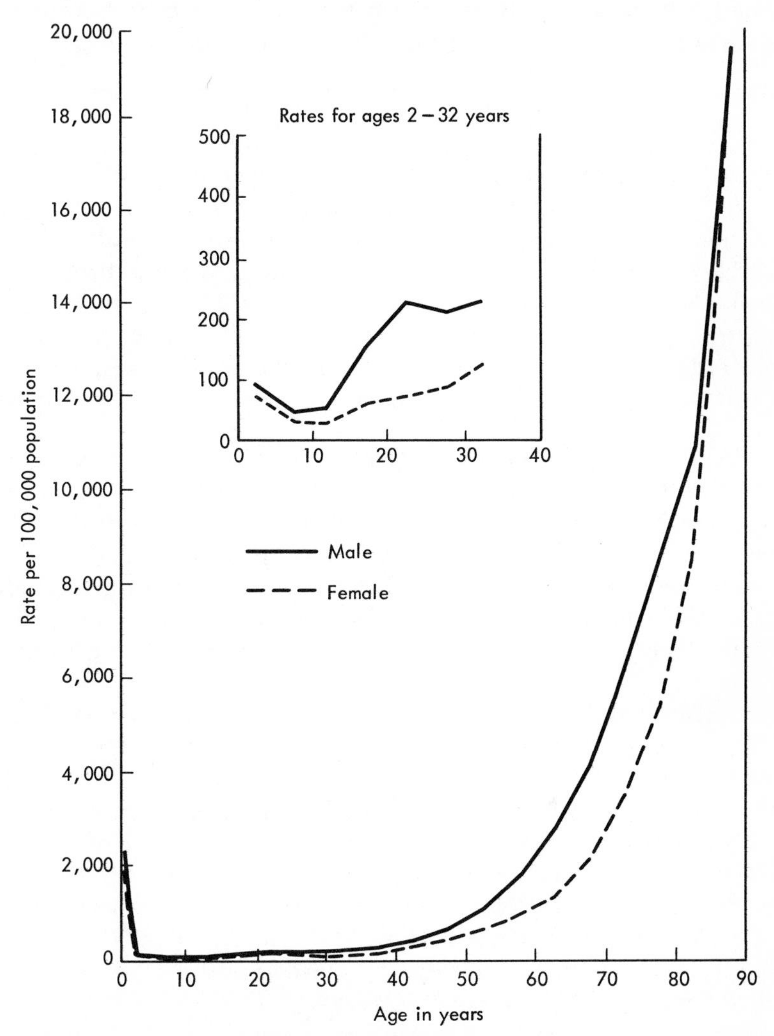

Figure 6.3 Death rates by age and sex: United States, 1969. *Source: U.S. Department of Health, Education, and Welfare,* Mortality Trends: Age, Color and Sex, U.S. 1950–69: Vital and Health Statistics, *Series no. 15 (Nov. 1973), Figure 4.*

ventionally called the *mortality schedule of a population;* and it is the variations and changes in mortality schedules which will be the focus of the next chapter.

Among the measures for summarizing the mortality schedule are the crude death rate, the standardized death rate, and the expectation of life at birth. These are explained in some detail in the Appendix. These summary measures may differ for two populations if mortality rates in the two populations differ either at every age or at only some ages.

Fertility

Human fertility, the direct antecedent of population growth and composition, has been the primary focus of population studies and speculations since Malthus. Today, particularly with the recent worldwide trend toward lower mortality and the widespread concern over rapid population growth, the analysis of fertility, childbearing, and family building has come to dominate population studies more than ever before. Accordingly, our introduction to fertility here and our discussions in subsequent chapters will be more extensive than our overview of mortality.

Practical concerns in the study of fertility. There are, of course, hosts of very practical reasons for recording and analysis of fertility data. Babies and their mothers need hospital facilities and products like diapers, formulas, cribs, and even new homes, and all of these consumption items require counts and projections of numbers of births. In addition, today's babies are tomorrow's toddlers, school children, soldiers, and labor force. And ultimately, they are the parents of the next generation of babies.

Fertility rates vary broadly from one society to the next and from one social group to the next. They also vary considerably over time. So beyond the immediate practical objectives noted above, numerous studies have sought to discover the causes, correlates, and consequences of variations and changes in fertility. The recent acknowledgment of the close relationship between population growth and levels of living, social welfare, and economic development has lent greater impetus and, indeed, considerable urgency to these investigations. And the recognition of these relationships has been accompanied by a widespread willingness to seek means of intervening in societal policies and in group and individual behavior in order to promote enhanced levels of social and economic well-being.

In the 1930s, the opposite was the case. Fertility was promoted by a variety of measures in Europe, ranging from taxes on bachelors in Italy to strongly enforced suppression of contraception and abortion in Germany. There were restrictions on abortion in the Soviet Union and both Sweden and France offered a variety of monetary inducements to have babies. Many such measures have recently been rescinded. For example, the French law prohibiting both abortion and all publicity and promotion of contraception was abolished in 1968.

In 1948, Japan adopted its Eugenic Protection Law which relaxed some of the previous restrictions on abortions, and in 1952 this law was amended to legalize abortion and free it from restrictions. At the same time, the government of Japan introduced a program to promote family planning. The first government-sponsored birth control clinic in the world was opened in Mysore, India, in 1930, and the government of independent India has had an official family planning program since 1951.

There are government-sponsored family planning programs in an increasing number of Asian and African countries including South Korea, Taiwan, Pakistan, Tunisia, and Egypt, and nonofficial programs are run by voluntary organizations in a number of Latin American countries. Nonofficial programs also exist in North America. In the United States the privately sponsored activities of Planned Parenthood-World Population and its affiliates are complemented in some areas by family planning services provided by local public health units and planned parenthood organizations operating without affiliation (See Figure 6.4).

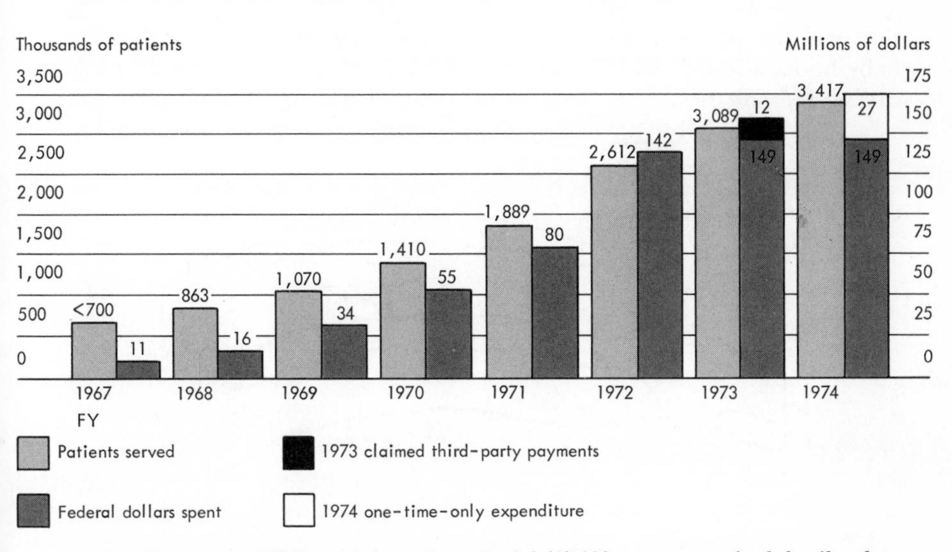

During Fiscal Year 1974, an estimated total of 3,417,000 women received family planning services in organized programs in the United States. This represents a fivefold increase in the number of patients served since 1967. The program grew rapidly so long as federal funding of family planning projects continued to increase during the late 1960s and early 1970s; but two years of frozen budgets have stalled program growth. (In 1974, as a result of court orders releasing previously impounded funds, HEW made a one-time-only expenditure of $30 million of family planning funds it had impounded in the previous year, limited to activities which would not recur in subsequent years.)

Figure 6.4 Patients served in organized programs, and federal expenditures for family planning services, Fiscal Year 1967 through Fiscal Year 1974. *Source: M. Corey, "U.S. Organized Family Planning Programs in Fiscal Year 1974,"* Family Planning Perspectives, *Vol. 7, no. 3, (May/June, 1975).*

Fertility studies in the twentieth century have echoed the thrust of the programs described above. In the first half of the century, they were closely connected to the attempt in Europe and the West to introduce national policies designed to combat aging, stagnation, or depopulation. But since the end of World War II, they have been directed toward helping us to understand and deal with the threat of overpopulation outside Europe and the West (Glass, 1965).

Measures of fertility. The most familiar measure of fertility is the *crude birth rate:* the number of births per thousand in the population. Birth rates vary markedly by age of women, and these variations are usually portrayed in age-specific birth rates. These rates are very high at ages 15–19 in populations where females marry early, but in the United States they are intermediate, with peak fertility between the ages of 20 and 24 instead. Fertility remains high through the ages of 25 to 29 in the United States; then it declines (see Figure 6.5).

We have earlier looked at trends in the United States crude birth rate and the post-World War II baby boom. Figure 6.5 shows that the baby boom affected mostly women aged 15 to 19, 20 to 24, and 25 to 29 during the post-1945 years. It affected women between the ages of 30 and

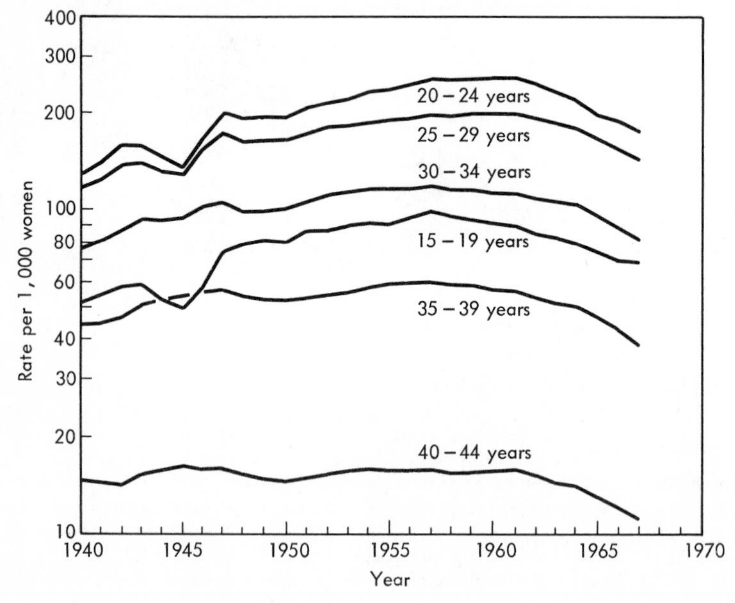

Figure 6.5 Birth rates by age of mother, 1940–67. Rates are based on births adjusted for underenumeration, semi-logarithmic scale. *Source: U.S. Department of Health, Education, and Welfare,* Natality Statistics Analysis, 1965–1967, *Series 21, no. 19 (May 1970).*

39 only briefly (apparently a reflection of births postponed during World War II), and it barely affected women older than 40.

Migration

Although world population growth ultimately depends on the balance of births and deaths alone, each individual population is subject to change —often very substantial—due to the comings and goings of migrants.

Definition and measurement in terms of the population balancing equation. The concepts of "migrant" and "migration" seem clearest when considered in the light of the population balancing equation:

$$P_1 = P_0 + B - D + I - O,$$

where

P_0 = population at the beginning of an interval
B = the number of births in the interval
D = the number of deaths in the interval
I = the number of in-migrants in the interval
O = the number of out-migrants in the interval
P_1 = population at the close of the interval

Following this equation, a migrant is a person entering (or added to), or leaving (subtracted from), the population of a given place or category by means other than birth or death (or aging, if the population category is an age group). The total gross and net increments caused by such entrances or departures comprise migration.

Unfortunately, there are some serious practical obstacles to this approach. In contrast to widely recorded phenomena like birth and death, only in very exceptional instances is entrance to, or departure from, a circumscribed population recorded. Metaphorically, the borders and boundaries of life itself are presided over by the recorders of vital statistics, but the borders and boundaries of communities and populations generally are not.

Of course, international frontiers are usually, although not always, exceptions to this rule. Indeed, there are routine and recurrent counts of numbers of border crossings and of international migrants. But the great bulk of migratory movements takes places unheralded, unremarked, and—worst of all for demographers and other social scientists—uncounted and unclassified. Indirect estimates of the volume of net migration can often be obtained by using the balancing equation and assuming that population change not accounted for by natural increase may be imputed to net migration (that $[P_1 - P_o] - [B - D] = [I - 0]$). However, this method, while very useful, is severely restricted in the range of information it gives us about either the causes and consequences of migration or the characteristics of migrants and nonmigrants.

Close to 20 percent of the American population changes residence every year. Most move to another house in the same county, and in conventional usage they are classified "local" or intracounty movers. But a substantial number, close to six or seven percent of the total population each year, are classified as "migrants" who move to a different county, roughly half in the state and half to a different state. Figure 6.6 shows

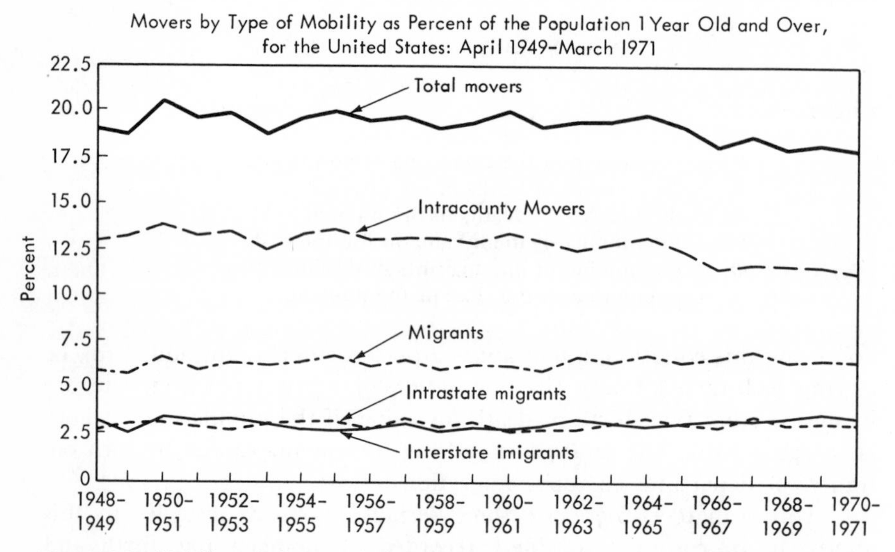

Figure 6.6 Mobility of the population of the United States, March 1948—March 1971. *Source: U.S. Bureau of the Census,* Current Population Reports, *Series P-20.*

that in the year from 1970 to 1971 an estimated 36.2 million Americans moved, including 13.1 million intercounty movers. About 6.2 million were migrants within the same state, and 6.9 million were interstate migrants.

SOURCES OF DATA

Modern demography and population studies have their origins in early studies which collected, analyzed, and interpreted data about numbers of deaths and births and discovered that there were regularities in these numbers over time and in relation to the numbers of total populations. The earliest questions posed concerned the regularities or fluctuations in the numbers of population, births, deaths, marriages, and migratory movements (see Lorimer, 1959; Thomlinson, 1976, pp. 10-11). Demography and population studies have since developed hand-in-hand, with ever more sophisticated and elaborate operations—usually administrative or legal in origin—for accumulating voluminous and detailed data about population size, characteristics, and vital events. The usual sources of data for population studies are censuses, sample surveys, vital registration systems, and population registers. In addition, the records of various public or private agencies—including school systems, social security administrations, hospitals, insurance companies—often serve as important sources of data.

Censuses

A population census is primarily a count of the number of inhabitants of a given area, but it usually includes the numbers of inhabitants in different population categories, also. Thus, most modern population censuses not only enumerate the total population, but they categorize it as well, by sex, age, and marital status; and by place of residence, administrative area, economic activity, and various other characteristics.

A census provides data on the size of the total population at the time of the census, on the composition of the population by major biological, ethnic, social, or economic characteristics, on the territorial distribution of the population with respect to key social or economic attributes. In principle, there is no limit to the variety and detail of information obtainable in a census. In practice, however, the scope is always limited by cost, the availability of resources, difficulties in developing reliable measuring instruments, and values which dictate what information is appropriate and in what format it should be published. A sample census schedule is presented in Appendix B (page 408). The kinds of information obtained in the census are best learned by careful inspection of the census schedule.

So great are the human and material resources required for carrying out a full-scale census enumeration that census coverage today is still far from universal. There are places in the world where the most elementary population data are lacking, and others for which we have only the barest demographic details. Sample survey techniques are, to be sure, contributing partial solutions to the problems of a worldwide census, but great gaps in our knowledge are likely to remain for a long time to come.

An important development in recent years has been the recording of entire censuses or samples from censuses on magnetic tapes or punch cards. These tapes or cards can be tabulated by the user according to his own needs. As this development matures, users of census data will have an unlimited range of tabulations, and census agencies will be able to reduce significantly their own tabulations and publications of data. Thus far it has been restricted largely to the United States census.

Sample Surveys

A sample survey is ordinarily used to estimate the compositional and distributional characteristics of a population on the basis of information on only a part, or sample, of that population. Recently, however, sample surveys have also been designed to estimate the number of inhabitants of a given area. Because it is so much less expensive and less time-consuming to enumerate only a fraction of the total population (and also because better quality of data is made possible by the increased expenditure allotted to each respondent), sample surveys have become increasingly important in data collection. Indeed, sampling has recently been done in conjunction with population censuses. By including many of the detailed questions in the sample survey only, it has reduced costs of enumeration and processing sharply and it has also resulted in better quality data.[4] Appendix C (page 419) shows a sample Current Population Survey (CPS) schedule.

The Current Population Survey (CPS) is conducted on an ongoing basis by the Bureau of the Census, primarily to obtain up-to-date information on the number of persons in the labor force (employed or not employed but seeking work), the numbers employed and unemployed respectively, and the characteristics—like sex, age, race, and occupation—of those employed and unemployed. In addition to employment information, the CPS is used to obtain other current information about the population. Thus, in the example of a CPS schedule shown in Appendix C, several questions pertain to living quarters and recent voting in Congressional elections.

Vital Registration Systems

In areas in which it is carried out at all, the registration of births, deaths, marriages, divorces, and related vital events ordinarily has some legal or administrative purpose. However, information based on vital records

[4] For a more extensive and detailed discussion of the use of sampling in censuses and population studies, see C. Taeuber, 1964. See also U.S. Bureau of the Census, "Procedural Report on the 1960 Censuses of Population and Housing, 1963; Taeuber and Hansen, 1964; and Alterman, 1969.

combined with census or sample survey data gives us a wide range of basic data about both the components of population change and the components of family formation (marriage and divorce).

The nationwide registration of vital events requires a permanent and comprehensive system of local registration offices and elaborate procedures to ensure the cooperation of government officials, medical personnel and others concerned with vital events, and of the population as a whole. Understandably, the procedure is carried out only in those countries which can afford it, and even then the records are not always complete. Nevertheless, data based upon vital records, even when incomplete, are very useful research aids. For they represent the most direct information obtainable on the components of population change. Examples of two kinds of registration forms, birth and death certificates, are shown in Figures 6.7 and 6.8.

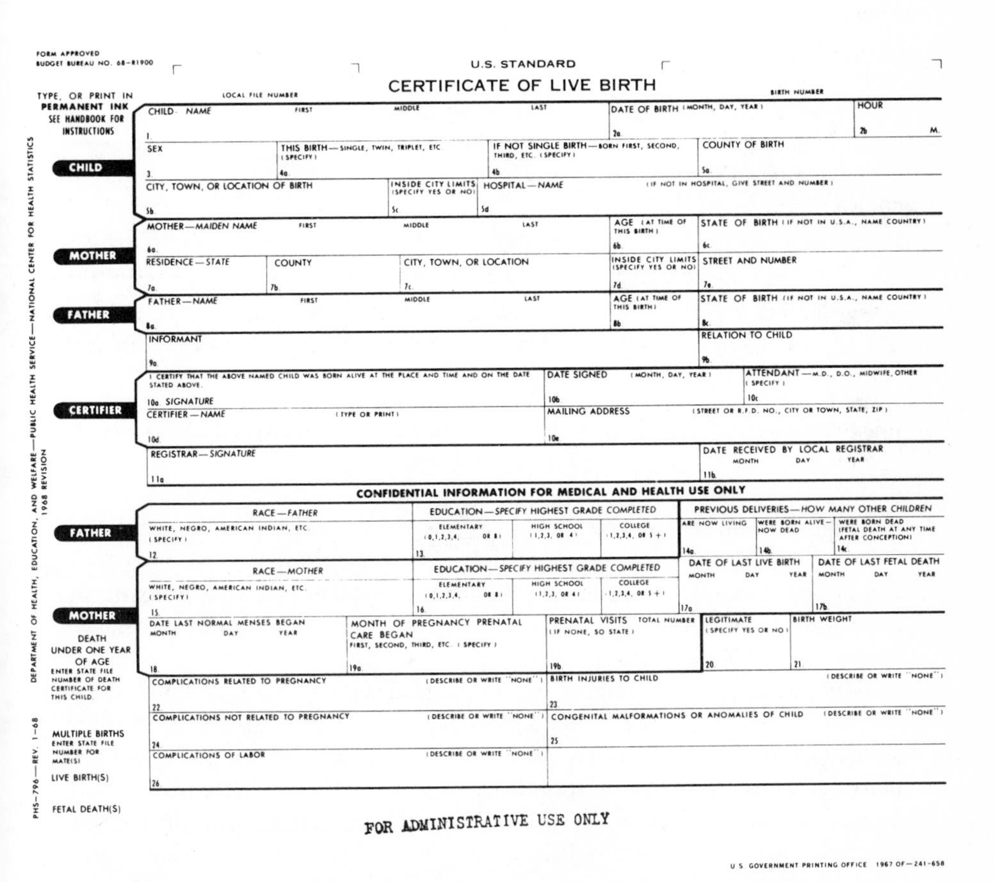

FORM APPROVED
BUDGET BUREAU NO. 68-R1900

U.S. STANDARD
CERTIFICATE OF LIVE BIRTH

TYPE, OR PRINT IN PERMANENT INK
SEE HANDBOOK FOR INSTRUCTIONS

LOCAL FILE NUMBER | BIRTH NUMBER

DEPARTMENT OF HEALTH, EDUCATION, AND WELFARE—PUBLIC HEALTH SERVICE—NATIONAL CENTER FOR HEALTH STATISTICS
1968 REVISION

CHILD
1. CHILD—NAME FIRST MIDDLE LAST
2a. DATE OF BIRTH (MONTH, DAY, YEAR)
2b. HOUR M.
3. SEX
4a. THIS BIRTH—SINGLE, TWIN, TRIPLET, ETC. (SPECIFY)
4b. IF NOT SINGLE BIRTH—BORN FIRST, SECOND, THIRD, ETC. (SPECIFY)
5a. COUNTY OF BIRTH
5b. CITY, TOWN, OR LOCATION OF BIRTH
5c. INSIDE CITY LIMITS (SPECIFY YES OR NO)
5d. HOSPITAL—NAME (IF NOT IN HOSPITAL, GIVE STREET AND NUMBER)

MOTHER
6a. MOTHER—MAIDEN NAME FIRST MIDDLE LAST
6b. AGE (AT TIME OF THIS BIRTH)
6c. STATE OF BIRTH (IF NOT IN U.S.A., NAME COUNTRY)
7a. RESIDENCE—STATE
7b. COUNTY
7c. CITY, TOWN, OR LOCATION
7d. INSIDE CITY LIMITS (SPECIFY YES OR NO)
7e. STREET AND NUMBER

FATHER
8a. FATHER—NAME FIRST MIDDLE LAST
8b. AGE (AT TIME OF THIS BIRTH)
8c. STATE OF BIRTH (IF NOT IN U.S.A., NAME COUNTRY)
9a. INFORMANT
9b. RELATION TO CHILD

CERTIFIER
I CERTIFY THAT THE ABOVE NAMED CHILD WAS BORN ALIVE AT THE PLACE AND TIME AND ON THE DATE STATED ABOVE.
10a. SIGNATURE
10b. DATE SIGNED (MONTH, DAY, YEAR)
10c. ATTENDANT—M.D., D.O., MIDWIFE, OTHER (SPECIFY)
10d. CERTIFIER—NAME (TYPE OR PRINT)
10e. MAILING ADDRESS (STREET OR R.F.D. NO., CITY OR TOWN, STATE, ZIP)
11a. REGISTRAR—SIGNATURE
11b. DATE RECEIVED BY LOCAL REGISTRAR MONTH DAY YEAR

CONFIDENTIAL INFORMATION FOR MEDICAL AND HEALTH USE ONLY

FATHER
12. RACE—FATHER: WHITE, NEGRO, AMERICAN INDIAN, ETC. (SPECIFY)
13. EDUCATION—SPECIFY HIGHEST GRADE COMPLETED: ELEMENTARY (0,1,2,3,4, OR 8) | HIGH SCHOOL (1,2,3, OR 4) | COLLEGE (1,2,3,4, OR 5+)
PREVIOUS DELIVERIES—HOW MANY OTHER CHILDREN
14a. ARE NOW LIVING
14b. WERE BORN ALIVE—NOW DEAD
14c. WERE BORN DEAD (FETAL DEATH AT ANY TIME AFTER CONCEPTION)

MOTHER
15. RACE—MOTHER: WHITE, NEGRO, AMERICAN INDIAN, ETC. (SPECIFY)
16. EDUCATION—SPECIFY HIGHEST GRADE COMPLETED: ELEMENTARY (0,1,2,3,4, OR 8) | HIGH SCHOOL (1,2,3, OR 4) | COLLEGE (1,2,3,4, OR 5+)
17a. DATE OF LAST LIVE BIRTH MONTH DAY YEAR
17b. DATE OF LAST FETAL DEATH MONTH DAY YEAR
18. DATE LAST NORMAL MENSES BEGAN MONTH DAY YEAR
19a. MONTH OF PREGNANCY PRENATAL CARE BEGAN FIRST, SECOND, THIRD, ETC. (SPECIFY)
19b. PRENATAL VISITS TOTAL NUMBER (IF NONE, SO STATE)
20. LEGITIMATE (SPECIFY YES OR NO)
21. BIRTH WEIGHT

DEATH UNDER ONE YEAR OF AGE
ENTER STATE FILE NUMBER OF DEATH CERTIFICATE FOR THIS CHILD.

22. COMPLICATIONS RELATED TO PREGNANCY (DESCRIBE OR WRITE "NONE")
23. BIRTH INJURIES TO CHILD (DESCRIBE OR WRITE "NONE")
24. COMPLICATIONS NOT RELATED TO PREGNANCY (DESCRIBE OR WRITE "NONE")
25. CONGENITAL MALFORMATIONS OR ANOMALIES OF CHILD (DESCRIBE OR WRITE "NONE")
26. COMPLICATIONS OF LABOR (DESCRIBE OR WRITE "NONE")

MULTIPLE BIRTHS
ENTER STATE FILE NUMBER FOR MATE(S)
LIVE BIRTH(S)
FETAL DEATH(S)

PHS-796—REV. 1-68

FOR ADMINISTRATIVE USE ONLY

U S GOVERNMENT PRINTING OFFICE 1967 OF—241-658

Figure 6.7 Certificate of Live Birth. *Source: U.S. Department of Health, Education, and Welfare,* Vital Statistics of the United States, 1967, *Vol. II, "Mortality."*

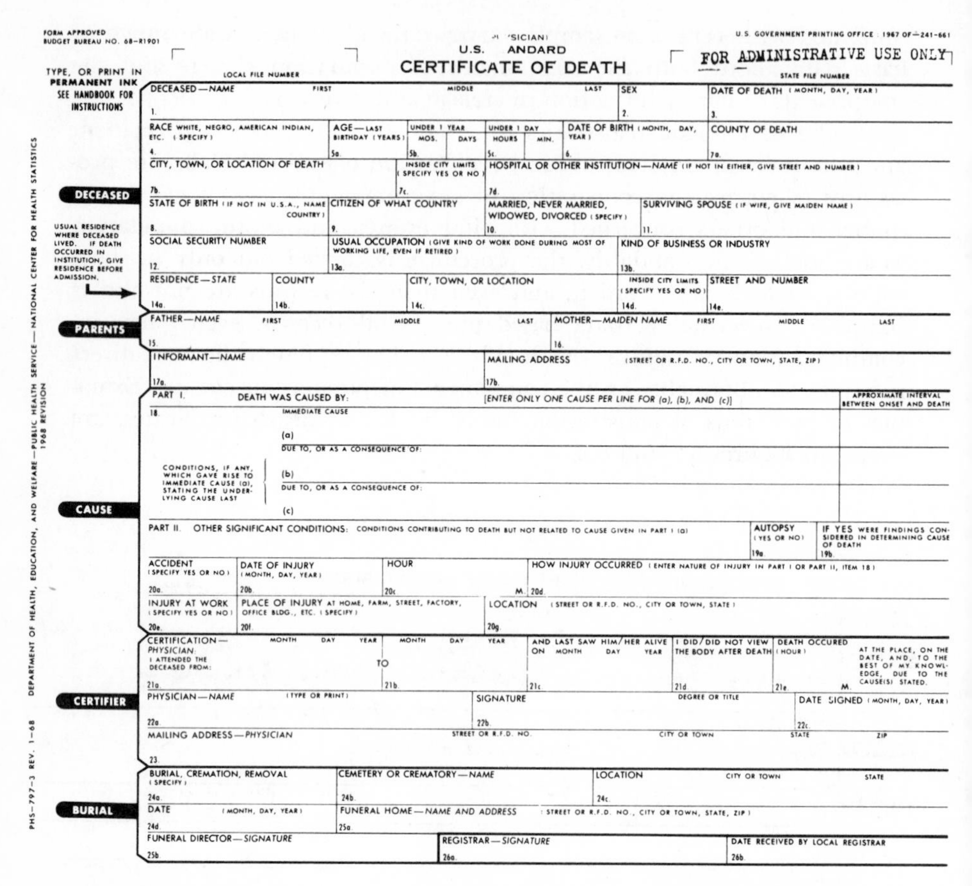

FORM APPROVED
BUDGET BUREAU NO. 68–R1901

U.S. GOVERNMENT PRINTING OFFICE : 1967 OF—241-661

PHYSICIAN
U.S. STANDARD
CERTIFICATE OF DEATH

FOR ADMINISTRATIVE USE ONLY

TYPE, OR PRINT IN PERMANENT INK
SEE HANDBOOK FOR INSTRUCTIONS

LOCAL FILE NUMBER

STATE FILE NUMBER

DECEASED

1. DECEASED—NAME FIRST MIDDLE LAST
2. SEX
3. DATE OF DEATH (MONTH, DAY, YEAR)
4. RACE WHITE, NEGRO, AMERICAN INDIAN, ETC. (SPECIFY)
5a. AGE—LAST BIRTHDAY (YEARS)
5b. UNDER 1 YEAR MOS. DAYS
5c. UNDER 1 DAY HOURS MIN.
6. DATE OF BIRTH (MONTH, DAY, YEAR)
7a. COUNTY OF DEATH
7b. CITY, TOWN, OR LOCATION OF DEATH
7c. INSIDE CITY LIMITS (SPECIFY YES OR NO)
7d. HOSPITAL OR OTHER INSTITUTION—NAME (IF NOT IN EITHER, GIVE STREET AND NUMBER)
8. STATE OF BIRTH (IF NOT IN U.S.A., NAME COUNTRY)
9. CITIZEN OF WHAT COUNTRY
10. MARRIED, NEVER MARRIED, WIDOWED, DIVORCED (SPECIFY)
11. SURVIVING SPOUSE (IF WIFE, GIVE MAIDEN NAME)
12. SOCIAL SECURITY NUMBER
13a. USUAL OCCUPATION (GIVE KIND OF WORK DONE DURING MOST OF WORKING LIFE, EVEN IF RETIRED)
13b. KIND OF BUSINESS OR INDUSTRY

USUAL RESIDENCE WHERE DECEASED LIVED. IF DEATH OCCURRED IN INSTITUTION, GIVE RESIDENCE BEFORE ADMISSION.

14a. RESIDENCE—STATE
14b. COUNTY
14c. CITY, TOWN, OR LOCATION
14d. INSIDE CITY LIMITS (SPECIFY YES OR NO)
14e. STREET AND NUMBER

PARENTS

15. FATHER—NAME FIRST MIDDLE LAST
16. MOTHER—MAIDEN NAME FIRST MIDDLE LAST
17a. INFORMANT—NAME
17b. MAILING ADDRESS (STREET OR R.F.D. NO., CITY OR TOWN, STATE, ZIP)

CAUSE

18. PART I. DEATH WAS CAUSED BY: [ENTER ONLY ONE CAUSE PER LINE FOR (a), (b), AND (c)] APPROXIMATE INTERVAL BETWEEN ONSET AND DEATH
IMMEDIATE CAUSE
(a)
DUE TO, OR AS A CONSEQUENCE OF:
CONDITIONS, IF ANY, WHICH GAVE RISE TO IMMEDIATE CAUSE (a), STATING THE UNDERLYING CAUSE LAST
(b)
DUE TO, OR AS A CONSEQUENCE OF:
(c)

PART II. OTHER SIGNIFICANT CONDITIONS: CONDITIONS CONTRIBUTING TO DEATH BUT NOT RELATED TO CAUSE GIVEN IN PART I (a)
19a. AUTOPSY (YES OR NO)
19b. IF YES WERE FINDINGS CONSIDERED IN DETERMINING CAUSE OF DEATH
20a. ACCIDENT (SPECIFY YES OR NO)
20b. DATE OF INJURY (MONTH, DAY, YEAR)
20c. HOUR M.
20d. HOW INJURY OCCURRED (ENTER NATURE OF INJURY IN PART I OR PART II, ITEM 18)
20e. INJURY AT WORK (SPECIFY YES OR NO)
20f. PLACE OF INJURY AT HOME, FARM, STREET, FACTORY, OFFICE BLDG., ETC. (SPECIFY)
20g. LOCATION (STREET OR R.F.D. NO., CITY OR TOWN, STATE)

CERTIFIER

21a. CERTIFICATION—PHYSICIAN: I ATTENDED THE DECEASED FROM: MONTH DAY YEAR
21b. TO MONTH DAY YEAR
21c. AND LAST SAW HIM/HER ALIVE ON MONTH DAY YEAR
21d. I DID/DID NOT VIEW THE BODY AFTER DEATH
21e. DEATH OCCURED (HOUR) M. AT THE PLACE, ON THE DATE, AND, TO THE BEST OF MY KNOWLEDGE, DUE TO THE CAUSE(S) STATED.
22a. PHYSICIAN—NAME (TYPE OR PRINT)
22b. SIGNATURE DEGREE OR TITLE
22c. DATE SIGNED (MONTH, DAY, YEAR)
23. MAILING ADDRESS—PHYSICIAN STREET OR R.F.D. NO. CITY OR TOWN STATE ZIP

BURIAL

24a. BURIAL, CREMATION, REMOVAL (SPECIFY)
24b. CEMETERY OR CREMATORY—NAME
24c. LOCATION CITY OR TOWN STATE
24d. DATE (MONTH, DAY, YEAR)
25a. FUNERAL HOME—NAME AND ADDRESS (STREET OR R.F.D. NO., CITY OR TOWN, STATE, ZIP)
25b. FUNERAL DIRECTOR—SIGNATURE
26a. REGISTRAR—SIGNATURE
26b. DATE RECEIVED BY LOCAL REGISTRAR

PHS–797–3 REV. 1–68 DEPARTMENT OF HEALTH, EDUCATION, AND WELFARE—PUBLIC HEALTH SERVICE—NATIONAL CENTER FOR HEALTH STATISTICS
1968 REVISION

Figure 6.8 Certificate of Death. *Source: U.S. Department of Health, Education, and Welfare,* Vital and Health Statistics of the United States, *"Mortality Trends," Series 20, no. 15 (Nov. 1973).*

Population Registers

A number of countries, including Denmark, Sweden, and Israel, maintain continuous population registers for various legal and administrative purposes. These registers are essentially lists of names, with each name accompanied by a number of personal characteristics. The population register in Israel lists every person in the population, giving his or her identity number, citizenship, nationality, religion, sex, date of birth, place of birth, date of immigration to Israel if born abroad, current marital status, and current address. The original purpose of the register was for the preparation of lists of eligible voters in the national and local elections and, during the 1948 conflict, for the administration of food rationing. The register has also been used in connection with military conscription, school enrollment, the issuance of passports, the carrying out of surveys and a population census, and for current estimates of the population.

A newborn child or a new immigrant to Israel is issued a birth or immigration certificate and an identity number and at the same time is entered into the population register. If the individual changes his marital status, he is required by law to inform the population register, a procedure actually done automatically through the register's connection to registrations for marriage and divorce. Similarly, the register is automatically informed of deaths through the required death registration and burial permits (which also inform the register of the change in marital status of the decedent's surviving spouse). In much the same way, emigrants are removed from the register either by declaring their intention to emigrate upon leaving the country, or after failure to return to the country after a specified time abroad.

In principle, persons who change their place of residence are also required by law to inform the population register. But in practice, changes of address in a population register are typically effected only after some time. Characteristically, the register is periodically brought up to date in preparation for some special undertaking: a forthcoming election, a census, or a legal change in eligibility for some welfare provision.

APPROACHES TO MEASUREMENT AND ANALYSIS

The most elementary quantitative representation of a population or a society is simply the total number of persons in that population. We have already looked at variations in population size; and we have mentioned some reasons why societies with small populations necessarily differ from societies with large populations, and why societies necessarily undergo changes as their populations grow in numbers.

The composition of a population with respect to two or more categories of some variable—like sex, place of residence, or age—can be represented by counts of the number of persons belonging to each category. The set of such counts over all the exhaustive, mutually exclusive categories of a variable is usually called a *frequency distribution,* thus, the age distribution or the occupational distribution. Frequency distributions and the measures that can be derived from them yield much more detailed quantitative representations of population than do total counts. And any derivative ratios which involve population in their numerators, denominators, or both are very often used to describe and compare different populations.

The measurement of components of growth of populations typically involves the computation of *rates:* measures of the frequency of events like marriages, births, deaths, or migratory moves relative to the number of persons exposed to the possibility, or "risk," of such an event. Thus, the crude death rate is the number of deaths per 1000 in the total population, the crude birth rate is the number of births per 1000 in the total population, and so forth.

Rates are calculated with data from two separate kinds of sources: vital statistics data on births and deaths (in the numerators), and census or survey statistics data on total populations (in the denominators). The rates are *crude* in that the specification of the population at risk is very broad and undifferentiated. In fact there are different risks of death, and even more differentiated risks of childbirth in various sex, age, or other subcategories of the population. Rates which are computed separately for specific subgroups of the population are called *refined,* or category-specific rates. The Appendix gives a more detailed discussion of rate measurement and analysis in population studies.

SUMMARY

In this chapter we have identified the components of population change, looked at some major types of change and variations over time, and indicated the ways in which these components are studied, measured, and analyzed. Population composition describes the numbers of persons of each type or category in a population: it is, in a nutshell, an inventory of a society's human resources. Since age, sex, marital status, and other compositional characteristics are also social roles, it is appropriate to view population composition as a society's role distribution, a key dimension of social structure.

The simple population balancing equation serves to identify the natural increase and net migration components of growth separately and to relate each to either the initial or the subsequent total population. A similar analysis of the components of growth can be used to study differential growth of given subgroups and sectors of the population.

The study of mortality, which began in the seventeenth century and gave rise to modern demographic analysis and population studies, remains a central topic both in view of the importance of mortality as an element in population growth and as the major indicator of overall and differential levels and conditions of health and well-being in populations and societies. Sex and age have bearing on the risks of death, as do other factors like marital status and social and economic conditions. Mortality rates have declined historically, but at different rates and under different conditions in each area and period. This is because the ability or willingness to combat mortality has varied through history among and within the different societies.

Fertility is now clearly the problematic component of the population growth equation. And, with nearly universally low or declining mortality and continued rapid population growth, fertility is receiving increasingly detailed attention and study. In particular, the increasing desire of private and government agencies to seek ways to intervene and influence numbers of births has given impetus to the study of variations and trends in fertility. Countries which exhibit low fertility today have experienced declines from previously high levels as part of their demographic transitions. The less developed countries tend to be high fertility countries today, though a number of these have experienced recent and significant declines.

International migration is a clearly defined topic of study. But the study of internal migration requires determination of criteria for identifying migrants and distinguishing between them and nonmigrant (within the same county) movers. Mostly because of definitional problems and ambiguities, it is difficult to assess trends over time in amount and directions of internal migration. But variations in migration rates do show that there are age, sex, and socioeconomic differences in the propensity to migrate.

The main sources of data on populations and population changes are censuses and surveys, vital statistics, and, in some countries, current population registers. The population census or survey is a one-time count of a population, typically seeking to enumerate each individual in each place of residence or a sample of individuals in a representative sample of areas. Vital statistics are records of vital events: births, deaths, marriages, and divorces. They are maintained for administrative and legal purposes, but are very important for population studies. Population registers are usually maintained in conjunction with vital statistics as a current inventory of population and citizens and record of places of residence.

Measurement and analysis of population data mainly involve counts, percent distributions, and rates and their comparison. Specialized statistical or mathematical models are often used in population analysis, but most studies of population variations and changes are carried out with the aid of crude and refined counts, percentages, and rates alone.

In the next chapter we turn to more detailed consideration of mortality analysis, of mortality trends, and of the social differentials in exposure to and protection from mortality.

7

The Social Structure of Death and Survival

In this chapter we examine in more detail the historical trends and current variations in levels of mortality. We will also consider the factors associated with the historical declines in mortality and with mortality differentials today. We will look first at recent mortality declines in Europe, European-settled countries, and the less developed countries. Then we will turn to the demographic and social factors which affect mortality rates. At the close of the chapter, we will analyze the way social structural factors are linked to differential exposure to illness and death risks and to differential access to health and medical treatment.

THE MODERN DECLINE IN MORTALITY RATES

A spectacular decline in mortality has taken place during the modern period in both Europe and countries of European settlement. How and why did this decline take place?

A New York graveyard. *(Wide World Photos)*

The Fall in Death Rates

Until the end of the seventeenth century, and even through the first decades of the eighteenth century, European populations had not only a generally high mortality rate but periodic population catastrophes, too, with fairly frequent famines, epidemics, and wars. While systematic data from this period are scanty, we do have genealogical records of certain European ruling families. And, since we assume that mortality in the general population must have greatly exceeded that of the aristocracy, the mortality records we have may be taken as lower bounds for the periods in question. Death rates among members of the European nobility born in the period between 1480 and 1789 have been computed by S. Peller (1965). In his analysis Peller was able to show that mortality was initially very high but began to fall in almost all age groups long before the age of modern medicine. Maternal mortality was one exception: it declined very little in the period.

A. M. Carr-Saunders estimated that the average annual crude death rate in the first half of the eighteenth century reached 30.4 per thousand in Sweden and between 28 and 36 per thousand in England and Wales (see Fig. 7.1). But from about 1750 onward, both countries enjoyed a virtually uninterrupted decline in crude death rates, and by about 1920

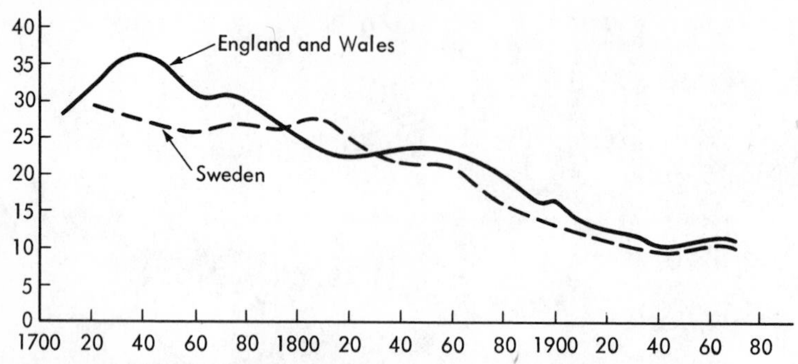

Figure 7.1 **Crude death rates in England, Wales, and Sweden, 1700–1970.** *Source: data for 1700–1930 from A. M. Carr-Saunders,* World Population *(Oxford: Oxford University Press), 1936; data from 1930–1970 from United Nations,* Demographic Yearbook, 1966, 1970.

the rates in both had diminished to less than 15 per 1,000 (Carr-Saunders, 1936, Chap. 5).

Even the high average rates of mortality at the beginning of the eighteenth century were obscured by the violent fluctuations in numbers and rates of deaths still characteristic of northwestern Europe. Such fluctuations had characterized all of Europe up to the close of the seventeenth century, and they continued to occur even later in countries in the east and south of Europe (Helleiner, 1965).

Crop failures, famines, wars, and epidemics are reported in Europe throughout the eighteenth century and in the nineteenth century as well. However, these crises were much more sporadic and less catastrophic than their predecessors had been. The overall picture of European mortality rates in that period parallels the declines in Sweden, England, and Wales, but with a lag of several decades. At the end of the nineteenth century, mortality was still substantially higher in southern and eastern Europe than in western and northwestern Europe. In the present century, mortality rates have continued to decline while life expectancy has increased substantially (see Tables 7.1 and 7.2).

Differential Declines by Time, Age Group, and Geographic Area

Life expectancy in Western Europe and the United States increased by some 20 years in the first half of the twentieth century. Judging from life tables for France (1817–1831) and Sweden (1816–1840), the average life expectancy at birth in Western Europe at the end of the first quarter of the nineteenth century was around 40 years. The data in Table 7.2

TABLE 7.1 Crude Death Rates in Europe, by Areas and Selected Periods

Area	*1900–1910*	*1935–1938*	*1945–1948*	*1955–1958*	*1975*
Britain, Netherlands, Scandinavia	14.1	10.7	10.3	9.7	9.8
Other countries in Western Europe	17.7	13.3	13.0	11.3	11.3
Southern Europe	21.7	15.6	12.7	9.4	9.2
Eastern Europe (excluding USSR)	24.5	15.7	10.0	10.0	10.2

Source: United Nations, Population Bulletin, *no. 6 (1962); and Endpapers.*

TABLE 7.2 Twentieth Century Gains in Life Expectancy at Birth

		Life Expectancy	
	Year	*Males*	*Females*
United States (Whites)	1900–1902	48.23	51.08
	1955	67.30	73.69
	1967	67.80	75.10
	1973	68.30	76.00
Sweden	1901–1910	54.53	56.98
	1951–1958	70.48	73.43
	1969	71.69	76.50
Netherlands	1900–1909	51.00	53.40
	1953–1955	71.00	73.90
	1971	71.00	76.70
France	1898–1903	45.74	49.03
	1950–1951	63.60	69.30
	1970	68.60	76.10
England and Wales	1901–1910	48.53	52.38
	1953–1955	67.52	72.99
	1969–1971	68.80	75.10

Source: Data for 1900–1958 from United Nations, Population Bulletin, *no. 6 (1962); for 1965–1967 from United Nations,* Demographic Yearbook *(1969); for 1973 from U.S. Bureau of the Census,* Statistical Abstract of the United States *(1974).*

show that, at the turn of the century, average Swedish life expectancy was just over 50 years and French life expectancy about 47 years. Thus, expectation of life increased by only about seven to ten years from the first quarter of the nineteenth century until the close of that century—but this increase was doubled in the following 50 years. Improvements in mortality conditions have been far from uniform for all age groups. The decrease in mortality rates has been most spectacular for ages 1–4 and 5–14 and for the one-year period following birth. Improvements have been substantial in adult ages, though less impressive after the age of 65.

The decline in mortality between 1750 and 1900 was, with the notable exception of Japan, confined largely to Europe and to areas of European settlement. As late as 1947, the crude death rates of Africa and South Central Asia were estimated to average about 25–30 per 1,000 of population. For the Near East and Far East (excluding Japan, whose crude death rate, just over 25 per thousand in 1920, had already declined to 16.5 per thousand by 1940 and to 7.6 per thousand by 1960), crude death rates averaged around 30–35 per thousand (U.N., 1953). Of course, these averages obscure crude death rates which reached or surpassed 40 per thousand in certain countries.

However, since the end of World War II, spectacular declines in mortality have been recorded for countries of Asia, Africa, and Latin America (see Table 7.3). For example, comparing crude death rates in 1935–1939 with those in 1955–59, Sri Lanka's rate declined from 24.5 to 9.9; Hong Kong's from 29.1 to 7.6; Chile's from 23.7 to 12.5; Mexico's from 23.3 to 12.5; and Mauritius's from 27.3 to 12.0 (Stolnitz, 1965). Similarly, expectation of life at birth increased for Egypt from 38 years in 1947 to 50 years in 1961; for females in India from 31.7 years in the forties to 42.1 years in 1956–61; and for females in Puerto Rico from 46.9 years in 1939–41 to 71.9 years in 1959–61 (Stolnitz, 1965).

TABLE 7.3 Decline in Crude Death Rates, by Continent, circa 1937 to 1965–71

	Crude Death Rate (estimate)	
Area	*circa 1937*	*1965–1971*
Africa	30–35	21
Asia	30–35	15
Latin America	20–25	10
Europe, United States, Soviet Union, etc.	13	9
World	24–27	14

Source: B. Berelson et al., "World Population: Status Report 1974. A Guide for the Concerned Citizen," Reports on Population/Family Planning, *No. 15, January 1974, p. 4. By permission of the Population Council.*

Causes of Declining Mortality

The causes of the decline in mortality are of both historical and practical significance. Since the search for collective and individual survival impels societies to pursue mortality control, any knowledge of the means by which such control has been achieved is of primary importance. Several factors are conventionally set forth as causes or conditions of declining mortality:

1. political circumstances, like internal order, absence of wars, and strife;
2. social and educational factors, including increased knowledge about clothing, shelter, and the production and exploitation of food;
3. sanitary factors, like improvements in water supply and drainage;
4. medical factors, including knowledge about the prevention, diagnosis, and cure of disease;
5. economic development, which has brought the replacement of subsistence food production, distribution with market mechanisms, investment in roads and communication, and rising income levels;
6. social reforms, like control of working conditions, establishment of minimum wages, and provision of services (Carr-Saunders, 1936; U.N., 1973).

However, there is considerable obscurity and controversy surrounding the question of the relative importance of these factors in the historical declines of mortality. The earliest studies of European mortality trends frequently held that social conditions, sanitary improvements, and scientific and medical advances were the primary causes of mortality decline. In part this hypothesis was based upon analyses of mortality by cause of death and upon the knowledge that mortality due to infectious and epidemic diseases declined spectacularly during the period when there were reforms in housing and working conditions, improvements in sanitation, discoveries in medicine, and the development of hospital and other treatment facilities.

More recently, however, it has become clear that the general declines in mortality in Western countries had already begun to take place during the eighteenth and early nineteenth centuries. This was substantially before the development of scientific methods of controlling individual diseases. Evidently, there were other major influences in the decline in mortality. These included rising levels of living, with wide improvements in diet (fundamental to the declining incidence of tuberculosis and the decrease in infant mortality); hygienic changes introduced by sanitary reforms (basic to the reduction of the typhus-typhoid and cholera diseases); and possibly a third factor, as well. There may have been favorable genetic developments connected with the declining incidence of scarlet fever and perhaps with the decrease in tuberculosis, typhus, and cholera. Thus, the declines in mortality were not due mainly to improvements in therapy. Instead, they were related more to the declining incidence of disease. The effects of treatment, therapy, medical discoveries, and the like seem to have been restricted to smallpox, and the effect of this improvement on the total reduction of death rates is a matter of some dispute (U.N., 1973; and especially McKeown & Record, 1962; McKeown & Brown, 1955; Helleiner, 1957; and McKeown, 1965).

In contrast to this, twentieth-century declines in mortality, especially the spectacular ones achieved in countries outside Europe or European settlement, are much more directly related to the deliberate introduction of public health aids and preventive medicine. Immunization programs, the introduction of DDT to kill malaria-carrying mosquitoes, and improved standards of sanitation in food and water distribution and sewage disposal have all helped to reduce mortality rates measurably. The underdeveloped countries, or LDCs, have been able to import and apply directly the knowledge and techniques which took years to develop in the European countries. The rapid reductions in mortality in the underdeveloped countries have also been obtained at relatively low cost, often with the help and direct subsidy of more developed nations. Low per capita income is no longer an insurmountable barrier to increasing longevity and lower mortality, though relatively higher income is always associated with greater longevity. But, of course, these same improvements in mortality, longevity, and population growth—unaccompanied as they are by many of the economic, social, and educational adaptations already made by Europe—may portend new and menacing problems for the underdeveloped countries and for the world as a whole. For they are a fundamental factor in the recent world population explosion.

DIFFERENTIAL MORTALITY

Historically, mortality studies have developed concurrently with life insurance and public health programs as well as alongside studies of population growth and dynamics. The originators of official mortality statistics envisaged them as major tools for improving the living conditions of the population. And, indeed, such studies have played this very role in the past two centuries in the West and in the twentieth century throughout the world. One of their major uses in this connection has been in *differential mortality studies:* the comparative analysis of living conditions and mortality in different countries and in different populations within any given country.

The study of differential mortality has played a key role in the discovery of the general correlates and causes of morbidity and mortality. It has also helped us understand the incidence of some specific maladies. The knowledge that a particular disease is more prevalent or more fatal in one population category than another is generally suggestive of the reasons for, or factors in, observed differences in mortality. A case in point is the study of perinatal mortality (infant deaths in the first week of life, which, in populations with relatively low infant mortality, may constitute more than half the total number of infant deaths). When it was discovered that perinatal mortality was strikingly lower among infants born to mothers who had lived in maternity homes before the delivery, and that it was inversely related to the amount of time before birth spent in such maternity homes, the new information received widespread attention and led to greater developments in obstetrics and prenatal care and nutrition.[1] Similarly, the discovery of great differences between smokers and nonsmokers in mortality rates due to lung cancer has stimulated research into the ways smoke, smoking, and air pollution are related to not just lung cancer, but a long list of other diseases as well.[2]

Types of Differential Mortality Studies

Mortality rates vary according to a number of different correlates. Geographic location, socioeconomic level, occupation, place of residence, and ethnic, racial, and religious characteristics have all been studied in the past, and they are still topics of current investigation. Each type of study presents certain methodological problems, and a few of these will be mentioned briefly along with examples of research results.

Differential mortality among nations. We have already noted the great gaps between the mortality rates of the developed and underdeveloped countries. In addition, within each of these two great categories there are many variations. Table 7.4 shows crude death rates, infant mortality rates, and expectation of life at birth for selected developed and underdeveloped countries during the 1960s and early 1970s.

There are a few limitations which we must keep in mind in comparing data like those in Table 7.4. In the first place, the several countries have different registration practices and definitions. Second, they enumerate and register data with different degrees of completeness. And finally, they may compute identical indexes in different ways. Thus, definitions of live birth, stillbirth, and infant death differ among the different countries. Deaths are recorded in some countries with refer-

1 For a detailed discussion of this, see Peller, 1948, pp. 405–56.

2 The major publications on this subject include Preston, 1970; Dorn, 1959, pp. 581–93; Hammond, 1966; and U.S. Department of Health, Education, and Welfare, Public Health Service Publication 1103, 1964.

TABLE 7.4 Mortality Indexes for Selected Developed and Underdeveloped Countries

	Crude Death Rate 1975	*Infant Mortality Rate 1975*	*Expectation of Life at Birth*[a]		
			Year	*Males*	*Females*
Developed Countries					
United States	9.4	18	1971	67.4	74.8
Canada	7.7	17	1965–67	68.8	75.2
France	10.6	16	1970	68.6	76.1
Netherlands	8.7	12	1971	71.0	76.7
United Kingdom	11.7	18	1969–71	68.8	75.1
Sweden	10.5	10	1969	71.7	76.5
USSR	7.9	26	1968–69	65.0	74.0
Underdeveloped Countries					
Chile	9.2	71	1969–70	60.5	66.0
India	15.7	139	1951–60	41.9	40.6
Sri Lanka	6.4	45	1962	61.9	61.4
Egypt	14.0	103	1960	51.6	53.8
Mauritius	6.8	65	1961–63	58.7	61.9
Upper Volta	25.8	182	1960–61	32.1	31.1

[a] Expressed e_0.

Source: Data on crude death rate and infant mortality rate from endpapers; data on life expectation from United Nations, Demographic Yearbook *(1973).*

ence to time of occurrence but in others with reference to time of registration. In some countries, the registration of death is voluntary, in others it is obligatory but incomplete, and in still others it is obligatory and virtually complete. Where registration is incomplete, statistics and indexes are often not corrected for underregistration of deaths or for underenumeration of the base populations. Finally, the different techniques of computation affect the calculation of mortality rates and of life expectation at birth (Shryock & Siegel, 1973).

Geographic, ethnic, religious, and racial variation within nations. Geographic variations in mortality within any nation are fairly clearly portrayed in a country's official statistics, and they are easier to compare than are international variations. However, the comparisons must be interpreted with great caution, for the population of any region, area, or place may include migrants. It may include relatively many or relatively few of them. And they may have arrived recently or long ago. Thus, it is still difficult to get a true reading of the mortality variations of any subpopulation within a larger society.

In many countries, national, ethnic, religious, or racial population groups are distinguished in official or other statistics, and there is often great interest in the mortality differences among them. In the United States, mortality rates among blacks are consistently higher than those of whites. And in Israel, mortality rates of non-Jews exceed those of Jews at most ages, though these differences are rapidly disappearing.

Variations by socioeconomic status. Perhaps the most difficult type of differential mortality study—and at the same time the one with the greatest popular and scientific interest—is that which seeks to relate mortality rates to different levels of socioeconomic status. There are many difficulties in both the collection and the interpretation of the data which represent mortality among different socioeconomic groups in a population. In the first place, it is not always easy to classify a population in terms of socioeconomic status. In the second place, the classification of numbers of deaths by the socioeconomic status of decedents is even more difficult. In particular, the classification of decedents whose socioeconomic status is determined by other related persons like wives, children, or other dependents, must be determined on the basis of information which isn't normally recorded in death certificates or other vital records. And finally, it is always difficult to impute status to decedents who have changed their socioeconomic level in the course of their lifetimes. This difficulty is especially evident in cases like retired persons or recently married persons. Nevertheless, information on socioeconomic differences in mortality is of great interest, and we shall describe three separate approaches to the collection and use of this kind of data.

The areal unit approach. The first approach involves an indirect computation: of mortality rates for areas or combinations of small areas characterized by different socioeconomic levels. (The combinations of small areas might be census tracts or wards in a city, townships, or other well-defined areas for which both base population data and death statistics can be obtained.) Classifications of census tracts or other areal units in terms of socioeconomic categories are usually based on characteristics like median income, median rental paid, median educational achievement, and percentage of the population in white-collar occupations.

An example of such an approach is Sauvy's study of Paris for the years 1891, 1936, and 1946 (Sauvy, 1954). The Parisian areal units, *arrondissements,* are classified according to whether they are "well off," "middle class," or "poor," and mortality rates are computed for each category of *arrondissement.* Table 7.5 shows that mortality is substantially lower in the well-off *arrondissements* than in the middle-class or poor ones, but that these differences have diminished slightly since 1891.

TABLE 7.5 Mortality by Socioeconomic Areas of Paris, 1891 to 1951

Areal Categories	*Standardized Death Rates*			*Infant Mortality Rate*			
	1891	*1936*	*1946*	*1891*	*1936*	*1946*	*1951*
Well off	16.8	9.6	9.5	91.9	47.2	47.1	24.1
Middle class	22.6	12.5	11.3	135.3	61.7	75.0	36.5
Poor	23.9	13.7	12.0	157.2	72.2	81.2	37.2
Total	22.5	12.2	11.2	136.3	63.5	71.7	34.4
Ratio: Poor / Well off	1.42	1.43	1.26	1.71	1.53	1.72	1.54

Source: Sauvy, 1954.

The socioeconomic gradient seems much steeper in the case of infant mortality than general mortality: between 1891 and 1936, infant mortality decreased spectacularly in Paris as a whole and in all three socioeconomic categories as well, and so did the ratio between infant mortality rates of the poor and well off. However, in the period of shortages and austerity just after World War II, infant mortality increased in the middle class and poor areas but remained stable in the well-off ones; and the ratio between the infant mortality rates of the poor to the well off increased. In the following postwar period, infant mortality in all socioeconomic categories again declined considerably, and interareal differences again diminished.

In a study based on Chicago census-tract data on population and mortality by age and color, A. J. Mayer and P. M. Hauser (1953) were able to compute life tables and expectations of life for white and nonwhite males according to economic status. In this study, census tracts were classified on the basis of median rentals. Table 7.6 shows the mortality differences between white and nonwhite males, along with differences in mortality among white high and low rental-tract categories. In the case of nonwhite males, the meaning of the difference between "high" and "low" rental-tract categories is often obscure and in any case not identical to that for whites. The reason for this is that, other things being equal, nonwhites have always been obliged to pay higher rents than whites for equivalent or less-than-equivalent housing. Thus, areal delineation on the basis of median rentals may reflect a double standard for measuring socioeconomic status. In other words, to the extent that poor or low-socioeconomic status persons are concentrated in low-rental census tracts, and rich or high-socioeconomic status persons are concentrated in high-rental census tracts, the area-type differences

TABLE 7.6 Expectation of Life at Birth by Color and Economic Status: Chicago, 1920, 1930, and 1940

Color and Economic Status	*1920*	*1930*	*1940*
White			
High-rental census tracts	61.8	65.0	67.8
Low-rental census tracts	51.8	53.7	60.2
Total	56.7	59.7	64.9
Nonwhite			
High-rental census tracts	—	45.4	55.9
Low-rental census tracts	—	40.0	49.9
Total	42.3	44.5	53.6

Source: A. J. Mayer and P. M. Hauser, Class differentials in expectation of life at birth, in R. Bendix and S. M. Lipset, eds., Class, Status and Power *(New York: Free Press, 1953), Table III, p. 283.*

do in fact reflect mortality differences between the poor and the rich, or between low- and high-socioeconomic status persons. But if poor or low-socioeconomic status nonwhites are forced—by the nature of the housing market and patterns of racial segregation—to pay high rents, this alone would cause many nonwhite neighborhoods to be classified as "high-rental" census tracts even if the people living there are actually quite poor.

The occupational mortality approach. A second approach to the analysis of mortality differences by socioeconomic status deals with occupational mortality. The study of occupational mortality is of considerable interest in its own right in that it reflects the different mortality and morbidity hazards associated with different occupations. Miners and teachers; executives and military officers; librarians and nurses all spend several hours a week exposed to different occupational conditions. Unfortunately, however, it is usually impossible to distinguish between mortality as it is connected with strictly occupational hazards and as it is linked to the lifestyle or socioeconomic status associated with any occupation.

Studies of occupational mortality generally seek to compute occupation-specific mortality rates. That is, they relate the mortality of individuals in a given occupation at or prior to death with the base population in that specific occupation. In addition, attempts are made to compute occupation-specific mortality rates for persons dependent upon, or otherwise attached to, the respective occupations and the socioeconomic categories associated with them. Thus, mortality rates are computed for wives and children in terms of the occupations of their husbands and fathers.

There is a long tradition of studies of this type in England and Wales. Here, as in other areas, mortality is highest in the lower social classes. But mortality from certain causes is higher in the higher social classes. Attempts have been made to carry out studies of occupational mortality differentials in the United States and in France as well. These have been much less detailed than the British studies, though for the United States in 1950, it was possible to classify male decedents between the ages of 10 and 64 by occupation or previous work experience for six different levels:

I. Professional workers
II. Technical, administrative, and managerial workers
III. Proprietors; clerical, sales and skilled workers
IV. Semiskilled workers
V. Laborers, except mine and agricultural workers
VI. Agricultural workers

These levels were compared by Moriyama and Guralnick (1956) within each age group, using ratios of mortality in each occupation-level group to the mortality of the total age group. These indexes, in turn, were compared to those of males in the respective socioeconomic groups in Britain in 1950. As Table 7.7 shows, the mortality of professionals (level I) in the United States in 1950 was lower than the mean for all levels, regardless of age; and the mortality of laborers (level V) was higher than the mean. In England and Wales, the departures from the average were smaller at all ages. In both countries the occupational-level differences in mortality were less at advanced ages (about 45 and over) than at younger ages.

The record linkage approach. The last approach to the study of mortality differences by socioeconomic status involves a technique known as record linkage. This entails the matching of vital statistics death reports for individuals with population census returns of the same individuals. The census information is then added to the information on the death certificates so that mortality rates may be computed for every population category identifiable in the census.

In large-scale record linkage studies of white mortality in the United States, E. M. Kitagawa and P. M. Hauser (1963; 1968; and 1973) established a strong inverse relationship between mortality and level of educational attainment. The higher the educational attainment, the lower the mortality risk for virtually all causes of death. This relationship is particularly pronounced for women, especially those aged 65 and

TABLE 7.7 Ratios of Death Rates by Occupation Level to Total Death Rates, by Age, for Men Aged 20–64: United States, England, and Wales, 1950

	Age					
Occupation Level	*20–24*	*25–34*	*35–44*	*45–54*	*55–59*	*60–64*
All Occupations						
United States	100	100	100	100	100	100
England and Wales	100	100	100	100	100	100
Occupation Level I						
United States	49	53	66	87	94	97
England and Wales	102	90	83	98	99	100
Occupation Levels II, III, and IV						
United States	80	84	91	96	99	101
England and Wales	94	95	96	97	99	101
Occupation Level V						
United States	190	232	219	178	146	128
England and Wales	122	138	143	129	115	106
Occupation Level VI						
United States	132	125	92	84	84	85
England and Wales	139	104	87	75	75	72

Source: Moriyama and Guralnick 1956.

over. Interestingly, it does not hold at all for men 65 and over. Table 7.8 shows the extent to which mortality differentials are associated with level of educational attainment. The indexes for each education level represent the ratios of the mortality rate in that sex-age-education group to the mortality rate for the total in the sex-age group.

As the authors point out (1973), education can hardly be considered the sole factor accounting for the variation in causes of death and in levels of mortality. However important it may be, the educational factor in such studies also reflects the socioeconomic variables with which education is closely associated: income, level of occupation, working conditions, lifestyle, diet and nutrition, quality of housing, and type of residence.

THE SOCIAL STRUCTURE OF MORTALITY CONTROL

In the earlier sections of this chapter we have touched on a point which deserves a more detailed discussion because of its implications for the analysis of the social structure of mortality control. Variations among

TABLE 7.8 Education Differentials in Mortality by Sex and Age: U.S. White Population, 1960 [a]

Number of School Years Completed	White Males: Total 25 years and over	White Males: 25–64 years	White Males: 65 years and over	White Females: Total 25 years and over	White Females: 25–64 years	White Females: 65 years and over
Total	1.00	1.00	1.00	1.00	1.00	1.00
Less than 8 years	1.03	1.15	1.01	1.16	1.30	1.09
Elementary, 8 years	1.01	1.06	1.00	1.05	1.08	1.03
High school, 1–4 years	1.00	0.97	0.98	0.90	0.89	0.94
College, 1 or more years	0.89	0.77	1.00	0.73	0.81	0.70

[a] Age-sex total = 1.00.

Source: E. M. Kitagawa and P. M. Hauser, Differential mortality in the United States: A study in socioeconomic epidemiology *(Cambridge: Harvard University Press, 1973). By permission of the President and Fellows of Harvard College.*

population groups as well as changes over time in mortality correspond to variations and changes in two distinct factors: in the exposure to the hazards that lead to mortality, like malnutrition, disease, and injury, and in both the quality of and the accessibility to treatment for diseases, malnutrition, and injury.

Problems of Mortality Control Among Societies

If we consider that the reduction of mortality must entail the reduction of exposure to hazards, or the improvement or expanded accessibility of medical technology, or both, it becomes clear that human societies do not universally take measures to reduce mortality. The practice of putting to death certain types of persons, or of systematically permitting them to die, is well documented for certain primitive societies and for a number of ancient civilizations. Societies are often slow or even unable to discard practices or institutions demonstrably associated with excessive mortality, or to adopt practices or institutions which can reduce mortality or exposure to disease and injury. For instance, even in the United States today it seems clear that neither alcoholic consumption nor cigarette smoking is likely to be discarded soon despite their association with many diseases. Again, both nationalized medical insurance plans and less powerful automobiles are capable of reducing mortality rates. Yet their adoption has encountered vigorous and determined opposition in the United States.

Differential Mortality Control Within Societies

Even in societies where every effort is made to control exposure to disease and injury, there are great variations in the nature, scope, and structure of the institutions and practices for medical treatment and cure. Within any society—regardless of its overall disease and mortality or the overall quality and scope of its medical technology—there are both social group differences in exposure to hazards and social group differences in access to medical treatment and cures.

Malaria relief field team at work. *(United Nations)*

Unfortunately, differential mortality studies and their data do not, and generally cannot, distinguish between differential exposure to disease and injury and differential access to medical technology. Nevertheless, there can be no doubt that there are two separate social processes operating here: the first is the distribution of individuals in the society so that they are exposed differentially to the risks of disease and injury; and the second is the differential access to institutionalized treatment facilities and medical technology. For instance, farmers, farm workers, and their families may be considerably less exposed than most people to lung diseases or to infectious diseases associated with urban life. But, on the other hand, they may have much less access than others to medical services, both because of their geographic isolation and because of their inability to afford expensive care. Military pilots are exposed to extraordinary daily hazards. But at the same time they may have unusually great access to medical care.

In the United States, mortality rates are closely associated with income. This is in part because people with higher incomes tend to have relatively little exposure to the hazards of undernutrition, disease, injury, and violent death. In addition, medical facilities and treatment are available primarily in a market, so that the people who are able or willing to pay more are the ones who receive more and better services. Of course, there are some special subgroups in the population, like members of the armed forces or of certain labor unions, who have access to superior medical treatment by virtue of their organizational associations. Others with the same income or socioeconomic status but without membership in comparable organizations may have considerably less access to such care.

The Institutionalization of Mortality Control

We have just seen that societies cannot, nor are they usually willing to, control mortality completely, and that even societies which have institutionalized widespread controls to reduce mortality have done so selectively rather than uniformly. As a tentative general hypothesis, we may suggest that the extent of institutionalized efforts to control mortality is inversely related to the "replaceability" of individuals in given social roles or positions. Thus, people in strategic or prestigious roles—those who are less easily replaced—are relatively well protected from hazards of illness or injury in their occupations, shelter, life style, and routine activities; they also have greater access to treatment, should illness or injury occur. Societies institutionalize means of controlling mortality to the extent that role differentiation and specialization put a premium upon role incumbents; and the replaceability of role incumbents decreases as roles become more differentiated and specialized. Conversely, to the extent that roles are not elaborately differentiated and the role incumbents are easily replaced, societies do not institutionalize means of mortality control.

Our hypotheses and analyses of differential mortality and the differential control of mortality must be far more detailed than they are at present if we are to understand, predict, and combat mortality. In addition, we need more detailed hypotheses and more detailed data bearing upon morbidity. The use of health surveys and detailed, large-scale analyses of insurance and health plan records are among the pursuits that seem to promise considerable progress in the analytical separation and better understanding of morbidity and mortality.

SUMMARY

In this chapter we have studied the historical declines of mortality in the West, the recent trends toward lower death rates in the newly independent and developing countries, and some patterns of differential

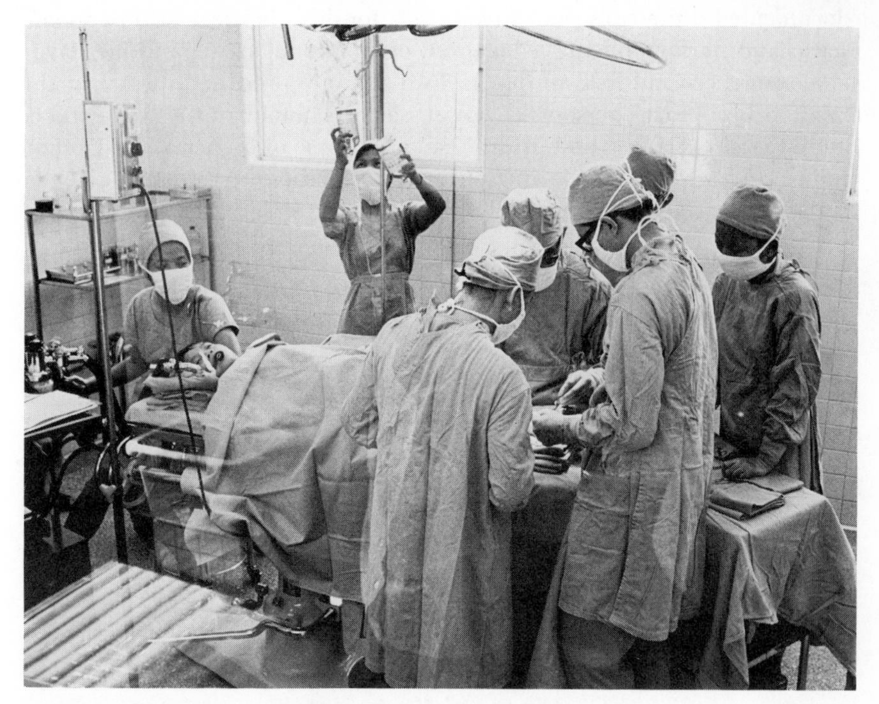

Life-saving tension and teamwork in Taiwan. *(United Nations)*

mortality. In Europe, crude death rates declined from levels of 30 per thousand or higher at the beginning of the eighteenth century to levels around or below 15 per thousand in the early decades of the twentieth century, and infant mortality has continued to decline through the century. Outside of Europe and European-settled countries, mortality remained high until about World War II; then it declined spectacularly in the postwar decades. Some areas in Africa and Asia still have high death rates.

The causes of the European historical declines in mortality include social and educational improvements, political stability, economic development, enhanced incomes and levels of living, social reforms, and sanitary and medical improvements. The more recent declines in mortality outside of Europe are accounted for largely by introduction of public health and preventive medicine measures rather than social, economic, or political development.

The study of differential mortality both among and within nations has served both to describe health and living conditions and to point to some causes of disease and death. The measurement of differential mortality has presented special difficulties, but a number of approaches have documented quite consistent inverse relationships between socioeconomic status and its components–education, occupational status, income, favorable residence–and risks of death. Two separate processes operate in this relationship. First, persons of lower socioeconomic status are exposed more to risks of illness and injury than are people of higher socioeconomic status; and second, people in the lower socioeconomic groups have generally limited access to medical knowledge, care, and treatment.

8

Matchmaking and Marriage

Marriage and divorce have long been a concern of population studies because of their recognized relationship to population composition and fertility. Next to age and sex, no characteristic is more basic to a population than its composition by marital status: its absolute and relative numbers of single, married, widowed, and divorced persons of each sex and at each age. Although children may be born outside of marriage, childbearing is always intimately associated with marriage, and it is generally viewed as both the object and a more-or-less immediate consequence of marriage.

While demographers and other students of population focused on population composition and fertility, they have been much less interested in the relationship of marriage patterns to family structure, kinship structure and social stratification. There have been a number of distinguished exceptions among demographers, but by and large it has been the sociologists and social anthropologists who have studied marriage and divorce with these relationships in mind.

Historically, marriage has been virtually universal and, especially in the case of the female, has taken place at early ages. Two reasons are generally advanced for this. First, under the conditions of high mortality which have characterized most populations throughout most of human history, universal or near-universal early marriage has been absolutely essential to assure the levels of fertility required for sheer population survival. And second, marriage is central both to the kinship structure, the fundamental dimension of social organization in most societies, and to the social integration and control of individuals.

While there are many demographic and social-structural questions about marriage and divorce, we will be concerned primarily with two kinds:

1. What are the variations and deviations from the pattern of universal early marriage? Under what conditions can societies allow, or even promote, bachelorhood and spinsterhood? What are the demographic and social-structural implications and consequences of such variations and deviations?
2. How is universal marriage—or for that matter, less-than-universal marriage—managed and sustained in populations and societies in which there are changing numbers of marriageable males and females of different ages, different personal characteristics, and often different social categories? What rules govern marriage markets? How do such rules change as populations and social structure and conditions change?

In this chapter, we shall consider the variations and changes in patterns of frequency of marriage (and of nonmarriage, or celibacy); of age at marriage; and of mate selection and its related arrangements.

PATTERNS OF COURTSHIP, MARRIAGE, AND FAMILY FORMATION

The manner in which marriages are contracted and families formed varies considerably among societies and among subunits within societies. Indeed, the very extent of marriage and family living, as opposed to celibacy and nonfamily residential arrangements, also varies widely. All societies require the formation of families or some other framework of reproduction for their survival. But some societies, and especially some subgroups within societies, have placed considerable emphasis and value upon social life and living arrangements outside the structure of the family. Societies with institutionalized monastic orders are a case in point.

Social Relationships Between the Sexes

Patterns of courtship, marriage, and family formation are influenced by the nature of social relationships between the sexes from the earliest ages. The manner in which children are socialized and educated, and the extent and nature of social interaction between boys and girls at every age, are connected with the eventual courtship styles and marriage partners chosen. In some societies, boys and girls are segregated from each other in infancy and remain segregated until marriage; this occurs, for example, among the ultraorthodox Jews in Jerusalem. In other societies, boys and girls may be brought up together at first but then segregated—in early childhood, like the Arapesh of New Guinea and the Teton Dakota of the American Great Plains, or at adolescence, like the Masai and Tallensi of Africa. In some societies, relationships between children or adolescents of opposite sex are characterized by shyness or shame, as in Victorian England. In others they are casual and matter-of-fact, as with the Samoans and the Trobriand Islanders of Melanesia.

In some societies premarital social relationships between adolescents of opposite sex are permitted only to persons already betrothed. In others a large variety of institutionalized relationships between the sexes may precede actual betrothal. Thus, while betrothal of children is very common in some societies, in others dating and other premarital social and sexual relationships of varying extent begin at different ages and continue into early adulthood, preceding actual betrothal and marriage.

Age at First Marriage

The range of ages at which marriages are contracted is narrow in some societies and wide in others. However, in every society the great majority of first marriages tend to be concentrated within a relatively narrow age span. This is particularly true for the ages at which females marry for the first time. Thus, while some females in a given society may marry for the first time at, say, 12 or 13 years of age, and others not until 29 or 30, the great majority are likely to enter into their first marriage at one of a much narrower band of ages, perhaps between 18 and 20. Finally, the modal (most frequent) age at first marriage varies among societies and between subgroups within societies. It is early in the United States and Canada and late in Eastern Europe. And it is later in the northeastern part of the United States than in the South.

Choice of Marital Partner

The choice of marital partner is most often in the hands of one or both parents of the young marriageable male or female. This is the case, for example, in traditional Islamic societies. However, in many societies the marriage choice and arrangements are made by some other kinsman or by the head of the extended family, lineage, or clan. The prospective bride or groom may or may not be consulted, may or may not know anything about the chosen spouse, and may or may not be allowed any say or veto rights over the choice. In some societies, the initiative, courtship, and choice all rest primarily with the young marriageable man or woman. The parents or other kin may or may not enjoy some initiative or power of veto in the matter.

The choice of marital partner, is, in every society, subject to some set of restrictions. In general, marriages tend to be homogamous: that is, they are contracted among persons of similar social characteristics or background. Restrictions upon choice of partner may be more or less formalized and rigid. They may be institutionalized in laws prohibiting marriages of certain types or in customs prescribing who is eligible to marry whom. Alternatively, restrictions may arise simply out of the opportunity, or lack of it, for social contact and interaction between the marriageable male and female or their families. For example, the opportunities for a coal miner's son to meet and interact with a banker's daughter are limited.

The restriction of marital partners to someone of the same group, clan, lineage, village, or ethnic category is called endogamy. Conversely, the restriction of the partner to someone from one or several different groups is called exogamy. Both endogamy and exogamy occur as a consequence of formalized or rigidly institutionalized rules and customs or as a consequence of less formal patterns of social contact and interaction. Thus, homogamous, endogamous, or exogamous restrictions may vary with respect to their content, range, and rigidity.

Marriage Transactions

Marriages in most societies entail some kind of material transaction between the families or kin groups of the bride and groom. Such transactions may be more or less important in determining the choice of partner. They take the form of bride-price, dowry, service obligations, or simply gifts. On the other hand, the exchange may involve only paper transactions or exchanges of equivalent items.

A bride-price is a gift or sum paid by a groom or his family to the

Bedouin couple with the bride's dowry. *(Wide World Photos)*

family of the bride, compensating the family for the loss of the bride's services. The bride's family may keep the bride-price, or give it to the bride herself. Or they may use it in contracting a marriage for a son, as a bride-price to be paid to the family of their son's bride. A dowry is a gift or sum paid by the family of the bride to the groom. The groom may be permitted to use the gift or sum as he pleases, or he may be obligated to leave all or part of it untouched. The latter assures the bride and her family that she will be treated well and adequately provided for: if the marriage is dissolved, the groom may be obliged to return all or part of the dowry to the bride or to her family.

THE FREQUENCY OF MARRIAGE AND NONMARRIAGE

The Historical Universality of Marriage

There seems to be no dispute among modern sociologists or social anthropologists about Ralph Linton's assertion that "practically all societies consider married life the most normal and desirable type of existence for adults" (Linton, 1936, p. 174). Indeed, so common is the assumption that marriage is universal or nearly universal in primitive societies that actual documentation is extremely rare.[1] True, in some ancient civilizations there were apparently high incidences of celibacy or prohibition of marriage among certain population subgroupings (Reinhard, Armengaud, & Dupaquier, 1968; chaps. 3 and 4), especially among slaves and certain upper-class groups. And celibacy among the Roman Catholic priesthood was institutionalized in medieval times. Nevertheless, marriage—or widowhood, for survivors of marital unions—seems historically to have been the dominant and almost universal pattern of existence for human adults.

The European Marriage Pattern

A major and extended deviation from the pattern of universal marriage occurred—and, to a considerable extent, continues—in Western Europe and in countries of Western European settlement beginning in about the sixteenth century. Western European marriages have typically been delayed to more advanced ages than in the rest of the world, and bachelorhood and spinsterhood have been an accepted, and statistically not infrequent, pattern of life.[2]

Table 8.1 shows the percentage of single men and women between the ages of 45 and 49 in selected countries of Western Europe, Eastern Europe, Asia, and Africa. The data, which cover various years between 1891 and 1952, show that the countries of Western Europe in that period had substantial percentages of unmarried adults. In Asia and Africa, on the other hand, marriage was virtually universal. Some countries of Eastern Europe also had nearly universal marriage, while in others the percentages remaining single were significant (but hardly ever as high as in Western Europe). As Table 8.2 shows, the United States has also been characterized by substantial percentages of single adults, but this has never been as pronounced as in Western Europe.

In Europe and the United States, and in other countries of European settlement, the period during and immediately following World War II witnessed a sharp increase in the annual numbers of marriages and in the annual marriage rates at all ages (Hajnal, 1956). Declines in the percentages of single persons aged 45 and over are already apparent in the United States data (Table 8.2) and they are becoming even more so in the countries that experienced the marriage boom.

[1] One exception is Krzywicki, 1934. See pp. 221–22 and p. 260 for documentation of his assertion that "every woman in primitive society is a wife."

[2] The research and writings of John Hajnal are the major sources for this review. See Hajnal (especially 1965, but also 1953a and 1953b).

TABLE 8.1 Percent Single at Ages 45–49, by Sex: Selected Countries in Western Europe, Eastern Europe, Asia, and Africa

Country and Date		Percent Single	
		Males	*Females*
Western Europe			
Austria	1900–1901	11	13
	1939	10	18
Belgium	1900–1901	16	17
Denmark	1900–1901	9	13
Finland	1900–1901	14	15
France	1900–1901	11	12
Germany	1900–1901	9	10
	1939	7[a]	15[a]
Great Britain	1900–1901	12	15
Holland	1900–1901	13	14
Iceland	1900–1901	19	29
Ireland	1891	20	17
Italy	1911	11	11
	1936	10	14
Norway	1900	11	18
Portugal	1900–1901	13	20
	1940	9	18
Spain	1900–1901	6[b]	10[b]
	1940	9	19
Sweden	1900–1901	13	19
Switzerland	1900–1901	16	17
Eastern Europe			
Greece	1907	9	4
	1928	7	4
Hungary	1900	5	4
	1941	6	9
Poland	1931	4	7
Romania	1899	5	3
Bosnia	1910	6[c]	2[c]
Bulgaria	1900	3	1
	1934	3	1
USSR	1897[d]	4	5
	1926	3[a]	4[a]
Serbia	1900	3	1
Yugoslavia	1931	5	5
Asia and Africa			
Morocco	1952 (Moslems)	2	2
Algeria	1948 (Moslems)	5	2

TABLE 8.1 Percent Single at Ages 45–49, by Sex: Selected Countries in Western Europe, Eastern Europe, Asia and Africa (*cont.*)

Country and Date			*Percent Single*	
			Males	*Females*
Tunisia	1946	(Indigenous population)	6	4
Egypt	1947		2	1
Mozambique	1950		4	3
Mauritius	1952		5	5
Turkey	1935		3	3
India	1931	(Including Pakistan)	4	1
Ceylon	1946		8	3
Thailand	1947		4	3
Malaya	1947		2	1
Formosa	1930		4	0
Korea	1930		1	0
Japan	1920		2	2
	1951		2	2

[a] Ages 40–49. [b] Ages 46–50. [c] Ages 41–50. [d] European Russia.

Sources: J. Hajnal, European marriage patterns in perspective, in D. V. Glass and D. E. C. Eversley, eds., Population in History *(London: Edward Arnold, 1965); J. Hajnal, The marriage boom, in J. J. Spengler and O. D. Duncan, eds.,* Demographic Analysis *(New York: Free Press, copyright 1956), with permission of Macmillan Publishing Co., Inc.*

TABLE 8.2 Percent Single at Ages 45–54, by Sex: United States, 1890–1974.

Year	*Males*	*Females*
1890	10.0	7.1
1900	10.3	7.8
1910	11.1	8.5
1920	12.0	9.6
1930	11.4	9.1
1940	11.1	8.7
1950	10.1	7.8
1955	8.5	6.8
1960	8.7	7.2
1969	7.1	4.9
1974	5.9	4.2

Source: D. J. Bogue, The Population of the United States *(New York: Free Press, 1959), p. 219; and U.S. Bureau of the Census,* Statistical Abstract of the United States, *1961, 1970, tables 27 and 36, respectively;* Current Population Reports *Series P20, no. 271, (October 1974).*

Socioeconomic Status and Marrying *vs.* Remaining Single

Educational achievement. In the United States in 1950, the percentage of single males between the ages of 45 and 54 varied inversely with level of educational achievement. About 16 percent of those with no schooling had never married, compared to less than seven percent of those with four or more years of college. The reverse was true of females of the same age group in the same year. Twenty-four percent of the women with four or more years of college remained single—compared to just under nine percent of those with no education at all, 4.5 percent of those with one to four years of elementary school, and five percent of those with five to eight years of elementary school (Taeuber & Taeuber, 1958, table 51; Bogue, 1959, Table 10-37).

Occupation and income. In 1957, some 6.4 percent of employed males between the ages of 45 and 64 were single. However, this figure was not representative across the board, for there were great variations among employment categories. According to Bogue (1959, Table 10-37), the designation "single" applied to 22 percent of farm laborers and foremen and to 20 percent of private household workers, but to only 2.5 percent of the sales workers. Single males included less than four percent of managers, officials, and proprietors or craftsmen, foremen, and kindred workers. In the same year, some 13 percent of employed women of the same ages were single. This proportion included 27 percent of professional, technical, and kindred workers and 19 percent of clerical and kindred workers. Finally, among United States urban and rural nonfarm males between the ages of 45 and 64, the percent single varied inversely and sharply by amount of income in 1956. Among those with incomes of under $2,000, some 23 percent were single. Conversely, the figure was only 1.7 percent for those earning $6,000 or more (Bogue, 1959, Table 10-38).

In later years the percentages remaining single have declined, especially in the groups which previously had high percentages of singles. And as the overall propensity to marry has increased, the socioeconomic status differences have tended to diminish. Thus, among American males aged 45–54 in 1974, some eight percent with elementary education only were single, compared to six percent of college graduates, 4.5 percent of those with one to three years of college, and five percent of those with high school education. Among males earning less than $3,000 in 1973, about 20 percent were single—compared to six percent in the $6,000–$9,999 income group and only three percent (in 1974) among males 45–54 years old with incomes $10,000 or over (U.S. Bureau of the Census, *Current Population Reports,* Series P-20, no. 271 [Oct. 1974] table 9).

Age at Marriage

From the point of view of its relationship to and its impact upon population growth and composition, the age at which people marry (especially females) is only slightly less important than the fact of marriage itself: a 35-year-old bride is not likely to produce as many children as an 18-year-old is. Yet anthropological and sociological studies of marriage mention age at marriage only in passing, if at all. And demographic studies of age at marriage have been severely limited in the range and scope of the societies and populations investigated.

Malthus: delayed marriage as a preventive check. In modern population studies, the question of age at marriage was most forcefully raised by Thomas Robert Malthus in the early nineteenth century, in the second and later editions of his famous *Essay on the Principle of Population* (see Malthus, 1958). In the first edition of his work, Malthus had concluded that vice, misery, famine, and war were the inevitable outcomes of the tendency of populations to grow beyond their means of sustenance; and, indeed that it was these factors that checked further population growth. But in his second and later editions, Malthus introduced "another check to population which does not come under the heading of either vice or misery." The newly recognized check was "moral restraint," by which Malthus meant primarily delayed marriage.[3] Malthus' ideas have provided food for both thought and research for many subsequent scholars. Yet, despite the controversy generated by these doctrines, and despite the studies and writings which they have stimulated, even demographers have been slow to follow Malthus' lead and analyze patterns of age at marriage. More research on the subject has recently been undertaken, however, largely because of the concern over rapid population growth and because of the interest in means and prospects of controlling it.

The universality of early marriage. There are good reasons to suppose that, in most societies in most places and at most times, marriage has been not only virtually universal but universally undertaken at very young ages—among girls either at or very close to puberty. The overwhelming picture from observations of travelers, administrators, missionaries, and anthropologists is that girls marry early in primitive or preliterate societies, and are often betrothed before puberty (see Krzywicki,

[3] For a fine discussion of the development of Malthus's ideas, see Petersen, 1971.

1934, p. 221; and Fortes, 1950). For ancient societies, there is literary and documentary evidence of similarly early betrothal and marriage (Reinhard, Armengaud, & Dupaquier, 1968, pt. I; Hopkins, 1965). This evidence takes the form of both actual accounts of early marriages, as in the Old Testament, and of enjoinments upon parents concerning the obligation or advisability of arranging marriages for their daughters and sons at an early age.

In addition, we have mentioned earlier that high mortality and low expectations of life have characterized most populations throughout history: this suggests that societies in which marriage and childbearing did not take place at early ages could not have survived over successive generations. The late French demographer Jean Fourastié (1959) showed that under conditions of high mortality, even with high and uncontrolled fertility, population growth and replacement are heavily dependent upon age at marriage. Thus, under mortality conditions characterized by life expectancies of no more than 25 years (which was the case in France from 1680 to 1725), a mean age of 25 years at first marriage for females would mean a population decline of about ten percent per generation—even taking into account remarriages after widowhood. Under the same mortality conditions, if the mean age at first marriage were 22.5 instead, this would result in a population increase of about six percent per generation. Improved mortality conditions (with life expectancies at birth reaching 30 years) would result in a growth rate of nine percent per generation if the average age at first marriage were 25 years, and in a growth rate of 34 percent per generation if the average age were 22.5.

The modern European deviation from early marriage. Just as there is a modern European deviation from the near universality of marriage, so there is a clear European pattern of relatively late marriage which deviates sharply from the early marriages common outside of modern Europe, especially among females. Table 8.3 covers selected years between 1891 and 1952, and it shows that in most countries of Western Europe only about one-third of the women between the ages of 20 and 24 were married—and this despite the fact that marriage before the age of 25 was substantially more frequent among females than males. In all the countries except Sweden, Iceland, and Ireland, the majority of women between the ages of 25 and 29 were already married. But very large minorities, from about 26 percent in Spain to about 45 percent in Switzerland, were still single. At around the turn of the century in Western Europe, the marriage of males before the age of 25 was infrequent. The percentages single among males between 20 and 24 years of age varied from just over 80 percent to more than 95 percent. In most countries not more than half the males aged 25 to 29 were already married.

In the Eastern European countries, a substantial majority of women aged 20 to 24 were married, as were all but a small minority of those aged 25 to 29. In three Eastern European countries, Poland, Hungary, and Greece, women of these age groups were relatively more likely to be single. As with women, larger minorities of Eastern European men than Western European men were married by age 20 to 24, as were quite substantial majorities of those aged 25 to 29.

Finally, male marriages in Asia and Africa were somewhat earlier than they were in Eastern Europe, and female marriages were almost universally earlier. In all of the countries shown in Table 8.3 except modern Japan, less than 30 percent of the women between the ages of 20 and 24 were still single. And even in Japan, this pattern is quite recent, for there has been a drastic change since 1920. In all countries of Asia and Africa, the overwhelming majority (85 percent or more) of the women between ages 25 and 29 were already married.

TABLE 8.3 Percent Single at Ages 20–24 and 25–29, by Sex: Selected Countries of Western Europe, Eastern Europe, Asia, and Africa

Country and Date		*Percent Single*			
		Males		*Females*	
		20–24	*25–29*	*20–24*	*25–29*
Western Europe					
Austria	1900–1901	93	51	66	38
	1939	89	60	68	42
Belgium	1900–1901	85	50	71	41
Denmark	1900–1901	88	50	75	42
Finland	1900–1901	84	51	68	40
France	1900–1901	90	48	58	30
Germany	1900–1901	91	48	71	34
	1939	91	51	64	31
Great Britain	1900–1901	83	47	73	42
Holland	1900–1901	89	53	79	44
Iceland	1900–1901	92	66	81	56
Ireland	1891	96	78	86	59
Italy	1911	86	46	60	30
	1936	91	54	69	39
Norway	1900–1901	86	54	77	48
Portugal	1900–1901	84	48	69	41
	1940	85	48	69	40
Spain	1900–1901	81[a]	34[b]	55[a]	26[b]
	1940	94	63	79	44
Sweden	1900–1901	92	61	80	52
Switzerland	1900–1901	91	58	78	45

TABLE 8.3 Percent Single at Ages 20–24 and 25–29, by Sex: Selected Countries of Western Europe, Eastern Europe, Asia, and Africa (*cont.*)

Country and Date		Percent Single: Males 20–24	Males 25–29	Females 20–24	Females 25–29
Eastern Europe					
Greece	1907	82	47	44	13
	1928	83	52	56	26
Hungary	1900	81	31	36	15
	1941	88	46	53	24
Poland	1931	83	41	61	30
Romania-Bosnia	1899	67	21	20	8
	1910	63[c]	31[d]	23[c]	6[d]
Bulgaria	1900	58	23	24	3
	1934	56	20	35	11
USSR	1897[e]	42 (20–29)		23 (20–29)	
	1926	51	18	28	9
Serbia	1900	50	18	16	2
Yugoslavia	1931	60	27	35	15
Asia and Africa					
Morocco (Moslems)	1952	59	28	8	3
Algeria (Moslems)	1948	68	37	23	10
Tunisia (indigenous population)	1946	73	46	29	13
Egypt	1947	69	35	20	6
Mozambique	1950	54	23	17	7
Mauritius	1952	72	33	24	12
Turkey	1935	49	24	18	6
India (including Pakistan)	1931	35	14	5	2
Ceylon	1946	80	43	29	12
Thailand	1947	61	24	30	11
Malaya	1947	54	17	7	2
Formosa	1930	52	19	15	4
Korea	1930	33	10	2	1
Japan	1920	71	26	2	1
	1951	83	34	55	15

[a] Ages 21–25. [b] Ages 26–30. [c] Ages 21–24. [d] Ages 25–30.

Sources: J. Hajnal, European marriage patterns in perspective, in D. V. Glass and D. E. C. Eversley, eds., Population in History (London: Edward Arnold, 1965); J. Hajnal, The marriage boom, in J. J. Spengler and O. D. Duncan, eds., Demographic Analysis *(New York: Free Press, copyright 1956), with permission of Macmillan Publishing Co., Inc.*

The data in Tables 8.1 and 8.3 are largely consistent with our hypotheses explaining the universality and early age of female marriage. Our first hypothesis was that conditions of high mortality make universal and early marriage mandatory for a society's survival. The countries of Asia and Africa have certainly been characterized by much higher mortality rates in this century than the countries of Western Europe. It can be reasoned that their extent of marriage and age at marriage have had immediate bearing not only on their population growth but on their survival as well. Conversely, mortality in Western European countries has long been low enough to assure quite considerable population growth even without universal or early marriage. As for Eastern Europe, its mortality and marital patterns have held an intermediate position between the Western European and Asian and African extremes.

Our second hypothesis held in part that marriage is central to the maintenance of kinship structure, which is central to the social organization of most societies. It is difficult to measure and compare the importance—and relative exclusiveness—of kinship as the basis of social organization. But the foregoing data may be one reason why the place of kinship in social structure is widely believed to have remained stronger and more central in Eastern Europe than in Western Europe, and stronger and even more totalistic in Asia and Africa.

THE POSTWAR MARRIAGE BOOM IN WESTERN EUROPE AND THE UNITED STATES: SOME FACTS AND SOME HYPOTHESES

A quick comparison of Tables 8.4 and 8.3 shows that age of marriage for both men and women in the United States has been substantially earlier than in Western Europe, but somewhat later than in most of Eastern Europe (see Hajnal, 1953a; Matras, 1965a and 1965b). However, Western Europe, the United States, and other countries of European settlement share one very important trend. In the post-World-War-II years in the United States, these has been a sharp drop in the proportions of single persons of both sexes at all ages between 20 and 29 (Rele, 1965). Similar sharp declines in the proportion of single persons have also occurred in virtually every country of Western Europe except France and Ireland, heralding a greatly increased tendency to marry and to marry at early ages (Hajnal, 1956, see especially table 3).

Very little is known about why people are marrying at earlier ages. One early hypothesis (Davis, 1956) holds that the decline is associated with the popularization of contraceptive techniques. According to this line of reasoning, individuals previously wishing to keep their number

TABLE 8.4 Percent Single at Ages 20–24 and 25–29, by Sex: United States, 1890–1974

	Males		*Females*	
Year	*20–24*	*25–29*	*20–24*	*25–29*
1890	80.7	46.0	51.8	25.4
1900	77.6	45.8	51.0	27.5
1910	74.9	42.8	48.3	24.9
1920	70.7	39.4	45.6	23.0
1930	70.8	36.7	46.0	21.7
1940	72.2	36.0	47.2	22.8
1950	59.1	23.8	32.3	13.3
1960	54.7	23.0	28.9	9.5
1969	54.6	18.0	35.4	11.0
1972	56.9	19.3	36.4	12.4
1974	57.0	22.6	39.6	13.1

Source: Bogue, 1959a; and U.S. Bureau of the Census, Statistical Abstract of the United States, *1961, 1970, 1975, tables 27, 36, and 47 respectively. Data for 1972 from U.S. Bureau of the Census,* Statistical Abstract of the United States, *1974. Data for 1974 from U.S. Bureau of the Census,* Current Population Reports, *Series P-20, no. 27 (Oct. 1974), table 1.*

of births in check did so by postponing marriage, just as societies institutionalized the delay of marriage until relatively advanced ages, very much as Malthus argued. Continuing along this line of reasoning, the development of contraceptive measures has rendered the postponement of marriage unnecessary. Coale (1969) finds support for this thesis in his historical study of fertility and marriage in Europe. Whether these two developments are universally linked we still can't say for sure; far more research must be done before we fully understand the reasons for this very important trend.

The Early Marriage Trend: Facts and Reasons

Earlier in this chapter we discussed characteristics associated with the likelihood of marriage. In the United States, there are a number of variables related to age at marriage.[4] Both males and females have tended to marry earlier in the South and later in the Northeast, than in other areas of the United States. Marriage is earlier among women from rural nonfarm areas than from rural farm areas. It is later in urban than rural areas, and later the larger the urban place. Marriage is later, too, among

[4] Our summary draws upon the materials presented in Taeuber and Taeuber, 1958, chap. 8; Bogue, 1959, chap. 10; and Rele, 1965.

rural farm males than among urban males. Nonwhites in the United States have tended to marry at younger ages than whites, and this difference is considerably more pronounced for females than for males. Native-born whites of native parents marry earlier than foreign-born whites, but native-born whites of foreign parents marry latest of all.

Both males and females with some education marry earlier than persons with little or no schooling, but persons with college education marry latest of all. Males who are employed as managers, officials, proprietors, craftsmen, foremen, or operatives (semiskilled machine operators) tend to marry fairly early, while men in sales occupations tend to marry late. Employed females who have managerial, sales, operative, or service jobs tend to marry early, while women in professional, clerical, craft, or foreman occupations are more likely to marry late. Among males, high income is associated with early marriage and low income with later marriage.

Recalling our earlier discussion of factors associated with likelihood of marriage and nonmarriage, it is evident that the socioeconomic characteristics associated with nonmarriage are generally also associated with delayed marriage. However, there are some important exceptions. For example, professional and highly educated males delay marriage to relatively late ages, but ultimately this group is characterized by a low percentage remaining single. Nevertheless, it is still appropriate to see both delayed marriage and nonmarriage as similar or even as two facets of the same phenomenon of deviation from the universal early marriage pattern.

Finally, it is important to note that the post-World-War-II marriage boom in Western Europe, the United States, and countries of Western European settlement has taken place especially among those population groups which had previously been characterized by the most consistent nonmarriage or postponement of marriage. Thus, the marriage boom has both lowered the average age at marriage and increased the percentages ever marrying in these groups. In this way it has reduced the overall differentials among regional, urban-rural, racial, nativity, and socioeconomic groups with regard to both age at marriage and incidence of marriage.

Changes in Marriage as a Social Institution

For societies in which marriage is voluntary—in other words, those where nonmarriage is a recognized, acceptable, and realistic alternative—and for societies in which age at marriage is variable rather than strictly prescribed, any number of social-psychological factors may be associated with an individual's marriage, nonmarriage, and age at marriage. But there are other important variables which influence the extent to which societies or social groups institutionalize universal and early marriage or, alternatively, nonmarriage or delayed marriage. In this area, we are most concerned with three important questions. Why do European societies and societies of European origin differ from non-European societies in patterns of frequency of marriage and age at marriage? What are the reasons for variations in marriage patterns among European societies? And what factors have been involved in the changes over time in marital patterns of both European and non-European societies?

Hajnal's analysis of the modern European marriage pattern. The British demographer John Hajnal has been a leader among contemporary students of marriage patterns. By way of explaining the patterns of modern Europe, Hajnal mentions two reasons already advanced by others (Hajnal, 1965). First, there are some peculiarly European difficulties in matchmaking. One of these is the widespread conviction that marriage should be decided upon only after the prospective spouses are well acquainted with one another. A second important factor is the surplus of marriageable women in modern Europe as opposed to the apparent shortages of such women outside Europe and in premodern Europe. This has combined with declining rates of marriage for males to decrease further frequency of marriage.

In addition to these factors, Hajnal hypothesizes that the unique European marriage pattern is closely connected to a third factor: the economic independence of the European stem family.[5] In Hajnal's words:

> It is tempting to see in this feature a key to the uniqueness of the European marriage pattern. In Europe it has been necessary for a man to defer marriage until he could establish an independent livelihood adequate to support a family; in other societies the young couple could be incorporated in a larger economic unit, such as a joint family. [Father and all sons, their wives and children, all in the same household.] This, presumably, is more easily achieved and does not require such a long postponement of marriage. This line of argument seems especially convincing if the larger economic unit is such that extra labour is often felt to be an economic asset. A system of large estates with large households as in Eastern Europe might thus be conducive to a non-European marriage pattern, while small holdings occupied by a single family and passed on to a single heir would result in a European pattern. (Hajnal, 1965, p. 133)

Hajnal argues further that the modern pattern may well have been closely connected to the uniquely European "take-off" into modern eco-

[5] The stem family consists of parents and the adult child who is to inherit the family property (in Europe, typically the family farm). If the inheritor is married, the stem family also includes his or her spouse and childen.

nomic growth (Hajnal, 1965, p. 132).[6] He observes that if the connection between European marriage patterns and the European stem-family system obtained, it must have led to a fundamental social and economic transformation of the society.

The details of such a transformation are far beyond the scope of this book. However, we may apply to Hajnal's analysis the idea that the change in Europe to non-universal and late patterns of marriage involved the institutionalization of these patterns as part of a new societal strategy of survival and adaptation. Perhaps the main feature of the new societal strategy was the shift from a localized subsistence pattern of agricultural production and distribution to a more differentiated regional market pattern. Incorporated in the shift were a greater differentiation of tasks and expansion of services and industries, accompanied by an increased demand for free labor (Weber, 1961; see also Hobhouse, 1966, pp. 281–92; and Bottomore, 1962, pp. 133–43). Apparently these very changes in societal strategies of survival and adaptation were related to the great decline in mortality that began in the eighteenth century (Eversley, 1965). Both this decline in mortality and rising standards of living may have been linked to widespread individual attempts to control fertility through postponed marriage or to institutionalized patterns of late marriage or nonmarriage (Hajnal, 1965; Eversley, 1965)—although we still aren't certain. Much remains to be learned about these transformations and their causes.

MATE SELECTION

The Variability of Rules and Patterns of Mate Selection

We can conceive readily enough of a mate-selection and marriage situation where any eligible male is as likely to marry any one of the eligible females in his society as he is to marry any other. We are equally able to imagine the converse situation, where any eligible female is equally likely to marry any one of the eligible males. Thus, if there are M eligible males and F eligible females in the society, there will be $M \times F$ possible and equally likely matches. In fact, however, such a situation hardly ever exists. There are always some constraints upon reciprocal mate selection that absolutely prohibit certain kinds of matches, make others so infrequent as to be virtually nonexistent, and render still others more or less frequent.

[6] The term "take-off" was used by Rostow, 1956 and 1960, in reference to an acceleration of economic growth.

In the United States, and elsewhere too, marriage between brothers and sisters is prohibited. In addition, some other kinds of marriages are unlikely. Marriages between 80-year-old women and 17-year-old boys, or between female college professors and male waiters, are rare enough to be virtually nonexistent. Marriages in which both partners are Protestant or both Catholic are considerably more common than those involving one Protestant and one Catholic, or one Christian and one Jew. And marriages in which both partners are white or both partners black are far more frequent than racially mixed marriages. French-speaking Swiss are more likely to marry other French-speaking Swiss than they are to marry Swiss who speak German, Italian, or Romansch. And French-speaking Canadians are more likely to marry French-speaking than English-speaking Canadians. In many states of the Union, eligible first cousins are prohibited from marrying one another. But in many other societies, it is understood that they ought to marry one another, and in some they must marry one another.

Thus age, race, religion, ethnic origin, place of residence, educational level, social status, kinship, language, and other social, economic, and cultural factors intervene in the process of mate selection. Such intervention always restricts and reduces the choice and number of potential mates, regardless of the total number and variety of eligible males and females in the marriage market at any moment in time. However, some factors do operate to widen the range of possible marital partners—for example, travel, going to college, commercial marriage brokerages, and lonelyhearts clubs.

The rules and patterns of mate selection in any society have far-reaching demographic and social structural implications. However, it is not always possible to plot these implications in exact detail, and they vary over societies and among different subgroups within societies. Similarly, those institutions which affect the processes of matchmaking and mate selection are different in one society than another. In this section, we have room to touch only briefly on the subject of variation and change in patterns of mate selection. We will focus on a few of the issues and problems that occupy research in this area.

Studying Patterns of Mate Selection

The norms, rules, and customs which influence the choice of a marriage partner may be more or less rigid, and they may be more or less explicit in different groups within societies. The study of patterns of mate selection is carried out typically through one or both of the following approaches:

1. the direct study of marriage rules, customs, and norms through observation, analysis of laws and literary sources, and use of informants or interview material. This approach has typically—although not exclusively—characterized anthropological and sociological studies of preliterate or primitive societies, historical studies, and field studies of single communities.
2. the quantitative analysis of different types of matches; that is, the study of differential frequencies of couples, comprising husbands from each given group, and wives from each of all the other respective groups.

The following discussion makes use of both approaches.

Some generalizations on age patterns in first-marriage mate selection. We can classify eligible bachelors and spinsters into three broad age categories: (a) "young"—under about 20 years of age; (b) "middle-aged"—over 20 but under 30; and (c) "old"—about 30 years of age or over. Given these categories, and reasoning on the basis of a variety of findings from many simple and complex societies, it is possible to arrive at some broad generalizations concerning age patterns in mate selection when both bride and groom are marrying for the first time. Men are more likely to be older than their brides than to be either the same age or younger. Acceptable or relatively frequent matches are those involving:

1. "young" (< 20) grooms and "young" (< 20) brides
2. "middle-aged" (20–29) grooms and "young" (< 20) brides
3. "middle-aged" (20–29) grooms and "middle-aged" (20–29) brides
4. "middle-aged" (20–29) grooms and "old" (30+) brides
5. "old" (30+) grooms and "old" (30+) brides
6. "old" (30+) grooms and "middle-aged" (20–29) brides

Less acceptable, unconventional, or relatively infrequent matches are those involving:

7. "young" (< 20) grooms and "middle-aged" (20–29) brides
8. "young" (<20) grooms and "old" (30+) brides
9. "old" (30+) grooms and "young" (< 20) brides

Of course, there are variations in the extent to which each type of match is acceptable. But variations and changes over time in the relative frequencies of the types often derive simply from variations in the population composition of the groups or societies in question. In other words, the relative frequencies of different kinds of matches are often dictated by the number of eligible males and females in each age group in the society. This number in turn varies according to the society's past patterns of fertility, infant and child mortality, and migration.

Conventions about age selection of mates tend to be more rigid for marriages of single, never-before-married brides and grooms than is the case for marriages involving previously married persons. Thus, the imbalances due to past demographic and social-structural factors are more likely to be resolved by flexibility in the patterns of age choices characteristic of remarriages rather than in those of first marriages.

Population Trends and Squeezes in the Marriage Market

Several kinds of population trends affect the marriage market. The marriage market's size and composition by age and by social strata at any point in time are governed by past fertility, past and recent migration, and recent patterns of marriage, divorce, and widowhood. Also, the composition of the marriage market can be affected by trends in education and even to some extent by occupational attainment. For example, through the 1950s and much of the 1960s, each year's new wave of young eligibles had a higher average level of educational attainment than had any previous marriage market in the United States.

The marriage squeeze. Certain population trends, in combination with mate-selection practices, can cause imbalances in the number of eligibles of the two sexes. This imbalance is often called a *marriage squeeze*. The mobilization of large numbers of young men into military service in wartime is one case in point, where eligible females in the market are confronted with a shortage of eligible males. Migratory streams also may generate imbalances in the numbers of unmarried persons in a community. One example of this kind of situation was the shortage of women in the Old West, a marriage squeeze which has been brought to popular attention in literature and motion pictures.

In addition to these causes, there may also be considerably more subtle sources of the marriage squeeze. In a society whose marrying couples are usually of different ages, for instance, where grooms are typically two or three years older than their brides, any inflection in fertility—either upward or downward—will be reflected by an imbalance in the marriage market some 20 years later. Males born in 1928 or 1929 in the United States would have married females born three or four years later (in 1931 or 1932) under normal circumstances. But the Great Depression caused a steep drop in fertility, so that relatively few babies—male and female—were born between 1929 and 1932. The result: males born in 1928 were confronted with a shortage in the marriage market 20 years later, and so there was a marriage squeeze in the early 1950s. Females who are born at the start of a great upward inflection in fertility will be faced with a marriage squeeze just like men born at the start of a low-fertility period. For example, women born at the beginning of the great American baby boom, between 1945 and 1947, confronted a shortage of males born two or three years earlier during World War II.

Another kind of marriage squeeze may be generated by shifting levels of educational attainment. Consider the "rule" that says that a girl ought to marry a man who (a) is two years older than herself, and (b) has as much or more education than she. If the number of college graduates, both male and female, increases every year, then the number of 22-year-old graduates exceeds the number of 23-year-old graduates, which in turn exceeds the number of 24-year-old graduates. Some 22-year-old women graduating from college will not find any 24-year-old male graduates left, for there simply aren't enough of them. The woman graduate caught in this kind of squeeze has two basic options: she can either delay marriage—for a short time or for a long time, depending on what the market allows—or, she can change the rules.

Demographic and Sociocultural Factors in Mate Selection

Demographic and social pressures on the marriage regime. If we examine together the two dimensions of the marriage regime—first, patterns of frequency of marriage and age at marriage, and second, patterns of matchmaking and mate selection—we find that the first is not compatible with the second over any very extended period of time. In other words, "marriage squeezes" are always present or in process. The patterns of mate selection prevailing in a society at any one time are eventually influenced by changing demographic and social conditions and must shift in response to them. These shifts, in turn, affect all the patterns of marital alliance and nonalliance, the entire marriage map, and, in turn, the nature of the relationships and distances among the social strata. These processes are not yet well understood. But there is now underway a great deal of theoretical research and some empirical research, too, which is likely to shed additional light on these relationships.

Sociocultural factors in nonarranged and arranged marriages. The effects of cultural and social factors on patterns and practices of mate selection differ according to whether or not, or within what more-or-less formalized limits, eligible males and females reciprocally choose their own marriage partners. In nonarranged marriages where individual reciprocal choice determines mate selection, marriage tends to be: (a) *homogamous*—that is, it takes place primarily between persons with similar social, economic, cultural, and other such characteristics; and

(b) *endogamous*–it takes place mostly between members of the same or similar ascriptive social subgroups or collectivities.[7] The acceptability of deviations from homogamous and endogamous marriage varies over societies and changes over time. These variations have both demographic and other social-structural origins and correlates.

One demographic factor in the extent of homogamous and endogamous mate selection appears to be that of sheer physical access to eligible partners. Patterns of mobility notwithstanding, there is a strong tendency for persons to choose their partners from among eligibles living in close geographic proximity to their own and their parents' homes–even among young persons temporarily away from home. Thus, homogamous and endogamous marriage follows, to a considerable extent, from the fact of residential segregation alone. However, as we shall demonstrate below, other factors also operate to promote homogamy and diminish heterogamy. Among nonhomogamous marriages, hypergamous marriages (where females of lower rank or social status marry males of higher rank or status) are much more frequent than hypogamous marriages (where the rank or status of the male is lower than that of the female).

Matchmaking institutions and arranged and nonarranged marriages. The social institutions that directly affect matchmaking and mate selection in social groups where people choose their own marriage partners are basically different from those where marriages are arranged. In the first category are all those institutions operating to structure and bound, or to catalyze, the random meetings and interaction of eligible males and females. As Zelditch has noted:

> Even where mate selection is free, and instrumental calculations are unconscious if they operate at all, some mechanisms of mate selection tend to ensure that mates are at least of similar social rank. The control mechanisms are to some extent managed by parents, to some extent the result of the way in which a society's system of stratification affects interaction, and to some extent the result of peer group control over the dating process. (Zelditch, Jr., 1964, p. 688)

Thus, colleges and beaches, churches and nightclubs, offices and assembly lines, street corners and parlors are all places at which eligible males and females can meet and court. At the same time they tend to encourage the matching of likes and to discourage the matching of unlikes. In contrast, other kinds of institutions like hospitals, political parties, conventions, and ocean cruises, may provide arenas for the meeting of eligible unlikes.

[7] For a summary and discussion of some findings on the tendency toward homogamous and endogamous marriages in the United States, see Zelditch, Jr., 1964.

A wedding in the field can reflect the couple's life style. *(Wide World Photos)*

Where marriages are typically arranged by persons other than the marital partners themselves, the circumstances and agencies of matchmaking may vary widely. In many societies, either fathers, or both parents, or uncles, or sometimes other relatives may be assigned the duty of arranging marriages. Alternatively, matchmaking may be one of the duties of the social group's political, religious, or other functionaries. In some cases, matchmaking is a recognized occupation in its own right.

In societies in which marriages are arranged, the range and efficiency of matchmaking institutions affect not only mate selection but also people's chances of eventual marriage and their age patterns at marriage. Indeed, the arrangement of marriages may in many situations overcome possible geographic and social-class barriers to mating, thus expanding both range and variety of the marriage market. Exogamous arrangements, transactions between families of different rank, and marriage among the European nobility are cases in point. The institutions and mechanisms of mate selection in societies in which eligibles choose their own partners also affect—although perhaps not so obviously—the chances of eventual marriage and patterns of age at marriage. And these, in turn, will affect patterns of fertility and population growth (Hajnal, 1965).

SUMMARY

The frequency of marriage, the frequency and acceptability of nonmarriage, and patterns of age at marriage have been the traditional concerns of marriage research in population studies. In this chapter we have reviewed trends and variations in frequency of marriage and in age at marriage. But in addition we have introduced the topics of matchmaking and assortative mating against the background of more general population trends and constraints.

In most societies and in most periods of history, marriage has been virtually universal as the normal, desirable mode of existence for adults. Modern Europe has deviated markedly from the universal marriage pattern for some three centuries, with significant numbers of men and women remaining single. While the historically common pattern has been one of quite early marriage, especially for girls, in modern Europe marriage has tended to occur relatively late in life, with age at marriage usually varying directly with educational achievement or socioeconomic status for both males and females. In the United States, Canada, and Australia, remaining single has always been less frequent than in Europe, although marriage has not generally been universal as in the non-European societies. And in North America and Oceania, marriage has been, on the average, much earlier than in Europe. But both Europe and the countries of European settlement experienced marriage booms, a return to more nearly universal marriage, and to earlier marriage, beginning in the 1940s and continuing through the 1960s. Some return to delayed marriage seems to have taken place in the late 1960s and 1970s, but it remains to be seen if the frequencies of marriage and nonmarriage will shift.

The major attempt to explain the European pattern of late marriage and frequent nonmarriage finds the central cause in the desire to avoid marriage and family formation in the absence of sufficient economic security. Thus, young persons with no property, occupation, or assured employment have traditionally delayed marriage or avoided it entirely. In the middle of the twentieth century, a similar line of explanation goes, birth control was sufficiently well known and extensively adopted to enable more young persons to marry, and to marry younger, without the immediate entailment of childbearing and its responsibilities.

Responsibility for determining a young person's eligibility for marriage, his choice of a spouse, the various conditions of the betrothal, and indeed the residential, employment, and lifestyle conditions of the newlywed couple have traditionally been in the hands of parents or relatives, instead of being left to the young persons involved. Even in modern marriage, parents are typically able to manipulate the settings in which young persons of opposite sex are likely to meet and court. Conventions governing choice of marriage partner have varied over different societies and in different social groups and strata within a society. But a principle of homogamy, where the choice of a partner is informally limited by similarities in social and cultural characteristics, is found very frequently. Choice of marriage partners may depend not only on social conventions but also on the availability of socially acceptable eligible unmarrieds of appropriate age. Fertility trends or social changes may generate a marriage squeeze, where there is an imbalance between the number of eligible males and the number of eligible females from the point of view of both age and social acceptability. Resolution of a marriage squeeze can take place by delaying marriage—either for a short period, until new eligibles enter the marriage market, or indefinitely—or by changing the rules of mutual acceptability.

In the next chapter we turn to the study of fertility. Not only is fertility the major component of population growth and structural change today; it is also the key component of population policy and action because it is manipulatable. As we shall see, frequency and age at marriage are of central importance in determining levels of birth rates. Matchmaking and marriage choices have a crucial influence on the pattern of fertility for both individual couples and entire populations and societies.

9

Fertility Trends and Differentials

Notwithstanding current hopes for zero population growth and the historical declines in fertility in the West, in most countries of the world today birth rates are high, families are large, and many of the children born are actually unwanted. With death rates at, or converging to, low levels throughout the world, our understanding of population growth now rests mainly on our knowledge and understanding of fertility. Since no one wants the death rate to increase, our hopes for resolving population-growth problems—whether for the entire world or for individual societies and communities—rest entirely upon controlling the birth rate.

In this chapter we will look in some detail at fertility trends and differentials. We will consider the most recent fertility trends in the United States and elsewhere, then turn to an analysis of differential fertility, focusing on the factors which work toward the convergence of fertility patterns over time. Finally, we will review and evaluate the analytical frameworks and theoretical schemes—both sociological and nonsociological—which have been put forth to explain long-term shifts in birth rates and differential fertility.

TRENDS AND VARIATIONS IN FERTILITY

How have patterns of childbearing and levels of fertility changed over time? How do they differ in different countries and among the different social groups? Our answers to these questions come from a variety of sources. For trends since 1900, an extensive comparative analysis has been prepared by the United Nations Population Branch, and we shall draw upon this work. For data concerning previous trends in fertility, it will be necessary to turn to a number of separate sources. In discussing historical trends in fertility, we shall confine ourselves to the crude birth rate only, that is, to the number of annual live births per thousand persons in the mean (average) population.

Trends and Variations Before 1900

The crude birth rate in northwest Europe, excepting France, fluctuated around 35 per 1,000 throughout most of the nineteenth century. It began to decline to lower levels only as the century ended. The rate for Eastern Europe was higher, fluctuating around 45 per 1,000 throughout the nineteenth century. But at around the turn of the century, it declined to levels slightly below 40 per thousand (Carr-Saunders, 1936). Birth rates in Italy and southern Europe in the eighteenth and nineteenth centuries were evidently somewhat higher than those of northwestern Europe (Carr-Saunders, 1936; Cipolla, 1965; Frederici, 1968). And the birth rate in France began to decline even before the close of the eighteenth century, remaining substantially lower than that of the rest of Western Europe throughout the nineteenth century (Bourgeois-Pichat, 1965).

Estimates of the crude birth rate in North America suggest exceptionally high fertility levels. In the Catholic population of Quebec, French Canada, the crude birth rate is estimated to have reached about 60 per 1,000 in 1670, declining to about 45 per 1,000 in 1690. It recovered again to over 55 per 1,000 between 1710 and 1750 and to over 60 per 1,000 between 1770 and 1780. The rates declined thereafter to levels closer to those in Europe (Carr-Saunders, 1936). The crude birth rate for the white population of the United States is estimated to have been as high as 55 per 1,000 in 1780. It remained above 50 per 1,000 until after 1830, and declined thereafter to levels characteristic of late nineteenth-century Europe (Thompson & Whelpton, 1933).

Fertility Trends in the Twentieth Century

In a comparative analysis of fertility levels and trends throughout the world in the twentieth century, the United Nations Populations Branch (United Nations, 1965) divided the countries of the world into "low fertility" and "high fertility" countries. The first group has crude birth rates of under 30 per 1,000 and the second has rates of 30 per 1,000 or above.

Low fertility countries. The low fertility countries divide into three subgroups. The first subgroup includes the majority of countries in northern, western, and central Europe, together with Argentina, Australia, Canada, Israel, New Zealand, and the United States. In these

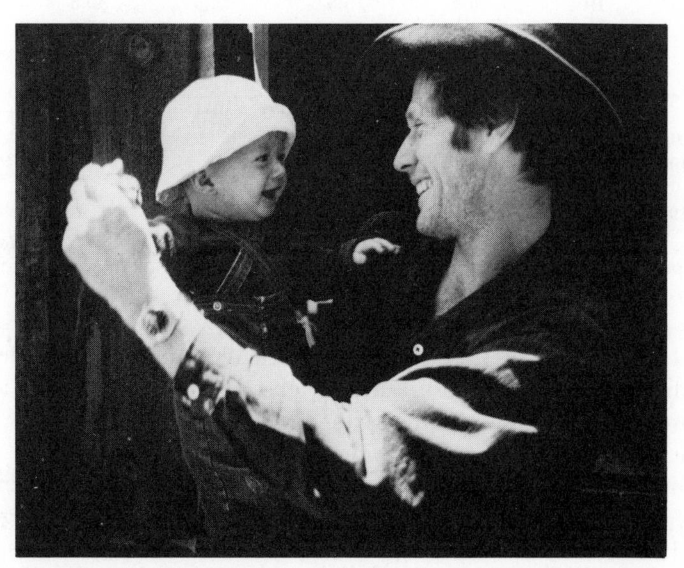

In a low-fertility country, one-child or two-children families are common. *(Ilka Hartman; Jeroboam, Inc.)*

countries fertility declined in the twentieth century until the 1930s, turned upward in the late 1930s or early 1940s, developed into a baby boom in the late 1940s and early 1950s, and then leveled off. In the United States, Canada, Australia and New Zealand, the baby boom extended somewhat longer, lasting through the 1950s and leveling off only in the 1960s. Table 9.1 covers selected countries of the first subgroup.

TABLE 9.1 Twentieth-Century Fertility Trends in France, Sweden, England and Wales, the United States, Israel, and Japan

Year	*France*	*Sweden*	*England and Wales*	*United States*	*Israel*	*Japan*
1900–1904	21.2	26.4	28.2	....	....	....
1905–1909	20.1	25.6	26.7	....	....	....
1910–1914	19.0	23.7	24.3	....	....	....
1915–1919	11.4	20.8	20.9	24.1	....	....
1920–1924	19.9	20.3	21.3	22.8	....	35.6
1925–1929	18.5	16.3	17.1	20.1	....	33.8
1930–1934	17.2	14.4	15.3	17.6	32.0[a]	....
1935–1939	15.1	14.5	14.9	17.2	24.7[b]	28.7[c]
1940–1944	14.6	17.7	15.5	19.9	25.1	....
1945–1949	20.2	19.0	18.0	23.4	29.0	33.7[d]
1950–1954	19.4	15.5	15.5	24.5	30.8	23.7
1955–1959	18.3	14.5	15.9	24.6	25.6	18.2
1960	17.9	13.7	17.2	23.7	23.9	17.2
1975	17.0	14.2	16.1	16.2	26.5	19.2

[a] 1930–1933
[b] 1938–1939
[c] 1937–1940
[d] 1947–1949

Source: 1900–1960: United Nations, Population Bulletin, *no. 7 (1963) table 6.2, Fig. 1.2, p. 5. 1975: Endpapers.*

The countries of the second low fertility subgroup include those of southern and southeastern Europe, except for Spain. They are for the most part less industrialized than those of the first subgroup. These countries were characterized by a more or less consistent decline in fertility throughout the 1930s, 1940s, and 1950s. Their average levels of fertility were much lower at the close of the 1950s than at the beginning of the 1930s. And, indeed, they were very close to the low levels of the first subgroup (see Table 9.2). In 1967, Romania adopted a policy severely restricting induced abortions, and a dramatic increase in the crude birth rate quickly ensued. However, the 1967 peak of almost 28 per 1,000 has since been followed by a declining crude birth rate, to 19 per 1,000 in 1975.

The last subgroup of low fertility countries includes only Japan and the Ryukyu Islands. They are both characterized by high fertility until the end of World War II, very sharply declining fertility in the 1950s, and some recovery of fertility most recently (U.N., Population Branch, 1965, table 4.4).

TABLE 9.2 Twentieth-Century Fertility Trends in Italy, Romania, Bulgaria, and Yugoslavia

Year	*Italy*	*Romania*	*Bulgaria*	*Yugoslavia*
1900–1904	32.6	39.6	40.7	. . . .
1905–1909	32.6	40.1	42.5	39.2
1910–1914	31.8	41.8	39.0	37.8
1915–1919	22.7	40.0	26.4	. . . .
1920–1924	30.1	37.6	39.6	35.3
1925–1929	27.3	35.4	34.2	33.9
1930–1934	24.5	33.7	30.3	33.0
1935–1939	23.2	30.2	24.1	27.9
1940–1944	20.8	23.2	22.1	. . . .
1945–1949	21.1	24.9	24.6	28.2
1950–1954	18.3	24.9	21.7	28.8
1955–1959	18.0	22.9	18.7	24.8
1960	18.3	19.1	17.8	23.5
1969	18.1	27.1	15.0	19.5
1975	16.0	19.3	16.2	18.2

Sources: United Nations, Population Bulletin, *no. 7 (1963), fig. 1.2, p. 5; United Nations,* Population Data Sheet *(1975); and 1975 data from endpapers.*

High-fertility countries. Virtually all the countries in the high fertility category are in Africa, Asia, Middle America, and South America. In these areas, all the countries except for Argentina, Cyprus, Israel, Japan, the Ryukyu Islands, Uruguay, and Zanzibar are in the high fertility category. Of the high fertility countries, only a few have reliable series of birth statistics extending back over a period of two decades or more. Thus, for the majority (including virtually all the countries of Africa), no historical series of birth data exist.

We can say merely that although some fluctuation is evident in these countries of high fertility, the overall picture is one of fairly stable birth rates at high levels. A number of countries, including Taiwan, Malaysia, Singapore, Mauritius, and Reunion, have experienced fertility declines since World War II. At least two countries in the Caribbean area, Jamaica and the dominion of Trinidad and Tobago, have experienced increasing fertility. Table 9.3 shows birth rates in some selected high fertility countries of Asia.

Geographic Variations in Fertility Levels

Differences among countries. There is a wide range of variation in current fertility levels of different countries, as Figure 9.1 shows. But some recent studies see an underlying trend in this variation over time

TABLE 9.3 Birth Rates in Selected Asian High Fertility Countries, 1955–1975

Year	*Taiwan*	*Hong Kong*	*Singapore*	*Malaysia*	*Sri Lanka*
1955	45.3	36.3	44.3	44.0	37.3
1956	44.8	37.0	44.4	46.7	36.4
1957	41.4	35.8	43.4	46.1	36.5
1958	41.7	37.4	42.0	43.3	35.8
1959	41.2	35.2	40.3	42.2	37.0
1960	39.5	36.0	38.7	40.9	36.6
1961	38.3	34.3	36.5	41.9	35.8
1962	37.4	33.3	35.1	40.4	35.5
1963	36.3	32.8	34.7	39.4	34.5
1964	34.5	30.1	33.2	39.1	33.1
1965	32.7	27.7	31.1	36.7	32.7
1966	32.5[a]	24.9	29.9	....	....
1969	29.0	23.0	27.0	....	32.2
1975	24.0	19.4	21.2	38.7	28.6

[a] Figure for 1966 is not comparable owing to more (i.e., earlier) registration of births in the latter part of the year in connection with the national census. This is reflected in very low birth rates reported for the first months of 1967.

Sources: Data for 1955 through 1966 from D. Kirk, Natality in the developing countries: Recent trends and prospects. In S. J. Behrman, L. Corsa, Jr., and R. Freedman, eds. Fertility and Family Planning: A World View *(Ann Arbor: University of Michigan Press, 1969), p. 80; United Nations* Population Bulletin, *no. 7 (1963), Fig. 1.2, p. 5; 1969 data from United Nations* Demographic Yearbook *(1969); 1975 data from endpapers.*

in at least some parts of the world, with the birth rates of different European countries converging in recent years (Glass, 1968).

In countries outside of Europe, however, birth rates are much less homogeneous. Moreover, there does not appear to be any readily identifiable set of factors with which to associate levels of crude birth rates in the high fertility countries of Asia, Africa, and Middle and South America.

Besides the national differences already noted, there are at least two other types of geographic variation in levels of fertility. These are regional variations, and variations by urban-rural designation or by size of place of residence.

Regional differences. Regional and state differences in fertility have been apparent in the United States from the earliest censuses. For instance, looking at child-woman ratios (numbers of children under five years of age per 1,000 women of childbearing age), the rates in the United States census of 1800 for rural white women aged 20 to 44 years were 1,319 for the entire country but 1,799 in the East South Central states and only 1,126 in the New England states. These regional differences were preserved throughout the nineteenth century and first decade of the

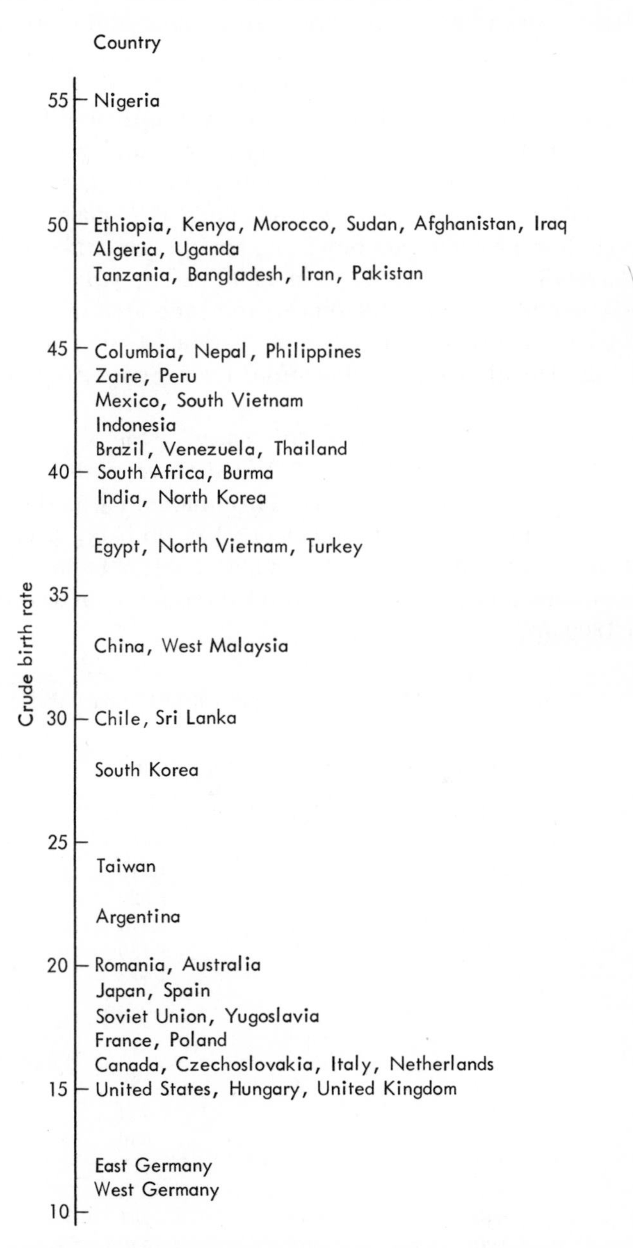

Figure 9.1 Countries by Crude Birth Rate, 1973. *Source: B. Berelson, "World Population: Status Report 1974"* Reports on Population, Family Planning, *no. 15 (January, 1974), p. 7. By permission of the Population Council.*

twentieth, a period of sharply declining fertility in the United States. In the 1940 census, when the national child-woman ratio had declined to its all-time low of 551 children per 1,000 rural white families, the rates in the New England and East South Central states were 443 and 648 respectively. With the rise in fertility in the 1940s, these differentials persisted. Thus, in 1950 the child-woman ratio for rural white women was 673 per 1,000 in the nation as a whole but 720 in the East South Central states and only 612 in the New England states. Regional variations have been much less pronounced, however, for the country's urban white women (Grabill, 1959). Moreover, in more recent years, and especially since 1960, overall regional differences from one area of the country to the next have notably diminished (U.S. National Center for Health Statistics, Public Health Service Publication, 1,000, Series 21 (1967), no. 11).

Rural-urban and size-of-place differences. One of the most widely recognized contrasts, especially in the United States, is that between high rural fertility and low urban fertility. This differential has been recorded in countries in Europe, but its incidence has probably been most pronounced in the United States and Canada. Table 9.4 shows the United States child-woman ratio by urban and rural residence for selected decades between 1800 and 1970.

TABLE 9.4 United States Urban and Rural Child-Woman Ratio, 1800–1970

Children Under 5 Years per 1,000 Females Aged 20–44				*Rural to Urban Ratio*
Year	*Total U.S.*	*Urban*	*Rural*	
1800	1,281	845	1,319	1.56
1810	1,290	900	1,329	1.48
1820	1,236	831	1,276	1.57
1830	1,134	708	1,189	1.68
1840	1,070	701	1,134	1.61
....	....	....	....	....
....	....	....	....	....
....	....	....	....	....
1910	609	469	782	1.67
1920	581	471	744	1.58
1930	485	388	658	1.70
1940	400	311	551	1.77
1950	551	479	673	1.41
1960	689	653	784	1.20
1970	520	501	579	1.16

Source: For 1850–1950, W. F. Grabill, The fertility of the United States population, in D. J. Bogue, The Population of the United States *(New York: Free Press, 1959); for 1960–1970, United States Bureau of the Census,* Characteristics of the Population, *Vol. 1, 1960, 1970.*

Within the United States and Canada there have been regional variations in the extent of urban-rural fertility differentials. Similarly, there are broad variations among the different countries of Europe (Glass, 1968, app. 3). Finally, there is now considerable evidence that urban-rural fertility differentials exist in the high fertility countries of Africa, Asia, and Latin America (U.N. Population Branch, 1965).

Fertility Differences Related to Socioeconomic, Religious, and Racial Characteristics

Other characteristics related to fertility are the socioeconomic, religious and racial, and psychological traits of individuals and couples. Studies about the relationship of fertility to these characteristics probably had their beginning with the post-World War I publication of fertility and child mortality data obtained in the 1911 census of England and Wales, and their number has been increasing steadily ever since. The main body of these studies has been concerned with the measurement and analysis of relationships between fertility and the components of socioeconomic status. However, a number of investigations have been concerned also with the influence on fertility of religion, race, and ethnicity.[1]

We will confine our present review to a summary of the findings of some of these studies; later in this chapter we shall see how some of these findings are incorporated into explanations and theories of individual fertility behavior and the fertility levels associated with some social institutions, practices, and behavior patterns.

Some findings on fertility and socioeconomic status. In the low fertility countries of Europe, North America, and Oceania, there was for some time a marked inverse relationship between fertility and some of the components of socioeconomic status, like income, education, and occupational level. This meant that people at the upper socioeconomic levels, or getting there, had fewer children than those in lower classes. More recently, however, considerable evidence has pointed to a growing convergence of fertility rates, or at least to substantially diminishing differentials, among the different socioeconomic categories (especially when certain other characteristics, like religion, rural-urban migration status, and socioeconomic background, have been held constant). At the same

[1] Among the most important summaries of differential fertility findings are Ryder, 1959; National Bureau of Economic Research, 1960; United Nations, "Recent Fertility Trends," 1958; United Nations, *Population Bulletin* No. 7-1963, (1965); Goldberg, 1965; Freedman, 1962; and Goldscheider, 1971. In addition, the summary in United Nations, *Determinants and Consequences,* 1953, remains a basic statement in this area, now supplemented by a new summary in the 2d Edition (1973) of that work.

time, in the upper socioeconomic groups, there has been growing evidence of a direct relationship between fertility and income, educational level, and occupational status.

While the convergence of fertility patterns among socioeconomic groups is usually believed to take place as a result of the lower groups adopting the low fertility patterns characteristic of the middle or higher groups, the opposite has been the case among fairly recent United States childbearing female cohorts (*cohort* refers to all women born in the same span of years). There was a decrease in fertility in the 1906–1910 cohort compared with the cohort born between 1901 and 1905. But from then on there were increases only. Among the least-educated group, the decline continued through the 1911–1915 cohort. But among the next two groups this decrease occurred only in the cohort of 1906–1910. Among the better-educated groups, those who had completed high school or more, the increase in fertility started very early, among those born between 1906 and 1910. And their fertility increase is much more marked throughout than is that of the less-educated women. The increases are especially sharp among college-educated women. Thus, the convergence of fertility levels has come about because of a sharp rise in fertility among the higher socioeconomic groups rather than because of a decrease among the lower groups (Campbell, 1965).

However, it seems very likely now that the completed family size of subsequent cohorts of American women will be substantially smaller. This trend is already reflected in current low birth rates. And the trend toward convergence of fertility among the different socioeconomic groups will continue, but at much lower levels. One kind of evidence is in reports of numbers of births expected by currently married women. In recent surveys it has been found that women currently in each childbearing age group have had fewer births, and *expect* to have fewer births, than women reaching the same ages in earlier years (see Table 9.5). Thus, for example, in Table 9.5, women between the ages of 18 and 24 in 1967 had already had an average of 1.173 births per women (1173 per thousand) and expected, on the average to have a total of 2.852 births per woman. But women of the same age in 1974 had had, on the average, less than one birth per woman (848 births per thousand). And they expected to have, on the average, only 2.165 births. Of this 1974 group, only about seven percent of white wives and eleven percent of black wives expect to have four or more children during their lifetimes, compared to one-third of white wives and almost half the black wives aged 35 to 39 (see Figure 9.2).

Some details of the shifts in fertility are available from a somewhat earlier (1971) survey which shows that one factor accounting for some of

TABLE 9.5 Average Number of Births to Date and Lifetime Births Expected by Wives 18 to 39 Years Old, by Age: 1967 to 1974

Year	Total 18 to 39 years	By Age at Date of Survey: 18 to 24 years	25 to 29 years	30 to 34 years	35 to 39 years
Lifetime Births Expected per 1,000 Wives					
1974	2,550	2,165	2,335	2,724	3,091
1973	2,638	2,261	2,386	2,804	3,233
1972	2,678	2,255	2,452	2,915	3,218
1971	2,779	2,375	2,619	2,989	3,257
1967	3,118	2,852	3,037	3,288	3,300
Births to Date per 1,000 Wives					
1974	1,973	848	1,691	2,539	3,063
1973	2,044	895	1,755	2,623	3,189
1972	2,090	928	1,807	2,749	3,173
1971	2,146	952	1,949	2,802	3,210
1967	2,427	1,173	2,312	3,050	3,214

Source: U.S. Bureau of the Census, Current Population Reports, *Series P-20, no. 269 (September, 1974).*

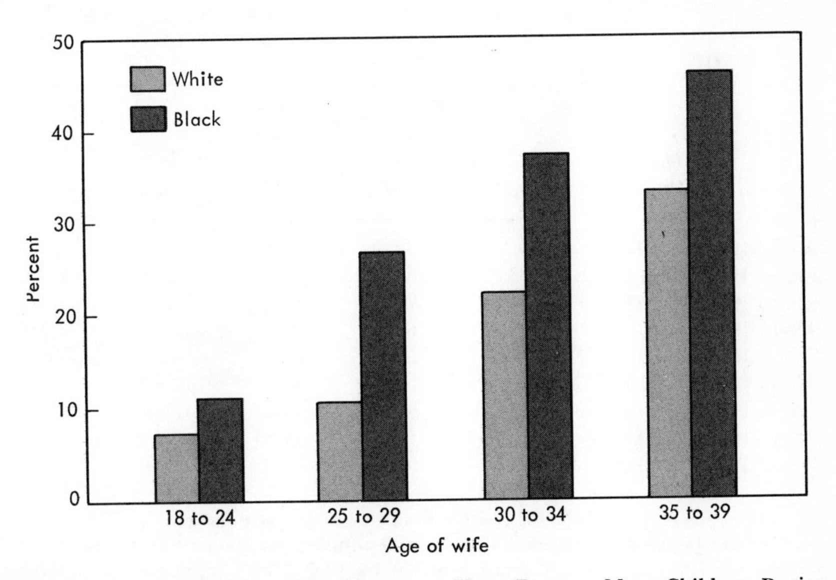

Figure 9.2 Percent of Wives Who Expect to Have Four or More Children During Their Lifetime. *Source: U.S. Bureau of the Census,* Current Population Reports *Series P-20, no. 269 (September, 1974).*

the decline in fertility levels is a trend away from early marriages and early childbearing (see Table 9.6). As the Census Bureau analysts report:

> One factor which accounts for some of the decline in fertility levels is a trend away from early marriages and early childbearing. The data indicate that the long-time trend toward earlier marriages was reversed 15 years ago; consequently, only 17 percent of the women born in 1950 to 1955 married by age 18, in contrast to approximately 30 percent of the women born in 1935 to 1939. The decrease in early marriages is paralleled by a drop in fertility levels for young women 18 years old and younger, from 204 per 1,000 women among those born in 1935 to 1939 down to to 104 per 1,000 women among those born in 1950 to 1955. The recent decline in fertility is not simply a result of changes in values and ideals among *young* women. Older cohorts of women have also begun to reduce their rates of childbearing. Data . . . show that women born in 1940 to 1944 are expected to have about 680 children per 1,000 women during the period when they advance from age 25 to age 30. Women born five years earlier in 1935 to 1939 added 800 children per 1,000 women from age 25 to 30, and the 1930 to 1934 cohort of women show 946 as a comparable

TABLE 9.6 Childbearing at Early Ages: Percent Who Married and Children Ever Born per 1,000 Women Ever Married, by Ages 18 and 25, for Cohorts of Women Born in 1900 to 1955 in the United States[a]

	By Middle of Age 18			*By Middle of Age 25*		
		Children			*Children*	
Year woman was born	*Percent married by this age*	*Per 1,000 women*	*Per 1,000 women ever married*	*Percent married by this age*	*Per 1,000 women*	*Per 1,000 women ever married*
1950 to 1955	16.6[b]	104[b]	627[b]	–[c]	–[c]	–[c]
1945 to 1949	21.2	135	637	82.8[b]	1,203[b]	1,453[b]
1940 to 1944	25.6	181	707	86.1	1,528	1,775
1935 to 1939	29.7	204	687	85.8	1,747	2,036
1930 to 1934	26.2	157	599	85.0	1,535	1,806
1925 to 1929	21.9	123	562	81.9	1,280	1,563
1920 to 1924	20.2	117	579	77.7	1,061	1,366
1910 to 1919	19.3	112	580	71.5	920	1,285
1900 to 1909	19.5	101	518	68.9	947	1,374

[a] Data as of June 1971, for civilian noninstitutional population.

[b] Data for 1950 to 1955 and 1945 to 1949 adjusted for the part of the cohort that had not reached the specified ages (18 or 25) by June 1971. See source for method of adjustment.

[c] – represents zero or rounds to zero.

Source: U.S. Bureau of the Census, Current Population Reports *Series P-20, no. 263 (April, 1974).*

figure. Similar trends toward lower fertility also appear in the number of additional children women have had from age 30 to 35. (U.S. Bureau of the Census [April, 1974], pp. 1–2)

Data from the same survey as well as other census materials show that similar trends are taking place among all the educational-level groupings of women, and among the several major racial and ethnic groups in the United States. Rindfuss and Sweet (1975) have shown that *all* these population categories have been characterized by a common historical pattern, featuring the rise in fertility immediately after World War II, a brief leveling off thereafter, the extended baby boom of the 1950s and early 1960s, and a sharp drop in fertility beginning the second half of the 1960s (see Figures 9.3 and 9.4).

These trends notwithstanding, there remain substantial differences in fertility among white American women classified by socioeconomic status, and there are even sharper socioeconomic differences among black women. In the 1971 Current Population Survey, it was found that the mean current parity (number of live-born children, up to the date of the investigation) of white American college-graduate women ages 25 to 34 was 1.2, compared to 2.8 births to white women with 1 to 3 years of high

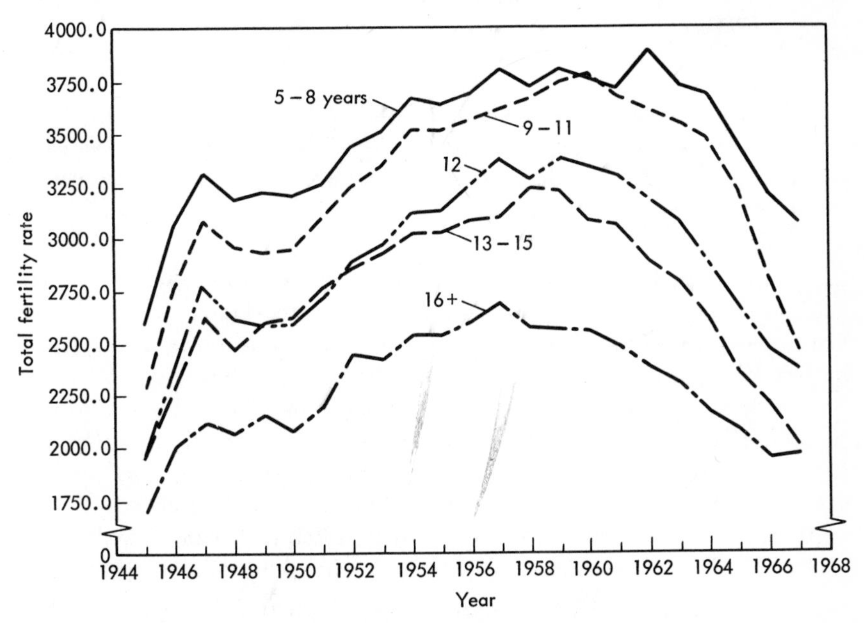

Figure 9.3 Total Fertility Rates for Five Education Groups: 1945–1967. *Source: Ronald Rindfuss and James Sweet, "The Pervasiveness of Postwar Fertility Trends in the United States," Center for Demography and Ecology, University of Wisconsin, Working Paper No. 75-24, August, 1975.*

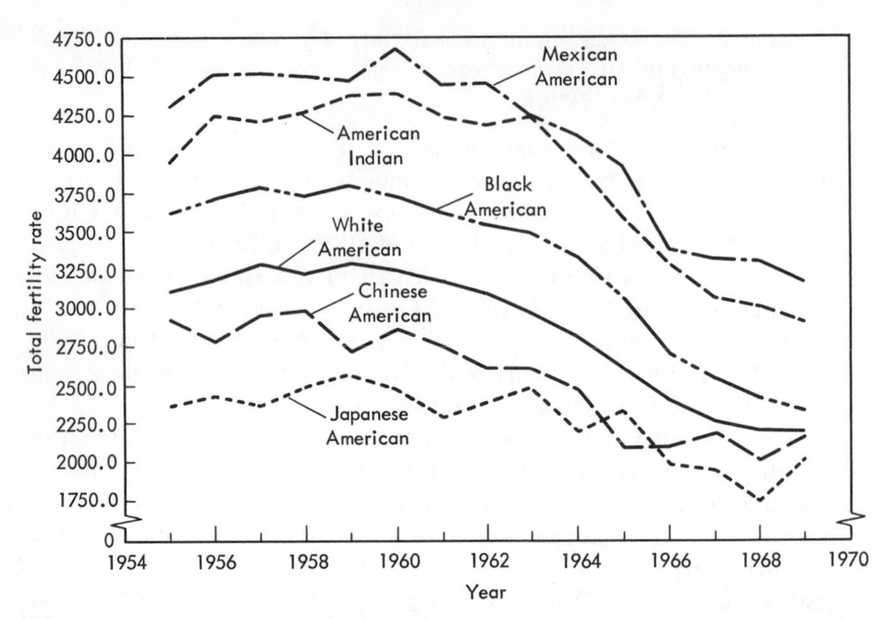

Figure 9.4 Total Fertility Rates for Six Racial or Ethnic Groups: 1955–1969. *Source: Ronald Rindfuss and James Sweet, "The Pervasiveness of Postwar Fertility Trends in the United States," Center for Demography and Ecology, University of Wisconsin, Working Paper No. 75-24, August, 1975.*

school (see Table 9.7). Mean current parity for black college-graduate women in the same age category was only 1.7, compared to 3.2 births to black women with 1 to 3 years of high school. We shall have occasion to cite other findings of this study in the present chapter.

Religious, racial, educational, and socioeconomic differentials. In the United States, Canada, Ireland, and the Netherlands, the fertility of Catholics has long been higher than that of non-Catholics. The fertility of Jews has generally been lower than that of Christians. In India, the Parsees have had much lower fertility rates than other religious groups, but the differences among those other groups are small. In Lebanon, the fertility of Moslem Arabs is higher than that of Christian Arabs.

A question frequently posed about religious differentials in fertility concerns the extent to which such differences simply reflect the socioeconomic status characteristic of each different religious group. Do Catholics have high fertility simply because their average educational attainment or occupational status is lower than that of Protestants? Is the lower fertility of Jews simply a reflection of their higher average educational attainment or occupational status?

TABLE 9.7 Children Ever Born per 1,000 Women 20 to 44 Years Old by Age, Race, and Years of School Completed, Specified Survey Dates: June, 1971; January, 1969; and April, 1960

Race and Educational Attainment	*Women 20 to 24 Years Old*				*Women 25 to 34 Years Old*				*Women 35 to 44 Years Old*			
	Number 1971 (thousands)	*Children ever born per 1,000 women*			*Number 1971 (thousands)*	*Children ever born per 1,000 women*			*Number 1971 (thousands)*	*Children ever born per 1,000 women*		
		1971[a]	*1969*[a]	*1960*[b]		*1971*[a]	*1969*[a]	*1960*[b]		*1971*[a]	*1969*[a]	*1960*[b]
White												
Years of school completed												
Elementary: Less than 8 years	138	1,406	1,345	1,433	386	2,642	3,000	2,705	609	3,665	3,814	3,101
8 years	149	1,383	1,500	1,581	457	2,860	3,164	2,548	616	3,515	3,311	2,686
High School: 1 to 3 years	950	1,444	1,483	1,539	1,815	2,842	2,904	2,461	1,810	3,225	3,171	2,511
4 years	3,689	704	677	912	5,620	2,090	2,197	2,099	4,878	2,843	2,777	2,244
College: 1 to 3 years	1,963	299	247	425	1,492	1,796	1,858	1,932	1,201	2,877	2,790	2,219
4 years or more	773	144	177	296	1,583	1,224	1,290	1,476	1,011	2,427	2,480	1,952
Black												
Years of school completed												
Elementary: 0 to 8 years	54	(B)	1,769	1,752	184	3,272	3,326	3,181	328	4,012	4,457	3,306
High school: 1 to 3 years	271	1,336	1,823	1,622	444	3,171	3,358	2,835	359	4,081	3,802	2,824
4 years or more	487	688	686	954	575	2,033	2,326	2,096	399	3,033	3,054	2,217
College: 1 year or more	237	312	323	459	248	1,750	1,542	1,504	170	2,182	2,335	1,747

[a] For the noninstitutional population.
[b] For the total population.
(B) Base less than 75,000 in 1971.
Source: U.S. Bureau of the Census, Current Population Reports, *Series P-20, no. 263 (April, 1974) table 51.*

Since United States censuses do not give us data on religion, it has not been possible to draw upon census fertility tabulations in studying religious differences. However, the findings of a sequence of nationwide fertility studies in the United States indicate that these differences in fertility remain even when socioeconomic status is taken into account.[2] Fertility of Catholic women is higher, and fertility of Jewish women lower, than would be expected simply on the basis of education, income, place of residence, husbands' occupation, or other indicators of socioeconomic status. Indeed for Catholics, there is some evidence of a direct relationship between socioeconomic status and fertility. The relationship between social class and fertility appears to be U-shaped among Catholics: higher and lower socioeconomic categories both have and expect higher fertility than do the middle categories.

Data comparing black and white fertility from the recent Current Population Survey are shown in Table 9.7. The data show that the lower the educational achievement level, the greater is the difference between black and white fertility. Among those with only grade school education, black women between the ages of 35 and 44 reported an average of four births, compared to 3.5 births for white women in 1971. Fertility differences between black and white women who completed high school or attended college are small, though black fertility remains measurably higher. But among those who graduated from college, fertility rates of white women are substantially higher than those of black women. This finding supports earlier findings of national surveys and also of the 1960 census.

In the 1960 data, the fertility of nonwhite women (primarily black, but including small proportions of other nonwhites which varied by region and types of communities) exceeded that of white women by 26 percent in the United States as a whole. However, this excess was very highly concentrated in the South, where nonwhite fertility exceeded white fertility by 42 percent. Outside of the South, nonwhite fertility was only moderately higher than white fertility: by seven percent in the Northeast, by 12 percent in the North Central regions of the country, and by ten percent in the West (Whelpton, Campbell, Patterson, 1966, table 184).

Reporting the findings of the 1960 Growth of American Families study, an investigation of family planning whose scope was comparable to that of a census, Whelpton, Campbell, and Patterson explored data from that study, from the 1960 census, and from previous studies bearing upon white-nonwhite fertility differentials in the United States. Their analysis of color differences in actual fertility in 1960 and in expected future fertility reported by white and nonwhite respondents has given us

[2] For a careful review, critical discussion, and extensive bibliography see C. Goldscheider, 1971, chap. 10, "Religion, Minority Group Status, and Fertility." See also Ryder and Westoff, 1971, pp. 66–86.

detailed information on these differentials. Examining the socioeconomic and regional variations in nonwhite-white fertility differentials, Whelpton, Campbell, and Patterson (1966) observed:

> When we come to nonwhite couples without any previous Southern farm residence, we find average past and expected numbers of births that do not differ significantly from those of . . . the white sample. In other words, by the time nonwhite couples are one generation or more removed from the rural South, their fertility is very much like that of the white population. (p. 342) [3]

> When we consider the white-nonwhite fertility differentials, we find that the largest differentials exist among couples who have relatively low educational attainment (grade-school or incomplete high school) and who have lived or are living on Southern farms. Among couples with no Southern farm background and among well-educated couples, white and nonwhite do not differ greatly in their fertility.
>
> We can present these facts more clearly by dividing the nonwhite and white samples into three main groups:
>
> I. Those who have completed high school or have had some college education and those with less education who have never lived on a Southern farm.
> II. Those who have a grade school or incomplete high school education and who have previously lived on a Southern farm.
> III. Those who have a grade school or incomplete high school education and who were living on a Southern farm when interviewed.
>
> Within Group I, nonwhites have very nearly the same past and expected fertility as whites . . . inasmuch as this group contains 63 percent of the nonwhite sample, we can say that a majority of nonwhite couples have and expect about the same number of children as white couples in similarly defined socioeconomic groups. . . .
>
> Within Group II, nonwhites have moderately higher past and expected fertility than whites . . . This group contains 11 percent of the nonwhite sample. Finally, within Group III, nonwhites have much higher fertility than whites. . . . This group contains 26 percent of the nonwhite sample.
>
> The most important facts brought out here are (a) that the fertility of a majority of nonwhites does not differ widely from that of whites in similar socioeconomic groups, and (b) that the differences that exist for the remainder of nonwhites are closely associated with characteristics that will have less influence in the future than they do now—previous and current Southern farm residence and low educational achievement. These findings give us reason to believe that fertility differences between whites and nonwhites will become narrower. (pp. 347–8) [4]

[3] Selections from Pascal K. Welpton, Arthur A. Campbell and John E. Patterson, *Fertility and Family Planning in the United States* (copyright © 1966 by Princeton University Press), p. 342.

[4] Selections from Pascal K. Welpton, Arthur A. Campbell and John E. Patterson, *Fertility and Family Planning in the United States* (copyright © 1966 by Princeton University Press), pp. 347–48.

These findings and conclusions are essentially supported and sustained in the 1965 sequel, the National Fertility Study. Indeed Ryder and Westoff, in reporting findings of this study, are able to assert that "with the ever-diminishing importance of rural life in this country, the rapid disappearance of racial differences in fertility seems imminent" (Ryder & Westoff, 1971; p. 91).

Socioeconomic differentials in less developed high fertility countries. Do Ryder and Westoff's conclusions apply to other countries besides the United States? If they do, we should expect that, as development, urbanization, and especially women's education proceed in less developed high fertility countries, lower fertility levels will result from changing patterns of marriage and adoption of family limitation practices in the higher social classes, among educated groups of women, and in the most developed geographic areas. Insofar as such differentials are actually found, special importance is attached to them. For they are commonly viewed by demographers and other population-watchers as indicators of the beginnings of fertility control and heralding a downward inflection in the birth rate and in the rate of natural increase.

In the high fertility countries of Latin America, Asia, and Africa, some signs of an inverse relationship between components of socioeconomic status and fertility have been found. But this relationship is much less consistent than in the low fertility countries. A number of studies reveal only few signs of such fertility differentials. Others yield convincing evidence at least of differentials associated with the educational achievement of women and the occupational status of husbands (see summaries in Beshers, 1967; and in United Nations, Population Branch no. 7, 1963).

The recent examples of declines in fertility in LDCs lend credence to the idea that there may be emerging geographic, ethnic and socioeconomic fertility differentials (Abu-Lughod, 1965; Yaukey, 1961). But this remains a topic for more intensive research as more detailed data become available for these countries.

EXPLANATIONS OF FERTILITY TRENDS AND VARIATIONS

The attempt to explain broad trends and variations in fertility turned early to the investigation of the social and cultural factors that influence fertility. Such explanations have in considerable measure been guided by the framework, proposed by Kingsley Davis and Judith Blake (1968), of several kinds of *intermediate variables* through which social and cultural factors are logically able to influence fertility:

I. Factors affecting exposure to intercourse
   A. Those governing the formation and dissolution of unions in the reproductive period, such as age of entry into sexual unions, extent of permanent celibacy, proportion of women entering sexual unions, and amount of reproductive period spent after or between unions.
   B. Those governing the exposure to intercourse within unions, such as voluntary abstinence, involuntary abstinence (from impotence, illness, and unavoidable but temporary separations), and coital frequency (excluding periods of abstinence).

II. Factors affecting exposure to conception, such as fecundity or infecundity, as affected by involuntary causes, use or nonuse of contraception, or fecundity or infecundity as affected by voluntary causes (for instance, sterilization, subincision, or other medical treatment).

III. Factors affecting gestation and successful parturition, including foetal mortality from involuntary causes and foetal mortality from voluntary causes like induced abortion. (Davis & Blake, 1956, p. 197)

In the view of Davis and Blake, *any* social or cultural factor affecting fertility must do so in some way which can be identified and classified under one of these intermediate variables. Accordingly, these variables provide a framework for assessing the weight, importance, or relevance of each social or cultural factor.

There is current research in process on all of Davis and Blake's intermediate variables. But two of these variables—age at marriage and extent of permanent celibacy, and use or nonuse of contraception—are central to many recent studies. We have already discussed the first of these variables, marriage, in the previous chapter. We will turn now to a very brief review of some of the most important findings concerning the second variable, contraception. This discussion will be extended even further in Chapter 13.

Voluntary Birth Control: A Brief Review of Selected Studies

The first studies bearing on the frequency of voluntary family limitation were undertaken in the United States in the 1930s. These studies yielded data indicating that the explanation of fertility differentials—and probably of trends over time in fertility—lay in voluntary, rather than biologically based, fertility restraints (see the summary in Kiser, 1967). These earliest studies were followed in the United States by the Indianapolis Study, which began in 1938 (Kiser & Whelpton, 1946–1958), and in England by a study in the early forties which was sponsored by the United Kingdom Royal Commission on Population (Lewis-Fanning, 1949). The

Indianapolis Study showed the widespread practice of family limitation, but the samples on which it was based were so limited that no assessment could be made of the extent of family limitation in the total population. In the Lewis-Fanning study, contraception was shown to the more widely used among younger couples. It was estimated that some type of contraception was practiced by about 66 percent of women who had married between 1935 and 1939, but by just 40 percent of those married in 1910–1919 and by only 15 percent of those married before 1910.

In the "Growth of American Families" study of 1955, 2,700 white wives between ages 18 and 39 years were interviewed. Seventy percent reported having used some method of contraception specifically to avoid conception (these women were called "motive users") and an additional eleven percent reported "douching for cleanliness only." These two groups combined were considered to be "action users" of contraception —a grand total of 81 percent of the subjects (Freedman, Whelpton, & Campbell, 1959). Of the women aged 35 to 39 (those closest to completed fertility in this study), a somewhat lower proportion, 65 percent, were "motive users." Some regional correlates were found to correspond to their use of contraceptives: 74 percent of all women residing in the suburbs of the largest cities, 69 percent of those residing in both small cities (2,500 to 50,000 inhabitants) and large cities (over 50,000 inhabitants), and 52 percent of the farm respondents were in this group of "motive users."

In a sequel to this study (Whelpton, Campbell, & Patterson, 1966), about eleven percent of the white couples were found to be sterile (mainly because of surgical sterilizations, about half of which had been indicated by pathological disorders and half for contraceptive purposes). Some 81 percent reported having practiced contraception already, and another six percent reported plans to practice it in the future (most of these were recently married couples wishing to have one or two children first). It was found that people of lower educational achievement (grade school only) were more likely to begin the practice of contraception only after several pregnancies, and that Catholics were more likely than Protestants to delay the practice of contraception or never to use it (see Table 9.8).

In a 1965 follow-up on the Growth of American Families study, high proportions of married women again reported the use of contraception (Ryder & Westoff, 1969). However, a new and important finding was that a majority of those planning their families had failed either to achieve the number of births desired or to time the births according to plan. Among those who had intended to have no more children, only 26 percent were successful on both these counts, with the rest experiencing either "number failure" or "timing failure." Among those intending to have more children, the probability of a "timing failure" was estimated at 67 percent (Ryder & Westoff 1969).

TABLE 9.8 Percentage of White Couples Who Have Used or Expect to Use Contraception, By Wife's Education and Religion: 1955, 1960, and 1965

	Total[a]			*Protestant*			*Catholic*		
Education	*1955*	*1960*	*1965*	*1955*	*1960*	*1965*	*1955*	*1960*	*1965*
Percent Have Used Contraception									
Total	70	81	84	75	84	87	57	70	78
College	85	88	88	90	93	90	62	67	81
High school, 4 years	74	83	86	80	86	88	61	73	82
High school, 1–3 years	66	78	83	70	80	86	59	73	75
Grade school	49	66	65	53	73	72	41	54	55
Percent Have Used or Expect to Use Contraception									
Total	79	87	90	83	90	91	67	80	87
College	88	93	94	92	96	95	71	82	89
High school, 4 years	83	90	92	88	92	92	71	83	90
High school, 1–3 years	76	85	88	79	87	90	68	80	85
Grade school	59	72	75	63	77	79	49	64	72
Number of Couples in Sample									
Total	2713	2414	2912	1817	1596	1902	787	668	845
College	417	427	584	306	284	399	73	79	136
High school, 4 years	1236	1153	1420	794	752	909	396	341	438
High school, 1–3 years	681	579	641	457	392	434	208	168	177
Grade school	377	255	267	260	168	159	110	80	94

[a] Includes women who are neither Catholic nor Protestant.

Source: C. F. Westoff and N. B. Ryder, Practice of contraception in the U.S.A. In S. J. Behrman, L. Corsa, Jr., and R. Freedman, eds., Fertility and Family Planning. A World View. *(Ann Arbor: University of Michigan Press, 1969), Table 12, p. 408.*

Table 9.8 shows other results of the 1965 study. By 1965, some 90 percent of white couples reported either past, or expected future, use of contraception—a figure which was up from the 87 percent in 1960 and 79 percent in 1955. In Table 9.8, two kinds of convergences in extent of use of contraception are evident: those between Catholics and Protestants, and those between groups of different education level. In the 1955 survey 83 percent of Protestant couples, but only 67 percent of Catholic couples reported past or expected future use of contraceptives. But by 1965, these percentages were markedly closer: 91 percent of Protestant and 87 percent of Catholic couples.

The 12 percentage point spread between the "college" and "high school 1-3-year" groups in 1955 (88 percent of the former and 76 percent of the latter reporting past or expected used of contraception in 1955) was reduced to a six percentage point difference by 1965. There were increases in both of these categories, but the increase for the "high school 1–3 year" group was much steeper. The "grade school" group increased its percentage of those expecting to practice contraception faster than any other category, similarly reducing the differences between the education category groups over the time period studied. Thus, the data from the sequence of national fertility surveys portray a movement on all color, religious, and social fronts in the direction of near-universal practice of contraception among American couples.

The Decline of Unwanted Fertility

In the 1970 National Fertility Study, the investigators probed still further into the issue of planned versus unplanned—or, more directly, of wanted versus unwanted—fertility in the United States. The study examined several aspects of this issue, including shifts in the numbers of children wanted over successive surveys in 1965 and 1970, and the degree of effectiveness in preventing unwanted births. In an analysis prepared for the Commission on Population and the American Future, Norman B. Ryder and Charles F. Westoff (1972) found that the number of children wanted has declined. These declines are most pronounced among white Catholic women, and group differences in wanted fertility are now very minimal. A second important finding was that the rate of unwanted births has declined dramatically, reflecting recent improvements in fertility regulation. The rate of unwanted births is calculated with reference to the number of "woman-years of exposure to risk." In Table 9.9, it is seen that the rates reported in the 1970 survey declined relative to those of the 1965 survey most dramatically among black and white Catholic women younger and relatively recently married. These are the groups which previously had highest levels of unwanted fertility.

TABLE 9.9 Unwanted Births per Thousand Woman-Years of Exposure to Risk, for Those with Consistent Histories, and Wanting at Least Two Births: Selected Cohorts, by Race and Religion, 1965 and 1970

	Age		*Duration of Marriage*		
	40–44	*35–39*	*10–14*	*5–9*	*0–4*
Total					
1965	35	60	78	130	167
1970	36	53	57	64	85
Black					
1965	96	186	211	236	258
1970	99	100	108	108	136
White					
1965	31	50	66	117	124
1970	32	47	53	59	74
White non-Catholic					
1965	30	46	64	99	101
1970	28	42	50	61	78
White Catholic					
1965	36	63	74	175	282
1970	46	66	60	54	65

Source: N. B. Ryder and C. F. Westoff, "Wanted and Unwanted Fertility in the United States: 1965 and 1970" in C. F. Westoff and R. Parke, Jr., Demographic and Social Aspects of Population Growth, *Vol. I of The Commission on Population and The American Future Reports (Washington, D.C.: Government Printing Office, 1972), p. 481.*

MICROANALYTIC AND MACROANALYTIC THEORIES OF FERTILITY

How are we to understand and explain the childbearing customs of societies and behavior of individuals and couples? How should we account for their change or, for that matter, for their persistence? A major issue in fertility research turns upon the relative promise and importance of microanalytic versus macroanalytic levels of investigation and explanation.

To render the issue more concrete, we may reconsider briefly the historical trends in fertility. The general form of these trends is mapped or depicted in Figure 9.5: initially high fertility rates (A); followed by a period of downward inflection (B); followed by a period of declining fertility (C); then a point or period ending the decline (D); and finally, a leveling off of fertility at lower rates (E). There are always variations in

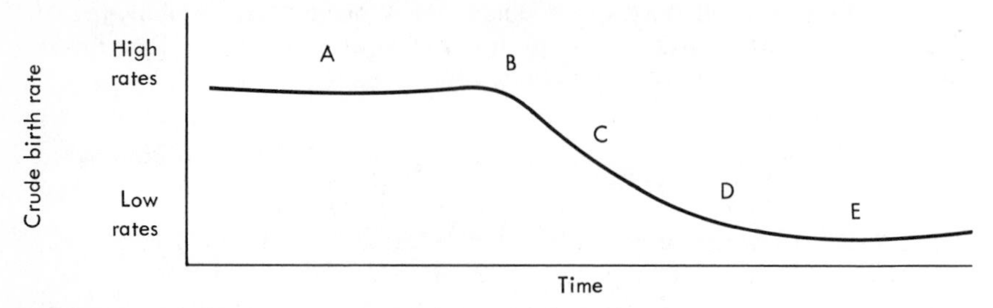

Figure 9.5 General Form of the Historical Trend in Fertility.

initial levels (A) of fertility, in the time and circumstances under which the downward inflection (B) occurs, and so on. Both microanalytic and macroanalytic theories of fertility bear upon the understanding of such variations.

Microanalytic theories of population growth are concerned with two major aspects of fertility. These are (a) individual survival or life span, variations in individual survival or life span, and the causes and correlates of both; and (b) the fertility of individuals or couples, variations in number and spacing of births, and causes and correlates of such variations. In contrast, the subject matter of macroanalytic theories of population growth consist of: (a) societal patterns of fertility and mortality; and (b) the structural and institutional features of societies which bear upon survival, mortality, and fertility. In particular, macroanalytic theories seek to account for societal variations in growth patterns in terms of structural attributes of entire societies or collectivities. We can review here only very briefly a few important examples of microanalytic and macroanalytic explanations of fertility, and a few notable attempts to reconcile them.

Microanalytic Theories

We shall present three examples of microanalytic theories of fertility. The first seeks to link individual fertility decisions and behavior to declining mortality; the second seeks to link individual fertility to the preservation or enhancement of social status; and the third links individual patterns to utility-cost considerations in the economic sense.

The declining mortality theory. The declining mortality explanation of declines in fertility has two key arguments. First, it holds that declining mortality implies a need for fewer children to be born. In order to assure a desired family size, or that children will survive to look after their elderly parents, or that a given number of children will survive to "continue the family line," parents no longer have to raise large families. The second argument is that declines in mortality actually impose objective hardship upon families having to support and educate ever-larger numbers of surviving offspring. There are simply more offspring surviving than used to be the case, and this means that today's families conceiving the same number of children as earlier families end up with more mouths to feed. Therefore, those people who are alert enough to recognize the implications of declining mortality, and those who have access to knowledge, means, and social support for controlling fertility, have taken steps to control their fertility.

Probably the most systematic formulation and exploration of the declining mortality theory is contained in a series of papers by D. M. Heer, D. O. Smith, and D. A. May (Heer, 1966; May & Heer, 1968; and Heer & Smith, 1969). Their argument goes as follows: suppose that most couples want to be quite certain that one male child will survive to the couple's old age. A computer simulation technique establishes the following relationships:

1. Conditions of high mortality (summarized by an expectation of life at birth of no more than about 20 years) require a very large number of births and very high birth rates. Childbearing must continue throughout the reproductive age span, so that the average age at motherhood must be quite high, 28.7 years. Even so, under conditions of such high mortality a substantial fraction of the women (nearly 39 percent) will never bear the number of sons needed to assure that at least one will survive to his parents' old age. However, the rate of natural increase in such a population over a long period of time (the "intrinsic rate" of natural increase) is fairly high, 1.7 percent annually (41 years to double).
2. Under conditions of moderate mortality, substantially lower birth rates are required. All but 2.5 percent of the mothers are able to bear enough sons to assure that at least one will survive to his parents' old age. Childbearing may slow down or stop late in the reproductive age span, and the average age at motherhood is younger—25.2 years. But under such conditions, a population would experience natural increase at a much higher rate—2.8 percent annually (25 years to double).
3. Under conditions of rather low mortality, a single male birth is almost certain to promise a male survivor. Therefore, the achievement of the goal requires that childbearing be continued over only a short part of the reproductive span, and so the mean age at motherhood is 20.4 years. Fertility rates would probably assure no more than a replacement of the population and certainly no substantial increase.

In sum, there is no reason for fertility to remain high when mortality levels are low. But other microanalytic theories give still other explanations for fertility declines.

The social status theory. The social status explanation of fertility, as originally formulated in 1890 by the French demographer Arsène Dumont, held that the ambition to rise to higher social positions is widespread, but that large families inhibit social mobility. Accordingly, people who seek to enhance their status will tend to control fertility and family size.

A modern formulation of the social status explanation by J. A. Banks (1954) attempts to account for the sharp decline in fertility in England between 1870 and 1900 by arguing that:

1. After a generation of prosperity, the British economy experienced a leveling off in the 1870s and 1880s.
2. To preserve their own newly acquired occupational and social status, and to assure its transmittal to their children (the latter entailing substantial investment in the education of the offspring) couples of the British salaried middle class restricted their births drastically.
3. The restriction of births became simpler and more socially acceptable during the period in question because of technological improvements in, and the promotion of, contraception.
4. As communication between the classes increased and as primary and postprimary education among the lower classes expanded, the pattern of family limitation started gradually to be diffused.
5. The further expansion of interclass communication and lower-class education intensified personal contacts and the motivation to acquire new prestige to such an extent that the pattern of family limitation came to permeate the entire social structure.

Variations of this analysis are sometimes formulated as explanations of fertility differentials, between, for example, urban and rural populations, Jewish and Christian ones, and foreign-born and first-generation native ones. Lower urban as compared to rural fertility; lower Jewish as compared to Christian fertility; and lower first-generation native as compared to foreign-born fertility are thus all explained in terms of attempts of the respective former categories to improve or assure socioeconomic status.

The utility-cost theory. The *utility-cost* explanation of fertility has received much attention and has been elaborated considerably in recent years. Its basic ideas were set forth by H. Leibenstein in 1957:

> It is not going too far to say that the essential element to be explained is the incentive or rationale behind the desire to have larger or smaller families. We have to visualize various contraceptive techniques as merely facilitating factors the utilization of which involves an economic or emotional cost of some sort. But the major burden of any theory must be on

> the explanation of the forces that create the necessary motivations for the creation of smaller rather than larger families.
>
> A distinction has to be made between the knowledge of alternatives and the choice among known alternatives. It seems reasonable to suppose that as incomes increase, the knowledge of the alternatives pertinent to family limitation also increases. But we still have to explain what determines the choice from among a range of known alternatives. The basic idea behind our theory is that motivations with respect to family size are, to a considerable extent, rational; that, on the whole, parents will want an extra child if the satisfactions to be derived from that child are greater than the "costs" that are involved—where "costs" are to be interpreted rather broadly. (Leibenstein, 1957, p. 159)

The utility-cost explanation of fertility assumes, first, that people behave rationally with respect to their own fertility. That is, people behave as if they were applying rough calculations to the problem of determining the desirable number of births. The second assumption of the utility-cost theory is that these calculations are directed toward balancing the satisfaction or utility to be derived from an additional child against the cost, both monetary and psychological, of having that child.

The theory distinguishes between three types of utility to be derived from an additional child. The first is the child's utility as a "consumption good,"—as a source of personal pleasure to the parents. The second is the child's utility as a productive agent, as a person who may be expected eventually to work and contribute to the family income. And the third is the child's utility as a potential source of security, for instance, in the parents' old age.

The costs of having an additional child are both direct and indirect. Direct costs are the usual expenses of maintaining the child until he is self-supporting, and indirect costs are those incurred when opportunities (for example, the wife's employment) are foregone because of the child's existence.

The utility-cost explanation of class differentials in fertility holds, in the first place, that since income varies over the different socioeconomic groups, different groups can afford more or fewer children (see Becker, 1960).[5] In the second place, the pattern of utilities and costs varies among the different socioeconomic groups. For example, the utility of an additional child is different for the farmer than for the clerk, just as the direct cost is different for the professor than for the unskilled laborer. Similarly, the indirect cost is different for the college-educated career woman than for the housewife (Duesenberry, 1960).

The utility-cost analysis also offers an explanation of changes in

[5] It was Becker's article that brought the utility-cost analysis of fertility to the attention of demographers.

fertility over time. Economic development, it reasons, can alter the pattern of utility and cost. For example, both the direct and indirect costs of an additional child probably rise as income increases, whereas the utility of the additional child as a source of security and as a contributor to family income probably diminishes. Families with higher incomes typically spend more directly on their children, for clothing, education, and medical services. And at the same time, the more highly educated mothers in such families forgo relatively greater income opportunities, and so they incur higher indirect costs. On the other hand, high income parents are less likely to need support from their children in their old age. Finally, in both high and low income families, the utility of the additional child as a consumption item is probably fixed (Leibenstein 1969, p. 162).[6]

The net effect of all the assets and debits in the utility-cost analysis is that the direct and indirect costs of raising children are higher in the more modernized societies where high proportions of the population (and women in particular) are educated. And so, we have witnessed fertility declines in the MDCs.

Macroanalytic Theories

We shall briefly discuss three macroanalytic theories of fertility. The first is Malthus's classic analysis of the relationship between food production, per capita income, and preventive checks on population growth. The second is the macroanalytic analysis of changing family structure as expressed in the emergence of the conjugal family, the establishment of the nuclear family couple as a decision making unit, and the rationalization of family formation. The third is the theory of population balance, which explains changes in population size, distribution, and other characteristics in terms of the availability of environmental resources, technological developments, and social organization.

Malthus's theory. The central historical personality in the recognition and formulation of a theory of interrelationships between population and social and economic change was Thomas Robert Malthus. Malthus is immortalized in demographic history for his *Essay on the Principle of Population* (1958), which appeared in no fewer than seven editions from 1798 to 1872, and for the controversy which raged and continues to rage around his ideas (Glass, 1953).

There are three central ideas in Malthus's analysis. First, since population tends to increase faster than food resources do, there is always

[6] F. Lorimer (1967) has carried out some hypothetical calculations showing variations in costs and utilities of children.

tension between population and subsistence. Second, this tension is resolved by the *positive checks* of mortality. That is, the increase in population to a level close to the limits of subsistence produces poverty, misery, vice, disease, and ultimately the mortality operating to restrain population growth. And finally, as Malthus allowed in second and subsequent editions of his *Essay,* a measure of population balance can be obtained by other means besides mortality checks. The *preventive checks* of moral restraint—like delayed marriage or continence in marriage—could replace positive checks to limit population growth.

Malthus felt that several of the social reforms advocated in his day would, if adopted, result only in increased population and higher levels of poverty, misery, and disease. At the same time they would diminish industry and thrift. He advocated preventive checks and, indeed, observed with approval the institutionalization of delayed marriage in increasingly broad sectors of the population (Malthus, 1829).

Diminished per capita income is, in Malthus's analysis, a structural attribute of a society which has experienced too rapid a population growth. The mortality and diminished fertility associated with the positive checks of vice, misery, wars, and famine affect all people in such societies, not just those who marry too early, or who bear too many children, or who do not earn enough. Further, the delayed marriage, solvency, and continence associated with preventive checks are primarily institutionalized means of diminishing fertility rather than individual acts of wisdom and foresight (Spengler, 1971). In Malthus's analysis, the key societal variable is the survival or nonsurvival of populations at subsistence levels. Malthus only implicitly took into account the possibility of survival at alternative levels of living. However, the more modern renditions of his theory have it that societies institutionalize preventive checks, not only upon threats to actual survival, but upon threats to survival at some acceptable minimum level.

The theory of changing family structure. The theory of changing family structure, formulated by W. J. Goode (1963) and others, holds that urbanization and industrialization are associated with the subversion and breakdown of the extended family system. In the extended family, the childbearing couple is not generally the decision making unit. Arrangements and decisions regarding matchmaking and marriage, residence, work and economic relations, and even the care and socialization of the young are not made by the couple affected, but instead by the most senior members of the extended family. Similarly, there is typically no discussion or decision about childbearing on the part of the couple. Children are conceived, born, and accepted as part of an inevitable life process rather than by decision.

In the relatively independent nuclear family, however, decisions are made by the couple, both before and after marriage. Each partner may decide to marry or not marry, each may choose his or her own spouse, and jointly the couple may make residential, occupational, and child-bearing decisions. Such decisions may be determined entirely by tradition; they may be entirely rational; or they may comprise some combination of these properties depending on the couple's individual characteristics like literarcy and socioeconomic status.

According to Goode's formulation, it is industrialization that causes and sustains the institutionalization of the conjugal, relatively small family. More precisely, industrialization undermines traditional family systems by rewarding mobility; by creating class-differentiated mobility within kin groupings; by organizing extrakinship institutions for meeting needs and problems previously handled by kinship institutions; by creating a value structure recognizing achievement; and by promoting specialization and differentiation, thereby diminishing the opportunities for kin to aid one another in occupational arrangements. It follows that industrialization promotes change in these specific aspects of family formation that concern the independence and mobility of newly formed families. For example, industrialization works to place marriage decisions and choice of spouse in the hands of the principal parties themselves, to diminish the rigidity and frequency of endogamous and exogamous practices, and to increase the frequency of neolocal residence (where the home of the new couple is located fairly independently of the locations of either of their parents' homes). Industrialization also works to make age at marriage, and variations of age, consistent with the increasing independence and mobility of the younger generation. And finally, industrialization promotes attempts to control fertility, primarily (but not exclusively) by making the couple the decision-making unit.

The theory of population balance. Elements of the *population balance* theory as formulated by human ecologists are found in modern sociology in the writings of Emile Durkheim, M. Halbwachs, W. F. Ogburn, and, particularly, A. H. Hawley (1950, especially chapter 9) and O. D. Duncan (1959). All societies are confronted by pressures created by their own tendencies to increase in number. Taking it as axiomatic that males and females in any human population mate and produce offspring, it follows that in the absence of social, institutional, physical, biological, or other inhibiting factors, populations tend to increase in size.

The pressures of population increase spell opportunity for some societies and disaster for others. The pressures of population growth bring about changes in the social organization and in the economic and technological arrangements of a population; alternatively they may also bring on institutionalized constraints upon mating and procreation. Thus, in any society there is an ongoing interaction between the population, its social organization, its technology, and its environment. As we saw earlier in the book, a society characterized by fixed technology and social organization must, when confronted by substantial growth in its own numbers, seek to expand its environment by settlement, cultivation, or exploitation of new areas. Otherwise it must suffer a decline in its per capita level of subsistence. On the other hand, a society with a fixed area can increase its production and look after its growing numbers by effecting changes either in its social organization, or in its technology, or both. But the society which is unable to alter its social or technological patterns, and which is also unable to expand its physical or geographical environment must either institutionalize means to control population growth, suffer substantial decreases in its levels of living, or—historically the most common case of all—lose all of its potential growth through high mortality.

This analysis differs from that of Malthus in that it explicitly incorporates the possibility that not just one technology and social organization, but various ones, affect the balance between population and resources and bear upon levels of subsistence and quality of life.

Some Attempts to Reconcile Microanalytic and Macroanalytic Analyses

Institutionalization of new fertility behavior. A number of attempts have been made to reconcile microanalytic and macroanalytic analyses of fertility and population growth. R. Freedman (1968) argues that when large numbers of persons exhibit characteristic patterns of decision making and behavior in response to changing typical exigencies (like changing mortality levels or changing modal utility and cost patterns), these behavioral patterns become institutionalized and normatively prescribed in the society. Thus, not only do diminishing mortality and increasing education have the effect, predicted by microanalytic analysis, of lowering the fertility of individuals. But these individual responses of lower fertility may be institutionalized and normatively supported in societies experiencing substantial decreases in mortality and increasing literacy and education.

Tastes as a sociological variable. R. A. Easterlin focuses upon the concept of *tastes* as a bridge between the microanalytic economic and macroanalytic analyses (Easterlin, 1969). Working with the utility-cost model of fertility behavior, he suggests viewing the formation of *tastes,* which determine utility and cost under a given pattern of income and prices, as a sociological as well as an economic variable:

> . . . . To turn to the formation of tastes, it is here that many of the fertility variables emphasized by the sociologists come to the fore. While it is attitudes . . . which together with resource and price constraints immediately determine fertility decisions, a host of other variables lie behind these attitudes. In general, one's preference system at any given time may be viewed as molded by heredity and past and current environment. The process starts with birth and continues through the life cycle. Religion, color, nativity, place of residence, and education enter into the shaping of tastes. So, too, does one's childhood and adolescent experience in one's own home with material affluence and family size. One reaches family-building age with preferences already molded by this heritage, but these preferences are subsequently modified by ongoing occupational, income, and family-building experiences, among others. Exposure to various information media influences tastes throughout the life cycle.
>
> Because of the important role of cumulative experience in the formation of tastes, it is probably correct that typically tastes change rather slowly over time. For some analytical purposes, this may justify the economist's usual assumption of constant tastes. But in areas of behavior such as fertility which involve a substantial time period or where cross-section differences among classes are of interest, such an assumption seems dubious.
>
> Nor can the economist dismiss taste phenomena as noneconomic in nature, for it is clear that economic variables enter into the shaping of tastes and affect behavior through this channel as well as via the resource and price constraints traditionally emphasized. Hence, an adequate framework for fertility analysis calls for explicit attention to preference phenomena and the factors entering into their formation.[7]

In an important critical review of recent research on fertility, G. Hawthorn (1970) adopts the Easterlin scheme and begins a systematization and summary of those findings that bear on variations in resources, costs, and tastes. These variations, in interaction with one another, are seen as determining fertility decisions and behavior. Religion, education, female employment, urbanization, race, and social mobility are all reexamined from the point of view of their influence on tastes in the utility-cost analysis. But the approach is still very novel and its concrete applications remain to be worked out and evaluated.

Multiphasic response to demographic and economic change. The well-known attempt by K. Davis to analyze fertility trends in modern demographic transitions in terms of a theory of change and response (1963) may also be viewed as an attempt to reconcile microanalytic and macroanalytic analyses. Davis points out that in countries experiencing

[7] Easterlin, R. A., Towards a socio-economic theory of fertility: A survey of recent research in economic factors in American fertility. In S. J. Behrman, L. Corsa, Jr., and R. Freedman, eds., *Fertility and Family Planning: A World View* (Ann Arbor: University of Michigan Press, 1969), p. 135.

a demographic transition there were typically more than a single means by which the birth rate was brought down following the lowered mortality and a period of sustained growth. These means generally included delayed marriage, international migration, sterilization, abortion, and the increasing use of contraception. Such *multiphasic responses,* according to Davis, represented reactions to the decline in mortality and to the sustained natural increase which ensued, but not to poverty or to crises of subsistence. They were prompted by personal, rather than by societal or national, goals and considerations.

The demographic transitions always took place under conditions of economic expansion and growth. Davis's theory seeks to explain personal strategies of marriage and family formation—concerns of the microanalytic analysis—in terms of the individual's location in the society's social and economic structure. Differential location, he argues, gives rise to differential opportunities for exploiting (or for avoiding the negative effects of) macroanalytic variables such as changes in the scope or structure of the society's economic activity. Davis presumes childbearing to be a normal activity, and he seeks to identify the circumstances under which childbearing is controlled or diminished.

According to this analysis, location in the social and economic structure makes for differences in the advantages to be reaped from the control of fertility in any given economic circumstance. Those individuals who stand to gain the most from adopting practices which diminish fertility will practice birth control; while those who are so located in the society and economy as to derive little or no reward from fertility control will not limit family size.

SUMMARY

In this chapter we have confined our discussion of fertility trends mostly to the period following World War II. We identified five types of trends, three for more developed countries and two for less developed countries. Among the MDCs, some had already reached very low levels of fertility by the onset of World War II. (Western Europe, Australia and Hungary, Northern America and Oceania, had crude birth rates not exceeding 20 per thousand.) With the exceptions of Germany and Hungary, all of these low-fertility nations experienced a baby boom following World War II. There were two kinds of baby booms. Short booms reflected mostly fertility which had previously been postponed. They brought about no change in patterns of completed family size for the most part, and they were followed by even lower birth rates. In contrast, extended baby booms reflected both "catching up" on previously postponed fertility and some increases in average numbers of children born per women or per couple. These occurred in the United States, Canada, Australia, and New Zealand, and they were followed in the 1960s and 1970s by sharp fertility declines. A third pattern was evident for MDCs. In this pattern, the trend toward lower fertility only began around or after World War I, and it had achieved only moderately low fertility by World War II (crude birth rates were over 20, as in some countries of Eastern and Southern Europe and Argentina). Countries with this pattern continued their steady fertility declines and, excepting the special case of Romania, all had crude birth rates under 20 per thousand by 1970.

Virtually all the LDCs had crude birth rates exceeding 35 per thousand on the eve of World War II. Two groupings of LDCs may now be identified as those in which there have been notable declines in birth rates since World War II, and those with continued high fertility.

The lower fertility MDCs which experienced baby booms after World War II have histories of regional, religious and ethnic, and socioeconomic differentials in fertility rates; but though some of these differentials remain pronounced the overall recent trend is of convergence of marriage, family building, and fertility patterns among the various subgroupings. In the MDCs only recently attaining low fertility on a national level, there remain substantial regional, ethnic, and socioeconomic differences. The LDCs were in the past characterized by uniformly higher fertility, with few signs of place-of-residence or socioeconomic differentials. However there is some evidence of differential fertility in the LDCs exhibiting recent declines in birth rates, especially among literate or educated as compared to illiterate women.

Remarkably, the MDCs with fertility approaching replacement or zero population growth levels exhibit very little in the way of articulated national population policies. And with a few exceptions, they have also had relatively few publicly sponsored efforts to introduce or promote the use of contraception. In some non-Catholic, capitalist countries of the West there have been commercial and sometimes medical-profession promotions of contraception, but even this has been absent in most of the low fertility MDCs. Thus, the origins of the small families and low birth rates in these countries seem not connected with public population policy or measures of intervention.

The extent to which national population policies or organized efforts to introduce family planning and birth control practices have been influential in those LDCs where birth rates have declined is a topic of lively debate, and there are currently efforts to develop systematic means of evaluation. The previously separate views—that these LDC fertility declines are a direct consequence of the introduction and promotion of birth control, or that they are a consequence of social and economic development—have drawn closer together. Most students of population today view modern social and economic development as including the introduction of new family values and means to achieve them, and they see the successful introduction and acceptance of family planning as depending upon some threshold of social and economic development sufficient to institutionalize new levels of living demands and expectations.

There are many theories about fertility variations and trends. Microanalytical theories stress the role of individual or household preferences and fertility decisions, and they inquire about the factors which influence individuals. Macroanalytical theories stress the role of social conditions in the very fact and acceptability of abstraction, evaluation, and decision making about marriage, family formation, and number of births.

In the next chapter we look at patterns of migration. As we shall see, there are special problems in the very definition of migration and identification of migrants. We will consider these problems, then turn to analysis of both individual and community factors in migration; and finally inquire about demographic, social, and individual consequences of migration.

10

Migration Patterns

Of all the components of population growth, migration may well be the most complex. Unlike birth or death, the definitions themselves of migration and migrant are always problematic, and this means that counting migrants is difficult. Again, because of the myriad alternative ways of grouping individuals, any one migratory move can be assigned a variety of origins and destinations. Also, unlike births and deaths, an individual's migration is a voluntary action. Thus, societal values and norms concerning movement, and the manner in which these are manifested in individual and collective behavior, must be studied in relation to both migration and nonmigration. Finally, migratory movements have consequences for the individual migrant, for the populations of origin and destination, and for the greater, more inclusive, societal unit within which the migration takes place. And all these consequences must be described and analyzed.

In the first section of this chapter, we will review problems of the definition and measurement of migration. Then, we will attempt to contrast patterns of migratory movements in and among societies to draw a contrast between one-time migrants and recurring migratory movements.

In the remainder of the chapter, we will consider migration, population redistribution, and differential migration from the points of view of the movers and nonmovers within a population, the communities of origin and destination, and the societies within which migration takes place. We conclude with a consideration of the individual, community, and societal consequences of migration.

INTERNATIONAL MIGRATION

Compared to internal migration, the concept of *international migration* seems unambiguous: it refers to changes of residence across international boundaries. In principle, the quantitative description of international migration should be straightforward by reason of its unambiguous definition. But in practice, this is not quite true. There are many gaps in the definition, reporting, compilation, and analysis of international migration statistics. And besides this, the exact status of a person crossing an international border—whether a legal or an illegal immigrant, a visitor, a student, a temporary worker, or a person related to one of these—is very often ambiguous.

For example, in Chapter 6 we discussed briefly the net civilian immigration component of population growth, which in the United States includes net alien immigration, net arrivals from Puerto Rico, net arrivals from abroad of civilian United States citizens, conditional entrants, and emigration totals. But this concept, even assuming reliable measurement of all its components, does not include *all* groups of persons entering the country. Students and their dependents, temporary workers, businessmen and exchange aliens and others admitted as nonimmigrants are not included, though effectively they are residents of the United States while here. In addition, aliens who are in the United States illegally are likewise not included (Keely, 1972). Similar problems exist for other countries, and so in general, our information about international migration is far from complete, despite the seeming simplicity of the concept.

International migration has been a major factor in redistribution of the world's population in certain periods of history, and indeed large areas of the world have been populated largely by international migrants and their descendants. The number of Europeans emigrating overseas from the beginnings of colonization until World War II has been estimated at more than 60 million by Dudley Kirk (1946), and according to United Nations estimates another ten million moved out of Europe between 1946 and 1963. The total number of international migrants within the European continent, as the totals in Asia and in Africa, is surely very large, but this figure is not readily estimated.

The major determinants of international migration are generally asserted to be economic and political factors, the first usually viewed as both "push" and as "pull" factors, the second exclusively as "push." Not very much is understood about the specific characteristics of international migrants, the implications of the circumstances or motivation for their moves, or the broader consequences of their migration.

An important outcome of international migration, however, is the diffusion of peoples and cultures to the extent that there are very few if any national populations which are entirely homogeneous with respect to national, religious, racial, and ethnic origins. The United States, populated almost entirely by immigrants and their descendants, is the classical case of the multiorigin (whether "melting-pot" or "pluralist" is a matter of learned debate) society. But other countries have large foreign-born components as well (see Figure 10.1) and even larger subgroups which are native born but of foreign origins. A major sociodemographic problem concerns the variations in mutual adaptation and integration of these groupings. For despite the ideals of folk sovereignty, national self-determination, and the quest for ethnic purity and independence, these very concepts have led, as Davis points out (1974), to both forced migration and restriction of movements. The improvements in communications and the sheer technology of travel and movement, combined with need for larger, more differentiated, and more flexible labor pools, are likely to lead to more, rather than less, international migration in the future.

INTERNAL MIGRATION: THE MOBILITY STATUS APPROACH OF CENSUSES AND SURVEYS

In search of direct information, researchers have turned increasingly to the *migrant status* or *mobility status* approach, which seeks to reconstruct past movements on the basis of information returned by individuals in census or survey inquiries. Persons are asked either where they resided at some previous date or whether or not they changed residences within some interval preceding the date of the census or survey. This yields information on both the volume and direction of migratory movements. In a variation of this approach, respondents are asked their place of birth. This information, together with data on current place of residence, also yields quantitative representations of migratory movements.

Examples of the mobility status approach include the migration

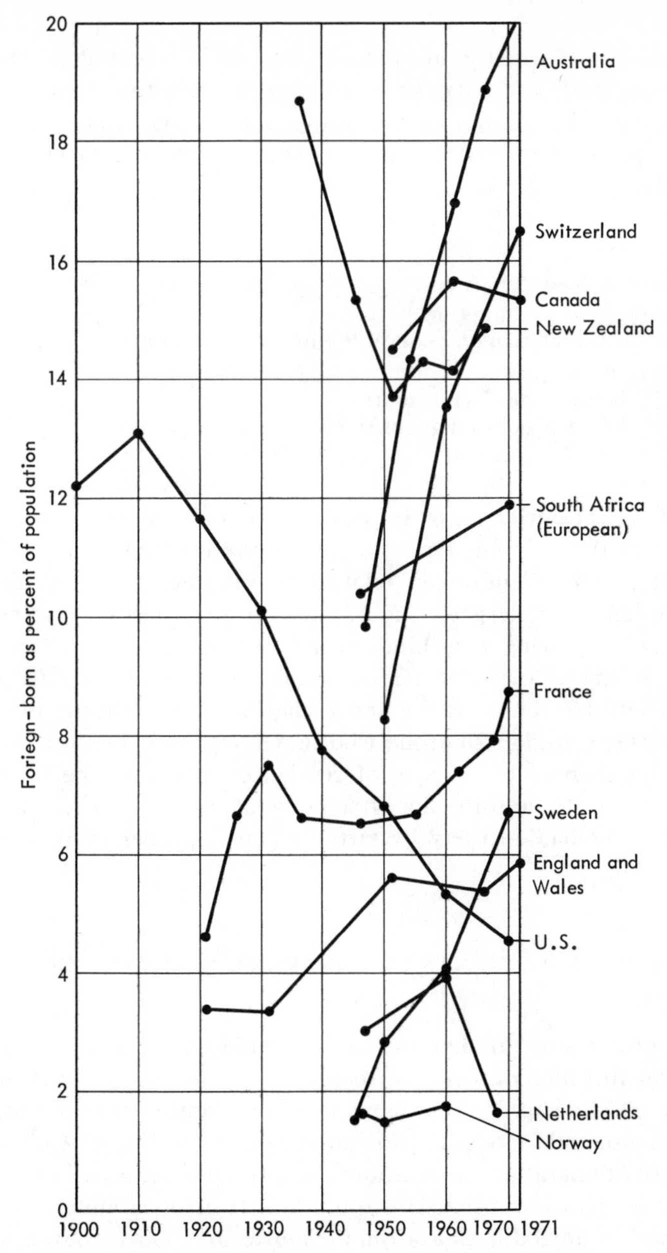

Figure 10.1 Percent Foreign-Born in Selected Countries, 1900–1971. Foreign-born populations of a selection of countries are plotted as a percentage of each country's total population. In most developed countries proportion has been rising, and in some older industrial countries of Europe it now exceeds the proportion in the United States. *Source: Kingsley Davis, "The Migration of Human Populations,"* Scientific American, *Vol. 231, no. 3, September 1974. Copyright © 1974 by Scientific American, Inc. All rights reserved.*

studies of both United States censuses and the Current Population Survey.[1] These studies classify the population by mobility status, determining this status by comparing the individual's current place of residence with his place of residence five years ago. The following classifications are used:

Same house
Different house in same county (intracounty movers)
Migrants (intercounty movers)
 different county, same state (intrastate migrants)
Interstate migrants
 between contiguous states
 between noncontiguous states
Movers from abroad (Shryock, 1964, p. 10)

These categories make it possible not only to count numbers of migrants of the different types but to analyze differential frequencies of the various types of moves in relation to any one, or any combination, of the other characteristics investigated in the census or survey. The problem of specifying what kinds of moves actually constitute migration, or who is and who is not a migrant, is solved differently in different research settings. Thus, as the above classifications indicate, the United States census considers someone who moves to a new house a "migrant" only if he changes his county of residence; otherwise, he is merely a "mover." For the anthropologist, however, an entire society may be a migrant or nomadic society by virtue of moving over even shorter distances.

MIGRATORY MOVEMENTS IN DIFFERENT KINDS OF SOCIETIES

An important step in deriving and formulating generalizations about migration in different kinds of societies is found in the work of Goldscheider (1971, chap. 7). He analyzes the relationship between migration and socioeconomic modernization in Africa. According to Goldscheider, the extent of migration in traditional societies (the term includes agrarian and also preagrarian societies) is quite low. It involves almost exclusively moves which are both short-distance moves and moves between homogeneous areas. Such moves tend either to involve whole populations (as in nomadic movements) or else they are idiosyncratic, without pattern.

Migration in traditional societies, in Goldscheider's view, may be

[1] Shryock (1964) offers a detailed description and analysis of these migration studies; see also Shryock and Siegel (1973).

related to any of three things: the development of new territories or new sources of sustenance; marriage, especially in exogamous networks of tribes, villages, or societies; or political causes like warfare or conquest. Both because of the limited volume of migration and because of its idiosyncratic nature, neither the origin nor the destination community is greatly affected by migration. The amount of migration in traditional societies is, in turn, constrained by (a) the rigidity of status-reward systems; (b) high community loyalty and low status of movers; (c) physical barriers to movement; and (d) high levels of solidarity and integration in such societies.

The propositions formulated by Goldscheider are tentative, and they will need to be examined and elaborated as better data become available. However, Goldscheider has been able to use his framework to contrast the migration characteristics outlined above with the quite different patterns of migration associated with socioeconomic development and modernization—under colonialism or under emerging nationalism. Migration and population redistribution have been integral parts of the modernization process. Under the economic and political changes of modernization, previous constraints on migration have been reduced. In addition, economic changes have generated expanded trade and production. Taxation has forced individuals to move from subsistence farming to wage employment, and new patterns of recruitment of workers have evolved. All these changes have been accompanied by changing attitudes about migration (Goldscheider, 1971, pp. 182–96). As we shall note below, these generalizations hold, for the most part, for migration and population redistribution in the United States as well.

Migration and Changes in the Regional Distribution of the United States Population Between 1870 and 1950

As Table 10.1 shows, there were some major population shifts in the United States between 1870 and 1950. The proportion of the total population residing in the Northeast dropped from 34.6 to 28.5 percent, and that of the north central region dropped from 33.7 to 29.5 percent. In the same period, the proportion of the population residing in the West increased greatly, from 2.6 to 13.0 percent. The proportion living in the South changed hardly at all.

In a monumental study at the University of Pennsylvania, a team of demographers and economists analyzed the 1870–1950 population redistribution and its relationship to simultaneous trends in the volume and structure of economic activity (Lee et al., 1957; Kuznets, Miller & Easterlin, 1960; Eldridge & Thomas, 1964). Population redistribution,

TABLE 10.1 Percent Distribution of United States Population by Regions, 1870–1950

	1870	*1880*	*1890*	*1900*	*1910*	*1920*	*1930*	*1940*	*1950*
Total U.S.	100.0	100.0	100.0	100.0	100.0	100.0	100.0	100.0	100.0
Northeast	34.6	31.4	29.9	29.9	30.1	30.1	30.0	29.4	28.5
South	29.2	30.4	29.5	30.1	30.0	29.3	28.9	29.6	29.0
North Central	33.7	34.6	35.6	34.7	32.5	32.2	31.4	30.5	29.5
West	2.6	3.5	4.9	5.4	7.4	8.4	9.7	10.5	13.0

Source: Eldridge and Thomas, 1964, Vol. III, Table 1.6.

viewed as differential regional population growth, was analyzed by natural increase (births minus deaths) and by net migration (total in-migrants minus total out-migrants) for each decade between 1870 and 1950. The data are summarized in Tables 10.2 and 10.3.

With the exception of the Northeast from 1900 to 1910 (the decade in which European immigration to the United States reached its peak) the main component of population growth in regions other than the West was natural increase. For the West, however, in every decade, net migration was much more important than natural increase.

The South shows negative net migration (in other words, net out-migration) in every decade after 1880, and the North Central region exhibits net out-migration during the decades from 1930 to 1950. The South has had consistently higher rates of natural increase, and the Northeast consistently lower ones, than the rest of the country. The West has consistently been characterized by spectacularly high rates of net migration, reaching close to 400 net migrants per 1,000 average population in both the 1880–1890 and 1900–1910 decades, and surpassing 100 net migrants per 1,000 average population even during the decade of the Great Depression, from 1930 to 1940.

Migration out of the South in all decades has included large proportions of blacks moving primarily to the Northeast and to North Central regions. The North Central areas have had a net in-migration of blacks in all decades, and particularly after 1920. In-migration to the West has been largely by native whites, with substantial black in-migration beginning only in the 1940–1950 decade (Eldridge & Thomas, 1964, chap. 4).

The redistribution of the population of the United States has been reflected not only in regional shifts but also in great increases in the number of urban places and in the size and density of urban places.

TABLE 10.2 Natural Increase, Net Migration, and Total Increase in the United States, by Regions, 1870–1880 to 1940–1950 (in thousands)

Decade	*Natural Increase*	*Net Migration*	*Total Increase*	*Average Population*
Northeast				
1870–1880	2,091	339	2,430	14,551
1880–1890	1,633	1,443	3,076	17,305
1890–1900	1,985	1,871	3,856	20,771
1900–1910	2,272	2,728	5,000	25,173
1910–1920	2,613	1,461	4,074	29,710
1920–1930	3,457	1,543	5,000	34,246
1930–1940	1,563	376	1,939	37,716
1940–1950	3,786	253	4,039	40,704
South				
1870–1880	3,895	112	4,007	13,254
1880–1890	3,368	–236	3,132	16,823
1890–1900	4,342	–91	4,252	20,626
1900–1910	4,698	–23	4,675	25,132
1910–1920	4,451	–985	3,466	29,202
1920–1930	5,983	–1,540	4,443	33,157
1930–1940	4,527	–1,091	3,436	37,097
1940–1950	6,947	–2,241	4,705	41,167
North Central				
1870–1880	3,392	991	4,383	15,173
1880–1890	3,341	1,660	5,000	19,864
1890–1900	3,400	529	3,929	24,315
1900–1910	3,151	400	3,551	28,047
1910–1920	3,063	1,072	4,135	31,890
1920–1930	3,982	572	4,554	36,234
1930–1940	2,266	–717	1,549	39,286
1940–1950	4,684	–577	4,107	42,114
West				
1870–1880	268	434	702	1,261
1880–1890	369	891	1,260	2,242
1890–1900	423	579	1,001	3,373
1900–1910	608	2,083	2,691	5,249
1910–1920	710	1,340	2,050	7,620
1920–1930	1,029	1,867	2,897	10,093
1930–1940	668	1,310	1,978	12,531
1940–1950	2,035	3,539	5,573	16,307

Source: Eldridge and Thomas, 1964, Vol. III, Table 1.13.

TABLE 10.3 Rates of Natural Increase and Net Migration per 1,000 Average Population, by Regions, 1870–1880 to 1940–1950

	Northeast		*South*		*North Central*		*West*	
Decade	*Natural increase*	*Net migration*	*Natural increase*	*Net migration*	*Natural increase*	*Net migration*	*Natural increase*	*Net migration*
1870–1880	144	23	294	8	224	65	213	344
1880–1890	94	83	200	−14	168	84	164	397
1890–1900	96	90	211	− 4	140	22	125	172
1900–1910	90	108	187	− 1	112	14	116	397
1910–1920	88	49	152	−34	96	34	93	176
1920–1930	101	45	180	−46	110	16	102	185
1930–1940	41	10	122	−29	58	−18	53	105
1940–1950	93	6	169	−54	111	−14	125	217

Source: Eldridge and Thomas, 1964, Vol. III, Table 1.14.

The proportion of the population in urban places increased from 5.1 percent in 1790 to 25.7 percent in 1870, and to 59.0 percent in 1950. The percentage of the population in cities of 100,000 or more increased from 10.7 percent in 1870 to 29.4 percent in 1950.

The Pennsylvania group were able to study the relationship between migration and urbanization only indirectly, since they were not able to study intrastate migration. Thus, they were able to conclude only:

> that migration is very likely a unified problem, that urbanization has been in large measure a migration phenomenon and that the two processes, interstate migration and urban growth, have tended to vary together because they have migration in common and because they have been associated with pervasive changes in social and economic organization. (Eldridge & Thomas, 1964, p. 226)

Redistribution of the United States Native-Born Population by 1958

Some data bearing directly upon the relationship between migration and population redistribution are available from a study by K. E. Taeuber and associates (Taeuber, Chiazze, Jr., & Haenzel, 1968). In a national sample of the United States population in 1958, persons aged 18 and over reported their residence histories. Their histories yielded a large amount of data concerning migratory moves, migrants, and places of origin and destination.

Table 10.4 shows the percentage distribution of the native-born population by size of birthplace and size of current residence. The diagonal cells represent persons whose 1958 place of residence was the same size as that of their birthplace and include 45 percent of the total native-born population. This percentage includes 29 percent who have always lived in the same place and 16 percent who have lived in at least two places. About 37 percent of the population reported moving to places larger than their birthplaces (the cells below the diagonal). And 18 percent reported moving to places smaller than their birthplaces (cells above the diagonal). Of the farm-born population (some 27 percent of the total) only a little more than one-third (35 percent) were in places classified as "farm" in 1958. Only a fourth (24 percent) were in "rural nonfarm" places; the rest (41 percent) were in cities. Of the total adult population in cities of 500,000 or more, about two-fifths were born in smaller places. Of the total in cities of 50,000-499,999 inhabitants, more than half were born in smaller places. As the table shows, the migratory shifts favored the metropolitan towns with populations between 2,500 and 499,999 (with 29.4 percent of the population in such places in 1958, compared to 20.0 percent born there). The table also reveals a very sharp decline

TABLE 10.4 Percentage Distribution of United States Native-Born Population, Aged 18 and Over, by Size of Birthplace and Size of Current Residence, 1958

	Size of Current Residence							
Size of Birthplace	*Total*	*(1)*	*(2)*	*(3)*	*(4)*	*(5)*	*(6)*	*(7)*
Total native population 18 years and over	100.0	15.2	19.5	9.9	12.3	15.7	15.6	11.8
(1) 500,000 or more	15.6	8.8	1.3	2.1	1.9	.6	.7	.2
(2) 50,000–499,999	14.8	1.4	7.9	1.5	1.9	1.0	.8	.3
(3) Metropolitan, 2,500–49,999	5.2	.3	.7	2.5	.8	.4	.3	.1
(4) Metropolitan, rural nonfarm	5.4	.3	.6	.4	3.3	.3	.4	.1
(5) Nonmetropolitan, 2,500–49,999	15.1	1.6	2.8	1.1	1.2	6.1	1.7	.6
(6) Nonmetropolitan, rural nonfarm	16.6	1.1	2.5	1.0	1.3	2.8	7.0	.9
(7) Farm	27.3	1.6	3.7	1.3	1.9	4.5	4.7	9.6

Source: Taeuber, Chiazze, Jr., and Haenszel, 1968, Table 51.

in the farm population (11.8 percent in 1958, compared to 27.3 percent born there).

Some Conclusions on Migration and Economic Differentials

The Pennsylvania research group, whose study we described earlier in this section, conducted a very intricate analysis of relationships between income, employment and occupations, and migration rates for the period

Migration—walking to the next job. *(Wide World Photos)*

between 1870 and 1950. They concluded: (a) the volume of net migration "responded positively and significantly" to swings in economic activity, increasing during periods of prosperity and diminishing during periods of depression; (b) all major color-nativity sectors of the population (for example, native-born whites, foreign-born whites, and blacks) responded to temporal variations in economic activity; (c) the directions of migration were related to income per worker in the different regions and subregions, with the overall migration pattern working toward a convergence of income levels and a decline of regional differences; but (d) some streams of migration took place in directions not consistent with income differentials; (e) finally, nonwhites seemed in general to be more responsive than whites to subregional income differentials (Eldridge & Thomas, 1964, pt. II, chap. 4, "Conclusions"). In other words, the migratory patterns were closely connected with differentials in income and economic opportunity, but not uniformly so for all population categories or groups.

DIFFERENTIAL MIGRATION

There are at least three different kinds of questions to be asked concerning differential migration in large-scale and relatively highly differentiated societies:

1. What kinds of persons, or groups, migrate with high frequencies, and what kinds migrate only rarely?
2. What kinds of communities attract large inflows of migrants, and what kinds of communities generate large outflows?
3. What kinds of societies sustain high volumes of migration and what kinds sustain low ones?

As we shall see, the search for generalizations has been somewhat disappointing.

Differential Migration Among Individuals and Groups

D. J. Bogue (1959b) has summarized research findings bearing on the first question as follows:

> Only one migration differential seems to have systematically withstood the test—that for age. The following generalization has been found to be valid in many places and for a long period of time. Persons in their late teens, twenties, and early thirties are much more mobile than younger or older persons. Migration is highly associated with the first commitments and acts of adjustment of adulthood that are made by adolescents as they mature [for example, entrance into the labor force, marriage, family formation]. (p. 504)

Support for this generalization has been found in many empirical studies in different social settings, rendering this one of the most accepted generalizations in the social sciences.

Other differentials holding for the United States are indicated by Bogue as follows:

> 1. Men are more migratory than women, especially over long distances and when conditions at the destination are insecure or difficult.
> 2. Persons with professional occupations are among the most migratory groups in the population, whereas laborers and operatives (semiskilled workers) have below average mobility.
> 3. Unemployed persons are more migratory than employed persons.
> 4. Negroes are less migratory than whites. (p. 504)

With regard to the last differential, Shryock (1964, table 11.1) notes that nonwhites have higher intracounty mobility rates than whites; he agrees, however, that they have lower migration rates, and he supports the rest of Bogue's conclusions. Similarly, a more recent study of differential migration in the United States (Morrison, 1972) generally supports Bogue's conclusions.

Types of Communities Stimulating In-Migration and Out-Migration

In comparison with the findings above, there have been even fewer conclusions made on the kinds of communities which attract in-migration or generate out-migration. Indeed, very little is known about this aspect of differential migration. Bogue (1959b) indicates that rates of out-migration from an area vary inversely with the general level of educational attainment in the area (the lower the area's educational level, the higher the out-migration, and vice versa). Also, rates of out-migration tend to be closely related to rates of in-migration. Geographic variations in rates of mobility in the United States are shown in some detail by Shryock (1964). But no association is proposed between these variations and any areal classification or population category. Similarly, rates of out-migration and in-migration have been shown to differ systematically by type of residence (urban, rural, metropolitan, nonmetropolitan) but only very recently has an attempt been made to classify cities on this basis (Morrison, 1972). Metropolitan areas characterized by unusually high rates of net in-migration between 1960 and 1966 were designated *spontaneous growth centers* (SGCs). The single factor identified with the attractiveness of these communities has been defense expenditures. The locations of the SGCs with highest rates of in-migration are shown in Figure 10.2.

In an investigation of gross and net migration in which in-migration, out-migration, and net migration were studied in relation to population

Figure 10.2 Location of 3M Spontaneous Growth Centers. *Source: Morrison, "Population Movements and the Shape of Urban Growth: Implications of Public Policy," in* Population Distribution and Policy, *ed. Sara Mills Mazie, Vol. 5, Commission on Population Growth and the American Growth Research Reports (Washington, D.C.: Government Printing Office, 1972), p. 317.*

composition, income levels, and the demand for labor, I. S. Lowry (1966) found no evidence that labor market conditions influence the rate of out-migration. Rates of out-migration are determined primarily by the composition of the population. The highest propensities to migrate are found among young single adults and among young adult couples with small children. Populations with high proportions in these categories tend to have high rates of out-migration. However, the choice of alternative destination is influenced by both distance to the destination and labor market conditions there. Thus, rates of in-migration are affected by employment and income.

Depressed communities and prosperous communities both experience out-migration, primarily in relation to their age composition. However, while prosperous communities attract in-migrants from the national pool of persons "on the move," and especially from nearby places, depressed communities do not attract enough in-migrants to replace their out-migrants. Hence, depressed communities are frequently characterized by net out-migration as well as by a shift in the age distribution toward higher proportions in the less mobile ages. By contrast, prosperous communities attracting an excess of in-migrants over out-migrants also may experience a shift in their age distributions over time toward higher proportions in the younger, mobile ages. It is thus that long-depressed communities eventually become characterized by low rates of out-migration, complementing their low rates of in-migration. And long-prosperous communities become characterized by higher rates of out-migration along with their higher rates of in-migration—a conclusion consistent with that of Bogue, cited above (Lowry, 1966, chap. 5).

Intersocietal Comparisons of Migration

The conceptual and practical difficulties in defining and measuring migration are compounded in the effort to carry out international comparisons. Nevertheless an important start has been made in this direction by Long (1970; 1973), who has compared census and survey data on changes of address for the United States, Canada, Great Britain, and Japan. Such percentages migrating—whether in the one-year or five-year period prior to the census or survey inquiry—prove to be highest in the United States, though the Canadian percentages are very close behind.

In his analysis Long points to three distinct levels of residential mobility around 1960: the highest level for North America, an intermediate level for Great Britain, and the lowest level for Japan. But when allowance is taken of differences between the countries in the proportions of their working forces in agriculture, a two-level division emerges. Comparison of migration percentages restricted to males in nonagricultural employment shows a high level for the United States and Canada: 52.4 percent of the nonagricultural male labor force in the U.S. and 53.0 percent in Canada, moved at least once in the five years preceding the respective inquiries (see Table 10.5). But a similar comparison eliminates the difference between Japan and Great Britain: the percentages of the nonagricultural male labor force that moved during the twelve months preceding the respective inquiries were 20.4 percent for the United States, but 12.1 percent in England and Wales and 13.4 percent in Japan (see Table 10.5).

TABLE 10.5 International Comparisons of Migration: Percent Reporting Change in Address in Period Preceding Inquiry, circa 1960

	All Males		*Males Employed Outside Agriculture*	
Country	*Males 5+: Migration Five Years Prior to Census*	*Males 1+: Migration Twelve Months Prior to Census*	*Migration Five Years Prior to Census*	*Migration Twelve Months Prior to Census*
United States	50.9	20.9	52.4	20.4
Canada	45.1	N.A.	53.0	N.A.
England and Wales	36.8	12.0	38.0	12.1
Scotland	36.9	11.2	N.A.	N.A.
Japan	N.A.	8.7	N.A.	13.4

N.A.: Not available.
Source: Long, 1970, Tables 1, 2, 4.

The age and sex patterns of percentage mobile seem generally similar in the four countries, though very detailed comparisons were not possible. Other similarities appear in Long's analysis of socioeconomic differentials in short-distance and long-distance moving in the four countries (1973, pp. 255–57). The major conclusions are: (a) blue-collar workers have higher rates of short-distance (*within* local areas) moving than white-collar workers; white-collar workers have higher rates of longer-distance movement (*between* local areas); and the greater the distance the greater the white-collar–blue-collar differentials; and (b) professional and technical workers had higher migration rates than other white-collar workers.

A Theory of Differential Migration

Thus, other than the correspondence between modal ages of migrants and modal ages of entrance into the labor force, marriage and earliest family formation, there is little basis for a theory of differential migration. Only the finding (for example, by Ladinsky, 1967) that professional workers are characterized by unusually high migration rates, and the conclusion that migration among professionals is related to occupational career mobility and to family life cycle may be suggestive of a "change and response" theory reminiscent of Davis's theory of differential intervention in marriage and family formation (see our discussion in Chapter 9).

Ladinsky's finding was that professionals whose careers are tied neither to equipment whose location is geographically fixed nor to clientele in a fixed locale very often move their places of residence in connection with job advancements. These movements, in turn, are concentrated in the early stages of their family life cycles—typically before deep involvement of children in their own educational and social locales. Thus, certain professionals may be so located in the social and occupational structure as to have access to special economic and occupational opportunities *if* they are able to move. The result is that these people do in fact move at rates higher than those of other occupational and social categories.

The hypothesis that there is a relationship between volume of migration and *numbers of opportunities* was orginally formulated by Stouffer in 1940, and it still appears repeatedly in the modern sociological and demographic literature on migration and mobility. In brief terms, such an hypothesis of differential migration patterns holds that individuals differently located in the social structure (a) have different degrees of knowledge about, and (b) are able to benefit to differing extents from, opportunities at places other than those in which they currently reside.[2]

Another hypothesis concerning differential migration focuses upon the predicament-resolving properties of migration. For example, Bogue (1959b, p. 499) has listed as stimulants to migration such predicaments as lack of an offer of marriage; loss of farm; loss of nonfarm employment; prolonged receipt of low income; retirement; death of spouse, parent, or other relative; onset of poor health; political, racial, or religious oppression and discrimination; disaster in the community; and forced movement resulting from legal enactments. To the extent that there are

[2] For a similar hypothesis case in terms of a theory of decision making, see Beshers and Nishiura, 1960; and Beshers, 1967, especially chapter 5.

differential frequencies of the various predicaments in different population groups, we would expect that there is also a differential tendency to migrate as a predicament-resolving tactic.[3]

Both of these hypotheses seem to find some support in such meager empirical materials as are available. But they still leave open the question of community and societal determinants of differential migration.

INDIVIDUAL, COMMUNITY, AND SOCIETAL CONSEQUENCES OF MIGRATION

The analysis of the consequences of geographic mobility is one pursuit of social research in which great emphasis is placed upon the contradictions of human social existence. For although few studies of geographic mobility conclude that there aren't individual or societal benefits to migration, a large number do stress the personal and community disorganization, the problems of adjustment and conflict, the anomie and alienation, associated with migration.

Individual Consequences of Migration

A literature so vast as to defy concise summary has arisen to describe and analyze the processes of adjustment and acculturation undergone by migrants in their new social settings. The first of such studies was probably the classic *Polish Peasant in Europe and America,* by W. I. Thomas and F. Znaniecki (1918–1920). This study and its successors have stressed the role segregation of migrants—their exclusion from certain spheres of activity and social life and their performance of specialized migrant roles in other spheres. They have also stressed the difficulties in adjustments and acculturation associated with the differences in norms, values, and customs of migrants and nonmigrants (see Wirth, 1945).

A very large number of studies has dealt with the relationships between migrants or migrant status and alienation, delinquency, family disorganization, mental illness, unemployment and poverty, and promiscuity; and also marriage, intermarriage, and fertility. Generally, findings have shown that migrants have higher frequencies of all these phenomena than does the general population, and there have been analyses in varying detail of several intervening variables and circumstances (Park, 1925). Similar themes are discussed in the more recent, popular-

[3] For discussions of differential frequencies of predicaments, see Matras, Rosenfeld, and Salzberger, 1969; also Rossi, 1955.

ized works such as Whyte's *The Organization Man* (1956) and Packard's *A Nation of Strangers* (1972). We will return to this theme later in this volume.

A closely related literature has sought to analyze the conditions under which adjustment and acculturation in varying forms and degrees takes place. Most authors dealing with this problem have treated it as a matter of individual learning, accommodation, or "resocialization" (see Germani, 1965). But more recently an increasing number, following S. N. Eisenstadt (1954), have viewed it as a problem of social change, of change in role distributions or systems of role allocation. We shall return to this approach shortly.

Recent research has shown that migration is widely associated with gains in income and occupational status (Blau and Duncan, 1967; Duncan, Featherman, and Duncan, 1972; Lansing and Morton, 1967; Morrison, 1972). But it has not been easy to determine whether these are favorable effects of migration per se or whether they are due to the selectivity of migration, that is, to the characteristics of the migrants themselves (see Long and Heltman, 1975). In other words, many migrants are persons, who without migrating at the time they did, would have achieved income or occupational status gain. Migration tends to take place in streams, and presumably there is a sufficient feedback of information from migrants to would-be migrants to suggest that repeated failures to find opportunities would have some effect upon the stream. The fact that migration streams continue suggests that some benefits are indeed obtained from moving to new grounds. On the other hand, there is considerable return migration along the path of any migration stream. This suggests that there may be high or variable rates of failure. The evidence, though, is still inconclusive, for although a large body of empirical data relate the volume of return migration to the volume or velocity of migration streams (Long and Hansen, 1975), these do not bear specifically upon the question of the migrant's success in his new setting.

Similarly, though there has been much concern with new predicaments presumably generated by, or at least associated with, migratory moves, there have been virtually no studies of the extent to which migration-stimulating predicaments are in fact resolved by migration.

Community Consequences of Migration

The community consequences of migration which have been studied are confined mainly to the areas of population size and composition, size and structure of the labor force, residential patterns, voluntary organizations, and political structure. In his analysis of the absorption of immigrants, Eisenstadt (1954) presents the problem of absorption as one of change in the role-allocation structures of both the migrant groups and the societies which absorb them. The absorption process thus generates change both in the migrant group and in the absorbing communities. The variables in question are: (a) the types of pluralistic structures (meaning the systematically different allocation of social roles) which arise from different types of migration; (b) the limits, in various kinds of absorbing communities, to which pluralistic structures may develop without undermining the social structure; and (c) the types of disintegrative behavior which may develop on the part of both migrants and nonmigrants, and the possibility of institutional disorganization and change taking place in the absorbing community.

Thus, Eisenstadt, in dealing primarily with migrant groups rather than with individuals, anticipated the study of what has since been called *chain migration*: the sequential migration of related or otherwise-connected individuals to the same destination.[4] In Eisenstadt's scheme, the formation on the one hand of *landsmannschaften* (groups sharing common geocultural origin) and specialized religious, educational, or other institutions serving migrants, and the existence on the other hand of community patterns of residential, occupational, or social segregation are both subsumed under the rubric of differences in roles allotted to, and performed by, migrants and nonmigrants respectively. The community change may tend either toward the convergence of role distributions or toward the stabilization and institutionalization of separate, pluralistic role structures.

Thus, Southern European immigrants to the large cities of the United States were initially segregated from the native-born population. They were concentrated in ethnic ghettos and unskilled occupations, and organized in ethnic church and mutual-aid associations. That is, they were initially allotted special "immigrant" roles in a pluralistic structure. Later, the immigrants or their offspring dispersed residentially, occupationally, and socially, although their role distributions may not yet have converged entirely with those of "old American" parts of the population.

In a somewhat similar manner, black, Puerto Rican, and Mexican immigrants to the large cities of the United States were initially segregated residentially, occupationally, and socially from the native white population. But far from undergoing a change in the direction of role distributions which converged with those of native whites, the evidence indicates an institutionalization of separate, pluralistic black and white role structures (See Taeuber & Taeuber, 1964).

[4] This concept was also extensively used in Price, 1964; and MacDonald and MacDonald, 1964.

Societal Consequences of Migration

The chief societal consequences of migration lie in the redistribution of the population, both areally and by type of community. Shryock summarizes the historical record of the United States up to 1964 as follows:

> The dominant trend in the geographic redistribution of the population was along the advancing frontier of settlement essentially in the Westward direction. . . . Beginning later than the Westward movement was the movement out of the South to the North, . . . involving both whites and Negroes. The out-migration of Negroes was particularly heavy during World War II. In recent years there have been counter-movements of whites from the Northwest to certain metropolitan and urban areas in the South.
>
> The current trend of geographic redistribution involves movement out of the heartland of the United States to the seacoasts and to the shores of the Great Lakes. There has apparently been a net migratory movement from rural to urban areas for a long time. Within metropolitan areas there is now a centrifugal movement of population, most large cities losing people in the interchange with their own suburbs. (Shryock, 1964, pp. 63–64)

More recently there has been net migratory movement away from metropolitan areas. Some of this represents continued suburbanization of population and employment around existing metropolitan areas (U.S. Bureau of the Census, *Current Population Reports,* Series P–20, no. 256, Nov. 1973). However, there have also been net gains for smaller cities and for rural places (Beale & Fuguitt, 1975). Of the four regions, the South and West continued in 1970–73 to experience net in-migration from other parts of the United States as was the case in 1965–70; and the Northeast and North Central regions continued to experience net out-migration.

Similar accounts can be put together for other countries as well. However, these descriptions do not complete the picture of the social and economic organizational effects of migratory movements. Typically, the migration streams tend to be selective—that is, they include certain types of people but exclude others. Far from being a simple redistribution of the total population, migratory movements involve a changing distribution of given types of people in distinct ways. Thus, for example, the interchange within metropolitan areas does not merely send net increases to the suburbs or metropolitan ring. Rather, it sends persons of higher income and status to the suburbs and persons of lower income and status from the suburbs to the cities, a process which operates to polarize cities and metropolitan rings (the surrounding suburbs) with respect to income and socioeconomic level (Schnore & Pinkerton, 1966). Similarly, there is some evidence that systems of migratory movements deepen racial segregation (Duncan & Hauser, 1960; Taeuber & Taeuber, 1965, chaps. 6 and 7; Hodge & Hauser, 1968).

The manner in which suburbanization trends have operated to concentrate higher-status population in the metropolitan ring and low-status persons in the central city is illustrated for the Chicago metropolitan area in Table 10.6. The table shows the composition of the

TABLE 10.6 Indexes of Disproportionate Change for Three Educational Classes in the Chicago Metropolitan Area, 1950–1960: A Methodological Illustration [a]

Population (aged 25 and over) by Years of School Completed[b]	*Percent of City Population, 1950*	*Percent of Ring Population, 1950*	*City Ring Difference, 1950*	*Percent of City Population, 1960*	*Percent of Ring Population, 1960*	*City-Ring Difference, 1960*	*Indexes of Disproportionate Change, 1950–60*
	(1)	*(2)*	*(3)*	*(4)*	*(5)*	*(6)*	*(7)*
							Col. (6) — Col. (3)
Total	100.00	100.00		100.00	100.00		
Grade	46.80	40.35	−6.45	42.92	30.13	−12.79	−6.34
High	39.99	41.41	+1.42	42.80	47.90	+ 5.10	+3.68
College	13.21	18.24	+5.03	14.28	21.97	+ 7.69	+2.66

[a] The 1950 Standard Metropolitan Area (and its equivalent, the 1960 Standard Consolidated Area) for Chicago and Northwestern Indiana.

[b] "Grade" = 0 through 8 years; "High" = 1 to 4 years of high school; "College" = 1 to 4 or more years of college.

Source: Schnore and Pinkerton, 1966, p. 494.

central city and metropolitan ring populations respectively by educational achievement categories in 1950 and in 1960, city-ring compositional differences in 1950 and 1960, and "indexes of disproportionate change" during the ten-year period. For the Chicago metropolitan area, the indexes of disproportionate change show that the suburbs enjoyed disproportionate increases in the percent of population who had gone to high school or college, and a disproportionate decrease in the percent who had attended grade school only. Schnore and Pinkerton (1966, p. 495) show that the same pattern occurred in 216 of the 363 United States metropolitan areas studied. Suburbanization generally operates to shift the more educated groups away from the central cities of metropolitan areas and to concentrate the lower-education groups inside the central cities.

In-migration from overseas and rural-to-urban movements have been responsible historically for another major societal consequence: the populating of the great cities of America and the building of the industrial labor forces of the nineteenth and twentieth centuries in Europe and in the United States. Whether migratory movements in the Western world and in the underdeveloped countries today have the same relationship to industrialization, or whether they bear any relationship at all to changing economic organization, is a topic of intensive current research.

SUMMARY

We have seen in this chapter that migration can be studied from demographic, geographic, general sociological, and sociopsychological points of view. In all instances, the volume, directions, distances, causes, and consequences of migration are important topics of concern. A classical demographic topic has been international migration and its bearing on the worldwide distribution of population. From the beginnings of colonization to the outbreak of World War II, more than 60 million Europeans emigrated overseas, including close to 33 million who moved to the United States alone. The number of European refugees and displacements between 1913 and 1968 has been estimated to be about 29 million, with another 46 million forced international immigrants migrating in Asia, Africa, or the western hemisphere in the same period. Net emigration has had the effect of moderating greatly the population growth of several European countries, with Ireland probably the best known example. Conversely, the populations of countries with high rates of immigration have included quite large foreign-born sectors. In the United States, the foreign-born population reached a peak of about 13 percent in 1910, declining thereafter to just over four percent currently. But other countries of immigration have had much larger percentages of foreign-born population, though the absolute numbers have been very much smaller. A few places, such as Israel, Hong Kong, and Kuwait, have populations that are more than half foreign born. Aside from the overall effects on population distribution, international migration has had a special role in redistributing populations of given attributes—of given national, religious, or ethnic origins; of given occupations or educational qualifications.

The effects of internal migration on population redistribution are evident in the example of the United States. The historical westward movement of the population involved large numbers of migrants, the overwhelming majority of them native born. While the Eastern Seaboard is still the most densely populated region of the country, California has replaced New York as the most populous single state. The growth of American cities in the nineteenth and twentieth centuries was achieved largely by rural-to-urban migration, though overseas immigrants were also important. The twentieth century expansion and spillover of large cities into suburbs, and the growth of metropolitan areas, were largely a consequence of migratory movements of families from central cities outward to nearby suburbs. Other countries have experienced similar population redistributions as a consequence of migratory movement.

Theories about the causes of migration have centered around two concepts: first, the pursuit of economic opportunity or enhanced levels of living; and second, people's age or life cycle propensities to move. In addition, political factors have been recognized as cause of much of international migration. Actual studies of the causes of migration have examined differential rates of migration, compared the characteristics—especially employment and economic—of communities from which migrants originate and to which migrants move, and inquired of migrants themselves the reasons for moving. The main explanatory principle invoked to account for or predict internal migration remains that of shifting of human resources in adaptation to the changing economic contingencies reflected in differential employment and wage and salary opportunities in different places, areas, or labor markets.

Migration has both individual and community consequences. There are indications that migrants who move out of an area obtain higher incomes and achieve higher occupational status than similar individuals remaining in the same place of origin. Data also show that rural-to-urban migrants have had lower fertility than those who remain in the country. In general, systematic investigation of the consequences of migration is still just beginning, and there are many other areas of this topic which have yet to be studied. One of these areas is deviance. Various types of deviance—crime, mental illness, family disorganization—have been thought to be more frequent among lower-class migrants than among nonmigrants. There still are few conclusive studies, however, isolating the migration factor from other influences.

The individual consequences of migration—income, fertility deviance, and so forth—are in the aggregate community consequences as well. In addition there are community consequences of special patterns of residence, association, and participation characterizing migrants. Thus, formation of migrant residential communities, churches and organizations, distinctive school attendance, and separate political inclinations are very common. The nature of the population of never-migrants and some-times-migrants in a community may be an important determinant of the axes of social solidarity and differentiation. Finally, communities, and all their organizations, must develop arrangements and institutions to assure continuity and stability of social interaction and relationships—whether work, neighborhood, political, or whatever—in the face of very considerable population turnover.

Large percentages of the population change residences each year—and many of these people move to a different county or farther. Aside from their population growth or decline due to net in- or out-migration, most American communities have experienced substantial population turnover in the recent past and may look forward to further population turnover due to migration. The societal implications of this movement—whether positive, in the form of efficient adaptation of populations to shifting technological and economic exigencies, or negative, in that the United States may be a "nation of strangers"—is a debate still in search of systematic and convincing research.

The components of population growth and change which we have discussed in the second part of this volume include those representing *entrance* into populations, i.e. births or in-migration to a given place; *departures* from populations, i.e. deaths or out-migration; and *changes in location*—whether changes in geographic location by migration, or in social location by aging or mobility. In Part III we turn to demographic, social, economic, and political responses to population growth and change.

Three

Responses to Population Growth and Change

11

The Impact of Population Changes on Social Systems

In the first part of this volume we suggested that variations in population size, density, and structure are closely related to variations in social structure. Surveying world populations, we concluded that societies with distinctly different populations tend to differ in systematic ways. We saw, for instance, that some of the important taxonomies of societies are closely connected to the sizes and densities of their populations. We suggested that population growth, the ways societies respond to actual or potential growth, and the strategies that societies adopt to assure their survival and adaptation in the face of population growth can be viewed as a fundamental cause of social change. In this connection we cited Durkheim's analysis, which sets forth the principle that the growth of population and social density gives rise to an increasing differentiation and division of labor.

In this chapter we shall return to these ideas, exploring them in more detail and considering possible directions for the further study of ways in which population growth and turnover generate changes in social structure. We will return to Durkheim's principle of the division of labor, exploring some of its reasons and some of its implications. In addition, we will attempt to formulate—at least tentatively—two additional principles relating population growth and population turnover to social change. These are the expansion of social boundary systems (the increase in size, number of participants, range, or scope of social, economic, or political units); and the adoption and institutionalization of innovations. We shall try to show that these responses to population changes—division of labor, expansion of social boundary systems, and institutionalization of innovations—occur singly or in combination in all types of societies. In every case, their effect is to improve or to assure survival and adaptation under conditions of increased numbers or shifting membership in the population. We turn first to some general considerations of social structure.

THE ELEMENTS OF SOCIAL STRUCTURE

For social scientists, the concept of "social structure" conveys some notion of stable or recurring patterns of social relationships. Many are content to use the concept without further definition or elaboration. There is, however, a tradition of developing the idea of social structure around the concepts of social role or social position. In this approach the *social structure* of a society is specified as:

1. The set of social roles and positions
2. The set of institutionalized relationships between pairs of roles and between larger combinations or subsystems of roles
3. The composition of the population with respect to social roles and to subsystems of social roles
4. The flow and exchange of social rewards and resources

The basic and most elementary concept in the analysis of social structure, and in sociological analysis generally, is that of *social role*. We shall say here simply that a social role is a set of socially prescribed behaviors and relationships. An individual occupies that role if his social behavior toward others and their behavior toward him *both* satisfy the prescriptions of the role. Some examples of social roles include the President of the United States, the hobo, the hippie, the school teacher, the ward politician, the mother, the bus driver, the child, the playmate, the bank clerk, the bricklayer, the uncle, or the steady girlfriend. Each role is characterized by a socially prescribed set of behaviors on the part of the incumbent and on the part of others in relationship to him.

A social role which recurs in a society, is recognized in the society, and whose set of behaviors is normatively prescribed in the society, is said to be *institutionalized* in that society. Such a role, together with the behaviors it prescribes for the incumbent and for others toward the incumbent, and the norms or rules governing these behaviors, comprises one of the society's *institutions*. Thus, we say that the mother-in-law is an institution in American society, that the matchmaker was an institution in agrarian European societies, and that the Emperor is an institution in Japanese society.

Social Systems and Institutionalized Role Relations

A second facet of social structure comprises the recurring patterned relationships between recognized or institutionalized social roles. This facet of social structure has received by far the most attention in sociological analysis. Relationships between incumbents of different social roles typically conform to socially prescribed patterns. Some examples are a few common two-person relationships: mother-child, husband-wife, employer-employee, or leader-follower. In any given society, these tend to conform to expected, socially prescribed, boundaries. On the other hand, the nature of the mother-child relationship and any other of these relationships may well vary from society to society.

Similarly, any given society has distinctive patterns which characterize relationships within groups, whether these be small groups (family, friendship club, work group) or larger ones (churches, businesses, factories, political parties). When a number of social roles are gathered into such *systems* of patterned relationships, the larger units are called *social systems* (or *subsystems*) of the society. The socially prescribed relationships between incumbents of a system's component social roles are said to be institutionalized relationships. Thus, a society's social systems may include any recognized system of social roles—the family, the church, voluntary organizations, businesses, neighborhood groups, the government, or political parties. In fact, the entire society is itself a social system.

Any social system which is recognized in the society and for which a set of relationships between role incumbents is prescribed in the society is said, like similar social roles, to be institutionalized in that society. In this sense, the family, the school, the church, and the political party are all institutions in American society, and they may be institutions in other societies as well.

A social system typically includes subsystems which are less complex but also characterized by institutionalized role relationships. For example, the family includes the mother-father subsystem, the brother-sister subsystem, the father-daughter subsystem, and so on—and these subsystems are all characterized by socially prescribed and recurring relationships. Again, the factory includes work-group subsystems, the board of directors subsystem, the office-staff subsystem, and the maintenance-staff subsystem.

Finally, any two or more social systems may be related to one another in a *system of social systems,* with stable or recurring relationships prescribed and recognized among them. The family, the school, and the police department comprise a system of social systems; the federal government, the United States Chamber of Commerce, and the American Federation of Labor comprise another system of social systems. A municipal administration, too, is a system of social systems.

Composition of the Population by Social Roles

The third facet of social structure is the composition of the society's population with respect to recognized social roles and key combinations of social roles. The composition of a population by social role and by combinations of social roles indicates (a) the relative frequency in the society of given social roles or types of roles and (b) the relative frequency of characteristic combinations of roles, that is the relationships between social roles as reflected by joint incumbency. Thus, in the first case, the roles of the unskilled laborer and the professional worker may both be recognized in two different societies, but the relative number of laborers in one society may be considerably different from that in the other. Similarly, rural occupancy may be a recognized role in many societies, but the relative number of rural folk may be greater in one society than in another. As for the relationships between social roles, being an unskilled laborer in one society may be related to rural residence, while being a laborer or a professional worker in another society may have nothing whatsoever to do with the urban or rural role.

In one society there may be many educated women, but in another there may be relatively few. Many women in society *A,* but not society *B,* have occupational roles outside the home; and in society *C,* but not society *D,* employment of women outside the home may be related to women's levels of education.

The Allocation and Exchange of Social Rewards and Resources

Different types of social interaction have different purposes, forms, and outcomes. There are kinds of products or outcomes of social interaction which are valued and desired by individuals or by groups—whether material outputs, emotional satisfactions, certain kinds of relationships, or simply a sense of order. Food, shelter, medical care, entertainment, and automobiles are all products of human interaction, as are all other products of production processes involving human interaction. Honor, prestige, and power are others. Individuals may receive, value, and consume such outputs of social interaction, and for this reason we may call them all *social rewards.*

Sometimes social rewards of one type can be exchanged or converted or otherwise used and maneuvered in order to receive other social rewards. A social reward which can be exchanged or converted as well as consumed can be called a *social resource.* Thus, money and barterable goods are social resources. So, sometimes, are friendship and kind words.

In terms of these concepts *social interaction* can be defined as the flow of social rewards and exchange of social resources among the roles and positions, and among the groupings and subsystems of roles and positions, in the social structure.

CHANGE IN SOCIAL STRUCTURE

Change in social structure will occur under four separate types of circumstance: (a) when the set of roles changes—by addition, subtraction, bifurcation, or differentiation of roles; (b) when one or more role relationships or subsystem relationships change; (c) when numbers or proportions of incumbents in the various roles, roles categories, or role systems shift, or when rules governing incumbency change; or (d) when allocation of social rewards, or rules governing conversion and exchange of social resources, change.

A central assertion of this volume is that population growth, turnover, or shifts *always* effect one or more of these changes in social structure, or, alternatively, that social systems *always* respond to population changes. We illustrate this idea in a simplified manner and formulate some preliminary generalizations in this chapter. And in the chapters which follow we try to expand the argument in more detail.

Dyad to Triad Transformations

The *dyad,* or two-person group, is the very simplest social system. The changes in this social system attending the addition of a single person to form a *triad,* or three-person group, is the simplest example of the response of a social system to population growth. The comparison of dyads and triads is a classical topic in sociological analysis.[1]

The most familiar example of the dyad is the married couple; the most familiar triad is the family of three—the couple and one child. The group transformation brought about by the birth of the child is familiar, but it is also profound. What was once a social system consisting of husband-wife relations now becomes a much more complex social system, with several added dimensions. It is now a system of husband-wife; mother-child; father-child; and husband/father-wife/mother-child relations. A significant property of the three-person family, as of triads generally, is the tendency to divide into a coalition of two members against the third. This tendency has attracted a great deal of attention among sociologists, social psychologists, and psychoanalysts. And it has also been the subject of a fairly elaborate and rapidly developing theory of coalitions in triads (Caplow, 1968).

In the transformation of the couple to a triad by virtue of the addition of a child, we can identify several shifts in relationships, and cast them in the social-structural terms presented earlier in this chapter. In the first place, there are both more individuals in the (now three-person) system, and there are also three two-person subsystems instead of the original single two-person system. There are new roles and role-relationships: wife not only remains wife in the wife-husband subsystem, but she also becomes mother in the mother-child subsystem. Finally, the nature of the earlier relationship, the husband-wife relationship is altered by the presence of the third person: the wife-husband relationship *also* becomes mother-father in the mother-father-child triad, and in this way its nature is changed.

Thus the birth of the child, and the transformation of the dyad to a triad implies new roles for each member of the original couple: husband and wife also become mother and father. It also implies new role relationships in the expanded system, as mother-child and father-child relationships become significant. In addition, the coming of the child demands a new allocation of time for both husband and wife and revisions in the flows and exchanges of rewards and resources. There are both rewards directed to the child and gratifications from interaction with the child.

The triad has new needs—for space, products, services, and interaction with other individuals and social units. And often this means

[1] The best known discussions are probably those of the German scholar, Georg Simmel (1858–1918) whose paper on "The Number of Members as Determining the Sociological Form of the Group" was translated and published in the United States as early as 1902 (*American Journal of Sociology,* Vol. 8, no. 1, July 1902). Many of Simmel's other papers were subsequently translated, entering the literature and forming a base for a developing line of study of group structure and social systems. See Simmel, 1950.

From dyad to triad. *(United Nations)*

shifts in employment, in residence, and in patterns of interaction with extended family, friends, neighbors, or others. The addition of a third person also brings on another change, as the family becomes a more permanent social unit. Even if one person should withdraw or die, the family can continue and eventually replace the loss—by remarriage or another birth. Not so the couple: loss or withdrawal of one member dissolves the entire relationship.

As the child and couple age, the relationships within the triad change. The child's knowledge, strengths, skills, and his weight, influence, and power increase relative to each separate parent and to both parents jointly. The parents' own skills, experiences, aptitudes, and physical capacities change as they age, as do their social relations outside.

The same kinds of changes occur in other dyad-to-triad transformations as we have seen in the case of the family unit. Consider, for example, the merchant and single clerk, or the craftsman and apprentice. Each of these working dyads is characterized by similarities of interest and by common orientation to the tasks at hand, by shared work experience and differentiation from those not so engaged. As Simmel noted, the addition of a clerk, apprentice, or employee means the transformation of a working dyad to a working triad, and this introduces two-employee solidarity vis-à-vis employer. At the same time, employers find it easier to keep two subordinates than one at a distance and to obtain their compliance. In all events, the transformation to a working triad introduces, in addition to the three-person subsystem, additional two-person subsystems and coalitions as well as altering the initial employer-employee subsystem.

More Complex Social Systems

Social systems more complex than dyads or triads are affected by population turnover, by changes in population distribution, and by changes in population composition, as well as by changes in numbers and by aging. *Population turnover* is replacement of a departing or withdrawing member of the social system by a new member. As we noted earlier, this can occur in triads as well, but it is more characteristic of larger, more complex social systems such as organizations, residential communities, or the labor force. By *population distribution* we mean the physical or geographic dispersion of individuals belonging to the system. This includes their density, distance or physical access to one another, to other social systems, to individuals, or to objects. The distribution of persons in a social system can change simply because people can move from one location to another.

Population composition is the sum total of the characteristics and attributes of individual members. It may change insofar as the characteristics of individuals entering or departing from the population are, in the aggregate, different from those of the total of the permanent population. But population composition may change also as a consequence of individual changes, like increased education, occupational shifts, marriage or divorce, or shifting social status.

Families. The sequence of events and changes over time which a family unit undergoes include marriage, the birth of first and subsequent children, the growth and eventually the departure of the children from the household and the dissolution of the couple by death of one member. This sequence is called the *family cycle.* The family cycle includes changing numbers of persons in the family unit, changing age, and changing marital status. In some instances there is turnover by virtue of death of a child and subsequent birth of another child. For larger or extended families there routinely is turnover by virtue of deaths and births as well as by marriage, divorce, and widowhood.

In the course of the family cycle, there are several changing constellations of role relations: husband-wife, father-child, mother-child, brother-sister, elder brother-younger brother, and so forth, with many triads and coalitions forming and reforming. In addition, the content of role behavior varies over time, and so do the allocation of time, attention, interest, and authority. Thus, the time of the wife may be initially taken up with work, then later with childrearing, and still later with work again. The couple may spend some part of the family cycle alone prior to birth of children and again after the children's marriages and departures—but this does not mean that the couple returns to its original relationship. The ages, as well as the accumulated experience and "time in the system" of the married couple, as well as their interests, abilities, tastes, and aptitudes change as part of the aging process.

Large families have different patterns of allocation of time and resources than do small families. But for all families, the addition of new members forces shifts in the allocation of time and resources and, sometimes, in the very mode in which sustenance and resources are assured. The growing family may send additional members to work, or the major earner or some other family member may seek new employment, perhaps in a different place of residence. Patterns of intrafamily authority and dominance also shift as the family grows, and new patterns develop as the family and its members age.

Organizations

Two features distinguish formal organizations from other social systems: these are identifiable boundaries or explicit membership criteria of an organization; and the organization's coordination of activities with reference to some explicit goal or set of goals. The corporation has stockholders, managers, and employees; its activities are oriented toward the production and sale of goods or services for profit. The Boy Scouts of America has national and local sponsor and advisory groups, an administrative structure, scoutmasters and leaders, and scouts of varying ages, ranks, sizes, shapes, and activity categories; and its activities are oriented to the goals of health, fellowship, good citizenship, and community integration and participation of the young scouts and sometimes of their parents. Organizations are widely studied both because so much of social life, interaction, production, and exchange of social rewards and resources takes place in the context of formal organizations, and because they are microcosms of society and social relations generally.

Sociology, the administrative sciences, and other related fields have studied organizations from many perspectives, looking at their internal structure, differentiation, and complexity; at the behavior of individuals and subgroups in organizational settings; at patterns of leadership, influence, and power in organized groups; and at the effectiveness of organizations in achieving their goals. The impact of an organization's size on its structure and other characteristics has received very considerable attention as well.

Comparisons of organizations of different sizes have suggested that the larger the organization, the greater its complexity in terms of specialization of positions and in terms of both horizontal and vertical differentiation. For example, the number of divisions within a specialized department of industrial organizations is greater the larger the number of employees in the organization. The number of authority levels within a division tends to be greater the larger the firm or organization. Moreover, the larger the organization, the greater the degree of formalization of authority structure, the greater the formalization of orientation and training of new members, and the more likely there is to be formal stipulation of sanctions for violation of rules (Hall, 1972).

The numbers of persons engaged in administrative tasks in organizations such as business and production firms, hospitals, schools and universities (the "administrative component") has been extensively studied in relationship to overall size. In general, the relative size of the administrative component is smaller in larger organizations. But for very large organizations, there is a direct relationship: the proportion engaged in administrative activities is enlarged to meet the demands of coordination and control for an organization of very great size. Thus, the United States Government's Department of Defense has a larger administrative component than General Motors.

Despite only limited research on organizational *growth* (as distinct from comparison of organizations of different sizes) it seems clear that as growth occurs in organizations there are processes of formalization, greater complexity, and redistribution of power and authority which take place by way of enabling the organization to handle its increased size. As Hall has summarized:

> Growth brings new members into the organization. They come in at all levels and with a variety of experience, expertise, motivations, and desires for the organization and themselves. An immediate consequence of their arrival is that they upset existing patterns of interaction and communications. Existing social relationships are altered as the new members find their niches in the social structure. For veteran members of the organization this is somewhat threatening, since the former power arrangements are now distorted and new alignments emerge. . . . [N]ew members are superimposed on the existing system and penetrate into it, with the frequent result of setting the "new guard" versus the "old guard."
>
> Communications patterns between the groups are often blocked or nonexistent; within groups heightened solidarity can develop, which further decreases between-group interactions. If the organizational arrangements are such that communication and cooperation are expected and necessary, such a development is clearly dysfunctional for the organization. When new members are absorbed into the existing system, disruption occurs as the previous system becomes no longer operative. The total membership has to learn what the new pattern is and react accordingly. In any case the social system is disrupted. (Hall, 1972, 135–36)

The business, the factory, the university, the local government, the veterans' organization, the church, and the political party are all examples of organizations whose internal relationships, interaction processes, and activities are disrupted by entrance of additional members. In addition, however, organizations experience disruptions even of ongoing relationships under conditions of rapid turnover of members. Moreover, it is often the case that expected or institutionalized turnover actually precludes the very development of deeply solidary relationships.[2]

Systems of social relations in organizations are basically unstable in the face of population turnover. At most, they can incorporate mechanisms for "handling" population turnover, for minimizing disruptions in ongoing relations, eliminating stoppages in flows of information, and building on impersonal, institutionalized, position-to-position rather than person-to-person relationships in continuing "business as usual" under all personnel movement contingencies. However, when Mr. Jones leaves the firm, or is transferred to the Siberia office, Mr. Smith, his replacement, cannot ever be an exact duplicate of Mr. Jones. Aside from his personality differences compared to Jones—whose relevance may be minimized as far as possible by the nature of the work and work rela-

[2] This theme has been expanded by numerous writers. See especially W. F. Whyte, *The Organization Man,* and Vance Packard, *A Nation of Strangers.* We will return briefly to this theme later on.

A crowded pineapple processing factory—a response to increased population. *(United Nations)*

tionships—Smith inevitably has some background or work experience characteristics that are different from Jones'. And in all events, the fact that he is a newcomer, and that even after five years he will have less time in the system than his prior-arrival colleagues, suffices to make him different from Jones. What is most important is that some part of the web of relationships, both formal and informal, around the social position filled by Jones must be altered in some manner with the advent of Smith. The university, the military installation, the oil exploration site, and often the plant or facility of a far-flung business empire are examples of organizations in which "moving on" is the frequent and expected pattern. And this state of flux is taken into account in the formation of friendships, work relationships, and patterns of authority and influence.

Finally, organizations are made up of members of different ages and seniority who play different organizational roles and fill different organizational positions, and who are sometimes located in physically different places. A business organization with given numbers of senior officials and junior employees; with given numbers of executives, clerks, and production employees; and with given numbers located in the several plants and distribution centers must be organized to coordinate the activities of all these persons to maximize production, sales, or profits. Changes in age, in seniority, in occupations and positions, and in locations of individual members entail not only individual adjustments to new settings and relationships. They also imply the need for new arrangements, relationships, and communications and authority networks to attain the goals of the group. Thus an organization which ages, or in which many shifts from unskilled or semiskilled to skilled or professional positions have taken place, must adopt new procedures for guiding and controlling its production flows, relationships, activities, and chains of responsibility and authority.

Marriage Markets and Recruitment Squeezes

We have earlier introduced the concept of the marriage squeeze, the imbalance between the numbers of males and females respectively available or eligible for marriage. We noted that there are basically two kinds of resolutions of marriage squeezes: staying single—for a short time, for a longer time, or indefinitely—and changing the rules of eligibility and choice of marriage partners. Thus we saw that whether our heroine finds her true love this year or has to wait for next year depends in part on the marriage market: the size and composition of the populations of marriageable men and competing marriageable women. Again, whether she marries a rich groom or has to settle for a less well-heeled mate; whether he will be a handsome specimen or a homely one; whether he will be of the "right" social characteristics or lesser origins, all depend in part on the nature of the male marriageables and female competitors. The couples that are ultimately formed, the families which these couples rear, and the social participation and social networks in which they move and interact are similarly influenced by the population shifts—growth, turnover, or changing composition—affecting the marriage market and marriage choices and options.

Similar kinds of demographic constraints operate in social situations involving mutual association choices or recruitment. Consider, for example, an informal friendship network like a bridge club. The members are all, in addition to being more or less expert at bridge, persons who are mutually agreeable to entertaining and visiting in one another's homes. Selection of members is not random: rather there are some *rules* of mutual desirability or acceptability. If some one or more of the group move away, a number of things can happen to the bridge club. First, the bridge club can continue with reduced numbers. If this is neither possible or desirable, the bridge club can recruit new members from among the old residents of the community. Or, it can recruit new members from among the newcomers to the community.

Each of these courses of action for the bridge club has its positive and negative aspects. The first course entails no change in the rules implicity or explicity adopted previously to govern acceptability. However, this could mean being short-handed, short-funded, or short of houses. Moreover, in the long run additional decrements are surely to be anticipated in the future. Therefore, this strategy promises the ultimate demise of the bridge club.

The second course implies changing the acceptability rules. A person presumably not previously deemed acceptable or desirable is now found to be desirable under the new circumstances. This shift in the rules assures survival of the group. The third course may allow survival without changing the rules, provided "outsiderness" is not a characteristic implying nonacceptability.

Sociologically we are interested in the conditions under which the first, second, or third courses are adopted; and if rules are changed, in what direction do they change under various circumstances? We can view this problem much more generally, looking at broader social networks or social systems; at the activities, tastes, and relationships involved; and at rules for acceptability or nonacceptability.

The community college, the state university, and the high-prestige university each have their standards of admission for freshmen and for continuing at subsequent levels. These vary in accordance with the size and composition of the pool of candidates for entrance. Centerville Normal College may have a distinguished faculty and an excellent academic reputation; but if it draws only from among a small pool of four or five hundred local high school graduates annually, it cannot possibly restrict enrollment to the very best students. In order to admit only the top ten percent its selection would be limited to a maximum pool of only forty or fifty students. In contrast, the high prestige university which draws from a pool of hundreds of thousands of national high school graduates can enforce all manner of admission standards and requirements. However, when numbers of high school graduates decline—whether because of fertility shifts 18 years earlier, because of migration, or because of increased dropout rates—the recruitment and admissions norms and policies must be reviewed and often revised. Conversely, when the numbers seeking admission increase rapidly—mostly because of population growth, as in the 1950s and 1960s—all the colleges and universities, local and national alike, can be more choosey, enforcing more rigid admissions and continuation standards and "flunking out" students who don't make the grade.

Similar demographic constraints influence recruitment to military service, both voluntary and selective service, and they affect parts of the job market, too. Employers can recruit employees from pools which differ in sizes, composition, skills, and geographical distribution, in accordance with *both* the kind of employment and the demographic constraints of the area in which they are operating. Thus employment want ads may seek employees for strictly local firms; but in some occupations and industries the recruitment effort is regional or nationwide, with the want ads in the local paper reflecting the variations.

SOCIAL SYSTEM RESPONSES TO POPULATION CHANGE

We can extend some of the ideas raised in the discussions of the dyad and triad, families, organizations, and the marriage market and other recruitment systems. In each of these examples we posited some ongoing social system which undergoes change in the wake of certain population changes. A full society is itself an ongoing social system, and as such it is also typically affected by population changes. Two major types of population changes are particularly relevant: turnover of population, which takes place by entrances and departures through migration and births and deaths; and growth of the population, which can also occur by increments or decrements deriving both from births and deaths and from migration. Population turnover *disorganizes* ongoing social systems, because the population replacements never exactly duplicate the departures. Population growth *expands* some or all of the units in the social system, and it also disorganizes the system because it typically occurs disproportionately to the existing composition.

Population Processes and Social Disorganization

Population processes may be direct or indirect causes of social disorganization. Both the changing size of population elements and the changing absolute or relative numerical relationships between them may render a group, an institution, or a social system unable to function or pursue its goals. Political institutions, decision making bodies, or political elites may be so affected by population growth or changing composition: for instance, the town meeting becomes unwieldy when communities become large. Again, legislative bodies, community councils and assemblies have difficulty operating with very heterogeneous constituencies. They must instead form coalitions, political machines, and political exchange and trade-off routines. These, in turn, will themselves become disorganized as population composition changes, and so they must periodically be revamped. Under conditions of population growth and changing composition, political elites must coopt new elements or give way to competitors.

Schools, churches, voluntary organizations, police forces, business and industry, and recreational institutions are other examples of social systems disorganized by population growth, turnover, or changing composition. The changing composition of a population, by age, race, ethnicity, religion, social class, or educational achievement, and changing size too, may well cause some institutionalized set of relationships to become disorganized. That is, they become unable to continue in their previous manner or direction. This forces change in the content of roles and in the nature of social relationships. Primary schools which have previously served pupils of some specific strata, or religious, ethnic, or racial origins must introduce changes in curricula, in teaching routines, and sometimes in personnel to meet the needs of new children of different origins and different socialization histories. Such a disorganization and reorganization process can extend to entire school systems in and outside ghetto areas. And it can extend to other educational institutions, like colleges or universities, as well.

Economic and production institutions routinely and recurrently become disorganized by the changing educational backgrounds of successive cohorts of new workers. Among males aged 25 to 29 in 1910, less than 20 percent completed high school. But by 1960, more than 74 percent were high school graduates (See Table 11.1 and Figure 11.1). No

TABLE 11.1 Educational Attainment of U.S. Males, 25–29 Years of Age, 1910–1960: Percentage Distributions

Date	*Total*	*Completed Less Than Five Years of School*	*Completed Five or More Years of School; Did Not Complete High School*	*Completed High School or Beyond; Did Not Complete College*	*Completed College; Four Years or More*	*Median Number of School Years Completed*
Census						
1960	100.0	3.4	22.5	59.7	14.4	12.3
1950	100.0	5.4	34.4	50.6	9.6	12.0
1940	100.0	6.9	50.2	36.0	6.9	10.1
Estimate						
1930	100.0	10.6	58.3	24.6	6.5	8.7
1920	100.0	16.7	59.2	19.2	4.9	8.4
1910	100.0	21.2	59.0	15.7	4.1	8.2

Source: Adapted from Folger and Nam 1964, table, 4.

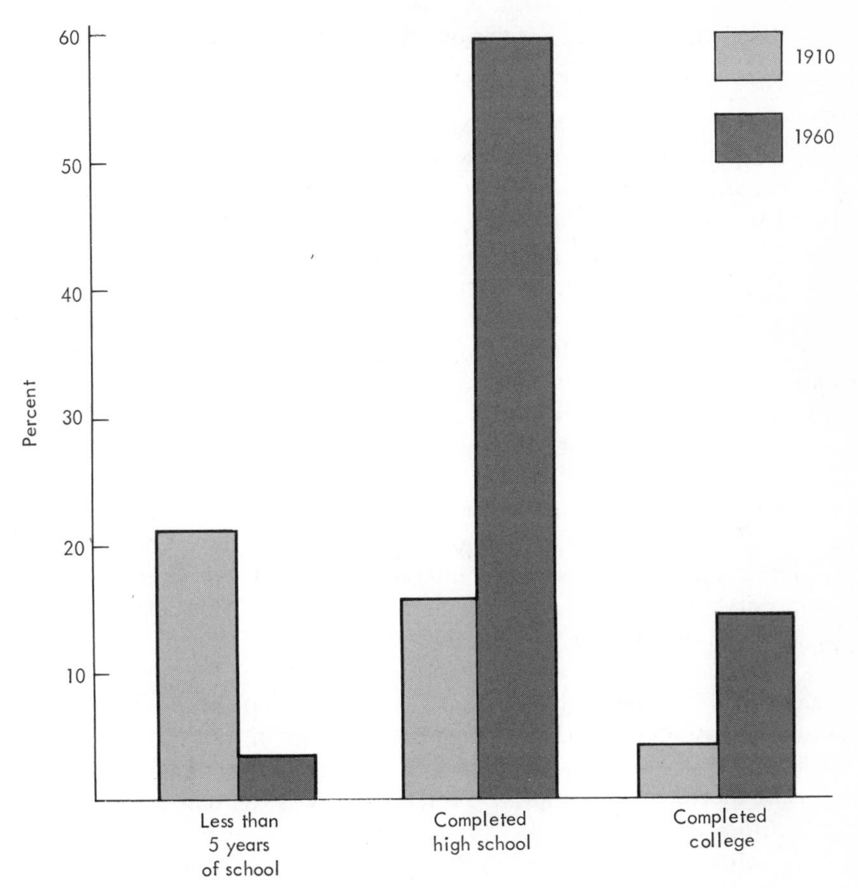

Figure 11.1 Educational attainment of U.S. males aged 25–29 in 1910 and 1960.

industry or economy can integrate young persons with university degrees into the kinds of occupations and production arrangements in which persons with only grade-school education have previously been functioning without making major changes. Factories are also disorganized by the need to integrate the city-born-and bred into occupations previously held by farm-born-and-bred workers. The economy, and all of its sectors, must innovate and introduce technological and organizational changes, just as other social systems must. Norman Ryder (1965) summarizes the process. "Social change occurs to the extent that successive cohorts do something other than merely repeat the pattern of behavior of their predecessors."

Division of Labor, Expansion of Boundary Systems, and Adoption of Innovation

Responses to increased social density. The proposition that societies respond to population growth, and to the increasing social density and competition entailed by such growth, was formulated by Durkheim. Durkheim saw the increase in human contacts and interaction, or *social density,* as distinct from *population density,* the number of persons per unit of area. Growth in social density derives both from population growth itself and from improvement in media systems like communications and transport. This intensified interaction or increased social density is accompanied by increased competition for all social rewards, and for sheer allocation of time and attention. The competition is, in turn, resolved productively by individual and institutional division of labor.

We can illustrate this by considering a small town of one thousand inhabitants which maintains ongoing arrangements for managing community business and for social interaction among the residents. The community's business includes taxation, managing whatever functions the local administration is charged with—school, police and fire protection, water and sanitation—and carrying on ongoing business with the larger administrative units of county and state. The social interaction among the residents includes neighborhood, retail trade, church and other relationships. In a community of this size, none of these arrangements is inordinately complex. This is because the number of *options for possible relationships* and connections and alliances in each social sphere, while not small or even readily countable, is clearly finite.

If we consider what will happen when 500 persons move into the community, we can see the implications for the social system's organization. Provision of housing and employment, school, professional, and shopping services will all engender organizational shifts in the community. In addition, however, the newcomers' participation in community affairs, decision making, and ongoing social interaction, will involve minimally a very large increase in the number of *options for possible relationships* in each social sphere. Choices about whom to associate with, whom to ignore, whom to do business with, whose help and political support to seek, or whose children should one's own children play with are now much more complex. All manner of mediating institutions may be needed to help organize the options and implicitly or explicitly lay out priorities for interaction. The same kinds of organizational implications apply to larger communities, or to the society as a whole, on a much broader scale.

Division of labor. Division of labor serves both to allocate social positions to the increment (not at the expense of the old timers, though many of them will also shift their positions) and to create new institutions which will organize the activities and social relationships in some coherent and productive manner. Thus the specialization of retail businesses and of professional services resolves the otherwise oppressive competition among businessmen and professionals both for status and success in their overlapping occupations and for the attention, patronage, and interaction with clients and customers. For their part, the clients and customers have fewer options and alternatives for direction of their interaction and patronage. Similarly, churches, clubs, recreational facilities multiply and differentiate, with the same effect—both providing less competitive social positions for an increasing population, and organizing the "dense" social interaction.

Expansion of boundary systems. Expansion of social boundary systems occurs when additional members are absorbed into the system, and when some position or set of positions has an enlarged number of incumbents. Expansion takes place especially when the number of component subsystems within the boundary system is increased. When a department store, an insurance office, a factory, a public utility, or a governmental unit adds a new section, department, or division, an expansion of a boundary system occurs. When banks and oil refineries merge, when a chain store buys out an independent grocer, when labor unions federate, expansion of boundary systems takes place.

Boundary systems are always associated with material and social resources and rewards. These resources and rewards are "scarce" in the sense that each system seeks to assure or enhance its own resources. Boundary systems of similar types—nations, regimes, industries, organizations, extended families, grocery stores—tend to compete with each other for scarce material and scarce social resources, and they seek to control or neutralize competing systems. Increasing numbers of populations permitting some economies of scale and enhanced efficiency improve the competitive position of a boundary system. Merger with an advantaged boundary system allows the less advantaged one to share and enhance the benefits of scale and efficiency.

Adoption of innovation. An important response to the disorganization attending population growth or turnover is adoption of some social or technological innovation. The industries recruiting new cohorts of highly trained employees can, and are usually well advised to, adopt productive, distributive, or organizational innovations. It is often the case that alternative ways of doing things are *known* in an organization or social system, but not adopted. Sheer inertia, or normative prescription of current, less efficient procedures may overcome purely instrumental criteria favoring the adoption of new ways of doing things. But population growth and turnover confront the organization, the business, the church, the bureaucracy, and the state with a kind of crisis—and the social system must make some sort of adjustment in its operations, activities, and relationships. These can include strictly technical improvements in such spheres as energy conversion, production, cultivation, and the development of new materials and crops and products, marketing, storage, transportation, or communication. But they can extend also to such spheres as systems of payment, work-sequence management, legal concepts, and systems and institutions of planning and control.

Other examples of innovative adaptations may include the substitution of nonfamily religious, educational, recreational, or welfare institutions for those needs which were previously met by the family. We may view a change from ascriptive to universalistic criteria in role allocation and social relations and the institutionalization of mobility processes as examples of social-structural innovation.

It is clear that changes in size or composition of the population have implications for the organization of societies and social relations; for the recruitment of individuals to the various power positions and social strata; and for the rules which govern access to positions, to social strata, and to the differential rewards and resources associated with them. The details of some of these interrelationships will be the subject of the next chapters.

SUMMARY

In this chapter we have introduced directly the idea of population change as a central factor in social change, showing that population shifts disorganize and force changes in ongoing social arrangements. We have seen how shifts in size or composition of family groups, schools, work settings, public services, and community political organizations render the continued operation of the social unit under its previous relationships and arrangements difficult or impossible. On a larger scale, population changes may render impossible the continued operation of fixed choice and selection institutions like university admissions, military recruitment, or the marriage market. In the family, the allocation of tasks, of space, of authority, and gratifications may change as family size and composition shift. In production organizations, turnover in the working force may entail new formal and informal relationships, new technologies or production processes, or new procedures for distributing products or rewards. In the marriage market, population growth and shortages of eligibles may cause the delay of marriage or changes in rules governing choice of mates. Even in the bridge club, population turnover causes the departure of players and cronies; they must be replaced either from among those previously ineligible, or else from among newcomers. In either case, new arrangements and relationships must be effected.

There are three general kinds of social system responses to population change: division of labor, expansion of boundary systems, and adoption of innovations. Division of labor includes the elaboration and institutionalization of new social roles or positions, or changes in content and behavior in existing positions. It also includes differentiation of new relationships between roles, or new organizational arrangements. Thus, expansion of universities has involved the development of new disciplines and departments; the growth of urban populations has seen rationalization and division of labor in manufacturing and services; and the growth of government has been accompanied by elaboration of additional agencies and bureaus and division of labor among them. Expansion of boundary systems can include not only growth of the population in a social system, but expansion of the system to include previously external subsystems. When a municipality annexes suburbs, when banks or factories or businesses merge, when organizations grow and their activities and responsibilities proliferate, expansion of boundary systems is taking place and new associative, production, or authority positions and interrelationships are evolving. The adoption of innovations can involve not only new technologies for production or communication, but also social and managerial innovations. Thus, bureaucratization is a social innovation; so are cost accounting and incentive pay in the factory, or pass-fail options in the university.

In the chapters which follow, we turn to a more specific discussion of demographic, economic, social, and political responses to population changes. In the next chapter, we examine the major demographic response of migration and urbanization.

12

Demographic Responses I: Migration and Urbanization

The responses of societies to actual or potential population growth may be social-organizational, economic, or demographic. Demographic responses to population growth can be distinguished according to whether they are *distributional responses,* which entail some change in the geographic or spatial distribution of the population, or whether they are *growth-control responses,* which entail some form of social intervention in the processes of population replacement and growth. We have talked about such responses before, although not precisely in those terms. In this and the next chapters we shall discuss and illustrate them in more detail, considering also the conditions under which one or another type of response is likely to occur.

We treat the demographic responses of population redistribution and growth control as separate from social and economic responses for analytic purposes only. It is particularly relevant here to note that such a distinction is in reality artificial: indeed, one of the purposes of this book has been to show that population changes themselves generate social structural changes. Accordingly, the abstraction here of "demographic responses" should be viewed in the context of our overall discussion of responses to population pressure, change, and growth.

Bearing this in mind, it is important to see that the two general demographic strategies of dealing with population growth are vastly different in nature. The first, redistribution, is basically a positive response, reflecting the society's institutionalized acceptance of population growth. The second, growth control, is basically a negative response, reflecting an institutionalized rejection, or at least only a qualified acceptance, of population growth. Unfortunately, we are still far from capable of analyzing satisfactorily the correlates and causes of institutionalized acceptance or rejection of population growth. Still, it is important to consider as far as possible the alternatives and circumstances which are associated with a society's choice of one or the other response.

OUT-MIGRATION AND BIFURCATION VERSUS INVOLUTION

Out-Migration and Bifurcation

We have already seen that a society confronted with population growth must either export or otherwise rid itself of the population increment or else expand its base of sustenance. Otherwise, it faces lower average levels of living, or worse. To the extent that a base of sustenance is closely circumscribed territorially, it is obvious that the expansion of settlement is one means of dealing with the problem. Another solution, the exportation of the population increment by emigration, is equivalent to the expansion of territorial settlement in the sense that the population increment is sustained by some territorial base of sustenance above and beyond that already existing for the initial population. Thus, out-migration or territorial expansion can be viewed as a generalized strategy for the survival of population increments.[1] This strategy may take a number of forms:

1. Expansion of the area of settlement or control;
2. Emigration of the population increment to join a different, already organized, population or society;
3. Migration of the population increment to form a new, separately organized, population or society.

Examples of areal expansion—either following or associated with population growth—are recorded for every type of society, from hunting and gathering bands to urban-industrial nation-states. However, regard-

[1] See Petersen's important analysis, "The General Determinants of Migration," 1969 and 1958, in which he elaborates upon connections between migration and population growth.

less of type, a society may find itself facing any one of a variety of contingencies with respect to the opportunities for expanding its area of settlement. Some of these have been mentioned already in Chapter 2 and need not be recapitulated. It suffices to note that only in the case of small, low density populations is the expansion of areas of settlement or control likely to be uncomplicated by the economics and politics of intersocietal relations. And it is only in low density areas comprising *only* small, low density populations that such areal expansions can go unchallenged.

Under even the most favorable conditions, the extent to which a society can expand areally is limited by the potentiality for transport, communication, and economic and political integration over the expanded area. Historically, societies have varied widely in their degrees of success in colonizing and in adapting their political, economic, and social institutions to greatly expanded areal settings. The social, economic, or political disorganization and disintegration associated with falure to extend the control and institutional arrangement of the mother society may bring to an end the very population growth that initiated the expansion. Spain in the modern period is a case in point.

Examples of the transfer and resettlement of parts of populations accompanying or following substantial population growth are known for virtually all types of societies. By *transfer and resettlement,* as opposed to expansion of settlement, we mean the effective departure of a population subgroup from membership in the mother society to somewhere outside that society's political control and institutional sphere. One example would be the Irish emigration to North America. Population subgroups so departing and transferring out of the original population may be more or less organized as social groupings; and after their departures they may or may not organize themselves.

Transferred and resettled population subgroups may join some already existing, relatively highly organized, society. The "great Atlantic migration" from Europe to America in the nineteenth and early twentieth centuries involved population subgroups joining, essentially, an existing and ongoing nation. Similarly, the extensive population transfers following World War II involved groups departing from their societies of origin and joining already existing societies of destination. For example, many Germans left Germany and moved to South American countries; and large numbers emigrated from countries of Southern Europe to Australia and to Canada. The directions and political and economic outcomes of population transfers are related to the sizes and densities of populations outside that of the home society, as well as to general intersocietal relationships, communication, and exchange. (Fig. 12.1)

Population transfer originating as an expansion of settlement or as colonization on the part of the home society has often resulted in *bifurcation*—the independence of the newly transferred and resettled population. At the same time, the newly settled societies, if small or sparsely populated, have often actually recruited or sought otherwise to promote substantial population transfers and increments (notable examples are Australia, Canada, and New Zealand).

In transferring and resettling themselves, population subgroups may reorganize into autonomous social groups or independent societies. The process of growth and bifurcation has occurred frequently among hunting and gathering bands, and even among settled tribal societies. It has also been the basic process associating much premodern and modern exploration, colonization, and population transfer with the founding of new societies and nations.

Clearly, both expansion of settlement and the territorial transfer of some segments of a population are demographic responses to population growth which permit problems of sustenance to be resolved without necessarily entailing immediate social reorganization or technological changes in the original society. But these responses are not always possible, for they depend on the availability of some territorial destination and the physical and political access to it. For the society confronted by a growing population, emigration is a relatively painless solution. But first, there must be a place to which to emigrate—and this is not always the case.

Involution

Exactly the opposite conditions from those described above characterize the second demographic response to population growth: *population involution*. This response involves increased density of settlement as well as an intensification of exploitation, and it has virtually immediate effects upon, and implications for, social and political organization. (Some of these have been discussed or touched upon earlier.) Population involution, unlike out-migration or bifurcation, may occur independently of the demographic and political relationships between neighboring societies.

Population involution involves the adaptation and extraction of sustenance for a larger population occupying the same territorial unit as that of the original population (or occupying progressively smaller territorial units). This alone implies some change in production, distribution, and exchange and in the processes of social control. Thus, theories or analyses which assume that societies "opt for" stability rather than

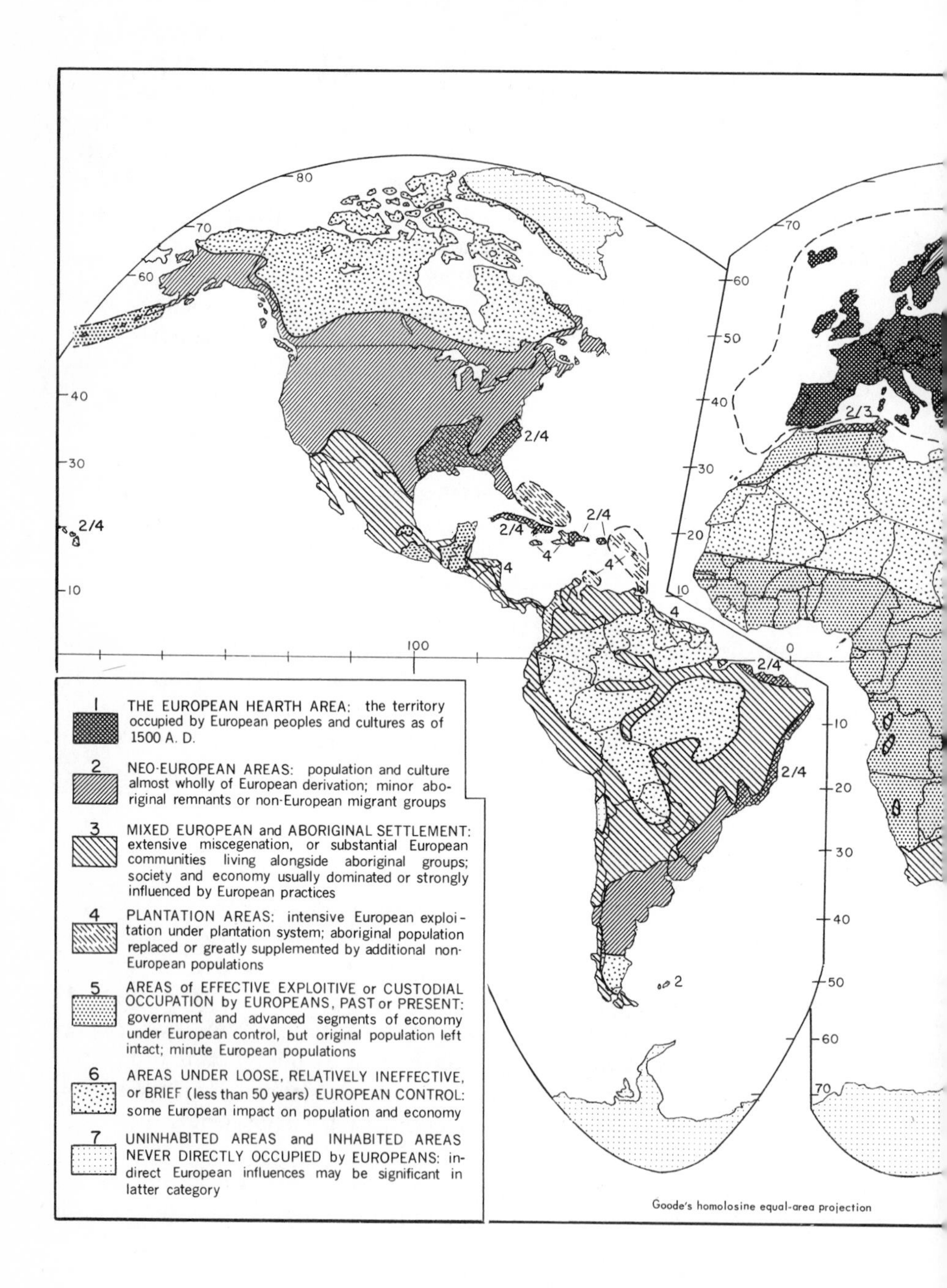

80
70
60
50
40
30
20
10
0
100
2/4
2/3
4
2
1
THE EUROPEAN HEARTH AREA: the territory occupied by European peoples and cultures as of 1500 A. D.
2
NEO-EUROPEAN AREAS: population and culture almost wholly of European derivation; minor aboriginal remnants or non-European migrant groups
3
MIXED EUROPEAN and ABORIGINAL SETTLEMENT: extensive miscegenation, or substantial European communities living alongside aboriginal groups; society and economy usually dominated or strongly influenced by European practices
4
PLANTATION AREAS: intensive European exploitation under plantation system; aboriginal population replaced or greatly supplemented by additional non-European populations
5
AREAS of EFFECTIVE EXPLOITIVE or CUSTODIAL OCCUPATION by EUROPEANS, PAST or PRESENT: government and advanced segments of economy under European control, but original population left intact; minute European populations
6
AREAS UNDER LOOSE, RELATIVELY INEFFECTIVE, or BRIEF (less than 50 years) EUROPEAN CONTROL: some European impact on population and economy
7
UNINHABITED AREAS and INHABITED AREAS NEVER DIRECTLY OCCUPIED by EUROPEANS: indirect European influences may be significant in latter category
Goode's homolosine equal-area projection

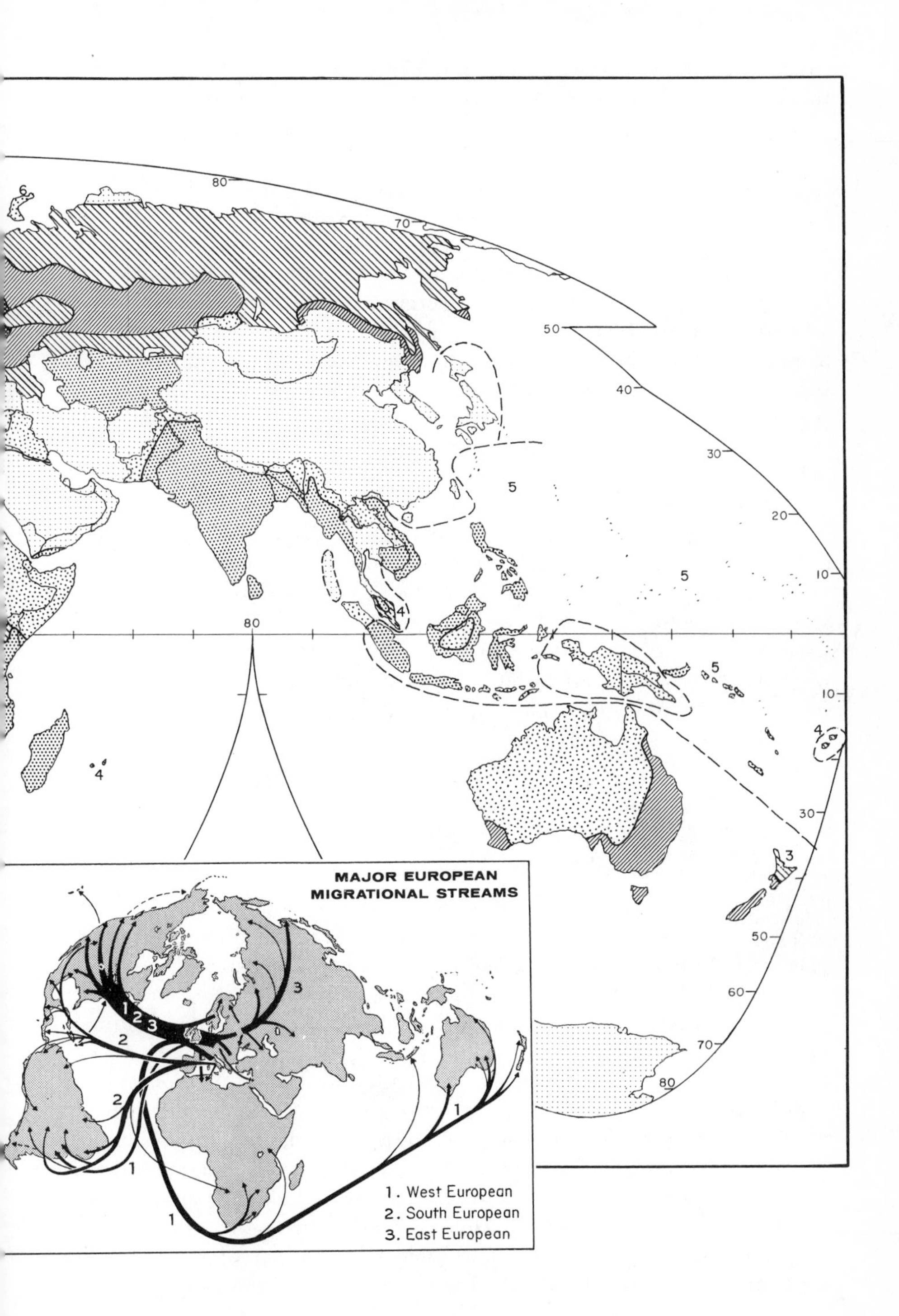

MAJOR EUROPEAN MIGRATIONAL STREAMS
1. West European
2. South European
3. East European

change, would indicate that population involution is a demographic response to population growth *only* where less disorganizing responses, such as out-migration, are ruled out on geographical, political, or other grounds.

But historically, as mankind has increasingly populated the earth, the alternatives open to population groups seeking to emigrate have become progressively narrower and more rigidly enforced. Thus, the societal strategy of survival and adaptation has increasingly entailed an involutional response to growth. However, as we have shown in the case of the United States, societies also may turn to involution as a demographic response to population growth despite the opportunities for further expansion of settlement. Thus, *some* societies do opt for the path of social-structural, economic, and political change connected with population involution despite the absence of constraints on the presumably preferred strategy of expansion of settlement.

The notion of population involution is extremely broad. It includes virtually every kind of change in population density. More intensive and more dense agricultural exploitation and settlement, as well as urbanization, metropolitanization, and megalopolitanization, can all be viewed as involutional responses to population growth. And, of course, these responses themselves vary widely over societies and over time.

We turn next to urbanization, which, along with increased longevity and family limitation, is among the three most significant sociodemographic processes of the twentieth century.

THE URBAN-METROPOLITAN REVOLUTION AS THE MODERN SOCIETAL STRATEGY

That a major sociodemographic, urban-metropolitan revolution is taking place is indicated by the principal population trends found throughout the world today. These include increasing population size, increasing density, increasing concentration and agglomeration, and the political organization and integration of large geographic areas. Virtually every facet of social life—from politics, to economics, to religion, to education—and many facets of private life, too, have been affected by this urban-metropolitan revolution. The societal strategy of adaptation is changing in the direction of increasing differentiation. But at the same time there is a greatly increasing interdependence among individuals, groups, and societies located great distances from one another.

Although there has been a considerable amount of investigation done on the histories of individual cities, estimates of the urban population of the world are available only for about the last 150 years. In 1800, an estimated three percent of the population of the world lived in cities or urban places of 5,000 inhabitants or more. Of these urban dwellers, only about 2.4 percent lived in cities of 20,000 or more, and a mere 1.7 percent lived in cities of 100,000 or more. However, between 1800 and 1970 the population of the world increased fourfold. And in this period, the population in urban places of 5,000 or more increased elevenfold and the population in cities of 100,000 or more increased almost fourteenfold. Thus, by 1970 more than a third of the world's population lived in urban settlements of 5,000 persons or more; and nearly a quarter lived in cities of 100,000 or more. (See Table 12.1)

In the United States, urbanization has far exceeded the world trend. In 1790 some five percent of the population of the United States lived in urban places (places of 2,500 or more inhabitants), and there were only 24 such urban places in the nation. By 1970, however, there were 6,435 urban places in the United States, and these contained about 70 percent of the total population. Some other countries—for example, Great Britain and Israel—have even larger urban percentages in their populations. But most have considerably smaller ones.

We have already talked about prehistoric and ancient urban settlement. Cities and urban living are older than recorded history itself. However, it should be clear that ancient and preindustrial urban residence cannot be viewed as a societal strategy of adaptation. While urban agglomerations were, and are, an integral part of state societies, nonagricultural production remained throughout most of human prehistory and history only a minute part of the population's total means of gaining sustenance. Indeed, nonagricultural production plays a relatively small part in many national economies even today.

Prehistoric, ancient, medieval, and even modern cities can be described in a variety of ways: as market centers; as fortresses, garrison cities, or points of political control; as centers of worship or ecclesiastical control; as loci of culture and the arts; or as combinations of any or all of these (Weber, 1968). But historically, urban population served (or exploited, as the case may have been) the mass of surrounding country folk engaged in agriculture and basic extractive occupations. The modern urban revolution—and it is not yet universal, for urban growth does not everywhere and inevitably have these characteristics—consists not merely in the increase in number and size of urban agglomerations. It reflects urban economic activity becoming the *major* part of national economies and the urban sector playing a progressively greater part in absorbing and providing sustenance to the new population increments.

As Friedlander (1969) shows in his study of migration and demographic transitions, England's industrial revolution was accompanied

TABLE 12.1 Percentage of World Population in Cities of 5,000+ and 100,000+ by Region, 1800–1970

	Total World Population (millions)	*Percent in Cities 5,000+*	*Percent in Cities 100,000+*							
			World total	*Europe* [a]	*Asia* [a]	*Russia-USSR*	*North America* [b]	*Latin America* [c]	*Africa*	*Australia-New Zealand*
1800	906	3.0	1.7	3.0	1.6	1.4	–	0.4	0.3	–
1850	1171	6.4	2.3	5.8	1.7	1.8	5.5	1.5	0.2	–
1900	1608	13.6	5.5	14.5	2.1	4.2	18.5	5.7	1.1	21.7
1950	2400	29.8	13.1	21.1	7.5	18.5	29.0	16.5	5.2	39.2
1960	2995	31.6	20.1	33.0	12.3	23.9	60.2	24.1	8.1	60.2
1970	3632	33.0 [d]	23.3	39.0	20.2	31.5	57.6	33.4	11.5	61.1

[a] Excluding Russia/USSR
[b] U.S.A. and Canada
[c] Western Hemisphere, excluding U.S.A. and Canada
[d] Rough estimate

Source: 1800–1960—E. E. Lampard 1965; 1970—Davis 1969, and "1970 World Population Data Sheet," Population Reference Bureau, Washington, D.C.

by an urban revolution in this very sense. The enormous population growth of the period was absorbed mainly by the urban centers and employed mainly in urban industrial and service sectors. Similarly, as we saw in Chapter 5, after 1860 the bulk of United States population growth was absorbed in urban places and occupations. Thus, although American cities are of much more recent origin than their European or Asiatic counterparts, they participated much earlier in a nationwide urban revolution of the modern sort indicated here.

The Urban Community: Differentiated, Complex, and Largely Migrant

Urban communities differ from rural communities, not only with respect to population size and density but also with respect to virtually all other facets of social structure.[2] It is clear that the recognized social roles of cities differ from those of rural places. The city is the locus of both a large number and a great variety of different social and economic roles. The psychiatrist, the hippie, the artist, the chorus girl, the corporation lawyer—these are typically found in the city and only very infrequently in the village. And while there are merchants, school teachers, ministers, divorcees, and teenagers in rural places, it is in the city where there are both large numbers and many different subtypes of merchants, school teachers, ministers, divorcees, and teenagers.

The nature of the urban revolution and of urban growth is such that urban residents are sharply differentiated according to whether they are recent arrivals, residents of long duration, born and brought up in the city, and so on. Urban populations typically contain a high proportion of migrants. The absorption and integration of successive waves of new residents, who are often initially strangers to city life altogether, is a central and recurring process of urban society.

In a 1958 survey taken in the United States, only a minority of white respondents 18 years of age or older reported having lived in the same place since birth. Percentages reporting different durations of residence varied by size of place, with those in the largest cities and in farm communities (43 percent and 40 percent respectively) most likely to report living in the same place since birth, and those in small cities in metropolitan areas reporting the shortest durations of residence (Taeuber, Chiazze, & Haenzel, 1968, pp. 19–20). Table 12.2 shows the results of this survey in detail.

This typically migrant nature of urban populations is found every-

[2] For a classic statement on this, see Wirth (1938); and for a more recent one, see Hauser (1965b).

TABLE 12.2 Duration of Continuous Residence of White Population in Current Place, by Size of Place

	Duration (years)					
Size of Place	*Total*	*Entire life*	*40 or more*	*10–39*	*1–9*	*Less than 1*
500,000 or more	100.0	42.7	9.9	28.5	16.7	2.2
50,000–499,999	100.0	25.1	8.7	36.1	25.2	4.9
Metropolitan, 10,000–49,999	100.0	14.7	5.0	32.5	40.0	7.8
Metropolitan, 2,500–9,999	100.0	10.6	2.8	28.2	51.0	7.4
Metropolitan, rural nonfarm	100.0	17.8	3.7	29.8	42.3	6.4
Nonmetropolitan, 10,000–49,999	100.0	19.4	6.3	36.6	31.2	6.5
Nonmetropolitan, 2,500–9,999	100.0	16.2	7.5	38.7	31.9	5.7
Nonmetropolitan, rural nonfarm	100.0	22.1	5.0	32.7	32.7	7.5
Farm	100.0	40.1	7.2	31.1	31.1	3.5

Source: Taeuber, Chiazze, & Haenszel 1968, table 7, pp. 19–20.

where. A great variety of urban social forms, institutions, and commercial services originate in the very "strangeness" of much of the population to the city and the urban setting. In response to the needs of population groups not native to the area, the city often spawns ethnically segregated communities who maintain separate institutions and formal and informal organizations like kinship and neighborhood groups, churches, social clubs, and settlement houses. Gangs, taxi-dance halls, lonely hearts clubs, bars, and red-light districts also arise out of the need to adjust to urban life.

"Time in the system" or length of residence in the city is evidently a major factor in the adjustment of individuals and groups to the urban setting. A number of indicators of socio-economic status are characteristically found to be positively associated with duration of residence in the city: age seems critical in this respect. Several variables affect duration of residence: these include region of origin, foreign birth, and occupation. Similarly, indicators of social participation, such as membership in organizations and voter registration, are also found to be related positively to length of residence (Shannon and Shannon, 1967).

A second factor crucial to the newcomer's adjustment to the city is his level of social and economic resources upon arrival. Level of education and occupational skill are particularly important. The ability of the newcomer to compete for access to urban social and economic roles, desirable urban space, and favorable urban associations is closely connected with the cultural, social, and economic resources represented by his occupational skills and education. Of immigrants in the nineteenth and early twentieth century, those from Germany and Scandinavia were at a great advantage compared with those from Eastern Europe, both by virtue of their earlier arrival and by virtue of their high average level of education and occupational skills. Among current urban immigrants, the professional and experienced skilled workers find adjustment to new surroundings much easier than do unskilled, "off-the-farm" migrants.

The urban institutional network is far more complex than its rural counterpart. A simple computation of the number of possible combinations of relations indicates the institutional complexity made possible simply by the size and density of the urban population. The institutions of economic production are much more varied, and so are the personal, business, public, and institutional services. Educational, religious, and cultural institutions are more varied and complex, and voluntary organizations vie with one another for membership and the participation of mutually shared members.

The rural community has its local school, church, bar, newspaper, civic club, and political organization. It has its stores and service station, its lawyers and its doctors. But the urban community may have whole systems of schools and educational institutions—day-care centers, universities, libraries, specialized academies, and vocational and professional schools—and these may be interrelated in a variety of ways and degrees. The city or metropolitan area also has systems of churches, indeed, often organizations and hierarchies of churches, church institutions, and clergy. And it has systems, too, of bars, lounges, and nightclubs.

Similarly the metropolis has many professional offices and organizations; wholesale and retail businesses; and processing, manufacturing, and fabricating industries. The city's recreational facilities and services, both free and commercial, are many and diverse; and its clubs and voluntary organizations range from neighborhood sewing circles to juvenile gangs to business associations and political organizations.

Spatial Patterns and Their Social Effects

Given the extraordinary diversity and complexity described above, a crucial task in urban sociology and ecology is the classification of social roles, groups, and institutions in the urban community and the plotting and analysis of actual patterns of social contact and relationships among them.

The physical layout, land use, and transport and communication arrangements and technology of the city are important in this respect. The social structure and the physical or spatial structure of a city are

City traffic in Rome—the result of the spatial structure of the city. *(United Nations)*

closely related: indeed, they reflect one another. Accordingly, a city's social structure may often be studied with the aid of data bearing upon its physical structure (see Hawley, 1950). For social relationships are mediated by physical proximity and accessibility. These, in turn, depend on patterns of settlement and the location of social institutions and social systems. By the same token, social proximity and accessibility may be the key factors in the competition among the various social and economic units for space or locations in the urban area. For this reason, patterns of settlement and location in the urban area are widely viewed as representations of the urban social structure. A long tradition of the study of spatial relationships in cities has shed light upon urban social structure in America.

Thus, in their classic study of occupational stratification and mobility in the Chicago area in 1950, Duncan and Duncan found that a "close relationship between spatial and social distances in a metropolitan community" was reflected in patterns of residential concentration and segregation of occupational groups. (Their focus of study was that area denoted as the "Chicago Metropolitan District" in the 1940 census.) The highest indexes of segregation were found for the professional and laborer groups, at both extremes of the occupational scale, and the lowest values for the clerical workers in the middle of the scale. This suggested that urban residential segregation is greater for those occupation groups with clearly defined status than for those whose status is ambiguous (Duncan and Duncan, 1955). Similar patterns have been found in later studies, most recently in Puerto Rico (Schwirian and Rico-Velasco, 1971).

The study of ethnic urban residential patterns, frequently carried out in connection with studies of ethnic assimilation, has a long tradition in sociological and human ecology. As Lieberson points out:

> . . . . [D]uring the heyday of European immigration to the United States, the propensity of immigrants to first locate in ghettoes and their later movements out of these areas of first settlement were frequently utilized as a measure or index of an ethnic group's assimilation. Studies of such diverse urban centers as Chicago, Durban, Montreal, Paris, and the major cities of Australia attest to the widespread existence of residential segregation and its usefulness as an indicator of ethnic assimilation. Indeed, during the twenties and thirties, ethnic residential patterns were a major research interest of sociologists and others. (Lieberson, 1961, p. 1)

Lieberson himself found that the extent of ethnic segregation influences citizenship status, ethnic endogamy and intermarriage, the ability to speak English, and intergenerational occupational mobility (Lieberson, 1961).

The maps of Figure 12.2 show the distribution of homes, by rental groups, and the distributions of immigrant ethnic groups and of blacks in the city of Chicago in 1930. Inspection and comparison of the maps reveal the closeness or distance of the ethnic groups relative to one another, as well as indicating their locations in terms of high or low rental areas. Thus, for example the black population was, already in 1930, very highly segregated in a "black belt" inhabited almost exclusively by blacks. Among the foreign born, those from Italy, from Russia, and from Poland were the most highly concentrated while the immigrants from Germany were very broadly dispersed throughout the city.

Areas of black residence were largely lowest rent areas. But a comparison of maps 1 and 4 shows that there were also a number of high rent areas with very high percentages of black residents. Some of the Russian-born immigrants and some of the German-born immigrants were concentrated in medium and high rent areas. But for the most part, areas of ethnic concentration in Chicago in 1930 also tended to be low rent areas.

In their study of black residential patterns in American cities, Taeuber and Taeuber found that in virtually all large cities, both in the North and in the South, the black population has always been highly

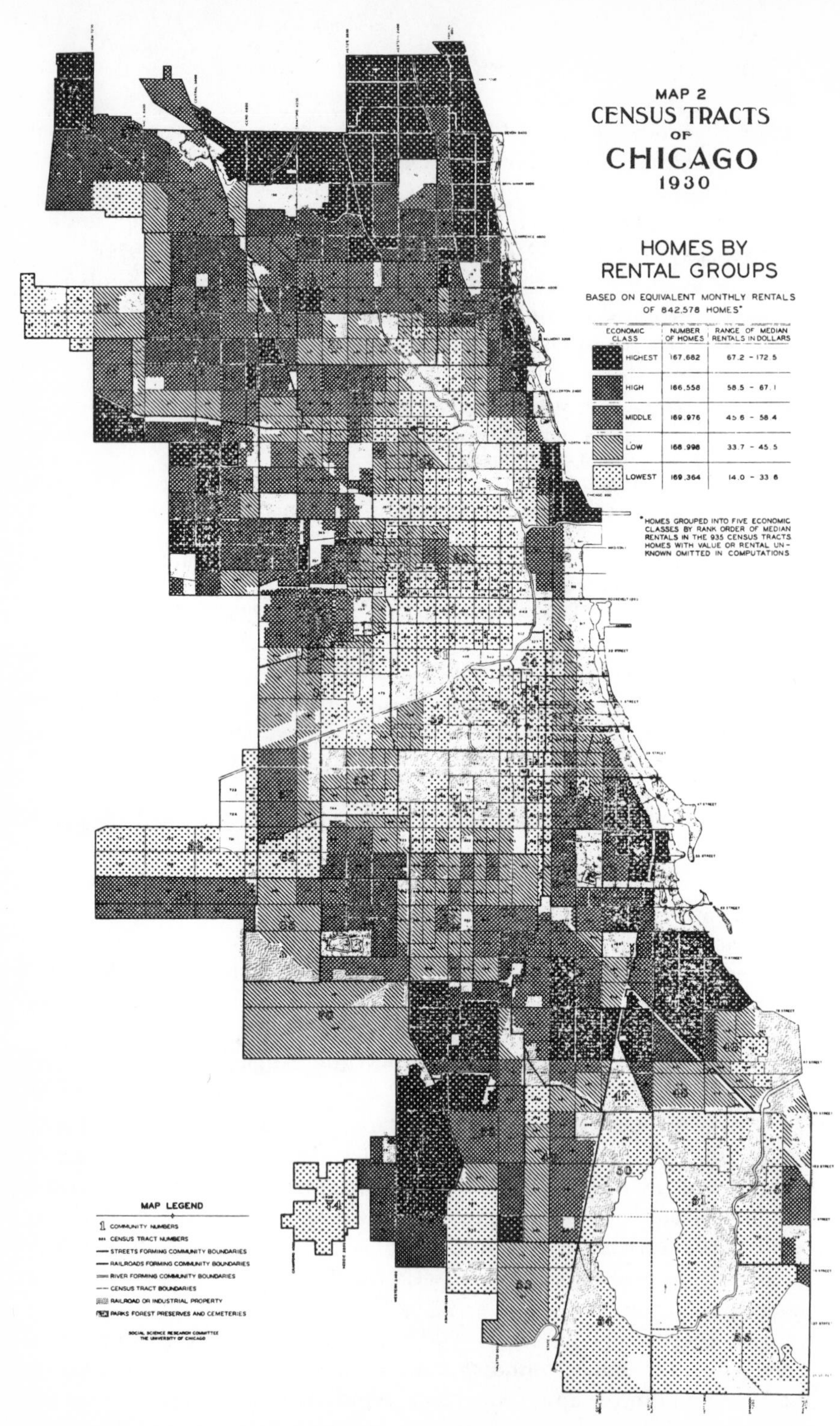

Figure 12.2 Census tracts of Chicago, according to selected characteristics. *Source: Reprinted by permission from E. W. Burgess and C. Newcomb,* Census of the City of Chicago, 1930 *(Chicago: University of Chicago Press).*

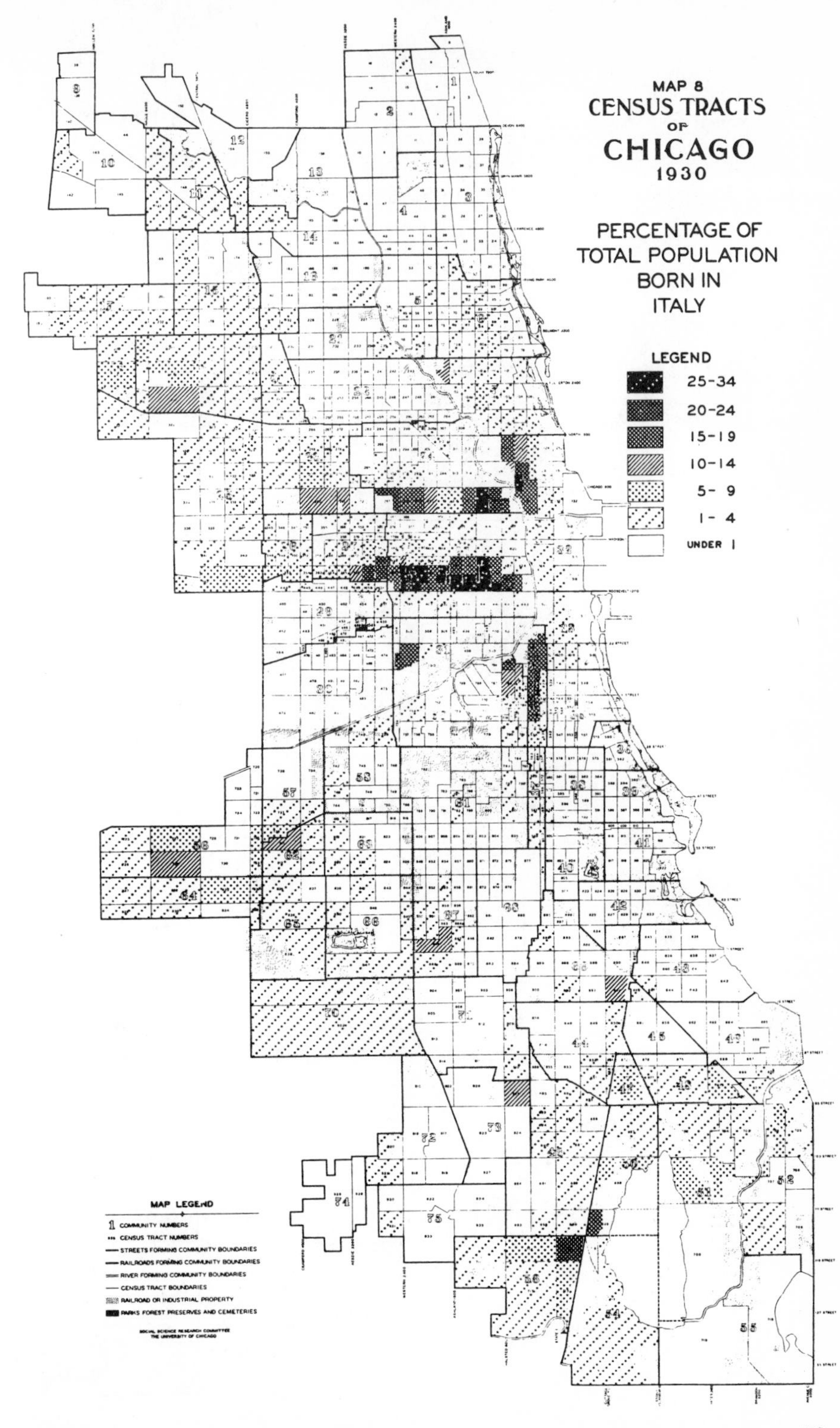
MAP 8
CENSUS TRACTS
OF
CHICAGO
1930
PERCENTAGE OF
TOTAL POPULATION
BORN IN
ITALY
LEGEND
25-34
20-24
15-19
10-14
5- 9
1- 4
UNDER 1
MAP LEGEND
COMMUNITY NUMBERS
CENSUS TRACT NUMBERS
STREETS FORMING COMMUNITY BOUNDARIES
RAILROADS FORMING COMMUNITY BOUNDARIES
RIVER FORMING COMMUNITY BOUNDARIES
CENSUS TRACT BOUNDARIES
RAILROAD OR INDUSTRIAL PROPERTY
PARKS FOREST PRESERVES AND CEMETERIES
SOCIAL SCIENCE RESEARCH COMMITTEE
THE UNIVERSITY OF CHICAGO

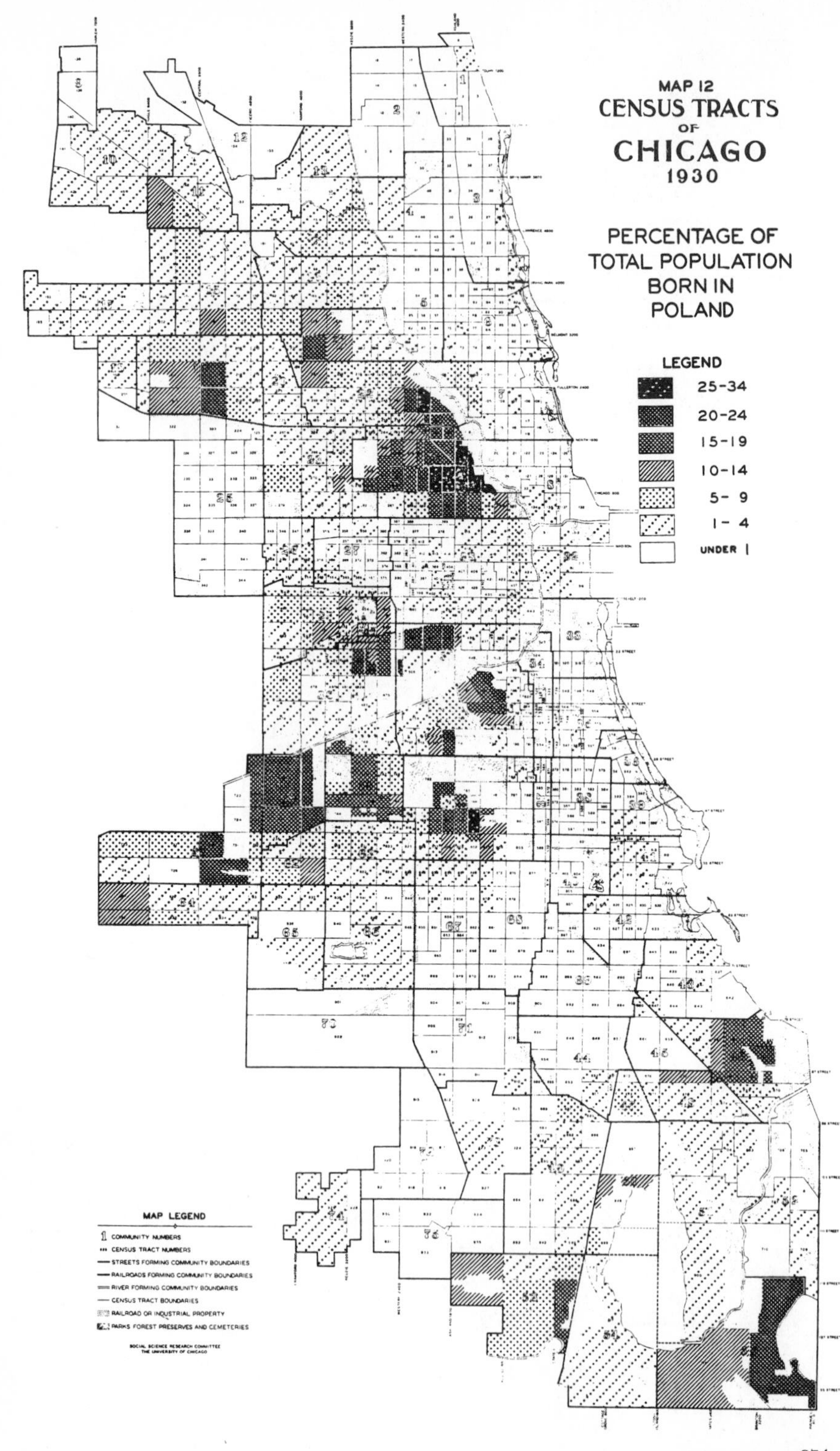
MAP 12
CENSUS TRACTS
OF
CHICAGO
1930
PERCENTAGE OF
TOTAL POPULATION
BORN IN
POLAND
LEGEND
25-34
20-24
15-19
10-14
5- 9
1- 4
UNDER 1
MAP LEGEND
COMMUNITY NUMBERS
CENSUS TRACT NUMBERS
STREETS FORMING COMMUNITY BOUNDARIES
RAILROADS FORMING COMMUNITY BOUNDARIES
RIVER FORMING COMMUNITY BOUNDARIES
CENSUS TRACT BOUNDARIES
RAILROAD OR INDUSTRIAL PROPERTY
PARKS FOREST PRESERVES AND CEMETERIES
SOCIAL SCIENCE RESEARCH COMMITTEE
THE UNIVERSITY OF CHICAGO

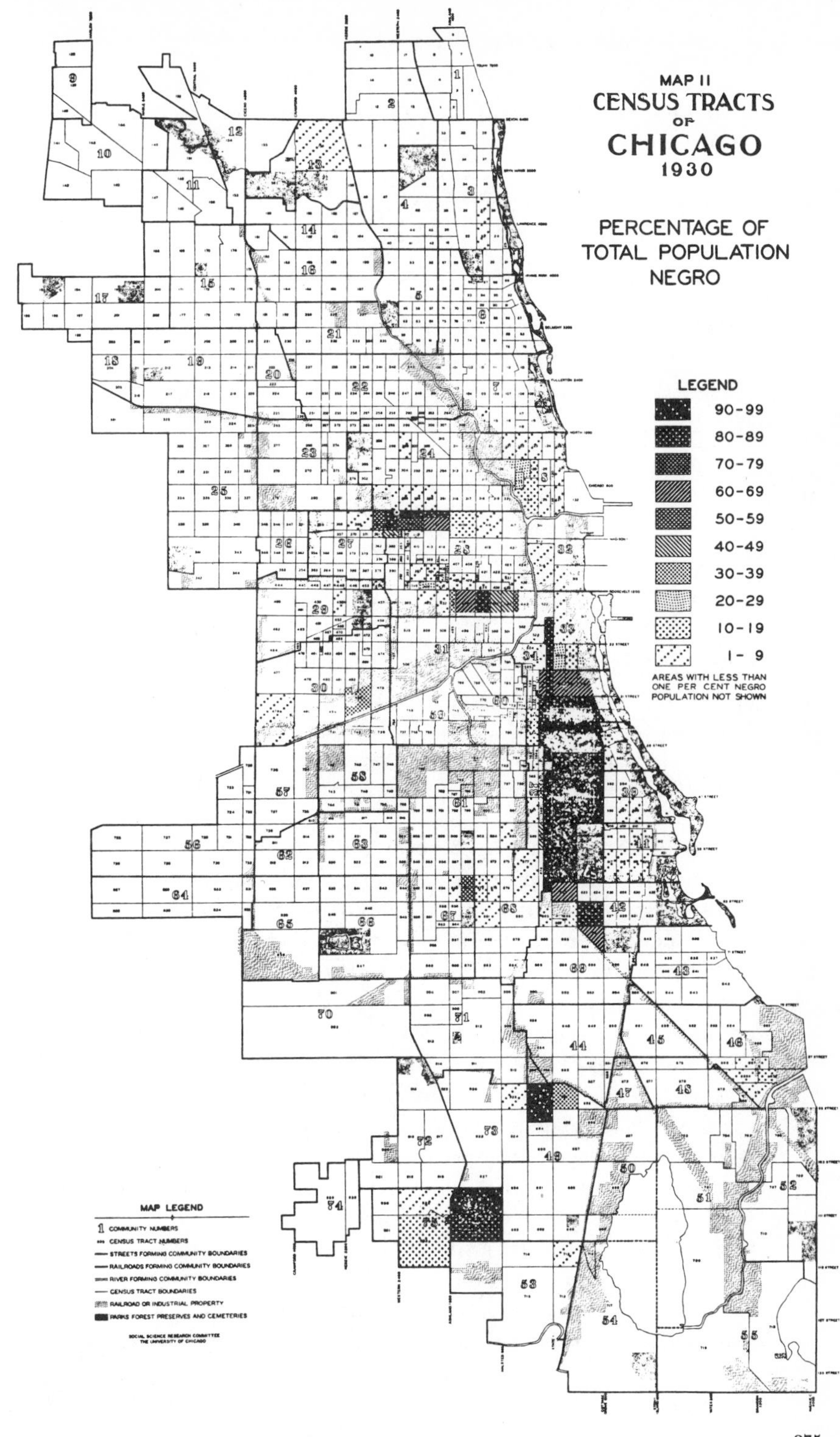
MAP II
CENSUS TRACTS
OF
CHICAGO
1930
PERCENTAGE OF
TOTAL POPULATION
NEGRO
LEGEND
90-99
80-89
70-79
60-69
50-59
40-49
30-39
20-29
10-19
1- 9
AREAS WITH LESS THAN
ONE PER CENT NEGRO
POPULATION NOT SHOWN
MAP LEGEND
COMMUNITY NUMBERS
CENSUS TRACT NUMBERS
STREETS FORMING COMMUNITY BOUNDARIES
RAILROADS FORMING COMMUNITY BOUNDARIES
RIVER FORMING COMMUNITY BOUNDARIES
CENSUS TRACT BOUNDARIES
RAILROAD OR INDUSTRIAL PROPERTY
PARKS FOREST PRESERVES AND CEMETERIES
SOCIAL SCIENCE RESEARCH COMMITTEE
THE UNIVERSITY OF CHICAGO

segregated and is still more segregated than are white ethnic groups. They also found that from the Civil War until World War II, there was a general tendency for residential segregation to increase with the growth of black populations (Taeuber and Taeuber, 1965). This tendency is shown clearly in Table 12.3.

TABLE 12.3 Indexes of Residential Segregation Between Negroes and Native Whites in Ten Northern Cities, 1910, 1920, 1930, and 1950

City	*1910*	*1920*	*1930*	*1950*
Boston	64.1	65.3	77.9	80.1
Buffalo	62.6	71.5	80.5	82.5
Chicago	66.8	75.7	85.2	79.7
Cincinnati	47.3	57.2	72.8	80.6
Cleveland	60.6	70.1	85.0	86.6
Columbus	31.6	43.8	62.8	70.3
Philadelphia	46.0	47.9	63.4	74.0
Pittsburgh	44.1	43.3	61.4	68.5
St. Louis	54.3	62.1	82.1	85.4
Syracuse	64.0	65.2	86.7	85.8

Source: Karl E. and Alma F. Taeuber, Negroes in Cities *(Chicago: Aldine Publishing Company); copyright © 1965 by Karl E. and Alma F. Taeuber; Table 19, p. 54.*

It is clear that variation of population in one respect is typically not unconnected with variation in some other respect. For example, cities with large proportions of the population employed in manufacturing and small proportions in services tend to have smaller proportions with secondary or higher educations. They tend also to have earlier marriages and higher fertility, than do cities with large proportions employed in services. Thus, economic differentiation among cities tends to entail a number of social structural differences.[3]

Historically, the urban community's greater variety of jobs, living styles, contacts, amusements, social relationships, and general opportunities in life has been accompanied by higher per capita income and by a much larger variety of comforts and consumption opportunities than is the case for small or more isolated rural communities. Thus, with few exceptions, the majority of migratory movements have been from rural to urban places and from smaller to larger urban places. Even the recent suburbanization trends—moves from New York City to Scarsdale, or from Chicago to Barrington—are properly viewed as the

[3] For a detailed analysis of this tendency, see Duncan and Reiss (1956).

redistribution of population *within* large agglomerations rather than as movements from larger to smaller places.

CITIES AND HINTERLANDS: THE METROPOLITAN COMMUNITY

Typically, the *hinterland* of a city is considered to be the area surrounding and including the city. This area has better or more ready access to that city, its institutions, and services than to any other city or urban center.

The concept of hinterland may refer to general access to a city, or it may be more specialized and refer to access to specific services of a city. The entertainment, cultural, and banking services of a large city typically have greater hinterlands than do the bakery or grocery services, for people will travel farther to see a play or transact a loan than they will to buy a loaf of bread or a quart of milk. Thus, a given rural area may be in the wholesaling hinterland of one city but in the educational hinterland of another. In general, however, hinterland is used in reference to the area served by the various commercial, cultural, communication, and other services of the urban center.

The Evolution of Cities and Their Hinterlands

The concept of hinterland has been of great value in accounting for the origins and evolvement of cities and for analyzing the social and economic relationships between cities and the total societies in which they are found. What follows is a more or less classical account of the origin of cities.

Consider a society of food growers, hunters, collectors, or other primary producers with individual families, extended families, or tribes settled over a fairly extensive area. The production of food is such that each family is able to produce some surplus product, like rice, in addition to its own immediate requirements. It may occur to one individual that by performing some service, like shoeing horses, for many primary producers in exchange for surplus food, he can both eat well and work less hard.

Accordingly, the blacksmith, who may have created a new role in the society, sets out wandering from place to place, shoeing horses in exchange for food. Before long, it will probably occur to him that he can shoe many more horses if he spends his time doing only that, and if the horses come to him rather than he to them. Besides, he reasons, there is much to be said in favor of a more permanent home and place of work. In such a contingency, the blacksmith will try to choose a place of work accessible to a maximum number of potential clients. He will look for a spot which is central to the entire area of the society's settlement, located on some path or crossroad, or otherwise conveniently situated with respect to the society's territorial distribution.

If some other members of the society follow suit and decide to produce and exchange shoes, weapons, or tools for the surpluses produced by farmers, fishermen, and hunters, they, too, will probably decide that establishing permanent workplaces is easier than peddling their wares in the countryside. If they are as rational as the blacksmith, they too will establish their places of work and exchange in the same easy-to-reach area as the blacksmith shop.

Eventually the blacksmith, shoemaker, toolmaker, and other tradesmen will have established a point of exchange, and an important change will have taken place. The agriculturists no longer shoe their own horses, make their own boots, or fashion their own tools. Instead, they depend upon the craftsmen at the exchange center for these goods and services. The craftsmen and manufacturers, in turn, depend for food upon the agriculturists in their hinterland—upon those to whom their services are accessible. Thus a simple reciprocal dependence has been established between two places of settlement: the nonprimary production or service area and its hinterland.

As agricultural and extractive activities become specialized, more exchange services are needed for marketing of surplus produce and the purchase of primary products. In other words, when Farmer Brown stops growing everything his family needs and raises only corn, he must depend on others to buy his surplus corn and sell him milk and eggs. In addition, as relatively more surpluses become available for exchange, manufactured and fabricated products are demanded in greater quantity and variety. Thus, new nonprimary economic roles and activities emerge. These, like the initial ones, tend to locate at points of maximum accessibility and, if the process continues, eventually develop into metropolitan agglomerations that grow, become further differentiated, and achieve an increasing metropolitan dominance over their rural and smaller urban hinterlands (Bogue, 1949).

THE MEGALOPOLITAN NETWORK

Under conditions of general population growth and improved technology, cities grow and absorb a large portion of the population's increase by virtue of both centripetal and centrifugal population movements. A centripetal movement is from the periphery to the center; a centrifugal one, from the center to the periphery. As agricultural techniques improve, rendering more and more rural workers superfluous, the rural population is attracted to city employment and urban styles of life. Conversely, as cities grow in size and density, the urban population moves outward from the city center. New areas are then annexed to the city, or independent suburbs and populations are established beyond it. Thus, the urban area is no longer limited to the political boundaries of one or several cities. Rather, it may comprise a number of different types of urban areas.

Various concepts have been introduced to represent and analyze such urban areas: "metropolitan areas," "urbanized areas," "conurbation," "central cities," and "metropolitan or suburban rings." Concepts such as these and their statistical representations reflect the fact that a great many persons, institutions, and activities are urban in character, have close spatial and social relationships with cities and urban centers, but are themselves located outside cities or outside the dominant city of the area.

When the outlying areas of two cities undergo continued suburbanization in the direction of each other, the process evolves along the major transport routes and leads eventually to dense settlement of the entire ribbon of land between the cities. Such urbanized ribbons have sometimes been called "strip cities." And in some areas, networks of interrelated and interconnected strip cities have emerged. For example, there is now a huge network of large cities connected by contiguous bands of urban settlement on the eastern seaboard of the United States. This network, stretching from around Boston in the North to the Washington-Norfolk area in the South, has been called *megalopolis* (Gottman, 1961). The term *megalopolis* has lately been used to denote an interconnected group of cities and connecting urbanized bands, and we shall call a network of such cities and bands a *megalopolitan network*.

The most important characteristic of the megalopolitan network is the kind of specialization and interdependence that obtains among its cities. Whereas the key interdependence in a regional economy is between the city and its rural hinterland, or between the metropolitan center and its smaller urban satellites and rural hinterland, the interdependence characterizing the megalopolitan network is between cities of different types, different functional specialization, and different economic bases (Duncan et al., 1960). The megalopolitan network includes agricultural and other primary-production hinterlands, which send their products into the urban areas for processing, manufacturing, fabrication, and distribution. But mainly, the megalopolitan network comprises urban populations living in cities, in suburbs of cities, or in or near urban bands connecting cities.

A careful inspection of maps and an analysis of the population, labor force, and economy of geographic units suggests that a number of megalopolitan networks may be identified in the United States (see Figure 12.3). There is the eastern seaboard network mentioned above, but three others as well. There is a ring of cities and urban settlements which stretches westward from the Boston-Albany region to the Great Lakes, eastward through the Cleveland-Youngstown-Pittsburgh-Washington area, and northward to Boston. In addition, a major urban line extends from Cleveland, to the Toledo-Detroit area, to Chicago, and finally to St. Louis. Finally, a California megalopolitan line starts in the Sacramento-San Francisco region and moves through to San Diego. The United States is by no means unique. Megalopolitan networks or lines can be identified in Great Britain, from the Liverpool-Manchester area to London-Dover; and in Western Europe, from Amsterdam to Milan, the latter crossing national boundaries. In Japan, such a network extends from the Tokyo-Yokohama area to Osaka. However, we still lack firm objective criteria for delineating megalopolitan networks; we also lack methods for describing, comparing and analyzing their geographic, demographic, social, and economic features.

Thus, population growth and agglomeration have been associated with the differentiation and mutual dependence attending the most recent societal strategy of survival and adaptation: megalopolitanization and the extension of megalopolitan networks across vast areas and sometimes across national boundaries. While a few of the social and political problems associated with this type of development have been recognized, we are still far from understanding the demographic, social structural, political, psychological, and economic correlates and consequences of the process.

SUMMARY

In this chapter we have discussed patterns of urbanization, the proliferation of metropolitan areas and metropolitanization of population, economy and social life, and the growth of megalopolis and megalopolitan networks. The urbanization pattern is one of the two current major demographic responses to population growth and change. The other response, out-migration and the bifurcation of the parent society, has always been a potential or actual demographic response to population growth. Population involution, consisting in increased density of settlement as well as intensification of exploitation and sustenance-yielding activities, is a more recent demographic response and has been possible since the neolithic or agricultural revolution. With increasing population

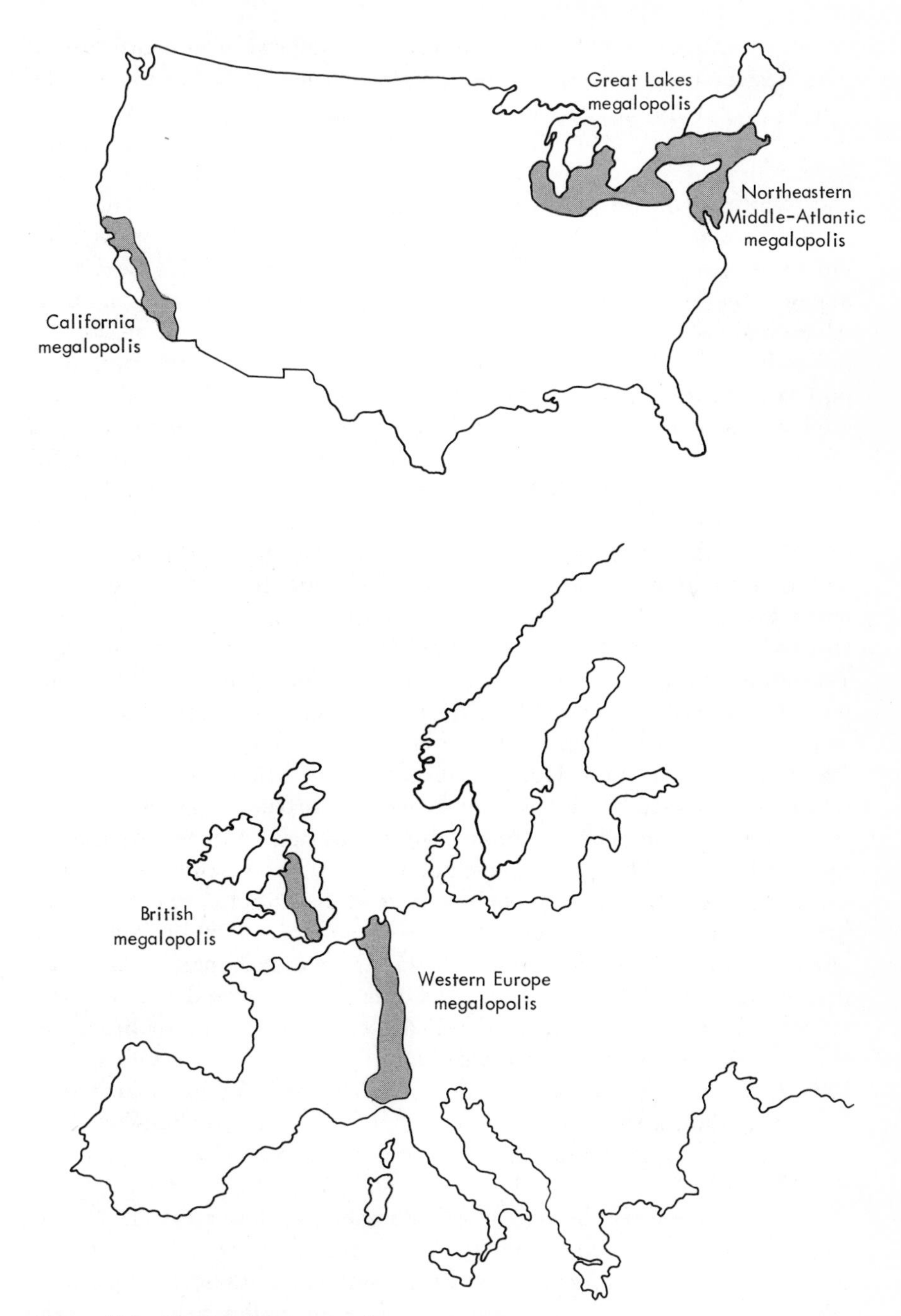

Figure 12.3 Megalopolitan networks.

on the earth's surface the opportunities for emigration and bifurcation have become progressively narrower, so that societal survival and adaptation have increasingly entailed an involutional response to growth, with more intensive agricultural settlement and exploitation: in other words, urbanization.

The proportion of the world's population living in its cities has grown enormously in less than two centuries, though this growth has not been uniform in the various continents and regions. In the United States, urbanization has exceeded the world trend by far, while in Africa and Asia it has lagged. But the modern urban revolution consists not only in the increasing number and size of urban places and their populations. It consists everywhere in a shift to nonagricultural, urban-economic activity as the major economic base, increasing dominance of urban social and political forms, and increasing orientation to urban life-styles and adoption of urban norms and values.

Heterogeneity of population and complexity of associations and organizations are the basic attributes of urban places. In addition, the fact that modern urban growth has been due in large measure to migration means that urban populations are differentiated by length of residence. Urban spatial patterns reflect closely the patterns of social associations and relationships. And physical layout, land use, and transportation configurations of the city reflect social proximity and mutual accessibility. A familiar example is that of residential segregation: racial segregation is the most familiar example, but ethnic and social class residential segregation are equally a part of urban social life.

The city and its surrounding hinterland are mutually dependent upon ongoing exchange, commercial, cultural, and political relationships. As very large urban centers have evolved, both smaller nearby urban places and surrounding rural areas are increasingly specialized and oriented to the single metropolitan-area regional exchange system, with the central city dominant and mediating exchange and relationships within the metropolitan area as well as between the metropolitan area and outside. As metropolitan areas have grown and multiplied, they have themselves become increasingly specialized and organized in systems of metropolitan areas, called the megalopolis or megalopolitan network.

Population growth in the United States since World War II has been characterized by growth of the coastal and Great Lakes megalopolitan networks and also by growth of inland metropolitan areas. But there has been some dispersal of population within these networks. Though surely affected by public policies of various types, these changes have taken place in the absence of internal migration policy per se. Whether population changes can be controlled through policies formulated to influence or restrict migration remains an open issue.

In the next chapter we turn to a second major demographic response to population growth: family limitation and population control. In the United States, the practice of birth control is nearly universal, although there are variations in means employed, timing, and effectiveness. Elsewhere, however, a crucial dimension of the population explosion still remains the conditions of acceptance and institutionalization of fertility control in societies in general and in LDCs in particular.

13

Demographic Responses II: Family Limitation and Population Control

CONTROL OF POPULATION GROWTH

In this chapter we will look at attempts to control natural increase as a response to population growth. We should note that such controls are not the only way of limiting population growth. In countries where migration has been an important factor in growth, the legislative or administrative control of migration is an important kind of demographic response. But for the world as a whole, population control is ultimately the control of natural increase, generally through control of marital fertility. The social circumstances under which intervention on the part of couples to delay or prevent births has occurred, or can be induced to occur, are matters of considerable debate and extensive scientific investigation. We will touch only briefly on the impact of population policy in inducing practice of fertility control, since we return to this issue in more detail in the closing chapter of our text.

It will be recalled that in our discussions of mortality, marriage, and fertility, we noted the variable extent to which societies institutionalize mechanisms to control mortality, timing and matchmaking in marriage, and fertility. We reconsider this variability now as a demographic response to population growth. In our previous discussions we mentioned social and economic factors such as place of residence, education, occupation and income in connection with this variability. And to these we now add one more factor: recent patterns of population growth.

Clearly, in virtually all societies today, the volume and rate of population growth are not ordinarily ignored, but are recognized and observed on a more-or-less ongoing basis. Moreover, the relationships between births, marriages, deaths, health and illness, and population growth are also recognized, if not always analyzed with the precision with which we like to credit ourselves. To the extent that technologies or social arrangements for intervening in the elements of natural increase are known by a society, it seems reasonable to hypothesize that one or a combination of these may be invoked in response to population growth or pressure. However, there is still no body of theory to predict whether or not a society confronted with a growing population will institutionalize intervention into natural increase, and if it does, what form the intervention will take and to what vital area (mortality, marriage, or fertility) it will be addressed.

The Noncontrol of Mortality

The classic Malthusian statement holds that since the production of sustenance cannot keep up with the growth of population, increases in population must inevitably be followed and balanced by the positive check of increased mortality. A much less rigid statement is suggested in Hawley's discussion of "population balance" (1950): *if* production or distribution of sustenance cannot keep up with population growth (and if no avenues of migration are possible), then mortality is likely to rise.

But our concern here is with another problem. If population growth is unaccompanied by increased production of sustenance, does it induce societies to intervene in the direction of increasing, or allowing, higher mortality? And does population decline induce societies to intervene in the direction of controlling and decreasing mortality? We considered the second part of the question in Chapter 7, when we speculated on the conditions under which societies do or do not institutionalize efforts to control mortality. That societies may also institutionalize the noncontrol of mortality—that they may arrange for, or not try to prevent the deaths of certain of their members—is consistent with the observation of (a) fluctuations in mortality in primitive societies and (b) patterns reflecting such intervention in agrarian and preindustrial societies. Kryzwicki has studied the subject. Although he notes the poor quality of the

The modern response to mortality, such as a heartbeat monitored by electrocardiograph, decreases its effect as a population control. *(Courtesy of the American Heart Association)*

data, he is nevertheless able to remark that while infant and child mortality in primitive tribes is higher than in European civilization, it is not uniformly high. He cites examples of both quite low and quite high mortality (Kryzwicki, 1934, pp. 226–43).

E. A. Wrigley (1968) has examined the preindustrial mortality history of Colyton, Devon, in England. He notes that there were instances and periods of extremely low as well as quite high infant and child mortality during the sixteenth, seventeenth, and eighteenth centuries. There was considerable variation in adult mortality as well. Wrigley suggests that these fluctuations may have been closely related to living standards; to short-term weather, harvest, or epidemic conditions; or to longer-term factors like economic circumstances, density of settlement, changes in virulence of diseases, or changes in genetic characteristics. We can add that, while Wrigley's conclusions may be true, such fluctuations in mortality may also have reflected responses to population growth and to the changing circumstances of the survival and adaptation of population increments.

Even societies which do not actually practice infanticide and similar means of population control may manipulate mortality: this is suggested in Colin Clark's characterization of 1953 Lebanese infant mortality rates (195 and 315 for males and females, respectively) as reflecting the operation of a principle on the order of "thou shalt not kill but need not strive officiously to keep alive" (Clark, 1967, p. 44). But while mortality can be a factor in population control, this concept is identified primarily with control of marriage and births. It is to these that we turn in the sections which follow.

Societal Control of Marital Fertility: Some General Considerations

Malthus's prescription for the control of population growth entailed, essentially, the control of marriage. We have already noted some of the factors in variation in patterns. However, there seems thus far to have been little or no attempt made to investigate the relationship—direct or indirect—between population growth and patterns of marriage. Nor has there been much attention paid to the relationship between patterns of migration, population redistribution, and marriage. Nevertheless, there can be little doubt that norms and practices of marriage, divorce, and remarriage are related to the societies' efforts to control population growth, although the exact connections remain to be determined. Perhaps the most convincing evidence is the declines in age at marriage and the increases in proportions ever married, both of which are associated, at least chronologically, with the recent spread and institutionalization of fertility control. In other words, with the advent of effective techniques of fertility control, marriage appears to have been freed from its bondage to the exigencies of societal control of population growth.

One of the great problems confronting contemporary population studies concerns the extent to which, and the manner in which, societies institutionalize control of marital fertility in response to population growth and other changes. In our early discussions of fertility, we argued that the recent widespread interest in individual behavior vis-à-vis fertility, and in individual responses to social, economic, or demographc contingencies to fertility is probably of only limited promise. Of more importance is the subject of the societal institutionalization of norms and patterns of marital fertility as a response to social, economic, or demographic contingencies. A. J. Coale has summarized the findings to date of what is probably the most extensive, ambitious, and geographically detailed historical study of marriage and marital fertility. He notes that there is still no possibility of formulating a "grand generalization that will provide a compact and widely valid explanation of the decline of marital fertility in Europe" (Coale, 1969). More precisely, although a relationship between declining mortality and fertility is often advanced, it is clear that in Spain, Bulgaria, and other southern and Eastern European countries fertility in fact declined in the last decades of the nineteenth and first decades of the twentieth centuries while mortality remained high.

Direct systematic study is still needed to determine the exact relationship between patterns of fertility control and changes in population size, density, distribution, composition, or mobility. Tentatively, we may view societal intervention to control marital fertility as a special case of social innovation. And we may hypothesize that population growth and increasing density are likely to promote the adoption of this particular—and demographically crucial—innovation.

THE GROWTH OF THE MOVEMENT FOR CONTRACEPTION, FAMILY PLANNING, AND POPULATION CONTROL

Evidence of the antiquity of knowledge and practice of means to prevent conceptions and births is easy to obtain, and so are indications of the wide range of such practices and the range of societies in which some form of contraception has been known and practiced. Indeed, a formidable compilation of such evidence was published by Dr. N. Himes more than a generation ago (Himes, 1936, reprinted 1963), and new evidence has since been added. Historical demographers have conjectured that there was systematic practice of family limitation in preindustrial European communities (Henry, 1956; Wrigley, 1966). And the hypothesis that the downward inflection of the birth rate in France as early as the eighteenth century was due to widespread practice of contraception is widely accepted.

Although some pamphlets and books published early in the nineteenth century advocated birth control in the wake of Malthus's treatise, organized efforts to promote practice of birth control do not seem to have emerged until the second half of the nineteenth century in England and a generation later in the United States. In each case these efforts were directed toward promoting individual welfare rather than societal interests. Although early authors who favored contraception—including Francis Place (1822), Robert Dale Owen (1830), and Charles Knowlton (1832)—did emphasize the dangers of excessive population growth as a reason for adopting contraception, the birth control movement subsequently developed as a feminist movement or a social reform movement rather than as a population control movement.

The founder of the American family planning movement was Margaret Sanger. As a trained nurse working in New York, she was exposed daily to the sufferings of women with pregnancies and babies they did not want and also to women risking their lives to abort unwanted pregnancies. Mrs. Sanger gave up nursing to devote herself to teaching women about contraception so they could escape the sorrows of unwanted pregnancies and the medical and legal dangers of illicit abortions. The rationale of the movement founded by Mrs. Sanger in 1913 held that women have the right to freedom from unwanted pregnancies. Moreover, families and existing children are better off—and have greater independence and social, economic, and educational opportunity—to the extent that further unwanted children are not born, and that, hence, society at large benefits.

The population control movement is virtually entirely a post-World War II phenomenon. Its genesis and development are connected with the person, concerns, and activities of John D. Rockefeller III more than any other individual. In the early postwar years Rockefeller became very much concerned about population growth in Japan and the Far East, and he began to promote multidisciplinary population studies. This was done primarily by encouraging the organization of, and thereafter vigorously supporting, the Population Council. This organization's stated purposes were:

> To study the problems presented by an increasing population of the world; to encourage and support research and to disseminate as appropriate the knowledge resulting from such research; to serve generally as a center for the collection of facts and information on the population questions; to cooperate with individuals and institutions in the development of programs; and to take the initiative in the broad fields which in the aggregate constitute the population problems.

In fact the Population Council did vigorously promote research and training in social scientific as well as in medical, biological, and pharmaceutical aspects of population, reproduction, and population control. Moreover, this organization mobilized the interest and commitment both of professionals and of other larger foundations, most notably the Ford and Rockefeller Foundations. It catalyzed and promoted the interest of foreign govenments—India and Pakistan first, then later many others—in population problems and in organization of programs of study and programs of action. It mobilized the interest and participation of other organizations and foundations in these activities and gave the population control movement a developing legitimacy in the face of indifference or organized opposition to birth control.

Meantime, the family planning movement, spearheaded by the Planned Parenthood-World Population organization, moved closer to the group of scientists and foundations concerned with the population explosion. In 1959, a Presidential committee on the American foreign aid program, chaired by General William Draper, devoted a full chapter of its report to the "population question" and recommended that the United States government assist foreign nations seeking to deal with their problems of rapid population growth; and that the government should support research on the question within the United Nations and elsewhere. President Eisenhower rejected the proposal as "a subject that is not a proper political or governmental activity or function or responsibility." But others, in Congress and in public life, publicly advocated positive American response to requests from foreign governments for aid in controlling population. President Kennedy reversed the earlier policy, but he did not commit the United States to providing such assistance. Rather, requests for aid for studying population trends and for developing population control programs were referred to private foundations and organizations such as the Population Council and the Planned Parenthood-World Population organization.

It was especially in the early 1960s, with the publication of results of the 1960 population censuses and the growing awareness of the research, training, and dissemination activities of the universities and private foundations, that increasing numbers of governments of developing countries (LDCs) began to initiate population studies, adopt population policies, and seek the aid of MDCs in effecting population control policies. Already in the 1950s, the United Nations had a technical assistance program and many MDC governments also had programs to provide such assistance. But it was only in 1964 that President Johnson committed the United States Government to an active role in population control, through the programs of the Agency for International Development (AID), the Office of Economic Opportunity (OEO) and the National Institutes of Health (NIH).

Meantime the population control movement, initially a "population coalition" comprising government officials, foundations, philanthropists, and demographers largely committed to a family planning solution to the world population problem, was joined (or perhaps outflanked) by the "environmental radicals" who viewed the population problem much more in terms of imminent crisis and saw little if any promise in voluntary family planning solutions. The latter, with apocalyptic visions and the zero population growth (ZPG) watchword, achieved considerable publicity victories in the 1960s. And the population control movement as a whole achieved a new victory with the appointment by President Nixon of The Commission on Population Growth and the American Future, the first such body. The deliberations and reports of this commission reflected mainly the approaches and commitments of the "population coalition"—in other words, voluntary family planning—and took note only parenthetically of the concerns and proposed solutions of the "environmental radicals."

The population control movement enjoyed a sequence of successes in the 1960s and early 1970s, including the commitment of governments and of the United Nations, and of both professional and lay opinion, to the goal of lowering the rate of population growth and to explicit policies and programs designed to achieve this goal. The United States Government commitment, and the appointment of the commissions were, of course, special achievements for the population control movement, and the promotion and organization of a World Population Year in 1974 and a World Population Conference to highlight it were to have been further achievements for the movement. As it turned out, the 1974 World Population Conference in Bucharest, Romania, proved highly critical both of the population control movement's analysis of the threat of population growth and of its program for dealing with it. Nonetheless, there was and remains wide consensus about the desirability of making available information and means of contraception. And there has been continuing expansion of practice of contraception in MDCs and LDCs alike.

FAMILY LIMITATION PRACTICES

To what extent do couples intervene in the natural processes of reproduction in order to control the number or timing of births? We may be able to conceive theoretically of societies in which no intervention at all takes place, but their actual existence is highly unlikely. Probably no society is completely free of practices inhibiting conception and birth. However, these practices may not be motivated by the desire to control the number and timing of births. On the contrary, intervention deliberately designed to limit and control fertility has been and remains exceptional among societies. And it is far from universal in those societies in which it is known and practiced. The data reviewed in Chapter 9 from the sequence of national fertility surveys portrays a movement on all color, religious, and social fronts in the direction of near-universal practice of contraception among American couples.

Among countries in which estimates of contraceptive use have been attempted, the percentages reporting family limitation practices are generally smaller than in the United States or in the United Kingdom. However, a pattern of association with socioeconomic status occurs in virtually every instance in which socioeconomic indicators are measured.[1] In the United States and Canada—but not in the United Kingdom—there are clear urban-rural and size-of-city differentials. Nevertheless, these and the socioeconomic-status differential have been diminishing over time (see Matras, 1965). A selection of findings on the extent of contraceptive practice around the world shows variations ranging from about two percent in Kenya, Nepal, and Turkey to over 75 percent (see Figure 13.1) in the United Kingdom. However, it is important to bear in mind that these estimates are of varying quality and reliability.

For the most part, studies of the extent of contraceptive practice have dealt separately, if at all, with induced abortion. However, it is necessary to recognize that in many societies induced abortion has been, and remains, the primary method used to limit fertility and control population growth. In Japan, Eastern Europe, and to a certain extent Scandinavia, abortion has been a major means of birth control (Tietze 1965). In other countries, too, the number and proportion of women who use induced abortion to prevent unwanted births are probably fairly large.

Impact and Methods of Voluntary Birth Control

In every case, family limitation has been shown to have a substantial impact upon fertility. Although there are variations in the extent to which individuals are successful in their contraceptive efforts, individual women or couples who practice family limitation generally do have fewer children than those who don't. And population groups with large proportions that practice family limitation have lower levels of fertility than those with only a small proportion using birth control.

Contraception may be practiced by any one or a combination of methods. One conventional distinction is that made between natural and artificial (mechanical or chemical) methods. One of the two primary methods in the first category is *coitus interruptus* (male withdrawal just before ejaculation). This is the method mentioned in the Old Testament. Apparently widely known and used throughout the Western world, it is probably largely responsible for the modern decline in European fer-

[1] See, however, the analysis of Westoff, Potter, and Sagi (1964) emphasizing that rural-urban background and religious differences may account for the inverse socioeconomic differential.

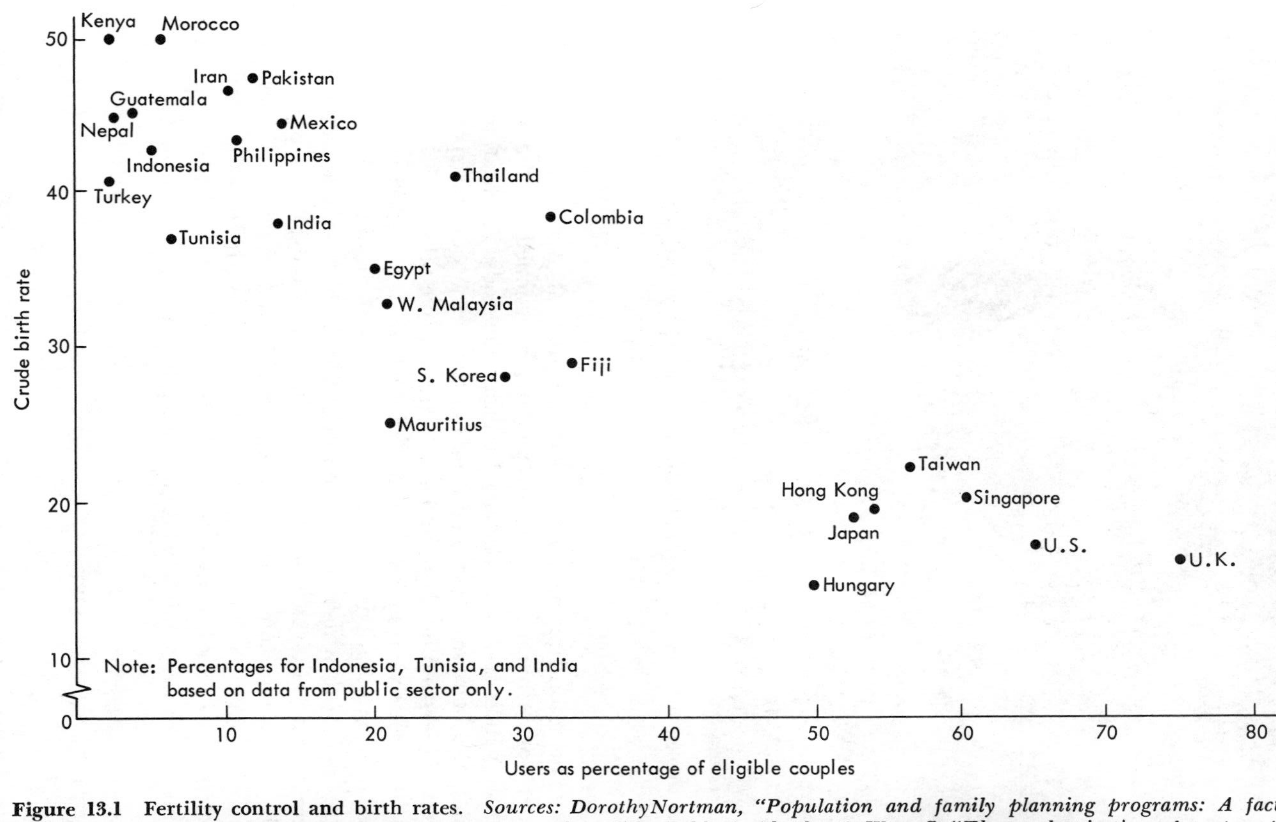

Figure 13.1 Fertility control and birth rates. *Sources: DorothyNortman, "Population and family planning programs: A factbook,"* Reports on Population/Family Planning, *September 1973, Table 4; Charles F. Westoff, "The modernization of contraceptive practice,"* Family Planning Perspectives *4, no. 3 (Summer 1972), p. 10. Reprinted with the permission of the Population Council from Bernard Berelson, "World Population: Status Report 1974,"* Reports on Population/Family Planning, *no. 15 (January 1974),* p. 34.

Italian women in a pro-abortion bill demonstration. *(Keystone)*

tility. The second primary method in the natural category is the "safe period," or "rhythm" technique currently sanctioned by the Catholic Church, which prohibits the use of other methods. Artificial methods include the condom, diaphragm, and intrauterine devices; spermicidal creams, jellies, and douches; and oral contraceptive pills.

The relative frequency of use of each of the respective methods varies over populations and over population subgroups. Similarly, the effectiveness with which any of the respective methods is used varies over different population groups. Finally, individuals and groups practicing family limitation vary in their pattern and timing of its use. Generally, we may distinguish initial undertakings of family limitation according to whether they occur before the first birth, after the first birth but before completion of the family, or after completion of the desired family size.

VALUES OF FAMILY SIZE

With evidence that fertility in certain populations has been increasingly subject to the direct control and wishes of parents, demographers have become progressively more interested in values about family size, in variations among these values, and in the relationship of expressed ideals of family size to expected and actual fertility. Indeed, one argument holds that the key to reducing fertility in high fertility countries lies not only in family planning programs and economic development but in the generation of a small family ideal (Blake, 1965).

This dimension of childbearing differs in an important way from the marriage and intervention dimensions and other factors listed by Davis and Blake (1956). The factors mentioned by Davis and Blake all represent behavioral characteristics which can be observed and measured for individuals, groups, or social collectivities, whereas the dimension of preferred family size is a value which we must infer indirectly. Nonetheless, it is of great importance to consider values of family size and to review, however briefly, some of the research results in this area.

Ideal Family Size

Our information on family size values comes almost exclusively from opinion and attitude surveys, some of whose data are summarized in Table 13.1. The average ideal number of children varies from two children in Austria in 1960 to 4.2 children in Canada in the same year. For most countries the average lies between about 2.5 and 3.5. Thus, countries of Europe and European settlement are fairly homogeneous with respect to average ideal family size. An unexpected finding is that ideal family sizes reported in countries outside Europe also center in the range of two to four children.

Reports such as these and data on actual fertility performances in different population groupings represent the only obvious clues we have to institutionalized values and patterns of family size in different communities, collectivities, and socioeconomic categories or ascriptive groups.

Some Pressing Questions Regarding Values of Family Size

An important kind of discrepancy has been recorded in some studies of family size preference between individuals' fertility ideals and their expectations of their own behavior. For instance, J. Blake (1965) has found that outside the higher social and economic classes, many Europeans expect to have, and actually do have, considerably fewer children than they consider ideal. Blake reasons that the fact that actual fertility is lower in the countries of Europe than in the frontier countries of European overseas settlement represents a coming to terms, in the case of Europe, with harsh economic realities. For the family size preferences in both cases are very similar—averaging at around three children. Given the similarity of family size preference in the face of disparate economic

TABLE 13.1 Ideal Number of Children Reported in Selected Countries of Europe and European Settlement

Country	*Date*	*Average Ideal Number Children*	*Percent Saying Four Children or More*
Austria	1960	2.0	4.0
Belgium	1952	2.64	25.0
Finland	1953	2.84	22.0
France	1944	3.17	34.0
	1945	2.92	24.0
	1946	2.70	20.0
	1947	2.77	23.0
	1948	2.88	23.0
	1959–1960	2.77	16.9
Italy	1951	2.80	19.0
Netherlands	1947	3.66	46.0
	1960	3.3	38.7
Norway	1960	3.1	25.0
Switzerland	1960	2.9	22.4
Great Britain	1938	2.94	25.0
	1939	2.96	29.0
	1944	3.00	33.0
	1947	2.84	25.0
	1952	2.84	26.0
	1960	2.8	23.2
Sweden	1947	2.79	22.0
West Germany	1950	2.21	11.0
	1953	2.28	11.0
	1958	2.6	12.0
Australia	1947	3.79	64.0
Canada	1945	4.06	60.0
	1947	3.91	55.0
	1960	4.2	70.1
United States	1936	3.17	34.0
	1941	3.42	41.0
	1945	3.61	49.0
	1947	3.37	43.0
	1949	3.91	63.0
	1953	3.33	41.0
	1960	3.6	50.6

Source: J. Blake, Demographic science and the redirection of public policy, Journal of Chronic Diseases, *Vol. 18, November, 1965. By permission of Pergamon Press Ltd.*

conditions, Blake also concludes that there is no a priori reason to expect modernization and economic development by themselves to bring small family values. Only direct policies affecting family structure and fertility behavior are likely, in Blake's opinion, to influence family size values and ultimately, actual fertility.

There is some question about whether, in fact, the attitudes expressed in surveys actually reflect societal norms and values about fertility or family size. Clearly, if such opinions really do reflect societal values and norms, we need an explanation of why there is such a discrepancy between ideal, expected, and actual fertility in so many areas. There surely seem to be more factors involved than economic circumstances.

For instance, the number of children reported as ideal is closely related to the number of children actually already borne, with two exceptions. Women or couples with no children are very likely to understate their desire to become parents, and parents with one child are very likely to indicate a desire for more (Bachi and Matras, 1964; Knodel and Prachuabmoh, 1973). We also know that the ideal family size reported in surveys typically increases with increasing age—as do the numbers of children borne. Over a large range of populations, the preferences are very highly concentrated at around two to four children, regardless of the patterns of cumulative total fertility which characterize the population in question. This striking similarity of results may be a consequence of studying—and averaging—cross sections of women or couples where almost everyone reported exactly the number of children born as the ideal or preferred number.

Thus, the exact meaning of the results of opinion surveys concerning preferred family size must be considered carefully; and alternative and additional representations of family size values and ideals must be sought. It seems quite clear that there do exist societies and subcultural groups in which the very concepts of "number of children desired" or "ideal number of children" are unknown (Bachi and Matras 1964). But even for those cultural settings in which the concept is meaningful, a model more realistic than that of the couple's fixed image of its desired family would be one in which the *image* of its desired family *may change* in time and over the couple's marital life cycle.

The Relationship Between Marriage, Intervention, and Values of Family Size

As a closing thought for this chapter's discussion, we should point out that the three dimensions of childbearing—marriage, societal intervention, and values of family size—are very closely interwoven. As we have already seen, Malthus first raised the possibility that population growth could be controlled by postponing marriage.[2] Hajnal has hypothesized that it was precisely the widespread desire to keep families small and assure their support which was responsible in large measure for the unique European pattern of delayed marriage and high proportions of singles. Finally, at least two of the three dimensions of childbearing, patterns of marriage and patterns of intervention to limit family size within marriage, have been widely shown to vary directly and jointly with levels of fertility (see Matras, 1965). The contraction over time of differentials in marriage and family limitation patterns corresponds to the contraction of fertility differentials among the various countries of Europe and among different subgroups in European national populations.

However, the exact role of family size values in the interaction between marriage, intervention, and fertility is yet to be assessed. The effects of marriage age and mate selection patterns on fertility have yet to be studied, too. Finally, and perhaps most important, we must study and describe in detail the manner in which societal strategies of survival and adaptation, and of population growth or nongrowth, are translated and reflected in individual decisions about marriage and family formation.

SUMMARY

In this chapter we have considered the second major demographic response to population growth, the attempt to control natural increase. We have studied especially the adoption of family limitation and the movements and policies promoting it throughout the world.

In the United States, the practice of birth control is nearly universal, and the numbers of unwanted children are low and declining in most population subgroups. The increasing acceptibility of abortion as a means of preventing unwanted births shows promise of bringing fertility even more under the control of couples involved, reducing fertility differentials in the various population groups and probably lowering overall birth rates. Whether such private successful family planning and couple control of fertility is consistent with national or worldwide control needs remains a matter of debate. In other Western countries, the practice of contraception is probably somewhat less prevalent and successful, but later marriage and widespread abortion combine to result in as low or lower birth rates in many of them. In LDCs, the practice of contraception remains infrequent, though this behavior is beginning in

[2] That postponement of marriage does indeed have this result has been clearly shown by Leasure (1963).

some countries and there is increasing evidence of inroads of values and preferences favoring small families coupled with an increasing awareness that small families are possible.

Although contraceptive means have been known and practiced for centuries, the family planning movement began in England and the United States primarily as part of women's liberation movements in the early decades of the present century. This movement has primarily sought to promote control of family size and prevention of unwanted children as beneficial to women, families, and society alike. Especially since World War II, family planning has come to be viewed as a response and partial solution to the world and national population growth problems. In recent years, public and private agencies and national governments have been alerted to the problems of excessive population growth, and to the kinds of policies that can be used to control population growth. National and international public and private agencies and organizations have undertaken a worldwide program of studies about current knowledge, attitudes, and practices in fertility control and family limitation; they are also attempting to introduce and promote family limitation where it has previously been unknown or insignificant. There also exists a dissenting point of view which holds that our resources are better turned to more general social, economic, and cultural development in these target areas. This argument holds that without development the family limitation programs will not succeed, but with development, family limitation will be spontaneously adopted.

In a number of LDCs, the adoption of family limitation has been strongly linked to significant declines in birth rates. While there was some past tendency for supporters of the birth-control promotion programs to claim credit for more general development trends, the more recent discussion has stressed the complementarity and natural dovetailing of the population control and development programs respectively.

In the following chapter, we will turn to a consideration of the economic responses to population growth and change. We shall see that there has been an extended debate surrounding past relationships between population and economic development and welfare; and that forms of this debate continue to surround the discussion of the economic impact of current population growth.

14

Economic Responses: Population, Development, and Welfare

It was Malthus who most impressed upon his contemporaries and subsequent generations the lesson that population and economic welfare comprise a mutually interacting system. The gloomy conclusion which Malthus reached was that populations tend to outgrow their resources and means of sustenance, and that inevitably population growth must be brought under control. As we saw earlier, this happens either by "positive checks" of increased mortality, like disease and violence, and the social disorders that accompany them; or by "preventive checks" like the postponement or foregoing of marriage or continence within marriage. Malthus also taught that even those happy periods of prosperity and high food production will inevitably produce enough additional people to exhaust the available resources. The result will be a return to original subsistence levels of living and to high death rates.

We have earlier alluded to this line of reasoning and also to the counter line of reasoning which holds that population growth enhances economic welfare. In this chapter, we will go into more depth in our evaluation of such arguments, examining more systematically the economic responses to population changes. Of course, any response which implies a shift in allocation or exchange of social rewards or resources can be considered an economic response, and indeed it may be so classified by economists under the rubric of welfare economics. But we shall confine our consideration here to a more conventional definition: economic responses are those responses in the areas of work and of production and distribution of exchangeable goods and services in the conventional sense.

We will look first at the responses that take place in the working force and employment market as population changes. Then, we will turn to the specific responses of savings and investment, and of productivity. In many instances it will be appropriate to deal with economic responses to population change in the more developed countries (MDCs) and in the less developed countries (LDCs) separately. As in the case of migration and population redistribution, we shall see that economic responses, too, are mediated in part by the sociopolitical context in which the population change is taking place.

POPULATION CHANGES AND THE WORKING FORCE

The working force is the part of the population normally available for employment in organized economic activity. Factory employees, office workers, farmers, proprietors, and unpaid workers in family farms or businesses and persons temporarily unemployed are all part of the working force; but young children and retired persons are not. The working force must produce the goods and services needed to satisfy the requirements of the whole population. Obviously, the size and characteristics of the working force, and the manner in which it is employed, bear very heavily on the total output of goods and services. Population growth and change affects output through their influence on (a) the growth of the working force; (b) the proportions employed or unemployed in the working force; and (c) all the factors which condition the output per employed member of the working force (this will be discussed in subsequent sections).

Growth of the Working Force

The ratio of persons of working age to the total population depends, of course, on the age composition of the population. The latter, in turn, is influenced both by births and deaths and by patterns of in-migration and out-migration. Spengler (1972 and 1974) and others have shown that the proportion of working ages in a population is maximized under conditions of relatively low natural increase, as when annual growth is about five per 1,000; and it declines as the rate of natural increase rises. The long-range trend of decreasing fertility in industrialized countries has worked generally to raise the proportion of the working age population over time, although the post-World War II baby booms reversed this trend temporarily. In less developed countries where the birth rates have remained at generally high levels, there has been relatively little change in population age structures. But in some countries there have been recent appreciable decreases in the proportions of adult population, probably as a result of decreasing mortality and, sometimes, increasing fertility.

For populations receiving net in-migrants, the in-migration contributes proportionately more to the growth of the working force than to population growth as a whole. This is because migration streams characteristically include a large proportion of young adults. Thus, the trans-Atlantic migration from Europe to the United States in the late nineteenth and early twentieth centuries made a major contribution to the American working force: about one-third of the working force in the four decades preceding World War I were foreign born. In Australia in the decade following World War II immigration was the major contributor to growth of the working force, while the working forces of Italy, Greece, Spain, Turkey, and Yugoslavia grew substantially less than they would have in the post-World War II decades because of the emigration of workers. The working forces of cities and metropolitan areas have been greatly augmented, and those of many rural communities greatly reduced, by rural-to-urban migration. Finally, the size of the working force in frontier areas—including the American West, the Argentine pampas, and Siberia—is typically very large relative to the total population, largely by reason of its large migrant component.

The size of the working force depends also on the extent or rates of participation at each age and for each population group (young persons, old persons, single females, married females) to seek and accept employment. Population factors may also affect rates of participation: high fertility implies reduced working force participation of women, and the opposite holds true as well. Rural-to-urban migrants may have lower participation rates than the nonmigrant population, while urban migrants are likely to have higher rates of participation. The long term trends in industrialized countries have involved declining rates of participation among young males and elderly males, and increasing rates of participation among married women.

Employment and Unemployment

Readiness to work must be matched by availability of employment if the productive potential of the working force is to be realized. The great increases in production and social welfare notwithstanding, the fear of unemployment and the fact of unemployment remain a major challenge to the fabric of Western society. At least since the 1930s, an important tradition of economic analysis has held that the rate of investment required to sustain full employment cannot be maintained under conditions of stationary or declining population. According to the Keynesian analysis, at least some minimal population growth is necessary to avoid excessive unemployment; in the absence of population growth governments must increase expenditures to offset the investment shortage occasioned by declining population growth and causing unemployment.

However, more recent analyses have viewed diminished rates of population growth as favorable to high levels of employment. A number of arguments have been marshalled by J. J. Spengler (1972). First, the employment of young people, who are new entrants into the working force, is more difficult when the population is growing at a rapid rate than when it is growing at a low rate or not at all. For under conditions of growth, large numbers of additional jobs are required each year; while under conditions of nongrowth the number of jobs made available by death or retirement of incumbents is close to the number needed for new entrants. Second, the rate of capital formation tends to be inversely related to the rate of population growth. In rapidly growing populations, the capital shortage will probably especially affect the employment-oriented investment, with the result that inputs complementary to labor will grow less rapidly than the working force, or not fast enough to maintain full employment. This means that under rapid population growth unemployment, underemployment, and "disguised unemployment" are likely to be high—a condition which is conspicuous in high fertility LDCs. Spengler's third point is that employment is facilitated by a low and nonfluctuating rate of natural increase. This is because these conditions (where the relative number of new entrants into the working force does not fluctuate) allow the physical and personal capital essential to the maintenance of health and employment to be formed at a relatively high and constant rate.

In developing countries, important dimensions of the economy are the very absence of capital; the shortage of land; and a general imbalance between the supply of labor and the supply of other factors of production which means that labor is typically underemployed to start with. In the LDCs, high population and working force growth may be conducive to higher unemployment and underemployment through factors such as the decrease in land per worker, recourse to land of inferior quality, or fragmented or overcrowded holdings. In the absence of employment opportunities outside agriculture, the migration of unemployed rural working force may simply imply the transfer of underemployment or unemployment to the cities.

Unequal economic and population growth in various parts of the world or within any given country are the rule rather than the exception. A basic hypothesis in population studies has been that migration is the major factor in bringing about an adjustment between different countries or regions. In MDCs, minimum degrees of migration and mobility are necessary for maintaining high levels of employment. But in the LDCs, employment problems may be created rather than resolved by rural-to-urban movements; for such movements often reflect not so much differential development and adjustments as much as chronic deficiency in the demand for labor. Low incomes and low levels of employment in agriculture, together with high density or high population growth rates, are among the main causes of out-migration from rural areas.

It is important to note that the discussion of relations between population change and employment rests largely on theoretical rather than on empirical analyses. Thus, the role of population factors in determining levels of employment is still difficult to evaluate precisely; and even the directions in which population changes influence employment remains a controversial matter.

POPULATION, SAVINGS, AND INVESTMENT RESPONSES

The effects of population growth and shifting age composition on the rate of savings and investments is one of the relationships between demographic factors and economic development most extensively analyzed and discussed. We may consider *savings* to be the excess of income over consumption; and *investment,* the commitment of savings to purchase of capital goods or training or knowledge for purposes of enhancing future production. The key elements of our analysis are:

1. The population in the working or labor force ages, usually taken as the population aged 15 to 64;
2. Dependency, taken usually as the ratio of persons under 15 and aged

Investment—a commitment to future production. Here, the New York Stock Exchange. *(Wide World Photos)*

65 or older, to the population aged 15 to 64, but sometimes represented by the ratio of the *total* population to the population aged 15 to 64;

3. Density of the population, taken usually as the number of persons per unit of land area, or persons per units of arable land, but sometimes viewed in terms of the number of persons in the labor force ages relative to land area or to other resources.

Population growth and the attendant changes in the labor force, dependency, and density affect the society's productivity and its levels of per capita income through (a) the proportion of current national income that may be set aside for investment, and (b) the effectiveness with which available investment can be used to raise the productivity per worker.

The study of actual and alternative hypothetical population changes in low income, underdeveloped countries suggests that rapid population growth per se inhibits economic development and increased per capita income in such countries.[1] The relationship is summarized very succinctly by F. Lorimer:

[1] The pioneer and still the most detailed example of such an analysis is that of Coale and Hoover, 1958.

> Rapid population growth tends to reduce the proportion of current production that can be allocated to investment in new capital equipment and other facilities due both to the larger volume of goods required for immediate consumption by individuals and to the larger public expenditures needed for transportation, communication, social services, etc. At the same time, in a population with a rapidly increasing labor force a larger proportion of current investment must be used *extensively,* to provide new workers with resources at the standards already in effect, so that less of current investment is available for *intensive* use in raising levels of productivity per worker. (Lorimer, 1969, p. 178)

Modern demographic analysis has shown conclusively that the central factor in the age distribution of a population is the schedule of fertility rates. High fertility implies a "young" age distribution (high proportions at preadult ages) and low fertility implies an "older" age distribution (high proportions at adult and older ages). Moreover, changes in mortality have only minor effects on the age distribution of a population, whereas changes in fertility have a significant and rapid effect on age distribution (Coale, 1956).

Until the middle of the twentieth century, most analyses of the effects of population upon the economy focused on the relationships between population and natural resources, population and the labor supply (primarily as this was affected by rates of economic activity or labor force participation among both sexes at different ages), and population and consumption and markets.[2] In these analyses, the concept of dependency was introduced primarily with reference to aged persons, with relatively little attention to the connection between fertility and dependent children.

The Case of India

In *Population Growth and Economic Development in Low-Income Countries* (1958), A. J. Coale and E. M. Hoover applied the analysis of the relationship between fertility and age distribution to measuring the effects of alternative patterns of fertility upon dependency and upon potentials for development and increase of per capita income. Carrying out alternative projections for India for 1951 through 1986, they show that the continuation of India's high fertility pattern implies *both* a continued rapid growth of the entire population and an increase in the already very high burden of dependency. If, however, fertility were reduced by 50 percent over a 25-year period, the rate of total population

[2] See especially the summary of such analysis in United Nations, *Determinants and Consequences of Population Trends,* 1953, Part 3.

growth would decline very sharply. No less important, the burden of dependency would diminish. Figure 14.1 and Table 14.1 illustrate these projections.

In Figure 14.1 we can see that under the assumption of unchanged fertility, the percent of the total population aged 14 and under rises somewhat (from just below 40 percent to just over 40 percent); the percent aged 65 and over also climbs slightly; and the percent aged 15 to 64 declines somewhat. In consequence, the dependency ratio and the estimated number of nonearning dependents per earner (shown in the high projection of Table 14.1) would rise over the same period. In contrast,

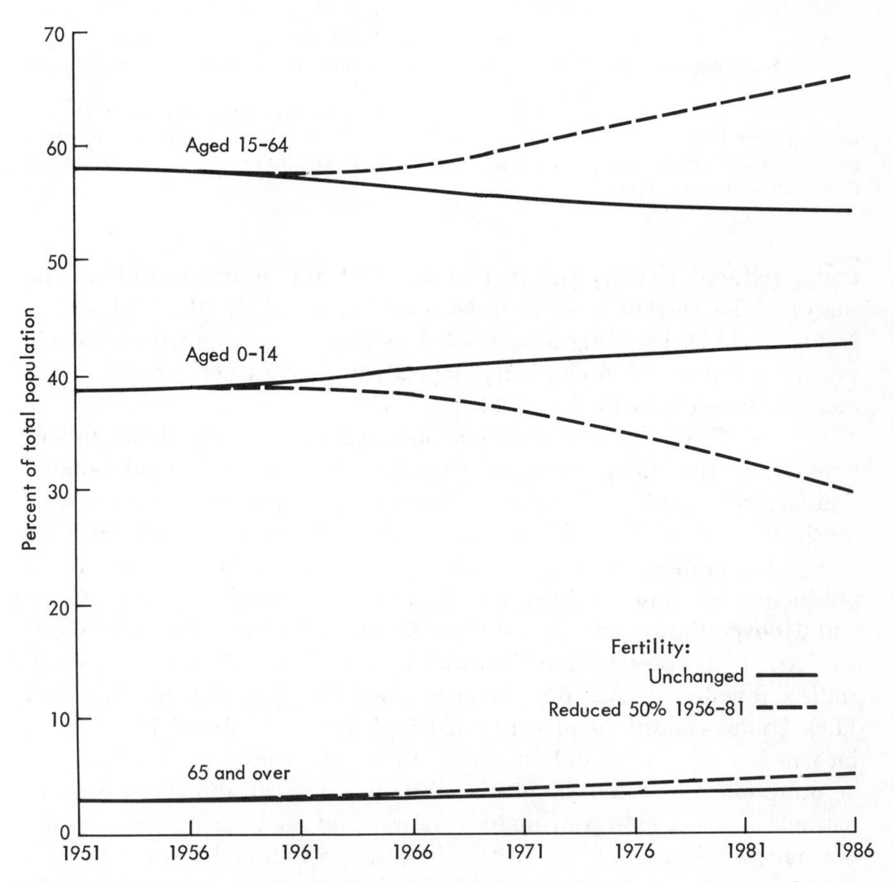

Figure 14.1 Percentage distribution of population by broad age groups under unchanged and reduced fertility assumptions, India, 1951–1986. *Source: Ansley J. Coale and Edgar M. Hoover,* Population Growth and Economic Development in Low-Income Countries: A Case Study of India's Prospects *(copyright © 1958 by Princeton University Press), chart #4, p. 41. Reprinted by permission of Princeton University Press.*

TABLE 14.1 Approximate Number of Nonearning Dependants per Earner under Alternative Population Projections, India, 1956–1986[a]

	Projection		
	Low	*Medium*	*High*
1956	1.51	1.51	1.51
1961	1.53	1.55	1.55
1966	1.52	1.60	1.60
1971	1.46	1.60	1.63
1976	1.37	1.51	1.65
1981	1.29	1.37	1.69
1986	1.24	1.25	1.71

[a] Assuming total number of full and part earners is 68.4 percent of number of persons aged 15–64, as in 1951.

Source: Ansley J. Coale and Edgar M. Hoover, Population Growth and Economic Development in Low-Income Countries: A Case Study of India's Prospects *(copyright © 1958 by Princeton University Press), table #32, p. 235. Reprinted by permission of Princeton University Press.*

under reduced fertility the percent aged 14 and under would decline sharply. The percent aged 15 to 64 would rise sharply (the broken line in Figure 14.1), implying a reduced dependency ratio and progressively smaller numbers of nonearning dependents per earner (the low and medium projections in Table 14.1).

As K. Davis (1951) had earlier observed in his study of the Indian population, the Indian subcontinent's high fertility and rapid population growth yields an "unusual burden of young-age dependency," much of which is "wasted" in that "women are pregnant, give birth to, and nurse millions of babies each year who die before they reach a productive age. Energy, food, and supplies are wasted on them." Coale and Hoover show that expenditures on the education, housing, social services, and consumption connected with high dependency drain India's investment and development capability (see Figures 14.2 and 14.3). Under conditions of continued high fertility, annual increases in income per consumer and in consumption per consumer are likely to be quite modest indeed, despite a substantial rate of annual increase in national income. However, under conditions of medium or low fertility, not only would the annual rate of increase in national income be substantially higher, but the rate of increase in income per consumer and in consumption per consumer would be three to four times higher than under conditions of high fertility (see Table 14.2).

Similar analyses have been carried out for other underdeveloped

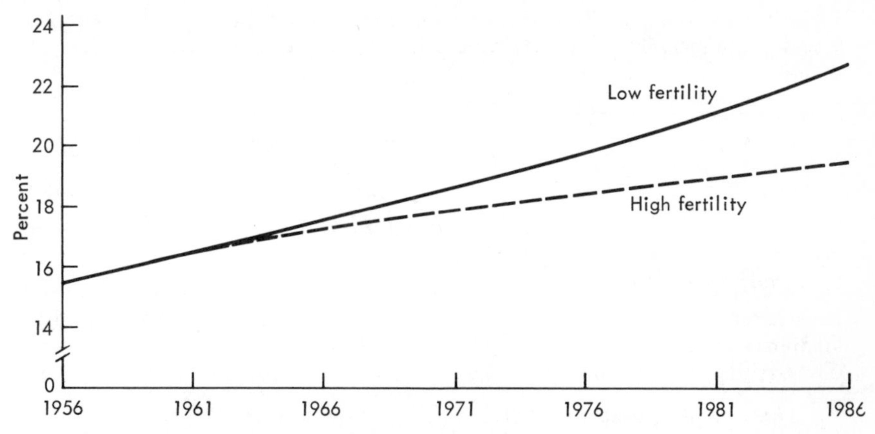

Figure 14.2 Developmental expenditures as a proportion of national income, with high and low fertility, India, 1956–1986. *Source: Ansley J. Coale and Edgar M. Hoover,* Population Growth and Economic Development in Low-Income Countries: A Case Study of India's Prospects *(copyright © 1958 by Princeton University Press), chart #11, p. 276. Reprinted by permission of Princeton University Press.*

Figure 14.3 Quinquennial increases in total population and in population of primary-schol age, with high and low fertility, India, 1956–1986. *Source: Ansley J. Coale and Edgar M. Hoover,* Population Growth and Economic Development in Low-Income Countries: A Case Study of India's Prospects *(copyright © 1958 by Princeton University Press), chart #9 (redrawn), p. 265. Reprinted by permission of Princeton University Press.*

TABLE 14.2 Annual Rates of Increase in National Income, per Consumer Income, and per Consumer "Consumption," by Five-Year Periods, India (Projection 1)

	Percentage Increase Per Annum					
	1956–1961	*1961–1966*	*1966–1971*	*1971–1976*	*1976–1981*	*1981–1986*
National Income						
High fertility	3.3	3.3	3.4	3.4	3.4	3.5
Medium fertility	3.3	3.3	3.4	3.5	3.7	4.0
Low fertility	3.3	3.5	3.7	3.9	4.2	4.5
Income per Consumer						
High fertility	1.4	1.2	1.0	1.0	0.9	0.9
Medium fertility	1.4	1.2	1.2	1.6	2.1	2.8
Low fertility	1.5	1.6	1.8	2.3	2.9	3.4
"Consumption" per Consumer						
High fertility	1.2	1.0	0.9	0.8	0.8	0.8
Medium fertility	1.2	1.0	1.0	1.4	1.9	2.5
Low fertility	1.3	1.4	1.6	2.0	2.6	3.0

Source: Ansley J. Coale and Edgar M. Hoover, Population Growth and Economic Development in Low-Income Countries: A Case Study of India's Prospects *(copyright © 1958 by Princeton University Press), table #38, p. 273. Reprinted by permission of Princeton University Press.*

areas, and in each case the policy implications seem clear: countries seeking to promote rapid development and increased levels of living must seek ways to reduce fertility. This conclusion has been widely adopted in both popular and the scientific discussions of the "world population explosion" and the "world population crisis."

Fertility Rates and Savings and Investment

The argument that population growth frustrates economic development and growth in per capita income because large numbers of children reduce the ability to save and invest has been challenged on a number of grounds. In the first place, the idea that children consume and fail to produce, hence are a social burden, has been questioned on both theoretical and empirical grounds. Studies have suggested that at the level of families and households, children do not necessarily lower the savings rate, and if they do the actual quantitative impact may be small.

Children substitute for other forms of consumption and are not necessarily increments to total family consumption. They may contribute directly to household income or their presence may stimulate one or both parents to work harder, longer hours, or more efficiently. If we view skills or education as investment, we can view children as encouraging capital accumulation in these forms of assets, and one analysis notes that children may provide stimulus to the amassing of estates.

In the second place, the importance of the origins of savings, and of the proportion of total savings originating within households and outside households respectively, remains to be assessed. The analysis of the negative influence of high fertility and population growth on economic development presumes, generally, that household or family savings are main sources of investment. But in the American case, for example, it seems clear that private capital formation in agriculture, nonfarm unincorporated businesses, and corporations has tended to be financed with resources internal to the respective sectors. On the other hand, a large proportion of household savings is in the form of residential construction, retirement funds, and insurance, and the proportion of private capital formation taking place in the corporate sector has increased steadily.

In the less developed countries, and in the more developed countries with planned economies, the level of savings depends more on tax policy and institutions in the public sector rather than on voluntary savings in the household sectors. The public sector is, of course, also responsive to population growth and the needs of the dependent population. But the exact effects of variations in the origins and locales of savings is yet to be determined conclusively.

POPULATION AND PRODUCTIVITY RESPONSES

Historically population growth has been linked not only to economic growth and increasing production, but also to increasing *productivity:* greater output per unit of input. Two kinds of explanations for this link have been advanced. The first explanation has involved the concepts of division of labor and *scale effects* (or economies of scale, or returns to scale) in production and in research and development, invention and adoption of innovation. The second kind has asserted that individuals and organizations work harder, improve efficiency, and adopt innovations under the pressure and threat of diminished per capita income implied by growing population.

Specialization and Scale Effects

There are several sources of economies of scale. First, within firms, larger size allows higher degrees of specialization and division of labor, enhancing technical efficiency of production processes and allowing lower unit costs. The classic example is, of course, the introduction of assembly line production—whether of bicycles, reapers, and cannons in the nineteenth century or automobiles, transistor radios, complicated cameras, and home appliances in the twentieth century. This kind of scale economy is, in turn, rendered practicable by increased size of markets, and indeed, initially by the very production for anonymous markets rather than fabrication to order for the individual consumer.

There are additional sources of economies of scale in quite large economies, and, to the extent that trade conditions permit, in the world economy. Here, economies of scale derive from the increased specialization and diversification between firms. When population and market reach a very substantial size, the firm initially designing and producing all the parts for its product, and indeed designing and building its own machine tools, may "disintegrate vertically" (or contract out) certain of its operations to other more specialized firms. A favorite public relations theme of General Motors revolves about the number of independent firms, not owned by GM, who produce parts used in General Motors vehicles, appliances, or equipment.

For quite large countries, the exploitation of natural resources, including agricultural exploitation, can be the more extensive as population grows and transport and communication allow geographic diversification, specialization, and exchange. Kelley (1972) cites estimates of the extent to which twentieth-century American growth in per capita output can be imputed to such economies of scale ranging from 10 percent in the 1929–1957 period to 50 percent in the period from 1909 to 1929.

The importance of invention and innovation in the historical growth of production and productivity is familiar to every schoolboy, and the names of the great inventors—Edison, Bell, Ford, the Wright Brothers, Westinghouse—are as familiar as their inventions. But there are thousands of lesser inventions and production processes, and their introduction, application, and exploitation in agriculture, industry, and commerce represent tens of thousands of adoptions of innovations. These, too, are behind the conversion of invention and innovation to enhanced output and higher per capita income. An emerging line of analysis in development economics and economic history views the *rates* of invention and innovation as related to population size and to population density.

The rate of invention, according to Kuznets (1960), increases with the number of inventors, which is in turn a fixed proportion of the population. An increase in the absolute number of inventors is likely to yield higher inventiveness per inventor. This is because new knowledge and its dissemination produces increasing returns per capita. Furthermore, the "density of the intellectual atmosphere" allows for more division of labor, as well as interrelatedness of knowledge and relatively low costs of communication. Indeed, studies by Higgs (1971a) and Kelley (1972) have shown both that the rate of invention is related to population size and the urban proportion in the population, and that invention tends to be highly concentrated in urban centers.

Aside from the rate at which inventions are produced, the rate at which they are adopted is also related to population size, to the size of firms, and to the size of their markets. Large firms apply new techniques more rapidly than do small firms, and the amount of sales per unit in research and development is greater for large firms than for small. The large firm, then, can spread the risk of adopting new inventions and processes; it can also spread the cost of developing or trying new processes.

Population Pressure and Productivity

The dominant theme in economic thought concerning the influence of population on productivity has been that of *diminishing returns to additional labor*: that each new pair of hands will not produce as much on the average as the hands already in existence because the amount of land is limited. But in fact, the history of Europe and the West from 1650 onwards show population growth occurring together with rising productivity. One type of explanation for this contradiction has been the view that population growth, whether at the level of the family unit or the community or the entire society, has been a challenge which has evoked the response of increased effort by individuals and societies (Simon, 1977, chap. 3).

This occurs in line with what Simon calls the "population-push" hypothesis:

> at a given point in time an agricultural people knows methods of obtaining higher yields from their lands than given by the methods they use. But the higher-yield methods demand more work. An increase of population then pushes people to adopt the new methods *despite* that they require more work. (Simon, 1977, chap. 6)

Simon contrasts the population-push hypothesis with the "invention-pull" hypothesis which is the Malthusian explanation of population growth:

> The argument begins with a society that is somewhat above subsistence level. Population expands until it reaches the subsistence limits of the technology in use. Then sometime thereafter population size becomes stationary, by mortality . . . or by mortality and/or birth control. . . . Someone then makes a discovery which permits more food to be produced on the same land area, and a shift to the new technology takes place. Population expands again until it reaches the subsistence limit of the newer technology, and so on. (Simon, 1977, chap. 6)

Simon does not find the two analyses mutually exclusive: rather, they complement one another. Nevertheless, he himself dwells at length on exposition of the former explanation. Increasing numbers of families and increasing size of families, both activated by population growth, are population-push mechanisms which bring about shifts in cultivation technologies as land becomes in short supply.

Probably the most important attempt to show this systematically is the one made by E. Boserup (1965), who characterizes agricultural technologies in terms of intensity of land use, as follows:

1. *Forest-fallow cultivation:* plots of land cleared in the forest are sown and planted for a year or two, after which they are to lie fallow for some number of years sufficient for the forest to regain them (about 20 to 25 years). Once regained by the forest, they are cleared and planted anew, the whole cycle beginning again.
2. *Bush-fallow cultivation:* the same procedure as above, but with a period of between six and ten years. After this time, the land is covered with bush or small trees.[3]
3. *Short-fallow cultivation:* same as above, but with a fallow period of only one or two years.
4. *Annual cropping:* although this is not usually considered a fallow-system, it may be classified as such since the land is left uncultivated for the months between the harvest of one crop and the planting of the next.
5. *Multicropping:* the most intensive system of land use, since the same plot bears two or more successive crops every year.

Analyzing patterns of agricultural development in Europe and elsewhere, Boserup concludes (a) that the typical sequence of development has been one of a gradual change from extensive to intensive types of land use, the change being more rapid in some regions than in others; and (b) that

[3] Forest-fallow and bush-fallow cultivation are often not distinguished but denoted together as "long-fallow" or "shifting" cultivation.

these shifts from extensive to intensive cultivation have occurred in the presence of increasing population size (Boserup 1965, pp. 16–18).

To show that changing agricultural methods are a consequence of population growth rather than the reverse (the latter being the Malthusian analysis), Boserup shows that virtually all cases of more intensive cultivation entail, at least initially, a greater input of labor per unit of output. Thus, more intensive cultivation is typically not adopted except under the pressure of a rising population (Boserup, chap. 5).

In addition to causing the introduction or adoption of innovations in cultivation, the pressures of rural population growth have also been responsible for the introduction, or expansion and development, of rural industry in otherwise preindustrial societies. Both full-time and seasonal agricultural unemployment due to population growth or labor-saving innovations may create permanent or temporary surplus labor, and under conditions of fixed land area, population pressure, and the resulting need to import food, such surplus labor can be mobilized into a rural industrial sector.

The short-term successes of such rural industrial sectors (due, for example, to improved terms of trade) have led to food surpluses for the rural population, and these, in turn, have encouraged earlier marriage and further population growth. Thus, population growth indeed results from improvements in the industrial sector, as Malthusian theory would have it, but it is the pressure of population growth itself that originally sets that very sector into operation. Such a process has been described and measured for preindustrial Flanders by F. F. Mendels:

> The Flemish population was thus embarked in an irreversible process of industrialization. Population pressure necessitated entrance into the nexus of foreign trade and the money economy; this caused an irreversible growth of population through a Malthusian process of myopic relaxation of restraints on marriage whenever a small surplus was left. (Mendels, 1969)

Population growth need not, of course, entail more intensive cultivation or industrialization if there are opportunities for expanding the area of production by extensive cultivation. Thus, Clark and Haswell point out that in Africa south of the Sahara, the amount of land cultivated in any one year is probably about one-thirtieth of the potential cultivable land. Africans cultivate very intensively indeed when they are hemmed in by topographical conditions, or by enemies, or when they are otherwise compelled to subsist on much smaller areas than they would like. But they prefer the system of shifting cultivation to that of more intensive cultivation. So long as abundant land is available, as it is in most of Africa, shifting cultivation yields better returns than settled agriculture in grain per unit of labor (Clark and Haswell, 1967, pp. 50–51).

A similar but more elaborate analysis is offered by Carneiro. He suggests several conditions under which population pressure does or does not engender political and social-structural differentiation and development (1961, Supplement 2; 1968, vol. 2). Carneiro points out that although shifting, "slash-and-burn," cultivation [4] is by far the most common system found in tropical rainforest environments, in fact (a) soils developed in tropical rain forests can support systems of cultivation more advanced than slash-and-burn; and (b) these more advanced systems do arise in response to the increasing pressure of human numbers on the land. To illustrate the two propositions, Carneiro refers to the various horticultural systems maintained by Melanesian tribal societies. These systems range from rudimentary slash-and-burn cultivation to an intensive, semipermanent system employing irrigation, terracing, and the use of fertilizers.

According to Carneiro, an intensification of agriculture follows population increase in those regions in which the area of cultivable land is distinctly circumscribed and limited—in "narrow valleys sharply confined and delimited by mountains or deserts. It is in such areas that early advances in agriculture, *and in other aspects of culture,* took place" (Carneiro, 1968, vol. 2, p. 141; italics supplied). In line with this conclusion, we remember that regardless of their fertility, areas with broad expanses of arable land, like the forested plains of northern Europe, the Russian steppes, and the eastern woodlands and prairies of the United States, were *not* the initial areas of agricultural advance. Rather, these regions lagged behind the narrow river valleys and coastal areas in both agricultural and cultural development. This is because extensive and unbroken agricultural land was available, so that population increase resulted in the dispersion of peoples instead of the intensification of agriculture.

In summary, we can see that theoretical considerations and historical developments converge to suggest that population size, growth and characteristics may all be important determinants of productivity levels. Population growth and shifting composition may create conditions favorable for economies of scale and for the introduction of new processes and techniques. An additional hypothesis which has not yet been

[4] Under the slash-and-burn method, a ring is cut through the bark and cambium layer of each tree. This causes the tree to die. Once dead, the trees are either burned down or left standing (the latter being as effective as burning, since the trees, now leafless, cannot shade the ground). At this point the farmers plant around the dead stumps or trunks. Because of the difficult task of weeding, the area of planting is often abandoned after a few years and a new area subjected to the slash-and-burn technique. See Hoebel, 1958, pp. 244–45.

investigated empirically is that population shifts give rise to new forms of industrial or commercial organization which, in turn, affect productivity greatly. For example, Rischin has speculated that the rise of corporate forms and "big business" in the United States, and the recruitment of the business elite, were closely related to patterns of overseas migration and shifting ethnic and nativity composition of the large cities:

> Once it became clear that political control of the big cities would inevitably pass into the hands of the immigrant groups, Big Business came to be regarded as a new preserve of the older Americans, where their status and influence would continue to flourish. (Rischin, 1965, p. 9)

The effect of population composition, and of race, nativity and ethnicity on the organization of entire industries and sectors of both the economy and individual firms (the garment industry, coal mining, cotton cultivation, and others) remains to be studied. Similarly, the effects of internal migration on the organization and productivity of agriculture and food processing industries, the aerospace industry, the colleges and universities, and a wide range of large-scale industrial sectors remain to be investigated. And even in more general terms, more information is needed for us to understand exactly how population shifts influence the organization of both production and distribution of products.

SUMMARY

The massive accumulation of studies, analyses, and literature notwithstanding, the major questions concerning economic responses to population change cannot yet be answered except in tentative and equivocal terms. The question of economic responses to population change has conventionally been cast in terms of its influence on savings and investment, employment, productivity, and income and income distribution.

A basic proposition dating from Malthus and the classical economists is the law of diminishing returns. Population density or the ratio of population density to natural resources leads to diminishing returns in production, assuming that supply of resources is fixed in quantity and quality, and that the possibility of far-reaching division of labor and technological progress is limited. If so, then when a certain level of density or utilization of cultivatible land is achieved, further increases in input yield diminishing returns per unit of input.

But the concept of economies of scale, first formulated by Adam Smith, virtually reverses this relationship. It asserts that a large economy should be more efficient than a small one. Economies of scale may be *internal,* secured within the firm or plant (by virtue of the size of the plant); or they may be *external,* benefiting the firm through the general development of the industry or economy that may reduce costs for all firms irrespective of their individual inputs.

A further hypothesis is advanced by Kuznets: population size exerts increasing returns to scale in the pace of inventive and innovative activity, and this has been a crucial factor in the growth of output per capita. While there is quantitative evidence relating inventiveness to population growth, and the location of inventivensss to population agglomerations, the evidence bearing on scale effects in production and in adoption of innovation is based primarily on case studies.

Our discussion about savings is generally restricted to private or household savings, excluding for the most part corporate or government savings. The major relationship examined has been that between the age distribution and savings. In general, when the age distribution favors high levels of labor force participation (the case where there is a low dependency rate with relatively large proportions aged 15–64 and lower proportions aged 0–14 or over 65), the savings potential is believed to be relatively great. Thus, age distribution affects savings most directly through the relative consumption needs of those not in the labor force. But it also bears indirectly on saving through its influence on household size and composition, on income and on income distribution.

Population growth per se and international and internal migration have also been seen to affect the level of savings, usually through their influence on age distribution, family or household size, or income. But empirical data on these relationships are not conclusive; indeed, they are sometimes contradictory. One argument links economic growth through the structure of investment to the age distribution of the population. It holds that the higher the dependency ratio, the greater the share of "not-directly productive" investments or social investment capital in the total investment, where not-directly productive (or demographic) investments include investments like schools, health facilities, social welfare, and residential housing needed for care and maintenance of the dependent population.

Keynes made an important analysis which today is known as the *stagnation theory*. It holds that declining population growth curtails investment opportunities because in the wealthy countries in which this occurs (a) a smaller proportion of the higher total income is consumed, leaving a larger proportion available for investment; and (b) the larger existing capital stock in a country with high income and low population growth means that good investment opportunities are hard to find. Declining population growth, and accompanying aging of the population, alter the relationship of consumption and savings to investment, and depress investment.

A second facet of the stagnation theory holds that employment responds negatively to declining rates of population growth. Widespread unemployment, the argument goes, can arise as a consequence of insufficient effective demand for goods and services in a stationary or declining population. In less developed countries, however, employment is said to respond negatively to higher rates of population and labor force growth, for the rapidly growing labor force causes a further deterioration in the already critical imbalance between the supply of labor and supplies of the other factors of production. Thus, economic growth theory treats MDCs and LDCs separately. In the LDCs, unemployment will be the response to population growth under a shortage of capacity; while in the MDCs there may be unemployment in response to population stagnation because demands are insufficiently high to utilize the production potential.

Overpopulation, under conditions of scarcity of land, generates unemployment or chronic underemployment. Deterioration of agricultural employment conditions is an important "push" factor in rural-urban migration; but in the absence of urban "pull" factors this may be simply a transfer of unemployment or underemployment to cities.

The United Nations presents a thorough examination of the economic effects of population changes in its *Determinants and Consequences of Population Growth.* Its general conclusion is that there are indeed significant population effects upon savings, investment, employment, and productivity; but these effects are very difficult to measure and even more difficult to assess in comparison with effects of nondemographic factors. The U.S. Commission on Population and the American Future concluded that a slowing of population growth will significantly raise per capita income by the year 2000 because of the shifting age composition and a rising percentage of women in the labor force, and that there is no convincing argument in favor of continued national population growth. The economists who prepared detailed papers for the commission acknowledged past positive effects of population growth on the output and per capita income—mainly through economies of scale in production, distribution, and adoption of innovations. But they doubt that any further economies of scale are possible in the future.

No conclusions have yet been drawn about fundamental relationships like the amount of work which is done as population conditions change. How much of what products are produced? How does the distribution of products respond to population change? Few conclusions have been drawn about the way savings and investment, employment, and products or productivity respond to population change either.

One important reason for this failure is that the economists frequently ignore the fact that economic responses to population changes always take place in some sociopolitical context, and the response is likely to vary in the different sociopolitical conditions. The ways in which individuals, groups, and economies respond to population change depends on at least three questions. First, who is organizing, mobilizing, or controlling the economy and making some key decisions? Second, how much constraint, or revision, can be exercised on each actor or economic unit? And third, how are payoffs, rewards, and sanctions structured? We turn to consideration of some of these issues in the concluding chapters. Because of the nature of the data available, much of our discussion will be a tentative formulation rather than definitive summary or analysis.

15

Social Responses to Population Changes

In this chapter we will look more closely at the various types of social-organizational responses to population growth, structural change, and population turnover. We noted earlier that population change exerts pressure on ongoing social systems and arrangements. In the present chapter, we will look at the specific ways this may take place: through the formation of large, dense settlements and agglomerations; through processes of migration and the turnover of social position and role incumbents; and through the creation of scarcities and surpluses of commodities, skills, and persons.

POPULATION GROWTH, SOCIAL ROLES, AND INSTITUTIONS

Population changes may often result in a restructuring of institutionalized relations between groups, social systems, and subsystems. Such shifts may or may not be accompanied by conflict. This is because changes in the numerical relationships between aggregates of role incumbents (which occur as byproducts of population processes) also operate to change the nature and content of the relationships between roles and between systems of roles. This occurs quite apart from the presence or absence of institutional or systematic disorganization.

Urban and Rural Residence

We may see this by considering the relationships between rural and urban populations as they have changed over time. Early in this century, the United States was predominantly rural. Urban places at that time, and the urban minority of the population, were organized basically to service the rural majority of the population—to provide commercial services and fabricated products and to coordinate networks of communication in a vast agricultural society.

In 1900, there were about two urban dwellers for every three rural dwellers in the United States. By 1960, however, there were about seven urban dwellers for every three rural inhabitants: the country had become largely an urban nation, serviced by a gradually shrinking rural population. What kind of effect has this shift had on our social roles and institutional relations? The change in numbers alone has occasioned a restructuring of the relationship between urban and rural dwellers. Today, the rural population is organized basically to service the urban majority population: it provides agricultural and other primary products; it also often provides food-processing services for the pervasive network of urban communities. Increasingly, however, the rural population also provides certain communications (road construction and maintenance, for example) and recreational services for the urban population as well. Both urban and rural economies and occupational structures, and the relationships between them, have been transformed in the wake of the numerical population transformation and redistribution.

Occupational Roles

Numerical changes in roles or occupations may also reflect (and have an influence on) shifts in social structure or social needs. In 1900, a total of 7,000 persons out of some 29 million in the working force reported their occupation as college teaching. The college professor at that time was a rarity. By 1950, however, there were 127,000 college teachers and professors, while the total working force had only doubled in size (to some 59 million). And by 1960 there were 177,000 college professors and teachers in working force of some 68 million. Other occupations shifted in numerical importance in our society. The number of gasoline station proprietors and managers, for instance, increased from 2,000 in 1900 to 190,000 in 1960. Other roles became less important: the number of blacksmiths, forgemen, and hammermen declined from 220,000 in 1900 to 33,000 in 1960 (U.S. Bureau of the Census, "Historical Statistics" 1960, and "Population Census" PC (2)-7A).

Between 1900 and 1960 the role of the college professor changed, and so did its relationship to the social structure. This was *in part* a result of the large increase in the number of college teachers employed. Similarly, the social role of a gasoline station operator or a blacksmith in the 1960s is different from what it was in 1900, in part because of the changing numbers in these occupations. All occupations or roles have not undergone such changes. Although the total number of physicians in the United States has increased in this century along with the rest of the population, the ratio of physicians to the rest of the population has changed but little. The nature of the physician's role, his status, and his relationship to the rest of the social structure varies in the different settings of the country, partly in accordance with the numerical physician-to-population ratio. This is an observation which clearly has not escaped the attention of those organized medical practitioners who oppose the expansion of medical education and an increase in the number of their colleagues.

Consider, finally, an urban community with a given occupational and place-of-origin distribution and a given racial composition. As population processes bring into this community a large number of rural migrants of different occupational skills and racial or ethnic backgrounds, the community will undergo changes both in general composition and in the relationships between its different occupational, ethnic, racial, duration-of-residence, and neighborhood groups. Regardless of whether community or institution disorganization occurs, the balance and institutionalized relationships between its subsystems will change. To the extent that one or more groups are dissatisfied with the changing relationships, social conflict may result.

Some social scientists have held that conflict always results in such a shifting of relationships between population groups and subsystems.[1] Whether or not this is true, it is important here to see that changes in the numerical relationships between population elements which occupy different social roles and subsystems may bring about changes in the nature and content of relationships between roles and between subsystems.

[1] The classic treatment of this problem is contained in the discussions of competition, conflict, accommodation, and assimilation in Park and Burgess, 1921.

Responses to Population Size

The sheer number of persons belonging to a society represents the totality of the society's human resources. It also represents the possibility, in quantitative terms, of its social role differentiation, division of labor, variety and complexity of social relationships, tolerance for deviations, and multiplicity of values and interests. The number of persons belonging to a society is also important in another way, for it is basic to the requirements of communication, the chain of power and authority, and the volume, range, and varieties of exchange.

Large population size renders individual eccentricities, idiosyncrasies, needs, and pursuits largely irrelevant to the survival, adaptation, and pursuit of the collective good which is the main business of any community as a community. If a total population represents a society's totality of human resources, then it follows that the larger the population, the greater are both the totality of human resources and the variety of human resources, abilities, needs, and wishes. Larger population size permits a heterogeneity and differentiation of skills and needs; it also may allow the deviant and nonconventional to coexist with the conventional.[2]

In large populations, mechanisms evolve to mobilize, organize, and exploit individual differences in taste, abilities, and activities. These help to enhance a community's potential for production, consumption, and survival and adaptation. Such mechanisms also help to catalyze and institutionalize the principle of division of labor. Relationships among individuals and among social units (including communities, cities, regions, and nations) become symbiotic or "exchange" relationships ("organic" rather than "mechanical," in Durkheim's terminology). Social institutions (which include everything from motherhood, to the factory, to the political organization, to the international oil development interests), which are as purposive as societies themselves, become more complex in larger populations. They can be analytically distinguished according to whether they are devoted to sustenance-producing activities (however elaborate the "sustenance" may turn out to be), or to the mediation of relationships among individuals and among specialized units or subsystems.

The multiplicity and mediational quality of institutions in large population groups reflects the division of labor. An immediate consequence of population size is the absolute number of individual role and

[2] Ogburn and Duncan, 1964, cite data in support of the idea that city size is directly related to tolerance of eccentricity, receptiveness to innovation, and overall inventiveness. See also the classic statement in Wirth, 1938.

The Chinese refugees in Hong Kong compete with other residents for the already limited space. *(United Nations)*

subsystem relationships which must be patterned and organized in some stable way so as to allow the uninterrupted conduct of social relationships and the society's affairs.

Social institutions are themselves confronted with conflicting exigencies as their population settings become larger and more differentiated. In a population which is small in size or in number of roles or role incumbents, individual eccentricities and differences in need, purpose, and behavior cannot be a matter of indifference. The reason for this is that individual institutions cannot sustain the scale of deviance that an entire society or community can tolerate: this is the case irrespective of the size of the population. If a child with unusual intelligence, abilities, and interests is bored in his classroom, he may disrupt it severely. Extramarital sex may be institutionalized in the society, but it disrupts smaller-scale family life. Different kinds of stresses also exist on a larger scale. A large absolute number of mediating institutions exist in societies with large populations. It is clear that any social institution in a highly differentiated, multi-institutional community is inevitably *in competition with* other, more or less similar, social institutions in the same community to the extent that participation is voluntary. Institutions which don't compete risk extinction.

This "market" of institutionalized subsystems competing with one another constitutes the setting for the interpersonal tensions and pressures on which Georg Simmel focused (Simmel, 1950, especially his famous "Metropolis and Mental Life"). According to Simmel, this competition (and the accompanying pressures) can be viewed as a direct output of population size and the institutionalization of differentiation or division of labor. We shall return to this topic briefly in our discussion of population density.

The point to be made here is that social institutions must respond and change if they are to survive under conditions of large, highly differentiated, populations and high institutional competition. More than this, they must build into themselves, or institutionalize, an ongoing awareness and evaluation of existing competition. Many institutions have not done this as society has changed. For example, a large variety of home institutions—including sewing and canning, Bible instruction for children, and musical recitals and songfests—have largely disappeared or have been transferred to other institutions. Other institutions, like sex and childbearing and the nurture of young children, remain in the family.

Responses to Population Density

If increasing population size creates the *possibility* of social differentiation, division of labor, and institutional variety and complexity, then clearly it is increasing population density which creates the *necessity* for differentiation and complexity. This is because high population density creates many social exigencies which do not necessarily attend large population size alone. These include (a) a high frequency of human contact which results simply from propinquity; (b) a competition for priority of attention and participation; (c) a competition for space and (d) a competition for access to places, activities, and institutions. High population density also operates to reduce costs and to simplify exchange, two factors which together directly promote specialization, production for markets, and market relationships and institutions.

Sorting contacts. The volume of possible daily contacts rises with increased population density.[3] This means that increasing population

[3] For more elaborate presentations, see Simmel, 1950, chap. 3; also Hauser, 1958.

In high-density communities, every available space is used, housing all social and economic groups. *(United Nations)*

density brings a greater need for institutionalized arrangements and relationships to mediate and regulate contacts and to assign priorities. Moreover, increases in volume and frequency of social contact work to enhance the specificity, shorten the duration, and diminish the information exchanged in each contact.

In low-density communities, the number of potential contacts is small. An individual may maintain contact with everyone "in contact range"—that is, with everyone in the community. Moreover, his contacts with another person may be long-lived over time and they may embrace different kinds of relationships. Thus, persons may be more or less well-organized over the years in their business, friendship, political, and neighborly contacts. But often contacts will cover several of these areas at the same time. Quite the reverse may be the case in high density communities. There the great majority of human contacts are specific in nature and purpose and very short-lived in time. Of course, some social relationships are more diffuse or more long-lived, even in high-density communities. But it is just such a process of sorting and assigning priorities to social relationships which, we said earlier, was an imperative of the high-density population.

For ten cents the New York City resident can pick up a telephone, dial a number, and say, "Good morning" or, "How are you?" to any of several million other New Yorkers. He can buy or sell stocks through any of the scores of stockbrokers or representatives. For the same price of a telephone call, he can order a sandwich, or reserve a dinner table, or have a new television set sent over, or arrange to try out the latest car model from Detroit—in each case through any of the several hundred establishments which exist for that specific purpose. He can invite any one of many of the other several millions who live in his community to attend his daughter's wedding or his son's bar mitzvah.

The system of institutions which exists to sort our social relationships and assign priorities to them is especially characteristic of high density communities. In big city neighborhoods, there are still family groups, schools, and jobs within which long-term, recurring, and diffuse relationships take place. But there are hundreds of other simple everyday transactions, like riding the subway or bus, buying the morning newspaper, and getting information on the telephone which all comprise patterned social relationships which typically are of short duration and have only small probability of recurring between the same role incumbents. These relationships produce the anonymity, isolation, and atomization which characterizes life in dense communities. There is, as Keyfitz has observed, a reciprocal assumption—rather than any actual knowledge—of the mutual competence of role incumbents engaged in social relationships and transactions with each other, but this remains unknown to each role player beyond the confines of the specific instance at hand (Keyfitz, 1965).

Space. Space becomes a scarce commodity in direct proportion to the degree of population density. Aside from the sheer amount of space which may be available to each person, group, or activity, it is usually the case that locations are differentially desirable to the different persons and groups and for different reasons. Thus, the allocation of space in a community is necessarily more rigorously regulated in high density populations. This allocation may be carried out through a number of institutionalized arrangements. A government may simply parcel out space on the basis of some specific criteria, or with no basis other than momentary fancy. Or, if private property is institutionalized in the society, there is likely to be a market and price mechanism which strongly influences the allocation of space.

In many communities there are customs, traditions, or zoning laws to regulate the use of space, regardless of whether or not there is a real property market. Thus, especially in high density communities, there tends to be a concentration and segregation of specific population types and of specific social and economic institutions and activities. There may be racial or ethnic segregation. And there may be residential areas, business or industrial areas, hotel and transient areas, areas of growing families, areas with high concentrations of educational institutions, and areas devoted largely to entertainment establishments.

Competition for space is reflected not only in the highest density communities but also in smaller urban and rural communities. However, in lower density communities the competition for space takes a distinctly different form. Here it is reflected primarily in different patterns of price, land use, and in rural communities, in the different crops grown and density of cultivation rather than in different occupancy patterns.

In the lowest density communities, nearly everyone can live in relatively uncongested surroundings. Regardless of the size or quality of the dwelling unit, it is likely to have windows and light on all sides and to be surrounded by at least some land unoccupied by other structures. Individual residential lots may vary in size, and dwellings may vary in size and facilities, but residential areas are not usually highly differentiated with respect to population or occupancy types. Similarly, business and industrial properties may vary in size and facilities. But beyond the general distinction between business center and industrial area, there are few further differentiations.

The highest density communities offer a sharp contrast. Here even persons or families who are quite well-off may not be able to afford the luxury of a "detached" dwelling unit, that is, of a unit surrounded by at least some unoccupied land area. Moreover, there tend to arise blocks of homogeneous dwelling unit types which attract concentrations of occupant types: young married couples, unattached persons, retired persons, the rich, the newly married, and so on. There also tend to be enclaves of homogeneous industrial or business properties—wholesalers, fish markets, garment industries, jewelers, importers, clothing retailers, book publishers—which tend to be located in distinctive areas. And among these dwelling units and commercial concentrations there are usually corresponding enclaves of institutions which serve (or are composed of) the type of people living or working there. Residential sections attract home-maintenance business, do-it-yourself stores, neighborhood improvement organizations, and "welcome wagon" clubs; schools may attract candy and ice cream shops, boys' clubs, and teen centers. The elderly may have golden age clubs and churches and health food stores and doctors' offices and group-practice clinics. And the young adults have eating places and clubs for nourishment, amusement, and conversation. And all of these businesses-of-a-kind have nearby purveyors and suppliers for their specialized services.

Access. Aside from the scarcity of space itself and the competition for occupancy of space in very high density communities, there is the further problem of access to key areas, institutions, or activities. The network of transportation and communication in any society typically renders some locations more accessible than others. As an institutionalized means of coping with problems of mutual accessibility, highways, public transportation, and communications media are more elaborate in denser population areas. Thus, high density communities may have a multiplicity of newspapers and magazines, each of which serves a particular neighborhood, or foreign-language group, or specialized industrial sector. There also exist specialized fleets of messengers and vehicles, specialized telephone and teletype networks, and an increasing body of private-frequency radio communications, all with large numbers of people engaged in their development and maintenance.

The institutions for mitigating differences and competition notwithstanding, there remains in high density communities considerable variation in accessibility to persons, institutions, activities, and information. Indeed, this variation constitutes an important axis of social differentiation in high density communities, and it is related to other dimensions of social differentiation. For example, in high density communities the lowest educational, income, or status groups may have little if any direct access to the polity, that is, to the decision-making, resource-controlling, or value-formulating subsystems and roles in the society. But other institutions, like the political "machine," settlement houses, labor unions, churches, or voluntary organizations, sometimes do afford access to the polity. In this way they may compensate in part for these groups' disadvantage in the competition for access to power. Analogous situations obtain with respect to access to jobs, education, medical services, shopping, recreation, and relatively unpolluted air, and we will return to these considerations in the next chapter.

Finally, we may note that while high population density entails a high frequency and great variety of social interactions and relationships, it also operates to reduce the costs of exchange. It operates more generally, too, to simplify social and economic transactions, the division of labor, and coordination and corporate ventures of every sort. Not only does high population density reduce the average costs of transferring commodities—but perhaps more important, it also reduces costs and delays in transferring information.

The low density community may have its builder or building contractor. But in communities of the highest density, even small structures are built by an elaborate system of architects, contractors, and subcontractors, each specializing in some particular facet of the operation. This kind of specialization and cooperation is not possible in very rural areas. In fact, it is possible only because the high population density has placed all elements in the transaction close to each other, so reducing the costs of meetings, informational exchange, and overall coordination.

MIGRATION, POPULATION TURNOVER, AND "TIME IN THE SYSTEM"

The concepts of familiarity and strangeness, of "old-timers" and "newcomers," of "insiders" and "outsiders" have come in and out of fashion in social and historical analysis. In the aftermath of the great waves of European immigration, these concepts were familiar in the analysis of community, employment, education, welfare, and politics. But with the growing passion for precise definition and measurement, some of these concepts lost some favor, at least among some social scientists. It is difficult to define and measure "familiarity" and "strangeness" as precisely as we might wish.

In spite of their difficulties, though, these concepts are still clearly pertinent to societies affected by large-scale migration and to communities experiencing extensive population turnover. The basic theme of familiarity vs. strangeness has been retained in the social scientific literature; indeed, it has achieved a certain popularity. In a widely read book, *A Nation of Strangers* (1972), Packard imputes to the frequency of migratory moves in the United States the upheaval of communities, the anonymity of neighborhood and apartment living, the fragmentation of family, and the uprooting of male-female relationships, religious beliefs, and vocational stability. One result of the modern "strangeness of neighbors" is a declining concern for the social consequences of behavior—which results, in turn, in high rates of divorce and malpractice, in indifference to local happenings, in "nomadic values," in personal isolation and helplessness, and in alienation of industrial workers and of students.

Though Packard has been taken to task both on technical grounds concerning his estimates of the frequency of migration and for overstating the consequences of migration (his professional colleagues may be even more annoyed at the popularity of the book), in fact he has reopened an issue which actually represents an intersection of important social and demographic problems. It is certainly true that today's intensive and sometimes frequently repeated migration has generated a large population which is rootless at least in the sense that individuals live in places different from those where they spent their childhood; and that often these individuals are unable to invoke neighborhood, kinship, or other ascribed loyalties or axes of solidarity.

Sometimes-Migrants and Never-Migrants

This sometimes-migrant group, of course, is not completely out in the cold. It is often the case that other values, interests, ideas, concerns, and commitments—which may derive from occupational activity, from educational background, or from cultural and media sources—provide long-term axes of social organization and solidarity. For many of the sometimes-migrant group of workers, executives, students, or professionals, and their families, these commitments have replaced racial, religious, ethnic, neighborhood, or kinship and crony-based solidarities. Also, sometimes-migrants are able to form new primary group relationships (often with other newcomers) and enter new organizational groups whether they move to New York, Houston, Los Angeles, Birmingham, Springfield, or Centerville.

The "well-rooted" group of never-migrants provides quite a contrast. And although it may be well-integrated, with closely overlapping kinship, religious, ethnic, occupational, and neighborhood ties, it also has its less favorable side. Communities in this group are bound by family and neighborhood-based values, concerns, and commitments and by narrow, ascriptively based solidarity. Never-migrants are typically strangers and estranged outside their own communities; and suspicious of outsiders generally. They may be reluctant to admit outsiders to claims on *their* job opportunities, on *their* housing opportunities, to participation in *their* neighborhoods, churches, and associations, and perhaps above all, to the attentions of *their* daughter, sister, or girl-next-door.

In all events, in all but the smallest communities, most social systems (and large industrial organizations and large universities, too) comprise a mix of both sometimes-migrant and never-migrant population elements. Each of these in turn is distributed over the various social strata or class groupings, and each is characterized by its own type of values, commitments, and axes of social differentiation and solidarity. Innumerable examples come to mind which suggest that the nature of this mix of sometimes-migrant and never-migrant elements bears heavily on the social, economic, and political relationships and activities in the respective communities, organizations, and social systems. But there is still a good deal of room for the systematic investigation of these effects at all levels of organization, from family and neighborhood to community and society.

Individual and Organizational Resocialization

The same theme applies to the more general turnover of incumbents in all types of social roles and positions, whether the turnover is occasioned by in- or out-migration or by life-cycle processes such as coming of age, marriage, or retirement. The new incumbent in a social position is inevitably different from the old incumbent in some sense. Inevitably, he is an "outsider" vis-à-vis old-timer incumbents of related social positions, and as such he must undergo some process of initiation, socialization, or absorption in the new role and in the new social system. There has been considerable social scientific attention to the processes of socialization, resocialization, absorption, and assimiliation of individuals and newcomers, though this has not frequently focused on the population processes that may give rise to them.

One topic which has not received much attention is the "resocialization" of organizations, institutions, and communities as they respond to population turnover. The bridge club, the school, the factory, and the university each has its crop of newcomers, and each undergoes resulting shifts in organization of tasks, in role relationships, in patterns of authority and allocation of rewards and gratifications. New elites arise and new rules are adopted in the wake of changing community composition and entrance of newcomers into community roles. New cliques and new criteria for popularity evolve in the high school or college as freshmen become sophomores, then juniors, and then seniors.

Thus, social organizations and social systems themselves change: they are themselves resocialized in the course of absorbing newcomers. This kind of shift is an important kind of social response to population growth and turnover. Persons with differing amounts of seniority may act according to their "time in the system": they frequently have different status, or they organize their activities and relationships differently, or they may receive different levels of rewards in group interactions. Organizations and social systems have built-in mechanisms which allow for differentiation according to "time in the system"; but it is important to remember that these mechanisms themselves undergo change under the pressure of population shifts.

POPULATION, SOCIAL INEQUALITY, AND SOCIAL STRATIFICATION

Population, Social Structure, and Social Rewards

The concept of *social inequality* describes the differential receipt of (and institutionalized claims on) income and wealth, influence and power, deference and prestige, and other social rewards. These are all commonly associated with either incumbency in the various social positions or with membership in the various social groups, strata, classes, or categories, or both. Males and females, bankers and miners, adults and adolescents, whites and blacks, leaders and followers, white-collar and blue-collar employees, farmers and urbanites, the educated and the illiterate, and high status groups or low status groups, all receive differing amounts of material and social rewards. We understand by *social rewards* any valued outcome of social interaction. These may include both material things (the outcomes of production processes) or nonmaterial satisfactions such as obedience, honor, influence and power, participation in valued associations, health, security, or simply a sense of social order. Some social rewards may only be consumed, either concretely or symbolically, but some can be exchanged for others. We may sometimes exchange money for power, love for influence, or obedience for security. We call social rewards which may be exchanged for others *social resources.* In general, there is a social structure of production of social rewards which organizes the participation of individuals and population groups in those interaction processes that yield social rewards and resources. There is also a social structure of distribution of social rewards which organizes the claims of individuals and groups on the available rewards and resources and the rules for their exchange (see Figure 15.1).

The top half of Figure 15.1 represents the distribution of social rewards to the population. The differential claims to rewards associated with social position and membership in groups or strata are what we call *social inequality,* while the process of attaining the various ranked positions, membership in the social strata, or the actual formation and ranking of positions and strata is called *social stratification.* The bottom half of the figure represents the production of social rewards, with differential contributions associated with the different social positions, memberships, and so forth. An important area of social research today is the measurement of different types of social rewards (our box B in the figure), the specifications of various types of social positions, strata, and

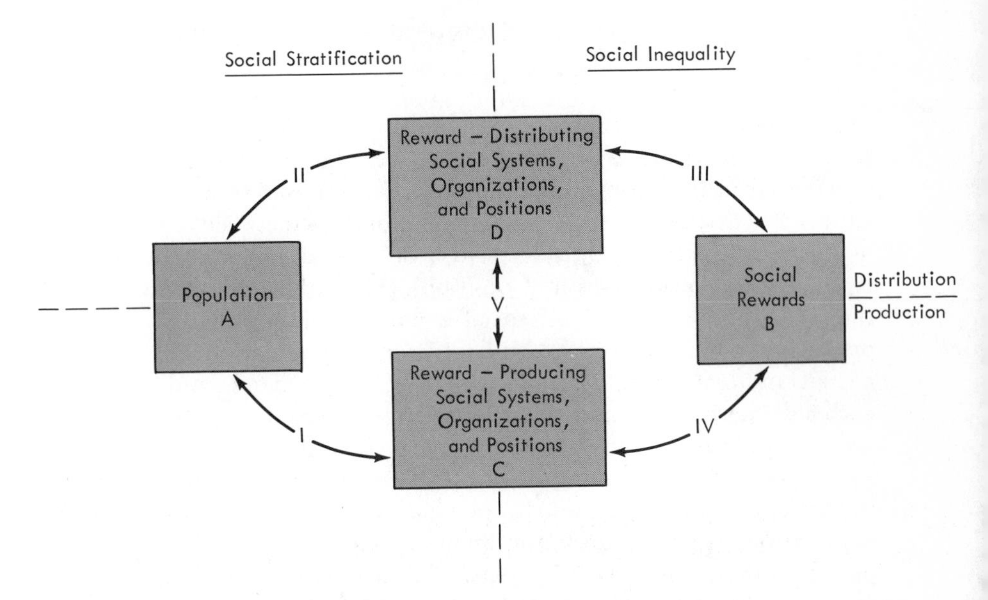

Figure 15.1 Population, Social Structure, and Social Rewards

subsystems which bear respectively on the production (box *C* and process *IV*) and on the distribution (*D* and *III*) of social rewards; the study of their overlapping and interrelationships (*V*), and of the rules and processes of access to and attainment of the various social positions (*I* and *II*) —in other words, the study of the mechanisms and operation of the system as of any moment in time. The study of occupations, income, and educational attainment, prestige and power, elites, social strata, and social classes all have important bearing on this investigation.

Effects of Population Change

It is clear, however, that the system itself undergoes changes over time. Comparisons of income distributions, the study of the rise and fall of social classes, and the analysis of technological change and changing industrial organization all provide insights into aspects and mechanisms of change; and changes in any one of these subsystems may catalyze shifts in the entire system. But the most obvious source of change in the system is clearly the change in size, composition, and characteristics of population. Such changes not only generate changing amounts and composition of social rewards produced, and changing demands on the distribution of rewards: they also cause strains and ultimately changes in the social organization of production and distribution and in patterns of social stratification.

Population growth per se puts strains on the structure of distribution of rewards. But population typically does not grow at an even pace throughout all its sectors. Instead, population growth tends to be differential in the various subgroups and categories. And it is this differential growth that causes changing relationships between the numbers of different types of people who are available as potential incumbents of the various social roles and positions. Thus, the relative numbers of the young and old, of higher social strata and lower social strata, or of urban and rural will change with differential population growth. This change in turn upsets systems of supply and demand, and associated exchange mechanisms and reward claims. And this forces shifts both in access to the various social positions and in reward claims and exchanges.

A basic understanding of the relationship between social differentiation and population growth opens a number of areas of inquiry to exploration. How has declining fertility influenced social mobility and opportunities for occupational status? We may also ask how the political and economic elites of newly independent LDCs have managed to retain power and status under the rapid growth and urbanization of their populations as claims on available rewards have shifted. If these elites have not been able to retain power, what role have population shifts played in their demise? Again, were there corresponding processes in the European population explosion?

This important area of inquiry is still in its infancy. Much more research on the relationship between population changes and social inequality and stratification is needed before we can even tentatively answer these questions with specific hypotheses and propositions.

SUMMARY

In this chapter we have reviewed some of the major types of social responses to population growth and change. We had earlier listed migration and urbanization as demographic responses to population change, and many of the social responses to population shifts do in fact concern migration and migrants and cities and urban agglomerations. In addition, however, we have seen that shifts in social exchange mechanisms and rules are also characteristic social responses to population growth and change, independent of the migration and urbanization factors. Population growth may render some commodities, values, or relationships in short supply either permanently or temporarily; it may also create surpluses of other items. Thus fixed-supply items like housing, space, privacy, and services such as medical care and government services may be made scarce under conditions of population growth. Spouses, bridge partners, school teachers, soldiers, and building contractors may be in short supply temporarily while population is undergoing a very rapid increase. Under the same conditions there may be surpluses (in number or proportion) of children, aged people, students, college graduates, widows, untrained labor, migrants, or sex-soldiers. The social responses to these population shifts are social innovations, and they typically involve changing values, rules of exchange, price mechanisms, and general shifts in conversion of social rewards and resources.

Finally, we have seen that population turnover may disorganize social systems even in the absence of growth or structural change. The incoming freshmen do not exactly replace the graduating seniors; the new army recruits have attributes different from those recently discharged; the new neighbors, employees, legislators, judges bring not only new faces but also new personal and social resources to the social systems into which they have been recruited. Conventional wisdom has the newcomers undergoing socialization processes, and this is indeed a central response to population turnover. But in addition, the social systems themselves undergo resocialization and change in the course of absorbing newcomers. And those organizations, social systems and institutional settings that continually or recurrently absorb newcomers must have built-in mechanisms to allow them to adjust and resocialize themselves as well as the newcomers. Mobility and promotion systems are the most widely recognized examples of such mechanisms.

In the next chapter we will look at political responses to population growth and change. We shall see that, as in the case of social responses in general, the study of political responses to population change is still in its infancy.

16

Political Responses: Participation, Influence, and Power

In this chapter, we will look at the kinds of political responses that may result from population change. This topic is still relatively unexplored, but it has recently received an important boost in the work of the United States Commission on Population Growth and the American Future. We shall review some questions about the political and administrative strains which population changes may produce. And we return to a subject we touched on before—that of the shifting political balance between heterogeneous population groups which accompanies changes in population size and structure. Finally, we shall raise some new questions about the implications of population change for recruitment to, and participation and mobility in, power groups like parties, organizations, cliques, and elites.

POPULATION GROWTH AND GOVERNANCE

The issue that is most frequently raised in discussions of political responses to population growth concerns the problems of maintaining effective government, with democratic constraints and imperatives, when population increases in size, density, and heterogeneity within a political unit of fixed territory. This is the central political issue raised in the deliberations and reports to the Commission on Population Growth and the American Future (Vol. 4, 1972). Typically, population changes will mean that political and administrative units which are organized to serve a population of given size and characteristics will be confronted with new needs for services, regulation, and constituent representation. These kinds of changes, and changing needs, are always taking place. Cities, townships, counties, or states grow in population; receive in-migrants or lose out-migrants; experience changes in age structure, family size, occupational skills, or educational levels; and experience shifts in population distribution. Such changes are usually followed by new demands on government by the citizens, and by new contingencies for government itself.

Provision of Services

The value of independence and self-sufficiency notwithstanding, Americans have always looked to government for at least some basic services. Although many Americans have cherished the right to bear arms (and popular culture often stresses individual self-sufficiency in this respect also), Americans have always looked to government for provision of basic security from outside threats and for the assurance of law and order within the society. Although many can and have made private arrangements for schooling, most Americans have looked to government for the organization and provision of basic education. Indeed, state institutions and local charters charge this service to local governments and make provisions for it. While individuals probably *could* build their own roads and transport networks, the provision of roads has also been expected of the government. In high density areas the government also organizes public water and sanitation systems to replace private wells and septic tanks; it provides public parks and libraries and recreation in addition to (and sometimes instead of) private facilities, and, it increasingly plays a role in the provision of public health, welfare, housing, employment, and transport services. Farm extension services, flood control, in some areas electricity, mental health, birth control, child care, and care of the aged are other kinds of services which are often provided by government. Political and administrative units with small populations can rarely organize, finance, or provide such services except with difficulty. In the past, individuals and families in small units either provided their own facilities and services, or did without. More recently as demands have increased, the smaller county, township, and small municipality governments have sometimes been able to draw on the resources of larger metropolitan, state, or federal governments in order to provide these kinds of services to citizens.

Government responses to the increasing demands and expectations of citizens have taken several forms: (a) the growth of government itself; (b) the increasing professionalization, specialization, and complexity of government; (c) a progressively more specialized, more compartmentalized, and more formalized communication between citizens and government which increasingly takes place through bureaucratic channels; (d) more taxation and more complex public financing; and, in the view of many, (e) decreasing control of elected officials over the specialized government bureaucracies. The number of civilian employees on the Federal Government payroll exceeded three million in 1969 (it has declined somewhat in subsequent years). The number of state and local government employees reached about 10.4 million in 1971 (including 5.5 million in educational services alone, and 5 million in all other employment). About 80 percent of federal employees are white-collar workers. About half of these are postal employees and employees in general administrative, clerical, and office services, but the other half include highly specialized personnel in engineering, medical and health, and business accounting and financial services and in all the scientific disciplines. (Blue-collar federal employees also tend to be highly skilled and specialized, but these are heavily concentrated in the Department of Defense.) Total government tax revenues, which were 67 billion dollars in 1950, reached a staggering 334 billion dollars in 1970, with per capita tax revenues rising from $386 to $1,341 in the same period (see Figure 16.1).

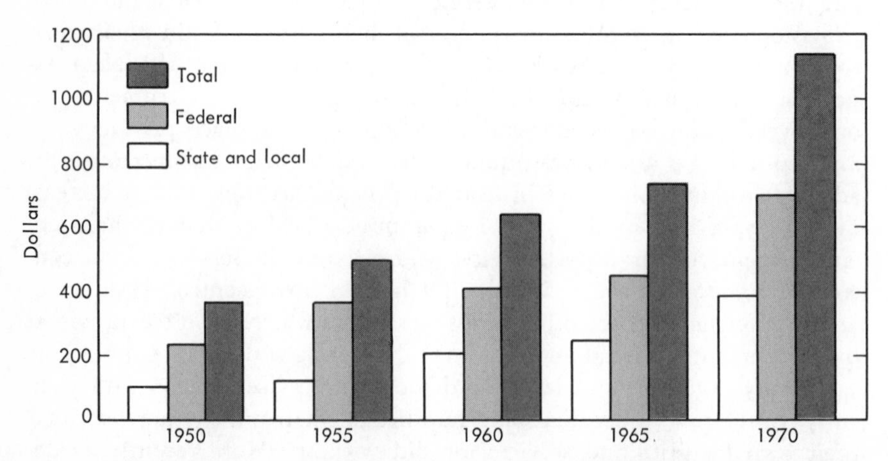

Figure 16.1 Per Capita Tax Revenue by Level of Government, 1950 to 1970. *Source: U.S. Bureau of the Census,* Statistical Abstract of the United States, *1972.*

The point is not so much that "government is big," or that "government is too big," but rather that government organized services become an integral part of society and economy as population grows in size and density. Government comes to involve not only the choice or election of popularly acceptable officials and their service while in office; but it also requires the provision of increasingly extensive, complex, and specialized services. It demands the increasing specialization and permanence of government services and the professionalization of politicians and elected officials as well.

But despite the growth, the increasing professionalization, and the institutionalization of government services and agencies, the growth of population size, density and diversity has also been accompanied by frequent expressions of inadequacy or breakdown in the provision of services. The ineffectiveness of cities and local governments in meeting needs for transport, housing, education, health, and welfare, and the financial and political difficulties these governments have encountered, have been viewed as indicators of the incongruence of political and administrative frameworks to the size, complexity, and diversity of their populations. Thus, in the era of metropolitan and megalopolitan settlement and economic organization, the municipal, township, county, and even state governmental frameworks are frequently seen as outmoded and inadequate for the populations' needs.

Regulation and Control

In small population groups, the activities or behavior of one individual may only infrequently impinge on those of another; and typically social groupings have mechanisms and devices for social control which may range from the entirely informal to those codified in literature, lore, or law. But as populations grow in size and density, less formal mechanisms of social control no longer suffice to protect individuals from the adverse consequences of the behavior, or indeed from the very diversity, of others. The result is that government is called upon to regulate all manner of behavior and activity, and to enforce agreed-upon rules and regulations.

In small, sparsely populated communities, the way individuals build their houses or the way they run their businesses may be a matter of indifference to their neighbors. Similarly, the way they dispose of their garbage or educate their children; their like or dislike for pets; the way they run their private lives; what kinds of plants they grow in their gardens or what kinds of beverages they concoct, may be largely a matter of indifference to others in the small population which has an abundance of space. In matters where neighbors and fellow townsmen *are* concerned, there are all manner of ways of conveying this to those offending the norms of the community or violating the rights, privileges, or freedoms of others, without resort to formal devices or regulating agencies.

But in the large, more densely populated community, the risks of violating the norms of community or the freedoms of others are magnified; and often both the community and the individual who are offended by another's actions may even be unknown to the individual offender (who in turn may not even be aware that his actions are offensive to anyone). Thus the regulation and control of behavior needs formal mechanisms and regulatory agencies as population grows in size, density, and diversity; and it is typically the legislative bodies and government agencies that are called upon to codify acceptable and unacceptable behavior, and to enforce the rules. Thus zoning laws,—along with legislation governing traffic and commerce, hunting and fishing, international currency exchange and gambling, standards of food packaging and cleanliness of restaurants, and licensing of physicians and lawyers and drivers and electricians—all work to regulate and control the behavior and diversity of individuals and to assure the safety, security, and health of others and of society.

Accordingly, the apparatus of modern government includes food inspectors, policemen, truant officers, licensing bureaus, building inspectors, traffic engineers, and game wardens in addition to legislators, judges, social workers, and teachers. These are organized in more or less elaborate agencies and institutions according to their functions and the size, diversity, and density of the populations they serve. But even the immense and complicated body of government employees is frequently asserted to be inadequate to meet the needs of growing and more dense populations. Law enforcement is often inadequate, and standards and licensing are often enforced only partially and sometimes corruptly as the populations outgrow the capacities of the various governmental agencies of regulation and control. The numbers of traffic accidents, unsolved crimes, backlogs of court cases, and the extent of unscrupulous if not downright illegal merchandising and other commercial practices, are all viewed as indicators of the government's inadequacy to meet the growing needs of the population.

POPULATION GROWTH AND POLITICAL REPRESENTATION

Virtually every American eighth-grader or high school student knows that the slogan of "no taxation without representation" was a battle-cry of the American Revolution. It is still an American political truism today that the legitimation of political decision-making activity, and especially demands on citizens—whether through taxation or military service or obedience to authority—rests formally on the representation of citizens and their wishes in legislative bodies and elective offices, and on the rights of citizens to organize to choose and elect candidates to office. But the legitimation of the political status quo is not all that rests on representation. The ability of citizens to communicate with their representatives and elected officials, to make their wishes and opinions known, and to influence the behavior of those in government also rests on the right to vote, to elect candidates or be elected, and to re-elect incumbents or to reject them. But population growth has meant that the size of constituencies—at the national congressional level, obviously, but at state and local levels as well—has increased to the extent of changing, if not destroying entirely, the meaning of "representation."

In 1790, the year of the first census of the United States, there were 106 representatives in Congress. The population totalled 3,929,000, so that average population of a congressional district was about 37,000. The 32 United States Senators at that time represented an average of 123,000 citizens each.

By 1970, the population had reached about 204,844,000, and the total number of representatives was 435 (the same number since 1910). The average congressional district now contained about 471,000 inhabitants. The 100 senators represented an average of 2,048,000 constituents. Obviously, for members of the United States Congress, even the attempt to ascertain the needs and interests of such large and usually diverse numbers of constituents on each issue before Congress is an enormous undertaking requiring large, complex staffs. At the state and local levels, of course, the numbers of constituents per legislator are smaller, but they are still very large.

Traditionally, elected officials and legislators have been the representatives of their constituents not only in their own legislative or administrative domains, but in national, state, or local government respectively as a whole. Thus, the constituent who wants information from, or assistance through, some federal government department has often sought the help of his United States senator or representative. Again the citizen who needs help in matters of state licensing or local building codes might turn to his state assemblyman, local alderman, or municipal council member. The legislator or elected official, in turn, exerts leverage and influence on nonelected government bureaus and employees, or at least he is able to pass information about constituents' needs, opinions, or demands to them.

Clearly the growth of population (especially the tripling of population in the present century while the form and size of most legislative bodies has remained constant), along with the growth of the legislative load itself, has rendered it impossible to sustain the traditional relationships and communication between representative and constituent. This relationship has become increasingly bureaucratized, and so the nature of "representation" is increasingly being confined for the average citizens to the act of voting or withholding votes. (A relatively small minority of citizens have somewhat more access to legislators and officials through membership in organizations and pressure groups.) Thus, the same population processes that have rendered government services and regulation and control functions inadequate have also rendered the representative relationship between government and governed more and more distant.

If government agencies' responses to population growth, redistribution, and diversity have mostly taken the form of a more-than-corresponding growth, specialization, and institutionalization, there have been other responses, as well. All manner of staffs, institutions, and establishments have evolved for the purpose of maintaining communication between representatives and constituents. Thus the administrative and specialized staffs of legislators and officials, as well as the public relations activities of the service and regulatory government agencies, have grown as rapidly as have government as a whole. Nonetheless, many observers view the growing isolation of citizens from their government representatives and officials as a problem as serious as the breakdown in services and regulation, and indeed some view it as a central causal factor in the ills of modern society. The increasing numbers of work disputes and strikes of teachers, police, firemen, and other government employees; the rise of radical right-wing and left-wing political and social movements; the antiwar movements, and the drug counterculture and its spinoffs can all be interpreted as indicators that there is a growing sense of alienation from government and political processes.

In his analysis of "Population Growth and the Federal System" prepared for the Commission on Population Growth and the American Future, D. Elazar introduces the concept of *critical mass* of population:

> Critical mass . . . refers to the range of population within the jurisdiction of a particular government that is sufficiently but not too large to enable that government to meet the appropriate needs, demands, and expectations of its citizens relative to political communication and governmental action, either directly through its own resources or by mobilizing sufficient power to gain the use of outside resources (human or economic) without losing its fundamental autonomy. (Elazar, 1972, p. 36)

Similarly, the notion of *less-than-critical mass* refers to jurisdictions with populations too small to meet those criteria, and the notion of *excess mass* describes the situation in which the population located within a particular governmental jurisdiction has increased beyond the possibility of effective political communication and government action desired or expected by the citizens.

Elazar goes on to point out that at all levels of government, the requisites for the respective services demanded (whether defense, education, communications, social welfare, and others) have changed drastically over time. This is due to changing technologies of warfare, transport, and so forth, and also to changing standards and expectations. Below the critical mass of populations, governments cannot mobilize the resources or the specialized personnel required for provision of services. But just as important, above the critical mass the sheer size of the governmental establishment required to meet the population's needs adds costs, limits coordination, and prevents communication with the public. Elazar suggests that the critical mass for states is about 2,000,000 population, and he places the threshold of excess mass at about 25 to 30 million. For local communities, a minimum population of 20,000 is essential for provision of services, while 250,000 is the maximum size for a community to sustain acceptable political communication. Elazar suggests that the United States as a nation state achieved critical mass at the turn of the century (with a population of 76 million), and that the federal government has already passed the threshold of excess mass in regard to exercising a direct role in providing domestic government services. Both political communication (between government and citizens *and* within government) and delivery of services are already impaired by excess mass of population.

Elazer's argument raises some serious questions about the very capacity of democratic government both to govern effectively and to remain democratic undercurrent and continuing population growth. Can New York City, or the state of California, or the United States for that matter, be governed? If they can, how can they be governed? A solution advanced by Elazar and other students of government is the strengthening of classical American Federalism. This mainly involves the transfer of initiative and authority to local jurisdictions without requiring them to depend only on local population and taxing powers for resources. Elazar suggests that such measures would restore responsibility and authority for provision of public services and regulation to jurisdictions large enough to operate effectively but small enough to assure political involvement, representation, and communication consistent with the democratic tradition and imperatives.

There have been recent attempts to effect such revival and strengthening of smaller jurisdictions. Some federal programs have been returned to state and local government administration and authority; and some great city functions have been decentralized, with borough, community, or neighborhood initiative and authority allowed to take over. These programs and attempts still remain to be analyzed and evaluated in full.

POPULATION CHANGE AND POWER-BALANCE CONSTELLATIONS

In the first chapter of this volume, we mentioned that one of the concerns about the world population explosion was that it was occurring unevenly in the various areas and continents, and that it had implications for shifts in the world balance of power which would be unfavorable to the West. We noted that in the pre-World War II decades, much of the European concern over population stagnation surrounded issues of power balances among nations on that continent. Finally, we noted that the problem of uneven growth is a much more general one, taking place on several fronts. Nations and provinces and cities and neighborhoods and communities and organizations of all types are very frequently comprised of different population types who may have different or even conflicting values, views, and interests. In organizational, community, and national affairs, some balance is struck between the aims and interests of different groupings, and this balance typically takes into account the relative size of the groups involved. Other considerations like wealth, knowledge, or pervasive or violent power may surely also enter into the balancing arrangements; but in most situations the sheer numbers and composition of the groups competing and cooperating are factors. Population changes impose strains on political balances by changing the relative sizes of population subgroups. The responses to such change, formulated in the simplest and most direct fashion, consist in formation of new political balance to ease the stresses of organizational or community conflict.

Ethnic Politics

The concept of ethnic politics is a familiar one to Americans. To some it reflects "un-American" group loyalties, even a kind of "tribalism," which contrasts with the American ideal of individualism. Ethnic politics may violate the image of the individual standing alone and free to make decisions without restraint from authority, tradition, or especially group loyalties. But for many, ethnic politics has been the key to acceptance and absorption into the mainstream of American life. If immigrants were initially underprivileged relative to native or older Americans with respect to jobs, education, social status, and mobility opportunities, at least they were equal in their enjoyment of the right to vote. And it is ethnic politics that has helped them to convert this right to other opportunities.

By *ethnic politics,* we mean the organization of political choices and appointments, the allocation of political and social rewards and resources, and the exercise of political powers and choices—all around the principles of rewarding past patterns of ethnic voting or affecting future patterns of ethnic voting. Ethnic voting is the preference of members of an ethnic group for a given political party, in consequence or expectation of that party being favorable to the ethnic group in some one or many senses. It is also the readiness to cross party lines to vote for or against a candidate belonging to a particular ethnic group (Wolfinger, 1968).

Waves of European "old immigrants" (Scotch-Irish, Irish Catholic, German, and Scandinavian) and "new immigrants" (Polish, Slavic, Italian, Jewish, and Greek) and their descendants have changed successively the political maps, coalitions, voting alignments, and salient issues in New England, the mid-Atlantic states, and parts of the north central states. The arrival of hundreds of thousands of Irish Catholic

Various ethnic groups exert much political influence. Here one group, the Irish of New York, demonstrates its solidarity in a St. Patrick's Day parade, one of the oldest gatherings of its kind. *(Wide World Photos)*

immigrants which began in the early nineteenth century triggered the formation of nativist movements which were initially simply antiforeign in orientation, but which soon became anti-Catholic, and later anti-Semitic as well. The existing political parties courted the votes of new immigrant voters, and so did entirely new political parties. Yankee Americans first joined forces to exclude the first waves of immigrants from sharing political power; eventually the "old immigrants" joined forces to protect their own newly won powers and privileges from inroads of "new immigrants." And most recently these once-new immigrants have formed coalitions to exclude blacks, Puerto Ricans, Chicanos, and other minorities from power.

The large ethnic groups have tended to develop stands and positions on the great issues in national, regional, or local politics in America. Yankees, Jews, Italians, and Poles have tended to support international involvement and commitment; Irish and Germans and Swedes have tended to oppose them. Locally Yankee, German, and Scandinavian Protestant fundamentalists have tended to oppose gambling (like bingo and off-track betting) and to support Prohibition; Irish, Polish, and Italian Catholics and Jews have found it easier to live with gambling, but not with Prohibition.

The administrations and political party machinery of many of the largest cities have historically been dominated either by a single ethnic group or by coalitions of ethnic groups. The success or local dominance of an ethnic group has often been measured by that group's electing a congressman, "taking over City Hall," or even nominating a candidate for an important office. Thus, the Irish and Italians have elected mayors in Boston, New York, and New Haven; and Germans and Scandinavians have elected mayors, senators, and governors in Wisconsin, Minnesota, and the Dakotas. Blacks have elected mayors in Gary, Indiana, Cleveland, Ohio, and Atlanta Georgia; and Chicanos have elected governors in New Mexico and Arizona. Ethnic voting is a factor both in the salience of issues and in the positions taken by candidates who don't belong to the ethnic group. Few candidates for Governor of New York or U.S. Senator from that state will take stands which might offend Irish or Italian interests; they should also be pro-Israel even if they are themselves white Anglo-Saxon Protestants (WASPs).

While the size, composition, and geographic distribution of an ethnic group is not, of course, the only factor in the appeals and trade-offs, coalitions and constellations that comprise ethnic politics, these population characteristics clearly do play a major role. Al Smith's nomination as the first Irish Catholic candidate for the presidency in 1928, and the bitterness and bigotry of the campaign and Smith's defeat by Herbert Hoover, were probably both due in large measure to the fact that during that period of our history, the proportion of foreign stock in the large American cities reached its maximum. Today, too, the shifts in ethnic composition of the populations of large cities like New York, Chicago, Detroit, Philadelphia, Cleveland, Boston have been a primary issue in political conflicts over housing, schools, transportation, and over political control of the city administrations and resources.

Other Power and Voting Blocs

Just as religious, racial, and national-origin blocs have been important elements in political coalitions, other population groupings have advanced or defended shared interest in common political causes. The United States Congress has long been an arena for regional and sectional blocs: North *vs.* South, East *vs.* West, inland *vs.* coasts. In each case these blocs are population categories or groupings whose representatives and senators have aligned themselves on questions affecting regional or sectional needs of their constituents. Currency issues, slavery, federal land policy, tariffs, off-shore oil exploration, agricultural price supports and flood control have all been issues which appealed differently to different regions of the country. And both the salience of the issues and the direction of policies ultimately adopted have been affected by trends in population size and distribution.

Another familiar type of political population group division has been that between rural and urban populations. In most state legislatures there are, at least on some issues, urban and rural blocs; the United States Congress as well has often been divided along rural-urban lines according to the constituencies and commitments of members; and large numbers of organizations and lobbies operate to promote rural and urban interests respectively both at state and at national levels. These blocs, the issues which activate them, and their more detailed composition and constituents have changed as the farm population has declined absolutely and relatively and the urban population has grown; and as the nature of agriculture and nonagricultured industries have been transformed.

The recent Supreme Court decision demanding reapportionment of congressional and legislative districts to achieve equality of representation promises to reverse the historic domination of legislatures and Congress by rural constituencies and their representatives. However, recent net urban-to-rural migration may operate both to slow down this reapportionment process, or to reverse some shifts that have already taken place.

In addition to ethnic, regional, and rural-urban politics, we may mention, finally, the advent of age-sex politics. Old age has long been a politically salient characteristic. Movements advocating rights and benefits for the aged have arisen throughout the present century at least; and some groups have organized voting campaigns, supported specific candidates or parties for election, and lobbied in the Congress and the legislatures. The most famous of these was probably the Townsend Movement which originated on the West Coast in the 1930s. With rapidly increasing numbers of aged in the population, political appeals are increasingly addressed to this bloc. We can particularly see this in states and areas like Florida, which have attracted large numbers of retired or elderly persons. Candidates, issues, and movements in these areas are closely linked to the concerns of the aged.

"Young age" as well as old age has become politically salient, especially since the period of the Vietnam War and the antiwar movement. The growing self-consciousness and, often, alienation of youth has had an influence in many areas of politics and government. The growing role of youth politics is highlighted by the recent constitutional amendment extending the right to vote to persons aged 18 years and over. While there have been relatively few political issues revolving around the interests of youth per se, a case can certainly be made for the assertion that the pressure to withdraw from Vietnam originated and was sustained among youth—and also that a contributing factor in the effectiveness of this pressure was the sheer numbers of youth (a product of the post-World War II baby boom).

Finally, the revival of women's rights and women's liberation ideas and movements has made sex politically salient. Women, like other voting blocs, have elected mayors and other officials and successfully pressed for appointment of additional female government officials. A big achievement of the women's movements has been the trend toward liberalization of abortion and the mobilization of political support for this trend. Support for the women's liberation movements and for sex politics is linked more to age composition and age turnover of the population than to sex composition: the sex composition is relatively stable over time; but it is largely the great young "baby-boom generation" of women who have supported and sustained the movement. And the growth of socially and politically involved cohorts of women has put women's lib on the social and political map.

Thus ethnic, sectional, rural-urban, and age and sex groups have sought influence and power, not simply through individual members who have become candidates or leaders but through the influence of the entire groups, too. These blocs have been more or less effective in achieving power and influence in accordance with salience of their characteristics, to be sure, and in accordance with objective factors and their rosters of activists and candidates. But an equally important factor may be the changing relative and absolute size, density, and distribution of these subgroups as a result of major population shifts.

POPULATION AND POWER GROUP RECRUITMENT, PARTICIPATION, AND MOBILITY

In the previous chapter we outlined a model of population, social rewards and resources, and social roles, subsystems, and strata which organize both the interactions and activities which produce rewards and the relationships which determine the distribution, allocation, and exchange of rewards and resources. In the same context we may now view *power groups* as those social systems, organizations, or groupings which have, seek, or actively compete for control or influence over the production, allocation, and distribution of rewards, or over the rules that regulate the conversion of resources.

Ruling elites, government, political parties and cliques, labor unions, businessmen's organizations, veteran's groups are all examples of social systems that have or explicitly seek power, control, or influence over resource production or distribution. Within other organizations and systems—universities, extended families, garden clubs, churches, or girl scout troops—there are typically groups and cliques that seek to influence resource allocation, too; and on a much smaller scale these are also power groups. But our concern here is with those groups which are active in the larger social arenas of communities, societies, and economic sectors.

The identification of power groups, the analysis of their sources of support and legitimacy, and the analysis of their modes of operation and activity are central problems in social stratification and also in political sociology. But, as we indicated earlier, the consequences of population change include both shifts in the amounts and composition of resources produced and shifts in the composition and interrelations between competing claimants. Thus, our particular interest here is the way in which power groups are affected by population changes and what these changes entail for production and distribution of rewards.

Ruling groups can both define the public good and mobilize and manipulate resources in pursuit of their formulation of the "public good." To do so, they need either legitimate authority and some minimum of consensus, or control of violent force, or both. Other power groups seek either to become ruling groups themselves or to influence the definition of public good and the manipulation of resources. There is always tension between rulers and at least some of the ruled. This is because rulers appropriate and allocate surplus production, and in doing this it is impossible to please everyone (see van den Berghe, 1974). In societies in which competition for ruling power is legitimized and institutionalized, both ruling groups (the "ins") and their competitors (the "outs") must compete for support for their respective definitions of the "public good" and for their rule. But even in societies in which there is no institutionalized competition for power, the ruling group tends itself to comprise competing subgroups, all of whom seek supporters, adherents, and consensus to legitimate their rule. And among those not in power there may be attempts either to displace those in power or to obtain some share of power.

Because ruling groups tend to identify the "public good" with their own interests and the interests of those close to them, and because rulers can and do allocate and distribute the sometimes-substantial part of the total product which is siphoned off as taxes or "public sector income," rulers and those close to them tend to be privileged groups. The ruled, in turn, are characterized by varying degrees of disprivilege, varying degrees of dissatisfaction, and varying degrees of militancy and insurgency.

In general, population growth tends to add to the numbers of "outs"—the disprivileged who are also the potential insurgents. If population growth is by natural increase, it consists primarily of increased numbers of youth and young adults. As Chamberlain (1970) has pointed out, in every society youth is shortchanged relative to middle-aged or older adults. Youth simply arrived later, after most of the benefits and good deals have already been taken by earlier arrivals. While youth are everywhere a threat to incumbent order, growing cities are particularly likely arenas for pools of youthful leaders. As population grows, the density of youth rises relative to the total population—this happened in the 1960s in the United States. This growing density increases their disadvantage because they must compete with one another for jobs and social positions. At the same time, though, it increases their political influence.

If population growth occurs mainly by net in-migration, it may comprise relatively privileged, high occupational status migrants and their families. But it is more likely to include primarily newcomers who—whatever their occupational, educational, or income levels—are outsiders and, as such, are generally disprivileged relative to old-timers in most respects, excluded from associations, opportunities, participation and control of rewards and resources.

Youth and migrants, both outsiders in different ways, are targets for recruitment to politically active "outs." According to Chamberlain (1970), insurgents are most likely to find allies in areas where population density has been increasing due to growth either in aggregate numbers or in the size of cities. These are situations in which there is growth in the population contained by an existing authority structure. The expanding population and the urbanizing population contain substantial numbers disproportionately disadvantaged by increased population density, and hence responsive to overtures and initiative from both indigenous and outside leaders.

But the recruitment of disprivileged youth and newcomers to the ranks of the active "outs" is by no means the only direction possible; it may not even be the most frequent course. The ruling group, or the "ins," may also try to recruit, or coopt, youth, newcomers and other disprivileged among the population increment. Indeed the group that is in power or close to being in power can very often provide individuals of disprivileged groups with opportunities for mobility in the framework of the political system. Their mobility, in turn, may be based on skills and ability to perform the work demanded; but it may also be based on the contacts and influence of these individuals in their own communities. Thus, the Chicago and Cook County Democratic Party organizations have retained power in that city and county over the decades of population growth and change largely by their ability to coopt, recruit, promote, and satisfy adherents hailing from Irish-Catholic, Polish, Jewish, Italian, and most recently, from black and from Spanish-American backgrounds and origins (Royko, 1971). By affording bureaucratic and political careers to thousands whose equal success in the conventional labor market might be in question, they have also been able to generate support for, and neutralize opposition to, their rule and influence in local Chicago politics. There is some evidence that this situation holds true in the reverse, as well. At least one student of the American upper class (Baltzell, 1964) has noted that this group's failure to recruit adherents and participants from outside the ranks of acceptable WASPs may spell the demise of this elite group itself.

SUMMARY

In this chapter we have examined the beginnings of study of political responses to population growth and change. Our discussion has concerned responses at all levels of the political organization: national, state, and local. A first general issue concerns the relationship between population growth and changes and the expectations and demands made upon local, state, or federal governments for services. Other issues concern the nature of political representation and the links between politician and constituency, and how these relationships, and how the size, composition and balances among constituencies themselves, are affected by population changes. The final topic raised has been the question of how participation in the political process responds to population changes.

Population growth, and especially the growth of densely settled agglomerations, generates disproportionate demands for government services, from sanitation, recreation, and health care to education services and facilities. Particular population groups create demands for specialized government services and facilities. Youth need schools, trained teachers, and job opportunities; the elderly need medical and social security programs; interested groups want cultural services; and the poor need welfare services. Because each group has specific needs, any group, as it increases in relative size, may become an actual or potential constituency whose needs and demands become politically salient issues to politicians and parties that seek to represent that constituency.

As population increases, the legislator or political representative represents progressively larger numbers of constituents. In 1800, the average population of a United States congressional district was 37,000. This number increased to 194,000 by 1900, to 471,000 by 1920, and it is likely to be well over 600,000 by the year 2000. The increasing size of congressional districts is accompanied by much greater heterogeneity as well. Legislative bodies have responded to increased legislative and constituent demands by developing leadership hierarchies, functional specializations, career professionalization, and procedural routinization; and individual legislators increasingly adopt the practices, and take on the characteristics, of professionalized bureaucrats.

In legislative bodies, in political parties, in public bureaucracies, and in all types of groups that exercise power, the political balance among racial, religious, ethnic, and social groups shifts in response to the differential growth and migration of these population groups. However, the extent to which political bodies reflect the composition of the population also depends on the articulation of the specific positions, demands, values, or ideologies of the various groups, and on their effectiveness in recruiting candidates and in mobilizing support. Alternatively, existing political power groupings can activate or mobilize the support of such constituencies by themselves by articulating the demands, values, and ideologies of the subgroups.

Individuals are probably less likely to participate actively in politics the larger the population and the higher the density of the community, other things being equal. The likelihood of personal acquaintance with active participants and with voters and constituents and supporters is both catalyst and reward for political activism; and this likelihood is lowest in large populations. However, it is probably the case that individuals involved in political activity will have greater opportunities for political mobility in larger population groups.

In Part III we have studied, often in a preliminary manner, the characteristic demographic, economic, social, and political responses to population growth, structural change, and turnover. Where possible, we have tried to formulate some principles governing such responses and examine the evidence supporting them. In many instances these relationships require further study, documentation, and elaboration, but their discussion even as hypotheses and conjectures can serve to make us aware of the issues involved, and perhaps to stimulate more detailed and systematic investigation.

In the concluding chapter, we will look at some of the direct responses of government to population changes as we take up the question of population policies and their probable effects on future population and social trends.

17

Population Policies and the Sociodemographic Utopia

In this chapter we will examine what population policy entails; we will also look at some attempts to formulate, adopt, and implement population policies. We review the work and recommendations of the Commission on Population and the American Future and extend our review to discussion, formulation, and attempts to implement population policies in several areas.

POPULATION POLICY AND POPULATION OBJECTIVES

Population policy is distinct from population theory and doctrine (on the latter, see Keyfitz, 1972; United Nations, 1973). It consists of both the formulation of, and articulation by, rulers, government, or legitimate authority, of some population objective or set of objectives that are associated with or serve the public good; and the commitment and manipulation of resources in pursuit of these population objectives, by means of direct or indirect intervention in mortality, fertility, or migration.

Population objectives may concern the size, growth rate, distribution, composition, or characteristics (often denoted as "quality" in discussions of public policy) of population. Population policy should be distinguished both from policies that bear on characteristics like the size, growth, or distribution of the population but adopted for other purposes and from policies that speak to other than demographic processes. The latter might include health policies which have the effect of reducing mortality and promoting population growth, but are adopted for their own sake; or educational policies which have the effect of improving population quality, but not through fertility, mortality, or migration.

Plato favored a population of fixed size of 5,040 landholders, on the grounds that this number assures defense capability and the various specialities a state requires, and at the same time it is within the capacity of the state to assure material provisions and to allow the personal acquaintance among citizens necessary for effective rule and civil order. Other thinkers have proposed fixed, optimum, population sizes as promising maximum welfare, happiness, power, or other value. But actual population policy almost never envisions a demographic objective cast in terms of some specific number or population form. Instead, it typically envisions and seeks some reasonably stable demographic situation different from that in which the society currently finds itself. Thus, some countries with slowly growing or stationary populations may adopt policies intended to promote growth; some countries with highly concentrated populations may adopt policies intended to promote population dispersion; and some countries experiencing in-migration of given characteristics have sought to restrict migration to those of other characteristics. Population policy is generally *not* determined in a single formulation by the ruling group that population should be of size *P,* distributed *A,B,* and *C,* composed *X,Y,* and *Z,* and with characteristics *Q,E,* and *D.* Rather, population policy is both less specific at any moment, and it evolves over time.

THE AMERICAN EXPERIENCE

Land Policy

American population policy before the twentieth century was primarily concerned with the *distribution* of population instead of its size, growth, or quality. The Northwest Ordinance of July 13, 1787 first set up provisions for governing new territories, establishing legislatures, admitting new states to the Union; it also set down a few basic political principles for the territories, like the prohibition of involuntary servitude, freedom of worship, trial by jury, and public support of education. A series of land acts, beginning with the Land Act of 1796 were passed by Congress to provide for the survey, division, and sale of lands in the public domain in the Northwest Territories. These acts also established the first land offices in Pittsburgh and Cincinnati, and later in other western settlements. They extended similar provisions of Spanish and French land grants and the Louisiana Purchase as the need arose, too.

Land became cheaper as more territory opened up. It was originally offered for sale in minimum sections of 640 acres at two dollars per acre. It subsequently became available first in half- and later in quarter-sections, and finally, under the Land Act of 1820, in minimum eighth-section tracts of 80 acres, with the minimum price reduced to $1.25 per acre. Where initial land acts favored revenue raising for the United States Treasury, subsequent land acts favored settlement. And between 1821 and 1832, some eleven relief acts were passed by Congress to meet western demands for cheap land and for preemption. This amounted to a legal confirmation of squatter claims on public lands. Subsequent acts continued to make concessions to settlers and also to grant both land and proceeds from federal land sales to new states.

A land reform movement arose between 1840 and 1860. It was led by Horace Greeley, and it advocated the granting of free homesteads to settlers and the limiting of land grants to large interests. On May 20, 1862, the Homestead Act, was passed offering any citizen or intending citizen family head over 21 years of age 160 acres of surveyed public domain land after 5 years of continuous residence and payment of a small registration fee. Alternatively, land could be acquired under the act after only 6 months residence at $1.25 an acre. Between 1862 and 1904, some 147 million acres were acquired free (except for registration fees) under the Act, and almost 611 million acres more were acquired by purchase. Another series of acts provided for land grants and homestead bonus to ex-soldiers, sales of coal lands, sales of desert lands, and sale and cutting rights on timberland, and separate forest and grazing homestead acts.

In 1862 and 1864, Congress passed the Pacific Railway Acts, authorizing a transcontinental railroad and land grants from the public domain on both sides of the railroad right of way. Earlier western canals and railroads were developed before the Civil War, with the Illinois Central Railroad (chartered in 1861) the first land-grant railway. The railroad received more than 2.5 million acres. When it sold these lands in the 1850s to cover construction costs of the railroad from Chicago to Cairo, Illinois, the Illinois Central carried out extensive colonization and promotion of settlement. The western railroads, chartered in the 1860s, included a central route from Chicago to San Francisco (the Union Pacific); a northern route from Lake Superior to Portland, Oregon (the Northern Pacific and later the Great Northern Line); a route along the 35th parallel (Atchison, Topeka, and Santa Fe Railroad) from Chicago to Los Angeles; and a southern route (the Texas and Pacific Railroad, which eventually combined right of way with the Southern Pacific). By 1884 some 155.5 million acres of public lands had been granted to railroads. Western states granted an additional 49 million acres, and loans totaling almost 67 million dollars were advanced to six companies to build the Pacific Route. In all, between 1607 and 1870 some 407 million acres of new land were occupied, including 189 million acres cultivated or improved. And in the 30 years between 1870 and 1900, no less than 430 million acres had been occupied. Two hundred twenty-five million acres were placed under cultivation, and the number of farms doubled from about 2.7 million in 1866 to 5.4 million in 1900. By 1840 half the population of the United States lived in the area west of the original thirteen states, and by 1900 about 28 percent lived west of the Mississippi.

Immigration Control

Immigrants were allowed into the United States largely without restriction through the nineteenth century, despite agitation on the part of nativist movements. Then the first exclusion act was passed in 1882 when Congress prohibited the immigration of Chinese laborers. A Federal Act of August 18, 1882, excluded criminals, paupers, the insane, and other undesirables from immigration to the United States and imposed a head tax of 50 cents (raised to two dollars in 1903 and to four dollars in 1907) on those entering. The Contract Labor Act of February 26, 1885, forbade further importation of contract laborers, but it exempted certain professional, skilled, and domestic labor. It was modified several times. In 1917, Congress imposed a literacy test on immigrants over 16 years of age; and in 1918 an act was passed to exclude anarchists and others who advocated the overthrow of the government.

On May 19, 1921, Congress passed the historic Quota Law. This limited immigration in any one year to three percent of the total number of each nationality, according to the census of 1910, with the maximum quota of 357,000 immigrants from each national group. On May 26, 1924, a new quota law was passed which used the earlier (1921) maximum quota, but limited immigration in any year to two percent of each nationality according to the census of 1890 (its purpose was to reduce quotas from eastern and southern Europe). The new law also banned Japanese and other Asian immigrants. It lasted until 1927. Thereafter

The United States moved from unrestricted immigration, as shown in an 1880 cartoon, to a "quota" system in an attempt to control population. Agitation for control began as early as the 1890s, evidenced here in a cartoon of 1893. *(Courtesy of the New-York Historical Society, New York City)*

the 1920 distribution of population by national origins was to serve as the basis for a maximum quota of 150,000 per annum. The quota rules did not apply to immigration from Canada or from Latin America.

Between 1945 and 1952 close to 250,000 European war refugees and displaced persons were admitted to the United States outside the quota system, by a special series of acts. In 1952 Congress passed the McCarran-Walter Act which codified United States immigration laws, retaining the quota system and the 1924 act provisions for maximum immigration. This act also dropped the ban against Asian and Pacific immigrants. The new act also sought to screen out "subversives" and other undesirables, giving the Attorney General the power to deport immigrants on the grounds of "communist and communist front" affiliations even after they had already acquired citizenship.

Most recently, the Immigration Act of 1965 abolished the national origins quota system. But for countries outside the Western Hemisphere, the act placed an annual ceiling of 170,000 on the number of immigrant visas to be issued (exclusive of parents, spouses, and unmarried children of United States citizens), with no more than 20,000 immigrants allowed annually from any one country. For countries in the Western Hemisphere, an annual ceiling was imposed for the first time of 120,000 visas. In addition, a preference system favoring the reunion of families was imposed, and a requirement of employment clearances was instituted (see Keely, 1972).

Family-Planning Assistance to Developing Countries

World population explosion alarms were first sounded in the United States even before World War II. In 1927, sociologist Edward Alsworth Ross published a book entitled *Standing Room Only* in which he warned of impending world population pressure, of its social, economic and political dangers, and especially of the coming "great barrier" of the peoples of Europe, the Americas, and Australia, against those of Africa and Asia:

> Here in a nutshell is the issue between the Occidentals and the Orientals. The former decline to be encumbered with the excess population of the latter, not altogether from a selfish unwillingness to oblige, but because it is certain that, the religion and family system of the latter being what they are, there will be an endless succession of surpluses from which the Oriental people will desire to be relieved. . . . It is not by drawing off the redundancy of the population after it is formed that we can uphold a well state of society, but by preventing formation of that redundancy. (Ross, 1927, p. 345)

W. S. Thompson, a pioneer American demographer, argued in his book, *Danger Spots in World Population* (1930) that the Japanese challenge to American hegemony in the Pacific in the 1920s had its basic cause in population pressure. In an earlier chapter, we saw that a similar theme raised after World War II, together with the findings of the early postwar censuses, led professional demographers and university and private research organizations and foundations to sound a much stronger and more persistent world population explosion alarm—an alarm largely ignored by the American government and the Congress until the early 1960s.

In fact, in the decade from 1959 (when President Eisenhower declared that "birth control . . . is not a proper political government activity or function or responsibility") to 1969 (when President Nixon issued a presidential message on population which acknowledged United States and world population growth and the need for family planning, and asserted that "this Administration does accept a clear responsibility to provide essential leadership") government policy moved from repudiation or indifference, to the promotion and subsidizing of family planning services and research both at home and abroad (see Piotrow, 1973 for details on this metamorphosis).

Beginning with the 1960 presidential election campaign, and continuing through the Kennedy, Johnson, Nixon, and Ford administrations, the United States has financed and supported research and the introduction of fertility control measures in developing areas of the world and among limited income groups in the United States. In the Foreign Assistance Act of 1961, Congress enacted the legislation which established the policy and priority for these foreign-aid programs, even while the executive agencies of the government remained cool. And in the authorizing legislation for the Office of Economic Opportunity (OEO) and Social Security amendments of 1967, the Congress provided for limited domestic family planning services as part of the antipoverty program and the maternal and child health activities.

Domestic Population Policy? The Commission on Population Growth and the American Future

In July of 1969, President Nixon proposed the establishment of a Commission on Population Growth and the American Future, and on March 16, 1970, Congress passed legislation (PL 91-213) which established this commission "to conduct and sponsor such recommendations as may be necessary to provide information and education to all levels of government in the United States, and to our people, regarding the broad range of problems associated with population growth and their implications for America's future." The duties of the commission set forth in the act were:

1. to examine the probable extent of population growth and internal migration between now and the end of the century.
2. to assess the impact that population change will have upon government services, on the United States economy, and on resources and the environment
3. to make recommendations on how the nation can best cope with that impact

The commission was chaired by John D. Rockefeller, III (who, as we already mentioned, was a central personality in the campaign to make known the problems of population growth and to seek technological and social solutions). Other members included university professors, physicians and public health administrators, businessmen, housewives, students, private foundation executives, two United States Senators, and two United States Representatives. The commission drew on a large administrative and professional staff and a great number of consultants. It deliberated, held public hearings, commissioned research reports (published in six separate volumes in 1972) and presented a summary report in March, 1972. In his letter of transmittal, Rockefeller highlighted the central findings and recommendations of the commission:

> . . . We have concluded that, in the long run, no substantial benefits will result from further growth of the Nation's population, rather that the gradual stabilization of our population through voluntary means would contribute significantly to the Nation's ability to solve its problems. We have looked for, and have not found, any convincing economic arguments for continued population growth. The health of our country does not depend on it, nor does the vitality of business nor the welfare of the average person.
>
> The recommendations offered by this Commission are directed to increasing public knowledge of causes and consequences of population change, facilitating and guiding the processes of population movement, maximizing information about human reproduction and its conseqences for the family, and enabling individuals to avoid unwanted fertility. (U.S. Commission, *Report,* 1972, p. 4)

Several major themes appear in the commission's report, and also to a greater or lesser extent in the subsequent recommendations. These included (a) the "unwanted child" theme, (b) the "social justice" theme, and (c) the crisis or ecological theme. The first theme emphasized the great need to help individuals, couples, or families control reproduction and avoid unwanted children through better information, education, and birth control services. The second theme insisted that priority must be given to equalizing the rights of minorities and of women. At the same time this theme tended to minimize the importance of other factors. The third theme emphasized the deteriorating environment; it called for basic changes in economic and other values to deal with this problem.

The commission concluded its report with a set of recommendations that dealt with population; sex education; child care; out-of-wedlock children and adoption; women's rights; access to contraception, voluntary sterilization, and abortion; programs to reduce unwanted fertility and the provision of family planning services; migration, population distribution, and urban and rural areas; help for minorities and the poor; and the adoption of population stabilization as a goal, with recommendations supporting research in population and in fertility control. Probably the most controversial of the recommendations were those that advocated liberalization of abortion and the provision of birth control information and services to minors and teenagers. Many persons concerned with ecology, resources, the environment, and the "quality of life" were disappointed by the commission's relative neglect of these issues and the absence of more specific economic and environmental recommendations. And many concerned with problems of population distribution, urban development, and the social and psychological consequences of migration were disappointed that the commission did not make more specific recommendations in this area.

President Nixon declined to act on the recommendations of the commission, and he explicitly rejected the most controversial recommendations dealing with abortion and distribution of family planning services to minors. The commission's report was not immediately followed by specific legislation, action, or programs. But, the preparation and submission of the report, the fanfare of publicity, the controversy surrounding its recommendations have provoked unprecedented public debate and discussion—but not policy.

But, as Phyllis Tilson Piotrow has pointed out (Piotrow, 1973, p. 198), in a literate and modern society like the United States, it is possible that the success or failure of a policy that deals with population and reproductive behavior depends not on the presence or absence of government programs but on the individual response:

> For American population policy in the field of reproduction the right people are not the President and his advisors, but rather the millions of young women and men who will reproduce in this and future generations During the late 1960's and early 1970's they were already deciding for more contraceptives, legal abortion, and lower fertility. Within the United

States the history of birth control policy may well be a series of non-self-fulfilling prophecies in which the informed public response to the crisis obviates the need for a more drastic policy. (Piotrow, 1973, p. 198)

THE EUROPEAN EXPERIENCE

In contrast to the novelty of population policy in the American experience, European countries have past histories of explicitly adopted population policies. The European population policy and nonpolicy histories reflect, in turn, a number of important historical traditions not found in America.

The European Traditions

Acceptability of government intervention. Europe has a long history of government intervention in social affairs. Such intervention has been strongly institutionalized throughout Europe: there is long-standing belief that government has the capacity to obtain and organize information, and the knowledge and skills to analyze social problems and to mobilize the resources, knowledge, and skills necessary to intervene in resolving them. To be sure, there have always been more-or-less alienated groups in Europe who have viewed themselves as underprivileged, ignored, or exploited by government and society. But there has not been the generalized suspicion of rulers and government per se, and the hostility to government initiative, that have so frequently been evident in America. Thus in Europe, government has been the natural "address" for problems of housing, health, poverty, or economic investment as well as other areas of regulation.

Political salience of demographic trends. A second point is that there has been in Europe—among statesmen, soldiers, and men of affairs as well as scholars—a long-standing awareness and recognition of the historical declines in fertility, in family size, and in population growth rate. There has been, correspondingly, long familiarity with the analysis and speculation about the political and military, economic, and moral consequences of these trends. In particular, these population developments, and the speculation and analysis that surround them, have taken place in the shadow of evolving and often conflicting nationalism, as is evidenced by a sequence of violent military confrontations within Europe (see Glass, repr. 1967). Thus, even if the pronatalism that was earlier the central theme of European population policies may be outmoded today, it is difficult for European policymakers to view themselves as entirely free of the considerations that led to such policies in the past. And it is even more difficult for them to adopt diametrically opposite policies today.

The role of established religion. In most countries of Europe, established religion has historically played a powerful role in the conduct of public and individual affairs alike. Established religions have had their own population doctrines, if not necessarily population policies in our sense in this book; and they have sought to subvert population policies not consistent with religious doctrine. Religion has not played the same kind of role in America. Although it has certainly been a very important factor in the personal affairs of Americans, and although organized religious denominations have certainly been influential in public affairs at local and national levels, there has been no established religion in the United States since colonial times. Thus, organized religion here has been involved in controversies over access to contraception and abortion through its participation in American political processes, on a more-or-less similar footing with the other actors in the political arena. But in Europe the religious establishments have typically been much more than equal players in the political arena. Rather, they have been more in the nature of both making the rules and being the referee.

Population distribution imperatives. Finally, European nations have been much more alert to the possibilities and to the desirability (if not absolute necessity) of policy intervention in population distribution than has been the case in the United States. Town and regional planning are probably much more developed in Europe than in the United States. In most of Western Europe this may be due to a very long-standing familiarity with population density: with dense urban settlement as well as dense rural and agricultural settlement. In contrast, densely populated agglomerations are a more recent development in the United States. In Eastern Europe, regional planning is related to the strong commitment of the communist regimes to rapid industrialization; and in the Soviet Union and in Germany during World War II, forced migration and settlement involving hundreds of thousands of persons was carried out for political as well as economic reasons. Some countries of Europe, especially the Mediterranean and Balkan countries, have actively promoted overseas emigration of their citizens. Italy, for example, had long encouraged overseas emigration, but this policy was reversed in the 1920s by the Fascist regime which both prohibited emigration and adopted strongly pronatalist policies. (After World War II overseas emigration was again encouraged.)

Population Trends and Policy Measures

In general, the measures which have resulted in lower fertility in Europe have not originated as population policies. Instead, they have evolved either entirely without government intervention, or as a consequence of policies introduced more in the context of social reforms or measures to expand social opportunity. The liberalization of induced abortion in the Soviet Union which followed the Revolution, the availability of abortion in central and eastern European countries, and the widespread availability of both abortion and contraception in the Scandinavian countries, evolved not as measures to control fertility but as elements of women's rights and social justice programs. Even today, the pressure to expand family-planning services in Europe is exerted in the name of "women's rights" rather than "population control." But measures intended to promote increased fertility—whether extensive propaganda, family allowances, taxation policies, housing and school subsidies, or prohibition of abortion and suppression of family planning information and supplies—*were* very often adopted as part of explicit pronatalist population policies. Similarly, measures which have explicitly supported and subsidized population redistribution, or which have encouraged existing trends toward centralization and agglomeration, have been attempted in France, the Netherlands, Britain, and Sweden. These programs have included planning activities, subsidized housing, employment, education, and services in planned communities.

Successes and Failures in Western Population Policy

In both Europe and the United States, we can claim some successes for population policy in the areas of population settlement and redistribution, international migration, and, in some cases, internal migration and redistribution. In numerous historical cases, new areas have been opened successfully to settlement and development; desired migrants have been attracted and undesired migrants have successfully been excluded; new or more numerous skills or labor power have been introduced through migration; and populations have been redistributed on either a local or national scale. There are also cases where surplus population or labor has been successfully encouraged to emigrate. And finally, cases also exist of forced emigration, migration, or settlement. All of these reflect the more-or-less effective use of policy measures by rulers and governments to achieve some explicit population goal.

It does not seem possible to claim any notable successes for population policies seeking to raise fertility (with the possible exception of some short-run successes for abortion suppression measures). While fertility did increase somewhat in the "pronatalist policy" countries around and subsequent to World War II, it also increased in countries which were less militantly pronatalist. There is no convincing analysis or evidence to support the idea that the pronatalist population policy measures were responsible for the fertility gains. On the contrary, there are good reasons to suppose that these gains would have taken place without the policy measures. It could, perhaps, be argued that the decline of fertility to its present low level in the "policy" countries (France, Belgium, Sweden, Germany, Italy, and to some extent Great Britain and Eastern European countries) was delayed somewhat by the programs of family allowances, housing subsidies, suppression of abortion and, in France and Italy, of contraception. But even this must remain largely a matter of conjecture, since there seems little promise that the analysis of empirical materials will be able to shed much light on the issue.

A CONTEMPORARY WORLD POPULATION POLICY: DIRECTIONS AND DILEMMAS

It is too early to speak of the "non-European experience" in population policy—except, perhaps, for Japan—other than to note that the source and driving force behind population policy has been the concern with too-rapid population growth rather than population stagnation. And population policies, to the extent they have been adopted outside Europe (see Nortman, 1974; Berelson, 1974) have been largely addressed to the problem of reducing fertility. But the concepts, directions, and dilemmas of fertility-lowering policy are not actually endemic to the developing countries nor to one or another category of areas or societies. Rather, they are inherent to intervention to reduce fertility as a political, social, and economic process.

Directions for Fertility Reduction Policies

Three basic kinds of policy directions are possible for countries wishing to reduce fertility. These include the reduction of unwanted fertility; the change or manipulation of fertility norms, values, and trade-offs;

and the reduction of fertility capacity. By far the most acceptable and "popular" concept is that of reduction of unwanted fertility.

Reducing unwanted fertility. This idea holds that a substantial part of fertility in most populations is unwanted. Here, the provision of means of preventing unwanted fertility is a great boon both to the couples and families who actually use it and to the community and population as a whole.

Earlier in this text, we have noted that there is an ongoing dispute over how far the reduction of unwanted births can go, even if it should be fully achieved, toward achieving zero population growth or even resolving the problem of excessive world population growth. Be that as it may, it is certainly the case that the objective of reducing unwanted fertility is to many an acceptable policy objective, (though not to all—for instance, not to the Catholic Church) both in MDCs and in LDCs; and policy measures aimed at reducing unwanted fertility have not had to rely on coercion. On the contrary, measures to reduce unwanted fertility enjoy the aura of "liberation." The possibilities for reducing unwanted fertility are essentially two: increasing abortions, and controlling or preventing conceptions. Each of these has its potential and its limitations as a policy measure.

Abortion has been, and can be, a major means of reduction and control of unwanted fertility where it is widely available, cheap, safe, and free of legal or social sanctions. Most modern societies have long histories of suppression of abortion, on religious, social, medical, or demographic grounds, though all have had substantial illicit abortion activity nonetheless. In countries with very advanced abortion technology the legalization of abortion has had a very rapid and measurable effect on fertility levels. Japan, and more recently Britain and the United States, are cases in point. Presumably, as other countries with large medical establishments and advanced abortion technology liberalize and legitimate this practice, it is likely to contribute very considerably to further reduction of unwanted fertility. Countries which have either modest medical infrastructures or technology, or with large parts of the population strongly opposed to abortion on moral or ideological grounds cannot find much immediate promise in abortion as a practical policy for reducing fertility. First, they must direct policy toward changing negative attitudes about abortion or expanding abortion technology and medical infrastructure, or both.

We now recognize that widespread practice of contraception has been an important factor in the historical declines in fertility where they have occurred; and that variations in fertility continue to be very closely related to variations in the extent and patterns of practice of contraception. In many countries, information about and access to contraception were long suppressed on various moral, religious, social, medical, or demographic grounds. Here, an important fertility reduction policy measure has been the very legalization and legitimation of distribution, dissemination, or sale of contraceptive devices and materials. Beyond this, many governments have gone a step farther by actively seeking to introduce and distribute contraceptive information, devices, and materials.

But, fundamentally, bringing condoms, pills, IUDs and the like into every home, hearth, and bedroom is more than even the most ambitious governments are able or care to take on alone. In Europe and North America, of course, governments have been relative late-comers to the activity of distributing contraception. Instead, the basic "selling" of contraception to physicians, patients, druggists, and their clients has been undertaken by private enterprise, the drug companies—with government moving in only to reach (through health services and the like) those who were not reached by commercial sales campaigns. In LDCs, governments or outside agencies cooperating with government have taken the initial promotion and sales roles—not private companies. But the diffusion of contraception on the part of government is typically limited by the scope and diffusion of government services generally: to the extent that there are health services, and that the population can and does avail itself of such services, the health service network is or can be a contraception distribution network as well. But in most areas of the world these are very limited indeed in reach.

It stands to reason that the task of governments will be made lighter if they seek to enlist private commercial distribution and sales networks to promote adoption of contraception. Indeed, this has taken place, with governments sometimes initiating, financing, and subsidizing the distribution of contraceptives through private-for-profit sales agencies. But these schemes, too, encounter limitations, which are of two kinds. In the first place, there are many subsistence agriculture communities which have not yet been reached by real commercial distributing networks. Their past isolation from education, modern market agriculture, and consumption has also meant isolation from trade and commerce in general, and from contraceptive promotion in particular. In the second place, the practice of contraception is conceived in many countries as a health measure. In these areas it is initiated and distributed by, and entrusted only to, officials or professionals or quasi-professionals of the health services, and not to be traded by peddlers, street vendors, or shopkeepers. Thus, the teaching, selling, and distribution of contraceptive information and means—while acceptable and indeed widely used—is in many areas being extended only very slowly beyond limited "project" or "target" populations.

Changing fertility and family norms, values, and trade-offs. The growing feeling that the reduction of unwanted births will not alone be enough to resolve world or national population problems has led to the expression of a need to change people's images, norms, and values about the number of children they want—indeed, about the desirability of marriage itself. To bring fertility to replacement or ZPG levels, according to analysts, the average number of children wanted by couples cannot exceed two, or thereabouts. Although on the average, individuals and couples in most countries express the desire for more than two children per family, there is nothing inevitable about these high-fertility preferences. It is quite possible, many analysts believe, to get persons and couples to want, and to be satisfied with, fewer children than they want now. An effort should also be made to persuade individuals that there are other acceptable and attractive life styles besides marriage and family-raising.

Two approaches are typically considered as possible policy measures to achieve these kinds of goals. They are (a) persuasion, propaganda, education, and the like, and (b) raising the "price"—in all senses—of children, and also of marriage. The idea of propaganda, advertising, and persuasion campaigns is self-explanatory. But we may add that, so far, there is very little evidence of the effectiveness of such efforts, and it is difficult to measure their effectiveness. We should mention that there are many testimonials to the effectiveness of this kind of persuasion in Mainland China.

The concept of manipulating the cost of either children or marriage is probably somewhat more complex. But we have earlier introduced the ideas of costs and utilities of children in our discussion in Chapter 9. The policy implications of changing the cost of children is simply government intervention in prices, taxes, and generally in the economy in ways which have the effect of *raising* the costs of children—making parents pay or pay more for health, education, or other services to children, especially for services to the third or fourth child and up. These kinds of policies might also be aimed at lowering the utility of children, prohibiting or delaying their entrance into the working force, cutting or abolishing family allowances or tax rebates for children. In other words, parents would be forced to pay a heavier price for not controlling their family size or for their preference for a larger number of children. Similarly, individuals can be financially penalized for marrying or marrying early.

These kinds of policies seem to border on coercion, but they do not actually cross this line. Persons are, after all, free to marry and have children as they please. But, as this line of reasoning goes, it is also reasonable to excuse the rest of society from the obligation to pay for these individuals' private preference for many offspring. In fact there are already some examples of the application of this type of approach in actual policy measures in India. Many economic and social measures conceived and debated in India today are evaluated, and sometimes adopted or rejected, from the point of view of their expected effect on the advantages or disadvantages to couples and individuals of preventing or delaying further births (see Raina, 1966).

Reduction of Fertility Capacity. By the reduction of fertility capacity we mean especially the extended delay of marriage; obstacles which might put off the remarriage of divorced or widowed women in fertile ages; and sterilization. Also included under this rubric could be the abstinance from sexual activity. Most of the science-fiction types of coercive controls on fertility envisioned by the more apocalyptic of the "environmental radicals" can also be included in this category.

Wherever there are laws to set minimum ages at which marriage is allowed, these laws have typically reflected some acceptable social norm rather than any attempt to influence fertility and population growth. Changing patterns of age at marriage have certainly affected fertility, and they have themselves, in turn, been affected by fertility practices. But even in Mainland China, where virtually all observers agree there is great pressure on young couples to delay marriage (and where, especially in the large cities, marriage *has* been characteristically late in recent years), there is no formal expression of policy or law to prohibit early marriage. Rather, educational and occupational considerations, housing shortages, and explicit demands of industrial committees all converge to render it wiser for young people to delay marriages. But although the raising of minimum ages of marriage would seem to be a fertility reduction policy option open to rulers and governments, in fact such a course seems unlikely except under the most drastic of circumstances. The deliberate manipulation of the costs and utilities of marriage, to induce spontaneous delay of marriage, seems a much less repressive, and therefore a more likely course. Whether or not this in fact has been the course of Mainland China we don't know for sure, although Tien (1975) has suggested that this is the case. The likelihood that governments will adopt population policy measures that would directly affect the frequency and age at marriage, or induce either sterilization or abortion even under conditions of very rapid population growth and serious economic difficulty seems very low at this point; and the discussion of such measures in some of the population crisis literature seems out of all proportion to their political feasibility.

Population Policy and Organized Promotion of Birth Control

The message of the population explosion is circulating—among individuals, and among private and public bodies, and among governments. And there has been extensive organization and mobilization of effort to introduce or promote birth control in the low fertility as well as in the higher fertility countries. To what extent are these programs responsible for the decline in fertility?

There is not yet an agreed set of criteria or procedures for assessing the impact of organized activity or of government policy on actual fertility, nor even on the extent to which birth control is practiced. Where measured practice of birth control has increased subsequent to organized efforts to promote it, it is always possible that it might have been adopted spontaneously, even without such efforts, under given social conditions. Where fertility has declined jointly with increased availability and use of contraceptive technology, it can be argued that fertility has elsewhere—and would here, too—decline under the given demographic and social circumstances even without availability of new technologies. Thus, although it seems probable that organized population control policies are linked to recent fertility declines, their exact relationship cannot yet be measured by statistics.

Population policy in developed countries. In a survey of population policy in developed countries, Bernard Berelson (1974) concludes that in these low fertility countries population policies have typically been implicit rather than explicit, and not adopted exclusively on demographic grounds. More often than not they are seen as part of more general social policy. Unlike the developing world, which is in a quite different demographic position, the political interest in these areas is to *sustain* population growth more than to limit it—but to sustain it at a low level. And here it is the variability, rather than the total magnitude, of demographic trends which is viewed as problematic. Thus a wide range of developed countries, including the United States, Canada, Great Britain, the Netherlands, Japan, Czechoslovakia, and Argentina, have appointed national commissions or retained permanent bureaus and panels for the purpose of examining population trends and making recommendations to their respective governments. Despite these, Berelson notes, remarkably few (only about a third) of the most advanced nations are characterized by widespread availability and practice of the full array of technologically and medically available means of modern fertility control. And the fact of the low rates of fertility in the developing countries appears to bear but little relation to population policy in these countries.

Population policy in less developed countries. The situation in less developed countries (LDCs) is somewhat different. Many of these nations have recently adopted policies with the explicit intention to reduce population growth rates. By 1974, some 33 LDC governments adopted official policies to reduce the population growth rate, and another 30 countries officially supported family planning activities for health, social, or other nondemographic reasons (Nortman, 1974). In Table 17.1 we can see that China, India, Pakistan, Indonesia, Bangladesh, and Egypt are among the larger nations which have adopted explicit policies to reduce population growth.

Government policies have generally been accompanied by concrete efforts to introduce or expand family limitation practices through education and information, through provision of health and social services and contraceptive devices, and through development of incentives for birth control. Evaluation of the programs has typically drawn on information concerning attitudes of the women or couples toward additional births; numbers of persons reached or contacted in the programs; numbers of women or couples accepting or agreeing to practice one or another method of birth control; numbers of personnel employed in the programs; or amount of funding for the programs.

Successful contraception programs are generally acknowledged to have been introduced in Hong Kong, Singapore, Taiwan, and South Korea. In addition, Berelson has claimed (1974) that favorable developments in family planning have also taken place recently in Colombia, Costa Rica, Fiji, Indonesia, Iran, Mauritius, the Philippines, Thailand, and Venezuela. And in Mauritius and Fiji as well as in Hong Kong, Singapore, Taiwan, and South Korea, according to Berelson, the sharp fertility declines of the 1960s may be credited at least in part to family planning programs.

The efforts of international agencies, private foundations, and governments to introduce and promote family planning have been attacked on the grounds that too often they are offered as substitutes for social improvements, which critics view as much more crucial for the countries in question. Bernard Berelson's summary of this controversy is instructive:

On the one side is the position that fertility will not decline to any

TABLE 17.1 LDCs Adopting Population Policies and Dates of Adoption, by Population Size and by Type of Policy

Population (in millions)	*Official Policy to Reduce Population Growth Rate*	*Official Support of Family Planning Activities for Other Reasons*	*Neither Policy Nor Support*
400 and over	China (1962) India (1952)		
100–400	Indonesia (1968)		Brazil
50–100	Bangladesh (1971) Pakistan (1960)	Nigeria (1970) Mexico (1972)	
25–50	Egypt (1965) Iran (1967) South Korea (1961) Philippines (1970) Thailand (1970) Turkey (1965)		Ethiopia Burma
15–25	Morocco (1968) Taiwan (1968) Colombia (1970)	Algeria (1971) South Africa (1966) Sudan (1970) Afghanistan (1970) North Vietnam (1962) South Vietnam (1971) Zaire (1973)	North Korea
10–15	Kenya (1966) West Malaysia (1966) Nepal (1966) Sri Lanka (1965)	Tanzania (1970) Uganda (1972) Iraq (1972) Chile (1966) Venezuela (1968)	Peru
10 and under	Botswana (1970) Ghana (1969) Mauritius (1965) Tunisia (1964) Laos (1972) Singapore (1965) Barbados (1967) Dominican Republic (1968) Jamaica (1966) Puerto Rico (1970) Trinidad and Tobago (1967) Fiji (1962) Gilbert and Ellice Islands (1970)	Dahomey (1969) Gambia (1969) Rhodesia (1968) Hong Kong (1956) Bolivia (1968) Costa Rica (1968) Cuba (early 1960s) Ecuador (1968) El Salvador (1968) Guatemala (1969) Haiti (1971) Honduras (1966) Nicaragua (1967) Panama (1969) Paraguay (1972)	Asia, 8 countries; North Africa and Middle East, 12; Sub-Saharan Africa, 28 countries; Latin America, 5 countries

Source: B. Berelson, "World Population: Status Report 1974," Reports on Population/Family Planning *No. 15, Jan. 1974, p. 24. Reprinted with permission of the Population Council.*

> appreciable degree without major changes in the social setting—popular education, standard of living, industrialization, liberation of women from traditional status, sharply reduced mortality especially in children, and so on. . . . In the extreme form of this view, family planning is unnecessary with social change and impossible without it.
>
> On the other side is the position that family planning properly administered can make a substantial difference in hastening the process of fertility decline by providing modern means to the nontrivial proportion of people ready for such measures and by encouraging the ambivalent. That may not be "enough" in itself, proponents of this position agree, but it is doable, needed in any case as means whatever the motive power, good in its own right on grounds of health and justice, contributory to such values as the liberation of women and popular education, and economic both in itself and as compared to the costs of social change, which proceeds as it can in any case. It appears to many observers that, as in most such broad disputes, both sides are in some sense correct and the issue is more a matter of combination (both are useful) and degree than of either/or. (Berelson 1974a, p. 30)

Berelson is seeking a truce and a coexistence of views and of policies and activities which will promote both population control and social development, holding implicitly that the two are complementary. At the same time he acknowledges that for the most part, the direct evaluation of the impact of family planning programs on actual fertility has not been possible. This is another way of saying that, so far, we have not been able to learn much from these programs about population trends and variations and their explanations.

The View from Bucharest, 1974

We close this discussion by reviewing, again, the 1974 World Population Conference in Bucharest, Romania, initiated by the United Nations as a conference of governments to discuss population and development. A "World Population Plan of Action" was drafted by the United Nations Population Division and revised by the United Nations Population Commission (an agency of the U.N. Economic and Social Council) for presentation to the conference. The draft "Plan of Action" sought recognition of world population growth as a global problem. It stressed the importance of world population policy in general, and of family planning in particular, to deal with the population problem, and it sought to set target dates for achieving certain demographic goals.

The proposed "Plan of Action" encountered very strong opposition to its very demographic emphasis, to its stipulation of target dates, and to its emphasis on population control and family planning solutions. (For accounts and different views, see Mauldin, et al. 1974; Tabbarah, 1975;

Concerned Demography, 1974). The "World Population Plan of Action," as finally adopted by the conference, viewed population variables as set in the context of socioeconomic development, and it stressed the integration of population growth and social and economic development. It declined to set targets for population growth, expectation of life, or family size; and while it supported "responsible parenthood," it also declined to set targets for implementing policies leading to such goals. More generally the plan, and the conference generally, chose to stress "development," de-emphasizing the concept of population control, and downgrading the urgency of the population explosion.

Thus the World Population Conference in Bucharest voiced a fair amount of skepticism about what had become conventional population explosion wisdom; it also voiced disenchantment with the cry for population policy and especially with population control as necessary prescriptions for dealing with world social and economic problems. There has been a sequence of "achievements" wherein numerous governments did in fact adopt national population policies. But the crowning world population policy achievement (which many expected to result from the conference) not only eluded its planners and pursuers; but its failure to materialize was so visible as to imply forthcoming reappraisals of both research and action—as well as of demographic theory and doctrine. In the long run this is sure to lead to new directions which can only prove fruitful for sharpening and adding to insights and understandings about populations, societies, and their interrelationships.

SUMMARY

In this concluding chapter we have examined population policies and tried to assess their promise and prospects generally and for the United States in particular. Although population policies relating to fertility and to international migration are most familiar, there have also been efforts to formulate, introduce, and implement policies regarding mortality, internal migration, and marriage. More generally, population composition and distribution is also a target for population policy.

Both before and immediately after World War II, the major thrust of population policy discussion and efforts was the attempt to stem the threat of population stagnation and decline, with regulation of international migration continuing as a long-standing objective. Declining rates of population growth were viewed in Europe and North America not only as serious economic and political concerns, but as a moral danger signal as well, and in some countries programs were developed to arrest the decline of fertility. In fact most countries of Europe experienced significant if brief baby booms during or immediately after World War II; but the actual role or effectiveness of deliberate policy and programs in these fertility booms is still challenged and debated.

Since 1950 major attention has been directed to the perils of continuing and rapid population growth. Very considerable efforts have been organized (a) to persuade individuals and governments of the dangers of such growth; (b) to introduce and promote ways to control this growth (in particular, this includes introduction of the concept and technologies of contraception); and (c) to persuade governments themselves to formulate, adopt, and implement policies and activities which will lower birth rates and control population growth. Many countries have indeed formally adopted such policies and sought to introduce and institutionalize the values, attitudes, knowledge and practices thought conducive to family limitation and population control. But many countries have resisted the adoption of formal population policies.

There does not appear to be a very clear-cut relationship between official population policies and the marriage and fertility behavior of individuals, couples, or groups. Thus, while the idea of population policy formulation and proposal is very highly developed and legitimated, in fact there is very little which can be called a national population policy in the United States. At the same time, the actual practice of fertility control is probably more extensive in the United States than in virtually any other country of the world, despite our failure to adopt a formal population control policy. Moreover, there are countries in which limitation of births by contraception or abortion is very extensive, while at the same time the country's official policy calls for increased fertility. Again, three of the very largest countries of the world (the United States, the Soviet Union, and Japan) have relatively moderate rates of natural increase which have experienced recent decline. But neither the United States nor the Soviet Union have formal population policies, and Japan has a mildly pronatalist policy.

We have little accurate information about trends of natural increase in Mainland China, nor do we have more than fragmentary details about population policy there. However, there are indications both of some formal policy favoring fertility control and of actual declines in birth rates in recent years. Brazil has no national population policy, and it is characterized by very high birth rate, low death rate, and very high rate of natural increase. India and Indonesia both have national policies and programs favoring fertility reduction; but both, so far, continue to have high rates of fertility and natural increase.

The recent revolutions in mortality, in access to knowledge and information, and in material aspirations and expectations have been taking place more or less simultaneously in most areas of the world. As these social, educational, and attitudinal trends and gains are consolidated, we may anticipate the eventual rationalization of family formation and institutionalization of intervention to control childbearing in all but the most remote societies. Something akin to population stabilization is likely to be attained in the most remote societies as well, though this may be a consequence of increasing mortality rather than control of fertility. But for most of the world's populations and societies, as knowledge is spread about fertility and its relationship to economic, social, and political factors, a significant degree of stabilization through fertility control seems a long-run likelihood—either with or without population policies. Population policies, however, will surely have bearing on the speed, smoothness, and comfort with which nations achieve stabilization, as well as on the ultimate sizes and levels of national and world populations.

Appendixes

Appendix A

Measuring and Comparing Population Size, Composition, and Change

In this appendix we present some techniques of quantitative description, measurement, and analysis of populations and their changes. The basic elements of modern demographic analysis are presented; their study should provide the reader with concepts and tools sufficient for reading and mastering the descriptions and analyses of the great majority of current demographic studies, articles, monographs, and texts.

COUNTS, RATIOS, AND FREQUENCY DISTRIBUTIONS

The most elementary quantitative representation of a population is simply the *total number of persons in that population.* And obviously, the most elementary quantitative representation of a society is the count of the number of persons in its population. We have already pointed to variations in population size; and we have mentioned some reasons why societies with small populations necessarily differ from societies with large populations, and why societies necessarily undergo changes as their populations grow in numbers.

The composition of a population with respect to two or more categories of some variable (sex, place of residence, age, and so forth) can be represented by *counts* of the number of persons belonging to each category. The set of such counts over all the exhaustive and mutually exclusive categories of a variable is usually called a *frequency distribution.* Frequency distributions and the measures derived from them yield much more detailed quantitative representations of population than do total counts. Finally, *ratios* involving population in their numerators, denominators, or both are very often used in describing and comparing populations.

We may illustrate counts, ratios, and frequency distributions by referring to Table A.1, which presents the size and some selected characteristics of the populations of New York and Wisconsin.

TABLE A.1 Size and Selected Characteristics of the Populations of New York and Wisconsin, 1970

	New York	*Wisconsin*
Area (sq. miles)	49,576	56,154
Total population	18,236,967	4,417,731
Population density per sq. mile	367.9	78.7
Males	8,715,339	2,167,373
Females	9,521,628	2,250,358
Sex ratio	91.5	96.3
Urban	15,602,486	2,910,418
Rural	2,634,481	1,507,313
Percent Distribution		
Total: all places	100.0	100.0
Urban	85.6	65.9
Rural nonfarm	13.4	24.7
Rural farm	1.0	9.4

Source: U.S. Bureau of the Census, Census of Population, 1970.

A glance at the *total populaton* of each state gives us our first basis for comparison: with 18.2 million in New York and 4.4 million in Wisconsin, the population of New York is about four times larger than that of Wisconsin. On the other hand, if we compare the land areas of the two states (about 49,600 square miles for New York and about 56,000 square miles for Wisconsin) we find that Wisconsin is somewhat larger than New York. The relationships between population and area are represented by *population density ratios* (the number of persons in the population divided by the number of areal units) and these are usually expressed as "population per square mile" or "population per square kilometer." Thus, in our data:

$$\text{New York population density} = \frac{18{,}236{,}967 = \text{total pop. of New York}}{49{,}576 = \text{total square miles in New York}} = 367.9 \text{ persons per square mile.}$$

This is compared to:

$$\text{Wisconsin population density} = \frac{4{,}417{,}731 = \text{total pop. of Wisconsin}}{56{,}154 = \text{total square miles in Wisconsin}} = 78.7 \text{ persons per square mile.}$$

It is clear that the population density of New York is almost five times that of Wisconsin.

The next figures, which classify and count the populations by sex, indicate that females are more numerous than males in both New York and Wisconsin. A somewhat more precise comparison between the two states is afforded by the *sex ratio,* computed as the ratio of males to females times some constant number, conventionaly 100 or 1,000. In the present case:

$$\text{New York sex ratio} = \frac{8{,}715{,}339 = \text{total males in New York}}{9{,}521{,}628 = \text{total females in New York}} \times 100 = 91.5 \text{ males per 100 females}$$

$$\text{Wisconsin sex ratio} = \frac{2{,}167{,}373 = \text{total males in Wisconsin}}{2{,}250{,}358 = \text{total females in Wisconsin}} \times 100 = 96.3 \text{ males per 100 females.}$$

Alternatively, a computation of the percentages of males and females in each of the respective states would provide another mode of description and comparison. From the data in Table A.1, we can compute the percentages of males in New York and Wisconsin as 47.8 percent and 49.1 percent respectively; their complements, of course, are the percentages of females—52.2 percent in New York and 50.9 percent in Wisconsin.

The table classifies places of residence according to three categories —urban, rural nonfarm, and rural farm—and gives the *frequency distribution* of each state's population by these categories. Thus, it is clear that some 15 million New Yorkers were urban residents in 1970, and, adding the counts of rural nonfarm and rural farm residents, that about 2.6 million lived in rural places. In Wisconsin, just under three million were urban and some 1.5 million were rural.

The rural population of New York exceeds that of Wisconsin in absolute numbers. Yet, looking at the percentage distribution of the populations of the two states by type of residence, it is clear that New York is overwhelmingly urban (with some 86 percent of the population residing in urban places), while Wisconsin is still partly rural (with 34 percent in rural places). Altogether, the percentage distributions by place of residence show that New York's population is about 86 percent urban, 13 percent rural nonfarm, and one percent rural farm, while Wisconsin's is about 66 percent urban, 25 percent rural nonfarm, and nine percent rural farm. Such percentage distributions, computed according to frequency distributions over sets of exhaustive and mutually exclusive population categories, are probably the most widely used quantitative representations in analytical studies of population.

In the sections that follow, we shall continue to see numerous examples of counts, ratios, absolute number distributions, and percentage distributions as quantitative representations of population size, structure, and composition. We proceed now to somewhat more specialized but still quite simple, quantitative representations.

COMPARISON OF DISTRIBUTIONS

For small-scale comparisons of frequency distributions or percentage distributions, it is possible and practical to make detailed component-by-component comparisons as we did in the place-of-residence distribution in the section above. However, for more extensive comparisons—for example, those involving a large number of populations or distributions over large numbers of categories—component-by-component comparisons quickly become unwieldy.

We shall describe two very different approaches to the summary comparison of distributions. The first uses measures of central tendency to summarize or characterize an entire frequency distribution. The second computes indexes that measure differences between pairs of distributions.

Measures of Central Tendency

The use and computation of measures of central tendency for comparing frequency distribution are discussed in most elementary statistics texts, and we will not repeat that material here. Some types of phenomena are easily measured on interval or numerical scales, while others must, with considerable difficulty, be differentiated and counted on ordinal (rank) or nominal (classificatory) scales. Age, weight, population density, and income are examples of the first (interval or numerical-scale) group; social status, occupational prestige, and academic diplomas and degrees may be measured on ordinal (rank) scales; and political identification, rural or urban residence, race, and marital status are examples of phenomena measurable on nominal (classificatory) scales only. And we may note that each of the respective scales has its own type of measure of central tendency.

Nominal scales: The mode. The appropriate indicator of central tendency for frequency distributions of variables measured on nominal scales (the variables of sex, race, region, and place of birth) is the *mode,* defined as the most frequent value. Thus, "urban" is the modal type of residence in Ohio, while "rural nonfarm" is the modal residence category in South Carolina.

Ordinal scales: The median. For frequency distributions of variables measured on ordinal scales (size of place, socioeconomic status, educational achievement, and occupational class) the most refined measure of central tendency available is the *median,* that value that divides a frequency distribution exactly in half. Thus, in Table A.2 we see that

TABLE A.2 Selected Characteristics of the Populations of New York and Wisconsin, 1970

	New York	*Wisconsin*
Median age	30.3	27.2
Median number of school years completed	12.1	12.1
Women aged 15–44		
Total	3,827,786	885,022
Ever-married	2,466,425	574,066
Percent ever-married	64.4	64.5
Number of live-born children	5,571,260	1,517,901
Per woman	1,455	1,715
Per ever-married woman	2,259	2,644

Source: U.S. Bureau of the Census, 1970.

the median age in 1970 was 30.3 years in New York and 27.2 years in Wisconsin. Similarly, the median number of school years completed among persons 25 years of age or older was 12.1 years in New York and 12.1 years in Wisconsin.

Interval scales: The mean. Frequency distributions for variables measured on interval scales (including age, income, number of hours worked, and number of liveborn children) are typically summarized and characterized using the arithmetic *mean,* or the average, as the measure of central tendency. Both "nominal variable" and "ordinal variable" measures of central tendency (mode, median) can also be used to summarize the distributions, but they are less refined than the mean. Table A.2 shows that the mean number of liveborn children for ever-married women age 15–44 was 2.26 in New York and 2.64 in Wisconsin.[1]

The Index of Dissimilarity

The comparison of distributions on the basis of measures of central tendency suffers from the discarding of information which is in the very nature of measures of central tendency. Thus, two very different frequency distributions with similar average, central, or modal values may be represented as essentially similar, as in the example of Table A.3. We can see that the use of medians or means to describe and compare the frequency distributions by educational achievement in Table A.3

TABLE A.3 Hypothetical Examples of Three Populations: Percent Distributions by Number of School Years Completed

School Years Completed	*Population A*	*Population B*	*Population C*
Total	100	100	100
0	20	10	30
1–4	20	20	15
5–8	20	40	10
9–12	20	20	15
13+	20	10	30
Median	6.5	6.5	6.5

would obscure the differences between the three hypothetical populations. For this reason, indexes of differences between entire distributions, such as indexes of concentration, indexes of segregation, and indexes of dissimilarity, are very often used to characterize and measure differences

[1] Note that this mean number of live-born children is equivalent to the ratio of live-born children per ever-married women aged 15–44 in 1960:

$$\text{Children per woman ratio} = \frac{\text{Total number live-born children for women aged 15–44}}{\text{Total number ever-married women aged 15–44}}.$$

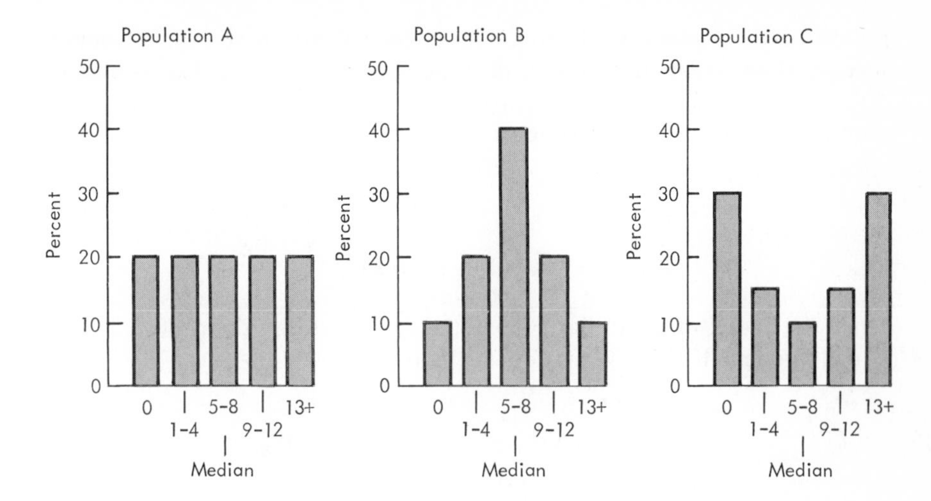

between distributions. Such indexes enjoy certain basic conceptual and computational similarities, and we shall confine our discussion here to what is currently the most widely used index of this form, the index of dissimilarity.

The *index of dissimilarity* measures the differences between two relative (proportional or percentage) distributions over a given set of categories by (a) summing over all categories the absolute values of the differences between the relative frequencies in each category, and then (b) halving that sum, so that the index will take a value between 0 and 1 or between 0 and 100 percent. Thus, comparing the urban-rural distributions of New York and Wisconsin given in Table A.1, the com-

WORKSHEET A Computation of the Index of Dissimilarity for Table A.1

	New York		*Wisconsin*		*Absolute*
Total	*Category Code* a_i	*Percent Distribution*	*Category Code* b_i	*Percent Distribution*	*Value of Difference* $\lvert a_i - b_i \rvert$
Urban	a_1	85.6	b_1	65.9	19.7
Rural nonfarm	a_2	13.4	b_2	24.7	11.3
Rural farm	a_3	1.0	b_3	9.4	8.4

$$\sum_{i=1}^{3} \lvert a_i - b_i \rvert = 39.4$$

$$\text{Index of Dissimilarity} = \Delta a,b = \tfrac{1}{2} \sum_{i=1}^{3} \lvert a_i - b_i \rvert = \tfrac{1}{2}(39.4) = 19.7\%$$

putation of the index of dissimilarity is carried out as shown in Worksheet A. The Summation sign Σ indicates that the absolute values of the differences $a - b$ are to be summed over all values of the subscript i beginning with $i - 1$ and through $i = 3$ inclusive:

$$\sum_{i=1}^{3} |a_i - b_i| = |a_1 - b_1| + |a_2 - b_2| + |a_3 - b_3| =$$
$$19.7 + 11.3 + 8.4 = 39.4$$

Since the index of dissimilarity denoted $\Delta\ a,b$ (read: "delta of *a*, *b*") is equal to one-half this summation, its value is

$$\Delta a,b = \tfrac{1}{2} \sum_{i=1}^{3} |a_i - b_i| = \tfrac{1}{2}\ (39.4) = 19.7$$

Put as simply as possible, the index of dissimilarity indicates the minimum proportion in one or the other population which would have to change categories in order for the two distributions to be identical. Thus, in the case at hand, the value of the index of dissimilarity between the urban-rural distributions of New York and Wisconsin is 19.7 percent (see bottom of the worksheet), interpreted as indicating that a minimum of 19.7 percent of *one* of the populations would have to move to a different type of residence in order for the two distributions to be identical.

Indexes of dissimilarity find their most extensive use in situations where large numbers of distributions must be compared either to one another or to some single standard distribution, or where large numbers of comparisons between pairs of distributions are in order.

MORTALITY ANALYSIS

Crude Death Rate

The simplest measure of the frequency of deaths in a population in a given time interval is the *crude death rate.* This is the ratio of the number of deaths in the population during the interval to the average population exposed to risk of death in that interval, multiplied by 1,000. The rate is conventionally computed with reference to single-year intervals. And the number of persons exposed to death is calculated by taking the average of that interval's fluctuating numbers. Thus:

$$\text{Crude death rate} = \frac{\text{Deaths in the population during the year}}{\text{Average population size during the year}} \times 1{,}000$$

or, alternatively:

$$\text{Crude death rate} = \frac{\text{Deaths in the population during the year}}{\text{Midyear population size}} \times 1{,}000.$$

The alternative is generally used because the midyear population is easier to obtain than the average population and is accepted as a good enough approximation of the average population. The crude death rate measures the number of deaths in a year per 1,000 persons in the population being studied.

Using the data in Table A.4, we can compute crude death rates in

TABLE A.4 Estimated Midyear Population and Total Marriages, Births, Deaths, and Infant Deaths for the United States, 1915, 1935, 1955, 1968, and 1969

	Estimated July 1 Population[a]	*Marriages*	*Births*	*Deaths*	*Infant Deaths*
1915	100,549,000	1,008,000	2,965,000	1,327,000[b]	296,000[b]
1935	127,250,000	1,327,000	2,377,000	1,393,000	120,000
1955	165,069,000	1,531,000	4,104,000	1,529,000	107,000
1968	199,870,000	2,059,000	3,502,000	1,923,000	76,000
1969	201,921,000	2,146,000	3,571,000	1,916,000	75,000

Source: U.S. Bureau of the Census 1970, tables 2 and 53.
[a] Total resident population
[b] Estimates

the United States for the years 1915, 1935, 1955, 1968, and 1969. These are as follows:

$$1915: \frac{1{,}327{,}000}{100{,}549{,}000} \times 1{,}000 = 13.2 \text{ per } 1{,}000$$

$$1935: \frac{1{,}393{,}000}{127{,}250{,}000} \times 1{,}000 = 10.9 \text{ per } 1{,}000$$

$$1955: \frac{1{,}529{,}000}{165{,}069{,}000} \times 1{,}000 = 9.3 \text{ per } 1{,}000$$

$$1968: \frac{1{,}923{,}000}{199{,}870{,}000} \times 1{,}000 = 9.6 \text{ per } 1{,}000$$

$$1969: \frac{1{,}916{,}000}{201{,}921{,}000} \times 1{,}000 = 9.5 \text{ per } 1{,}000.$$

It is obvious that crude death rates may vary considerably over different populations or in the same population in different years. Indeed, they may also vary among different subgroups or categories within a single population. We can always compute category-specific death rates as we do the crude death rate, using the ratio of the number of deaths in the category to the average number of persons in that category during the year. Thus:

$$\text{Category-specific death rate} = \frac{\text{Deaths of persons in the given category}}{\text{Average or midyear population in the given category}} \times 1{,}000.$$

Age-Specific Death Rates

Age-specific death rates are almost always computed separately for males and females. The set of age-specific death rates (for instance, the male and female age-specific death rates for ages 0, 1, 2, . . . , or for age intervals 0–4, 5–9, 10–14, . . .) observed in a population for a given year is called the schedule of age-specific death rates, or the *mortality schedule*. This schedule is the most commonly used detailed representation of mortality conditions obtaining in given populations in given years.

Estimates of the midyear population of the United States by sex and age for 1967 are given in Table A.5. These are the denominators for computation of age-specific death rates. Numbers of deaths to white and nonwhite males in each age group in 1967—the numerators for computation of white and nonwhite male age-specific death rates—are shown in Table A.6.

Age-specific death rates in 1967 for United States males by color are given in Table A.6, and the pattern of age and color differences is shown in Figure A.1. The death rate drops sharply after the first year of age and begins to climb again between ages 15 and 19. Death rates of nonwhites are consistently higher than those of whites until ages 70 to 74. From ages 75 to 79 and over, death rates of white males substantially exceed those of nonwhite males.

Infant mortality rate. A special age-specific death rate is the infant mortality rate. It commands particular interest both because of its magnitude relative to other age-specific death rates and because of its great sensitivity to socioeconomic conditions obtaining in the community. Since infant deaths tend to be highly concentrated in the interval just after birth, the denominator of the infant mortality rate is convention-

TABLE A.5 Estimates of Total Resident U.S. Population by Age, Color, and Sex, July 1, 1967

Age	*Total*			*White*			*Nonwhite*		
	Both sexes	*Male*	*Female*	*Both sexes*	*Male*	*Female*	*Both sexes*	*Male*	*Female*
Total: all ages	197,863,000	96,694,000	101,169,000	173,920,000	85,127,000	88,793,000	23,942,000	11,567,000	12,376,000
0–1	3,539,000	1,806,000	1,733,000	2,933,000	1,501,000	1,432,000	607,000	306,000	301,000
1–4	15,652,000	7,989,000	7,664,000	13,084,000	6,695,000	6,390,000	2,567,000	1,293,000	1,274,000
5–9	20,910,000	10,642,000	10,268,000	17,771,000	9,071,000	8,700,000	3,139,000	1,571,000	1,568,000
10–14	19,885,000	10,101,000	9,784,000	17,074,000	8,696,000	8,378,000	2,811,000	1,405,000	1,406,000
15–19	17,693,000	8,909,000	8,784,000	15,325,000	7,732,000	7,592,000	2,368,000	1,176,000	1,192,000
20–24	14,572,000	7,042,000	7,530,000	12,817,000	6,202,000	6,616,000	1,754,000	840,000	914,000
25–29	11,958,000	5,875,000	6,083,000	10,531,000	5,202,000	5,329,000	1,427,000	673,000	753,000
30–34	10,860,000	5,323,000	5,538,000	9,561,000	4,721,000	4,839,000	1,300,000	601,000	699,000
35–39	11,506,000	5,609,000	5,897,000	10,173,000	5,002,000	5,172,000	1,333,000	607,000	725,000
40–44	12,332,000	5,992,000	6,340,000	11,005,000	5,378,000	5,627,000	1,327,000	614,000	713,000
45–49	11,816,000	5,719,000	6,096,000	10,625,000	5,161,000	5,464,000	1,190,000	558,000	632,000
50–54	10,772,000	5,217,000	5,556,000	9,724,000	4,723,000	5,001,000	1,049,000	494,000	555,000
55–59	9,524,000	4,572,000	4,951,000	8,642,000	4,153,000	4,484,000	881,000	419,000	462,000
60–64	8,048,000	3,798,000	4,250,000	7,327,000	3,452,000	3,875,000	721,000	346,000	374,000
65–69	6,501,000	2,958,000	3,543,000	5,983,000	2,714,000	3,269,000	518,000	244,000	274,000
70–74	5,177,000	2,236,000	2,941,000	4,793,000	2,067,000	2,726,000	384,000	169,000	214,000
75–79	3,785,000	1,587,000	2,198,000	3,500,000	1,462,000	2,038,000	285,000	125,000	160,000
80–84	2,160,000	874,000	1,286,000	1,995,000	800,000	1,195,000	165,000	74,000	91,000
85 and over	1,174,000	446,000	727,000	1,057,000	396,000	661,000	116,000	50,000	66,000

Source: *U.S. Bureau of the Census,* **Vital Statistics of the United States,** *1967, Vol. I, Natality Table 3-2.*

TABLE A.6 Male Deaths and Death Rates by Age and Color, United States, 1967

Age	*Total*		*White*		*Nonwhite*	
	Number	*Rate*	*Number*	*Rate*	*Number*	*Rate*
Total	1,045,945	.010817	919,514	.010802	126,431	.010930
0–1	45,442	.025162	33,565	.022362	11,877	.038814
1–4	7,651	.000958	5,687	.000849	1,964	.001519
5–9	5,191	.000488	4,158	.000458	1,033	.000658
10–14	5,170	.000512	4,243	.000488	927	.000660
15–19	13,047	.001464	10,839	.001402	2,208	.001878
20–24	14,138	.002008	11,348	.001830	2,790	.003321
25–29	11,217	.001909	8,376	.001610	2,841	.004221
30–34	11,701	.002198	8,449	.001790	3,252	.005411
35–39	17,472	.003115	13,179	.002635	4,293	.007072
40–44	28,273	.004718	22,171	.004123	6,102	.009938
45–49	42,771	.007478	35,368	.006853	7,403	.013267
50–54	62,592	.011998	53,106	.011244	9,486	.019202
55–59	85,994	.018809	74,608	.017965	11,386	.027174
60–64	106,492	.028039	94,252	.027304	12,240	.035376
65–69	122,632	.041458	108,534	.039990	14,098	.057543
70–74	138,250	.061829	125,434	.060684	12,816	.075834
75–79	132,744	.083645	123,104	.084202	9,640	.077120
80–84	103,919	.118900	97,690	.122113	6,229	.084176
85+	90,906	.203825	85,191	.215129	5,715	.114300
Age Unknown	343	—	212	—	131	—

Source: U.S. Bureau of the Census, Vital Statistics of the United States, *1967, Vol. II, Part A, tables 1–8 and 1–25.*

ally taken as the number of births during the year. The numerator, which corresponds to those of other age-specific death rates, is restricted to the first year of life, since in this case the category of "infant" is defined as including all ages below the age of one year. Thus:

$$\text{Infant mortality rate} = \frac{\text{Number of deaths of infants under one year of age in the year}}{\text{Number of births in the year}} \times 1{,}000.$$

Table A.4 provides us with the data we need for computing U.S. infant mortality rates for 1915, 1935, 1955, 1968, and 1969:

$$1915: \frac{296{,}000}{2{,}965{,}000} \times 1{,}000 = 99.8 \text{ per thousand}$$

$$1935: \frac{120{,}000}{2{,}377{,}000} \times 1{,}000 = 50.5 \text{ per thousand}$$

$$1955: \frac{107{,}000}{4{,}104{,}000} \times 1{,}000 = 26.1 \text{ per thousand}$$

$$1968: \frac{76{,}000}{3{,}502{,}000} \times 1{,}000 = 21.7 \text{ per thousand}$$

$$1969: \frac{75{,}000}{3{,}571{,}000} \times 1{,}000 = 21.0 \text{ per thousand.}$$

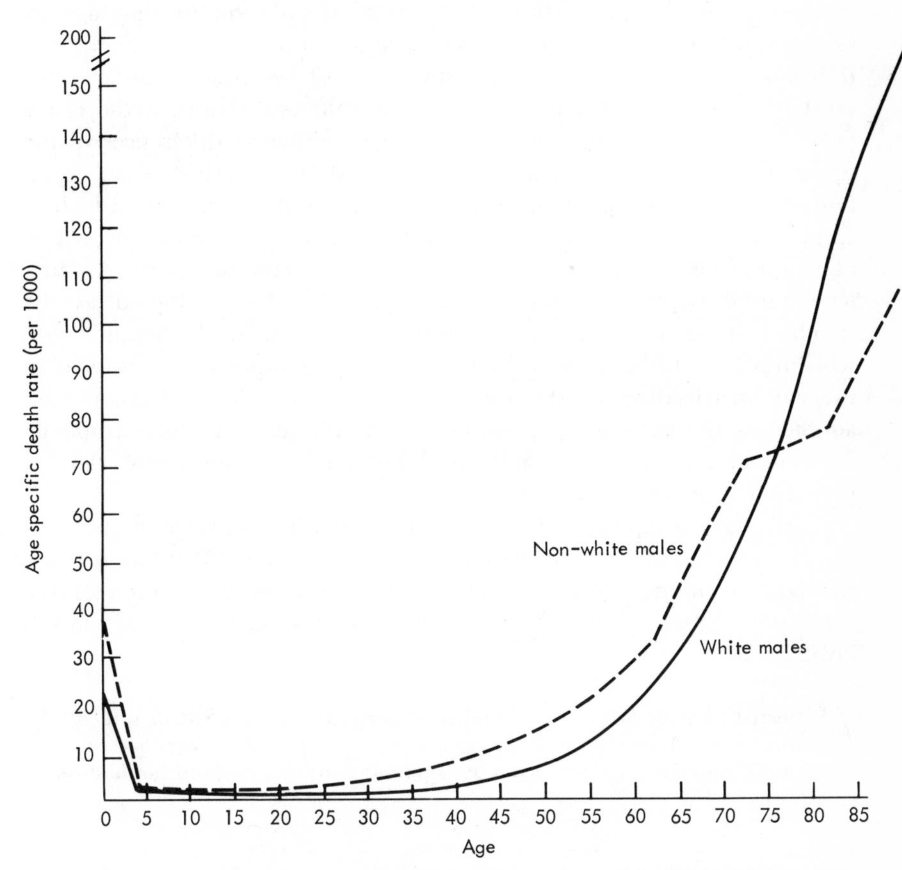

Figure A.1 Age-specific death rates for males, white and nonwhite, United States, 1967.

Standardization

We very often wish to compare mortality conditions in two different populations or in the same population at two different times. If the schedule of age-specific death rates is known for each of the communities, it is possible to compare the communities by comparing their age-specific death rates for each age-sex category. But the comparison of complete mortality schedules tends to be very detailed and awkward.

Comparison of crude death rates for two communities does enable the researcher to make some inferences about comparative mortality conditions in the respective communities. However, careful analysis of the relationship between the schedule of age-specific death rates and the crude death rate indicates that while the crude death rate is, in fact, an average of the various age-specific death rates, it weights each age-specific death rate by the proportion of the total population in that age-sex category. Thus, *the crude death rate measures the overall death rate as it is affected jointly by the age distribution of the population and the mortality schedule.* As a consequence, the difference between the crude death rates of two communities may be due either to differences in the schedules of age-specific death rates, or to differences in the age composition of the two populations, or to both. *Standardization,* which is employed quite extensively in demographic studies, controls the effects of composition by applying a schedule of specific rates to a corresponding schedule of population characteristics that has been adopted as the standard for a particular comparison. For example, if the mortality schedules for United States urban and rural populations were applied to the age distribution of the total population (the latter having been adopted as the standard population), standardized death rates could be determined for the urban and rural populations respectively. An explanation of this procedure follows.

We first compute and sum for all ages the "expected number of deaths" which *would* occur at each age in the standard population if the standard population were subject to the age-specific death rates of the given population. This computation and summation is done in the following way:

$$\begin{pmatrix}\text{Expected number of}\\ \text{deaths at ages 0–4 in}\\ \text{standard population}\end{pmatrix} = \begin{pmatrix}\text{Number of persons}\\ \text{aged 0–4 in}\\ \text{standard population}\end{pmatrix} \times \begin{pmatrix}\text{Death rate at}\\ \text{ages 0–4 in}\\ \text{given population}\end{pmatrix}$$

$$\begin{array}{ccccc} \bullet & = & \bullet & \times & \bullet \\ \bullet & = & \bullet & \times & \bullet \\ \bullet & = & \bullet & \times & \bullet \\ \bullet & = & \bullet & \times & \bullet \end{array}$$

$$\begin{pmatrix}\text{Expected number of}\\ \text{deaths, at ages 85 and}\\ \text{over, in standard}\\ \text{population}\end{pmatrix} = \begin{pmatrix}\text{Number of persons}\\ \text{aged 85 and over in}\\ \text{standard population}\end{pmatrix} \times \begin{pmatrix}\text{Death rate at ages}\\ \text{85 and over in}\\ \text{given population}\end{pmatrix}$$

Total expected number of deaths at all ages in standard population if subject to the schedule of age-specific death rates in the given population

We can now determine the *age-standardized death rate* of the given population. The death rate is the product of the crude death rate of the standard population times an adjustment factor consisting of the ratio of (a) the total expected number of deaths in the standard population if subject to the age-specific death rates of the given population, and (b) the total actual number of deaths in the standard population:

$$\begin{pmatrix}\text{Age-standardized}\\ \text{death rate for}\\ \text{given population}\end{pmatrix} = \begin{pmatrix}\text{Crude death rate}\\ \text{of standard}\\ \text{population}\end{pmatrix} \times \frac{\begin{pmatrix}\text{Total expected number}\\ \text{of deaths in standard}\\ \text{population if subject}\\ \text{to the schedule of}\\ \text{age-specific death rates}\\ \text{of given population}\end{pmatrix}}{\begin{pmatrix}\text{Total actual number}\\ \text{of deaths in standard}\\ \text{population}\end{pmatrix}}$$

The comparison of two age-standardized death rates entails the following computations:

$$\begin{pmatrix}\text{Age-standardized}\\ \text{death rate for first}\\ \text{given population}\end{pmatrix} = \begin{pmatrix}\text{Crude death rate}\\ \text{of standard}\\ \text{population}\end{pmatrix} \times \frac{\begin{pmatrix}\text{Total expected deaths in}\\ \text{standard population if}\\ \text{subject to age-specific}\\ \text{death rates of first}\\ \text{given population}\end{pmatrix}}{\begin{pmatrix}\text{Total actual number of}\\ \text{deaths in standard}\\ \text{population}\end{pmatrix}}$$

and

$$\begin{pmatrix}\text{Age-standardized}\\ \text{death rate for second}\\ \text{given population}\end{pmatrix} = \begin{pmatrix}\text{Crude death rate}\\ \text{of standard}\\ \text{population}\end{pmatrix} \times \frac{\begin{pmatrix}\text{Total expected deaths in}\\ \text{standard population if}\\ \text{subject to age-specific}\\ \text{death rates of second}\\ \text{given population}\end{pmatrix}}{\begin{pmatrix}\text{Total actual number of}\\ \text{deaths in standard}\\ \text{population}\end{pmatrix}}$$

Since (crude death rate of standard population) has in its numerator (total actual number of deaths in standard population), it is equivalent and simpler to write the equation as follows:

$$\begin{pmatrix}\text{Age-standardized}\\ \text{death rate for}\\ \text{given population}\end{pmatrix} = \frac{\begin{pmatrix}\text{Total expected deaths in standard}\\ \text{population if subject to age-specific}\\ \text{death rates of given population}\end{pmatrix}}{(\text{Total standard population})}.$$

TABLE A.7 Computation of Standardized Death Rates for White and Nonwhite Males, United States, 1967

Age *(1)*	*Standard Population, Total U.S. Males, July 1, 1967* *(2)*	*White Male Age-Specific Death Rates, 1967* *(3)*	*Column (2) × Column (3) Expected Deaths in Standard Population on Basis of White Male Rates* *(4)*	*Nonwhite Male Age-Specific Death Rates, 1967* *(5)*	*Column (2) × Column (5) Expected Deaths in Standard Population on Basis of Nonwhite Male Rates* *(6)*
0–1	1,806,000	.022362	40,386	.038814	70,098
1–4	7,988,000	.000849	6,783	.001519	12,135
5–9	10,642,000	.000548	4,874	.000658	7,002
10–14	10,101,000	.000488	4,929	.000660	6,667
15–19	8,909,000	.001402	12,490	.001878	16,731
20–24	7,042,000	.001830	12,887	.003321	23,386
25–29	5,875,000	.001610	9,459	.004221	24,798
30–34	5,323,000	.001790	9,528	.005411	28,803
35–39	5,609,000	.002635	14,780	.007072	39,667
40–44	5,992,000	.004123	24,705	.009938	59,548
45–49	5,719,000	.006853	39,192	.013267	75,874
50–54	5,217,000	.011244	58,660	.019202	100,177
55–59	4,572,000	.017965	82,136	.027174	124,240
60–64	3,798,000	.027304	103,701	.035376	134,358
65–69	2,958,000	.039990	118,290	.057543	170,212
70–74	2,236,000	.060684	135,689	.075834	169,565
75–79	1,587,000	.084202	133,629	.077120	122,389
80–84	874,000	.122113	106,726	.084176	73,570
85+	446,000	.215129	95,948	.114300	50,978
Total: all ages	96,695,000		1,014,793		1,310,198

$$\text{White Male Standardized Death Rate} = \frac{\sum [\text{column (4)}]}{\sum [\text{column (2)}]} \times 1{,}000 = \frac{1{,}014{,}793}{96{,}695{,}000} \times 1{,}000 = 10.495$$

$$\text{Nonwhite Male Standardized Death Rate} = \frac{\sum [\text{column (6)}]}{\sum [\text{column (2)}]} \times 1{,}000 = \frac{1{,}310{,}198}{96{,}695{,}000} \times 1{,}000 = 13.558$$

Source: Figures in column (2) from our table A.5; figures in columns (3) and (5) from our table A.6.

This is done in the computation of Table A.7, which uses age-standardized death rates to compare white and nonwhite male mortality in the United States in 1967. Taking the total male population of 1967 as the standard population, the standardized death rates for white and nonwhite males are 10.5 per thousand and 13.6 per thousand respectively.

The symbols at the bottom of Table A.7 of the form

$$\frac{\sum \text{[column (4)]}}{\sum \text{[column (2)]}}$$

mean:

$$\frac{\text{Summation of all the values in column (4)}}{\text{Summation of all the values in column (2)}},$$

which equals:

$$\frac{40{,}386 + 6{,}783 + \ldots + 133{,}629 + 106{,}726 + 95{,}948}{1{,}806{,}000 + 7{,}988{,}000 + \ldots + 1{,}587{,}000 + 874{,}000 + 446{,}000}.$$

But these sums are themselves given at the bottoms of the respective columns:

$$\sum \text{[column (4)]} = 1{,}014{,}793$$

and

$$\sum \text{[column (2)]} = 96{,}695{,}000.$$

FERTILITY ANALYSIS

As in the measurement of mortality, the chief focus in the measurement of fertility is the frequency of incidence of a vital event (in this case births) among the population exposed to the risk of that event. Certain analogies to the measurement of mortality will be immediately evident in the measurement of fertility.

Crude Birth Rate and Crude Rate of Natural Increase

The simplest measure of fertility is the crude birth rate, which is thoroughly analogous to the crude death rate. Thus:

$$\text{Crude birth rate} = \frac{\text{Number of births during the year}}{\text{Average or midyear population}} \times 1{,}000.$$

Using data from Table A.4, we can compute crude birth rates for the United States for 1915, 1935, 1955, 1968, and 1969:

$$1915: \frac{2{,}965{,}000}{100{,}549{,}000} \times 1{,}000 = 29.5 \text{ per thousand}$$

$$1935: \frac{2{,}377{,}000}{127{,}250{,}000} \times 1{,}000 = 18.7 \text{ per thousand}$$

$$1955: \frac{4{,}104{,}000}{165{,}069{,}000} \times 1{,}000 = 24.9 \text{ per thousand}$$

$$1968: \frac{3{,}502{,}000}{199{,}870{,}000} \times 1{,}000 = 17.5 \text{ per thousand}$$

$$1969: \frac{3{,}571{,}000}{201{,}921{,}000} \times 1{,}000 = 17.7 \text{ per thousand.}$$

The difference between the crude birth rate and the crude death rate is called the *crude rate of natural increase* and is a widely used measure of population growth. In the previous section of this chapter we calculated the crude death rates in the United States for the same years as above, also using data from Table A.4. With these two sets of data—crude birth and crude death rates—we can compute crude rates of natural increase for the corresponding years:

1915: 16.3 per thousand
1935: 7.8 per thousand
1955: 15.6 per thousand
1968: 7.9 per thousand
1969: 8.2 per thousand.

General Fertility Rate

It is obvious, of course, that the entire population is not exposed to the risk of births. For example, a theoretical population composed entirely of males, very young girls, and very old women would be exposed to no risk at all. And a population including a large proportion of women of childbearing age would be exposed to substantially greater risk than one with a smaller proportion. This being the case, the measurement of fertility can be refined considerably by limiting the denominator to the population more directly exposed to risk, namely, the female population in the reproductive ages. Thus, we have a second simple rate, the *general fertility rate:*

$$\text{General fertility rate} = \frac{\text{Number of births during the year}}{\text{Midyear or average number of women in reproductive ages (usually 15–44 or 15–49)}} \times 1{,}000.$$

In 1967, the general fertility rate for American women aged 15 to 44 was 87.6 per thousand. (We determined the number of women in the age group from Table A.5; the number of births, from Table A.8.) Figure A.2 shows the trend of the United States general fertility rate and crude

TABLE A.8 Births by Age and Color of Mother, United States, 1967

Age of Mother	*Total*	*White*	*Nonwhite*
Total: all ages	3,520,959	2,922,502	598,547
Under 15	8,593	2,761	5,832
15–19	596,445	435,239	161,206
20–24	1,310,588	1,116,686	193,902
25–29	867,426	749,997	117,429
30–34	439,373	370,069	69,304
35–39	227,323	189,322	38,001
40–44	67,053	55,045	12,008
45–49	4,158	3,383	775

Source: U.S. Bureau of the Census, Vital Statistics of the United States, *1967 (1969a: Vol. I Natality).*

birth rate in the period 1935 to 1970. Note that the movements and changes are virtually parallel throughout the 35-year period.

Category-Specific Birth Rates

Although recent years have witnessed a certain amount of interest in male fertility rates, *category-specific birth rates* ordinarily refer only to the women in the categories in question. In other words, their denominators indicate only the number of women in that category.

Age-specific birth rates are the most commonly used of the category-specific birth rates. For example, the age-specific birth rate for women aged 20 to 24 would be:

$$\frac{\text{Births during the year to women aged 20–24}}{\text{Average or midyear number of women aged 20–24 in the population}} \times 1{,}000.$$

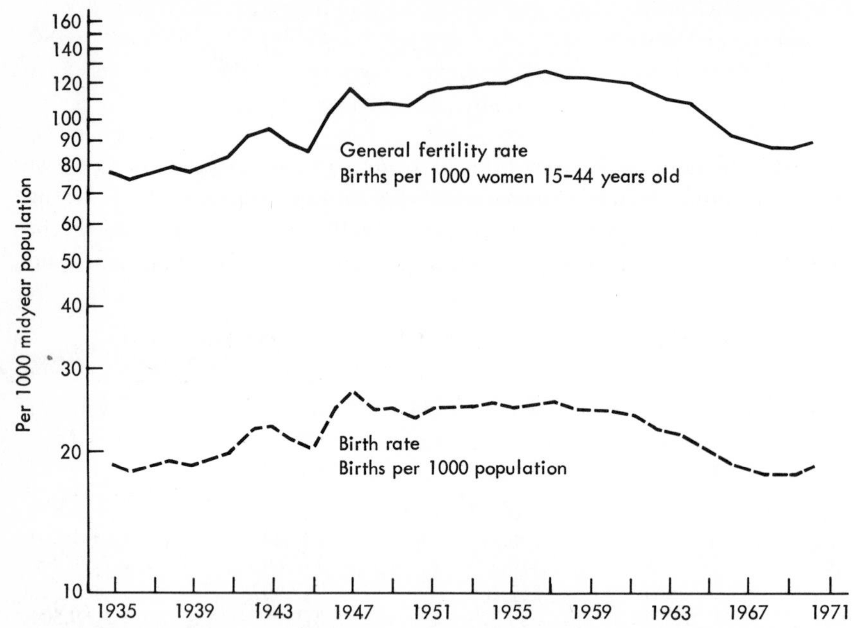

Figure A.2 U.S. annual crude birth rate and general fertility rate, 1935–1970. *Source: U.S. Bureau of the Census,* Current Population Reports, *"Population Estimates and Projections," Series P-25, no. 465 (Sept. 8, 1971) figure 2.*

Using data from Tables A.5 and A.8, we can determine age-specific fertility rates for all U.S. women in 1967:

Age	Rate per 1,000
10–14	0.9
15–19	67.9
20–24	174.0
25–29	142.6
30–34	79.3
35–39	38.5
40–44	10.6
45–49	0.7

A further refinement obviously is to compute age-specific birth rates for married women only. The *marital fertility rates* (or *legitimate fertility rates*) are calculated by dividing the number of children born to married women in each age group by the number of married women in each age group. Such rates are in fact routinely computed and used in fertility analyses in countries maintaining detailed estimates of the population by marital status (like France). Corresponding *illegitimate fertility rates* (number of children born to unmarried women in each age group divided by number of unmarried women in each age group) are also often computed. In the United States, the use of marital fertility rates has been severely restricted by the absence of appropriate statistics on marriage and marital status.

Age-specific birth rates and age-specific marital fertility rates for Poland around 1960 are shown in Figure A.3. Marital fertility rates are, of course, higher than the age-specific birth rates at all ages. For married women, the rate of fertility declines consistently with advancing age. Clearly the reason for the sharp climb in age-specific birth rates between ages 15 and 20 or 24 is that the proportion married among the total females increases sharply in this age range. Thus, comparison of curves

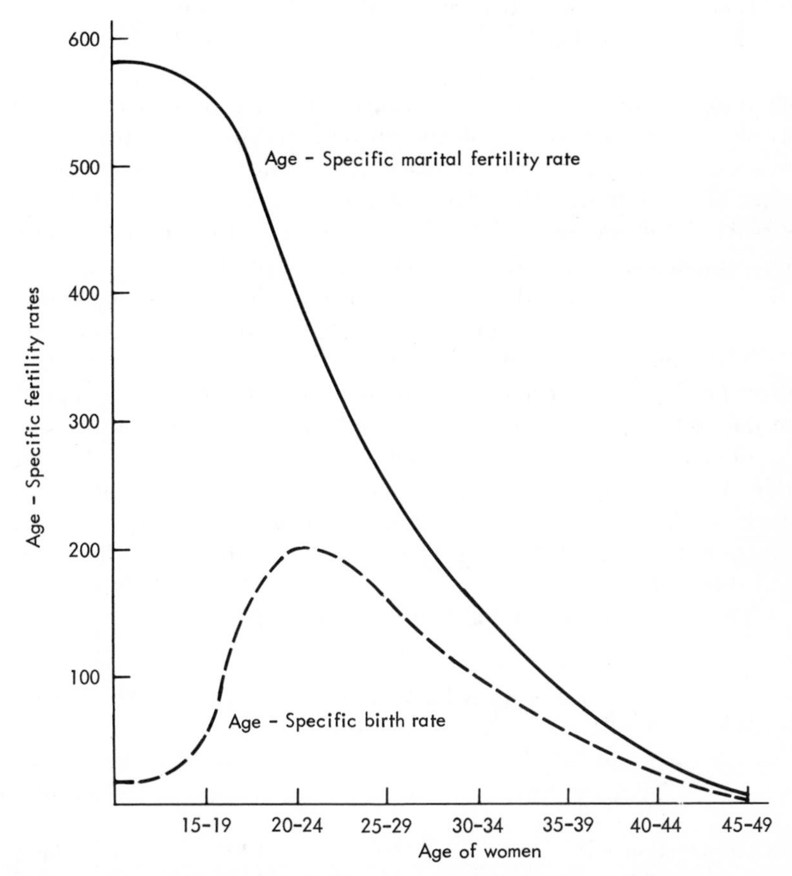

Figure A.3 Age-specific marital fertility rates (live births per 1,000 married women) and age-specific birth rates (births per 1,000 women in each age group), Poland, c. 1960. *Source: United Nations 1963b, p. 103; Berent 1970, p. 253.*

of age-specific birth rates for two populations may be confounding the effects of differences in proportions married at each age with differences in levels of fertility at each age.

Comparison of patterns of age-specific marital fertility rates may confound the effects of marriage with those of fertility levels only at the youngest ages—since large proportions of girls marrying at earliest ages are already pregnant at marriage, and, presumably, might well have remained single but for the fact of being pregnant. However, at most ages the comparison of marital fertility rates is free of effects other than actual marital fertility levels. Hence it is most satisfactory for fertility analysis where available.

Comparison of Fertility: Standardized Birth Rates and Reproduction Rates

The comparison of fertility conditions obtaining in two communities presents the same kinds of problems encountered in comparing mortality conditions. In particular, the comparison of crude birth rates presents the danger of confounding the effects of age-sex composition with those of the schedule of age-specific birth rates—precisely the pitfall inherent in comparing crude death rates. However, in a manner entirely analogous to the procedure described for age-standardized death rates, age-standardized birth rates can be computed and compared for two populations.

Two commonly employed summary measures of fertility are the *gross reproduction rate* and *net reproduction rate*. The gross reproduction rate, on which we shall concentrate here, is often interpreted as the ratio of mothers to daughters implied by the observed schedule of age-specific birth rates. The net reproduction rate is interpreted as the same ratio but takes into account the mortality conditions to which females in the population are subject up to and including their reproductive ages (see Table A.9).

The computations in Table A.9 adhere strictly to the definition of

TABLE A.9 Reproduction Rates for Women by Color, United States, 1967 (per 1,000 women)

	Total	*White*	*Nonwhite*
Gross reproduction rate	1,255	1,193	1,676
Net reproduction rate	1,213	1,158	1,582

Source: U.S. Bureau of the Census, Statistical Abstract of the United States, *1968.*

gross reproduction rate as the sum of the age-specific female birth rates (rate of births of daughters) over all childbearing ages. However, since the proportion of females among all births tends to be quite stable over time and with respect to the age of the mothers (about 0.485 of all children born are female, no matter what maternal age group is considered) the gross reproduction rate is usually computed as:

Proportion females among births ×
Sum of age-specific birth rates over all ages.

When computing the gross reproduction rate, age-specific birth rates given for five-year age groups (15–19, 20–24, etc.), are each assumed to be the same for each single age in every age group. The computation is:

(0.485 × (5) × $\sum$ (five-year age-group, age-specific birth rates) where the symbol $\sum$ means "summation".

The gross reproduction rate for all American women in 1967 is computed in the following way:

Age		Age-specific birth rate per woman
10–14		.0009
15–19		.0679
20–24		.1740
25–29		.1426
30–34		.0793
35–39		.0385
40–44		.0106
45–49		.0007
	Summation	0.5145

(5) × (Summation) = 2.5725.
(gross reproduction rate = (.485) × (5) × (Summation) = 1.248 (which is very slightly under the 1.255 rate given in Table A.9).

A measure called the *total fertility rate* is often used as a summary gauge of age-specific fertility rates. This rate is simply the summation of fertility rates (male and female births together) over all ages:

(5) × (Summation of five-year age-group fertility rates).

It can readily be seen that we have already computed the United States *total fertility rate* (TFR) for 1967 in the above example:

TFR = (5) × (Summation) = 2.5725.

Procedures for deriving the net reproduction rate and other refined measures of fertility, reproduction, and replacement of generations are given in more specialized texts and manuals.

Measures Based on Census or Survey Data Alone

The measures of fertility described so far are all based upon the numbers of registered births and cannot be used where births are not registered. There are, however, important measures of fertility which can be derived from census or population survey data, and these do not presuppose an effective system of birth registration. Of these, the simplest and most widely used is the *child-woman ratio,* a measure requiring only a detailed enumeration or estimate of the population by age and sex. It is defined in the following way:

$$\text{Child-woman ratio} = \frac{\text{Number of children under 5 years of age in population}}{\text{Number of women in reproductive ages (usually 15–44 or 15–49) in population}} \times 1{,}000.$$

Using data in Table A.5, we can compute the child-woman ratio for the United States in 1967 as is shown in Table A.10.

TABLE A.10 Child-Woman Ratios, United States, 1967

	Children Under 5 Years (1)	*Women 15–44 (2)*	*Child-Woman Ratio (per 1,000 women) (3)*
Total	19,191,000	40,172,000	477.7
White	16,017,000	35,175,000	455.4
Nonwhite	3,174,000	4,996,000	635.3

Finally, when census or survey data give numbers of children ever born to the women enumerated, the researcher can analyze the distribution of women by number of children ever born, both for women with completed fertility and for women with incomplete fertility (usually by age). Derivative measures, such as the proportion of childless women or the mean and median numbers of children ever born, can also be analyzed.

The various age-specific birth rates ordinarily have reference to different age groups of women all present in the population during the period in question. However, most of the measures can also be applied to the study of real cohorts of women—for example, women born in the same year or marrying in the same year. In *cohort fertility analysis,* the fertility of each cohort is measured in terms of successive ages or in terms of different durations of marriage, and the resulting analyses compares the fertility histories of women entering the fertile population at different times.

Appendix B

U.S. 1970 Census of Population and Housing Schedule

Page 1

This leaflet shows the content of the questionnaires being used in the 1970 Census of Population and Housing. See explanatory notes on the page 1 flap.

UNITED STATES CENSUS

This is your Official Census Form

Please fill it out and mail it back on Census Day, Wednesday, April 1, 1970

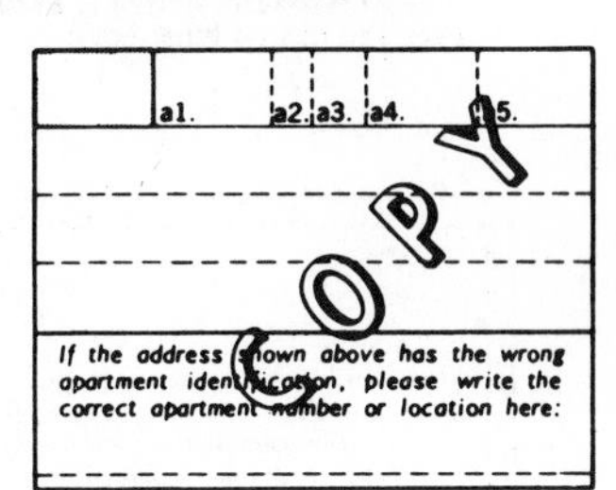

a1. a2. a3. a4. a5.

If the address shown above has the wrong apartment identification, please write the correct apartment number or location here:

How To Fill This Form

1. **Use a black pencil to answer the questions.**

   This form is read by an electronic computer. Black pencil is better to use than ballpoint or other pens.

   Fill circles "○" like this: ●

   The electronic computer reads every circle you fill. If you fill the wrong circle, erase the mark completely, then fill the right circle.

   When you write an answer, print or write clearly.

2. **See the filled-in example on the yellow instruction sheet.**

   This example shows how to fill circles and write in answers. If you are not sure of an answer, give the best answer you can.

   If you have a problem, look in the instruction sheet.

   All instructions are numbered the same as the questions on the Census form.

   If you need more help, call the Census office.

   You can get the number of the local office from telephone "Information" or "Directory assistance."

3. **Your answers are CONFIDENTIAL. The law (Title 13, United States Code) requires that you answer the questions to the best of your knowledge.**

   Your answers will be used only for statistical purposes and cannot, by law, be disclosed to any person outside the Census Bureau for any reason whatsoever.

   The householder should make sure that the information is shown for everyone here.

   If a boarder or roomer or anyone else prefers not to give the householder all his information to enter on the form, the householder should give at least his name, relationship, and sex in questions 1 to 3, then mail back the form. A Census Taker will call to get the rest of the information directly from the person.

4. **Check your answers. Then, mail back this form on Wednesday, April 1, or as soon afterward as you can. Use the enclosed envelope; no stamp is needed.**

   Your cooperation in carefully filling out the form and mailing it back will help make the census successful. It will save the government the expense of calling on you for the information.

U.S. Department of Commerce
Bureau of the Census
Form D-60

PLEASE CONTINUE

5. Answer the questions in this order:

Questions on page 2 about the people in your household.

Questions on page 3 about your house or apartment.

6. In Question 1 on page 2, please list each person who was living here on Wednesday, April 1, 1970, or who was staying or visiting here and had no other home.

EXPLANATORY NOTES

This leaflet shows the content of the 1970 census questionnaires. The content was determined after review of the 1960 census experience, extensive consultation with many government and private users of census data, and a series of experimental censuses in which various alternatives were tested.

Three questionnaires are being used in the census and each household has an equal chance of answering a particular form.

80 percent of the households answer a form containing only the questions on pages 2 and 3 of this leaflet.

15 percent and **5 percent** of the households answer forms which also contain the specified questions on the remaining pages of this leaflet. The 15-percent form does not show the 5-percent questions, and the 5-percent form does not show the 15-percent questions. On both forms, population questions 13 to 41 are repeated for each person in the household but questions 24 to 41 do not apply to children under 14 years of age.

The same sets of questions are used throughout the country, regardless of whether the census in a particular area is conducted by mail or house-to-house canvass. An illustrative example is enclosed with each questionnaire to help the householder complete the form.

80, 15, and 5 percent (100 percent)

Page 2

DO NOT MARK THIS COLUMN

1. WHAT IS THE NAME OF EACH PERSON who was living here on Wednesday, April 1, 1970 or who was staying or visiting here and had no other home?

Line No.

Print names in this order:
- *Head of the household*
- *Wife of head*
- *Unmarried children, oldest first*
- *Married childen and their families*
- *Other relatives of the head*
- *Persons not related to the head*

2. HOW IS EACH PERSON RELATED TO THE HEAD OF THIS HOUSEHOLD?

Fill one circle.

If "Other relative of head," also give exact relationship, for example, mother-in-law, brother, niece, grandson, etc.

If "Other not related to head," also give exact relationship, for example, partner, maid, etc.

Line No.	1. Name	2. Relationship
1	Last name / First name / Middle initial	○ Head of household ○ Wife of head ○ Son or daughter of head ○ Other relative of head—*Print exact relationship* → ○ Roomer, boarder, lodger ○ Patient or inmate ○ Other not related to head—*Print exact relationship*
2	Last name / First name / Middle initial	○ Head of household ○ Wife of head ○ Son or daughter of head ○ Other relative of head—*Print exact relationship* → ○ Roomer, boarder, lodger ○ Patient or inmate ○ Other not related to head—*Print exact relationship*
3	Last name / First name / Middle initial	○ Head of household ○ Wife of head ○ Son or daughter of head ○ Other relative of head—*Print exact relationship* → ○ Roomer, boarder, lodger ○ Patient or inmate ○ Other not related to head—*Print exact relationship*
4	Last name / First name / Middle initial	○ Head of household ○ Wife of head ○ Son or daughter of head ○ Other relative of head—*Print exact relationship* → ○ Roomer, boarder, lodger ○ Patient or inmate ○ Other not related to head—*Print exact relationship*
5	Last name / First name / Middle initial	○ Head of household ○ Wife of head ○ Son or daughter of head ○ Other relative of head—*Print exact relationship* → ○ Roomer, boarder, lodger ○ Patient or inmate ○ Other not related to head—*Print exact relationship*
6	Last name / First name / Middle initial	○ Head of household ○ Wife of head ○ Son or daughter of head ○ Other relative of head—*Print exact relationship* → ○ Roomer, boarder, lodger ○ Patient or inmate ○ Other not related to head—*Print exact relationship*
7	Last name / First name / Middle initial	○ Head of household ○ Wife of head ○ Son or daughter of head ○ Other relative of head—*Print exact relationship* → ○ Roomer, boarder, lodger ○ Patient or inmate ○ Other not related to head—*Print exact relationship*
8	Last name / First name / Middle initial	○ Head of household ○ Wife of head ○ Son or daughter of head ○ Other relative of head—*Print exact relationship* → ○ Roomer, boarder, lodger ○ Patient or inmate ○ Other not related to head—*Print exact relationship*

9. *If you used all 8 lines* **—Are there any other persons in this household?** ○ Yes ○ No
Do not list the others; we will call to get the information.

10. Did you leave anyone out of Question 1 because you were not sure if he should be listed—for example, a new baby still in the hospital, or a lodger who also has another home? ○ Yes ○ No
On back page, give name(s) and reason left out.

3. SEX *Fill one circle*	4. COLOR OR RACE *Fill one circle.* *If "Indian (American)," also give tribe.* *If "Other," also give race.*	DATE OF BIRTH 5. Month and year of birth and age last birthday *Print*	 6. Month of birth *Fill one circle*	 7. Year of birth *Fill one circle for first three numbers*	 *Fill one circle for last number*	8. WHAT IS EACH PERSON'S MARITAL STATUS? *Fill one circle*
Male ○ Female ○	○ White ○ Japanese ○ Hawaiian ○ Chinese ○ Korean ○ Negro or Black ○ Filipino ○ Other– *Print race* ○ Indian (Amer.) *Print tribe* →	Month ____ Year ____ Age ____	○ Jan.-Mar. ○ Apr.-June ○ July-Sept. ○ Oct.-Dec.	○ 186- ○ 192- ○ 187- ○ 193- ○ 188- ○ 194- ○ 189- ○ 195- ○ 190- ○ 196- ○ 191- ○ 197-	○ 0 ○ 5 ○ 1 ○ 6 ○ 2 ○ 7 ○ 3 ○ 8 ○ 4 ○ 9	○ Now married ○ Widowed ○ Divorced ○ Separated ○ Never married
Male ○ Female ○	○ White ○ Japanese ○ Hawaiian ○ Chinese ○ Korean ○ Negro or Black ○ Filipino ○ Other– *Print race* ○ Indian (Amer.) *Print tribe* →	Month ____ Year ____ Age ____	○ Jan.-Mar. ○ Apr.-June ○ July-Sept. ○ Oct.-Dec.	○ 186- ○ 192- ○ 187- ○ 193- ○ 188- ○ 194- ○ 189- ○ 195- ○ 190- ○ 196- ○ 191- ○ 197-	○ 0 ○ 5 ○ 1 ○ 6 ○ 2 ○ 7 ○ 3 ○ 8 ○ 4 ○ 9	○ Now married ○ Widowed ○ Divorced ○ Separated ○ Never married
Male ○ Female ○	○ White ○ Japanese ○ Hawaiian ○ Chinese ○ Korean ○ Negro or Black ○ Filipino ○ Other– *Print race* ○ Indian (Amer.) *Print tribe* →	Month ____ Year ____ Age ____	○ Jan.-Mar. ○ Apr.-June ○ July-Sept. ○ Oct.-Dec.	○ 186- ○ 192- ○ 187- ○ 193- ○ 188- ○ 194- ○ 189- ○ 195- ○ 190- ○ 196- ○ 191- ○ 197-	○ 0 ○ 5 ○ 1 ○ 6 ○ 2 ○ 7 ○ 3 ○ 8 ○ 4 ○ 9	○ Now married ○ Widowed ○ Divorced ○ Separated ○ Never married
Male ○ Female ○	○ White ○ Japanese ○ Hawaiian ○ Chinese ○ Korean ○ Negro or Black ○ Filipino ○ Other– *Print race* ○ Indian (Amer.) *Print tribe* →	Month ____ Year ____ Age ____	○ Jan.-Mar. ○ Apr.-June ○ July-Sept. ○ Oct.-Dec.	○ 186- ○ 192- ○ 187- ○ 193- ○ 188- ○ 194- ○ 189- ○ 195- ○ 190- ○ 196- ○ 191- ○ 197-	○ 0 ○ 5 ○ 1 ○ 6 ○ 2 ○ 7 ○ 3 ○ 8 ○ 4 ○ 9	○ Now married ○ Widowed ○ Divorced ○ Separated ○ Never married
Male ○ Female ○	○ White ○ Japanese ○ Hawaiian ○ Chinese ○ Korean ○ Negro or Black ○ Filipino ○ Other– *Print race* ○ Indian (Amer.) *Print tribe* →	Month ____ Year ____ Age ____	○ Jan.-Mar. ○ Apr.-June ○ July-Sept. ○ Oct.-Dec.	○ 186- ○ 192- ○ 187- ○ 193- ○ 188- ○ 194- ○ 189- ○ 195- ○ 190- ○ 196- ○ 191- ○ 197-	○ 0 ○ 5 ○ 1 ○ 6 ○ 2 ○ 7 ○ 3 ○ 8 ○ 4 ○ 9	○ Now married ○ Widowed ○ Divorced ○ Separated ○ Never married
Male ○ Female ○	○ White ○ Japanese ○ Hawaiian ○ Chinese ○ Korean ○ Negro or Black ○ Filipino ○ Other– *Print race* ○ Indian (Amer.) *Print tribe* →	Month ____ Year ____ Age ____	○ Jan.-Mar. ○ Apr.-June ○ July-Sept. ○ Oct.-Dec.	○ 186- ○ 192- ○ 187- ○ 193- ○ 188- ○ 194- ○ 189- ○ 195- ○ 190- ○ 196- ○ 191- ○ 197-	○ 0 ○ 5 ○ 1 ○ 6 ○ 2 ○ 7 ○ 3 ○ 8 ○ 4 ○ 9	○ Now married ○ Widowed ○ Divorced ○ Separated ○ Never married
Male ○ Female ○	○ White ○ Japanese ○ Hawaiian ○ Chinese ○ Korean ○ Negro or Black ○ Filipino ○ Other– *Print race* ○ Indian (Amer.) *Print tribe* →	Month ____ Year ____ Age ____	○ Jan.-Mar. ○ Apr.-June ○ July-Sept. ○ Oct.-Dec.	○ 186- ○ 192- ○ 187- ○ 193- ○ 188- ○ 194- ○ 189- ○ 195- ○ 190- ○ 196- ○ 191- ○ 197-	○ 0 ○ 5 ○ 1 ○ 6 ○ 2 ○ 7 ○ 3 ○ 8 ○ 4 ○ 9	○ Now married ○ Widowed ○ Divorced ○ Separated ○ Never married
Male ○ Female ○	○ White ○ Japanese ○ Hawaiian ○ Chinese ○ Korean ○ Negro or Black ○ Filipino ○ Other– *Print race* ○ Indian (Amer.) *Print tribe* →	Month ____ Year ____ Age ____	○ Jan.-Mar. ○ Apr.-June ○ July-Sept. ○ Oct.-Dec.	○ 186- ○ 192- ○ 187- ○ 193- ○ 188- ○ 194- ○ 189- ○ 195- ○ 190- ○ 196- ○ 191- ○ 197-	○ 0 ○ 5 ○ 1 ○ 6 ○ 2 ○ 7 ○ 3 ○ 8 ○ 4 ○ 9	○ Now married ○ Widowed ○ Divorced ○ Separated ○ Never married

Make no mark in this margin

Make no mark in this margin

11. Did you list anyone in Question 1 who is away from home now—for example, on a vacation or in a hospital?	○ Yes ○ No *On back page, give name(s) and reason person is away.*	12. Did anyone stay here on Tuesday, March 31, who is not already listed?	○ Yes No *On back page, give name of each visitor for whom there is no one at his home address to report him to a census taker.*

26:1

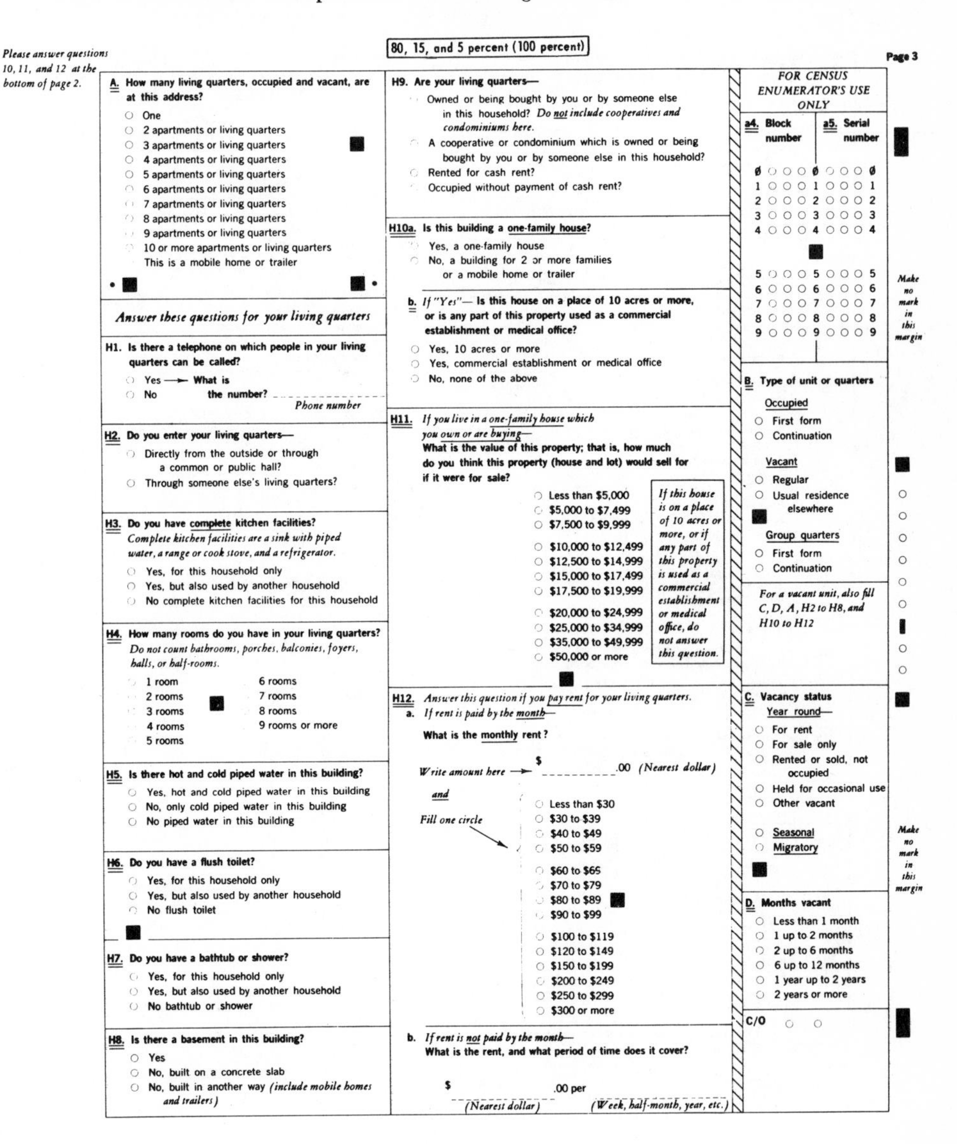

Please answer questions 10, 11, and 12 at the bottom of page 2.

80, 15, and 5 percent (100 percent)

Page 3

A. How many living quarters, occupied and vacant, are at this address?
- ○ One
- ○ 2 apartments or living quarters
- ○ 3 apartments or living quarters
- ○ 4 apartments or living quarters
- ○ 5 apartments or living quarters
- ○ 6 apartments or living quarters
- ○ 7 apartments or living quarters
- ○ 8 apartments or living quarters
- ○ 9 apartments or living quarters
- ○ 10 or more apartments or living quarters
- ○ This is a mobile home or trailer

Answer these questions for your living quarters

H1. Is there a telephone on which people in your living quarters can be called?
- ○ Yes → **What is the number?** ________ *Phone number*
- ○ No

H2. Do you enter your living quarters—
- ○ Directly from the outside or through a common or public hall?
- ○ Through someone else's living quarters?

H3. Do you have complete kitchen facilities?
Complete kitchen facilities are a sink with piped water, a range or cook stove, and a refrigerator.
- ○ Yes, for this household only
- ○ Yes, but also used by another household
- ○ No complete kitchen facilities for this household

H4. How many rooms do you have in your living quarters?
Do not count bathrooms, porches, balconies, foyers, halls, or half-rooms.
- ○ 1 room
- ○ 2 rooms
- ○ 3 rooms
- ○ 4 rooms
- ○ 5 rooms
- ○ 6 rooms
- ○ 7 rooms
- ○ 8 rooms
- ○ 9 rooms or more

H5. Is there hot and cold piped water in this building?
- ○ Yes, hot and cold piped water in this building
- ○ No, only cold piped water in this building
- ○ No piped water in this building

H6. Do you have a flush toilet?
- ○ Yes, for this household only
- ○ Yes, but also used by another household
- ○ No flush toilet

H7. Do you have a bathtub or shower?
- ○ Yes, for this household only
- ○ Yes, but also used by another household
- ○ No bathtub or shower

H8. Is there a basement in this building?
- ○ Yes
- ○ No, built on a concrete slab
- ○ No, built in another way *(include mobile homes and trailers)*

H9. Are your living quarters—
- ○ Owned or being bought by you or by someone else in this household? *Do not include cooperatives and condominiums here.*
- ○ A cooperative or condominium which is owned or being bought by you or by someone else in this household?
- ○ Rented for cash rent?
- ○ Occupied without payment of cash rent?

H10a. Is this building a one-family house?
- ○ Yes, a one-family house
- ○ No, a building for 2 or more families or a mobile home or trailer

b. *If "Yes"*— **Is this house on a place of 10 acres or more, or is any part of this property used as a commercial establishment or medical office?**
- ○ Yes, 10 acres or more
- ○ Yes, commercial establishment or medical office
- ○ No, none of the above

H11. *If you live in a one-family house which you own or are buying—*
What is the value of this property; that is, how much do you think this property (house and lot) would sell for if it were for sale?
- ○ Less than $5,000
- ○ $5,000 to $7,499
- ○ $7,500 to $9,999
- ○ $10,000 to $12,499
- ○ $12,500 to $14,999
- ○ $15,000 to $17,499
- ○ $17,500 to $19,999
- ○ $20,000 to $24,999
- ○ $25,000 to $34,999
- ○ $35,000 to $49,999
- ○ $50,000 or more

If this house is on a place of 10 acres or more, or if any part of this property is used as a commercial establishment or medical office, do not answer this question.

H12. *Answer this question if you pay rent for your living quarters.*
a. *If rent is paid by the month—*
What is the monthly rent?

Write amount here → $ ________.00 *(Nearest dollar)*

and

Fill one circle
- ○ Less than $30
- ○ $30 to $39
- ○ $40 to $49
- ○ $50 to $59
- ○ $60 to $69
- ○ $70 to $79
- ○ $80 to $89
- ○ $90 to $99
- ○ $100 to $119
- ○ $120 to $149
- ○ $150 to $199
- ○ $200 to $249
- ○ $250 to $299
- ○ $300 or more

b. *If rent is not paid by the month—*
What is the rent, and what period of time does it cover?

$ ________.00 per ________
(Nearest dollar) *(Week, half-month, year, etc.)*

FOR CENSUS ENUMERATOR'S USE ONLY

a4. Block number | **a5. Serial number**

Ø ○ ○ ○ Ø ○ ○ ○ Ø
1 ○ ○ ○ 1 ○ ○ ○ 1
2 ○ ○ ○ 2 ○ ○ ○ 2
3 ○ ○ ○ 3 ○ ○ ○ 3
4 ○ ○ ○ 4 ○ ○ ○ 4
5 ○ ○ ○ 5 ○ ○ ○ 5
6 ○ ○ ○ 6 ○ ○ ○ 6
7 ○ ○ ○ 7 ○ ○ ○ 7
8 ○ ○ ○ 8 ○ ○ ○ 8
9 ○ ○ ○ 9 ○ ○ ○ 9

B. Type of unit or quarters

Occupied
- ○ First form
- ○ Continuation

Vacant
- ○ Regular
- ○ Usual residence elsewhere

Group quarters
- ○ First form
- ○ Continuation

For a vacant unit, also fill C, D, A, H2 to H8, and H10 to H12

C. Vacancy status

Year round—
- ○ For rent
- ○ For sale only
- ○ Rented or sold, not occupied
- ○ Held for occasional use
- ○ Other vacant
- ○ Seasonal
- ○ Migratory

D. Months vacant
- ○ Less than 1 month
- ○ 1 up to 2 months
- ○ 2 up to 6 months
- ○ 6 up to 12 months
- ○ 1 year up to 2 years
- ○ 2 years or more

C/O ○ ○

Make no mark in this margin

Make no mark in this margin

Page 4

15 and 5 percent

H13. *Answer question H13 if you pay rent for your living quarters.*

In addition to the rent entered in H12, do you also pay for—

a. Electricity?
- ○ Yes, average monthly cost is → $ ______.00 *Average monthly cost*
- ○ No, included in rent
- ○ No, electricity not used

b. Gas?
- ○ Yes, average monthly cost is → $ ______.00 *Average monthly cost*
- ○ No, included in rent
- ○ No, gas not used

c. Water?
- ○ Yes, yearly cost is → $ ______.00 *Yearly cost*
- ○ No, included in rent or no charge

d. Oil, coal, kerosene, wood, etc.?
- ○ Yes, yearly cost is → $ ______.00 *Yearly cost*
- ○ No, included in rent
- ○ No, these fuels not used

H14. How are your living quarters heated?
Fill one circle for the kind of heat you use most.
- ○ Steam or hot water system
- ○ Central warm air furnace with ducts to the individual rooms, or central heat pump
- ○ Built-in electric units *(permanently installed in wall, ceiling, or baseboard)*
- ○ Floor, wall, or pipeless furnace
- ○ Room heaters with flue or vent, burning gas, oil, or kerosene
- ○ Room heaters without flue or vent, burning gas, oil, or kerosene *(not portable)*
- ○ Fireplaces, stoves, or portable room heaters of any kind
- In some other way—*Describe* → ______
- ○ None, unit has no heating equipment

H15. About when was this building originally built? *Mark when the building was first constructed, not when it was remodeled, added to, or converted.*
- ○ 1969 or 1970
- ○ 1965 to 1968
- ○ 1960 to 1964
- ○ 1950 to 1959
- ○ 1940 to 1949
- ○ 1939 or earlier

H16. Which best describes this building?
Include all apartments, flats, etc., even if vacant.
- ○ A one-family house detached from any other house
- ○ A one-family house attached to one or more houses
- ○ A building for 2 families
- ○ A building for 3 or 4 families
- ○ A building for 5 to 9 families
- ○ A building for 10 to 19 families
- ○ A building for 20 to 49 families
- ○ A building for 50 or more families
- ○ A mobile home or trailer
- Other—*Describe* ______

H17. Is this building—
- ○ On a city or suburban lot?— *Skip to H19*
- ○ On a place of less than 10 acres?
- ○ On a place of 10 acres or more?

H18. Last year, 1969, did sales of crops, livestock, and other farm products from this place amount to—
- ○ Less than $50 (or None)
- ○ $50 to $249
- ○ $250 to $2,499
- ○ $2,500 to $4,999
- ○ $5,000 to $9,999
- ○ $10,000 or more

15 percent

H19. Do you get water from—
- ○ A public system *(city water department, etc.)* or private company?
- ○ An individual well?
- ○ Some other source *(a spring, creek, river, cistern, etc.)*?

H20. Is this building connected to a public sewer?
- ○ Yes, connected to public sewer
- ○ No, connected to septic tank or cesspool
- ○ No, use other means

H21. How many bathrooms do you have?
A complete bathroom is a room with flush toilet, bathtub or shower, and wash basin with piped water.

A half bathroom has at least a flush toilet or bathtub or shower, but does not have all the facilities for a complete bathroom.
- ○ No bathroom, or only a half bathroom
- ○ 1 complete bathroom
- ○ 1 complete bathroom, plus half bath(s)
- ○ 2 complete bathrooms
- ○ 2 complete bathrooms, plus half bath(s)
- ○ 3 or more complete bathrooms

H22. Do you have air-conditioning?
- ○ Yes, 1 individual room unit
- ○ Yes, 2 or more individual room units
- ○ Yes, a central air-conditioning system
- ○ No

H23. How many passenger automobiles are owned or regularly used by members of your household?
Count company cars kept at home.
- ○ None
- ○ 1 automobile
- ○ 2 automobiles
- ○ 3 automobiles or more

The 15-percent form contains the questions shown on page 4. The 5-percent form contains the questions shown in the first column of page 4 and the questions on page 5.

H24a. How many stories (floors) are in this building?

- ○ 1 to 3 stories
- ○ 4 to 6 stories
- ○ 7 to 12 stories
- ○ 13 stories or more

b. *If 4 or more stories—*
Is there a passenger elevator in this building?

○ Yes ○ No

H25a. Which fuel is used most for cooking?

Gas — From underground pipes serving the neighborhood ○ / Bottled, tank, or LP ○
Electricity ○
Fuel oil, kerosene, etc. ○
Coal or coke ○
Wood ○
Other fuel ○
No fuel used ○

b. Which fuel is used most for house heating?

Gas — From underground pipes serving the neighborhood ○ / Bottled, tank, or LP ○
Electricity ○
Fuel oil, kerosene, etc. ○
Coal or coke ○
Wood ○
Other fuel ○
No fuel used ○

c. Which fuel is used most for water heating?

Gas — From underground pipes serving the neighborhood ○ / Bottled, tank, or LP ○
Electricity ○
Fuel oil, kerosene, etc. ○
Coal or coke ○
Wood ○
Other fuel ○
No fuel used ○

H26. How many bedrooms do you have?
Count rooms used mainly for sleeping even if used also for other purposes.

- ○ No bedroom
- ○ 1 bedroom
- ○ 2 bedrooms
- ○ 3 bedrooms
- ○ 4 bedrooms
- ○ 5 bedrooms or more

H27a. Do you have a clothes washing machine?

- ○ Yes, automatic or semi-automatic
- ○ Yes, wringer or separate spinner
- ○ No

b. Do you have a clothes dryer?

- ○ Yes, electrically heated
- ○ Yes, gas heated
- ○ No

c. Do you have a dishwasher *(built-in or portable)*?

○ Yes ○ No

d. Do you have a home food freezer which is separate from your refrigerator?

○ Yes ○ No

H28a. Do you have a television set? *Count only sets in working order.*

- ○ Yes, one set
- ○ Yes, two or more sets
- ○ No

b. *If "Yes"—* **Is any set equipped to receive UHF broadcasts, that is, channels 14 to 83?**

○ Yes ○ No

H29. Do you have a battery-operated radio?
Count car radios, transistors, and other battery-operated sets in working order or needing only a new battery for operation.

○ Yes, one or more ○ No

H30. Do you (or any member of your household) own a second home or other living quarters which you occupy sometime during the year?

○ Yes ○ No

5 percent

Page 6

The 15-percent and 5-percent forms contain a pair of facing pages for each person in the household (as listed on page 2). Shown on each pair of pages in the 15-percent form are the questions designated as 15-percent here on pages 6, 7, and 8. Shown on each pair of pages in the 5-percent form are the questions designated as 5-percent here on pages 6, 7, and 8.

Name of person on line (1) of page 2

Last name ______ First name ______ Initial

15 and 5 percent

13a. Where was this person born? *If born in hospital, give State or country where mother lived. If born outside U.S., see instruction sheet; distinguish Northern Ireland from Ireland (Eire).*

○ This State
OR
______ *(Name of State or foreign country; or Puerto Rico, Guam, etc.)*

5 percent

b. Is this person's origin or descent— *(Fill one circle)*

○ Mexican ○ Central or South American
○ Puerto Rican ○ Other Spanish
○ Cuban ○ No, none of these

15 percent

14. What country was his father born in?

○ United States
OR
______ *(Name of foreign country; or Puerto Rico, Guam, etc.)*

15. What country was his mother born in?

○ United States
OR
______ *(Name of foreign country; or Puerto Rico, Guam, etc.)*

5 percent

16. *For persons born in a foreign country—*

a. Is this person naturalized?

○ Yes, naturalized
○ No, alien
○ Born abroad of American parents

b. When did he come to the United States to stay?

○ 1965 to 70 ○ 1950 to 54 ○ 1925 to 34
○ 1960 to 64 ○ 1945 to 49 ○ 1915 to 24
○ 1955 to 59 ○ 1935 to 44 ○ Before 1915

15 percent

17. What language, other than English, was spoken in this person's home when he was a child? *Fill one circle.*

○ Spanish ○ Other— *Specify* ______
○ French
○ German ○ None, English only

18. When did this person move into this house (or apartment)? *Fill circle for date of last move.*

○ 1969 or 70 ○ 1965 or 66 ○ 1949 or earlier
○ 1968 ○ 1960 to 64 ○ Always lived in this house or apartment
○ 1967 ○ 1950 to 59

19a. Did he live in this house on April 1, 1965? *If in college or Armed Forces in April 1965, report place of residence there.*

○ Born April 1965 or later } *Skip to 20*
○ Yes, this house .... }
○ No, different house

b. Where did he live on April 1, 1965?

(1) State, foreign country, U.S. possession, etc. ______

(2) County ______

(3) Inside the limits of a city, town, village, etc.?
○ Yes ○ No

(4) *If "Yes,"* name of city, town, village, etc. ______

15 percent

20. Since February 1, 1970, has this person attended regular school or college at any time? *Count nursery school, kindergarten, and schooling which leads to an elementary school certificate, high school diploma, or college degree.*

○ No
○ Yes, public
○ Yes, parochial
○ Yes, other private

15 and 5 percent

21. What is the highest grade (or year) of regular school he has ever attended?

Fill one circle. If now attending, mark grade he is in.

○ Never attended school— *Skip to 23*
○ Nursery school
○ Kindergarten

Elementary through high school (grade or year)
1 2 3 4 5 6 7 8 9 10 11 12
○ ○ ○ ○ ○ ○ ○ ○ ○ ○ ○ ○

College (academic year)
1 2 3 4 5 6 or more
○ ○ ○ ○ ○ ○

22. Did he finish the highest grade (or year) he attended?

○ Now attending this grade (or year)
○ Finished this grade (or year)
○ Did not finish this grade (or year)

23. When was this person born?

○ Born before April 1956— *Please go on with questions 24 through 41.*

○ Born April 1956 or later— *Please omit questions 24 through 41 and go to the next page for the next person.*

5 percent

24. *If this person has ever been married—*

a. Has this person been married more than once?

○ Once ○ More than once

b. When did he get married? ______ *Month* ______ *Year*

When did he get married for the first time? ______ *Month* ______ *Year*

c. *If married more than once—* **Did the first marriage end because of the death of the husband (or wife)?**

○ Yes ○ No

15 and 5 percent

25. *If this is a girl or a woman—*
How many babies has she ever had, not counting stillbirths?
Do not count her stepchildren or children she has adopted.

1 2 3 4 5 6 7 8
○ ○ ○ ○ ○ ○ ○ ○
9 10 11 12 or more None
○ ○ ○ ○ ○

15 percent

26. *If this is a man—*

a. Has he ever served in the Army, Navy, or other Armed Forces of the United States?

○ Yes
○ No

b. Was it during— *(Fill the circle for each period of service.)*

Vietnam Conflict *(Since Aug. 1964)* .... ○
Korean War *(June 1950 to Jan. 1955)* .... ○
World War II *(Sept. 1940 to July 1947)* .... ○
World War I *(April 1917 to Nov. 1918)* .... ○
Any other time .... ○

5 percent

27a. Has this person ever completed a vocational training program? *For example, in high school; as apprentice; in school of business, nursing, or trades; technical institute; or Armed Forces schools.*

○ Yes ○ No— *Skip to 28*

b. What was his main field of vocational training? *Fill one circle.*

○ Business, office work
○ Nursing, other health fields
○ Trades and crafts *(mechanic, electrician, beautician, etc.)*
○ Engineering or science technician; draftsman
○ Agriculture or home economics
○ Other field– *Specify* ______

28a. Does this person have a health or physical condition which limits the kind or amount of work he can do at a job? *If 65 years old or over, skip to question 29.*

○ Yes
○ No

b. Does his health or physical condition keep him from holding any job at all?

○ Yes
○ No

c. *If "Yes" in a or b—* **How long has he been limited in his ability to work?**

○ Less than 6 months ○ 3 to 4 years
○ 6 to 11 months ○ 5 to 9 years
○ 1 to 2 years ○ 10 years or more

15 and 5 percent

QUESTIONS 29 THROUGH 41 ARE FOR ALL PERSONS BORN BEFORE APRIL 1956 INCLUDING HOUSEWIVES, STUDENTS, OR DISABLED PERSONS AS WELL AS PART-TIME OR FULL-TIME WORKERS

29a. Did this person work at any time last week?

○ Yes– *Fill this circle if this person did full- or part-time work. (Count part-time work such as a Saturday job, delivering papers, or helping without pay in a family business or farm; and active duty in the Armed Forces)*

○ No– *Fill this circle if this person did not work, or did only own housework, school work, or volunteer work.* *Skip to 30*

b. How many hours did he work last week (at all jobs)? *Subtract any time off and add overtime or extra hours worked.*

○ 1 to 14 hours ○ 40 hours
○ 15 to 29 hours ○ 41 to 48 hours
○ 30 to 34 hours ○ 49 to 59 hours
○ 35 to 39 hours ○ 60 hours or more

15 percent

c. Where did he work last week? *If he worked in more than one place, print where he worked most last week. If he travels about in his work or if the place does not have a numbered address, see instruction sheet.*

(1) Address *(Number and street name)* ______
(2) Name of city, town, village, etc. ______
(3) Inside the limits of this city, town, village, etc.?
○ Yes
○ No
(4) County ______
(5) State ______ (6) ZIP Code ______

d. How did he get to work last week? *Fill one circle for chief means used on the last day he worked at the address given in 29c.*

○ Driver, private auto ○ Taxicab
○ Passenger, private auto ○ Walked only
○ Bus or streetcar ○ Worked at home
○ Subway or elevated ○ Other means– *Specify* ______
○ Railroad

After completing question 29d, skip to question 33.

15 and 5 percent

30. Does this person have a job or business from which he was temporarily absent or on layoff last week?

○ Yes, on layoff
○ Yes, on vacation, temporary illness, labor dispute, etc.
○ No

31a. Has he been looking for work during the past 4 weeks?

○ Yes ○ No— *Skip to 32*

b. Was there any reason why he could not take a job last week?

○ Yes, already has a job
○ Yes, because of this person's temporary illness
○ Yes, for other reasons (in school, etc.)
○ No, could have taken a job

32. When did he last work at all, even for a few days?

○ In 1970 ○ 1964 to 1967 ○ 1959 or earlier
○ In 1969 ○ 1960 to 1963 ○ Never worked } *Skip to 36*
○ In 1968

– continued –

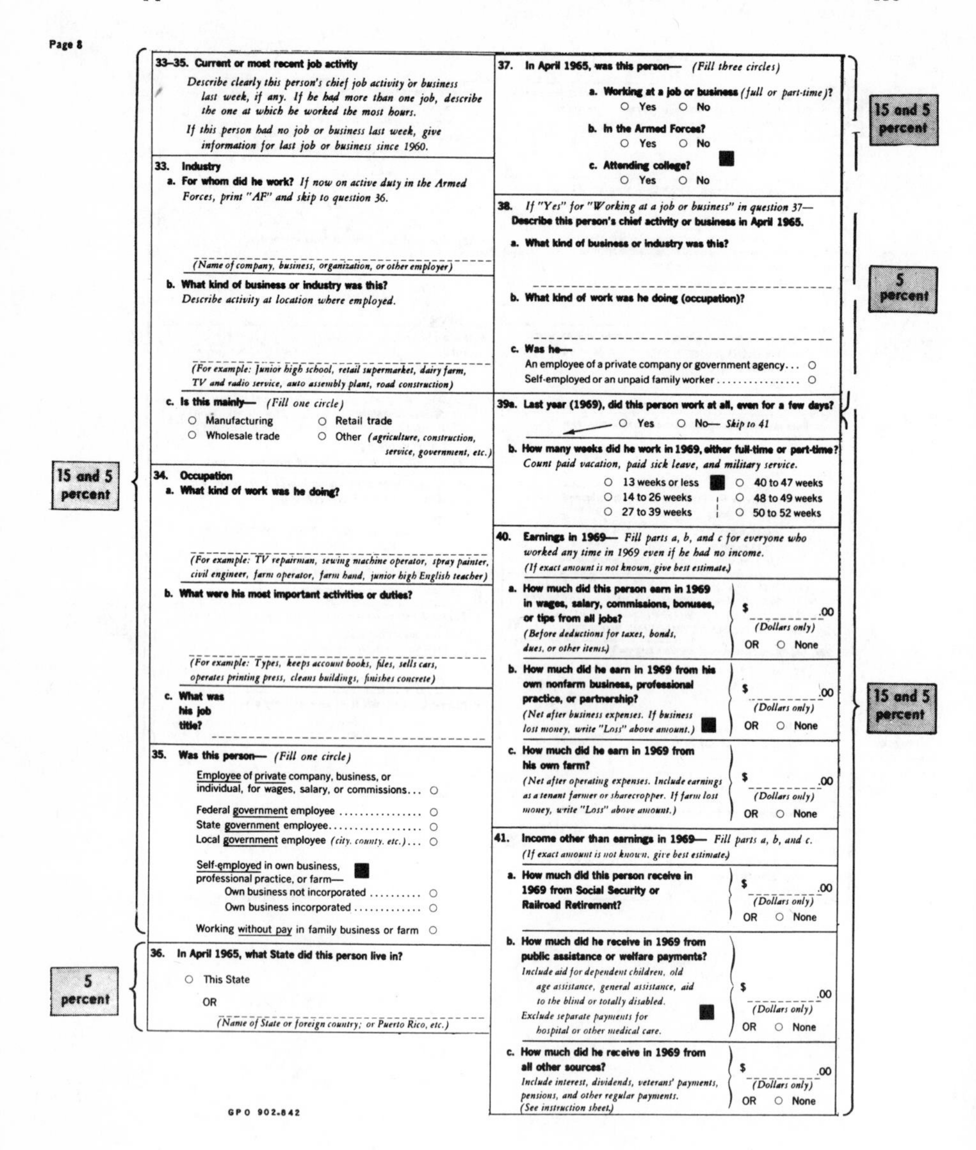

Page 8

15 and 5 percent

33–35. Current or most recent job activity

Describe clearly this person's chief job activity or business last week, if any. If he had more than one job, describe the one at which he worked the most hours.

If this person had no job or business last week, give information for last job or business since 1960.

33. Industry

a. For whom did he work? *If now on active duty in the Armed Forces, print "AF" and skip to question 36.*

(Name of company, business, organization, or other employer)

b. What kind of business or industry was this?
Describe activity at location where employed.

(For example: Junior high school, retail supermarket, dairy farm, TV and radio service, auto assembly plant, road construction)

c. Is this mainly— *(Fill one circle)*

○ Manufacturing ○ Retail trade
○ Wholesale trade ○ Other *(agriculture, construction, service, government, etc.)*

34. Occupation

a. What kind of work was he doing?

(For example: TV repairman, sewing machine operator, spray painter, civil engineer, farm operator, farm hand, junior high English teacher)

b. What were his most important activities or duties?

(For example: Types, keeps account books, files, sells cars, operates printing press, cleans buildings, finishes concrete)

c. What was his job title?

35. Was this person— *(Fill one circle)*

Employee of private company, business, or individual, for wages, salary, or commissions ... ○

Federal government employee .... ○
State government employee................... ○
Local government employee *(city, county, etc.)*... ○

Self-employed in own business, professional practice, or farm—
Own business not incorporated .... ○
Own business incorporated .... ○

Working without pay in family business or farm ○

5 percent

36. In April 1965, what State did this person live in?

○ This State

OR

(Name of State or foreign country; or Puerto Rico, etc.)

15 and 5 percent

37. In April 1965, was this person— *(Fill three circles)*

a. Working at a job or business *(full or part-time)*?
○ Yes ○ No

b. In the Armed Forces?
○ Yes ○ No

c. Attending college?
○ Yes ○ No

5 percent

38. *If "Yes" for "Working at a job or business" in question 37—*
Describe this person's chief activity or business in April 1965.

a. What kind of business or industry was this?

b. What kind of work was he doing (occupation)?

c. Was he—
An employee of a private company or government agency... ○
Self-employed or an unpaid family worker .... ○

15 and 5 percent

39a. Last year (1969), did this person work at all, even for a few days?

○ Yes ○ No— *Skip to 41*

b. How many weeks did he work in 1969, either full-time or part-time?
Count paid vacation, paid sick leave, and military service.

○ 13 weeks or less ○ 40 to 47 weeks
○ 14 to 26 weeks ○ 48 to 49 weeks
○ 27 to 39 weeks ○ 50 to 52 weeks

40. Earnings in 1969— *Fill parts a, b, and c for everyone who worked any time in 1969 even if he had no income.*
(If exact amount is not known, give best estimate.)

a. How much did this person earn in 1969 in wages, salary, commissions, bonuses, or tips from all jobs?
(Before deductions for taxes, bonds, dues, or other items.)
$ ____.00 *(Dollars only)* OR ○ None

b. How much did he earn in 1969 from his own nonfarm business, professional practice, or partnership?
(Net after business expenses. If business lost money, write "Loss" above amount.)
$ ____.00 *(Dollars only)* OR ○ None

c. How much did he earn in 1969 from his own farm?
(Net after operating expenses. Include earnings as a tenant farmer or sharecropper. If farm lost money, write "Loss" above amount.)
$ ____.00 *(Dollars only)* OR ○ None

41. Income other than earnings in 1969— *Fill parts a, b, and c.*
(If exact amount is not known, give best estimate.)

a. How much did this person receive in 1969 from Social Security or Railroad Retirement?
$ ____.00 *(Dollars only)* OR ○ None

b. How much did he receive in 1969 from public assistance or welfare payments?
Include aid for dependent children, old age assistance, general assistance, aid to the blind or totally disabled.
Exclude separate payments for hospital or other medical care.
$ ____.00 *(Dollars only)* OR ○ None

c. How much did he receive in 1969 from all other sources?
Include interest, dividends, veterans' payments, pensions, and other regular payments.
(See instruction sheet.)
$ ____.00 *(Dollars only)* OR ○ None

GPO 902.842

Appendix C

Current Population Survey Schedule

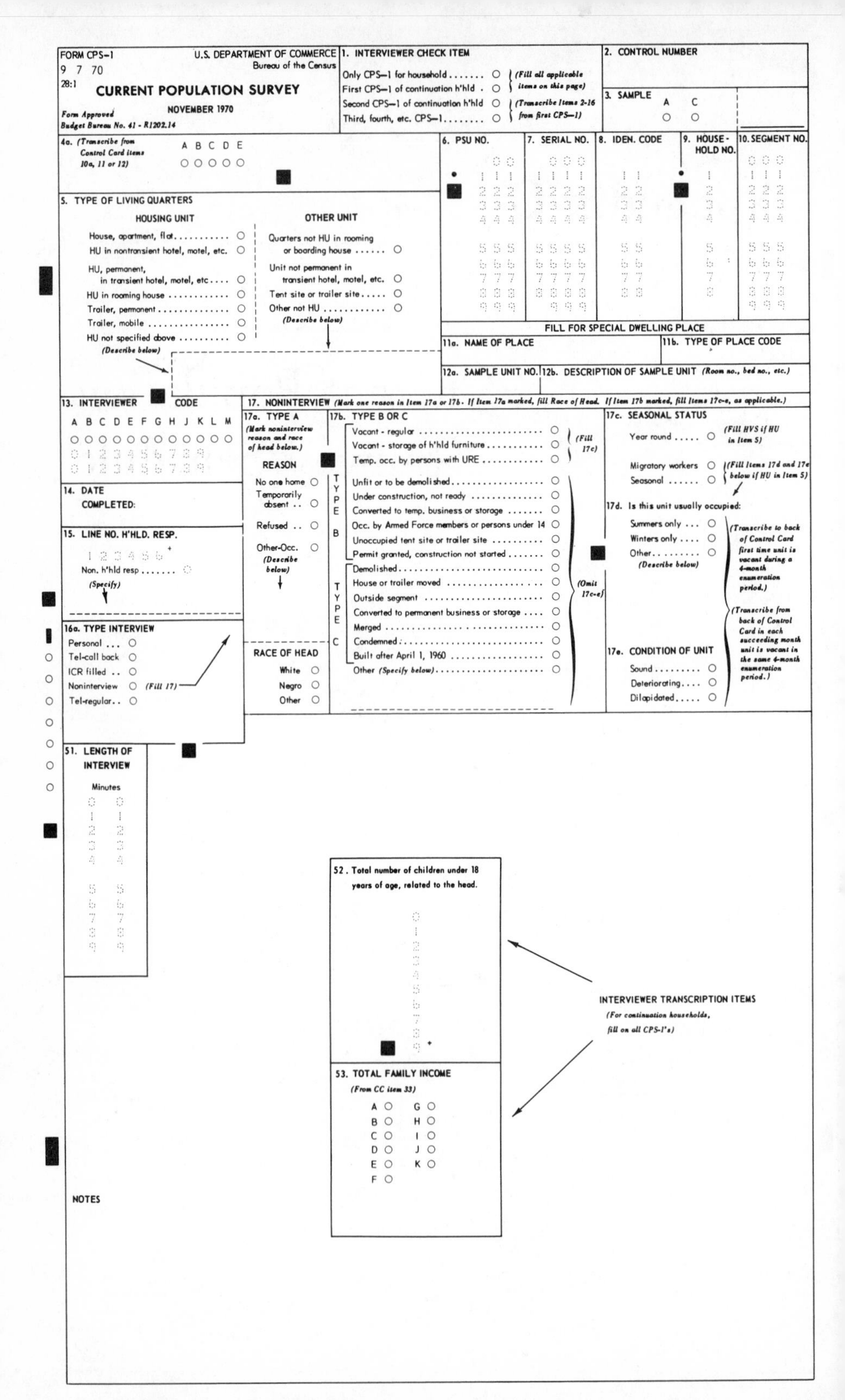

FORM CPS-1 U.S. DEPARTMENT OF COMMERCE Bureau of the Census
9 7 70
28:1
CURRENT POPULATION SURVEY
NOVEMBER 1970
Form Approved Budget Bureau No. 41 - R1202.14

1. INTERVIEWER CHECK ITEM
Only CPS–1 for household ○
First CPS–1 of continuation h'hld ○ *(Fill all applicable items on this page)*
Second CPS–1 of continuation h'hld ○
Third, fourth, etc. CPS–1 ○ *(Transcribe Items 2-16 from first CPS–1)*

2. CONTROL NUMBER

3. SAMPLE A ○ C ○

4a. *(Transcribe from Control Card items 10a, 11 or 12)* A B C D E ○ ○ ○ ○ ○

6. PSU NO.
7. SERIAL NO.
8. IDEN. CODE
9. HOUSEHOLD NO.
10. SEGMENT NO.

5. TYPE OF LIVING QUARTERS

HOUSING UNIT
House, apartment, flat ○
HU in nontransient hotel, motel, etc. ○
HU, permanent, in transient hotel, motel, etc ○
HU in rooming house ○
Trailer, permanent ○
Trailer, mobile ○
HU not specified above ○
(Describe below)

OTHER UNIT
Quarters not HU in rooming or boarding house ○
Unit not permanent in transient hotel, motel, etc. ○
Tent site or trailer site ○
Other not HU ○
(Describe below)

FILL FOR SPECIAL DWELLING PLACE
11a. NAME OF PLACE
11b. TYPE OF PLACE CODE
12a. SAMPLE UNIT NO.
12b. DESCRIPTION OF SAMPLE UNIT *(Room no., bed no., etc.)*

13. INTERVIEWER CODE
A B C D E F G H J K L M

14. DATE COMPLETED:

15. LINE NO. H'HLD. RESP.
Non. h'hld resp ○
(Specify)

16a. TYPE INTERVIEW
Personal ○
Tel-call back ○
ICR filled ○
Noninterview ○ *(Fill 17)*
Tel-regular ○

17. NONINTERVIEW *(Mark one reason in Item 17a or 17b. If Item 17a marked, fill Race of Head. If Item 17b marked, fill Items 17c-e, as applicable.)*

17a. TYPE A *(Mark noninterview reason and race of head below.)*
REASON
No one home ○
Temporarily absent ○
Refused ○
Other-Occ. ○ *(Describe below)*

RACE OF HEAD
White ○
Negro ○
Other ○

17b. TYPE B OR C
TYPE B
Vacant - regular ○
Vacant - storage of h'hld furniture ○ *(Fill 17c)*
Temp. occ. by persons with URE ○
Unfit or to be demolished ○
Under construction, not ready ○
Converted to temp. business or storage ○
Occ. by Armed Force members or persons under 14 ○
Unoccupied tent site or trailer site ○
Permit granted, construction not started ○

TYPE C
Demolished ○
House or trailer moved ○
Outside segment ○
Converted to permanent business or storage ○
Merged ○
Condemned ○
Built after April 1, 1960 ○
Other *(Specify below)* ○
(Omit 17c-e)

17c. SEASONAL STATUS
Year round ○ *(Fill HVS if HU in Item 5)*
Migratory workers ○
Seasonal ○ *(Fill Items 17d and 17e below if HU in Item 5)*

17d. Is this unit usually occupied:
Summers only ○
Winters only ○
Other ○
(Describe below)
(Transcribe to back of Control Card first time unit is vacant during a 4-month enumeration period.)

17e. CONDITION OF UNIT
Sound ○
Deteriorating ○
Dilapidated ○
(Transcribe from back of Control Card in each succeeding month unit is vacant in the same 4-month enumeration period.)

51. LENGTH OF INTERVIEW
Minutes

52. Total number of children under 18 years of age, related to the head.

INTERVIEWER TRANSCRIPTION ITEMS
(For continuation households, fill on all CPS-1's)

53. TOTAL FAMILY INCOME
(From CC item 33)
A ○ G ○
B ○ H ○
C ○ I ○
D ○ J ○
E ○ K ○
F ○

NOTES

18. Line No.

19. What was . . . doing most of LAST WEEK-
- Working
- Keeping house
- Going to school
- or something else?

Working *(Skip to 20A)* . . WK ○
With a job but not at work J ○
Looking for work . . . . . LK ○
Keeping house . . . . H ○
Going to school. . . . . . . S ○
Unable to work *(Skip to 24)* U ○
Other *(Specify)* . . . . OT ○

20. Did . . . do any work at all LAST WEEK, not counting work around the house?
(Note: If farm or business operator in hh., ask about unpaid work)

Yes ○ No ○ *(Go to 21)*

20A. How many hours did . . . work LAST WEEK at all jobs?

0 1 2 3 4 5 6 7 8 9 | 0 1 2 3 4 5 6 7 8 9

20B. INTERVIEWER CHECK ITEM

49+ ○ *(Skip to item 23)*
1-34 ○ *(Go to 20C)*
35-48 ○ *(Go to 20D)*

21. *(If J in 19, skip to 21A.)* Did . . . have a job or business from which he was temporarily absent or on layoff LAST WEEK?

Yes ○ No ○ *(Go to 22)*

21A. Why was . . . absent from work LAST WEEK?

Own illness . . . . ○
On vacation . . . . ○
Bad weather . . . . ○
Labor dispute . . ○
New job to begin within 30 days ○ *(Skip to 22B and 22C2)*
Temporary layoff *(Under 30 days)* ○
Indefinite layoff *(30 days or more or no def. recall date)* ○ *(Skip to 22C3)*
Other *(Specify)*. . ○

22. *(If LK in 19, skip to 22A.)* Has . . . been looking for work during the past 4 weeks?

Yes ○ No ○ *(Go to 24)*

22A. What has . . . been doing in the last 4 weeks to find work? *(Mark all methods used; do not read list.)*

Checked with-- pub.employ.agency ○
pvt.employ.agency ○
employer directly . ○
friends or relatives ○
Placed or answered ads . . . . ○
Nothing *(Skip to 24)* . . . . ○
Other *(Specify in notes, e.g., MDTA, union or prof. register, etc.)* ○

24. INTERVIEWER CHECK ITEM

Unit in rotation group:
(Mark one circle only)

○ 2, 3, 4, 6, 7 or 8 *(End questions)*
○ 1 or 5 *(Go to 24A)*

24A. When did . . . last work for pay at a regular job or business, either full- or part-time?

Within past 12 months ○
1 up to 2 years ago ○
2 up to 3 years ago ○
3 up to 4 years ago ○
4 up to 5 years ago ○ *(Go to 24B)*
5 or more years ago ○
Never worked . . . . . ○ *(Skip to 24C)*

20C. Does . . . USUALLY work 35 hours or more a week at this job?

Yes ○ What is the reason . . . worked less than 35 hours LAST WEEK?
No ○ What is the reason . . . USUALLY works less than 35 hours a week?
(Mark the appropriate reason)

Slack work . . . . ○
Material shortage . . . . ○
Plant or machine repair . . . . . ○
New job started during week . ○
Job terminated during week . . ○
Could find only part-time work ○
Holiday *(Legal or religious)* . . ○
Labor dispute . . . . ○
Bad weather. . . . . ○
Own illness . . . . ○
On vacation . . . . ○
Too busy with housework, school, personal bus.,etc. ○
Did not want full-time work . . ○
Full-time work week under 35 hours . . . . ○
Other reason *(Specify)* . . . . . ○

(Skip to 23 and enter job worked at last week)

20D. Did . . . lose any time or take any time off LAST WEEK for any reason such as illness, holiday or slack work?

Yes ○ How many hours did . . . take off?
(Correct 20A if lost time not already deducted; if 20A reduced below 35, correct 20B and fill 20C; otherwise, skip to 23.)
No ○

20E. Did . . . work any overtime or at more than one job LAST WEEK?

Yes ○ How many extra hours did . . . work?
(Correct 20A and 20B as necessary if extra hours not already included and skip to 23.)
No ○
(Skip to 23)

21B. Is . . . getting wages or salary for any of the time off LAST WEEK?

Yes . . . . ○
No . . . . ○
Self employed ○

21C. Does . . . usually work 35 hours or more a week at this job?

Yes ○
No ○

(Skip to 23 and enter job held last week)

22B. Why did . . . start looking for work? Was it because . . . lost or quit a job at that time *(pause)* or was there some other reason?

Lost job . . . . ○
Quit job. . . . . ○
Left school . . . . ○
Wanted temporary work ○
Other *(Specify in notes)* ○

22C.
1) How many weeks has . . . been looking for work?
2) How many weeks ago did . . . start looking for work?
3) How many weeks ago was . . . laid off?

0 1 2 3 4 5 6 7 8 9 | 0 1 2 3 4 5 6 7 8 9

22D. Has . . . been looking for full-time or part-time work?

Full ○ Part ○

22E. Is there any reason why . . . could not take a job LAST WEEK?

Yes ○ → Already has a job ○
No ○ Temporary illness ○
Going to school . ○
Other *(Specify in notes)* ○

22F. When did . . . last work at a full-time job or business lasting 2 consecutive weeks or more?

1965 or later *(Write month and year)* . . ○
(Month and year)
Before 1965. . . . . ○
Nev. worked full-time 2 wks. or more ○
Never worked at all . . . . ○

(Skip to 23 and enter last full-time civilian job lasting 2 weeks or more, job from which laid off, or "Never Worked")

OFFICE USE ONLY

INDUSTRY		OCCUPATION	
0 ○ ○	A ○	0 ○ ○ ○	N ○
1 ○ ○	B ○	1 ○ ○ ○	P ○
2 ○ ○	C ○	2 ○ ○ ○	Q ○
3 ○ ○	D ○	3 ○ ○ ○	R ○
4 ○ ○	E ○	4 ○ ○ ○	S ○
5 ○ ○	F ○	5 ○ ○ ○	T ○
6 ○ ○ ○	G ○	6 ○ ○	U ○
7 ○ ○ ○	H ○	7 ○ ○	V ○
8 ○ ○ ○	J ○	8 ○ ○	W ○
9 ○ ○ ○	K ○	9 ○ ○	X ○
	L ○		Y ○
	M ○		Z ○

24B. Why did . . . leave that job?

Personal, family *(Incl. pregnancy)* or school . . ○
Health. . . . . ○
Retirement or old age . . . . ○
Seasonal job completed . . . . . . ○
Slack work or business conditions . . . . ○
Temporary nonseasonal job completed. . . . . ○
Unsatisfactory work arrangements *(Hours, pay, etc.)* ○
Other. ○

24C. Does . . . want a regular job now, either full- or part-time?

Yes. . . . . . . ○ *(Go to 24D)*
Maybe-it depends *(Specify in notes)*. ○
No . . . . ○ *(Skip to 24E)*
Don't know . . . . ○

24D. What are the reasons. . . is not looking for work? *(Mark each reason mentioned)*

- Believes no work available in line of work or area . . . ○
- Couldn't find any work . . . . . ○
- Lacks nec. schooling, training, skills or experience . . . . . ○
- Employers think too young or too old . . . . ○
- Other pers. handicap in finding job . . . . ○
- Can't arrange child care . . . . . . ○
- Family responsibilities . . . . . ○
- In school or other training . . . ○
- Ill health, physical disability ○
- Other *(Specify in notes)* . . . . . ○
- Don't know . . . . ○

23. DESCRIPTION OF JOB OR BUSINESS

23A. For whom did . . . work? *(Name of company, business, organization or other employer.)*

23B. What kind of business or industry is this? *(For example: TV and radio mfg., retail shoe store, State Labor Dept., farm.)*

23C. What kind of work was . . . doing? *(For example: electrical engineer, stock clerk, typist, farmer.)*

23D. Was this person

An employee of PRIVATE Co., bus., or individual for wages, salary or comm P ○
A GOVT. employee *(Federal, State, or local)* . . . . G ○
Self-empl in OWN bus., prof. practice, or farm. . . . . O ○ *(If not a farm)* Is the business incorporated? Yes ○ No ○
Working WITHOUT PAY in fam. bus. or farm . . . . WP ○
NEVER WORKED. . . . . NEV ○

24E. Does . . . intend to look for work of any kind in the next 12 months?

Yes. . . . . ○
It depends *(Specify in notes)* ○
No . . . . ○
Don't know . . . . ○

(If entry in 24B, describe job in 23)

25. LINE NO.

0 1 2 3 4 5 6 7 8 9 | 0 1 2 3

26. RELATIONSHIP TO HOUSEHOLD HEAD

Head with other relatives *(incl. wife)* in household ○
Head with no other relatives in household . . . . ○
Wife of head. . . . . ○
Other relative of head . . . . . ○
Non-rel. of head with own rels. *(incl. wife)* in h'hld. ○
Nonrelative of head with no own relatives in h'hld . . ○

27. AGE

0 1 2 3 4 5 6 7 8 9 | 0 1 2 3 4 5 6 7 8 9

28. MARITAL STATUS

Married-civilian spouse present . . . ○
Married-Armed Force spouse present . . . ○
Married-spouse absent-- *(include separated)*. . . ○
Widowed or divorced. . ○
Never married . . . . . . ○

29. RACE

White ○
Negro ○
Other ○

30. SEX AND VETERAN STATUS

Male
Vietnam Era . ○
Korean War . . ○
World War II. ○
World War I. . ○
Other Service ○
Nonveteran . . ○

Female . . . . ○

31. HIGHEST GRADE ATTENDED

E H C
1 2 3 4 5 6 7 8 + None

32. GRADE COMPLETED

Yes ○
No ○

33.

DO NOT WRITE IN THIS SPACE

34. INTERVIEWER CHECK ITEM *(Mark one item and proceed accordingly)*

- ○ Entry in item 20A and P or G *(including Incorp. "Yes")* in item 23D *(Ask item 35)*
- ○ Entry in item 20A and O or WP *(excluding Incorp. "Yes")* in item 23D *(Ask item 39)*
- ○ Entry in item 21A *(Ask item 41)*
- ○ All other cases *(Skip to 45)*

35. How much does ... usually earn per week at this job before deductions?

Under $25	○	$80–$89	○
$25–$39	○	$90–$99	○
$40–$49	○	$100–$124	○
$50–$59	○	$125–$149	○
$60–$69	○	$150–$199	○
$70–$79	○	$200+	○

(Ask 36)

36. Did ... work for more than one employer LAST WEEK?

Yes ○ *(Skip to 42)*
No ○ *(Ask 37)*

37. In addition to working for wages or salary, did ... operate his own farm, business, or profession LAST WEEK?

Yes ○ *(Skip to 42)*
No ○ *(Ask 38)*

38. Did ... have any other job LAST WEEK at which he did not work at all?
(If "Yes," indicate whether paid for time off.)

Yes-Paid . . . ○ } *(Skip to 42)*
Yes-Not Paid ○ }
No . . . . ○ *(Skip to 45)*

39. In addition to this work, did ... do any work for wages or salary LAST WEEK?

Yes ○ *(Skip to 42)*
No ○ *(Ask 40)*

40. Did ... have a job LAST WEEK at which he did not work at all?
(If "Yes," indicate whether paid for time off.)

Yes-Paid . . . ○ } *(Skip to 42)*
Yes-Not Paid ○ }
No . . . . ○ *(Skip to 45)*

41. In addition to this job, did ... have some other job LAST WEEK at which he did not work at all?

Yes ○ *(Ask 42)*
No ○ *(Skip to 45)*

DESCRIBE 2ND JOB IF "YES" IN ANY OF 36 – 41

NOTE: Mark whether second job is same as or different from job in item 23B-D. Describe if different.

42. What was ...'s second job LAST WEEK?

Same as 23B-D ○ *(Skip to 13)*
Different from 23 B-D ○ *(Describe below and go to 43)*

A. NAME OF EMPLOYER

B. INDUSTRY

C. OCCUPATION

D. CLASS OF WORKER

Private . . . . ○
Gov't . . . . ○
Self-emp . . . . ○
(If not a farm) Inc. { Yes ○ / No ○
Without Pay . . . . . . ○
} *(Ask 43)*

43. How many hours did ... work at his second job LAST WEEK?

Ø ○ ○
1 ○ ○
2 ○ ○
3 ○ ○
4 ○ ○
5 ○ ○
6 ○ ○
7 ○ ○
8 ○ ○
9 ○ ○

(Ask 44)

44. How many hours did ... work at his principal job *(Item 23)* LAST WEEK?

Ø ○ ○
1 ○ ○
2 ○ ○
3 ○ ○
4 ○ ○
5 ○ ○
6 ○ ○
7 ○ ○
8 ○ ○
9 ○ ○

(Skip to 45)

FOR OFFICE USE ONLY

INDUSTRY

Ø ○ ○ A ○
1 ○ ○ B ○
2 ○ ○ C ○
3 ○ ○ D ○
4 ○ ○ E ○
5 ○ ○ F ○
6 ○ ○ ○ G ○
7 ○ ○ ○ H ○
8 ○ ○ ○ J ○
9 ○ ○ ○ K ○
L ○
M ○

OCCUPATION

Ø ○ ○ ○ N ○
1 ○ ○ ○ P ○
2 ○ ○ ○ Q ○
3 ○ ○ ○ R ○
4 ○ ○ ○ S ○
5 ○ ○ ○ T ○
6 ○ ○ U ○
7 ○ ○ V ○
8 ○ ○ W ○
9 ○ ○ X ○
Y ○
Z ○

45. INTERVIEWER CHECK ITEM

In what State is this household located? *(Mark one circle and proceed accordingly)*

All states except Georgia, Kentucky, Alaska, or Hawaii ○	Georgia or Kentucky ○	Alaska ○	Hawaii ○
Is this person 21 years old or over?	**Is this person 18 years old or over?**	**Is this person 19 years old or over?**	**Is this person 20 years old or over?**
Yes ○ *(Ask 46)* / No ○ *(Go to next person)*	Yes ○ *(Ask 46)* / No ○ *(Go to next person)*	Yes ○ *(Ask 46)* / No ○ *(Go to next person)*	Yes ○ *(Ask 46)* / No ○ *(Go to next person)*

46. This month we have some questions about whether people voted in the recent Congressional election. Did ... vote in the election held on November 3rd *(pause)* **or did something keep . . . from voting?**

Voted ○ *(Skip to 49)*
Did not vote ○ *(Ask 47)*
Don't know ○ *(Ask 47)*

47. Was ... registered to vote in that election?

Yes ○ *(Skip to 49)*
No ○ *(Ask 48)*
Don't know ○ *(Skip to 49)*

48. What was the main reason ... was not registered to vote? *(Mark one circle)*

- Not a citizen of the United States . . . . ○
- Had not lived here long enough to be qualified to vote . . . . ○
- Not interested, just never got around to it, dislikes politics, etc. . . . . . . ○
- Unable to register because of illness, no transportation, couldn't take time off from work, etc. ○
- Other reason *(Specify below)* . . . . ○
- Don't know . . . . ○

(Ask 49)

49. Thinking back to 1968, did ... vote in the Presidential election that year?

Yes ○
No ○
Don't know ○
} *(Fill 50)*

50. INTERVIEWER CHECK ITEM

Who reported on voting for this person?

Self ○
Other ○
(Go to next person)

Appendix D

U.S. Population Data Sheet

U.S. POPULATIO

(population figures in thousands[1])

	Area (Sq. Mi.)	Date of Admission	First Census After Admission[1]	1900	1910	1920	1930	1940	1950
United States	3,615,122	—	3,929	76,212	92,228	106,022	123,203	132,165	151,3
Alabama	51,609	1819	128	1,829	2,138	2,348	2,646	2,833	3,0
Alaska	586,412	1959	226	64	64	55	59	73	1
Arizona	113,909	1912	334	123	204	334	436	499	7
Arkansas	53,104	1836	98	1,312	1,574	1,752	1,854	1,949	1,9
California	158,693	1850	93	1,485	2,378	3,427	5,677	6,907	10,5
Colorado	104,247	1876	194	540	799	940	1,036	1,123	1,3
Connecticut	5,009	1788	238	908	1,115	1,381	1,607	1,709	2,0
Delaware	2,057	1787	59	185	202	223	238	267	3
D. of Columbia	67	—	8	279	331	438	487	663	8
Florida	58,560	1845	87	529	753	968	1,468	1,897	2,7
Georgia	58,876	1788	83	2,216	2,609	2,896	2,909	3,124	3,4
Hawaii	6,450	1959	633	154	192	256	368	423	5
Idaho	83,557	1890	89	162	326	432	445	525	5
Illinois	56,400	1818	55	4,822	5,639	6,485	7,631	7,897	8,7
Indiana	36,291	1816	147	2,516	2,701	2,930	3,239	3,428	3,9
Iowa	56,290	1846	192	2,232	2,225	2,404	2,471	2,538	2,6
Kansas	82,264	1861	364	1,470	1,691	1,769	1,881	1,801	1,9
Kentucky	40,395	1792	221	2,147	2,290	2,417	2,615	2,846	2,9
Louisiana	48,523	1812	153	1,382	1,656	1,799	2,102	2,364	2,6
Maine	33,215	1820	298	694	742	768	797	847	9
Maryland	10,577	1788	320	1,188	1,295	1,450	1,632	1,821	2,3
Massachusetts	8,257	1788	379	2,805	3,366	3,852	4,250	4,317	4,6
Michigan	58,216	1837	212	2,241	2,810	3,668	4,842	5,256	6,3
Minnesota	84,068	1858	172	1,751	2,076	2,387	2,564	2,792	2,9
Mississippi	47,716	1817	75	1,551	1,797	1,791	2,010	2,184	2,1
Missouri	69,686	1821	140	3,107	3,293	3,404	3,629	3,785	3,9
Montana	147,138	1889	143	243	376	549	538	559	5
Nebraska	77,227	1867	123	1,066	1,192	1,296	1,378	1,316	1,3
Nevada	110,540	1864	42	42	82	77	91	110	1
New Hampshire	9,304	1788	142	412	431	443	465	492	5
New Jersey	7,836	1787	184	1,884	2,537	3,156	4,041	4,160	4,8
New Mexico	121,666	1912	360	195	327	360	423	532	6
New York	49,576	1788	340	7,269	9,114	10,385	12,588	13,479	14,8
North Carolina	52,586	1789	394	1,894	2,206	2,559	3,170	3,572	4,0
North Dakota	70,665	1889	191	319	577	647	681	642	6
Ohio	41,222	1803	231	4,158	4,767	5,759	6,647	6,908	7,9
Oklahoma	69,919	1907	1,657	790	1,657	2,028	2,396	2,336	2,2
Oregon	96,981	1859	52	414	673	783	954	1,090	1,5
Pennsylvania	45,333	1787	434	6,302	7,665	8,720	9,631	9,900	10,4
Rhode Island	1,214	1790	69	429	543	604	687	713	7
South Carolina	31,055	1788	249	1,340	1,515	1,684	1,739	1,900	2,1
South Dakota	77,047	1889	349	402	584	637	693	643	6
Tennessee	42,244	1796	106	2,021	2,185	2,338	2,617	2,916	3,2
Texas	267,338	1845	213	3,049	3,897	4,663	5,825	6,415	7,7
Utah	84,916	1896	277	277	373	449	508	550	6
Vermont	9,609	1791	154	344	356	352	360	359	3
Virginia	40,817	1788	692	1,854	2,062	2,309	2,422	2,678	3,3
Washington	68,192	1889	357	518	1,142	1,357	1,563	1,736	2,3
West Virginia	24,181	1863	442	959	1,221	1,464	1,729	1,902	2,0
Wisconsin	56,154	1848	305	2,069	2,334	2,632	2,939	3,138	3,4
Wyoming	97,914	1890	63	93	146	194	226	251	2
Puerto Rico	3,435	—	—	953[2]	1,118	1,300	1,544	1,869	2,2

Population totals to the nearest thousand.

1790-1970 data from U.S. Bureau of the Census, U.S. Census of Population: 1970 Number of Inhabitants, Final Report PC(1)-A1 United States Summary, U.S. Government Printing Office, Washington, D. C. 1971. (1970 Official Counts as corrected.)

Provisional statistics for state and national birth, death, and total infant mortality rates for 1971 are from U.S. Department of Health, Education and Welfare, Public Health Service, Health Services and Mental Health Administration, National Center for Health Statistics, Rockville, Maryland, Monthly Vital Statistics Report, Provisional Statistics, Annual Summary for the United States, 1971 (HSM) 73-1121, Vol. 20, No. 13, August 30, 1972.

[1] 1812 admission date would mean 1820 Census population, etc., United States population is for 1790, the first National Census; District of Columbia data is for 1800; California, Idaho, Maine, Rhode Island, Wyoming population is the year of admission; Florida and Texas, 1850.

Territorial population data for Alaska (1900-1950), Arizona (1900), Hawaii (1900-1950), New Mexico (1900), Oklahoma (1900).

[2] Population: 1899 figure; birth and death rates: 1970 figures.

Source: Population Reference Bureau Inc., Washington, D.C.

)ATA SHEET

60	1970	Percent of Change 1960-1970	Net Migration 1960-1970 (Percent)[3]	Percent Urban 1970[4]	Annual Births per 1,000 Population 1971	Annual Deaths per 1,000 Population 1971	Total Infant Mortality 1971[5]	Population Estimates Mid-1972[6]	Population Projections 1980[7]
9,323	203,235	13.3	1.7	73.5	17.3	9.3	19.2	208,232	226,934
3,267	3,444	5.4	−7.1	58.4	19.1	9.7	23.6	3,510	3,565
226	302	32.8	7.1	48.4	22.9	5.0	18.3	325	352
1,302	1,772	36.0	17.5	79.6	21.0	8.6	18.3	1,945	2,164
1,786	1,923	7.7	−4.0	50.0	18.1	10.6	19.9	1,978	2,052
5,717	19,953	27.0	13.4	90.9	16.8	8.5	16.8	20,468	24,226
1,754	2,207	25.8	12.3	78.5	18.1	8.1	18.0	2,357	2,636
2,535	3,032	19.6	8.5	77.4	14.6	8.5	15.5	3,082	3,551
446	548	22.8	8.5	72.2	17.7	9.0	14.4	565	655
764	757	−1.0	−13.1	100.0	33.8	13.9	28.5	748	—
4,952	6,789	37.1	26.8	80.5	16.5	11.2	20.7	7,259	8,280
3,943	4,590	16.4	1.3	60.3	20.4	9.0	21.3	4,720	5,191
633	770	21.5	1.7	83.1	20.1	5.7	18.1	809	874
667	713	6.8	−6.2	54.1	19.1	8.4	16.6	756	761
0,081	11,114	10.2	−0.4	83.0	17.2	9.6	20.7	11,251	12,256
4,662	5,194	11.4	−0.3	64.9	18.3	9.3	18.0	5,291	5,782
2,758	2,825	2.4	−6.6	57.2	16.1	10.3	17.0	2,883	2,908
2,179	2,249	3.1	−6.0	66.1	15.1	9.6	19.8	2,258	2,334
3,038	3,219	5.9	−5.0	52.3	18.1	10.3	20.4	3,299	3,372
3,257	3,643	11.8	−4.0	66.1	20.1	9.2	22.1	3,720	3,975
969	994	2.4	−7.2	50.8	17.3	10.7	16.3	1,029	1,016
3,101	3,922	26.5	12.4	76.6	14.3	7.9	18.0	4,056	4,782
5,149	5,689	10.5	1.4	84.6	15.7	9.9	17.1	5,787	6,277
7,823	8,875	13.4	0.3	73.8	17.9	8.5	19.2	9,082	10,031
3,414	3,805	11.5	−0.7	66.4	16.3	8.9	17.8	3,896	4,245
2,178	2,217	1.8	−12.3	44.5	21.7	10.4	26.6	2,263	2,245
4,320	4,677	8.3	—	70.1	17.1	10.9	19.0	4,753	5,070
675	694	2.9	−8.6	53.4	17.2	9.5	20.7	719	721
1,411	1,484	5.1	−5.2	61.5	17.0	10.2	17.2	1,525	1,570
285	489	71.3	50.4	80.9	18.9	8.3	22.9	527	673
607	738	21.5	11.3	56.4	16.6	9.8	15.6	771	878
6,067	7,168	18.2	8.0	88.9	15.1	9.2	18.0	7,367	8,300
951	1,016	6.8	−13.6	69.8	21.6	7.5	20.9	1,065	1,088
6,782	18,241	8.7	−0.6	85.6	15.5	10.1	18.6	18,366	19,789
4,556	5,082	11.5	−2.1	45.0	18.6	8.8	22.2	5,214	5,482
632	618	−2.3	−14.9	44.3	17.5	9.2	15.3	632	600
9,706	10,652	9.7	−1.3	75.3	17.7	9.2	18.2	10,783	11,675
2,328	2,559	9.9	0.6	68.0	17.2	9.6	18.4	2,634	2,787
1,769	2,091	18.2	9.0	67.1	15.8	9.3	18.1	2,182	2,421
1,319	11,794	4.2	−3.3	71.5	15.2	10.5	18.1	11,926	12,157
859	950	10.1	1.5	87.1	15.8	9.8	18.9	968	1,027
2,383	2,591	8.7	−6.3	47.6	20.2	8.8	22.5	2,665	2,731
681	666	−2.2	−13.9	44.6	17.0	9.9	17.1	679	658
3,567	3,924	10.0	−1.3	58.8	19.1	10.0	21.6	4,031	4,259
9,580	11,197	16.9	1.5	79.7	20.1	8.1	19.5	11,649	12,812
891	1,059	18.9	−1.2	80.4	25.8	6.8	14.1	1,126	1,234
390	445	14.0	3.8	32.2	17.1	9.7	15.0	462	504
3,967	4,648	17.2	3.6	63.1	16.9	8.2	20.8	4,764	5,229
2,853	3,409	19.5	8.7	72.6	15.7	8.8	18.6	3,443	3,958
1,860	1,744	−6.2	−14.2	39.0	18.0	11.5	21.9	1,781	1,634
3,952	4,418	11.8	0.1	65.9	16.0	9.1	15.7	4,520	4,930
330	332	0.7	−11.9	60.5	17.4	8.9	21.1	345	342
2,350	2,712	15.4	—	58.1	25.4	7.5[2]	24.5[2]	—	—

inmigration and outmigration as a percentage of the 1960 ulation, U.S. Department of Commerce News, Release CB71-85, 17, 1971.

an population comprises all persons living in urbanized areas ally containing at least one city of 50,000 or more and that ion of surrounding territory which meet specified criteria relating population density) and places of 2,500 inhabitants or more side urban areas. (1970 Census definition.) U.S. Bureau of the sus, U.S. Census of Population: 1970, Number of Inhabitants, al Report PC(1)-A1 United States Summary, U.S. Government ting Office, Washington, D. C. 1971.

[5] Annual deaths to infants under one year of age per 1,000 live births.

[6] July 1, 1972 population estimates from U.S. Bureau of the Census, Estimates of the Population of States: July 1, 1971 and 1972, Series P-25, No. 488, September 1972, U.S. Government Printing Office, Washington, D. C. 1972.

[7] 1980 population projections (Series I-E) from U.S. Bureau of the Census, Population Estimates and Projections, March 1972, Series P-25, No. 488, U.S. Government Printing Office, Washington, D. C. 1972.

Bibliography

ABU-LUGHOD, J. 1965. The emergence of differential fertility in urban Egypt. *Milbank Memorial Fund Quarterly,* Vol. 43, No. 1, Part 1.

ALTERMAN, H. 1969. *Counting People: The Census in History.* New York: Harcourt, Brace, & World.

BACHI, R. and J. MATRAS. 1964. Family Size Preferences of Jewish Maternity Cases in Israel. *Milbank Memorial Fund Quarterly,* April.

BALTZELL, E. 1964. *The Protestant Establishment. Aristocracy and Caste in America.* New York: Vintage Books.

BANKS, J. A. 1954. *Prosperity and Parenthood: A Study of Family Planning Among the Victorian Middle Classes.* London: Routledge & Kegan Paul.

BEALE, C. L. and G. V. FUGUITT. 1975. The new pattern of non-metropolitan population change. Presented at Conference on Social Demography. University of Wisconsin, Madison, July 15-16.

BECKER, G. S. 1960. An economic analysis of fertility. In the *National Bureau of Economic Research, Demographic and Economic Change in Developed Countries.* Princeton: Princeton University Press.

BERELSON, B. 1974. World Population: Status Report 1974. A Guide for the Concerned Citizen. *Reports in Populations/Family Planning,* No. 15, January.

BERENT, J. 1970a. Causes of fertility decline in Eastern Europe and the Soviet Union. Part I. The influence of demographic factors. *Population Studies,* Vol. 24, No. 1, March.

BERENT, J. 1970b. Causes of fertility decline in Eastern Europe and the Soviet Union. Part II. Economic and social factors. *Population Studies,* Vol. 24, No. 2, July.

BERGMAN, E. et al. 1974. *Population Policymaking in the American States.* Lexington, Mass.: D. C. Heath.

BERRY, B. J. L. 1973. *Human Consequences of Urbanization.* New York: St. Martin's Press.

BESHERS, J. M. 1967. *Population Processes in Social Systems.* New York: Free Press.

BESHERS, J. M. and E. N. NISHIURA. 1960. A theory of internal migration differentials. *Social Forces,* Vol. 39.

BLAKE, J. 1965. Demographic science and the redirection of public policy. *Journal of Chronic Diseases,* Vol. 18, November.

BLAKE, J. and P. DAS GUPTA. 1975. Reproductive motivation versus contraceptive technology: Is recent American experience an exception? *Population and Development Review,* Vol. 1, No. 2, December.

BLAU, P. M. and O. D. DUNCAN. 1967. *The American Occupational Structure.* New York: John Wiley.

BOGUE, D. J. 1969. *Principles of Demography.* New York: John Wiley.

BOGUE, D. J. 1959a. *The Population of the United States.* New York: Free Press.

BOGUE, D. J. 1959b. Internal migration. In P. M. Hauser and O. D. Duncan, eds., *The Study of Population.* Chicago: University of Chicago Press.

BOGUE, D. J. 1953. *Population Growth in Standard Metropolitan Areas, 1900–1950.* Washington: Government Printing Office.

BOGUE, D. J. 1949. *The Structure of the Metropolitan Community. A Study of Dominance and Subdominance.* Ann Arbor: Horace H. Rackham School, University of Michigan.

BOSERUP, E. 1965. *The Conditions of Agricultural Growth.* Chicago: Aldine.

BOTTOMORE, T. B. 1962. *Sociology.* London: Allen & Unwin.

BOURGEOIS-PICHAT, J. 1965. The general development of the population of France since the 18th century. In D. V. Glass and D. E. C. Eversley, eds., *Population in History.* Chicago: Aldine.

BURGESS, E. W., and C. NEWCOMB. 1930. *Census of the City of Chicago, 1930.* Chicago: University of Chicago Press.

CAMPBELL, A. A. 1965. Recent fertility trends in the United States and Canada. United Nations World Population Conference, Belgrade, September, 1965, *Proceedings,* Vol. II.

CAPLOW, T. 1968. *Coalitions in the Triad.* Englewood Cliffs, New Jersey: Prentice-Hall.

CARNEIRO, R. L. 1968. Slash and burn cultivation among the Kuikura and its implications for cultural development in the Amazon Basin. *Anthropologica,* Supplement No. 2, September. Reprinted in Y. A. Cohen, ed., *Man in Adaptation.* Vol. 2. Chicago: Aldine.

CARR-SAUNDERS, A. M. 1936. *World Population.* Oxford: Oxford University Press.

CHAMBERLAIN, N. W. 1970. *Beyond Malthus Population and Power.* New York: Basic Books.

CHASE, H. C. 1969. Registration completeness and international comparisons of infant mortality. *Demography,* Vol. 6, No. 4, November.

CIPOLLA, C. M. 1965. Four centuries of Italian demographic development. In D. V. Glass and D. E. D. Eversley, eds., *Population in History.* London: Edward Arnold.

CLARK, C. 1967. *Population Growth and Land Use.* London: Macmillan.

CLARK, C. and M. HASWELL. 1967. *The Economics of Subsistence Agriculture.* 3rd Ed. London: St. Martin's Press.

COALE, A. J. 1974. The History of Human Population. *Scientific American,* Vol. 231, No. 3, September.

COALE, A. J. 1969. The decline of fertility in Europe from the French Revolution to World War II. In S. J. Behrman, L. Corsa, Jr., and R. Freedman, eds., *Fertility and Family Planning: A World View.* Ann Arbor: University of Michigan Press.

COALE, A. J. 1956. The effects of changes in mortality and fertility on age composition. *Milbank Memorial Fund Quarterly,* Vol. 34, No. 1, January.

COALE, A. J. and E. M. HOOVER. 1958. *Population Growth and Economic Development in Low Income Countries.* Princeton: Princeton University Press.

Concerned Demography. 1974. *Emerging Population Alternatives,* Vol. 4, No. 2, Winter.

COREY, M. 1975. U.S. Organized family planning programs in fiscal year 1974. *Family Planning Perspectives,* Vol. 7, No. 3, May/June.

DAVIS, K. 1974. The migrations of human populations. *Scientific American,* Vol. 231, No. 3, September.

DAVIS, K. 1973. Zero population growth: The goal and the means. *Daedalus,* Fall, 1973: *The No-Growth Society.*

DAVIS, K. 1969. *World Urbanization, 1950–1970. Vol. 1. Basic Data for Cities, Countries and Regions.* Berkeley: Institute for International Studies, University of California. Reprinted by Greenwood Press 1976.

DAVIS, K. 1967. Population policy: Will current programs succeed? *Science,* Vol. 158, November 10.

DAVIS, K. 1963. Theory of change and response in modern demographic history. *Population Index,* Vol. 29, No. 4, October.

DAVIS, K. 1950. Statistical perspective in marriage and divorce. *Annals of the American Academy of Political and Social Science,* Vol. 272, November. Reprinted in J. J. Spengler and O. D. Duncan, eds., *Demographic Analysis.* New York: Free Press, 1956.

DAVIS, K. 1951. *The Population of India and Pakistan.* Princeton: Princeton University Press.

DAVIS, K. and J. BLAKE. 1956. Social structure and fertility: An analytic framework. *Economic Development and Cultural Change,* Vol. 4, April. Reprinted in Charles B. Nam, ed., *Population and Society*. Boston: Houghton Mifflin, 1968.

DEEVEY, E. S., JR. 1960. The human population. *Scientific American,* September.

DEMENY, P. 1974. The populations of underdeveloped countries. *Scientific American,* Vol. 231, No. 3, September.

DEMOS, J. 1968. Families in colonial Bristol, Rhode Island: An exercise in historical demography. *William and Mary Quarterly,* Vol. 25.

DORN, H. F. 1963. World population growth. In P. M. Hauser, ed., *The Population Dilemma,* The American Assembly. Englewood Cliffs, N.J.: Prentice-Hall.

DORN, H. F. 1959. Tobacco consumption and mortality from cancer and other diseases. *Public Health Reports,* Vol. 74.

DRAKE, M., ed. 1969. *Population in Industrialization.* London: Methuen & Co.

DUESENBERRY, J. S. 1960. Comment. In National Bureau of Economic Research, *Demographic and Economic Change in Developed Countries.* Princeton: Princeton University Press.

DUNCAN, B. and P. M. HAUSER. 1960. *Housing in Metropolis-Chicago.* New York: Free Press.

DUNCAN, O. D. 1964. Social organization and the ecosystem. In R. E. L. Faris, ed., *Handbook of Modern Sociology.* Chicago: Rand McNally.

DUNCAN, O. D. 1959. Human ecology and population studies. In P. M. Hauser and O. D. Duncan, eds., *The Study of Population.* Chicago: University of Chicago Press.

DUNCAN, O. D. and B. DUNCAN. 1955. Residential distribution and occupational stratification. *American Journal of Sociology,* Vol. 60, March.

DUNCAN, O. D., D. L. FEATHERMAN, and B. DUNCAN. 1972. *Socioeconomic Background and Achievement.* New York: Seminar Press.

DUNCAN, O. D. and H. W. PFAUTZ. 1960. Translator's Preface to M. Halbwach's *Population and Society: Introduction to Social Morphology.* Translated by O. D. Duncan and H. W. Pfautz. New York: Free Press.

DUNCAN, O. D. and A. J. REISS. 1956. *Social Characteristics of Urban and Rural Communities,* 1950. New York: John Wiley.

DUNCAN, O. D., et al. 1960. *Metropolis and Region.* Baltimore: Johns Hopkins University Press.

DURKHEIM, E. 1933. *The Division of Labor in Society.* Translated by George Simpson. New York: Macmillan.

EASTERLIN, R. A. 1969. Towards a socio-economic theory of fertility: A survey of recent research in economic factors in American fertility. In S. J. Behrman, L. Corsa, Jr., and R. Freedman, eds., *Fertility and Family Planning: A World View.* Ann Arbor: University of Michigan Press.

EBLEN, J. E. 1965. An analysis of nineteenth-century frontier populations. *Demography,* Vol. 2.

EHRLICH, P. 1968. *The Population Bomb.* New York: Ballantine.

EISENSTADT, S. N. 1954. *The Absorption of Immigrants.* New York: Free Press.

ELAZAR, D. J. 1972. Population growth and the federal system. In *Governance and Population: The Governmental Implications of 0 of Population*

Change. U.S. Commission on Population and the American Future, Research Papers, Vol. 4. Washington: Government Printing Office.

EL-BADRY, M. A. 1969. Higher female than male mortality in some countries of South Asia: A digest. *Journal of the American Statistical Association,* Vol. 64, December.

ELDRIDGE, H. T. and D. S. THOMAS. 1964. *Population Redistribution and Economic Growth, United States, 1870–1950, Vol. III, Demographic Analyses and Interrelations.* MEMOIRS of the American Philosophical Society, Vol. 61. Philadelphia: American Philosophical Society.

EVERSLEY, D. E. C. 1965. Population, economy, and society. In D. V. Glass and D. E. C. Eversley, eds., *Population in History.* London: Edward Arnold.

FEDERICI, N. 1968. *Lezioni di Demografia.* 3rd Ed. Rome: Edizioni E. DeSantis.

FOLGER, J. K. and C. B. NAM. 1964. Educational trends from census data. *Demography,* Vol. 1, No. 1. Reprinted in C. B. Nam, ed., *Population and Society.* Boston: Houghton Mifflin, 1968.

FORDE, C. D. 1964. *Habitat, Economy and Society.* London: Methuen & Co.

FORTES, M. 1950. Kinship and marriage among the Ashanti. In A. R. Radcliffe-Brown and D. Forde, *African Systems of Kinship and Marriage.* London: Oxford University Press.

FOURASTIÉ, J. 1959. De la vie traditionelle à la vie tertiare. *Population,* Vol. 14, No. 3.

FREEDMAN, R. 1968. Norms for family size in underdeveloped areas. *Proceedings of the Royal Society,* B. Vol. 159. Reprinted in D. M. Heer, ed., *Readings on Population.* Englewood Cliffs, N.J.: Prentice-Hall.

FREEDMAN, R. and B. BERELSON. 1974. The human population. *Scientific American,* Vol. 229, No. 9, September.

FREEDMAN, R., P. K. WHELPTON, and A. A. CAMPBELL. 1959. *Family Planning, Sterility and Population Growth.* New York: McGraw-Hill.

FREJKA, T. 1973. The prospects for a stationary world population. *Scientific American,* Vol. 228, No. 3, March.

FREJKA, T. 1973. *The Future of Population Growth: Alternative Paths to Equilibrium.* New York: Wiley Interscience.

FREJKA, T. 1972. Demographic paths to a stationary population: The U.S. in international comparison. In R. Parke, Jr. and C. F. Westoff, eds., *Demographic and Social Aspects of Population Growth.* Research Reports of the Commission in Population and the American Future, Vol. 1. Washington: Government Printing Office.

FREJKA, T. 1970. United States: The implications of zero population growth. *Studies in Family Planning,* No. 60.

FREJKA, T. 1968. Reflections on the demographic conditions needed to establish a U.S. stationary population growth. *Population Studies,* Vol. 22, No. 3, November.

FRIEDLANDER, D. 1969. Demographic responses and population change. *Demography,* Vol. 6, No. 4, November.

GERMANI, G. 1965. Migration and acculturation. In P. M. Hauser, ed., *Handbook of Research in Urban Areas.* Paris: UNESCO.

GIBBS, J. P. and K. DAVIS. 1958. Conventional versus metropolitan data in the international study of urbanization. *American Sociologiccl Review,* Vol. 23, No. 5, October.

GIBBS, J. P. and L. F. SCHNORE. 1960. Metropolitan growth: An international study. *American Journal of Sociology,* Vol. 66.

GLASS, D. V. 1968. Fertility trends in Europe since the second World War. *Population Studies,* Vol. 22, No. 1, March.

GLASS, D. V. 1967. *Population Policies and Movements in Europe.* Reprinted. London: Frank Cass.

GLASS, D. V. 1965. Population growth and population policy. In M. C. Sheps and J. C. Ridley, eds., *Public Health and Population Change.* Pittsburgh: University of Pittsburgh Press.

GLASS, D. V., ed. 1953. *Introduction to Malthus.* New York: John Wiley.

GOLDBERG, D. 1965. Fertility and fertility differentials: Some observations in recent changes in the United States. In M. C. Sheps and J. C. Ridley, eds., *Public Health and Population Change.* Pittsburgh: University of Pittsburgh Press.

GOLDSCHEIDER, C. 1971. *Population Modernization and Social Structure.* Boston: Little, Brown.

GOLDSCHMIDT, W. 1959. *Man's Way: A Preface to the Understanding of Human Society.* New York: Holt, Rinehart & Winston.

GOODE, W. J. 1963. *World Revolution and Family Patterns.* New York: Free Press.

GORDON, M. M. 1964. *Assimilation in American Life.* New York: Oxford University Press.

GOTTMAN, J. 1961. *Megalopolis: The Urbanized Northeastern Seaboard of the United States.* New York: Twentieth Century Fund.

GRABILL, W. F. 1959. The fertility of the United States population. In D. J. Bogue, *The Population of the United States.* New York: Free Press.

GREELEY, A. M. 1974. *Ethnicity in the United States: A Preliminary Reconnaissance.* New York: John Wiley.

GREVEN, P. J., JR. 1970. *Four Generations: Population, Land and Family in Colonial Andover, Massachusetts.* Ithaca: Cornell University Press.

GUILLAUME, P. and POUSSOU, J. P. 1970. *Démographie Historique.* Paris: Armand Colin.

HAJNAL, J. 1965. European marriage patterns in perspective. In D. V. Glass and D. E. C. Eversley, eds., *Population in History.* London: Edward Arnold.

HAJNAL, J. 1953a. The marriage boom. *Population Index,* Vol. 19, No. 2. Reprinted in J. J. Spengler and O. D. Duncan, eds., *Demographic Analysis.* New York: Free Press, 1956.

HAJNAL, J. 1953b. Age at marriage and proportions marrying. *Population Studies,* Vol. 7, No. 2.

HALL, R. 1972. *Organizations: Structure and Process.* Englewood Cliffs, N.J.: Prentice-Hall.

HAMMOND, E. C. 1966. Smoking in relation to the death rates of one million men and women. In W. Haenszel, ed., *Epidemiological Approaches to the Study of Cancer and Other Diseases.* National Cancer Institute Monograph No. 19. Washington: Government Printing Office.

HAUSER, P. M. 1967. Family planning and population programs. A book review article. *Demography,* Vol. 4, No. 1.

HAUSER, P. M., ed. 1965a. *Handbook of Social Research in Urban Areas.* Paris: UNESCO.

HAUSER, P. M. 1965b. Urbanization: An overview. In P. M. Hauser and L. F. Schnore, eds., *The Study of Urbanization.* New York: John Wiley.

HAUSER, P. M. 1963. Statistics and society. *Journal of the American Statistical Association,* Vol. 58, No. 301.

HAUSER, P. M. 1958. On the impact of urbanism on social organization, human nature, and the political order. *Confluence,* Vol. 7, No. 1, Spring.

HAUSER, P. M. and L. F. SCHNORE, eds. 1965. *The Study of Urbanization.* New York: John Wiley.

HAWLEY, A. 1959. Population composition. In P. M. Hauser and O. D. Duncan, eds., *The Study of Population.* Chicago: University of Chicago Press.

HAWLEY, A. 1950. *Human Ecology: A Theory of Community Structure.* New York: Ronald Press.

HAWTHORN, G. 1970. *The Sociology of Fertility.* London: Collier-Macmillan.

HEER, D. M. 1966. Births necessary to assure desired survivorship of sons under different mortality conditions. Presented to Annual Meeting, Population Association of America, New York, April.

HEER, D. M. and D. O. SMITH. 1969. Mortality level, desired family size, and population increase: A further variant on a basic model. *Demography,* Vol. 6, No. 2, May.

HELLEINER, K. F. 1957. The vital revolution reconsidered. *Canadian Journal of Economics and Political Science,* Vol. 23, No. 1. Reprinted in D. V. Glass and D. E. C. Eversley, eds., *Population in History.* London: Edward Arnold, 1965.

HENRY, L. 1956. *Anciennes familles genevoises.* Paris: Presses Universitaires de France.

HIGGS, R. 1971a. "American inventiveness, 1870–1920." *Journal of Political Economy,* Vol. 79, May/June.

HIGGS, R. 1971b. *The Transformation of the American Economy, 1865–1914: An Essay in Interpretation.* New York: John Wiley.

HIMES, N. E. 1963. *Medical History of Contraception.* Reprinted. New York: Gamut Press.

HOBHOUSE, L. T. 1924. *Social Development, Its Nature and Conditions. Hobhouse's Principles of Sociology,* Vol. IV. New York. Reprinted. London: Allen & Unwin, 1966.

HOBHOUSE, L. T., G. C. WHEELER, and M. GINSBERG. 1915. *The Material Culture and Social Institutions of Simpler Peoples.* Reprinted. London: Routledge & Kegan Paul, 1965.

HODGE, P. L. and P. M. HAUSER. 1968. *The Challenge of America's Metropolitan Population Outlook 1960–1985.* New York: Praeger.

HOEBEL, E. A. 1958. *Anthropology.* New York: McGraw-Hill.

HOPKINS, M. K. 1965. The age of Roman girls at marriage. *Population Studies,* Vol. 18, No. 3, March.

KEELY, C. B. 1972. Immigration: Considerations in trends, prospects, and policy.

In R. Parke and C. F. Westoff, eds., *Demographic and Social Aspects of Population Growth.* U.S. Commission on Population and the American Future, Research Reports, Vol. 1. Washington: Government Printing Office.

KELLY, A. C. 1972. Demographic changes and American economic development: Past, present, and future. *Economic Aspects of Population Change.* U.S. Commission on Population Growth and the American Future, Research Papers, Vol. 2. Washington: Government Printing Office.

KEYFITZ, N. 1972. History of population theory. In W. Peterson, ed., *Readings in Population.* New York: Macmillan.

KEYFITZ, N. 1965. Population density and the style of social life. *Bioscience,* Vol. 16, No. 12, December.

KIRK, D. 1969. Natality in the developing countries: Recent trends and prospects. In S. J. Behrman, L. Corsa, Jr., and R. Freedman, eds. *Fertility and Family Planning: A World View.* Ann Arbor: University of Michigan Press.

KIRK, D. 1946. *Europe's Population in the Interwar Years.* League of Nations. Princeton: Princeton University Press.

KISER, C. V. 1967. The growth of American family planning studies: An assessment of significance. *Demography,* Vol. 4, No. 1.

KISER, C. V., W. H. GRABILL, and A. A. CAMPBELL. 1968. *Trends and Variations in Fertility in the United States.* Cambridge: Harvard University Press.

KISER, C. V. and P. K. WHELPTON, eds. 1958. *Social and Psychological Factors Affecting Fertility.* Vols. 1-5. New York: Milbank Memorial Fund.

KITAGAWA, E. M. and P. M. HAUSER. 1973. *Differential Mortality in the United States. A Study in Socio-economic Epidemiology.* Cambridge: Harvard University Press.

KITAGAWA, E. M. and P. M. HAUSER. 1968. Education differentials in mortality by cause of death, United States, 1960. *Demography,* Vol. 5, No. 1.

KITAGAWA, E. M. and P. M. HAUSER. 1963. Methods used in a current study of social and economic differentials in mortality. In *Emerging Techniques in Population Research.* New York: Milbank Memorial Fund.

KNODEL, J. and V. PRACHUABMOH. 1973. Desired family size in Thailand: Are the responses meaningful? *Demography,* Vol. 10, No. 4, November.

KNOWLTON, C. 1832. *Fruits of Philosophy.* Boston: A. Kneeland.

KOLB, J. H. and E. S. DE BRUNNER. 1935. *A Study of Rural Society, Its Organization and Changes.* Boston: Houghton Mifflin.

KRZYWICKI. L. 1934. *Primitive Society and Its Vital Statistics.* Warsaw: Mianowski Institute.

KUZNETS, S. 1960. Population change and aggregate output. In National Bureau of Economic Research, *Demographic and Economic Change in Developed Countries.* Princeton: Princeton University Press.

KUZNETS, S., A. R. MILLER, and R. A. EASTERLIN. 1960. *Population Redistribution and Economic Growth, United States, 1870–1950.* Vol. 2. *Analyses of Economic Change.* Philadelphia: American Philosophical Society.

LADINSKY, J. 1967. Sources of geographic mobility among professional workers: A multivariate analysis. *Demography,* Vol. 4, No. 2.

LAMPARD, E. 1965. Historical aspects of urbanization. In P. M. Hauser and L. F. Schnore, eds., *The Study of Urbanization.* New York: John Wiley.

LANSING, J. B. and J. N. MORGAN. 1967. The effect of geographic mobility on income. *Journal of Human Resources,* Vol. 2, No. 4, Fall.

LEASURE, J. W. 1963. Malthus, marriage, and multiplication. *Milbank Memorial Fund Quarterly,* Vol. 41, No. 4, October.

LEE, E. S., et al. 1957. *Population Redistribution and Economic Growth, United States 1870–1950.* Vol. 1. *Methodological Considerations and Reference Tables.* Philadelphia: American Philosophical Society.

LEIBENSTEIN, H. 1969. Pitfalls in benefit-cost analysis of birth prevention. *Population Studies,* Vol. 23, No. 2, July, pp. 161-70.

LEIBENSTEIN, H. 1957. *Economic Backwardness and Economic Growth.* New York: John Wiley.

LEWIS-FANNING, E. 1949. Report on an inquiry into family limitation and its influence in fertility during the past fifty years. *Papers of the Royal Commission in Population.* Vol. 1. London: HMSO.

LIEBERSON, S. 1961. The impact of residential segregation in ethnic assimilation. *Social Forces,* Vol. 40, No. 1, October.

Life. April 17, 1970. Vol. 68, No. 14.

LINTON, R. 1936. *The Study of Man.* Englewood Cliffs, N.J.: Prentice-Hall.

LOCKRIDGE, K. B. 1968. Land, population, and the evolution of New England society. *Past and Present.* Vol. 39, April.

LONG, L. H. 1973. Migration differentials by education and occupation: Trends and variations. *Demography,* Vol. 10, No. 2, May.

LONG, L. H. 1970. On measuring geographic mobility. *Journal of the American Statistical Association,* Vol. 65, No. 331, September.

LONG, L. H. and K. A. HANSEN. 1975. Trends in return migration to the South. *Demography,* Vol. 12, No. 4.

LONG, L H. and L. R. HELTMAN. 1975. Migration and income differences between black and white men in the North. *American Journal of Sociology,* Vol. 80, No. 6, May.

LORIMER, F. 1969. Issues in population policy. In P. M. Hauser, ed., *The Population Dilemma,* 2nd Ed. Englewood Cliffs, N.J.: Prentice-Hall.

LORIMER, F. 1967. The economics of family formation under different conditions. United Nations World Population Conference, Belgrade, 1965, *Proceedings,* Vol. II. New York: United Nations.

LORIMER, F. 1959. The development of demography. In P. M. Hauser and O. D. Duncan, eds., *The Study of Population.* Chicago: University of Chicago Press.

LOWRY, I. S. 1966. *Migration and Metropolitan Growth: Two Analytical Models.* San Francisco: Chandler Publishing.

MACDONALD, J. S. and L. D. MACDONALD. 1964. Chain migration, ethnic neighborhood formation, and social networks. *Milbank Memorial Fund Quarterly,* Vol. 62, No. 1, January.

MCKEOWN, T. 1965. Medicine and world population. In M. C. Sheps and J. C. Ridley, eds., *Public Health and Population Change.* Pittsburgh: University of Pittsburgh Press.

MCKEOWN, T. and R. G. BROWN. 1955. Medical evidence related to English population changes in the eighteenth century. *Population Studies,* Vol. 9, Part 2, November.

McKeown, T. and R. G. Record. 1962. Reasons for the decline of mortality in England and Wales during the nineteenth century. *Population Studies,* Vol. 16, Part 2, November.

Malthus, T. R. 1829. *A Summary View of the Principle of Population.* Supplement to Encyclopedia Britannica.

Malthus, T. R. 1958. *An Essay on the Principle of Population.* 2 Vols. Everyman's Library. London: Dent (reprinted).

Matras, J. 1973. *Populations and Societies.* Englewood Cliffs, N.J.: Prentice-Hall.

Matras, J. 1965a. The social strategy of family formation: Some variations in time and space. *Demography,* Vol. 2.

Matras, J. 1965b. Social strategies of family formation: Some comparative data for Scandinavia, the British Isles, and North America. *International Social Science Journal,* Vol. 17, No. 2.

Matras, J., J. M. Rosenfeld, and L. Salzberger. 1969. On the predicaments of Jewish families in Jerusalem. *International Journal of Comparative Sociology,* Vol. 10, No. 3.

Maudlin, W. P. et al. 1974. The World Population Conference and the Population Tribune, August 1974. *Studies in Family Planning,* Vol. 15, No. 12, December.

May, D. A. and D. M. Heer. 1968. Son survivorship and family size in India: A computer simulation. *Population Studies,* Vol. 22, No. 2, July.

Mayer, A. J. and P. M. Hauser. 1953. Class differentials in expectation of life at birth. In R. Bendix and S. M. Lipset, eds., *Class, Status and Power.* New York: Free Press.

Mendels, F. F. 1969. Population pressure and rural industrialization in a preindustrial society. Paper read at General Assembly, International Union for Scientific Study of Population, London, September, 1969.

Moriyama, I. M. and L. Guralnick. 1956. Occupational and social class differences in mortality. In *Trends and Differentials in Mortality.* New York: Milbank Memorial Fund.

Morrison, P. A. 1972. Population movements and the shape of urban growth: Implications for public policy. In S. M. Mazie, ed., *Population Distribution and Policy.* U.S. Commission on Population and The American Future Research Papers, Vol. 5. Washington: Government Printing Office.

Murdock, G. P. 1949. *Social Structure.* New York: Macmillan.

Newsweek. September 2, 1974.

Nortman, D. 1973. Population and family planning programs: A handbook. *Reports on Population/Family Planning,* No. 2, 5th Ed., September.

Notestein, F. W. 1970. Zero population growth. *Population Index.* Vol. 36, No. 4, October.

Ogburn, W. F. and O. D. Duncan. 1964. City size as a sociological variable. In E. W. Burgess and D. J. Bogue, eds., *Contributions to Urban Sociology.* Chicago: University of Chicago Press.

Ottenberg, S. and P. Ottenberg. 1960. *Cultures and Societies of Africa.* New York: Random House.

Owen, R. D. 1830. *Moral Physiology.* New York: Wright and Owen.

Packard, V. 1972. *A Nation of Strangers.* New York: David McKay.

Park, R. E. 1925. Community organization and juvenile delinquency. In R. E.

Park, E. W. Burgess, and R. D. MacKenzie, *The City*. Chicago: University of Chicago Press.

PARK, R. E. and E. W. BURGESS. 1921. *Introduction to the Science of Sociology*. Chicago: University of Chicago Press.

PELLER, S. 1965. Births and deaths among Europe's ruling families since 1500. In D. V. Glass, *Population in History*. London: Edward Arnold.

PELLER, S. 1948. Mortality past and future. *Population Studies,* Vol. 1, No. 4, March.

PETERSEN, W. 1975. *Population*. 3rd Ed. New York: Macmillan.

PETERSEN, W. 1971. The Malthus-Godwin debate, then and now. *Demography,* Vol. 8, No. 1, February.

PETERSEN, W. 1969. *Population*. 2nd Ed. New York: Macmillan.

PETERSEN, W. 1961. *Population*. New York: Macmillan.

PETERSON, W. 1958. A general typology of migration. *American Sociological Review,* Vol. 23, No. 3, June. Reprinted in W. Peterson, *The Politics of Population*. New York: Doubleday, 1964.

PIOTROW, P. T. 1973. *World Population Crisis: The United States Response*. New York: Praeger.

PLACE, F. 1822. *Illustrations and Proofs of the Principle of Population*. Reprinted by Houghton Mifflin, Boston, 1930, ed. N. E. Himes.

Population Information Program. 1974. *Population Report,* Series 5, No. 2, August.

PRESSAT, R. 1972. *Demographic Analysis*. Chicago: Aldine.

PRESTON, S. H. 1970. *Older Male Mortality and Cigarette Smoking: A Demographic Analysis*. Berkeley: Institute of International Studies, University of California.

PRICE, C. A. 1963. *Southern Europeans in Australia*. Melbourne: Oxford University Press.

RAINA, B. L. 1966. India. In B. Berelson, *et al.,* eds., *Family Planning and Population Programs*. Chicago: University of Chicago Press.

REINHARD, M. R., A. ARMENGAUD, and J. DUPAQUIER. 1968. *Histoire generale de la population mondiale*. 2nd Edition. Paris: Editions Montchrestien.

RELE, J. R. 1965. Trends and differentials in the American age at marriage. *Milbank Memorial Fund Quarterly,* Vol. 43, No. 2, April.

RINDFUSS, R. and J. SWEET. 1975. The pervasiveness of postwar fertility trends in the United States. Working Paper No. 75-24, Center for Demography and Ecology, University of Wisconsin.

RISCHIN, M., ed. 1965. *The American Gospel of Success: Individualism and Beyond*. Chicago: Quadrangle Books.

ROSS, E. A. 1927. *Standing Room Only?* New York: Century.

ROSSI, P. H. 1955. *Why Families Move*. New York: Free Press.

ROSTOW, W. W. 1960. *The Stages of Economic Growth, A Non-Communist Manifesto*. Cambridge: Cambridge University Press.

ROSTOW, W. W. 1956. The take-off into self-sustained growth. *Economic Journal,* March.

ROWNTREE, G. and R. M. PIERCE. 1961. Birth control in Britain. Parts I and II. *Population Studies,* Vol. 15, Nos. 1 and 2, July and November.

ROYKO, MIKE. 1971. *Boss: Richard J. Daley of Chicago*. New York: New American Library.

RUPRECHT, T. K. and C. WAHREN. 1972. *Population Programmes and Economic and Social Development*. Paris: OECD.

RYDER, N. B. 1965. The cohort as a concept in the study of social change. *American Sociological Review,* Vol. 30, December.

RYDER, N. B. and C. F. WESTOFF. 1972. Wanted and unwanted fertility in the United States; 1965 and 1970. In R. Parke, Jr. and C. F. Westoff, eds., *Demographic and Social Aspects of Population Growth,* Research Reports of the Commission on Population Growth and the American Future, Vol. 1. Washington: Government Printing Office.

RYDER, N. B. and C. F. WESTOFF. 1971. *Reproduction in the United States 1965*. Princeton: Princeton University Press.

RYDER, N. B. and C. F. WESTOFF. 1969. Fertility planning status: United States 1965. *Demography,* Vol. 6, No. 4, November.

SAUVY, A. 1954. *Théorie génèrale de la population*. 2 Vols. Paris: Presses Universitaires de France.

SCHNORE, L. F. 1958. Social morphology and human ecology. *American Journal of Sociology,* Vol. 63.

SCHNORE, L. F. and J. R. PINKERTON. 1966. Residential redistribution of socioeconomic strata in metropolitan areas. *Demography,* Vol. 3, No. 2.

SCHWIRIAN, K. P. and J. RICO-VALASCO. 1971. The residential distribution of status groups in Puerto Rico's metropolitan areas. *Demography,* Vol. 8, No. 1, February.

SHANNON, L. W. and M. SHANNON. 1967. The assimilation of migrants to cities. In L. F. Schnore, ed., *Social Science and the City: A Study of Urban Research*. New York: Praeger.

SHRYOCK, H. S., JR. 1964. *Population Mobility Within the United States*. Chicago: Community and Family Study Center.

SHRYOCK, H. S. and J. SIEGEL. 1973. *The Methods and Materials of Demography*. U.S. Bureau of the Census. Washington: Government Printing Office.

SIMMEL, G. 1950. *The Sociology of George Simmel*. Translated and edited by K. H. Wolf. New York: Free Press.

SIMON, J. L. 1977. *The Economics of Population Growth*. Princeton: Princeton University Press.

SJOBERG, G. 1964. The rural-urban dimension in pre-industrial, transitional, and industrial societies. In R. E. L. Faris, ed., *Handbook of Modern Sociology*. Chicago: Rand McNally.

SPENGLER, J. J. 1974. *Population Change, Modernization, and Welfare*. Englewood Cliffs, N.J.: Prentice-Hall.

SPENGLER, J. J. 1972. Declining population: Economic effects. *Economic Aspects of Population Change*. U.S. Commission on Population Growth and the American Future, Research Papers, Vol. 2. Washington: Government Printing Office.

SPENGLER, J. J. 1971. Malthus on Godwin's 'Of Population'. *Demography,* Vol. 8, No. 1, February.

STEWARD, J. H. 1955. *Theory of Culture Change*. Urbana: University of Illinois Press.

STOLNITZ, G. J. 1965. Recent mortality trends in Latin America, Asia, and Africa. *Population Studies,* Vol. 19, No. 2.

STOUFFER, S. 1940. Intervening opportunities: A theory relating mobility and distance. *American Sociological Review,* Vol. 5.

SYMONDS, R. and M. CARDER. 1973. *The United Nations and the Population Question 1945–1970.* London: Sussex University Press.

TABBARAH, R. 1975. Bucharest revisited. *People,* Vol. 2, No. 3.

TAEUBER, C. 1964. Taking an inventory of 180 million people: The U.S. Census. In R. Freedman, ed., *Population, The Vital Revolution.* New York: Anchor Books.

TAEUBER, C. and M. H. HANSEN. 1964. A preliminary evaluation of the 1960 Census of Population and Housing. *Demography,* Vol. 1, No. 1.

TAEUBER, C. and I. B. TAEUBER. 1958. *The Changing Population of the United States.* New York: John Wiley.

TAEUBER, I. B. 1972. Growth of the population of the United States in the twentieth century. In R. Parke and C. F. Westoff, eds., *Demographic and Social Aspects of Population Growth.* Research Reports of U.S. Commission on Population Growth and the American Future, Vol. 1. Washington: Government Printing Office.

TAEUBER, I. B. and C. TAEUBER. 1971. *People of the United States in the 20th Century.* U.S. Bureau of the Census, A Census Monograph. Washington: Government Printing Office.

TAEUBER, K. E., L. CHIAZZE, JR., and W. HAENZEL. 1968. *Migration in the United States: An Analysis of Residence Histories.* Public Health Monograph No. 77. Washington: Government Printing Office.

TAEUBER, K. E. and A. F. TAEUBER. 1965. *Negroes in Cities.* Chicago: Aldine.

TAEUBER, K. E. and A. F. TAEUBER. 1964. The Negro as an immigrant group: Recent trends in racial and ethnic segregation in Chicago. *American Journal of Sociology,* Vol. 69, No. 4.

TEXTOR, R. B. 1967. *A Cross Cultural Summary.* New Haven: Human Relations Area Files Press.

THOMAS, W. I. and F. ZNANIECKI. 1918–1920. *The Polish Peasant in Europe and America.* 2 Vols. New York: Owen Publications. Reprinted 1958.

THOMLINSON, R. 1976. *Population Dynamics Causes and Consequences of Population Change.* 2nd Ed. New York: Random House.

THOMPSON, W. S. and P. K. WHELPTON. 1933. *Population Trends in the U.S.A.* New York: McGraw-Hill.

TIEN, H. YUAN. 1975. Planned reproduction, family formation, and fertility decline. *Modern China,* Vol. 1, No. 3, July.

TIETZE, C. 1965. Induced abortion and sterilization as methods of fertility control. In M. C. Sheps and J. C. Ridley, eds., *Public Health and Population Change.* Pittsburgh: University of Pittsburgh Press.

TILLY, C., ed., 1974. *An Urban World.* Boston: Little, Brown.

Time. 1974. September 16, 1974.

UNITED NATIONS. 1973. *Determinants and Consequences of Population Trends.* 2nd Ed. New York: United Nations.

UNITED NATIONS. Annual. *Demographic Yearbook.* New York: United Nations.

UNITED NATIONS. 1953. *The Determinants and Consequences of Population Trends.* New York: United Nations.

UNITED NATIONS, POPULATION BRANCH. 1965. *Population Bulletin No. 7, 1963.* New York: United Nations.

UNITED NATIONS, POPULATION BRANCH. 1962. *Population Bulletin No. 6, 1962.* New York: United Nations.

U.S. BUREAU OF THE CENSUS. Annual. *Statistical Abstract of the United States 1973.* Washington: Government Printing Office.

U.S. BUREAU OF THE CENSUS. 1971. *Census of Population 1970.* Vol. 1. *Characteristics of the Population.* Part. 1. U.S. Summary Section. Washington: Government Printing Office.

U.S. BUREAU OF THE CENSUS. *Current Population Reports,* "Population Estimates" Series P-25. Various Numbers and Dates. Washington.

U.S. BUREAU OF THE CENSUS. *Current Population Reports,* "Population Characteristics" Series P-20. Various Numbers and Dates. Washington.

U.S. BUREAU OF THE CENSUS. 1963. Working Paper No. 16. *Procedural Report in the 1960 Censuses of Population and Housing.* Washington: Government Printing Office.

U.S. BUREAU OF THE CENSUS. 1960. *Historical Statistics of the United States.* Revised Edition. Washington: Government Printing Office.

U.S. BUREAU OF THE CENSUS. 1950. *U.S. Census of Population, 1950,* Vol. II.

UNITED STATES COMMISSION ON POPULATION GROWTH AND THE AMERICAN FUTURE. 1972. *Population and the American Future.* Washington: Government Printing Office.

U.S. DEPARTMENT OF HEALTH, EDUCATION, AND WELFARE. 1973. *Mortality Trends: Age, Color, and Sex, U.S. 1950–69.* Vital and Health Statistics, Series 20, No. 15, November.

U.S. DEPARTMENT OF HEALTH, EDUCATION, AND WELFARE. 1970. *Natality Statistics Analysis 1965–1967.* Public Health Service Publication 1000, Series 21, No. 19, May.

U.S. DEPARTMENT OF HEALTH, EDUCATION, AND WELFARE. 1967. *Vital Statistics of the United States, 1967, Vol II,* "Mortality."

U.S. DEPARTMENT OF HEALTH, EDUCATION, AND WELFARE. 1967. U.S. National Center for Health Statistics, Public Health Service Publication 1000, Series 21, No. 11.

U.S. DEPARTMENT OF HEALTH, EDUCATION, AND WELFARE. 1964. Report of the Advisory Committee to the Surgeon General of the Public Health Services. Public Health Service Publication 1103. *Smoking and Health.* Washington: Government Printing Office.

UTTERSTRÖM, G. 1965. Population in eighteenth-century Scandinavia. In D. V. Glass and D. E. C. Eversley, eds., *Population in History.* Chicago: Aldine.

VAN DEN BERGHE, P. 1974. *Man and Society.* New York: Elsevier.

WEBER, M. 1968. *The City.* Translated by D. Martindale and G. Neuwirth. New York: Free Press.

WEBER, M. 1961. *General Economic History.* Translated by F. H. Knight. New York: Collier Books.

WESTOFF, C. F. 1974. The populations of the developed countries. *Scientific American,* Vol. 229, No. 9, September.

WESTOFF, C. F. 1972. The modernization of contraceptive practice. *Family Planning Perspectives,* 4, no. 3, Summer.

WESTOFF, C. F., R. G. POTTER, and P. C. SAGI. 1964. Some selected findings of the Princeton Fertility Study, 1963. *Demography,* Vol. 1, No. 1.

WESTOFF, C. F. and N. B. RYDER. 1969. Practice of contraception in the U.S.A. In S. J. Behrman, L. Corsa, Jr., and R. Freedman, eds., *Fertility and Family Planning. A World View.* Ann Arbor: University of Michigan Press.

WHELPTON, P. K., A. A. CAMPBELL, and J. E. PATTERSON. 1966. *Fertility and Family Planning in the United States.* Princeton: Princeton University Press.

WHYTE, W. F. 1956. *The Organization Man.* New York: Simon and Schuster.

WIRTH, L. 1945. The problem of minority groups. In R. Linton, ed., *The Science of Man in the World Crisis.* New York: Columbia University Press.

WIRTH, L. 1938. Urbanism as a way of life. *American Journal of Sociology,* Vol. 44, July.

WOLFINGER, R. E. 1968. The development and persistence of ethnic voting. In L. H. Fuchs, ed., *American Ethnic Politics.* New York: Harper Torchbooks.

WOYTINSKY, W. S. and E. S. WOYTINSKY. 1953. *World Population and Production, Trends and Outlook.* New York: Twentieth Century Fund.

WRIGLEY, E. A. 1969. *Population and History.* London: George Weidenfeld and Nicolson.

WRIGLEY, E. A. 1968. Mortality in pre-industrial England: The example of Colyton, Devon, over three centuries. *Daedalus,* Historical Population Studies, Spring, pp. 546-80.

WRIGLEY, E. A. 1966. Family limitation in pre-industrial England. *Economic History Review,* 2nd Series, Vol. 19, No. 1, pp. 82-109.

YAUKEY, D. 1961. *Fertility Differences in a Modernizing Country.* Princeton: Princeton University Press.

ZELDITCH, M., JR. 1964. Family, marriage, and kinship. In R. E. L. Farris, ed., *Handbook of Modern Sociology.* Chicago: Rand McNally.

ZELINSKY, W. 1966. *A Prologue to Population Geography.* Englewood Cliffs, N.J.: Prentice-Hall.

Index

A.L. OLIVEIRA MEMORIAL LIBRARY
3 1782 00069 5466
HB871 .M28
Introduction to population : a
sociological approach / c1977

POPULATION INFORMATION FOR [illegible] COUNTRIES (continued from front end papers)

Region or Country *	Population Estimate Mid-1976 (millions) †	Birth Rate ‡	Death Rate ‡	Rate of Population Growth (annual, percent) §	Number of Years to Double Population ¶	Population Projection to 2000 (millions) ‖	Infant Mortality Rate **	Population under 15 Years (percent) ††	Median Age (years) ††	Life Expectancy at Birth (years)	Urban Population (percent) ‡‡	Per Capita Gross National Product (USA) §§
United States	215.3	15	9	0.8	87	262.5	17	27	28.1	71	74	6,640
LATIN AMERICA	**326**	**37**	**9**	**2.8**	**25**	**606**	**75**	**42**	**18.9**	**62**	**59**	**940**
MIDDLE AMERICA	**81**	**45**	**9**	**3.4**	**20**	**172**	**65**	**46**	**16.9**	**62**	**56**	**900**
Costa Rica	2.0	28	5	2.3	30	3.6	45	42	18.2	69	41	790
El Salvador	4.2	40	8	3.2	22	8.8	54	46	16.9	58	39	390
Guatemala	5.7	43	15	2.8	25	11.1	79	44	17.6	53	34	570
Honduras	2.8	49	14	3.5	20	6.2	117	47	16.5	54	28	340
Mexico	62.3	46	8	3.5	20	134.4	61	46	16.8	63	61	1,000
Nicaragua	2.2	48	14	3.3	21	4.8	123	48	15.7	53	49	650
Panama	1.7	31	5	2.6	27	3.2	44	43	18.2	66	49	1,010
CARIBBEAN	**27**	**31**	**9**	**2.1**	**33**	**44**	**71**	**41**	**19.9**	**64**	**43**	**820**
Bahamas	0.2	22	6	4.2	16	0.3	32	44	18.7	66	58	2,460
Barbados	0.2	21	9	0.8	87	0.3	38	34	22.3	69	4	1,110
Cuba	9.4	25	6	1.8	38	14.9	29	37	22.4	70	60	640
Dominican Republic	4.8	46	11	3.0	23	10.8	98	48	16.1	58	40	590
Grenada	0.1	26	8	0.4	173	0.1	32	47	—	63	8	300
Guadeloupe	0.4	28	7	1.5	46	0.5	44	40	19.2	69	9	1,050
Haiti	4.6	36	16	1.6	43	7.1	150	41	18.8	50	20	140
Jamaica	2.1	31	7	1.9	36	2.8	26	46	17.3	68	37	1,140
Martinique	0.3	22	7	0.5	139	0.5	32	41	19.0	69	33	1,330
Netherlands Antilles	0.2	25	7	1.8	38	0.4	28	38	—	73	32	1,530
Puerto Rico	3.2	23	6	2.4	29	4.0	23	37	21.6	72	58	2,400
Trinidad & Tobago	1.1	26	7	1.5	46	1.4	26	40	19.3	66	12	1,490
TROPICAL SOUTH AMERICA	**178**	**38**	**9**	**2.9**	**24**	**338**	**82**	**43**	**18.1**	**60**	**58**	**840**
Bolivia	5.8	44	18	2.6	27	10.6	108	43	18.3	47	35	250
Brazil	110.2	37	9	2.8	25	207.5	82	42	18.6	61	58	900
Colombia	23.0	41	9	3.2	22	44.3	76	46	16.9	61	64	510
Ecuador	6.9	42	10	3.2	22	14.0	78	47	16.3	60	39	460
Guyana	0.8	36	6	2.2	32	1.2	40	44	17.2	68	40	470
Paraguay	2.6	40	9	2.7	26	5.1	65	45	16.6	62	38	480
Peru	16.0	41	12	2.9	24	30.9	110	44	17.6	56	60	710
Surinam	0.4	41	7	3.2	22	0.9	30	50	15.1	66	49	870
Venezuela	12.3	36	7	2.9	24	23.1	54	44	17.4	65	75	1,710
TEMPERATE SOUTH AMERICA	**39**	**24**	**9**	**1.5**	**46**	**52**	**67**	**32**	**25.7**	**67**	**80**	**1,540**
Argentina	25.7	22	9	1.4	50	32.9	64	29	27.4	68	81	1,900
Chile	10.8	28	8	1.7	41	15.9	78	39	20.5	63	76	820
Uruguay	2.8	21	10	1.1	63	3.4	45	28	29.4	70	80	1,060
EUROPE	**476**	**15**	**10**	**0.6**	**116**	**540**	**22**	**24**	**32.2**	**71**	**64**	**3,680**
NORTHERN EUROPE	**82**	**13**	**12**	**0.2**	**347**	**91**	**15**	**24**	**33.4**	**72**	**73**	**3,960**
Denmark	5.1	14	10	0.4	173	5.4	12	23	32.5	73	80	5,820
Finland	4.7	13	10	0.4	173	4.8	10	24	30.1	69	58	4,130
Iceland	0.2	20	7	1.3	53	0.3	11	32	24.7	74	86	5,550
Ireland	3.1	22	11	0.7	99	4.0	17	31	26.8	72	52	2,370
Norway	4.0	15	10	0.6	116	4.5	12	24	32.4	74	45	5,280
Sweden	8.2	13	11	0.4	173	9.3	9	21	35.3	75	81	6,720
United Kingdom	56.1	13	12	0.1	693	62.3	16	24	34.0	72	76	3,360
WESTERN EUROPE	**153**	**13**	**11**	**0.5**	**139**	**171**	**10**	**24**	**33.1**	**72**	**77**	**5,460**
Austria	7.5	13	12	0.1	693	8.1	23	24	33.7	71	52	4,050
Belgium	9.8	13	12	0.3	231	10.7	16	23	34.3	71	87	5,210
France	53.1	15	10	0.8	87	61.9	12	24	32.6	73	70	5,190
Germany (Federal Republic of)	62.1	10	12	0.2	347	66.5	21	23	34.4	71	88	5,890
Luxembourg	0.4	11	12	0.7	99	0.4	14	21	35.2	71	68	5,690
Netherlands	13.8	14	8	0.9	77	16.1	11	27	28.9	74	77	4,880
Switzerland	6.5	13	9	0.7	99	7.3	13	24	32.1	73	55	6,650
EASTERN EUROPE	**107**	**17**	**10**	**0.7**	**99**	**122**	**26**	**23**	**31.4**	**70**	**55**	**2,670**
Bulgaria	8.8	17	10	0.7	99	10.0	25	22	33.5	72	59	1,770